States of Anxiety

The attitude of many Russian soldiers to continuing the war in 1917 was ambiguous at best. Some indication of their feelings can be seen in this celebration of May 1 at the front. The banner reads "Long Live the International Holiday of the Proletariat!!"

States of Anxiety

Scarcity and Loss in Revolutionary Russia

WILLIAM G. ROSENBERG

OXFORD
UNIVERSITY PRESS

Oxford University Press is a department of the University of Oxford. It furthers
the University's objective of excellence in research, scholarship, and education
by publishing worldwide. Oxford is a registered trade mark of Oxford University
Press in the UK and certain other countries.

Published in the United States of America by Oxford University Press
198 Madison Avenue, New York, NY 10016, United States of America.

© Oxford University Press 2023

All rights reserved. No part of this publication may be reproduced, stored in
a retrieval system, or transmitted, in any form or by any means, without the
prior permission in writing of Oxford University Press, or as expressly permitted
by law, by license, or under terms agreed with the appropriate reproduction
rights organization. Inquiries concerning reproduction outside the scope of the
above should be sent to the Rights Department, Oxford University Press, at the
address above.

You must not circulate this work in any other form
and you must impose this same condition on any acquirer.

CIP data is on file at the Library of Congress
ISBN 978-0-19-761015-2

DOI: 10.1093/oso/9780197610152.001.0001

Printed by Integrated Books International, United States of America

To Mollie, Cole, and Nadia, my three grandchildren, whom I love very much, and without whom this book might have been finished much sooner.

Contents

Preface   xi

Introduction: "Beyond the Great Stories" of Russia's Wars
and Revolutions   1
   The Past and Present in Three "Great Stories"   1
   Material Conditions, Emotional Fields, Power, and Their "Voices"   6
   Historical Imagination and Its Mindsets   8
   The Focus of This Study   14
   A Methodological Challenge: Reading beyond Description   21
   Putting the Revolution in Its Place: Great Stories and
      Historical Explanations   24

PART I: THE IMPERIAL MEANINGS OF SCARCITY AND LOSS

1. "Fighting with God" and the Languages of Loss   29
   Assessing Patriotism   32
   Surveilling Loyalty   38
   Early Losses and Their Implications   40
   At the Front: The Shocks of War   43
   Reading Soldiers' Moods   50
   Military Censorship and the Galician Disaster   57

2. Was Russia Prepared?   60
   "Embedded" Underdevelopment, Russia's Peasants, and
      the Market Problem   64
   Fault Lines of Economic Mobilization   71
   Russia's Railroad Lifeline   77
   The Strains of State Finance   84
   Assessing Loss   92

3. "Dying of Hunger": Representations and Realities of Scarcity   98
   Early Voices of "Extreme Need"   99
   The Military Zone of Violence   102
   "Dying of Hunger": Procurements, Prices, and the Rising
      Cost of Living   109
   "Extreme Need" in the Workplace   115
   Food Insecurities and the "Baba" Question   118

4. Empowering "Responsible Publics" and the Emergence of War
   Capitalism ... 122
   War Industries Committees and the Special Councils ... 123
   Devolving Authority, Engaging the Localities ... 125
   The Progressive Bloc and the Question of Autocratic Power ... 129
   Funding Production, Regulating Distribution ... 133
   Contesting Authorities: The Emissary Problem ... 136
   Militarization vs. Mediation: The "Worker Question" ... 140
   War Capitalism and Its Cultures ... 146
   Rising Anxieties with the Coming of Winter ... 152

5. Seeking Solutions, Drowning in Blood ... 157
   Winter and Spring of 1916: Anxieties about Mismanagement and
     Malfeasance from Below ... 159
   Contending Anxieties: Confusion and Chaos from Above ... 162
   The Vexing Problems of Rationing and Fixed Prices ... 165
   State Finance as a "Bacchanalia of Corruption" ... 170
   Political Dilemmas ... 176
   Scarcity, Railroads, and the Labor Question: Militarization as Solution ... 183
   "Brusilov's Breakthrough" as Tragic Romance ... 190
   The Soldiers' Story: "Drowning in Blood" ... 195

6. Scripting Revolution ... 199
   "Literally Facing Starvation" ... 200
   Extending Compulsory Labor: From World War to Civil War ... 203
   The Rittikh Confiscation ... 206
   Subsistence Protests and the October Strikes ... 210
   Russia's Revolutionary Situation ... 216
   Scripting the Revolution ... 220

PART II: REVOLUTIONARY IMPERATIVES

7. "Responsible Men in Whom the Country Has Confidence": The
   Challenges of Revolutionary Governance ... 231
   Writing the "Truth" in the Third Winter of War ... 232
   Scarcity and Anxiety on the Home Front ... 235
   Uprising, Insurrection, Revolution ... 237
   Locations and Forms of Power and Questions of Political Legitimacy ... 244
   Scarcity and Social Identity ... 249
   Loss and the Meanings of War ... 251
   The Challenges of Revolutionary Governance ... 254

8. Addressing Scarcity, Confronting Loss ... 259
   Food Anxiety and the Grain Monopoly: Legitimacy and Function ... 260
   Food Supply, Land Redistribution, and Democratic Practice ... 268

  Democratizing the Railroads and the Concept of "Statization"   271
  Controlling the Cost of Living: Revolutionary State Finances, War
    Capitalism, and the Liberty Loan   276
  Giving Meaning to Loss: Politics, Passions, and the April Crisis   285

9. Social Conflict, Mediation, and the Revolutionary State   307
  Politics and the First Coalition   308
  Coalition Governance and the Weighty Actor Thesis   311
  Seeking Security and Dignity in the Spring Strike Wave   313
  The Ministry of Labor as a Site of Mediation   319
  Activism in the Countryside   324
  Once More "on the Brink of Catastrophe"   331

10. "Slaughter" at the Front, the July Insurrection, and a
   "Government to Save the Revolution"   335
  Brusilov Redux: The Kerensky Offensive   335
  Threats to "Great Russia" and the Liberals' Retreat   341
  The July Insurrection   344
  The "Real Demands of Russian Life"   347
  The "Government to Save the Revolution"   351
  Once Again "on the Brink of Catastrophe"   354

11. The Collapse of War Capitalism   359
  Village Sovereignty   360
  Who Owns the Workplace?   363
  Summer Strikes   368
  Beleaguered Ministries: Labor, Trade and Industry, and Finance   371
  War Capitalism and the Revolutionary State   375

12. Democratic Predicaments and the Bolshevik Coup   382
  Scarcity, Loss, and Politics at the Moscow State Conference   382
  Kornilov, the Front, and the Countryside   389
  "Radical Dictatorships," Autonomous Nationalities   394
  The Railroad Republic   399
  The Anxieties and Predicaments of October   403

PART III: FROM WORLD WAR TO TOTAL WAR: SCARCITY, LOSS, AND DYSFUNCTIONAL DICTATORSHIPS AFTER OCTOBER

13. Circumstance, Ideology, and Bolshevik Power   413
  Rhetoric, Realities, and the Limits of Bolshevik Power   414
  Illusions of Peace   417
  Land and Bread as Metaphors of Hope   422

  Nationalization from Below, Refinancing Production from Above,
   Repudiating Debt   424
  "Still Starving" Workers and Increasingly Hungry Peasants   429
  Dictatorship as the Primary Task of Soviet Power   439

14. "Our Lives Have Become Unbearable!": Dictatorships in the
  "Fight against Hunger"   445
  Extreme Need as Counterrevolution   445
  Once Again, "the Revolution Is in Danger!"   449
  Once Again, Mobilizing "Solutions"   451
  Scarcity and the Anti-Bolshevik Dictatorships   454
  The Bolsheviks' "Fight against Hunger"   458
  The Normalization of Concealment   463
  Losing the "Hunger War"   470

15. Violence, Loss, and the Collapse of War Communism   474
  "Vectors of Social Violence"   474
  Scarcity, Loss, and the Trauma Question   478
  Losing Great Russia: Paramilitary Violence and the Defeat
   of the Whites   482
  The Fight against Desertion   489
  Rabkrin and the Obligation to Work   495
  "All for Transport!" Tsektran and the Labor Armies   503
  The Collapse of War Communism: "Bolshevism without the
   Bolsheviks!"   510

Epilogue: Scarcity, Loss, and Soviet History   517
  Soviet Russia's Long Civil War   517
  Stalin's Assaults and Soviet "Redemption"   521
  Loss and Scarcity after the "Great Patriotic Struggle"   524
  Challenges and Adaptations: Reform, Stability, and Stagnation   526
  Archiving the Soviet Great Story   529
Bibliography   537
Index   565

Preface

Long in gestation, this study reflects an even longer interest in revolutionary Russia, one that goes back well before Richard Pipes suggested I study the dilemmas and plights of Constitutional Democratic liberals in this period. Young and naïve, I initially understood this period as one of great hopes and expectations, as well as even greater disappointments when the problems of revolutionary change got the better of those with the best of intentions. At that long ago time, politics, parties, and political ideologies dominated our conceptions of revolutionary upheaval. They also centered a great deal of the available evidence. (My army career took a nosedive when I continued my subscription to *Pravda*.) The closest I could get to a topic that might gain me access to materials in the USSR was the "crisis of those at the top": *krizis verkhov*. The Lenin Library in Moscow and the Saltykov-Shchedrin Library in Leningrad contained a wealth of relevant material, even if archives for the period and all that followed were tightly shut. I well remember one librarian in Moscow who refused to give me the copies of the Kadet Party's journal in 1917 until she had finished reading them. Censorship was not the issue. Curiosity and the excitement of discovery was.

Much older now (if not necessarily much wiser), I continue to admire the remarkable and progressive changes many tried to effect in the revolutionary period in areas like penal theory and the law, civil marriage, and the emancipation of women from the church and their husbands, and even (or even especially) literature, theater, art, and architecture. Some utopian visions were clearly quite admirable in the first and short-lived phase of Russia's and the Bolsheviks' cultural revolution. A print of the Malevich painting *Peasant Women* still adorns one of my walls. (A print of Jack Kollmann's remarkably spiritual Russian photographs adorns another.) The nature and magnitude of individual and collective catastrophe in this period became an ineffable background noise, something to be recognized statistically but for which the necessary evidence for full description was not readily at hand. Politics continued to dominate much of our thinking, especially during the 1960s, when the antiwar protests focused overwhelmingly on political change, their social and cultural elements still largely marginal in importance.

My own thinking began to change as I struggled in this period with the dilemmas of Russian liberals, hoping they might give some insight on the contemporary upheavals. What was clear as I finished that book was not that Kadet efforts to create a democratic political order and institutionalize the values of civil rights and liberties were not admirable. It was that their politics had increasingly little relation to the socioeconomic actualities of Russia's revolutionary moment, nor to the effects the most destructive war in history may have had on the revolution's culture of violence. As a result, Charles Tilly's informal gatherings at Michigan and Leopold Haimson's seminal work and his seminars at Columbia both drew my attention. Joining an increasing (and increasingly perspicacious) cohort, I began seriously to work on Russian labor activism with Diane Koenker. By the time that book was finished, Soviet Russia was again in a full-fledged political revolution, although just as in the period 1914–22, its social, economic, and cultural dimensions—and especially the current and future effects of scarcity and loss—were not readily apparent.

It should be obvious that this study reflects the influence of many teachers, scholars, and students, far too many people to acknowledge individually. While the bibliography lists only cited sources, many more first-rate books and articles have clearly influenced my thinking. Students at Michigan over the course of almost fifty years stimulated me greatly with their insights and critiques. Many subsequently had fine careers of their own, publishing (at last count) some forty volumes. I am gratified to think that my work with them was not likely the impediment I sometimes feared. A monthly interdisciplinary seminar by a small group of faculty throughout the 1990s kept me constantly alert to different conceptualizations and theories of social change. The remarkable series of colloquia organized by Leopold Haimson at the Institute of History in St. Petersburg brought me together with many fine Russian and non-Russian scholars who presented works in progress as well as often controversial interpretations. I am very grateful to Nikolai Smirnov, Vladimir Cherniaev, Nikolai Mikhailov, Boris Kolonitskii, and others who worked hard to ensure the seminar met regularly every three years around themes of broad historical interest. It is a great loss to many of us that the colloquia series is yet another casualty among so many of Vladimir Putin's horrific and unconscionable war against Ukraine.

Over the course of many years Leopold Haimson was a constant source of insight, critical thinking, and friendship. That I owe loyalties to the two very different historical schools represented by Columbia and Harvard might come as a surprise to some, but the friendships and collegiality of faculty and colleagues in both places broadened my thinking despite (or perhaps because of) differences of view. So has the work I've done with Francis Blouin around reading archives as well as their documents. Our yearlong Sawyer Seminar brought leading post-Soviet scholars and archivists together in Ann Arbor with those from many other countries. I feel confident in saying that the collection of essays and proceedings from the seminar handsomely published by the University of Michigan Press is a volume of unique value to historians and archivists alike. During the anniversary events of 2017 I had the opportunity to present parts of this study to colleagues in Cambridge, England, as well as Cambridge, Massachusetts, and in Paris, St. Petersburg, New York, Princeton, Wellesley, and the Kennan Institute in

Washington. I am grateful for the comments and criticisms I received, many of which I have taken to heart. All of the photographs come from the Central State Archive of Kinophoto Documents in St. Petersburg (TsGA KFFD SPb). I greatly appreciate the help of Alevtina Serveevna Zagorets and Oksana Igorevna Morozan in selecting and preparing them for publication.

Dan Orlovsky has read all of my chapters, Heather Hogan those on 1917. I shared notes on the esoterica of state finance in the revolutionary period with Ekaterina Pravilova, both of us much encouraged in our work by the late and revered St. Petersburg Academician Boris Vasil'evich Anan'ch. Boris Kolonitskii and Alfred Rieber gave me valuable advice as well. I am very fortunate to have had such good and supportive colleagues.

As I am for having Nancy Toff as my editor at Oxford, who encouraged me early on to make this additional contribution to a vast literature. She has been a wonderfully supportive colleague for this project as well as for an earlier volume on authority in history and the archives that originated Oxford's History and Archives Series. Brent Matheny at Oxford has also been a great help in overseeing the production process, as were Oxford's anonymous readers who raised important questions for me to consider. I'm very appreciative. This book is clearly much better for all these time-consuming efforts and encouragement.

As has often been the case with historians of faraway places, my family has had to tolerate my preoccupation with this project, my many absences on research trips, and the anxieties familiar to most émigré Jews originally from the region. (My mother-in-law Dora Borenstein, who left Ukraine by foot in 1920, was always relieved that I had not been "detained.") My assurances that the greatest danger for me lay in crossing the street was to little avail. I have been blessed that for more than sixty years my remarkable wife, Elinor, stoutly resisted my efforts early on to make her into a Russianist, despite getting A's in her Russian-language courses. Her clear-headed intelligence about this and so many other matters has allowed us to pursue two quite different and equally rewarding careers in ways that greatly enhanced both our lives and, for me, at least, provided a number of important subjects and issues to think carefully about. I am deeply in her debt.

As I am indebted to my children and grandchildren, but for different reasons. From them I've learned a great deal about the advantages of different life trajectories as well as impediments overinvolved parents sometimes put in their way. The same is true with the social and cultural understandings their different generations have provided. Peter and Sarah have both taught me much in very different ways. My three grandchildren, one of whom has taken to referring consistently to my "so-called" work, have given me more pleasure than they realize (along, of course, with occasional sleepless nights). As proof positive, it is a joy to dedicate this "so-called" book to them.

Islesboro, Maine, August 2022

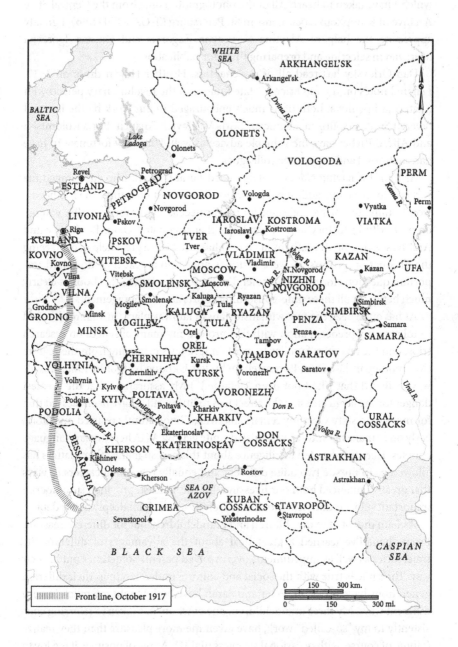

Introduction

"Beyond the Great Stories" of Russia's Wars and Revolutions

The hundredth anniversary of the Russian Revolution in 2017 passed virtually without notice. Several good new syntheses appeared in print, scholarly conferences and lecture series were held at leading institutes and universities, and a range of new and not so new details were added to our knowledge about what is still generally regarded as a seminal event of the twentieth century. Unlike the revolution's seventieth anniversary in 1987, there were no animated debates about its historical meaning. Nor were there any new arguments about its worldwide implications or more than an occasional nod in the direction of its possible importance to understanding our contemporary world. Not surprisingly, this was especially the case in the Russian Federation. Lenin still lay outside the Kremlin in Red Square, preserved and observed as a historical curiosity but no longer linked in any clearly defined ways to historical memory. Sightseers passed through, poorly if at all informed about the ten days once thought to have shaken the world. In Vladimir Putin's ahistorical regime, ceremonial linkages were more readily drawn to the imagined greatness of Imperial Russia than to the reality of Soviet gods who failed.

The Past and Present in Three "Great Stories"

The 1987 anniversary, by contrast, came at a seminal moment in Soviet history. Mikhail Gorbachev's *perestroika* involved hitherto unimaginable levels of openness (*glasnost*') that soon challenged the party's formal monopoly on power, enshrined in the notorious Article Six of the Soviet Constitution. The 1987 anniversary itself was momentous in this regard not as celebration of what the Communist Party had accomplished in seventy years but precisely the reverse. The linkage between the party's political monopoly and its legitimacy was fundamentally historical, based on an officially irrefutable conception of how history was destined to progress. Soviet socialism was imagined and secured by Leninists, but party rule was ordained and legitimized by history itself as the necessary and inevitable stage toward the ultimate communist world order. The

States of Anxiety. William G. Rosenberg, Oxford University Press. © Oxford University Press 2023.
DOI: 10.1093/oso/9780197610152.003.0001

Great Story of Bolshevik triumphalism was a literally prescriptive history, now demonstrably gone wrong. Indeed, it is not too much to say that the collapse of historical essentialism in the Great Soviet Story was both the cause and the consequence of the collapse of the USSR as a functional state: cause, because the formal legitimacy of the Party's right to rule rested on the verities of a particular understanding of history and its purported laws that was increasingly thought to be false; consequence, because having failed to serve its legitimizing purpose, the narrative itself was deemed to have no historical merit.

The origin of the Soviet Great Story preceded the revolution that enshrined it, its well known ideological and political roots stemming from nineteenth-century radical Russian populism and the spreading wave of European Marxism. So did a second Great Story that was also under siege in the 1980s, this time in connection with the two-hundredth anniversary in 1989 of the French Revolution. Here the assault involved leading French conservatives, including distinguished historians like the ex–Communist Party member François Furet, who saw revolutionary France not only in terms of its democratic and socialist underpinnings but as a source of the brutal authoritarianism reflected in the French Great Terror. Among others, Furet was soon joined by the prominent Princeton historian Arno Mayer, who linked the French and Soviet terrors to their common revolutionary origins in his heralded volume *Furies*. The German historian of fascism Ernst Nolte and Harvard's Richard Pipes, who was just completing his own prodigious study of the Russian Revolution, took the argument one big step further, identifying Bolshevism as the primary source of Nazism and the Holocaust. As Queen Elizabeth came to Paris representing monarchy during the 1989 anniversary, the popular magazine *Figaro* insisted it was time for France to get over its revolutionary illusions. "The French Revolution is finished," its editor wrote, "the left is dead."[1]

The concept that revolution could bring democratic socialism and fulfill the unrealized promises of 1789 was also a Great Story for many leading figures in revolutionary Russia. It was articulated forcefully by the social democrat Nikolai Chkheidze, who led the moderate Menshevik faction in the Imperial State Duma before being president of the Petrograd Soviet from February to September 1917; his colleague Irakli Tsereteli, the prominent Georgian Menshevik and leading party spokesman in 1917 who joined the Provisional Government in its first coalition; and Alexander Kerensky, prime minister and minister of war in 1917

---

[1] See, e.g., François Furet, *The Passing of an Illusion: The Idea of Communism in the Twentieth Century* and *Interpreting the French Revolution* (Cambridge: Cambridge University Press, 1981); Arno Mayer, *Furies: Violence and Terror in the French and Russian Revolutions* (Princeton, NJ: Princeton University Press, 2000); François Furet and Ernst Nolte, *Fascism and Communism*, trans. K. Golsan (Lincoln: University of Nebraska Press, 2001); Richard Pipes, paper presented to International Conference on the Russian Revolution, Jerusalem, 1987; *Figaro*, April 25, 1992. The French commemoration is fully discussed in Steven L. Kaplan, *Farewell, Revolution: Disputed Legacies, France 1789–1989* (Ithaca, NY: Cornell University Press, 1995).

and the revolution's best known personage after Lenin. For Russia's democratic socialists, Hegelian and Marxist concepts of causality rooted in socioeconomic class interests and relations also structured the optimistic logic of Imperial Russia's historical future, although, in contrast to the Bolsheviks, hardly determined it. A progressive democratic socialist future was predictable in "normal" times, but it could readily be altered by extraordinary circumstances like the First World War. Behind the democratic socialist Great Story was thus a much greater pessimism about how history might actually (as opposed to logically) unfold. Great catastrophes like the war could provoke a revolutionary upheaval before the social and cultural maturation that was necessary to sustain social democracy on politically democratic foundations. For many democratic socialists in Russia, this was the essential failure of 1789 that had ultimately brought political liberty and the possibility of equality after a tumultuous and inhumane period of upheaval whose legacies were never fully extinguished.

When the Soviet Union disappeared in 1991, only one Great Story of Russia's revolution was left standing: that of the possibility of liberal social progress in Russia through responsible representative politics and full civil liberties. This narrative, too, was deeply rooted in the Russian past. Although it never gained massive popular support, the various strains of Russian liberalism developed in the aftermath of Russia's Great Reforms in 1861 in representative rural welfare institutions (*zemstvos*) and city and town assemblies (*dumas*) and especially with the development of the legal profession and the modernization of Russia's leading universities. When political parties emerged in Russia during the revolutionary upheaval of 1905, Russian liberals in the Constitutional Democratic Party (Kadets) briefly took center stage. Their leader was the prominent historian Pavel (Paul) Miliukov, well known internationally for his work on the reforms of Peter the Great and his articulation of the "statist" position in Russian historiography: the centrality of the state itself to the processes of socioeconomic modernization and political reform.

Alongside Miliukov were other notables, reflecting the various strains of the liberal movement: the progressive physician, finance specialist, and agrarian expert Andrei Shingarev, who had rocked Russia in the 1890s with his volume *The Dying Village*; the conservative jurist and brilliant orator Vasili Maklakov, brother of the tsar's minister of interior; the provincial railroad expert Nikolai Nekrasov; and Alexander Manuilov, economist and rector of Moscow University. All would become ministers in 1917. Vladimir Nabokov, father of the famous writer, was also a member of the Kadet Central Committee. So were Maksim Vinaver and Sophia Panina, the first a leading advocate for Jewish rights who with others was expelled from the new State Duma in 1906 after protesting its early dissolution from across the Finnish border at Vyborg, the second renowned as a social activist and founder of the Peoples' House (Narodnyi Dom) in St. Petersburg who would be acquitted of anti-Soviet subversion in a riveting public trial after the Bolsheviks took power. At the core of the Kadet program were demands for universal civil rights, more democratically elected assemblies, a comprehensive resolution of the vexing question of land use and ownership, and the relaxation of impediments to industrial development and economic modernization. These were shared by liberal industrialists and others in what was called the Progressist Party, led by the Moscow textile manufacturer Alexander Konovalov, and Alexander Guchkov's more conservative liberal party, the Octobrists, who supported the tsar's constitutional reforms of 1905 as an important step in the right direction. In 1917, Konovalov would become Russia's first democratic minister of trade and industry, Guchkov its first minister of war.

As it gained new traction with the Soviet fall in the 1980s and 1990s, the liberal Great Story echoed Miliukov's statism and the broad liberal commitment to civil liberties. Firmly grounded in private property rights, the social importance of economic growth, and untethered individualism, the liberal Great Story stressed the historical necessity of a strong state to assure the equality of rights and socioeconomic opportunity against an entrenched and resistant landed gentry. In its more focused "neoliberal" forms that took hold in the Russian 1990s, even the moderate democratic socialist narrative was flawed because it imagined economic goods and social services could be equitably distributed by regulating market exchange and limiting the accumulation of personal wealth.

Here, too, the Russian Revolution was a crucible not simply of Soviet authoritarianism but of the fate of political liberty and democratic rights in circumstances of social upheaval where there was no strong state to protect them. Inside Russia and out after 1991, this neoliberal appropriation was written as a Great Story of political conspiracy, ruthless political ambition, and human tragedy, leaving no room whatsoever for celebration. In studies within and outside Russia the tropes of power, conspiracy, violence, and inhumanity were soon refashioned from their longer term antisocialist uses into elements of an older conservative narrative about revolution itself. In this old/new understanding, all sociopolitical revolutions had again become inherently problematic Great Revolutions, greatly bad. The determining effects of materiality or social and cultural mentalities and emotional states were said to be endlessly amenable to human agency, that is, ideologically conditioned politics. Everywhere revolutions occurred they were made by self-conscious, power-hungry, and ideologically driven revolutionaries, whose actions validated Hannah Arendt's famous assertion that "freedom has been better preserved in countries where no revolution ever broke out, no matter how outrageous the circumstances of the powers that be."[2]

---

[2] Hannah Arendt, *On Revolution* (New York: Viking Press, 1965), 41.

In their more recent iterations, variants of the three Great Stories of 1917 are also exercises in historical appropriation that read the past through presentist lenses and assign it meaning for presentist purposes. Unless they are carefully based on new evidence, most such "reassessments" wrongly assume that current events like the end of the Soviet Union somehow change the contextualized meanings of past events, in this case Russia's vast and traumatic upheavals between 1914 and 1922, when Lenin's regime temporarily postponed its goal of creating communism from the ashes of world and civil war. Consciously or not, most grand narratives weave these contextualized meanings into prefigured teleologies. They create and re-create social memories of the past that are often more important as artifacts of contemporary political cultures than points of entry into really lived experience. It is the narrative telling itself that is paramount, in other words, rather than its empirical foundations. Reassessments argue that previous historians got the story wrong. Grand narratives argue that the big picture can be understood only by arguing its (big) political causes and (usually bigger) political consequences, that is, by placing it within a teleological frame.

What is wrong with reassessments and appropriations is not their presentism per se or their often undisguised moralism. All good historians try to get their stories right in part so that meanings for the present can be rightly drawn. Rather, what is wrong is the ways presentist perspectives subordinate the complex actualities of lived experience to a narrative of deliberate political or ideological purpose. The interpretative differences well known to historians of Russia between Richard Pipes (who organized his understanding of the period around political conspiracy) and Martin Malia (who focused on Marxist-Leninist ideology) are, in fact, part and parcel of the same (or very similar) perspectives. While few would deny that the Russian Revolution of 1917 was an event of great importance in the history of the twentieth century, the very recognition of what our French colleagues would call its *événementiel* significance conflates the complex processes of its constitution into simplifying reductions. Great events privilege grand narratives. Their focus tends to be on politics and ideology in part because these are most readily discernible within the complexities of the moment, most easily described and documented, and most readily linked to outcomes. Individual and collective social, cultural, and emotional experience is rendered unimportant, or at best relatively unimportant, to historical outcomes.[3]

In this connection, in an interesting historical conjuncture of its own, the breakdown of the Great Soviet Story also occurred in the midst of a prodigious outburst of postmodernist critical theory. The footnote as a scholarly device came

---

[3] Richard Pipes, *The Russian Revolution* (New York: Knopf, 1990); Martin Malia, *The Soviet Tragedy: A History of Socialism in Russia, 1917–1991* (New York: Free Press, 1994); Claude Romano, *L'événement et le monde* (Paris: Presses Universitaires de France, 1998), translated into English by Shane Mackinlay as *Event and World* (New York: Fordham University Press, 2009).

into particular scrutiny, as did the ways historical archives themselves structured the stories their documents evidenced through processes of acquisition, cataloging, and access. Among other challenges, this confronted the very integrity of narrative history itself as an objective telling of the past "as it really was." Prominent American historians such as Gertrude Himmelfarb and Lawrence Stone thought critical historical theory could destroy the profession itself.[4]

An important if less noticed contribution to this argument in the 1990s was Robert Berkhofer's *Beyond the Great Story*, referenced in this introduction's subtitle. Taking up the challenges postmodernism was presenting to established understandings of "historical representation and truthfulness," Berkhofer expanded on the work of Hayden White and others on the roles of narrative, rhetoric, and contextualization as implicitly historical methodologies. He focused particularly on the transition "from rhetoric to politics through the roles of voice and viewpoint in history."[5]

Although Berkhofer did not stress it, the configuration of historical archives themselves illustrates his point. In Moscow, the Central State Archive of the October Revolution became the Soviet Union's new national archive, pointing its users to the ways the revolution itself determined everything of historical importance that followed. Any document mentioning Lenin or Stalin was labeled "of exceptional value." When the U.S. National Archives was formally created in the 1930s, Herbert Hoover dedicated its new building "to the romance of history [which] will have living habitation here in the writing of statement, soldiers, and all the others, both men and women, who have built the great structure of our national life." Great national stories in both places were thus constructed around essential people, political parties, and their documents, as well as the institutions that supported them.[6]

Material Conditions, Emotional Fields, Power, and Their "Voices"

How are these issues relevant to our understanding of revolutionary Russia? With the barriers to archival access largely knocked away in Russia, and all sorts of new evidence available on the period concerning events in the provinces, the

---

[4] See the journal pieces by Gertrude Himmelfarb and Lawrence Stone from *Times Literary Supplement* and *Past and Present*, among other contributions in Keith Jenkins, ed., *The Postmodern History Reader* (London: Routledge, 1997); Anthony Grafton, *The Footnote: A Curious History* (Cambridge, MA: Harvard University Press, 1999); Mary Poovey, *A History of the Modern Fact* (Chicago: University of Chicago Press, 1998).

[5] R. F. Berkhofer, *Beyond the Great Story: History as Text and Discourse* (Cambridge, MA: Harvard University Press, 1996), vii, xii.

[6] D. McCoy, *The National Archives* (Chapel Hill: University of North Carolina Press, 1978), 72. See the discussion in Francis X. Blouin and William G. Rosenberg, *Processing the Past: Contesting Authority in History and the Archives* (New York: Oxford University Press, 2011), ch. 2.

disintegration of empire, gender issues, the mobilization of nationalities, and the like, the historiography has thickened even as popular interest everywhere seems to have declined. The answer proposed by this study's contribution to an already vast literature is twofold. First, there is the nature and effects of increasing material scarcity and physical loss between 1914 and 1922 and the complex emotional fields of insecurity and anxiety that accompanied them in a variety of ways. The actual circumstances here are difficult to assess. Material conditions varied substantially in different times and localities and even within different communities. The ostensible objectivity of statistics often cloaked inadequacies in the way they were gathered and radical differences in localities that bedeviled contemporary analysts. Moods, emotions, and emotional fields—those conditions where one's feelings are determined in part by those perceived to be experienced by nearby others, like the patriotism of soldiers marching in parades or the contagious anger of striking workers—are inherently difficult to discern in real time, much less historically. Moreover, the key issues here are not simply, and in some ways not even primarily, the social and emotional circumstances in which Russia's wars and revolutions were situated during this awful period of sociopsychological dislocation and political upheaval, but in the ways these conditions, in all of their uncertainties, presented very real and very complicated problems that every one of the familiar contenders for power was forced to confront. Here, too, consequently, the forms and locations of power itself become a central part of the problems themselves. Power came "out of the barrel of a gun" in revolutionary Russia, but it was also embedded in the ability to bring vital production to a halt, control the means of transport that were essential to the distribution of scarce goods, and rearrange village social relations by consensual agreement rather than laws or degrees: that fertile and unsewn land should not be private property, for example, and that peasants who had separated their holdings from community possession had to be brought back into the fold.

Second, there is the closely related matter of the languages in which these matters were expressed and addressed: the importance of understanding the roles of "voice and viewpoint," as Berkhofer put it, in the ways leading individual and collective actors expressed or reflected them, how they might have been heard or translated into political acts and policies, and their relationship to historically imagined possibilities about Russia's rational and logical progress toward full-fledged modernity and well-being. In ways the first few chapters of this study will describe, the very scale of the war's carnage and its effects destabilized historical mindsets from the moment Imperial Russia entered the conflict in July 1914. It also engendered powerful new voices of its own. Scarcity, grievous loss, and the anxieties of need and insecurity themselves created an increasingly urgent need to explain and describe what for many was increasingly inexplicable and indescribable, to bring narrative coherence, in other words, to the individual and collective convulsions on the territories of Imperial Russia's dissolving empire.

Although important work has been done on some of these issues, especially by younger British, German, and American scholars as well as a small group of Russian historians in the post-Soviet period liberated from earlier analytical constraints, none of the Great Stories of war and revolution in Russia focuses principally on these convulsions in terms of the range of solutions that were available to political actors of all persuasions or the forms of power and languages in which they were addressed. In their various iterations, the liberal, democratic socialist, and Soviet Great Stories all maintain implicitly or directly that agency, reason, and the longer-term processes of modernization constituted the elements of progressive historical change and allowed the possibility of correcting what in Russia after 1914 seemed to go terribly wrong. In fact, modern war brought increasing dissidence, uprisings, radical political change, and the unrestrained violence of civil war. Scarcity, loss, and their accompanying anxieties grew steadily into "life in catastrophe," as the Russian historian Igor Narskii has emotively described it, presenting contemporaries and historians alike with the daunting task of understanding and explaining how this could have happened.[7]

Historical Imagination and Its Mindsets

Throughout the revolutionary period in Russia one of the striking aspects of what Berkhofer calls "voice and viewpoint" was the commonality of historical thinking itself among leading political activists. In contrast to the way 1917 was marked in 2017, this seems like a quaint anachronism. Putin's Russia and Trump's America lack historical perspective and historical understanding. Neither looks forward or back in any clear way. For a short time after 1991, "Where is Russia going?" (*Kuda idet Rossiia?*) was a common question, a residue of institutionalized Soviet teleology and the title of an annual publication. By 2017, variants of Francis Fukuyama's notion of the "end of history" seemed so firmly rooted that the question was no longer given serious attention.[8] The United States and Russia both relied on presentist ideologies of social stability and individual wealth untethered by any ideologized sense of progressive historical change. For Putin and his supporters an uninformed nostalgia for an imagined past "greatness" substituted for informed understanding and even rudimentary knowledge of historical origins. Teleology was Greek philosophy. In sharp contrast, virtually

---

[7] Igor Narskii, *Zhizn' v katastrofe* (Moscow: Rosspen, 2001).
[8] Francis Fukuyama, *The End of History and the Last Man* (New York: Free Press, 1992).

all of the principal political figures in revolutionary Russia thought historically about their circumstances and positions. Their viewpoints were situated teleologically in a clear sense of how history could and should develop, including those of the sadly incapable tsar who saw himself bearing the god-given values and three-hundred-year-old Romanov traditions borne by his "unforgettable" father, the notoriously repressive Alexander III, as he expressed it at his coronation in May 1986.

One useful way of understanding these historical mindsets is to resist distilling them into distinct political ideologies, although they are certainly amenable to such reductions, and to think of them instead as variants on what the intellectual historian and theorist Hayden White has elegantly described as "deep structures of historical imagination": modes of thought that, consciously or not, prefigure ways historical stories are written.[9] White carefully explores nineteenth-century European historical writing in these terms, focusing on Hegel, Michelet, Ranke, Tocqueville, and Burckhardt, none of whom was politically engaged in creating the histories they analyzed. During the Russian revolutionary conjuncture, in contrast, the historical imaginations of leading actors shaped the contending ways the revolutionary story was understood as it developed, as well as the ways it was initially told in documents, memoirs, and participant histories. With the presumed authority of personal experience, the renowned historian and publicist Paul Miliukov, who served briefly as foreign minister in 1917, joined Lenin's commissar of foreign affairs and head of the Red Army Lev Trotsky and others in writing their own early versions of the Great Stories. Miliukov and Trotsky both wrote three-volume studies objectively titled *History of the Russian Revolution*. The populist socialist revolutionary and minister of agriculture in 1917, Viktor Chernov, went a step farther and labeled his four-hundred-plus pages *The Great Russian Revolution*. In the defensive and self-aggrandizing Kerensky's case, it was *The Crucifixion of Liberty* and *Russia and History's Turning Point*, both titles connoting that a victimized Kerensky himself stood at the apex of world-historical change.[10]

These and other historically minded activists wove the documentation they helped produce into powerful and variously convincing narratives, filtering both sources and events through the perceptions and languages of their own historical imaginations and experience. Moreover, there was an interesting commonality between them despite their sharp political differences, a consequence

---

[9] Hayden White, *Metahistory: The Historical Imagination in Nineteenth Century Europe* (Baltimore, MD: Johns Hopkins University Press, 1973).

[10] Paul Miliukov, *The Russian Revolution* (Gulf Breeze, FL: Academic International Press, 1978–87); Leon Trotsky, *The Russian Revolution* (London: Routledge, 1961); Viktor Chernov, *The Great Russian Revolution* (New Haven, CT: Yale University Press, 1936); Alexander Kerensky, *Russia and History's Turning Point* (New York: Duell, 1965).

of their mutual upbringing during a modernizing age of scientific reason and discovery. For historians, the nineteenth-century Rankean seminar with its devotion to archives and textual evidence offered a science of history, Hegel's writing the laws of history itself. Auguste Comte and the new field of sociology distilled communities and social relations in connection with the dialectical logics of change, especially (but not only) in its Marxian variants. Science was also creating maps of the mind in addition to poison gas, airplanes, and long-range artillery. Freud was popular. Russian physicians and others would soon use psychology's new insights to invent the concept "shell shock" as they treated the unprecedented traumas of modern war.[11] For virtually all of the major political actors in revolutionary Russia, historical progress was not simply a secular metaphor for social and political life. It was a shared conviction in the scientific possibility of social betterment, civil liberties, and intelligent rule.

In the liberal historical imagination broadly defined, progress was realized by rational governance, competent and well-informed officials capable of effectively managing the state. The proper use of reason and rationality moved history in a progressive direction toward individual and collective liberty and socioeconomic improvement. Reason and rationality also gave possibility to the historically inherent logics and processes of socioeconomic betterment and individual freedom. Among other elements these involved the institutional mediation of competitive social interests, the rationalization of economic production and distribution, and the structuring of state institutions to support the individual rights and legal structures rationality required—all familiar parts of liberal political programs. In its Russian revolutionary context, the liberal Great Story eschewed any notion of divine intervention or fatalism. Looking through Peter the Great's "window on the West," it also rejected any notion of historical inevitability or divine ordination, even if its underlying logic forecast the likelihood, not simply the desirability, of certain kinds of social and political change.

Politically, Russian liberals during the revolutionary period can be divided into conservative, centrist, and left-leaning groups, but central to their common historical imagination was thus a strong notion of historical agency that privileged the roles of history's Napoleons and Rasputins as well as "responsible" monarchs and prime ministers. Toward this end, the authority of an enlightened autocrat could use state power to overcome the resistance of antiquated officials, outmoded social formations, ineffective economic practices, antiquated traditions, and underdeveloped cultural and socioeconomic conditions. A major step in this progressive direction occurred during the upheavals of 1905, when Nicholas was pressured into establishing a representative State Duma with

---

[11] See esp. Jan Plamper, "Soldiers and Emotions in Early Twentieth Century Russian Military Psychology," *Slavic Review* 68, no. 2 (2009): 259–83.

significant power especially over the nonmilitary state budget, albeit on a highly restricted franchise. In principle, constitutional monarchy was fully achievable in Russia, and for many, especially after the war began in 1914.

As Russia's major liberal party, Kadets included activists of various inclinations, largely held together by a forceful Miliukov. Together they presented themselves as above partisan social interests (*nadpartiinost'*) and committed to progressive and enlightened statesmanship (*gosudarstvenost'*). Along with their more conservative liberal colleagues in the Octobrist Party they saw a strong state as a vital guard against the destructive potential of mass activism, a guarantor of law and formal authority. Centrist and more conservative liberals saw themselves struggling *for* the disadvantaged and less cultured social sectors whom Miliukov in 1905 urged therefore to "stay peaceful and calm."[12] For more left-leaning liberals, both within and outside the Kadet Party, their voices of reason also had to be extended toward Russia's vital social forces (*zhivye sily*) as a whole, working with their democratic socialist colleagues to support worker and peasant trade unions and other associations that would ensure popular needs were rationally articulated and pursued.

In terms of social partisanship, the democratic socialist historical imagination differed sharply. This was not only because it linked state institutions to particular social (class) interests but also because its various parties and tendencies emphasized the possibility of social welfare, civil liberties, and liberal political reforms pressured from below by rational organization, social mobilization, and a leadership capable of using the instruments of state power in coalition with others to assure a stable democratic socialist order.

Here, too, there were various strains of thought and political inclination, from Menshevik social democrats tied to Russia's rapidly growing proletariat and close to liberals in matters like civil liberties, to those like Trotsky's mentor Iulii Martov and others who were close to Lenin's radical internationalists. Democratic socialists also included the center and right factions of Chernov's peasant-based Socialist Revolutionary Party, which had its roots in Russian populism. Together they commonly recognized, as all socialists did, a complementary source of power outside the purview of the state: that of the ability of workers or peasants to withhold labor to achieve political goals by strikes and protest demonstrations, or otherwise apply pressure from below to secure essential reforms from above. In this the more radical Left Socialist Revolutionaries saw themselves as heirs of the populist terrorist of the 1880s who succeeded in assassinating the Tsar Emancipator Alexander II in an effort to inspire a peasant uprising. The historically determined processes of modernization, in other

[12] A full discussion is in my "Representing Workers and the Liberal Narrative of Modernity," *Slavic Review* 55, no. 2 (1996): 245–70.

words, made socially instituted power a formidable rival to the monopoly on power claimed and legitimized by the state.

Underlying the democratic socialist imagination was also an explanation in events through the ways they related to each other and the more formal "laws" of historical change: Hegelian and Marxian laws of dialectical causality rooted in class interests and relationships. Thus the question of agency was also a point of difference between most democratic socialists and liberals. The argument of many moderate socialists that Russian workers and peasants had to "mature" into full consciousness of their circumstances for democratic socialism to take root limited for some the kinds of activism they and their parties should pursue. Social power had to be effectively deployed to assist in the realization of civil rights and political freedoms, not simply mobilized and unleashed.

Here the events of 1905 held broader implications than those related only to the possibilities of constitutional democracy. The tsar's October Manifesto establishing the Duma and granting other limited rights was the consequence of massive strikes in September and October 1905, coordinated in part by a council (*soviet*) of delegates from many leading St. Petersburg factories. The power immanent in mass social action was demonstrable and irrefutable. But so was the power of the state to repress it with the coercive military and police forces held exclusively at its command. When strikes and demonstrations continued in Moscow after the October Manifesto, tsarist authorities bombarded the working-class districts with artillery. Casualties were extensive. When peasants pressed their demands for land and the end of burdens imposed by the 1861 reforms, Prime Minister Peter Stolypin declared martial law. Military courts-martial in the villages hanged as many as five thousand, most likely more. In this respect, behind the democratic socialist Great Story was a strong appreciation of the (dialectical) power of reaction. Ideological optimism about the historical eventuality of socialism was tempered by a recognition of the roles malevolent actors and conspiracies could play, although these were not trivial, but of the strength and staying power of those who had so much to lose from the end of the autocratic order. Throughout the revolutionary period, socialist as well and liberal memories of 1905 strengthened the grip of history itself on viewpoints and voices.

In terms of White's "deep structures of historical imagination," however, many democratic socialists had much in common with their democratic liberal counterparts during Russia's wars and revolutions after 1914. For both, teleologies of historical progress were rooted in processes of modernization: the institutional rationalization of competitive social interests, the economic processes of production and distribution, and the technological competence of the state institutions that oversaw them. The centrality of reason and rationality to historical progress thus lay behind the democratic socialist Great Story as it did the democratic liberal one, even (and perhaps especially) in understanding and struggling against thoughts and behaviors they deemed "irrational." Fatalism and anything remotely resembling divine intervention also had no place. More passively than in the liberal imagination, but still central as well, was the role of parties composed of politically conscious and clear-thinking activists, midwives rather than parents to progressive historical change.

Here, too, consequently, the overwhelming bulk of historical documentation produced and assembled by democratic socialists closely resembled that of the liberals. This was not simply because evidence about workers' and peasants' attitudes and behaviors was intrinsically difficult to collect, but because the democratic socialist Great Story was also structured around party policies, programs, actions, and the perspectives of their members. The rich trove of Menshevik materials stored unread for years in the Central Party Archive in Moscow until the 1990s contained exactly the kind of documents found in the archives of Russian liberals: official protocols of party meetings, resolutions in multiple variants, and the like.[13] In Stanford, Amsterdam, and elsewhere, these materials are augmented by private correspondence, memoir materials, various brochures, and other memorabilia from private collections, all immensely valuable but almost none that inform historians about the social subjects of democratic socialist concerns.

These sorts of materials, so valuable to social historians, were brought to the foreground only in the construction of the Soviet Great Story, systematically collected and archived by the Bolsheviks after Lenin nationalized all Russian archives and private document collections in June 1918. For Lenin and his supporters, of course, the Great Story was historically determined by the social position and power of workers and poor peasants even in Russia's relatively underdeveloped capitalist order. Radically contending against all others, it nonetheless was also centered in a mindset that imagined reason and rationality governing a socialist/communist utopia once the laws of history ran (or were pushed along) their course. For Lenin and his followers, reason was *embedded* in history, following Hegel and Marx, not simply applied by historical actors, and based on historical laws of causality. Agency mattered not in terms of an inevitable longer-term trajectory but in the timing of its realization. History could be shoved, and shoved forcefully, in the direction it was ordained to take if its pushers had the power to effect the radical changes it ordained. In brief, the creation de novo of Soviet-style socialism, the ultimate historicist project, validated in its revolutionary enactment both the formally rational theories of

---

[13] See the important article by Ziva Galili, "Archives and Historical Writing: The Case of the Menshevik Party in 1917," in *Archives, Documentation, and Institutions of Social Memory*, ed. F. X. Blouin and William G. Rosenberg (Ann Arbor: University of Michigan Press, 2006), 443–50.

nineteenth-century Marxism and the most irrational elements of their brutal Leninist enactment.

As the Leninist and then Soviet Great Story ideologized Marxian rationality into historical law, scientific documentation not only became the essential verification of historical explanation. It also constituted the scientific foundations of Bolshevik political legitimacy, the party's historically determined right to rule. Evidence to the contrary was thus intrinsically dangerous. Nationalizing the archives in 1918 was also the nationalization of historical description, explanation, and truth, along with Soviet historical memory. What became the world's largest cohort of state archivists sorted hundreds of thousands of documents or more into prescribed categories in ways that turned the radical Bolshevik historical imagination into Soviet historical reality, even as laws making the unauthorized destruction of documents a crime against state property would prove to be a huge if unintended gift to historians after the Soviet regime and its Great Story both collapsed.[14]

The Focus of This Study

This study goes beyond the Great Stories of the Russian Revolution by exploring 1914–22 as a period of increasingly difficult sets of problems that each successive government and each contending form of power were forced by circumstances to address. The most pressing of these had to do with the actualities and perceptions of increasing scarcities in a wide range of essential goods: food especially and other goods of "primary necessity," as they were called in Russian; fuel for heating and industrial production; military equipment and supplies for armies and paramilitary forces; capital to sustain wages and industry; and functioning locomotives and freight cars to distribute goods. The role and effectiveness of markets and market exchange itself were closely related here, as we will see, and the difficult problem of effectively regulating prices.

A second set of problems related to the enormous scale of loss throughout the revolutionary period in all of its many dimensions: physical loss in unimaginable and unprecedented military causalities; the corresponding losses of civilians and purported enemies murdered or displaced from their homes and communities; the loss for many of social place and position; and the loss of a common sense of security in a revolutionary world described variously at the

---

[14] See the materials in Blouin and Rosenberg, *Archives,* esp. those by V. V. Lapin, former director of the Russian State Historical Archive (RGIA) and his mentor, the academician B. V. Ananich. The story of Istpart, the Bolsheviks' special historical commission in the 1920s, is told by Larry Holmes, *Revising the Revolution: The Unmaking of Russia's Official History of 1917* (Bloomington: Indiana University Press, 2021).

time and afterward as one of great grief, anxiety, fear, derangement, and turmoil (in Russian, *gore, trevoga, strakh, ogorchenie, smuta*). All of this involves traumas of various sorts and finds expression in mourning and nostalgia, despondency and despair, and sometimes fearsome rage.[15] For many who survived, loss of this magnitude changed their very conception of right and wrong, empowering various sorts of violent behavior. For others, like the great writer Vladimir Nabokov, the Bolsheviks took away their childhood.[16]

There were, of course, other kinds of problems during these tumultuous years that political actors of all stripes had to face, many well treated in the literature: the very scale of the Great War itself, for example, as well as the bloody civil wars that followed; the ethnic and national diversity of the empire, in which all political institutions were vulnerable to continuous pulls toward autonomy and independence, especially those of political democracy; the position of revolutionary Russia in a bitterly contentious international order and the threats and effects of foreign intervention; the sharp disparities between formal and popular cultures that reinforced social difference and impeded the sense of national unity and purpose so important to Germany, France, and Britain during these difficult years. The problems related to scarcity and loss, however, were of a different nature and order of magnitude. They joined the actualities of circumstance to individual feelings and common emotional fields. They were articulated in powerful voices and violent, coercive actions. They demanded attention to perceptions as well as actualities. And most important, they defied in their scale and complexity effective solutions that correlated to the mindsets and historical imaginations of the period's major political actors, even the most ideologized.

In this conceptualization, the political revolutions of 1917 were the consequence of a popular uprising and a successful if unexpected military insurrection. Its proximate origins began with the world war in July 1914, although, as much of the literature has rightly argued and as this study will also discuss in relevant places, its socioeconomic and cultural dimensions had deeper structural roots in Russia's efforts to modernize politically, socioculturally, and economically, especially after the emancipation of the serfs and other important reforms of the 1860s. In important ways Russia's first revolutionary experience in 1905 also carried residues that very much affected political and historical mindsets after 1914, as well as key events like the organization of the Petrograd Soviet in February and the network of local committees and soviets that followed. But as the first part of this study will argue, the outbreak of world war radically altered the context and circumstances of Russia's future development, as did the brief

---

[15] An excellent discussion is in David L. Eng and David Kazanjian, eds., *Loss: The Politics of Mourning* (Berkeley: University of California Press, 2003).

[16] Vladimir Nabokov, *Speak Memory*, rev. ed. (New York: Putnam, 1966), 73.

historical moment of political democracy between February and October 1917 and the vicious conflicts and destruction of total civil war.

How were the early military disasters processed and understood at the front as well as the high places of state power, when the Imperial Russian Army, the largest in Europe, was sent to fight "for tsar and country"? Between July and December 1914, Russia mobilized 5.1 million men into a standing army of 1.4 million. By the summer of 1915, an additional 2.3 million had been drafted, bringing the total number of men under arms in the first year of war to a staggering 8.8 million. By 1917 that number had nearly doubled.[17] A small but significant number of women also managed to become soldiers between 1914 and 1916, some mobilized after the February revolution into the celebrated "Battalion of Death" in part to shame their male comrades into staying in the fight.[18] According to the best available information, between the outbreak of war and January 1, 1917, Russia suffered almost 3 million battlefield casualties. Many of those listed at the front as "seriously wounded" died soon afterward, including many of the 32,000 severely incapacitated by poison gas attacks. More than 2.7 million others were taken prisoner or otherwise unaccounted for. Thus, 40 percent of the Russian army was lost in thirty months of fighting, an average of almost 200,000 men a month. Some 1.5 million were missing. More than 3 million civilians became refugees—a "whole empire walking," as Peter Gatrell has described it so well. By January 1917 the cumulative total of war refugees reached 6 million; by July it was 7.4 million. Total military casualties themselves by the time the world war ended for Russia were above 7 million as well.[19] How were these "shocks of war" expressed? How were they discerned and assessed and filtered into state politics and public perceptions? Was Russian society and its political economy adequately prepared for a conflict of this magnitude? Were losses of this magnitude related to deficits in goods or morale or the strident voices of "extreme need" that began to spread even more rapidly than scarcity itself, obscuring actualities and becoming a problem in itself?

As Imperial Russia moved toward February 1917, how were the related issues and arguments over production, distribution, inflation, and the difficult questions of markets and prices increasingly understood? How and why were these matters also related to the administration of state finances, on one hand,

---

[17] Tsentral'noe Statisticheskoe Upravlenie [henceforth TsSU], *Rossiia v mirovoi voine, 1914–1918 goda (v tsifrakh)* (Moscow, 1925), 17, 30.

[18] See Laurie S. Stoff, *They Fought for the Motherland: Russia's Women Soldiers in World War I and the Revolution* (Lawrence: University of Kansas Press, 2006); Melissa Stockdale, "'My Death for the Motherland Is Happiness': Women, Patriotism, and Soldiering in Russia's Great War, 1914–1917," *American Historical Review* 109, no. 1 (February 2004): 78–116; P. P. Shcherbinin, *Voennyi faktor v povsednevnoi zhizni russkoi zhenshchiny v XVIII–nachale XX v.* (Tambov, 2004), 424–44.

[19] Peter Gatrell, *A Whole Empire Walking* (Bloomington: Indiana University Press, 1999), citing E. Z. Volkov, *Dinamika narodonaseleniia SSSR za vosem'desiat let* (Moscow, 1930), 212; TsSU, *Rossiia v mirovoi voine*, 30.

and value systems, on the other, that were reflected in the ways requisition, confiscation, and markets themselves attempted to address them as scarcities and their accompanying anxieties continued to increase? Between 1914 and 1917 the prices of essential goods rose everywhere in Russia, as they did in other warring powers. They found increasing expression in food riots and other forms of protest: a crowd of "mostly women" shouting that they were starving and throwing rocks at shops that refused to honor ration cards, for example.[20] The financial costs of the war were also proving to be immense, far more than even the most knowledgeable people in Russia (or elsewhere) could have predicted, greatly aggravating inflation. In the beginning of 1916, Finance Minister Peter Bark and his forceful liberal critic Andrei Shingarev were in fierce conflict over the likely costs and consequences of two more years of fighting, something no one thought possible when the war first began. By November Bark reported that the cost of the war had exceeded 15 billion rubles and might have been as high as 25 billion, largely financed by loans and unbacked currency emissions.[21] How (and whether) the state could meet these obligations remained unclear. In the meantime, its printing presses had to keep churning. By the fall of 1917, after Shingarev himself as minister of finance in the Provisional Government had done his best to stop the flow, state outlays were a staggering 1.5 billion rubles a month, almost all financed by the printing press.[22]

How did new public organizations like the War Industries Committees and the city and rural (*zemstvo*) organizations discussed in chapters 4 and 5 relate these issues to faults in tsarist state administration and its centralization of power before liberals and democratic socialists had to confront them head-on in 1917? Was tsarist state finance actually a "bacchanalia of corruption," as the newspaper *Birzhevye Vedomosti* (*Stock Market News*) insisted in January 1916?[23] Were the state's efforts to "militarize" the workforce appropriate solutions? Did the front-line experience itself and the obscuring objectivity of statistics cloud the actual levels of individual and collective deprivation, and even more so their accompanying anxieties, perhaps especially (but certainly not only) for women burdened as well by the loss of husbands, sons, and fathers and various levels and forms of grief? At high levels as well as in towns and villages, speculation and market manipulation also caused great concern. Conservative liberals within or close to government circles like Peter Struve and Alexander Krivoshein wanted fixed prices extended to all foodstuffs. Duma president Mikhail Rodzianko

---

[20] RGIA, f. 1276, op. 11, d. 167, ll. 254–55, 272, 281, 297.
[21] RGIA f. 565, op. 2, d. 555 ll. 1–2; G. Demetr'ev, *Gosudarstennye dokhody i raskhody Rossii i polozhenie gosudarstvennago kaznacheistva za vremia voiny s Germaniei I Avstro-vengriei do kontsa 1917 god* (Petrograd 1917), 31.
[22] A. I. Shingarev, *Finansovoe polozhenie Rossii* (Petrograd: Synod, 1917), 1011.
[23] *Birzhevye Vedomosti*, Jan. 24, 1916.

and the leader of the tsar's loyal conservative liberal Octobrist Party, Alexander Guchkov, pressed for nationalizing major military suppliers remaining in private hands, particularly the gigantic Putilov complex in Petrograd, whose striking workers would rapidly expand the popular uprising that ended Romanov rule. How did Andrei Shingarev, speaking in the Duma as the liberals' voice of conscience, characterize the increasing gulf between Russia's moneyed social elites, who could access scarce goods, and those "below," the *nizy*, many of whom in urban areas lost their jobs or were otherwise penalized when they left work to search for food? And what were the likely connections between the practices and cultures of "war capitalism," popular resistance, and contending notions of fairness?

By the winter of 1916 virtually all leading political figures thought Russia was already "approaching catastrophe," as the tsarist minister of interior himself was warning.[24] An important event in both practical and symbolic terms was the failure of General Aleksei Brusilov to break through the Austrian and German lines in the late spring of 1916 in an effort to force them out of the war. The heralded Brusilov offensive was also a catastrophe in terms of the losses it inflicted. Against almost all of the prescriptions of contending historical imaginations in late 1916, Imperial Russia seemed to be lurching toward upheaval and "drowning in blood."[25] By October, scarcity and "the food question" preoccupied all leading actors, public forums, and the press. In these circumstances, prescriptive "solutions" became the primary scripts for the revolutionary events that followed.

How, then, should we place the story of the political changes of 1917 within the socioeconomic and sociocultural circumstances that lay behind them—the multiple conditions and dimensions of scarcity and loss that continued to exacerbate under Russia's first historic experiment with political democracy? The roles of perceptions as well as actualities, of anxieties over scarcities and prices as well as their material levels, continue to ground the discussion. So does the complex question of loss, now expressed openly and clearly in the quest to give the First World War some comprehensible and acceptable meaning. Here, the radical political changes so thoroughly described in the literature affected the ways and locations in which these and other issues were approached. The devolution of state authority downward from the center that animated efforts by Russia's "responsible publics" to empower special plenipotentiaries and local officials before 1917 were now institutionalized in unexpected ways. Railroads were democratized from above to empower administrative committees on the lines. Trade unions and factory committees were formally authorized to negotiate

[24] RGIA f. 457, op. 1. d. 209 l. 3 ob.
[25] Russian State Military History Archive [RGVIA] f. 2003, op. 1, d. 1486 ll. 190, 222.

workers' interests with factory owners in order to increase productivity and rationalize wages. Liberals and democratic socialists both agreed that successful mediation was essential to stem escalating social conflict.

With the formation of the first liberal-socialist coalition government in early May 1917, a new Ministry of Labor was created under the prominent Menshevik and vice chair of the Soviet Executive Committee Matvei Skobelev, who served in the position through September. The democratic socialist economist Vladimir Groman, meanwhile, a leading member of the prestigious Chuprov Society for the Development of Social Science at the University of Moscow, became head of the Soviet's own Economic Commission. The venerable social democrat Georgi Plekhanov headed another commission under the Kadet engineer and minister of transport Nikolai Nekrasov to address the wage levels for railroad workers.

Groman also played an active role in the government's Special Council for Defense in 1915 and 1916 and led the Union of Cities in publicly addressing the problems of markets and prices. In 1917 he found himself charged by the Petrograd Soviet Executive Committee to solve them. Faced with a similar task as they related to Russia's railroads, the country's "lifeline," as they were called, Plekhanov essentially threw up his hands. Perhaps most dramatic in terms of the ways the Great Stories of 1917 would develop, the firebrand socialist Alexander Kerensky added the post of minister of war to his responsibilities as minister of justice. Immediately Kerensky began working closely with General Brusilov on plans for another offensive, one that both mistakenly insisted would protect the revolution by finally bringing the war to a successful end. Even before its launching in June, Kerensky had become the first cult figure of the revolutionary period, as the Russian historian Boris Kolonitskii has detailed, eclipsing for a brief moment the recently returned Lenin and everyone else in public recognition and popular support.[26]

Why, then, did the problems of scarcity and their accompanying anxieties not diminish? Why was Shingarev, so sharply critical of tsarist minister Bark, unable to effectively address inflation and come to despair of his efforts? Why were Groman and others unable to present the Soviet and Provisional Government with a workable plan to fix prices and regulate exchange? And what were the implications of Labor Minister Skobelev's failed efforts in his newly created Special Division for the Resolution of Conflict between Management and Labor, as well as those of Plekhanov in his work with railroaders? How in this context did the irregular solutions to the problem of scarcity and the distribution of goods before 1917 gain a stronger hold, despite the efforts of Skobelev, Plekhanov, Gromon, and others to contain them? In the process, both the formal

---

[26] Boris I. Kolonitskii, *Tovarishch Kerenskii: Antimonarkhicheskaia revoliutsiia i formirovanie kul'ta "Vozhdia Naroda" mart–iiun' 1917 goda* (Moscow: NLO, 2017).

exercise of state and soviet power and the increasing (and increasingly bitter) competition between political parties and social formations were contrasted to the ways power of a different sort was exercised in strikes and demonstrations. In contrast to the Great Stories in each of their variations, however, focus here is on the *limits* of addressing effectively the material and emotional needs that underlay the revolutionary uprising itself, the "democratic predicament" of October.

Understanding Russia's revolutionary processes in these ways should allow us to resituate the familiar story of Lenin and his Bolsheviks capturing what was left of state power in October quite differently from the narratives of political chicanery and personal will—the "only way," Kerensky wrote in *Crucifixion of Liberty*, that civil liberties and political democracy were prevented from coming to Russia.[27] Lenin's political machinations and rather incredible will to power are vitally important here, of course. The securing if not simply the seizing of state power obviously became the instrument through which the Bolshevik dictatorship was successfully institutionalized, at least in terms of its total monopoly on formal power and its ultimate control over the informal power immanent in demonstrations and other forms of social protest. But the socioeconomic and sociocultural circumstances of October still need further attention: from the brief but prescient life of the "Railroad Republic" in September and the increasing spread of well-honed practices of confiscation and requisition to resolve problems of scarcity and distribution, to the violent implications of the cumulative effects of material and emotional loss, among its other probable causes. In the narrative here, Lenin and his comrades came to power imagining their understanding of historical progress would enable these problems finally to be solved, at least for workers, peasants, and those few others determined by the Bolsheviks' historical imagination entitled to enjoy them.

The argument here is that these themes can be followed to their logical, if devastating, conclusions in both the socioeconomic and political complexities of civil war. Why "war communism" was even less able than "war capitalism" to deal effectively with Russia's revolutionary circumstances is a point of entry into some of the neglected aspects of the Bolsheviks' quest to rule, including the "flying inspections" that avidly if futilely sought to uncover the huge suspected quantities of hoarded goods, as they did again in the goods famine following the dissolution of the Soviet Union, and the comprehensive institutionalization of requisition, confiscation, and militarization of labor that tsarist authorities had also thought might ease the problems of scarcity and loss. The difficult issue for historians of this period is not only to find words to adequately reflect the material and emotional deprivations of life in catastrophe after 1918. It is also to sift

---

[27] Alexander Kerensky, *The Crucifixion of Liberty* (New York: John Day, 1934).

through the causes and nature of the unrestrained violence that reached every corner of the former tsarist empire as demobilized soldiers and deserters found their way back to cities, towns, and villages and became Reds, Whites, and multiple shades of Green in ferocious struggles for retribution and survival, and those both within and outside Bolshevik control fought to secure or avoid the Leninist historical vision of Russia's past and future.

A Methodological Challenge: Reading beyond Description

If the effects of scarcities and loss constitute a key part of experience during the Russian revolutionary period, how are historians to access them in analytically useful ways? The sources for this study include letters, speeches, protest demands, descriptions of actions, and other primary sources that express a range of feelings, especially those of soldiers and their families who experienced the effects of loss almost as a matter of routine. To reduce the filtering effects that historical narration inevitably brings to the ways sources are used, it is largely based on archival documents. But how can one be sure that the feelings described in archival documents and other primary materials themselves accurately reflect what was actually felt, that archival descriptions do not themselves filter individual or shared feelings through the social and cultural norms they also engage, or the possible expectations of their readers, including military censors and the police?

There is also a problematic relation between the expression of individual emotions and what are presented here and in other studies as collective feelings: those that are thought reductively to be experienced as if the collective were an organic emotional whole. Are there circumstances wherein individual emotions might reasonably be described as reflecting those of a larger group? And can the ways particular events and their descriptions configure collective feelings also be as important in some ways as the actual array of feelings themselves, as for example during military parades, patriotic celebrations, peasant protests, or labor strikes? At various points throughout this exploration an argument is made that the ways feelings were expressed and described carried significant weight in and of themselves, however accurately they reflected what was actually felt. One might readily understand the likely connections between anxiety and the actual or anticipated scarcity of food, which has earned its own category as "food insecurity" in the psychological repertoire of anxiety disorders given how widespread hunger is felt. This is especially challenging with primary materials alluding to or describing the effects of loss. Evidence like soldiers' letters have to be read with particular attention to the likely filters that affected their expression, as well as the reasons why.

Even the most poignant descriptions in letters and memoirs, moreover, often filter experience into language that conceals as much as it reveals. "We clearly saw they were leading us like cattle to the slaughter," as one soldier wrote home in 1916, almost certainly masks an enraging and humiliating helplessness, even if some military censors read "waiting for death" as expressive of patriotic stoicism. Well into 1917, soldiers wrote about the horrific conditions and neglect of the wounded, longing to be home, their anger toward workers and others who were "betraying" their "sacrifice" ("Hang the rats!"), murderous feelings toward corrupt officers who sold precious food and clothing, outrage that "they have shot thousands of women in Moscow" and at the way they themselves were treated ("like dogs!"). After soldiers and workers both were allowed to organize in 1917, to be treated with dignity became everywhere a nonnegotiable demand.[28] Here almost certainly was the emotional cauldron of anger and loss that helped set the revolutionary trajectory on its violent course.

Yet the analytical difficulty of accessing emotional states and the relationship between individual and collective violence does not diminish the importance historically of the problem of loss itself. Even more so than the huge problems of scarcity and finance in revolutionary Russia's faltering political economy, the nature and effects of loss were difficult to measure in any but the objective terms of casualty statistics or reports on the number of refugees towns and villages now had to support. State-sanctioned violence is always clear in its behaviors, always murky in its subjective effects, as the first discussions of shell shock during the Great War suggest. Common violence is almost always defined by the brutality of its actions rather than the social or psychological brutalization that conditioned it.

Especially among a small number of Russian historians liberated from the restrictions of the Soviet Great Story, there have been serious efforts at delineating the emotional mindsets of the revolutionary period. Vladimir Buldakov and Tatiana Leont'eva especially have made impressive contributions to the literature and have influenced my thinking on the subject.[29] For their colleague Aleksandr Astashov, a defining element of peasant life on the eve of World War I was "the feeling of belonging to the specific place of one's birth," a "sacralization" of an intimate "homeland" that peasants took with them to defend the abstracted homeland at the front.[30] For Olga Porshneva, the sensibilities of peasant soldiers were

[28] For example, RGVIA f. 2003, op. 1, d. 1486, l. 56; f. 2067, op. 1, d. 3853, l. 73 ob.; Diane Koenker and William G. Rosenberg, *Strikes and Revolution in Russia, 1917* (Princeton, NJ: Princeton University Press, 1989), 18, 72–75, 172–74, 275–81.

[29] Among other of their many publications see esp. Vladimir Buldakov, *Krasnaia Smuta* (Moscow: Rosspen, 2010); and "Revolution and Emotions: Toward a Reinterpretation of the Political Events of 1914–1917," *Russian History* 45 no. 2–3 (2018): 196–230; Vladimir Buldakov and Tatiana Leont'eva, *Voina porodivshaia revoliutsiia* (Moscow: Novyi Khronograf, 2015).

[30] A. V. Astashov, "Russkii krest'ianin na frontakh pervoi mirovoi voiny," *Otechestvennaia Istoriia* 2 (Mar. 2003): 72–73.

structured by the instability of the traditional land commune and fraught with hostility toward landowners and state officials thought responsible for keeping the village poor. In her view these feelings combined in a near-constant struggle against the cross-generational pressures of a modernizing and industrializing economy, which were also weakening traditional peasant religiosity and further exacerbating tensions. The French and Canadian historian Corinne Gaudin has taken this argument an important step further, showing how the drawing of soldiers from their villages challenged notions of fairness, service, and sacrifice and displaced peasant anger onto relations with the state and its representatives. The French historian Alexandre Sumpf, meanwhile, has explored every experience at the front that could not help but create profound emotional reactions, from the devastating effects of artillery and machine-gun fire for those caught in the "no man's zone" between the lines to the dangerous and emotionally fraught practices of retrieving bodies, recovering body parts, and burying what was left of the dead.[31]

Especially in connection with the rampant forms of violence that perforated the Russian revolutionary experience from start to finish, however, one can only make reasonable deductions about the likely mix of sources. Why Jews especially were viewed with such suspicion within and around the war zone before 1917 can be easily explained by presumptions that they logically favored more tolerant Austrian and German administrations than Russian ones, but not the brutality with which they were so cruelly assaulted or the apparent pleasure many seemed to find in their distress. We must situate the question of violence within Russia's socioeconomic circumstances in 1919 and 1920, but there is no convincing explanation of why some 100,000 Jews were killed during these years, largely at the hands of marauding anti-Bolsheviks.

We can also recognize that soldiers' letters and other documents expressing emotions that go "against the grain" of shared or common stories, as the anthropologist Ann Stoler has phrased it, can also usefully be read in this regard, as can documents and other sources.[32] Stoler developed the concept with particular attention to archives like the former Central State Archive of the October Revolution in Moscow, where letters and documents contradicting official narratives were nonetheless preserved in special closed repositories. These materials reflect suppressed counter- or "secondary" narratives, as Samuel Hynes has described them, in both their composition and their preservation.[33] At least

---

[31] O. S. Porshneva, *Mentalitet i sotsial'noe povedenie rabochikh, krest'ian i soldat Rossii v period pervoi mirovoi voiny* (Ekaterinburg: Ur. ORAN, 2000); Corinne Gaudin, "Rural Echoes of World War I: War Talk in the Russian Village," *Jahrbücher für Geschichte Osteuropas* 56, no. 3 (2008): 391–414; Alexandre Sumpf, *La Grande guerre oublié: Russie 1914–1918* (Paris: Perrin, 2014).

[32] Ann Stoler, *Along the Archival Grain* (Princeton, NJ: Princeton University Press, 2009).

[33] Samuel Hynes, *The Soldiers' Tale: Bearing Witness to Modern War* (New York: Lane, 1997).

until February 1917, for example, soldiers wrote against the tsarist patriotic grain at their peril. Repression of subversive views was usually brutal and swift. Even sanctions against slandering the tsar and the members of the royal family were quite severe. Similar practices were activated again in both the Red and White armies.

Yet there is ample evidence that secondary or counternarratives were current in some form among Russian soldiers from the moment of mobilization until the end of the civil wars, telling a different story than patriotic loyalty to "Tsar and Fatherland" and "cheerful spirits," as tsarist military censors characterized the soldiers' dominant mood at the front throughout the war. These counternarratives were also sure to engage at some point the radically new experiences the revolution brought to Russia, even if they were not easily or safely written out: the feelings of astonishment, fear, panic, uncertainty, and emotional confusion that sometimes begged labeling. Here, too, one can partly overcome the problem of teasing feelings from texts by recognizing that the sources themselves, especially soldiers' letters home, may also have created the emotions they described. But in contrast to the common story, the risks of going "against the grain" at the front, in factories, in villages, and in the many fraught meetings that animated so much of political life during and after 1917 also authenticate their emotional expressions by giving them a greater "ring of truth." While the problem for historians of accessing feelings remains, this suggests that at least some letters and documents of this sort can carry readers convincingly to the emotions they are read as reflecting, making the problem of access itself less an impediment to emotional understanding.

Putting the Revolution in Its Place: Great Stories and Historical Explanations

The staying power of Great Stories is not in their capacity to describe the past. Embedded in carefully documented scholarly narratives by historians or laid out in books intended to inform social memories, Great Stories always involve explanations for what occurred, a linking of events and people through historical imaginations in ways that give their narrative structures explanatory meaning. Why the revolution occurred is part of the telling how. Why the Bolsheviks came to power positions cause and effect to show how radical social transformations can occur. Implicit in political biography is a theory of history, an explanation based on agency. What this study tries to demonstrate is not that politics and biography are in any way unimportant to historical outcomes, but how the effects of the actualities and emotions of loss and the socioeconomic anxieties and deprivations contextualize the limits of political agency itself—how, for example, conceptualizing demonstrations as emotionally charged sociocultural activism instead of "riots" helps locate the possibilities of social and political transformation in terms of the kinds of power latent in sociocultural formations and its relation to socioeconomic and political contingency.

In its broader conception, Lenin and his party's turn away from War Communism in 1921 marked the end of Russia's revolutionary period—a modern-day "time of troubles," as it was widely described to evoke the period of death and destruction just before the start of the Romanov dynasty in 1613, when Russia lost a third of its population. How, then, should we understand the horrific famine that followed after the fighting largely stopped in late 1921 and 1922, when some 5 million more casualties were added to the more than 20 million military and civilian deaths since the start of the world war in 1914? Were rain and other food supplies actually exhausted? Did the problem continue to lie in the insufficiencies of railroad transport, as many had argued since 1914? And what happened to money itself in this period that impaired Bolshevik efforts to control or eliminate its use as a medium of exchange? Especially during the time of the White armies advances in 1919 and 1920 and the Bolshevik counteroffensives, how were prospects of victory affected by urgent concerns over food as well as politics and military competence? How was it that even in Bolshevik Russia workers describing themselves as "conscious" and "patiently starving revolutionaries" telegraphed from Ivanovo-Voznesensk to protest the center's policies, "Everything is taken from us, nothing is provided.... We have not a pound of reserves.... We can accept no responsibility for what happens if our needs are not met"?[34] As many or more died from all causes in this brutally formative period of Soviet rule as during the Second World War. And why did deprivation and loss continue despite the New Economic Policy Lenin introduced in 1921? When the tenth anniversary of 1917 was celebrated in 1927, Trotsky and other would-be agents of change were certain the revolution's hopes for security and well-being could never be realized under Stalin. What, then, by way of epilogue, were the possible connections, if any, between the effects of scarcity and loss a decade earlier and the revolution's last "Great Leader" unleashing the power of the revolutionary state itself against the peasants and workers whose interests it supposedly represented, the fierce turns to forced draft collectivization and militarized industrialization that gave history another violent push in the "right direction"?

Is this then, finally, why the democratic liberal Great Story took such hold outside Soviet Russia in the revolution's aftermath? Part of the reason rests on the kinds of documents that provide its evidence and suggest the possibility of

---

[34] *Ekonomicheskaia Zhizn'*, Nov. 16, 1918.

its promise. One cannot read through the invaluable series of liberal and democratic socialist party documents published since 1991 without being reinforced about the centrality of politics and possibility in this period. The often remarkable speeches and party protocols encourage one to neglect the complex socioeconomic and sociopsychological issues in which their revolutionary politics were set, and which insistently demanded resolution. Part of the reason as well, perhaps, is because the democratic liberal story is compatible with general Western understandings of historical agency and what are considered to be the inherent dangers of revolutionary circumstance, as Arendt suggested. Certainly this helps explain the authority attributed to works like Pipes's *The Russian Revolution*, published with exquisite timing just as Soviet Russia itself discarded its own Great Story in favor of the neoliberal version he advanced.

In sum, what is lacking in the ways the Great Stories of Russia's war and revolution have largely been told, and what this study tries to remedy, is an understanding of how complex and historically contextualized effects of scarcity and loss related to the revolution's course of development and its outcomes, situating politics and power first and foremost as a set of efforts to address them. It thus attempts to contribute to a further understanding of these enormously difficult problems, including the emotional states that they engendered, problems that every successive holder of any kind of power during this period had somehow to address, and which other large-scale revolutions before and since have struggled with as well. In other words, the effort here is to show how key elements of this seminal historical moment may have been socially and emotionally, as well as politically, constituted, and in this way better situate revolutionary Russia in its historical place.

PART I

THE IMPERIAL MEANINGS OF SCARCITY AND LOSS

1
"Fighting with God" and the Languages of Loss

Just after the Austrian invasion of Serbia on July 14, 1914 (by the Russian calendar), a huge throng gathered in St. Petersburg at the great Kazan Cathedral on Nevskii Prospekt, Russian Orthodoxy's vague replica of St. Peter's Basilica in Rome. What occurred in the capital and elsewhere in Russia has been well described by witnesses and historians alike. In St. Petersburg the crowd cheered the priestly injunction that "to retreat from the dangers of war" would be for Russia an "unthinkable moral rejection of the great historical task of defending the blood interests of the entire Russian people." The "dignity" of an organic Russian state was threatened, along with the "mutuality" of all Slavs.[1] When the handsome forty-six-year-old tsar Nicholas II issued his Imperial Manifesto several days later calling on his subjects to defend their Fatherland, his setting was the great St. Georges Hall in the Winter Palace and his forum was a solemn Holy Mass. The hall itself memorialized the Great Patriotic War against Napoleon in 1812. The Holy Mass, conducted before the miracle-working icon of the Virgin of Kazan specially transported to the palace for the ceremony, blended the sacredness of historical tradition, sacrifice, and national commitment with divine will and intervention. Nicholas deeply believed in his divinely ordained role as the protector of the Orthodox Russian state. According to the French ambassador Maurice Paleologue, the tsar prayed "with a holy fervor that gave his pale face a movingly mystical expression."[2] After the ceremony, an enormous crowd greeted his appearance on a palace balcony, joining on their knees his call for God's blessing on Russia's guns.

Shortly afterward, the tsar convened an extraordinary one-day session of Russia's two parliamentary chambers, the State Council and State Duma. For some the day became one of the most "historical and unforgettable" moments in all of Russian history, "the realization of the holy dreams of the best of our people."[3] Nicholas had always regarded the Duma with resentment and contempt, a dangerous threat to his own God-given powers. Facing the quite

---

[1] RGIA f. 1470 op. 1 d. 391, ll. 2–6.
[2] Maurice Paleologue, *An Ambassador's Memoirs*, 2 vols. (New York: Doran, 1927), 1:74–95.
[3] RGIA, f. 1470, op. 1, d. 391, ll. 18–19.

different challenge of war, the tsar now reached out to an institution he detested on the counsel of his frail and easily tired seventy-five-year-old prime minister, Ivan Logginovich Goremykin, "so as to be in full unity with His people."[4] Even the most oppositional Duma figures responded in kind, declaring their unqualified commitment to "following our tsar in defense of our Fatherland," since it "simply could not be otherwise."[5]

The assembled delegates represented a broad range of experience and outlooks. They applauded the elderly Goremykin when he promised the Duma would be convened into session before its next scheduled assembly six months hence "if events deemed it necessary"; they cheered even louder when he proclaimed, rather fatefully, "[W]e will carry through this war, however it turns out to be, to the very end!"[6] Then, following speeches by Foreign Minister Sergei Sazonov and Finance Minister Peter Bark, fifteen delegates themselves were allowed to speak, representing every major faction in the Duma except the Bolsheviks.

However surprising it might seem in retrospect, each speaker without exception dwelt in some way on the *opportunities* the war was bringing to Russia, albeit with some references to the "noble" and "necessary" sacrifice soldiers and their families would have to endure. Minister of Finance Bark, a former director of one of Russia's leading banks who had long complained about the general stagnation of Russian industry and the need for the state to stimulate investment, seized the opportunity to speak forcefully of the need to "mobilize" Russia's financial resources, a process which required major reforms, as liberals and others had long demanded. Bark's first duty would be to assure the state could provide the massive resources the war would require. To applause and shouts of "Bravo!" he announced the first step in this direction: the right of the state bank to issue short-term treasury notes to the extent required to meet the war's needs. Russia could be "completely confident that the government is ready to bear the broadest costs to meet this urgent need."[7]

The tropes of opportunity and unity dominated every subsequent speech. On behalf of Russia's Jews, "who have always considered themselves citizens of Russia and have always been true sons of their Russian fatherland [*otechestvo*]," Deputy Naftali Fridman pledged that the Jewish people would stand beneath Russia's banners and "fulfill our duty to the very end!" From the extreme right, the notorious reactionary Nikolai Markov II from Kursk, who believed the Talmud forbade Jews taking oaths of service and had fought to exclude them from the military, declared that war would only strengthen and purify holy Russia. He had already seen "with this own eyes" women walking along with their sons and

---

[4] Gosudarstvennaia Duma, *Stenograficheskii otchet*, July 26, 1914, col. 1.
[5] RGIA f. 1470, op. 1, d. 391, l. 18.
[6] Gosudarstvennaia Duma, *Stenograficheskii otchet*, July 26, 1917, cols. 11–12.
[7] Ibid., col. 17.

husbands going to war, "never perhaps to return, without a single reproach or complaint, a single questioning of why, praying for the gift of victory."[8] The most notable speeches, however, came from two men who in 1917 would become leading actors in the drama just begun: Paul Miliukov, the influential historian, publicist, and leader of Russia's liberal Constitutional Democratic Party, who would become foreign minister in 1917; and Alexander Kerensky, the histrionic democratic socialist from Saratov, who would become minister of war and then, from July to October, serve as democratic Russia's last prime minister and most iconic personage.

Miliukov's struggles to make Russia a modern European constitutional democracy in the aftermath of the revolution of 1905 were well known.[9] In the midst of contentious debates about how best to advance this goal, he held firmly to the view that the tsar could eventually be persuaded that rational liberal reforms were vital to Russia's social and economic modernization, and hence its ability to defend and advance its interests as a world power. The outbreak of war gave Russia's liberals an extraordinary opportunity to assert to the tsar himself their support for the state and the need to guide it in a spirit of national unity to the progressive reforms that victory required.[10] Whatever his party's relationship had been to the government's policies in the past, the liberals' first task now was to preserve and protect "one and indivisible" Russia. In its expression of the opportunity the war held for the Russian state, Miliukov gave full voice to the optimistic liberal belief in the power of rational agency to turn the regime in a progressive historical direction. For the first time in his long parliamentary career, he received, according to the transcripts, "stormy applause" from the entire chamber.[11]

This mindset sharply separated the liberal leader from the thirty-three-year-old firebrand Kerensky. Elected to the Fourth Duma as one of only ten moderate Trudoviks, a party loosely linked to the peasant-centered Socialist Revolutionaries, Kerensky positioned himself as an indispensable link between the interests of Russia's rural and urban workers. For him as well as other socialists who rejected the radicals' appeal to vote against war credits and forcefully oppose the war, Kerensky hoped workers and peasants would mobilize to pressure the regime into political and social reform. Seizing the rostrum with the passion he would later display so insistently in 1917, he gave rhetorical flourish to the idea that "great suffering on the field of battle" would "strengthen the brotherhood of all peoples of Russia." In his historical imagination, the power latent in peasant

---

[8] Ibid., cols. 12, 27–28.
[9] The story has been well told by Melissa Stockdale, *Paul Miliukov and the Quest for the Liberal Russia, 1880–1918* (Ithaca, NY: Cornell University Press, 1996).
[10] Paul Miliukov, *Taktika fraktsii narodnoi svobody vo vremia voiny* (Petrograd: PNS, 1916), 2–6.
[11] Gosudarstvennaia Duma, *Stenograficheskii otchet*, July 26, 1914, col. 24.

and worker activism was a necessary element of effective political struggle. His appeal was not to the tsar and his audience but to the broad ranks of peasants and workers he hoped would lead Russia through the "inhuman sufferings, destitution and hunger of war [and] by defending the country, to liberate it."[12]

At this historic moment, at least, the future head of the Provisional Government felt sure he had Imperial Russia's full attention. He was right. In the days that followed, a transcript of the Duma session was printed in a separate edition of 1 million copies.[13] Every leading Russian newspaper and journal parsed and reparsed the delegates' speeches, most reading them back as an opportunity for "fundamental changes" in the relationship between government and society, as the leading newspaper *Russkiia Vedomosti* (*Russian Gazette*) put it: a historic opportunity to review outmoded attitudes and out of necessity create like the French a "union sacrée" to assure military victory and Russian national renewal.[14] For the moment, at least, Lenin and his Bolsheviks, whose internationalist opposition to the war would soon echo from various European sanctuaries, seemed utterly irrelevant to Russia's future. The most famous print of the war, entitled *Holy War*, was soon circulating, representing the tsar in armor on a white steed illuminated by a rising sun and brandishing a sword and shield proclaiming, "God is with Us!"[15] Patriotic feeling seemed to roll outward from St. Petersburg, now renamed Petrograd to reinforce its Russianness, rippling through the European provinces, the Urals, and the vastness of Siberia all the way to Vladivostok some five thousand miles from the capital and soon to be the only major port for foreign military aid.

Assessing Patriotism

For many supporters of Imperial Russia's political and social regimes, no event during the reign of Russia's last tsar seemed more propitious for the future of the autocracy than the outbreak of the First World War—"those wonderful early August days," as the British ambassador Sir George Buchanan later described them.[16] In the first six months of 1914, labor unrest had escalated to levels not seen since the revolutionary turmoil of 1905, a scant nine years before. The massacre (as it was soon known) of Lena gold field workers in 1912 had lit what many worried was a new revolutionary fuse. In 1913 almost 900,000 industrial

---

[12] Ibid., cols. 18–19.
[13] *Istoricheskii Den' 26 Iulia 1914 g.* (Moscow, 1914).
[14] *Russkiia Vedomosti*, Aug. 9, 1914; *Rech'*, July 27, 1914.
[15] Stephen M. Norris, *A War of Images: Russian Popular Prints, Wartime Culture, and National Identity, 1912–45* (DeKalb: Northern Illinois University Press, 2006), 146, 150.
[16] George Buchanan, *My Mission to Russia and Other Diplomatic Memories*, 2 vols. (Boston: Little, Brown, 1923), 1:213.

workers had engaged in more than twenty-four hundred strikes to protest wage and living conditions. In the seven months between January and the end of July 1914, these numbers had grown to more than 1,300,000 workers and thirty-four hundred strikes.[17] Areas of industrial concentration were rife with dissidence, especially the Vyborg district in St. Petersburg across the Neva River from the tsar's Winter Palace. The Presnia district in Moscow, shelled by the regime in December 1905, was again a scene of agitation and protest. Workers, students, members of the intelligentsia, and public figures in and outside the major parties pressed for change.

The countryside was also awash in unrest. The efforts of Peter Stolypin, who would come to be known as Russia's last great statesman, to carve separate households out of traditional village communal holdings as a way to modernize Russian agriculture ran counter to traditional peasant values. It was resented and in some areas strongly resisted. Social democratic activism in both its moderate (largely Menshevik) and radical (largely Bolshevik) inclinations was growing. In many places the differences between these contentious groupings were also blurring, increasing the confidence among followers that the Great Social Democratic Story—a historically determined transition to democratic socialism—would soon be realized. So was peasant support for the broader-based Socialist Revolutionaries who boycotted the Duma to protest a discriminatory franchise that radically underweighted peasants. Even the liberal Constitutional Democrats and the more conservative Octobrists were recalibrating their political strategies on the eve of the war. Some demanded their parties form tactical alliances with groups to their left. Some contemplated a return to the more militant actions that had brought Russia's parliament itself into being in 1905. As Leopold Haimson has notably argued, Imperial Russia was in a state of serious social instability on the eve of the war, in sharp contrast to Germany and Austria.[18]

All of this appeared to dissolve overnight with the outbreak of war. A wave of patriotism unprecedented since the victory over Napoleon one hundred years earlier seemed to flood the country. Suddenly the regime seemed presented with an opportunity to displace festering conflict onto a unifying hostility toward the foreign invader. A collective sense of Russian identity would be nurtured from an ethnically diverse empire around the core beliefs of Orthodoxy and Slavic brotherhood. The tsar himself fervently believed his rightful place was at the head of his troops. Only with great reluctance did he accept the High Command's

---

[17] Diane Koenker and William G. Rosenberg, *Strikes and Revolution in Russia* (Princeton, NJ: Princeton University Press, 1989), 58.
[18] Leopold Haimson, "The Problem of Social Stability in Urban Russia, 1905–1917," *Slavic Review* 4 (1964): 619–42; 1 (1965): 1–25.

insistence that his uncle, Grand Duke Nikolai Nikolaevich, be appointed commander in chief. Within months, Tolstoy's *War and Peace* became a bestseller.

An optimistic national feeling welled up everywhere in Europe in July 1914. The *union sacrée* was hardly a Russian convention. But in contrast to the demonstrations in Paris, Berlin, and elsewhere in Europe, all of Russia seemed united not simply in a sacred union but behind a sacred cause. In Germany, the war poet Paul Enderlich wove "holy purpose" into his paeans to German sacrifice. There were echoes of this as well in France and Britain. But only in Russia were the holy foundations of tsarist autocracy directly linked to Russia's military destiny. "Sons of Russia," Archbishop Arsenii proclaimed, "the future is known only to God. The fate of the reign and its people is in God's hands. But we believe without a doubt that, as has been the destiny of our Fatherland in the past, God is and will be with us. We must look at this war as a Holy Crusade."[19] No wonder Ambassador Buchanan thought the war was a "godsend" for Nicholas and his regime.[20]

With the opening of archives in post-Soviet Russia, historians began to readdress the question of Russian patriotism in 1914 and throughout the war, parsing its dimensions in terms of symbolic representations, emotions, and manifest behaviors. As Hubertus Jahn and others have shown, the visual artifacts of patriotism played a central role in creating the images of patriotic feeling, as they did elsewhere in Europe.[21] Widely read magazines like *Sinii Zhurnal* (*Blue Journal*) were filled with photographs of hearty-looking Russian troops in cheerful poses. Popular block prints (the Russian *lubok*) displaying the evil enemy in a variety of forms flooded the countryside. Drama and film soon played important roles as well, as did new literature and popular classics. Well-known artists and writers like Kazimir Malevich, Vladimir Mayakovskii, and Leonid Andreev contributed to this effort. Heroism represented as a Russian dragon slaying Teutonic knights joined more imaginative depictions of Germans as spiders, scorpions, and killers of women and children.[22]

When the emotions these patriotic artifacts were designed to reflect are visually represented, they are easily read: love for tsar and country; willingness to sacrifice to protect land and loved ones; pride in past victories and heroic traditions; confidence and reassurance through individual identification with a collective effort. So were the values they depicted. These left as little to the imagination as the scenes created to reflect them. We can trace the volume and popularity

---

[19] Gosudarstvennaia Duma, *Stenograficheskii otchet*, July 26, 1914, cols. 4–5.
[20] Buchanan, *My Mission*, 213.
[21] Hubertus Jahn, *Patriotic Culture in Russia during World War I* (Ithaca, NY: Cornell University Press, 1995); Melissa Stockdale, *Mobilizing the Russian Nation: Patriotism and Citizenship in the First World War* (Cambridge: Cambridge University Press, 2016); Igor Arkhipov, "Patriotizm v period krizisa 1914–1917 godov," *Zvezda* 9 (2009): 177–204.
[22] Norris, *A War of Images*, ch. 7; V. Denisov, *Voina i lubok* (Petrograd: Izd. Nov. Zhurnala, 1916).

of these artifacts throughout the war as well as across the revolutionary divide. Before 1917, they universally reflected the dominant tropes of Great Russian nationalism in their symbolism and their content. As the war progressed, these were joined by references to the unpatriotic actions of those in and outside the regime who were "betraying" the war effort. After the February revolution, the symbolic representations of patriotic culture depicted a constancy of purpose that shifted easily from "tsar and country" to the defense of Russian "freedom" and patriotic appeal to buy Liberty Bonds.

Massive demonstrations like the ones that occurred in Petrograd and elsewhere with the outbreak of war also seemed easy to understand. Flags, parades, anthems, broadsides, and patriotic speeches are all languages of attachment to regimes, nations, and states: "for tsar and country" or "my country 'tis of thee." For marching soldiers and onlookers alike, a collective elan seems to displace possible anxieties with confidence and hope, often reinforced by weaponry that appears more powerful than it might later prove to be. The event itself creates what might be called an emotional field on which the languages of patriotism claim hegemony, linking forthcoming sacrifice to the common good and rationalizing in advance the losses that are certain to come. Whether hoist on a standard, engraved on a lapel pin, or held in one's hand, a national flag connotes a superordinate identity, loyalty, and attachment, a patriotism that is readily seen and felt.

But how can one go beyond these readings to discern or measure the depth of patriotic feeling in any accurate or useful way? Accepted definitions of patriotism frame it as emotional identity with particular conceptions of the state, love of country, or, in Leonard Doob's phrase, the "more or less conscious convictions" that one's individual or group welfare is dependent on preserving the functional and protective power of an existing state.[23] The demonstration or ascription of patriotic feelings thus provides legitimacy even to very unpopular regimes, enabling the mobilization of those caught in its emotional grip even if its expressions confuse national defense or popular welfare with imperial aggression or the squandering of human life. Rejecting patriotic language is also difficult ("unpatriotic") or even dangerous ("treasonous"). Among the troops going to war the tropes of patriotic languages—stoicism, fatalism, and a heroic (masculine) readiness to die for one's country—defend against its inevitable costs and collectivize personal feelings in ways that make individual anxieties socially unpalatable. They construct and dehumanize enemies and elevate political leaders in the name of the state and the organicity of the nation. Patriotism is thus a set of

---

[23] Leonard Doob, *Patriotism and Nationalism: Their Psychological Foundations* (New Haven, CT: Yale University Press, 1964), 5–6.

languages, practices, and emotions that can themselves stimulate these feelings even within those most resistant to their collective appeal.

What was historically most important about the massive wave of patriotism apparently so clear to observers at the beginning of the war, moreover, was not simply the feelings it seemed to reflect but the assumptions and beliefs it encouraged in high places about popular support for the tsarist regime and the "holy war" it had just declared. In this way the much heralded "sacred union" in Russia was an intoxicating fiction. Its cultivation was particularly important to those in and outside the government who thought that what was needed most to prosecute the war was an effective concentration of state authority; a well-functioning autocracy was simply the most desirable form of government for Russia at war, just as the perceived need for strong, centralized power in France and Britain led to special war powers acts and the suspension of some democratic practices.

Yet it is difficult to imagine that the demonstrated militance of striking Russian workers throughout the spring of 1914 suddenly dissolved into patriotism with the outbreak of war. Nor could war erase the many thousands of peasant families' memories of the brutal repressions against them a scant eight years earlier in the wake of the war against Japan. The American historian Joshua Sanborn divides popular reaction to mobilization around the country in 1914 into three categories: a private response to the dangers of war expressed more in silence and weeping than demonstration; patriotic demonstrations often encouraged or staged by the authorities, if not directly in support of the war per se at least in support of the tsar, the army, and the tasks they were now assuming; and active public opposition in the form of draft riots and other kinds of protests, most of which involved looting. In places like Tomsk and Barnaul draft "riots," as they were called in the press, grew into full-fledged battles between the police and those being mobilized.[24] Reports preserved in archives of the Ministry of Internal Affairs document "bloody clashes" between police and draftees in Perm, Ekaterinoslav, Simbirsk, Minsk, and Stavropol and throughout Tomsk province. More than a thousand took place in Tomsk itself. In what was described in Barnaul as a pogrom, thirty-three "wealthy houses" were torched, along with the Russian Bank for Foreign Trade. In Novonikolaevsk, seven draftees were killed at the railroad station as they assembled to report for duty. These protests were undoubtedly fueled by drinking in the early weeks of the war, an acting out of anger against the new ban on sales of alcohol as well as the anxieties of being called to

---

[24] Joshua Sanborn, *Drafting the Russian Nation: Military Conscription, Total War, and Mass Politics 1905–1925* (DeKalb: Northern Illinois University Press, 2003), 29–31, and his "The Mobilization of 1914 and the Question of the Russian Nation: A Reexamination," *Slavic Review* 2 (2000): 267–89.

battle. There is also evidence, however, of state offices being set on fire and rioters ripping up the Russian flag.[25]

In the countryside, meanwhile, many peasants may have been ready to defend their land from foreign invasion, but there was little support for and perhaps even less understanding of the imperial purposes of war, just as during the war against Japan. Olga Porshneva suggests that peasant fatalism therefore superseded patriotism in any modern sense. Vladimir Buldakov and Tatiana Leont'eva agree. They see the concept of patriotism itself as directly related to a sense of citizenship, which "did not and could not exist" in the communal countryside.[26] For Viatka province, Aaron Retish suggests, the strongest feelings were deep anxieties about the war's likely effects on the village.[27]

The more important historical question, however, was not whether or how soldiers and new recruits reflected patriotic feelings. As they do everywhere, military parades and ceremonial language in Russia created the *image* of loyalty to state and nation, a Tolstoian sense of organic unity, and the ineluctable movement of history beyond any individual's control. Marching off to war is always a mix of carnival, celebration, swagger, and concern. It requires a particular *vocabulary* of emotion, a language of bravado that engages and defines notions of masculinity, pride, and courage, among others, while also cloaking anxieties, sadness, and the immediate loss from separation. Studies have also shown that for soldiers facing the mortal risks of battle, fear and bravery often go together, as do homesickness and camaraderie, passivity and aggression, anxiety and moments of inner calm, subordination and great anger, even hatred, toward superiors who force them into danger.[28] Even some contemporary observers saw little sign of anything but resistance and resignation in the countryside. From inside the army, one even described new recruits as responding sullenly to the enthusiastic welcome of their commander: "One could see that the appeal of a quick victory over the Germans was not met with sympathy in the soldiers' hearts. Everyone looked gloomy and stressed, and listened to the speech as if they had to."[29]

---

[25] RGIA f.1292, op. 1, d. 1729, ll. 24–27 ob., 43–43 ob.; Iu. Iu. I. Kirianov, "Ulichnye besporiaki i vystupleniia rabochikh v Rossii," *Istoricheskii Arkhiv* 12 (1994): 91–99, 1 (1995): 65–102.

[26] Olga Porshneva, *Mentalitet i sotsial'noe povedenie rabochikh, krest'ian i soldat Rossii v period pervoi mirovoi voiny (1914–mart 1918)* (Ekaterinburg: UrO RAN, 2000), 80–124.

[27] Aaron Retish, *Russia's Peasants in Revolution and Civil War: Citizenship, Identity, and the Creation of the Soviet State, 1914-1922* (Cambridge: Cambridge University Press, 2008), 24; Joshua Sanborn, "Besporiadki sredi prizyvnikov v 1914 g. i vopros o russkoi natsii: Novyi vzgliad na problem," in *Rossiia i pervaia mirovaia voina*, ed. N. N. Smirnov (St. Petersburg: Izd. Bulanin, 1999), 202–15; Colleen M. Moore, "Demonstrations and Lamentations: Urban and Rural Responses to War in Russia in 1914," *The Historian* 71, no. 3 (2009): 355–75; and her "Vino kazennoe, i my kazennye': Krestiane-prizyniki i zapret prodazhi spiritnykh napitok v Rossii 1914 g.," in *Malen'kii chelovek i bol'shaia voina v istorii Rossii*, ed. T. A. Abrosimova (St. Petersburg: Bulanin 2014), 161–74.

[28] See esp. Richard Holmes, *Acts of War: The Behavior of Men in Battle* (New York: Free Press, 1986).

[29] D. P. Os'kin, *Zapiski soldata* (Moscow: Federatsii, 1929), 75.

In both their anticipation and their actuality, the patriotic languages and what we might call the emotional fields they engender cultivate feelings in tension with those they work to suppress. The valiant call to die for one's country readily stirs up a possibility one may be struggling to deny. By "emotional fields" we thus mean contexts that link feelings to particular kinds of physical acts or behaviors, like fear on the battlefield with military assaults, or anxiety and depression with suicidal carelessness and disobedience. The important questions about patriotic emotion and national unity as the war began in Russia, therefore, were about the relationship between image and actuality: the degree to which the celebrated imaginary of patriotic and stoic peasants ready and willing to die for Tsar and Fatherland would reflect the actual emotional fields of battle soldiers found themselves in, and the implications if it did not. The patriotic image itself was a powerful underpinning of military strategy and public posture. What, then, would Russia's stoic peasant soldiers actually think and feel when parade ground bravado met the new technologies and awful brutalities of modern war?

Surveilling Loyalty

For the tsarist regime and its military command, this was not an abstract question. No regime taking its country to war in 1914 was more fearful of popular unrest than Russia's. The revolution of 1905 lived large in social memory throughout the country but nowhere more sharply than the Winter Palace and Stavka, the army's military headquarters. The war Russia launched against Japan in 1904 was intended in large part to quell growing political dissent by displacing its passion onto a foreign enemy. It resulted instead in the disastrous loss of the Baltic Fleet at Tsushima, the mobilization of a forceful liberal as well as radical political opposition, massive strikes in September and October that brought the country to a halt, and the concession wrenched from a reluctant tsar to create some semblance of parliamentary governance to prevent the full-fledged revolution many feared would occur. The great wave of industrial strikes in 1913–14 and peasant resistance to replacing communal with individual ownership of land was clear evidence that strong currents of dissidence had again begun to flow. As the "holy war" began, the mood of the country remained of paramount importance. It had to be closely watched and carefully measured.

More than any warring power, surveillance in 1914 was deeply ingrained in Russian administrative culture, and thoroughly institutionalized. From the time of Peter the Great Russian political culture was molded in the wariness of insecurity. The Ministry of Interior's not so secret "secret police," the Okhrana, had offices in sixty cities and agents everywhere, even abroad. The Kadet Party leader Paul Miliukov warranted the full attention of the highest ranking officials at the Okhrana's Petrograd headquarters on the Fontanka canal. So did Andrei Shingarev, the liberals' leading figure in the Duma and the author of *The Dying Village*, whom the Okhrana began to spy on as early as 1891.

With the start of the war, the Okhrana's focus expanded from political surveillance to counterintelligence. Labor organizers were closely followed and arrested when they attempted to unionize workers or organize strikes. (Strikes were legal, organizing them was not.) Within the army surveillance had special importance. A wave of mutinies had occurred in November and December 1905, well after the Portsmouth Peace had been signed; some 130 more between January and June 1906. The best known, like that on the battleship *Potemkin*, mixed protests over food with resistance to authority, but everywhere a chaotic lack of discipline accompanied the brutality with which urban and rural protests were suppressed, amplifying the humiliation of military defeat. The years between 1905 and 1914 consequently saw efforts to improve the coordination and control of Russia's army and strengthen its training. Efforts were made to address the problem of distrust officers had for their soldiers, revise the curriculum at the military academy, strengthen the competency of the General Staff, and especially improve the training and literacy of recruits.[30] More than two-thirds of the army could read and write at some level.[31] Increasing literacy brought political awareness.

The means for tracking soldiers' thoughts and feelings was the office of the military censor. As the war progressed, all warring powers imposed some degree of censorship over mail coming to and from the front. Only in St. Petersburg, however, did the regime issue a comprehensive decree setting up military censorship in all of its forms as early as July 20, 1914, the day after declaring war.[32] And only in Russia were the goals of military censorship immediate and explicit: first and foremost to track soldiers' emotional and mental states. In the Russian censors' lexicon, the task was to measure *nastroenie*, best translated as "mood" rather than "morale" (*moral'noe sostoianie*, which connotes morality as

---

[30] John Bushnell, *Mutiny amid Repression: Russian Soldiers in the Revolution of 1905-1906* (Bloomington: Indiana University Press, 1985); Bruce W. Manning, *Bayonets before Bullets: The Imperial Russian Army, 1861-1914* (Bloomington, Indiana University Press, 1992), chs. 6-7; John W. Steinberg, *All the Tsar's Men: Russia's General Staff and the Fate of the Empire 1989-1914* (Washington, D.C.: Woodrow Wilson Press, 2010), chs. 5-7.

[31] A. B. Astashov, "Russkii krest'ianin na frontakh pervoi mirovoi voiny," *Otechestvennaia istoriia* 2 (Mar. 2003): 72-86.

[32] *Sobranie uzakonenii i rasporiazhenii pravitel'stva, izdavaemye pri Pravitel'stvuiushchem Senate* 192 (July 20, 1914): 3017-31, published in *Pochtovo-telegrafnyi zhurnal* 31 (1914): 458-70 as "Vremennoe polozhenie o voennoi tsenzure." See also John T. Smith, "Russian Military Censorship during the First World War," *Revolutionary Russia* 1 (2001): 71-95; Irina Davidjan, "Voennaia tsenzura v Rossii v gody grazhdanskoi voiny," *Cahiers du Monde Russe et Sovetique* 1-2 (1997): 117-25; A. B. Astashov, "Russian Military Censorship during the First World War," in *Military Affairs in Russia's Great War and Revolution*, ed. Laurie Stoff, Antony Heywood, Boris Kolonitskii, and John Steinberg (Bloomington, IN: Slavica, 2019), 241-64.

well as feeling). What the censors were seeking was something that blends the boundaries between emotions and attitudes, between culturally defined feelings like patriotism ("For Tsar and Fatherland!") or "cheerful and in good spirits" (*bodrost'*) and the far less certain feelings associated with the experience of battle. It is thus stronger than the English "morale," both in terms of the range of feeling it represented and its implications for how reliable individuals and units might be. Alone among the warring powers, Russian commanders would be informed from the start whether their troops were loyal. If dissent occurred, the censors would keep it from spreading outward from the army to soldiers' villages, towns, and factories, just as they would assure civilian dissidence did not penetrate the front. There would be no more *Potemkin* mutinies. Commanders would use this information to control their troops and, importantly, to make tactical decisions about how they should be deployed. At least in this area in 1914, the Russian High Command thought itself thoroughly prepared.

Early Losses and Their Implications

The total number of Russian soldiers who came under arms in the first eleven months of war was a staggering 8.8 million. A small number of women were among them, as Melissa Stockdale and Laurie Stoff have detailed, accepted into the ranks in part to stimulate the heroism of their male comrades. (In 1917 the Women's Battalion of Death would be formed to set a national "heroic" example.)[33] Nurses also played a critical role on the front, and while they are not included in official casualty lines, certainly should be thought of as part of Russia's overall military force.[34] Sizable mobilizations were intended to assure Russian numerical superiority over Germany and Austria. In part, this related to the greater emphasis in Russia on a seemingly limitless source of patriotic and stoic peasants from the countryside rather than advanced military technology. In part, it was also intended to deter Germany from reinforcing its troops in the West, as the regime had promised France and England.

Both tasks were soon made urgent by the extraordinary losses the Russian military endured in the very first weeks of war, as the First and Second Armies under Generals Samsonov and Rennenkampf attacked into East Prussia in the

---

[33] TsSU, *Rossiia v mirovoi voine 1914–1918 (v tsifrakh)* (Moscow, 1925), 18; Melissa Stockdale, "'My Death for the Motherland Is Happiness': Women, Patriotism, and Soldiering in Russia's Great War, 1914–1917," *American Historical Review* 1 (2004): 78–116; Laurie Stoff, *They Fought for the Motherland: Russia's Women Soldiers in World War I and the Revolution* (Lawrence: University Press of Kansas, 2006).

[34] Laurie Stoff, *Russia's Sisters of Mercy and the Great War: More Than Binding Men's Wounds* (Lawrence: University Press of Kansas, 1915).

hope of reaching Berlin and quickly bringing the war to a victorious end. In the two earliest battles, at Tannenburg and the Mazurian Lakes, Russians suffered as many as 140,000 killed and wounded. Some 120,000 were taken prisoner, although precise figures are impossible to obtain, and the number may have been much higher. Samsonov's entire Second Army was decimated. As many as 70,000 of Russia's best-trained troops were lost, pounded by new German artillery. Almost 100,000 more managed to survive only by throwing away their weapons and surrendering. The despairing Samsonov took to the woods and shot himself. The act was quickly interpreted as contrition for his ineptitude. With most of the Second Army gone on his southern flank, Rennenkampf, too, suffered awful casualties and was forced to retreat.

These early disasters were not easily reversed. For much of the late fall the Russian army dug in along the Northern Front in central Poland, west of the Vistula River. Battles here and at Lodz did not significantly alter the lines in either direction despite their intensity. Efforts turned instead to Austrian Galicia. Here Russians began to fight successfully along a broad front under Generals Ivanov, Ruzskii, and Brusilov, widely thought to be more competent than their colleagues to the north. Despite their own early disasters in August and September, when the Russian Fifth Army was almost surrounded and took heavy casualties, the Galician armies were able to regroup, replenish their casualties, and move forward. In September the region's historical capital, the well-fortified city of Lemberg (L'vov/L'viv), was captured. By November, most of the Galician region was under Russian control. With casualties on both sides now numbering more than 500,000, the Russian armies settled into a long siege of the Austrian fortress at Przemyśl, a gateway to the Carpathians and through the mountains to Budapest and Vienna.

Less than four months into the war, more Russian soldiers had been killed or wounded than in any previous Russian conflict, including Napoleon's invasion in 1812. In an even shorter period of time, more soldiers may have surrendered than in all previous Russian wars put together. It was now also clear that the war would not end quickly. Like public figures in London, Paris, and Berlin, prominent Russians in and outside the government expressed surprise and disappointment. The respected publicist and Kadet Party founder A. M. Koliubakin, who was soon himself to die at the front, wrote in the party's newspaper *Rech'* (*Speech*) about what he called the great disillusionment. *Novoe Vremia* (*New Times*) echoed this view. More than four thousand factories and plants in the Warsaw region had come under German control. All of this did nothing to compromise the official Russian cause. With respect to manpower as well as space, Russia's resources seemed unlimited. Only the timetable and costs of victory required recalculation. Rather than raising fundamental questions about how to pursue the huge and unexpectedly ferocious war itself, the defeats served mainly to shift public focus from the heralded opportunities of war to the familiar Russian question of who was guilty for Russia's defeats: *Kto vinovat?*

There were several possible answers. The most obvious implication was the incompetency of Russia's military command. How was it that Samsonov and Rennenkampf were so badly outmaneuvered? Why was coordination between the two commands so poor? Why did the High Command itself not correct deficiencies that earlier training maneuvers had revealed, and repeat almost exactly the plans of attack that had shown themselves deficient during exercises the previous spring? It was also apparent from the start that there needed to be drastic improvements in the supply of munitions and food as well as transport operations. Incompetence here as well was inferred. The British military liaison General Alfred Knox witnessed some of the battle up close. Coordination and communication between Russia's forces was poor or nonexistent. Essential supplies were lacking. Commanders were utterly unprepared to evacuate the huge numbers of wounded. Most seriously, Rennenkampf himself, an overly confident old-line cavalry officer whom Knox thought a dangerous anachronism best fit for the Napoleonic wars, failed to provide the support in men and equipment that Samsonov and the Second Army desperately needed, to the surprise of the Germans themselves.[35]

An additional and even more worrisome possible cause of the debacle, however, related to the soldiers' loyalty. How well were the soldiers fighting? What was the army's mood? And especially after the stunning defeats, how much did these disasters compromise the commitment of soldiers and their families to Tsar and Fatherland? Knox also recorded, with apparent surprise, that one of Samsonov's principal commanders, General Torklus, was "more interested in the psychology of his men than any preparation for their advance." He "delighted with their spirit" and saw "no trace of nerve strain" in the soldiers marching past his window. Knox himself saw disorder, confusion, and, as the Germans advanced, even panic as soldiers fled ferocious bombardment.[36]

In fact, throughout this awful fall the censors' reading supported the view of General Torklus. As the censors read soldiers' correspondence in the fall of 1914, the disasters at Tannenberg and the Mazurian Lakes reportedly had little effect on soldiers' emotional state. According to reports, "a huge majority" at the front remained "in good spirits and feeling patriotic [*bodrym i patrioticheskim*]." Russia's efforts to conquer East Prussia had come to an ignominious halt, and with them the hope that the war would be short. Yet soldiers at the front were reported ready and determined to "drive the cursed Germans completely from

---

[35] Alfred Knox, *With the Russian Army 1914–1917*, 2 vols. (London, 1921), 1: ch. 2.
[36] Ibid., 1:66.

Russia." "The *nastroenie* of the army is excellent," headquarters was secretly informed. "[T]he huge majority wants only to smash the enemy."[37]

At the Front: The Shocks of War

By the New Year's holiday, the Great War so many Russians welcomed jubilantly in July 1914 had already brought on the greatest human catastrophe in modern Russian history. Like the struggle itself, the front that had opened up was unprecedented in its extent, its nature, and the startling range of experiences it brought to Russian soldiers, especially new recruits. Comparisons can be made with the far better known front-line experience in France, especially as the German offensive turned into relatively static although equally deadly warfare. But while the attrition may have been vicious on both the Western and Russian Fronts, the very scale of the Russian Front set the situation there apart. There were also the effects of fierce winter conditions, extended lines of supply, difficulties of removing and caring for the wounded, and advanced German weaponry, especially aircraft and artillery. All intensified the nature of the front-line struggle in what has been called the "forgotten war" in the East.[38]

The Russian military zone as a whole was a vast area occupying much of what is now Belarus and Ukraine, officially designated as the primary region in which grain and other resources could be requisitioned to support the army. The term "front" itself is a complex signifier for the thin shifting line of actual combat, the literal borderline for many soldiers between life and death. As such it constituted an emotional field of individual and collective anxiety, variously expressed in language and action, repressed or managed in other ways in the service of emotional and psychological stability and physical survival. In contrast to the Western Front in France, the Russian Front stretched at times more than one thousand miles along changing German, Austrian, and in 1916 Romanian borders. Russia was also soon fighting like Germany on two distant fronts, with some 100,000 troops initially engaging Germany's Turkish allies in the Caucasus in the fall of 1914. The Caucasian battle zone, however, was never central to the war's outcome. Nor did the circumstances of battle against the Turks engage the same level of advanced weaponry or physical conditions even in the trenches, given the climate and the limitations of Turkish artillery. After the defeats at Tannenburg and the Mazurian Lakes the High Command even reduced Russian forces in the Caucasus to some sixty thousand, transferring almost half the troops to fight the Germans. Arriving just before the hardships of winter set in,

---

[37] RGVIA f. 2067, op. 1, d. 3853, ll. 6, 72–73, 260.
[38] Alexandre Sumpf, *La Grande guerre oublié: Russie 1914–1918* (Paris: Perrin, 2014).

the new arrivals found themselves facing the unexpected perils of a far better trained and equipped enemy in a radically different climate.

In the narrow sense, of course, the front was the thin area of personal combat that included the no man's killing zone between Russian and enemy forces as well as the more static trench warfare that framed the slaughter in northern France. In both places experience in the trenches involved unprecedented assaults to every possible sensory nerve, as it has again more than one hundred years later in Russia's war against Ukraine: the deafening noise of extended artillery bombardment, long and eerily silent periods of anxious anticipation of what was to come, weeks or longer in wet clothes, and unremitting stench. When either side took the offensive, the no man's land between them became a scene of utter and unutterable carnage, a landscape of unimaginable sights, sounds, and smells of sudden and slow death, a level of bestiality that surely for many dislocated faith and whatever conceptions they may have brought to the front about the nature of humanity. The French historian Alexander Sumpf has described it as a "dangerous desert," a physical, emotional, and psychological space where soldiers "lost each other as well as themselves" when "time ran out." To his American colleague Eric Leed, approaching the issue with the help of Erik Erikson's theory of ego development, no man's land during the First World War brought a combat fatigue in which the very notion of ego-identity dissolved, destroying the fibers keeping personalities whole.[39]

Trench life on the front line also meant poor rations, intestinal discomfort, incontinence, long days of frozen boredom suddenly interrupted by fierce bombardments or charges toward enemy positions. As the first winter of war wore on, soldiers on the front went weeks and sometimes months without a change of underwear that, as one soldier wrote home, "drove us out of our minds."[40] Dysentery and other diseases spread easily. Bitter cold assaulted freshly mobilized troops as early as November 1914. Russian trenches and bunkers were initially poorly constructed. Even after their engineering improved later in 1915, they generally provided little protection from shells that fell nearby. Troops on the Northern and Northwestern Fronts under frequent bombardment in near zero temperatures during the first winter of war found themselves "living in hell," surrounded by dead bodies "stacked like firewood."[41] Long-range guns kept the human face of the enemy at some distance, as did the airplane. Sudden bombardments were particularly fearsome. Aging Russian commanders like

---

[39] Alexandre Sumpf, "Russian Perception of No Man's Land during the First World War," in *Military Affairs*, ed. Stoff, 17–38; Stumpf, *La Grande guerre oublié*, 74–83 and passim; Eric J. Leed, *No Man's Land: Combat and Identity in World War I* (London: Cambridge University Press, 1979), 3–4.

[40] RGVIA f. 2067, op. 1, d. 3853, l. 542.

[41] M. Vol'fovich and K. Medvedeva, eds., *Tsarskaia armiia v period mirovoi voiny i fevral'skoi revoliutsii* (Kazan: Tatizdat, 1932), 21 (documents from the Central Archive of the Tatar Republic).

General Ruzskii still thought concentrating the maximum number of troops in a small area across the front strengthened the army's ability to attack. Instead, packing such salients only provided German artillery with easy targets. Shrapnel volleys caused ghastly wounds and mutilations.

As Jan Plamper has described, the expression of fear expanded strikingly at the turn of the century in European soldiers' texts for several reasons, not least the emergence of technologically modern warfare.[42] Russia was no exception. Whether they came from villages or factories, and regardless of their rank, many soldiers and officers feared the sudden death that came from new artillery, tanks, and flying machines. Witnessing unprecedented carnage, many feared being wounded more than being killed. Those many who fell wounded in offensive charges were left for hours in great pain and amid the most gruesome of scenes, despite the efforts of a perpetually understaffed medical corps. Retrieving them was always hazardous. Countless numbers heard and watched their comrades die.[43] The Germans' use of gas in 1915 added additional horrors to the front line. Russian soldiers and officers were ill prepared despite widely reported warnings. In one attack, some nine hundred men, almost a whole battalion, was destroyed, its soldiers instinctively running from the approaching clouds and unable in the process to affix their masks properly. The army had not been taken by surprise. Commanders were simply unable to prepare because they lacked adequate equipment and trained personnel.[44] "Only fifty escaped, bedraggled, haggard, so dazed by their experiences *that they were unable to tell us anything*" (my italics).[45]

Here precisely is one of the earliest and clearest descriptions of "shell shock," the condition that familiarly became a lasting consequence of the war everywhere in Europe and to which so much useful attention has been paid ever since to its nature and treatment, if not its political and social implications. Those rendered mute by the gas attack joined thousands or more who were similarly disabled by their battlefield experience. Shell shock in all of its occurrences was an affliction of survivors. Many who perished at the front almost certainly had the condition as well, leaving statistics on its extent necessarily understated.

The degree to which soldiers were being disabled in this way was already of concern to medical personnel during the Russo-Japanese War, when military doctors set up the first small clinics for what they initially diagnosed as "depressive stupor" and "nervous exhaustion." Most victims were thought to have suffered from head injuries of some sort. Many officers thought their afflictions

---

[42] Jan Plamper, "Fear: Soldiers and Emotion in Early Twentieth-Century Russian Military Psychology," *Slavic Review* 68 (2000): 259–83.

[43] RGIA f. 1088, op. 2, d. 164, l. 1; RGVIA f. 2067, op. 1, d. 11, l. 164; f. 2048, op. 1, d. 905, l. 269 ob.; f. 2067, op. 1, d. 2937, l. 32.

[44] Andrei Lobanov-Rostovsky, *The Grinding Mill: Reminiscences of War and Revolution in Russia, 1913–1920* (New York: Macmillan, 1935), 133; RGVIA f. 2003, op. 2, d. 669, ll. 13ff.

[45] RGVIA 2067, op. 1, d. 2937, l. 50; Lobanov-Rostovsky, *The Grinding Mill*, 133.

were signs of cowardice and unmasculine weakness. Indeed, the Russian word for "shell shock" at the time, *kontuziia*, referred to those suffering concussions or strikes to the head.

As Irina Sirotkina suggests, Russian military physicians may well have been more receptive to the diagnosis than their colleagues in the West, in part because they were more critical of the Russian regime but also because they resisted the still unsympathetic perspectives of many officers.[46] While this prejudice remained at the start of the war, shell shock by 1915 had become shorthand in Russia and elsewhere for the variety of psychiatric traumas industrial warfare was producing on all fronts. Russian military doctors addressed the problem at conferences in early May 1915 and in more detail when they gathered again in June. Recognizing the importance of the syndrome even without fully understanding its physiological dimensions, they acknowledged Russia's lack of expertise and trained personnel.[47] In any event the number of Russian victims was already substantial, however inaccurately recorded, as it was in France as well. By May 1915 there were some 13,000 cases officially designated as shell shock; by the end of 1915, the number had more than tripled, leading *Psikhiatricheskaia Gazeta* to argue strongly for special wards for traumatized soldiers.[48] An additional 53,185 victims would later be recorded for 1916.[49]

Yet current studies situate the overwhelming source of battle stress and its subsequent effects not on the full-blown neurological trauma associated with artillery bombardment or gas attacks, but on the more subtle if equally insidious effects of "ordinary" life on the front: the commonplace anxiety and fear the vast majority of Russia's 15 million mobilized soldiers must have felt in some form between 1914 and the fall of 1917. In the overwhelming majority of such cases, what we now know as posttraumatic stress disorder (PTSD) stems from such seemingly benign experiences as sustained periods of sleep deprivation, the discomfort of being constantly wet or cold, hunger, and a deep and constant emotional fatigue brought on by living passively on the edge of death, as well as witnessing and experiencing the literal wounds of combat. Its sociopathic effects,

---

[46] Irina Sirotkina, "The Politics of Etiology: Shell Shock in the Russian Army, 1914–1918," in *Madness and the Mad in Russian Culture*, ed. Angela Brintlinger and Ilya Vinitsky (Toronto: University of Toronto Press, 2015), 118–21.

[47] RGVIA, f. 2003, op. 2, d. 669, ll. 13ff.; Kim Friedlander, "Neskol'ko aspektov shellshok'a v Rossii 1914–1916," in *Rossiia v pervaia mirovaia voina*, ed. N. N. Smirnov, 315–24.

[48] *Psikhiatricheskaia Gazeta* 19 (1916), cited by Catherine Merridale, "The Collective Mind: Trauma and Shell-Shock in Twentieth Century Russia," *Journal of Contemporary History* 1 (2000): 41.

[49] *Rossiia v pervoi mirovoi voine v tsifrakh*, 30. In one of the few careful examinations of the subject in the Soviet Union, N. I. Bondarev records 82,124 cases of soldiers treated for mental and nervous disorders on the Northwestern Front between October 1, 1914, and September 30, 1917. N. I. Bondarev, "Zatrudeniia voiskogo vracha v sluchaiakh psikiatricheskoi diagnostiki," *Voenno-Meditsinskii Zhurnal* 5–6 (1931): 31–32.

in other words, are not simply from the episodic horrors of individual battle experiences but develop as a result of the constant strain of their expectation, especially in the arduous physical conditions in which the dangers of battle are constantly anticipated over long periods of time. A careful study by Peter Watson argues that in this and other ways, battlefield stress is so severe "as to be totally different" from the kind of stress one experiences from the "normal" vicissitudes of life.[50]

First among these conditions on the Russian Front might well have been the simple but often deadly condition of exhaustion.[51] Certainly exhaustion characterized much of the Russian army from the first battles at the Mazurian Lakes and Tannenberg onward. One element contributing to these early losses was the numbing fatigue produced by more than three weeks of sustained marches through difficult terrain in near constant contact with the enemy. The Mazurian Lakes region presented formidable physical challenges, but Samsonov's soldiers were pressed into the offensive with heavy packs and weapons without adequate periods of rest or relief and virtually no sleep. When Rennenkampf's First Army was then also ordered forward without adequate rest the consequences were similar, as they were when his troops were forced to retreat over some two hundred kilometers under conditions of near constant bombardment, reeling physically and, one can deduce, emotionally as well. The language of lost battles has never accepted "I'm tired" as a legitimate excuse.

Exhaustion also affected Russia's armies on the vast Southwestern Front during their more successful campaigns in the fall of 1914, "fighting without respite," as General Brusilov himself described it.[52] Commanders at army headquarters seemed to transfer popular images of sturdy Russian peasants onto strategies and operational orders that not only were physically unrealistic but severely damaged their soldiers' physical and emotional well-being. As they did with Samsonov and Rennenkampf, the generals at army headquarters resisted any notion of resting troops in the Southwest. They continually pressed Brusilov and other field commanders to sustain their drives in part to compensate for the disasters in East Prussia. Soldiers constantly on the move had little time or energy to protect themselves effectively from shelling. The advance here continued relentlessly even as the open Galician plains turned horrifically bloody. Rain, snow, and mud were suffered without adequate food and clothing; corporal punishments became severe. Indeed, some soldiers from the Northern Front wrote home about rumors of widespread desertion. Some units were even reported to have "gone

---

[50] Peter Watson, *War on the Mind* (London: Hutchinson, 1978).
[51] Terry Copp and Bill McAndrew, *Battle Exhaustion* (Montreal: McGill-Queen's University Press, 1990), 109–27. See also Roy Brook, *The Stress of Combat, the Combat of Stress* (Brighton: Alpha Press, 1999).
[52] A. A. Brusilov, *A Soldier's Notebook* (1930; Westport, CT: Greenwood Press, 1970), 96.

on strike." The language itself was a worrisome reminder to commanders that drafted workers could bring a different kind of militancy to the front. Many also wrote openly on postcards about the "horrors" of combat itself, disorganized flight in the face of the enemy's advance, the chaos and fear of bombardment, and the shocking effects of "whole regiments" being taken prisoner. Those who had written to their families earlier in the fall not to send warm underwear because they would soon be home now sent plaintive appeals for clothing because there was no end to the war in sight. Being cut off from their families seemed particularly hard on those who were away from home for the first time. The hardships of life at the front were clearly written out, disturbing even some censors and helping them understand why some soldiers wrote of their longing for surrender. As long cold nights blended with short fearsome days, some censors reported that depression and anguish (*toska*) were becoming widespread.[53]

Winter fighting by exhausted troops in the forests of the Western and Northern Fronts thus took its psychological as well as physical toll. Russian military doctors were soon differentiating symptoms they attributed to exhaustion from what they began to call "trench psychoses": the collapse of adaptive and resistance mechanisms that led especially to manic depression and dementia. And while soldiers on the Western Front developed similar symptoms, the physical distress of trench warfare in the East was almost certainly worse than in France's milder climate. Bitter cold, inadequate clothing, and especially the shortage of food amplified the torments of artillery bombardment and the constant dangers for those who left the trenches. Even the relatively long periods of inaction during the winter may have made matters worse in this regard, pitting brief inconclusive fighting against long periods of boredom made more intense by physical and emotional discomfort.

Soldiers' letters contained ample evidence of these miseries even as fighting temporarily subsided. Dampness and flooding ("Water everywhere in the trenches, we can scarcely pull our feet out of the muck it creates"); snow, ice, and frostbite ("We had 850 men in our battalion, almost 400 had frostbitten fingers and feet"); the stench of waste and unwashed bodies sometimes endured for weeks as troops waited for replacements that did not come ("We sit in the front-line trenches like animals, bullets whistling over our heads, deafened by the noise, despondent"); and shortages of nearly inedible food ("we are hungry and exhausted"; "they give us only half a bowl of some kind of porridge and a *funt* of bread each once in twenty-four hours").[54] "Our life is a prison," one soldier wrote home, but "even worse."[55] Grievances on the extended Galician

---

[53] RGVIA f. 2067, op. 1, d. 3853, ll. 22, 40–41, 73.
[54] RGVIA f. 2067, op. 1, d. 2932, ll. 16, 208; f. 2067, op. 1, d. 2935, ll. 2–8; f. 2031, op. 1, d. 1184, l. 35.
[55] RGVIA f. 2067, op. 1, d. 2937, l. 428.

Front in late 1914 were less focused on the hardships of winter, although these were severe here as well: rain snow, and mud suffered without adequate food and clothing; wounded left without care for long periods of time; doctors who looked only after officers and considered "soldiers worse than cattle."[56] Soldiers here wrote letters home about commanders stealing money and goods, trading openly with "Jew-spies," and then showing themselves so willing to surrender that the enemy stopped shooting, the "only thing that saved those of us who resisted by giving us time to retreat."[57] There is "a mass of problems that I cannot write about," a captain from the Belorussian regiment of the 7th cavalry wrote from the Galician Front, "that for me, and really for all of us are so difficult and enraging ... and make us all want to disappear away from the horrors of this war, this bloody nightmare ... [where] we live like beasts: filthy, hungry, cold, and ready every moment for death in battle with the enemy."[58]

From these letters one can readily understand why desertion was already a huge problem in the first months of the war, as it continued to be thereafter, and why some 1.5 million Russian soldiers were taken prisoner between July 1914 and May 1, 1915, 45 percent of all military loses for the period.[59] As A. B. Astashov has shown in his careful studies, desertion had run high among peasant soldiers longing for home even before 1914. The numbers are uncertain, but more than thirteen thousand were detained by police serving the Southwestern Front late in the winter of 1914–15, and desertion soon became commonplace among newly recruited troops going to the front as well as those already there. Among the latter were many with self-inflicted wounds who jumped off hospital trains to escape, reportedly in droves. A substantial number of deserters were soldiers on leave who simply failed to return. The army command, meanwhile, commonly applied sanctions against those higher in the chain of command thought responsible for letting desertion or surrender occur. When thirty thousand soldiers were taken prisoner from the Tenth Army near Konigsberg, its commander General Sivers was cashiered for letting it happen.[60] Yet as Solzhenitsyn describes in *August 1914*, surrender was often an act of moral courage on the part of commanders who understood the alternative would be their soldiers' annihilation.

---

[56] RGVIA f. 2031, op. 1, d. 1184, ll. 6–7ff.
[57] Ibid., ll. 74–76.
[58] RGVIA f. 2067, op. 1, d. 3853, ll. 40–41.
[59] TsSU, *Rossiia v mirovoi voine*, 30.
[60] A. B. Astashov, "Dezertirstvo i bor'ba s nim v tsarskoi armii v gody pervoi mirovoi voiny," Rossiiskaia Istoriia 4 (2011): 44–46; RGVIA f. 2067, op. 1, d. 2932, l. 27; Lobanov-Rostovsky, *Grinding Mill*, 9. An excellent comparative overview is Paul Simmons, "Desertion in the Russian Army, 1914–1917," in *Military Affairs*, ed. Stoff, 393–415.

Reading Soldiers' Moods

If the task of "elucidating the mood of the troops and their spirits" was so important to army commanders, why did "in good spirits and feeling patriotic" remain the dominant trope of censors' reports? Through all this carnage military censors consistently reported that the mood of the overwhelming number of Russian soldiers was very good, even excellent. "Our soldiers do not close their eyes to ... the obstacles that lie ahead, but duty to Tsar and Fatherland overcomes all difficulties"; "[S]oldiers go smartly [*likho*] on attack, waiting only for the order to smash the enemy further"; "[T]he mood is good, excellent. The soldiers literally do not hold back, do not accept any delays. In terms of their psychology and mental outlook they are one. ... They do not want to delay their victorious march forward."[61] Censors who wrote these reports did not lack sensitivity or intelligence. We have no collective information on their backgrounds, but the evidence suggests their ranks included career officers whose training had been strengthened since the war with Japan and other able personnel from in and outside the military, including some with high positions in the police.[62] Some clearly struggled with these broad patriotic categorizations. When one soldier wrote openly about "the horrors of this war, about our huge losses, about being taken prisoner, and not only about whole regiments but whole corps that fled from the advancing enemy and could not adjust to military life," it left a "very heavy impression" on the censor, "dissipated only when one realized that within the huge volume of letters they represented only a small percent."[63]

At first glance one might imagine Russia's military censors were actively involved with the High Command in systematic self-delusion. Yet one reason for the pervasive descriptions of spirited and patriotic troops was simply that so many letters actually expressed these sentiments, reflecting especially in 1914 the spirited and patriotic mobilization narratives that greeted recruits and infused military assemblies. The great demonstrations of support for Tsar and Country when the war began were emotionally empowering at various levels, but especially in the army and the offices of the state. The regime, its soldiers, and many censors alike were essentially caught in a circulation of emotional presumption and expectation. Soldiers' correspondence and censors' reports largely reflected notions of how soldiers were now *supposed* to feel, rather than revealing the concerns that underlay the elaborate censorship apparatus in the first place. For Stanley Washburn and Andrei Lobanov-Rostovsky, both of whom had close

---

[61] RGVIA f. 2067, op. 1, d. 2945, ll. 2, 30.
[62] Otdel Rukopisei State Public Library, St. Petersburg, f. 11152, op. 3, d. 98; A. A. Beloborodova, "Zashchita gosudarstvennoi tainy v rossiiskoi imperii: Deiatel'nost' voennoi tsenzury v 1914–17," *Voenno-istoricheskii zhurnal* 6 (2011), http://history.milportal.ru/2011/06.
[63] Beloborodova, "Zashchita," l. 73.

relations with censors, their descriptions of stoic peasant defenders of Tsar and Country loyally and in good spirits fulfilling their duty thus reflected the conflicts of hope and denial within and beyond the army's High Command. In other words, censors' summary accounts of soldiers' moods reflected what they thought they should be reading, what many soldiers and their officers thought (and were told) they should be feeling, and which many may actually have felt. In William Reddy's suggestive phrase, the Russian army, in effect, was constituted as a "community that attempted to manage emotions," as well as one determined to know what they were.[64] While patriotic narratives may well have expressed many of the troops' real feelings, the emotions they described may also have reflected broader cultural values and emotional expectations rather than actual feelings. As Laurie Stoff has discussed, these may also impact assumptions about gender that combat may destabilize. Soldiers must be "brave." "Anxiety" is a woman's affliction. "Fear" is cowardly.[65]

Prescriptive injunctions against emotional openness came in various places and in different ways. High morale was normalized, even insisted upon, an injunction that almost certainly served to discipline the expression of alternative feelings. When so many cards and letters included sensitive military information in the fall of 1914, the High Command issued special directives ordering troops to write "more carefully."[66] Many must have taken this to mean they had to write in a positive vein if they wanted their letters to reach home. Some censors clearly knew this, complicating how they should prepare their reports. They understood that illiterate soldiers in particular were restrained not only in terms of expressing their feelings but because it was "impossible to write the truth" if they wanted their letters to reach home.[67] Anthony Giddens has termed this "reflexive monitoring": when individual soldiers and officers suppress their feelings and conceal their experience in an effort to conform to what they thought good soldiers were expected to feel and experience. (Illiterate soldiers commonly dictated letters to comrades from their own villages or regions who could read and write. Wounded and hospitalized soldiers dictated theirs to nurses.)[68] Plamper has thoughtfully elaborated this idea in terms of accessing what may be suppressed through the "hermeneutics of silence."[69]

The complexities of "historical experience" itself complicates the issue. While many tend to regard "experience" as the bedrock of historical understanding ("I

---

[64] "AHR Conversation: The Historical Study of Emotions," *American Historical Review* 5 (2012): 1510.
[65] Stoff, *Russia's Sisters*, 142–43.
[66] RGVIA f. 2067, op. 1, d. 3853, ll. 72–73.
[67] Ibid., d. 2937, l. 377.
[68] Anthony Giddens, *Modernity and Self-Identity: Self and Society in the Late Modern Age* (Cambridge: Cambridge University Press, 1991).
[69] Jan Plamper, in "AHR Conversation," 1529.

was there, so I know!"), the scare quotes here warn that what is often described as the experience of others may well be more about the feelings and perceptions of the one doing the describing than of those being described. As with the problem of discerning patriotism or describing soldiers' moods from observing parades or reading letters, the core of the difficulty is the very problem of accessing past feelings and rendering the experience they constitute into coherent historical narratives. Iurii Lotman has described this process succinctly: an event may seem to those who live through it to be something "disorganized, chaotic, or without any broader meaning or historical logic. But when an event is told and retold through language, it inevitably acquires a structural unity. This unity, which in fact belongs only to the level of expression, is naturally transferred to the level of content as well."[70]

Lotman's insight has particular relevance to soldiers in war, and especially to the unprecedented nature of modern warfare experienced with such brutality in the fall and winter of 1914–15 and continued unabated thereafter. To narrate experience here in letters or memoirs, the emotional aspects of engaging the unprecedented technologies and brutalities of the war had to find some coherent expression, the "unimaginable imagined," as Aaron J. Cohen has put it.[71] A related problem is what Samuel Hynes described in *The Soldiers' Tale* as the "enthusiastic story": a reduction of literally dread-full experience into positive and socially encouraged tales of masculine courage and composure. Soldiers' tales necessarily struggle in some ways with emotions their writers are understandably reluctant to reveal: fear, indifference, cowardice, even the moments of incontinence that are inevitable aspects of modern battle. The awful horrors of war become patriotic sacrifice. Leaping out of trenches is narrated as an act of bravery, largely devoid of the fears, anxieties, or fatalistic defenses that accompanied the action.[72] Soldiers writing home as well as newspaper reporters and public figures cut against this grain at their peril.

How, then, can historians be sure the feelings described in their sources reflect what was actually felt? Thoughtful memoirists and biographers may tease these out in ways that seem wholly convincing. Brilliant writers like Solzhenitsyn or Erich Maria Remarque can evoke a credible sense of understanding by a convincing depiction of emotionally charged situations and scenes, even if for literary scholars an issue here is also how this engages or creates the readers' own feelings rather than those their subjects were supposed to have felt. For memoirists, writers, and correspondents, their "firsthand" accounts are also

---

[70] Iurii Lotman, *Universe of the Mind: A Semiotic Theory of Culture* (Bloomington: Indiana University Press, 1990), 221.

[71] Aaron J. Cohen, *Imagining the Unimaginable: World War, Modern Art, and the Politics of Culture in Russia, 1914–1917* (Lincoln: University of Nebraska Press, 2008).

[72] Samuel Hynes, *The Soldiers Tale: Bearing Witness to Modern War* (New York: Lane, 1997).

subject to the same waves of emotional camouflage that help send soldiers into battle. "Stoic peasant soldiers," the "most good natured, child-like, playful creatures in the world," whose capacity to attack was a "marvel," was a common trope of the Russian Front's best known foreign war correspondent, Stanley Washburn, who did not know Russian, as well as the memoirs of the far more restrained and insightful Guards officer, Prince Andrei Lobanov-Rostovsky, who served on the Southwestern Front and later taught at UCLA and Michigan.[73] Much of the contemporary newspaper and memoir literature describing the Russian Front before 1917 echoed these perspectives. The defensive tropes of stoicism, fatalism, and patriotic willingness to sacrifice for one's country filtered individual experience into socially and culturally acceptable representations of collective feeling.

Stoicism and fatalism have also been seen more broadly as characteristics of Russian peasant mentality, a perspective that has some merit. In the view of Porshneva, whose work has centered on the ambitious goal of analyzing the "mechanisms and content of the psychological changes, moods, and instincts [*avtomatizm*]" of Russian soldiers and "the role in their formation of the mental particularities of the peasantry," peasant soldiers brought from the countryside a fatalistic attitude to the front, an instinctive sense that its disasters were unavoidable. Their worldviews did not readily encompass the political reasons for war, whose rituals and discipline made more sense to them in religious terms, and their exposure to violence not only made them more cruel themselves but somewhat fearful of ever being able to return to "normal" life.[74] In Astashov's view, peasants held deep attachments to the "near world" of family and village, in contrast to the alien world of the front. In his and Porshneva's view, the "little fatherland" (*otechestvo*) of one's birth was all-important to a peasant but only loosely merged with attachment to the national Fatherland (*Otechestvo*) for which he had been called on to fight.[75]

Porshneva's and Astashov's important work reflects a widespread popular belief in 1914 that appeared in many of their sources. A widely circulated report in the press shortly after the war began, for example, described an entire unit, including its officers, who witnessed a vision in the sky over their position of the Holy Mother with Baby Jesus in her arms and one arm pointed toward the West, urging them to fight. The ranks fell to their knees, and then watched as the apparition changed into a large cross and disappeared.[76] The censors' reports certainly

---

[73] Stanley Washburn, *Field Notes from the Russian Front* (London: Andrew Melrose, 1915), 167 and *The Russian Advance* (New York: Doubleday, 1917), 49 and passim; Lobanov-Rostovsky, *The Grinding Mill*, passim.

[74] O. S. Porshneva, "Sotsial'noe povedenie soldat russkoi armii v gody pervoi mirovoi voiny," *Sotsial'naia istoriia: Ezhegodnik* (2001–2): 355–98 relying partly on S. Fedorchenko, *Narod na voine* (Petrograd, 1917).

[75] Astashov, "Russkii krest'ianin," esp. 72–74.

[76] RGIA f. 1062, op. 1, d. 5, entry of Sept. 18, 1914.

make it clear that peasant soldiers were lonely, heartsick, constantly worried about how their families were managing, and desperate for leave. ("Almost every letter expresses a passionate wish to see one's family, one's home ... a wish whose fulfillment depends on how long it will take for there to be peace.")[77] As the war continued, soldiers increasingly expressed anxieties about the rising cost of living in their villages and its implications for their family's welfare, a principal reason for desertion, as we have noted. ("With the cost of living so high, my heart is sick with worry when I think about how you must be living.")[78] One report even suggested soldiers volunteered for dangerous intelligence-gathering missions for the same reason, and once they left the lines just kept walking.[79]

Undoubtedly, the fact that some 80 percent of Russia's soldiers came from peasant villages is important to understanding social relationships and cultural perspectives at the front, including perhaps the fatalism with which many faced the possibility of death. Deeply felt village hostility toward gentry landowners may well have found reflection in anger about scarcities, bribes, and corruption in their units, and perhaps especially strong feelings about officers thought responsible for unnecessary casualties or who imposed harsh disciplinary measures unfairly, including courts-martial followed by immediate executions. Yet contemporary observers and later historians alike disseminate some of the same misconceptions that army commanders themselves had about the physical strength and stamina of their hearty peasant soldiers, whose collective mentality, insulated by religion and hard village life, they imagined protected these troops from much of the stress of war. Their Orthodox faith or lack of education did not mean a lack of intelligence or perception. Religious soldiers angrily blamed their officers and commanders for tactical military errors, for not recognizing their urgent need for rest, and for useless casualties that competence could have avoided. Many wrote of their outrage that they lacked adequate weaponry, that they were given leg wrappings (*botinki*) instead of boots, that officers and sergeants both were stealing and selling their food and equipment. They also railed against the humiliating way they were treated, even by the nursing corps, raising even in the degrading conditions of the front the issue of their dignity.[80] As leaves became more difficult to obtain, and then ended entirely in some units unless soldiers paid for them, some talked and wrote openly of the benefits of being wounded, especially during the hardships of winter.[81]

---

[77] RGVIA f. 2067, op. 1, d. 3853, ll. 572–572 ob.
[78] Ibid, l. 160.
[79] Ibid.
[80] RGVIA f. 2067, op. 1, d. 2937, l. 5; d. 2932, ll. 21, 36.
[81] RGVIA f. 2067, op. 1, d. 2935, l. 576, 578; d. 2932, ll. 7–8, 33; f. 2003, op. 1, d. 1486, ll. 194–205; f. 2067, op. 1, d. 3853, ll. 73–75.

If the dominant grain of soldiers' correspondence was some contrived level of "cheerfulness" and devotion to Tsar and Country, there is thus a strong implication of authenticity in the letters that can be read against this grain to reveal the complexities of feeling and anxiety at the front. The very distance in letters of this sort from the filtered prescriptions of loyalty, courage, and stoicism in the face of privation rings true in their unsuppressed admissions. "I find it difficult to get used to the endless sea of blood each day and which tears my heart from my chest"; "I find myself in the hands of fate, fearful and trembling, because blood is flowing and the ground shakes and there is always the smoke of gunfire"; "[W]e clearly saw they were leading us like cattle to slaughter."[82] As Reddy has suggested, for others the very process of writing despite these fears that they were "in good spirits" or "eager to crush the enemy" may also have made them feel that way, at least for the moment, just as marching to war before cheering crowds can make anxious soldiers feel "patriotic."[83]

Memoirs like those of Florence Farmborough can also be read most fruitfully against the grain of dominant contemporary discourse.[84] The historian Karen Petrone has done this in her thoughtful reading of a controversial memoir on the first year of the war that was written and published in the 1920s (and republished in 1998) by the Jewish psychologist L. N. Voitolovskii, who was drafted into the medical services both in the Russo-Japanese War and in 1914.[85] While the Soviet editors who published it praised it for its insights, the distinguished contemporary historian Igor Narskii has dismissed it as a fiction based not on firsthand experience but on various stories he had heard.[86] Voitolovskii, however, seems to have had the capacity to understand the conflicted emotions presented by some of the soldiers he interacted with and treated. Yet discerning his ability to do so is as much the historian's task as weighing the importance of his observations.

Sensitive to the filters through which Voitolovskii understood his patients as well as his own experience, Petrone is able to show how his accounts engage the conflicts of commitment and resistance, of anguish as well as the efforts to suppress anxiety in the service of adequate performance. There is authenticity in the complexities of the feelings he describes as well as his distance from others'

---

[82] RGIA f. 1088 op. 2 d. 164, l. 1; RGVIA f. 2048, op. 1, d. 905, l. 269 ob.; f. 2067 op. 1, d. 2937, l. 32; d. 3856, ll. 164.

[83] William M. Reddy, *The Navigation of Feeling: A Framework for the History of Emotions* (New York: Cambridge University Press, 2001), 96–111, 128. I appreciate Jan Plamper stimulating my thoughts on this issue.

[84] Florence Farmborough, *Nurse at the Russian Front: A Diary 1914-1918* (London: Constable, 1974).

[85] Lev Naumovich Voitolovskii, *Po sledam voiny: Pokhodnye zapiski, 1914–1917*, 2 vols. (Leningrad: Gosizdat, 1925, 1927); See also his *Vskhodil krovavyi mars: Po sledam voiny* (Moscow: Voenizdat, 1998), http://militera.lib.ru/memo/russian/voitolovsky_ln/index.html.

[86] Igor V. Narskii, "The Frontline Experience of Russian Soldiers in 1914–1916," *Russian Studies in History* 4 (Spring 2013): 32–34.

strong prescriptions of loyalty, courage, and stoicism in the fact of privation. His and others' struggles ring true in their very admission, as does his discussion of loneliness, his own inability to intervene against the brutality of looting and violence against especially Jewish civilians, and perhaps especially his fears after being away of returning to the awful conditions and dangers at the front.[87] The remarkable observations of the Jewish ethnologist and writer S. Anskii (aka Solomon Rappoport) are similarly most revealing when read with a sensitivity to their contrast to the perspectives of most of the officers he confronts.[88]

A final part of this difficult puzzle concerns the ways all lived experience acquires coherence as its fragments are passed into narrative forms, as we have discussed, and how these forms then acquire individual and social meaning in various (and variously structured) languages of expression.[89] (A related literature has amply demonstrated that social memory also works this way.)[90] What is contextually important here is that the world war that emerged in the fall of 1914 was unprecedented in its scale and scope, unimaginable in both literal and figurative ways. Much experience at the front in this sense had little connection to everyday life in the past or even to expectations about what it might be like. How totally new levels of experience could be processed and described was empirically as well as epistemologically uncertain. To extend this idea in Reddy's terms, the narration of war's horrors into patriotic sacrifice (or dreadful human waste, or even both) may actually link the certainties of expression to the *uncertainties* of feeling. For many soldiers, in other words, perhaps especially those who were illiterate and had to dictate how they felt to others, the safe use of patriotic or "spirited" (*bodrye*) narratives, prefigured everywhere during the war on posters and cards, in films, newspapers, books, and journals as well as in countless military ceremonies, may simply have reflected a longing to connect with the familiarities of home rather than a concurrence of expression and actual feeling.

It is, of course, empirically impossible to say precisely what the effect of all of this horror was on the behavior of Russian soldiers and officers, or to identify clearly the emotional and psychological conflicts peasant soldiers and others experienced after they found themselves at the front. Preoccupied with other pressing matters, Russian and Soviet authorities did not collect the information that may have been available. There was also little literature in Russia comparable

---

[87] Karen Petrone, "'I Have Become a Stranger to Myself': The Wartime Memoirs of Lev Naumovich Voitolovskii," in *Military Affairs*, ed. Stoff, 199–220.

[88] S. Ansky, *The Enemy at His Pleasure: A Journey through the Jewish Pale of Settlement during World War I*, ed. and trans. J. Neugroschel (New York: Henry Holt, 2002).

[89] Frank Ankersmit, Ewa Domanska, and Hans Kellner, eds., *Re-figuring Hayden White* (Stanford, CA, 2009); James Chandler et al., *Questions of Evidence* (Chicago: University of Chicago Press, 1991), 363–509.

[90] Maurice Halbwachs, *On Collective Memory*, trans. and ed. Lewis Coser (Chicago: University of Chicago Press, 1992). Kerwin Lee Klein reviews the literature in "On the Emergence of *Memory* in Historical Discourse," *Representations* 69 (2000): 127–50.

to that on "broken men" in the West after 1918, nor anything resembling what George Mosse has described as the "cult of the fallen soldier."[91]

At the same time, as we will discuss further later in this volume, it is well known that the emotional traumas of war can be readily expressed nonverbally through individual and collective acts of violence rather than through writing, especially of course by soldiers with limited literacy. These may reflect raw anger and rage as well as deep and conflicted longings and anxieties. They can smother fear of being brutalized through the act of doing violence to others. They can restore a sense of bravery by confronting a helpless antagonist. The very acting out of emotions can also reflect social or sociocultural conventions. Participating even reluctantly in even the more horrific forms of group violence like rape and pillage may be a way of assuring one remains a respected member of the group. From the very beginning of Russia's wars and revolutions the question of "mood" was not simply one of the soldiers' "fighting spirit."

Military Censorship and the Galician Disaster

Armed with these consistently positive reports about soldiers' moods, the Russian High Command remained consistently optimistic about the fighting capacity of the army. In early February 1915, the Germans launched a new offensive in East Prussia. The Russian command again badly underestimated the enemy's forces, but initial German gains did not significantly change the battle lines. Again, Russian losses were fierce. The Russian Tenth Army suffered more than fifty thousand casualties. Echoing the earlier Russian disaster, Ludendorff pumped up the German thrust as a second Tannenberg. By the end of February, however, Russian counterattacks had stabilized the area. Russian military fortunes seemed on the verge of improving. While the number of desertions was high and growing, and a worrisome number of soldiers had been taken prisoner—two matters that were almost certainly related—military censors continued to see few hints of possible disorders of the kind that had wracked the army and navy both less than ten years earlier in the war against Japan. The reported loyalty and enthusiasm of the soldiers communicated to headquarters by military censors gave no cause to revise the winter plan to strike Austria through the Carpathians and onto the Hungarian plain.

With this in mind, and with German troops in East Prussia defensively digging in, the Russian High Command continued to press an offensive against Austria in Galicia, building on the successes of Brusilov and others in the fall. The Russians would concentrate their forces here under what were regarded as

---

[91] George Mosse, *Fallen Soldiers* (New York: Oxford University Press, 1990), esp. ch. 5.

more competent field commanders against a less well equipped Austrian army whose Slavic soldiers from the Balkans were thought to be of uncertain loyalty. The Austrian army seemed all the more vulnerable when an ill-advised and poorly planned late winter offensive in the Carpathians by the bellicose Austrian chief of staff Count Franz Conrad von Hötzendorf proved an unmitigated disaster. During the last week of February, thousands of Austrian soldiers died from frostbite, sickness, and lack of medical care alone. If Austria-Hungary could be taken out of the war, Russia's superior numbers could possibly press Germany to end the fighting, especially considering the carnage in the West. In mid-March, the Russians overran the fortress at Przemyśl. Some 120,000 garrison troops surrendered, opening the way for a full-scale Russian offensive into the Carpathian Mountains.[92]

For a brief period of time in early April, expectations of success filled Russian newspapers. Trips to the front by war correspondents were carefully managed. Reports continued to emphasize discipline and high morale. To the London *Times* correspondent Washburn, for example, everyone seemed "contented and happy, especially when the weather was good. . . . The soldiers themselves go on from battlefield to battlefield, from one scene of carnage to another. They see their regiments dwindle to nothing, their officers decimated, three-fourths of their comrades dead or wounded, and yet each night they gather about their bivouacs apparently undisturbed by it all." Washburn did not see "a single sign among the soldiers of any disorder whatsoever" on the front in April 1915. Any reports to the contrary were "utterly distorted."[93] The popular illustrated journal *Niva* and others reinforced these perceptions.

Russian optimism was complemented by German anxiety. To Ludendorff and others, it was becoming increasingly clear that the Southwestern Front could not hold without German help. In some analyses, the threat of Italian intervention made German assistance all the more urgent, but the issue was pressing as well because Austria's collapse threatened destabilization throughout all of central Europe. After the Austrians lost Przemyśl, therefore, Germany redeployed long-range artillery and substantial numbers of troops to defend against Russia's advancing armies. Many new Russian recruits found themselves for the first time under ferocious bombardment. In mid-April, additional numbers of German troops moved into Western Galicia; in early May, the German command launched its own massive offensive.

Again German artillery decimated Russian positions. The winter lessons had not been learned. There were few reserves. Supplies dwindled and ran

---

[92] The story is told in detail by Alexander Watson, *The Fortress: The Siege of Przemysl and the Making of Europe's Bloodlands* (New York: Basic Books, 2020).
[93] Telegram from Washburn in RGIA f. 2067, op. 1, d. 3853, l. 366, and his *Field Notes from the Russian Front: The Russian Campaign* (London: Melrose, 1915), 169–70, 205.

out. Roads were clogged. Communication was faulty. General Ruzskii, calling for retreat, declared the situation to be hopeless. Russian troops were forced to pull back all across the front. Przemyśl, so recently captured at great cost, was evacuated. When fresh German forces were redeployed from the Balkans, the Galician retreat turned into a rout far worse even than Tannenberg and the Mazurian Lakes. By June 1915, the grand Galician capital of L'viv was once again occupied by the Germans and Austrians and promptly renamed Lemberg. As many as half a million Russian soldiers may have been captured or were otherwise missing. By May 1, 1915, Russia losses were almost 1.2 million, the number of family members bearing these losses as many as three or four times larger.[94]

While many military censors continued astonishingly to write that the retreat had not affected the soldiers' mood, some reports were far more ominous. What was soon known as the Great Retreat again reflected the consequences of the Russians' exhaustion, among its other brutal effects. Soldiers were "exhausted beyond words, too exhausted to groan as their wounds were dressed," as the British nurse Florence Farmborough described them; a "chaos of gigantic proportions," in Brusilov's words, where officers and men both "did not know what to do themselves or what their neighbors were doing."[95] Many soldiers expressed great bitterness toward officers for ordering them into battle without adequate weapons. Unit commanders were blamed for broken supply lines and the lack of food and munitions. Galician towns were plundered without mercy by soldiers increasingly "yearning for peace," a feeling one censor now reported in almost a third of all letters he was reading. And despite the threat of severe punishment, soldiers and officers both continued to reveal in their correspondence "entire plans of marching routes, positions, everything," as if they no longer cared: "almost every letter expresses their passionate wish to see one's family again, one's home."[96]

As the Great Retreat from Galicia became a rout, the heroic qualities of fighting for Tsar and Fatherland seemed to dissolve as legions of survivors carried the shocks of war back to whoever and whatever they found in their villages, cities, and towns, and into the further catastrophes of the war itself. So did the war's tenuous boundaries between the sacred and profane. "We Russians are fighting with God," one lamented, "the Germans fight with long-range artillery."[97]

---

[94] A. N. Iakhontov, "Tiazhelye dni (sekretnyia zasedaniia Sovieta Ministrov 16 Iiulia–2 Sentiabria 1915)," *Arkhiv Russkoi Revoliutsii* 18 (1926): 66; TsSU, *Rossiia v mirovoi voine*, 30; David R. Stone, *The Russian Army in the Great War: The Eastern Front, 1914–17* (Lawrence: University Press of Kansas, 2015), ch. 7.
[95] Farmborough, *Nurse*, 38; Brusilov, *Soldier's Notebook*, 136.
[96] RGVIA f. 2067, op. 1, d. 3853, ll. 433–34; f. 2031, op. 1, d. 1184, ll. 1–3.
[97] Vol'fovich and Medvedeva, *Tsarskaia armiia*, 27.

2
Was Russia Prepared?

In July 1914 all warring powers, as we know, expected the Great War to be short, a few months at most. At worst, the near universal expectation was that all belligerents would be physically and economically exhausted within a year, even if there was no outright victory for either side. Russia's vice minister for military supply, the decorated general of the infantry A. A. Polivanov, had prepared for a war lasting from two months to not more than twelve. Peace would be arranged on the basis of territories the armies then occupied, as it had been after the Franco-German War in 1870, the Russo-Turkish conflict in 1878, and the recent war with Japan. Few if any imagined that one year later Russia would have to support an army of more than 11 million fighting against Germany and Austria on a front extending more than a thousand miles while also fielding an army in the Caucasus against Germany's Turkish allies.

Part of the reason for this optimistic scenario was that the relatively limited needs of the recent Russo-Japanese War seemed appropriate models for mobilization and the formation of adequate military reserves. There was little thought that private industry might need to join with state factories in supplying the army in case of a more extended conflict. In 1913 a program had begun to strengthen the work of the all-important Main Artillery Administration, created in 1910, and the "Great Program" for building up the military, debated for several years before becoming law in June 1914, set in motion the planning and funding designed to make Russia's army not only the largest in Europe but the most powerful as well. Between 1908 and 1911 the State Duma budgeted less for the military than the War Ministry requested, but in 1912, 1913, and 1914 it allocated three times more. Despite reductions in some parts of the budget, more than 2.5 billion rubles in "ordinary" expenditures for the military was approved by the Duma between 1909 and 1913. In 1912 and 1913, the allocation rose more than 17 percent. Additional "extraordinary" expenditures authorized directly by the Council of Ministers assured that the Russian army in 1914 was receiving more funding than the German army and would soon become three times as large, a factor some historians view as accelerating the pace toward war.[1]

---

[1] A. L. Sidorov, *Finansovoe polozhenie Rossii v gody pervoi mirovoi voiny 1914–1917* (Moscow: Nauka, 1960), 60; Norman Stone, *The Eastern Front, 1914–1917* (London: Hodder and Stoughton, 1975), 37–38; Sean McMeekin, *The Russian Origins of the First World War*

How well prepared was the imperial Russian economy to sustain a modern war? And how seriously was the unexpected scale and scope of the war straining Russia's ability to defend itself in the late spring of 1915, as its armies retreated in chaos from the disastrous Galician offensive? In terms of broader historical interpretation, the question is least of all an economic one. It engages key issues of understanding the 1917 revolution and the origins of the Bolshevik system. Was the weakness of the last tsarist regime rooted more in economic difficulties or political ineptitude? Was the economic collapse that was to occur in 1917 rooted in the effects of the war or precipitated by the overthrow of tsarism itself and the concerted effort of Bolsheviks and others to undermine the legitimacy of the provisional regime? And to what extent were the policies of Bolshevik "war communism" after October driven by Leninist ideology as opposed to (or together with) the need to address the socioeconomic residues of longer-term economic failure? At their core, in other words, Russia's economic circumstances after 1914 relate directly to questions about the effectiveness of policies, practices, and the politics that set them in place.

Russia's relative underdevelopment as a modern economic power in comparison to Germany, Austria, England, and France has long been regarded as a key factor undermining its military capabilities in the First World War. Economic and social historians have emphasized the strains inherent in the processes of transitioning from an overwhelmingly agrarian economy to a partly industrialized one, especially in the 1890s before the Russo-Japanese War, and between 1908 and 1913, when industrialization was pressed with an eye on Russia's competitive international position and its importance to defense. Many see the origins of the revolution in these longer historical terms rather than the world war itself. Both the democratic liberal and democratic socialist Great Stories are grounded in the notion that without the war, their historicized vision of how Russia would modernize would have been realized. Indeed, a leading European economic historian even argues that the roots of 1917 are to be found in the *global* processes of late nineteenth-century socioeconomic transformation rather than that within Russia alone.[2]

Among the most powerful of these strains, rapid industrial growth confronted low levels of productivity, comparative inefficiencies in technology, and relatively low levels of training in rational industrial management and organization. As war approached, the Russian economy was in the midst of an inherently destabilizing

---

(Cambridge, MA: Harvard University Press, 2011), 33–37; V. L. Malkov, ed., *Pervaia Mirovaia Voina* (Moscow: Nauka, 1998), 12–105.

[2] Alessandro Stanziani, "The Russian Revolution in Global Perspective," unpublished ms. cited with the author's kind permission. See also his masterful study *Le économie en révolution: Le cas russe, 1870–1930* (Paris: Albin Michel, 1998).

period of transition. The intensification of industrial strikes between 1912 and July 1914 and unrest in the countryside as the Stolypin reforms moved to replace communal with individual holdings in ways that challenged traditional rural values may not have signaled a coming revolution even without the war, as some historians believe. But they clearly marked a political economy in distress. In this sense, at least, the war was something of a godsend to the tsarist regime, as the British ambassador George Buchanan suggested.[3]

The most knowledgeable Soviet historian of the question, A. L. Sidorov, considered that Russia's military resources were both insufficient and not well spent, a "very miserable and pitiful picture of the army's lack of preparedness for mobilization."[4] One can certainly argue in retrospect that spending huge sums to improve the stationary fortresses at places like Kovno and Brest-Litovsk along the East Prussian and Galician frontiers reflected a serious failure of political and military imagination, especially in light of the capacities of new and more mobile field artillery. However, such failure was characteristic of many high-ranking figures in every European power before 1914, including Germany and Austria, which poured similar resources into great fortresses like Przemyśl in Galicia. Investments in expanding Russia's cavalry also had obvious implications for sustaining a mobile infantry and artillery. Horses needed to be fed and supply lines set to accommodate their substantial appetites. It is also certainly the case that the defenders of what was called the "fortress system" were strongly at odds with War Minister Vladimir Sukhomlinov, who wanted them scrapped, and that this dissonance reflected cultural differences between aristocratic traditionalists like Generals Vladimir Dragomirov and Paul von Rennenkampf and the younger, upwardly mobile military "technicians" whom Sukhomlinov favored. According to a thorough study of the General Staff on the eve of the war, these younger officers had much to do with the generally positive reports about the army's capabilities prepared by British military attachés and other observers even after serious problems became apparent during strategic war games in the spring of 1914. As of 1912, slightly fewer than half of Russia's 45,582 officers were of aristocratic background.[5]

There was also cause for optimism in terms of Russia's industrial production. Here, too, the government's resistance to political liberalization now seemed to provide significant advantages in terms of state control over military production. While the Duma retained an important role in budgetary matters, it was prohibited from initiating or amending budget estimates. Military outlays were

---

[3] George Buchanan, *My Mission to Russia and Other Diplomatic Memories*, 2 vols. (London: Cassell, 1923), vol. 1, 212–15.
[4] Sidorov, *Finansovoe polozhenie*, 81–82.
[5] John Steinberg, *All the Tsar's Men: Russia's General Staff and the Fate of the Empire, 1898–1914* (Washington, DC: Woodrow Wilson Press, 2010), 258–69, 280–82.

strongly pushed by the tsar and his advisors, driven by the images of historic military glory that played such an important role in the dynasty's three-hundredth-anniversary celebrations in 1913. Huge investments were also made in rebuilding and expanding the Baltic and Black Sea fleets. Peter Gatrell has described the government's budgetary estimates as "ironclad" because the appropriations themselves were already in force. Between 1907 and 1913 these grew more than 40 percent.[6]

Defense production was almost entirely in state-owned factories, even if many of these depended on private suppliers. The largest was in Petrograd and Moscow. The Tula armaments complex a hundred miles south of Moscow, was a key site, as was the large Sormovo plant in Nizhnii Novgorod. Between 1900 and 1913 the private sector had doubled its share of defense production, but historical animus toward private entrepreneurship had only intensified with the emergence of manufacturers associations and other rudiments of civil society. The tsar himself was particularly adamant against depending for military goods on private manufacturers, the owners of which he distrusted as a social group, many of whom were foreigners. Production goals in state plants could be planned and executed by the Ministry of War without regard to cost or profit. Labor conditions and production problems could be cloaked from public scrutiny. There was little chance that plant managers could be accused of profiteering.

In these circumstances and given the near universal expectations about the short length of any future war, it is hardly surprising that officials in the War Ministry or the Main Artillery Administration had given little thought to mobilizing additional defense production. In the unexpected case of shortages, extra shifts in state plants could easily be added to production schedules. At the moment war broke out, production at the Tula complex had even been scaled back. The major issues of concern had instead to do with command and unit management, communication, and the distribution of military supplies, which all largely depended on effective administration of the railroads, especially lines closest to the fronts. On July 26, 1914, the same day the Duma met in its famous special session, Professor Peter Petrovich Migulin, a conservative economist widely recognized as an authority on Russian agriculture and finance, argued in the respected journal *Novyi Ekonomist* (*New Economist*) that Russia would have little difficulty withstanding a year of war with its current economic resources. Some 100 million rubles in funds were soon transferred from Berlin to St. Petersburg. A moratorium was declared on the exchange of currency for gold and the payment of foreign loans. Monetary exchange elsewhere had been suspended. According to the finance minister's calculations, even the suspension of

---

[6] Peter Gatrell, *Government, Industry, and Rearmament in Russia, 1900–1914* (Cambridge: Cambridge University Press, 1994), 139–52.

vodka sales demanded by the tsar would not reduce the state's income by more than 2.5 million rubles. This could be compensated by a readjustment of railroad tariffs.[7]

Other prominent industrial and commercial figures were equally confident that Russia's economy was resilient enough to meet the challenges of war. Although the Russian stock market had declined somewhat in the spring of 1914, the Eighth Congress of Representatives of Trade and Industry in June saw no signs that economic conditions would change significantly in the near future.[8] Between 1908 and 1913, the number of industrial enterprises had increased by some 30 percent, to almost thirty thousand. Coal production grew by 38 percent, iron ore by almost 30 percent between 1911 and 1913 alone.[9] Agricultural production, which provided some 80 percent of Russia's exports, was increasing, along with rural productivity in general and the availability of foodstuffs on the domestic market. Many thought optimistically that this was a consequence of the shift from communal to private landownership, the keystone of the Stolypin agrarian reform.[10] For Migulin and others, including Russia's leading financial newspaper, *Birzhevye Vedomosti* (*Stock Market News*), the growing role of the state was a powerful and welcome stimulus to further economic development and maybe even the war itself.

"Embedded" Underdevelopment, Russia's Peasants, and the Market Problem

In the aggregate, statistics showing Russia's economic performance between the start of the war in 1914 and the February revolution suggest that these expectations were at least partly borne out, especially in comparison to Germany. For 1917, S. N. Prokopovich, a well-respected contemporary economist with liberal social democratic leanings, measured only a 9.3 percent decline in agricultural production between 1913–14 and 1916–17, and a 30 percent drop in industrial production, measured in fixed rubles. Much of this was attributable to the loss of Poland. Two Soviet-trained experts on Russian agrarian production during the war, T. M. Kitanina and A. M. Anfimov, estimate the decline in sown land in seventy-two provinces between 1914 and 1917 at only around 11 percent, largely because of lost manpower.[11] The most comprehensive Soviet study of the wartime

---

[7] *Novyi Ekonomist* 31 (Aug. 2, 1914): 1–6.

[8] A. L. Sidorov, *Ekonomicheskoe polozhenie Rossii v gody pervoi mirovoi voiny* (Moscow: Nauka, 1973), 334.

[9] P. A. Khromov, *Ekonomicheskoe razvitie Rossii* (Moscow: Nauka, 1967), 405.

[10] A. N. Antsiferov, A. Bilimoviich, M. O. Osipovich, and D. N. Ivantsov, *Russian Agriculture during the War* (New Haven, CT: Yale University Press, 1930), ch. 2.

[11] S. N. Prokopovich, *Voina i narodnoe khoziaistvo*, 2nd. ed. (Moscow: Delo, 1918), 172–73; T. M. Kitanina, *Voina, khleb, i revoliutsiia* (Leningrad: Nauka, 1985), 21ff. See also A. M. Anfimov,

economy, by Sidorov, estimates the gross grain harvest rose in 1915 before declining about 15 percent in 1916 and only 3.5 percent more in 1917. Domestic machine building central to the war effort increased from 160 million to 302 million rubles, partly compensating for the sharp drop in imports. The productivity of industrial workers in Russia's Central Industrial Region also increased each year from 1914 to 1917, albeit by a small amount and only for large-scale industry, according to the Menshevik statistician Stanislav Strumilin, a student of Tugan-Baranovskii and a leading figure after 1921 in Gosplan. Gatrell calculates a 31 percent decline.[12] Most important, official figures for 1915 prepared and presented to the Council of Ministers by the State Chancery showed only a 7 percent reduction in sown land, caused mainly by fighting on the Southwestern and Northwestern Fronts, and a total output only 5 percent less than the five-year prewar average. These figures made it evident, the Chancery reported, that the harvest for 1916 would also be comparable to the prewar average despite the loss of production in particular regions. Chancery statistics for 1915 also predicted revenue of 1.8 billion for 1916, an increase of almost 65 percent.[13]

While Andrei Shingarev, Vladimir Groman, and other prominent economists and Duma members at the time complained that accurate data was impossible to come by, the well-known Russian social historian Boris Mironov has mustered aggregate data compiled by the Central Statistical Administration during and after the Civil War to argue that Russia's economy performed well between 1914 and 1917.[14] Gatrell has offered a similar, if more nuanced picture. The loss to Imperial Russia of 14 western provinces, including Warsaw and other industrial centers in Poland, clearly affected the national economy, as did a drastic reduction in exports. Yet Gatrell and his colleagues Mark Harrison and Andrei Markovich show some aggregate growth in the first two years of the war, largely as a result of state investment in defense production. Using statistics on industrial production compiled in 1918, they suggest that the production of sugar, salt, linen, and cotton cloth all increased between 1913 and 1916 and that "aggregate

---

Rossiiskaia derevnia v gody pervoi mirovoi voiny (1914–1917) (Moscow: Sotsialnaia i Politicheskaia Istoriia, 1962), chs. 2 and 3; Stanziani, *Le économie en révolution*, 101–26. The figures developed by Steven Wheatcroft and Peter Gatrell for agriculture are comparable. See Peter Gatrell, *Russia's First World War: A Social and Economic History* (London: Pearson-Longman, 2005), 166.

[12] S. Strumilin, "Ushcherb v proizvoditel'nosti truda vyzvannyia grazhdanskoi voiny i blokadoi," in *Izbrannye proizvedeniia*, 5 vols. (Moscow: Nauka, 1963), 2:190–96, first published in *Vestnik Truda* 3 (1921); Gatrell, *Russia's First World War,* 116. The problem of financing industry was extensively discussed throughout 1915 by an interministerial committee. See RGIA f. 1276, op. 12, d. 224 and 225, passim.

[13] RGIA f. 1276, op. 12, d. 225, ll. 20–21, 42.

[14] B. N. Mironov, *The Standard of Living and Revolution in Russia 1700–1917* (New York: Routledge, 2012).

production" of household goods "held up well."[15] Looking broadly at Russian national income, Markevich and Harrison argue that serious economic decline did not begin until 1917, at least in statistical terms.[16] Mironov is also convinced statistics show that Russia's economy did not begin to degenerate until after the February revolution. His argument makes the revolution itself the cause of Russia's subsequent economic collapse.[17]

Arguments about relative economic well-being based on statistics, however, can also be seen from different perspectives. Their very aggregation obscures significant differences between as well as within many provinces. The situation in different cities and towns varied widely depending in part on their access to resources and the nature of their industries. Towns and villages relatively close to railroad lines usually performed better than those at some distance for various reasons, including transport problems. In the deep countryside, as we will see, some village communities began to function essentially as self-contained autarchies as their regional economies faltered in the production and distribution of manufactured goods as well as the availability of foodstuffs in grain deficit localities like Tambov.

In addition, arguments about Imperial Russia's relative economic existence during these years reflect what Karl Polanyi termed in the theoretical language of economic anthropology the "economistic fallacy": a "formalist" approach that objectivizes socioeconomic processes as statistically measurable and understandable first and foremost in terms of their inherent (and hence "scientific") economic logics and rationality.[18] The error here is not the lack of rationality in processes of economic exchange nor the inaccuracy of aggregate statistics if they are presented with appropriate cautions. It is an assumption about the relationship between objective statistical indicators, market exchange, and the actual experiences of everyday life. Economically well-off societies commonly harbor large populations living at subsistence levels or below. In conditions of scarcity, or anticipated scarcities, the substantive anxieties and actualities of scarcity, as well as the perceived differences in economic well-being, are not statistically reducible and hence not proper components of economic measurement. Nor are the changing processes of both production and distribution, their perceived inequities, and the competing conceptions of "fairness" they engendered.

---

[15] Peter Gatrell and Mark Harrison, "The Russian and Soviet Economies in Two World Wars: A Comparative View," *Economic History Review* 3 (1993): 439–40.

[16] Andrei Markevich and Mark Harrison, "Great War, Civil War, and Recovery: Russia's National Income, 1913–1928," *Journal of Economic History* 3 (2011): 680.

[17] B. N. Mironov, "Cannon Fodder for the Revolution: The Russian Proletariat in 1917," *Kritika: Explorations in Russian and Eurasian History* 2 (Spring 2017): 389–400. B. N. Mironov, *Rossiiskaia imperiia: Ot traditsii k modernu*, 3 vols. (St. Petersburg: Bulanin, 2014).

[18] Karl Polanyi, "The Economy as Instituted Process," in *Economic Anthropology*, ed. E. LeClair and H. Schneider (New York: Holt, Rinehart, 1968), 122–42.

In other words, Polanyi and others have argued instead that production and exchange are always embedded in social and cultural processes that they also reflect: the social and cultural relations of plant owners and workers, for example, or how different villages interact as they exchange goods with each other. These processes also affect how goods are produced and exchanged. They reflect and reproduce the values and value systems different exchange practices engage. In the formal economic sense, markets and market prices are always about "scarcity": the relation between supply and demand, however abundant the supply. Prices balance availability and "need" when need is defined as the willingness to pay, not the necessity for essential goods like food. But whether markets are perceived to act "rationally" or "fairly" in these regards depends not only on the ways transactions occur and the level of commercialization they reflect but on the material, emotional, and ideological elements that define "scarcity" and "need," especially for individuals and communities facing deficits in essential goods and financial resources and find themselves under significant stress.

In the terms of economic anthropology, the operative concepts here can be reduced to "substantivism" and "embeddedness."[19] "Rational" actions and the formal logics of economic exchange also reflect substantive understandings of gain and loss embedded in contextualized cultural values and social relations. These affect the ways economies behave, and goods are produced and exchanged as much as or more than the logics of rational economic maximization used by economic "formalists." Simplifying the complex debates between formalists and substantivists, we can say with some confidence that along with actual conditions reflected in accurate and objective statistics, substantive values and socially and culturally embedded economic processes also affect how economies distribute goods, manage material well-being, and understand the meanings of need and social welfare.[20]

Thus, in substantivist terms, Russia's spurt of industrial modernization before the First World War was the result not only of rational investments but also of efforts to apply particular understandings of "rational" production, that is, a concerted effort to rationalize workplace practices and relations to make them more productive. As Heather Hogan has shown in an important study, the invention of the time clock and the imposition of so-called Taylor processes based on time and motion studies radically restructured work experience in many enterprises.[21] So did the further capitalization of private industry, which pressed

---

[19] See, e.g., Mark Granovetter, "Economic Action and Social Structure: The Problem of Embeddedness," *American Journal of Sociology* 19, no. 3 (1985): 481–510; A. Jenkins, "'Substantivism' as a Comparative Theory of Economic Forms," in *Sociological Theories of the Economy*, ed. Barry Hindess (London: Palgrave Macmillan, 1977), 66–91.

[20] Karl Polanyi, *The Livelihood of Man* (New York: Academic Press, 1977), ch. 1.

[21] Heather Hogan, *Forging Revolution: Metalworkers, Managers, and the State in St. Petersburg, 1890–1914* (Bloomington: Indiana University Press, 1993).

the importance of low wages and other costs in an effort to maximize profits, and the extension of commercial marketing practices like those famously introduced by itinerant Singer (Zinger) sewing machine salesmen. In these terms Russia's economy was still only partly commercialized by 1914. On a longitudinal scale between "primitive" and "highly commercialized" market systems, it was a "mixed" system characterized by the presence alongside regional or national commercial markets of minimally or noncompetitive local forms of highly gendered exchange—all peasant women selling the same or similar goods at the same place on the same day, for example, and "fairly," that is, at essentially the same price.[22]

As economic historians and anthropologists have characterized them, highly commercialized systems are distinguished by fully monetized exchange, long-distance trading patterns, highly developed forms of management and administration, and relatively impersonal processes of exchange. Production and distribution of goods especially in urban centers are interlocked with national politics and political authorities. In highly commercialized market systems, the processes of market exchange spread over a range of economic and socioeconomic functions. Labor is commoditized and exchanged; investing and the capitalization of business are brokered; and commodities as well as commoditized labor are fungible through well-developed monetary systems. All of this increases the production and distribution of goods and reduces scarcities. In the process, the concept "market" is valorized as an essential social good in itself.[23]

In contrast, less or minimally competitive market systems (and thus in economic terms more "primitive") are characterized by direct personal exchange built on trust, limited productivity, and essentially inelastic demand. What is produced is consumed or exchanged for other essential goods. The marketplace here is a center of barter or other relatively personal transactions. The very term "market" generally connotes the social gathering of the market*place* and is likely to encompass a range of activities and practices not directly associated with trade. In partly commercialized market systems local gateway communities also tend to channel goods in various ways into monopolistic systems of distribution, including black or gray markets that function most profitably for closely

---

[22] V. S. Diakin, B. V. Anan'ich, R. Sh. Ganelin, and B. B. Dubentsov, eds., *Krizis samoderzhaviia v Rossii, 1895–1917* (Leningrad: Nauka, 1984), esp. 358–59; B. Kerblay, *Les marchés paysans en U.R.S.S.* (Paris: Mouton, 1968), esp. 90–98; For a full discussion, see my "The Problem of Market Relations and the State in Revolutionary Russia," *Comparative Studies in Society and History* 2 (Apr. 1994): 356–96.

[23] G. William Skinner, "Marketing and Social Structure in Rural China," *Journal of Asian Studies* 24 (1964): 343; 25 (1965): 195–228; S. Plattner, "Markets and Marketplaces" in *Economic Anthropology*, ed. S. Plattner (Stanford, CA: Stanford University Press, 1989), ch. 7; Carol Smith, "Exchange Systems and the Spatial Distribution of Elites," as summarized in Richard Hodges, *Primitive and Peasant Markets* (New York: Blackwell, 1988); W. Christaller, *Central Places in Southern Germany* (Englewood Cliffs, NJ: Prentice-Hall, 1967); Roy Dilley, "The Notion of the Market in Social Anthropological and Sociological Perspectives," in Plattner, *Markets and Marketings*, ch. 1.

knit networks of traders when goods are scarce. Some of these might be the result of production cartels or other kinds of syndicates, especially in the area of natural resources, as they were in Russia in 1914. Others might be the result more simply of local interests or even personal and family relations that supersede the "objective" and "rational" practices of competitive market exchange. In either case the government was, in Gatrell's words, the "regulator of demand."[24]

In the view of the historical sociologist Teodor Shanin, Russia's problems relating to a partially commercialized economy found particular reflection in the tensions between producing for the market and producing to meet community needs, that is, the reluctance of peasant households to abandon personal and reciprocal ties for more impersonal and less controllable market relations. Especially in villages at some distance from railroads or river transport, production continued to be constrained by collective responsibilities, redistributive practices, and the virtual absence of internalized notions of land as private property. This did not mean communal villages necessarily resisted innovation nor that Russian peasants were not self-interested producers. Yet reorganizing production for the commercial market on the basis of predictions about future demand engaged social and cultural values quite different from those that structured production to meet household and community needs.[25] Producing for an uncertain commercial market displaced the relative security experienced in more personal and familiar kinds of exchange. There was also what the contemporary Russian historian Olga Porshneva describes as the securities of a communal way of life, with its shared responsibilities and welfare as well as its privations.[26]

In different ways, Peter Stolypin and Sergei Witte both understood this as prime ministers before 1914: Stolypin in his effort to confront Russia's subsistence agrarian culture head-on, Witte in his anxieties about Russia's underdeveloped industry and commercial economy more generally. Both also understood that the social and cultural marginalization of commercial activity had a long history in Imperial Russia. So did the direct role of the state in some branches of industrial manufacture, transport, and banking. Formal monopolies and monopolistic practices in metallurgy and metals production, oil, textiles, and other industries had long been condoned and in some cases directly facilitated by a state more concerned with securing the materials it needed than encouraging competitive markets and commercial cultures. In the metals and metallurgy branch

[24] Sidorov, *Ekonomicheskoe polozhenie*, 371–72; Peter Gatrell, *The Tsarist Economy* (London: Batsford, 1986), 177.
[25] T. Shanin, "Nature and Logic of the Peasant Economy," *Journal of Peasant Studies* 1 (1973): 64–80. See also E. Kingston-Mann and T. Mixter, eds., *Peasant Economy, Culture, and Politics of European Russian, 1800–1921* (Princeton, NJ: Princeton University Press, 1991), esp. chs. 1, 3, and 4.
[26] O. S. Porshneva, *Mentalitet i sotsial'noe povedenie rabochikh, krest'ian i soldat Rossii v period pervoi mirovoi voiny* (Ekaterinburg: UrO RAN, 2000), 84–85.

so important for military production, for example, twelve leading Petrograd producers had formed their own production syndicate as early as 1902 and moved aggressively over the years against nonmember firms. By 1911, the syndicate (officially the Society for the Sale of Metallurgical Products, or Prodamet) controlled 90 percent of sheet iron sales, 96 percent of construction steel, and 74 percent of all pig iron production.[27] As Witte insisted, these impediments had to be overcome for Russia to advance as a world economic power.

At the same time, Petrograd, Moscow, Nizhnii Novgorod, Odessa, and several other cities in the empire, along with the regions around them, clearly reflected a very high degree of commercial activity on the eve of the war, comparable in some sectors to that of Germany and Western Europe. Large metalworking and electro-technical enterprises well integrated into European business networks balanced to some extent the monopolistic practices of the syndicates. Yet they also stood side by side with hundreds of small enterprises operating in relative isolation from the commercial mainstream, and with employees who retained close ties to their village. More than half of Russia's nonagricultural workforce in 1914 labored as artisans or workers in shops with fewer than fifteen employees. They produced some 34 percent of Russia's total industrial output.[28]

Commercial market forces also shaped behaviors and expectations in some areas of the countryside as much as they did in more fully commercialized societies, especially in the Volga region and southern Ukraine, where the Stolypin reforms had produced a large number of separators from the traditional communes. Here the processes of modernization may well have had the most effect on peasant communities, intensifying hostility toward large landowners who could produce for export because the peasants' low standard of living provided cheap hired labor. Still, they had not managed on the eve of the war to improve significantly either the yields of vital foodstuffs or commercial crops like flax or cotton. Only some 25 percent of all rural households had been carved out of the traditional village commune into private landholdings by 1914. The remainder continued to live and work in variegated but still highly localized communal villages where the limits of the world (*mir*) still generally conformed in social and cultural terms not only to the limits of the commune itself but to notions of social stability. (In Russian, significantly, the same word for both "a rural commune" and "peace" is also *mir*.)[29]

Entrepreneurial activities also flourished in many rural areas in 1914, especially those engaged in handicraft production. Large numbers of grain merchants,

---

[27] Gatrell, *Tsarist Economy*, 178–79.
[28] V. G. Groman, ed., *Dinamika rossiiskoi i sovetskoi promyshlennosti*, 2 vols. (Moscow: Gosizdat, 1929–30), vol. 1, pt. 3, 176–77; Alex Nove, *An Economic History of the U.S.S.R.* (New York: Penguin, 1988), 17.
[29] Diakin, *Krizis samoderzhaviia*, 358.

petty traders, police, tax collectors, and minor bureaucrats collectively served as the social linkages between Russia's very different (and internally variegated) urban and rural worlds as well as with the state. Russian provincial towns and trading centers may be said to have constituted what the economic anthropologist G. William Skinner has termed "central places" of interaction between the highly commercialized environments of cities like Moscow and Petrograd and the much less commercialized political economies of the *mir*. Demand for manufactured goods was limited by poverty and the traditions of household self-sufficiency. Commodity production and grain marketing had both increased in the years before the war, but so had the amount of foodstuffs retained by the village for its own consumption, a sign of some resistance to commercialization. As peasant maxims had it, "tears flowed through gold" and "when money speaks, truth is silent."[30]

At the beginning of 1914, Russian per capita income remained little more than 100 rubles according to the best estimates, approximately one-third of what it was in Germany and less than one-sixth the level in the United States.[31] In essence, "partial commercialization" had created a "market problem" for wartime Russia: how to assure the distribution of scarce commodities and resources in ways that met basic local needs in the countryside as well as Russia's cities and towns while also satisfying the army's increasingly insatiable demands.[32]

Fault Lines of Economic Mobilization

The period between July 1914 and the spring of 1915 brought some social and economic dislocation almost everywhere. Within a relatively short period of time, however, the needs of the war itself began to have a strengthening effect on some industries and plants. By the summer of 1915, as new resources were mobilized to support defense production and a reasonable system of deferments and exemptions for skilled workers was finally in place, a complex process of industrial segregation began to unfold, separating industries favored for their

---

[30] Paul R. Gregory, "Grain Marketings and Peasant Consumption in Russia, 1885–1913," *Explorations in Economic History* 17 (1980): 135–64; Kerblay, *Les marchés*, 90–98; Porshneva, *Mentalitet*, 98, 352.

[31] Paul R. Gregory, "1913 Russian National Income," *Quarterly Journal of Economics* 3 (Aug. 1976): 445–49. See also the difficulties regarding this calculation in the reviews of his book *Russian National Income 1885–1993* (Cambridge: Cambridge University Press, 1983) by Geoffrey Jones in *Slavonic and East European Review* 64, no. 3 (1986): 473–75; Martin Spechler in *Journal of Economic History* 3 (1875): 737–38; Charles Feinstein in *Economic History Review* 38, no. 2 (1985): 330–31; and Olga Crisp in *Canadian Slavonic Papers* 2 (1984): 248–49.

[32] For a broad discussion, see Mark Harrison and Andrei Markevich, "Russia's Home Front 1914–1922: The Economy," in *Russia's Home Front in War and Revolution*, bk. 3, ed. Christopher Read, Peter Waldron, and Adele Lindenmeyr (Bloomington, IN: Slavica, 2018), 23–44.

importance to the war effort from those state officials were unable or uninterested in supporting, and identifying particular branches of production and particular plants within the favored category for financial and other kinds of assistance.

One of the features of this segregation was related to the exceptional degree of industrial concentration in Imperial Russia, both in geographical terms and in terms of the structure of production units. Russia's vast geography and relatively underdeveloped systems of commerce and communication had historically encouraged development near centers of wealth and power. So did the cultural proclivities of Russia's relatively small cohort of industrial entrepreneurs, which had few shared economic interests with provincial gentry. There were also pressures from the 1890s onward for economies of scale, an important element of both industrial growth and industrial concentration before the war.[33]

As a result, more than 60 percent of the country's workforce (excluding Poland) in 1914 was concentrated in the Moscow and Petrograd industrial districts, some 400,000 workers in the capital itself. More than half worked as metallists in large iron and steel fabricating plants making military equipment after 1914, some 80 percent in plants with more than five hundred employees. Metalworkers were a significant proportion of Moscow's industrial workforce as well, but Moscow province as a whole had a much larger concentration of textile workers, almost a half-million in Vladimir and Kostroma. Kiev province and the Donbas industrial region held the overwhelming number of mining and mineral extraction enterprises and workers. In 1913, the central industrial region stretching out from Moscow, the northern region around Petrograd, and the southern industrial region around the Donbas accounted for more than 60 percent of Russia's gross industrial output and employed more than 500,000 persons.[34] The concentrations of other industrial sectors were comparable. Almost 85 percent of Russia's oil production was centered in Baku; southern Russia produced 75 percent of the country's iron; almost 71 percent of all coal was mined in the Donets region, a figure which grew to almost 88 percent with the loss of Polish mines in 1914. By 1914, moreover, more than 55 percent of Russia's industrial workers were in large plants employing more than a thousand workers, subdivided into smaller shops to meet different production needs; almost 83 percent were in plants of more than one hundred.[35]

---

[33] A. J. Rieber, *Merchants and Entrepreneurs in Imperial Russia* (Chapel Hill: University of North Carolina Press, 1982).

[34] A. G. Rashin, *Formirovanie rabochego klassa Rossii* (Moscow: Sotsial-Ekonomicheskaia Literatura, 1958), 189.

[35] *Chislennost' i sostav rabotnikov zheleznodorozhnogo transporta k kontsu 1920 g.* (Moscow: Gosizdat, 1921), 98; P. A. Khromov, *Ekonomicheskaia istoriia SSSR: Period promyshlennago i monopolisticheskogo kapitalizma v Rossii* (Moscow: Vyshaia Shkola, 1982), 399ff.

How important was this in substantive terms? One obvious consequence was that grievances about wages were broadly shared. So were those relating to dignified treatment, especially in textile plants with large numbers of women workers but where almost all foremen were male. Large metals and machine building plants also tended to aggravate workplace relations and intensify disputes over wage differentials. Grievances did not have to be uniformly shared to affect productivity and production lines. The shutdown of only two or three plants in the Vyborg district of Petrograd, for example, even if stimulated by a relatively small number of workers, could turn thousands into the streets. The same was true for Moscow, the huge textile complexes in Ivanovo and Kostroma, and other significant industrial centers.

One additional result of this concentration was the unevenness of Russia's industrial production as a whole. Although total output for the fifty-eight provinces of European Russia increased between 1913 and 1916 by some 21 percent, in aggregate terms this was almost entirely due to metals and chemicals production and the production of guns and ammunition. Among all other industrial branches, only leather, linen, hemp and jute, and some clothing plants (including shoes) showed any increase at all and may have totaled only a little more than 8 percent of new production. Everywhere else, output declined, in some branches quite sharply. Most important were the declines in Russia's two largest industrial sectors in numbers of workers, excluding the railroads: food processing, where output may have fallen as much as 35 percent between 1914 and 1916, and cotton textiles, where the decline was reported to be around 17 percent.[36]

Reasons for these declines are not difficult to identify. Textiles and other sectors declined because in addition to its relatively weak internal markets Russia suffered from an overall shortage of domestic investment capital, a corresponding dependency on foreign banks and the cost of its indebtedness, and in some branches a serious weakening of exports, especially with the loss of German and Austrian markets. By the spring of 1916 all of these seemed serious enough to the editors of *Birzhevye Vedomosti* to worry that with the war's incalculable losses of blood and money, Russia still would not gain its economic independence from the more fully commercial markets and industries of western Europe.[37]

Yet this imbalance was also closely related to the state's focus on defense production, with little concern for how these changes were more broadly experienced in both material and substantive terms. By the time of the Galician disaster, the regime had already bestowed the largest and most lucrative military

---

[36] Tsentral'noe Statisticheskoe Upravlenie [TsSU], *Fabrichno-zavodskaia promyshlennost' v period 1913–1918*, vol. 26, no. 1 (Moscow ,1926), 404–13; N. Ia. Vorob'ev, "Izmeneniia v Russkoi promyshlennosti v period voiny i revoliutsii," *Vestnik Statistiki* 14 (1923): esp. 150–53.

[37] *Birzhevye Vedomosti*, Apr. 2, 1916.

contracts to a relatively small number of major producers. In the fall of 1914 contracts worth some 66 million rubles for shells and shrapnel were placed with only sixteen plants, led by the Putilov, Baltic, Obukhovskii, Nevskii, and Petrograd metal works in Petrograd.[38] In contrast, not surprisingly, both the output and profitability of less favored plants and industrial sectors quickly suffered. Materials they needed for production became increasingly scarce. So did private investment. Many smaller enterprises that lost out in the competition for contracts found themselves forced to scale back. Others closed their gates. While output increased over 50 percent in metalworking plants receiving state contracts between 1914 and 1915, the number of metalworking enterprises was reported to have contracted dramatically, from 2,420 to 1,977 (or 18.3 percent). Even in the favored chemicals industry, responsible now for meeting the army's massive need for gunpowder and explosives, the number of plants may have fallen from 504 at the beginning of 1914 to fewer than 390 by the end of 1915, and the number of chemical workers by some 21 percent.[39] In total, again according to data published by the Central Statistical Administration in 1926, some 929 major enterprises closed or ceased production in 1914 and 1915, and almost 300 more in 1916. Some of these plants reopened, but the overall effect of the shift to military production even in favored industrial sectors remained highly destabilizing.[40] In the meantime, the demand for defense production continued to grow. "Rationalization" and aggressive foremen ratcheted up the pace of work. "God save you to talk with a neighbor, take a smoke, leave the bench, sit in a group, or even worse, glance at a paper!"[41] It was hardly surprising that the substantive tensions and workplace stress even in the most favored industrial sector continued to intensify. But so did shop floor tensions in less favored industries, where strains came from declining production, a fall in real wages, and the threat of closing down rather than pressures to ramp up output.[42] Meanwhile the need to replace workers lost to the war helped drive raw and poorly educated rural labor into industrial centers far faster than they could be readily absorbed.

This was especially the case for women, many of whose well-being in the countryside was threatened by the loss of a husband or son. Women poured into the industrial workforce between 1914 and 1917, especially in Petrograd and Moscow. Textile, chemical, and paper industries continued to employ the largest share of women, as they had before the war, but changes in gender ratios occurred

---

[38] Sidorov, *Ekonomicheskoe polozhenie*, 28–29.
[39] TsSU, *Fabrichno-zavodskaia promyshlennost'*, vol. 26, no. 1, 34–36.
[40] Ibid.; Vorob'ev, "Izmeneniia," 26.
[41] Hogan, *Forging Revolution*, 196.
[42] TsSU, *Fabrichno-zavodskaia promyshlennost'*, vol. 26, no. 2, tables 14, 15, 71. Hogan, *Forging Revolution*, 182, 236, 266.

in every industrial group, including metals. By 1914, as many as 600 of the 1,250 workers in the important Aivaz machine shops in St. Petersburg were women. They earned a base pay of ninety kopecks compared to the one ruble fifty kopecks earned by men. When large numbers of women workers at the Treugol'nik rubber plant in Moscow fell ill from toxic fumes in March 1914, management dismissed their complaints as hysteria and "mass psychosis."[43] (Metalworkers supported them with a solidarity strike.) Women's life in the workplace was also aggravated by inadequate housing and other living conditions. Dignity emerged as a pressing issue along with wages, even as the risk of protest increased. Still, women managed in various ways to make their anger felt. In many shops and factories they were regarded as more militant than men, capturing the attention of Bolsheviks and other radical social democrats and further contributing to the range of tensions with male foremen and management. As a way of asserting control, some plant owners resisted granting wage increases to women despite expanding profits.[44]

In all these regards the fault lines of Russia's economic mobilization in the late spring of 1915 amplified the underlying distortions of its "partly commercialized" system of distribution. It became unprofitable for some mechanical plants, even in the metals sector, to continue production of nonmilitary goods, despite the fact that many other plants depended on such equipment to fulfill their own military contracts. Industrial output in Petrograd expanded more rapidly than in any other place in the empire after the war began, but so did competition for new defense orders and the rate of factory closings. Only the Moscow industrial region had as many plants shut down during the war as Petrograd.[45] Declining productivity particularly affected textile plants and their large numbers of women workers. By the end of 1914, some 18 percent of all textile enterprises had been forced to shut down as a result of inadequate supplies despite the state's demand for uniforms, reducing the workforce in this sector by almost 200,000.[46]

Here both symbolically and materially were perhaps the most dramatic consequences of the war's uneven effect on Russian industrial production: its substantive effect on dislocations and social relations within the workforce as well as the relation to the marketplace of those who lost their jobs temporarily or

---

[43] Hogan, *Forging Revolution*, 182, 236, 266.

[44] Diane P. Koenker and William G. Rosenberg, *Strikes and Revolution in Russia* (Princeton, NJ: Princeton University Press, 1989), 34–36. Among other works, see especially Rochelle Goldberg Ruthchild, *Equality and Revolution: Women's Rights in the Russian Empire, 1905–17* (Pittsburgh, PA: University of Pittsburgh Press, 2010).

[45] TsSU, *Fabrichno-zavodskaia promyshlennost'*, vol. 26, no. 1, 35–38; M. M. Shmukker, *Ocherki finansov i ekonomiki zhel.-dor. transport za 1913–1922* (Moscow: Naridnoe Komissariat Putei Soobshchenia, 1923), 95–102.

[46] Koenker and Rosenberg, *Strikes*, 43–46.

more permanently, and who found themselves cut off from everyday necessities by drastic changes in their income as well as by rising prices. While Petrograd, Moscow, and several other industrial centers saw huge increases in the number of industrial workers in a relative handful of plants working for defense, many areas of southern Russia, central Ukraine, and the textile towns of the Central Industrial Region experienced significant losses, undermining local economies and creating widespread hardship. The five largest Petrograd factories soon employed more than 80,000 workers, the seventeen largest more than 165,000. Housing was soon stretched to the limit.[47]

Perhaps more important, the evidence suggests that at least one-third of all employed workers in Russia left their jobs for one reason or another during the first two years of the war: because their plants shut down, because they were fired for "organizing" or "agitating" for strikes, because they were locked out, and, most stressful of all, because they needed instead to look for food or other necessary goods.[48] Women, again, were particularly vulnerable, targeted in many cases by foremen and other factory officials with whom they had had some form of altercation. According to a survey taken in Moscow at the beginning of 1915, metalworkers were spending some 74 percent of their family wages on food and clothing, textile workers even more than their recorded income.[49] At the Treugol'nik rubber plant in Petrograd, the site of protests over toxic fumes in March 1914, the number of workers replaced in 1915 exceeded ten thousand, a startling figure by any account. During the first nine months after it opened in July 1915, the new Moscow labor exchange saw more than 300,000 workers file through its offices.[50] Even in favored industrial enterprises and shuttered plants elsewhere that managed to reopen, their workers (and others) suffered the anxieties and deprivations of scarcity, social dislocation, and the constant threat of unemployment. In "formalist" terms, Russia's industrial economy grew significantly after the concerted efforts at economic mobilization in the late spring and early summer of 1915. In "substantive" terms, the process was embedded in deteriorating workplace relations and conditions, an increase in passive as well as more overt hostility between managers and workers, growing imbalances between those in favored and unfavored industries and even within them, and new levels of anxiety throughout the mobilizing industrial economy as a whole.

---

[47] Sidorov, *Ekonomicheskoe polozhenie*, 341; I. P. Lieberov, "Petrogradskii proletariat v bor'ba za pobedu fevral'skoi burzhuazno-demokraticheskskoi revoliutsiia v Rossii," *Istoriia SSSR* 1 (1957): 43.
[48] RGIA f. 1276, op. 11, d. 168, esp. ll. 3, 37–38.
[49] N. Balabanov, "Rabochii klass nakanune revoliutsii," in *Professional'noe dvizhenie v Petrograde v 1917 godu*, ed. A. Anskii (Leningrad: Soviet Professional'nykh Soiuzov, 1928), 15–16.
[50] K. F. Sidorov, "Rabochee dvizhenie Rossii v godu imperialisticheskoi voiny," in *Ocherki po istorii oktiabr'skoi revoliutsii*, 2 vols., ed. M. N. Pokrovskii (Moscow: Gosizdat, 1927), 1: 217–26.

Russia's Railroad Lifeline

In critical ways, each of the fault lines of Russia's economic mobilization was related to the performance of the transport system, especially railroads. As in the United States at the time, Russia's forty-three thousand miles of rail lines were considered the huge country's "lifeline" (*zhiznennyi nerv*), the single most important element in fostering and sustaining economic well-being and in facilitating the country's defense.[51] By late 1914 this was literally as well as figuratively true. The army depended on railroads for almost all of its military supplies, even those that field commanders or their agents requisitioned or confiscated. Wounded soldiers needed hospital trains. Refugees clambered on overflowing cars to take them from danger zones. The vast bulk of food and raw materials coming to Russia's cities and its industrial plants was carried by the railroads and stored in railroad depots. With the closing of the western frontier and after Turkey entered the war and access to the Mediterranean through the Dardanelle Straits was closed off, the Trans-Siberian line running almost fifty-five hundred miles from Moscow to Vladivostok was the empire's major route for imported goods. The British effort to relink Russia to the Mediterranean at Gallipoli was a well-known disaster.[52]

As late as 1913 commentators waxed eloquent about the financial, administrative, and strategic importance of Russia's railroads to the future of the empire. They urged the state to invest millions of additional funds in new construction, especially on private lines. A few argued that this would only increase already large private profits at the expense of the state's own interests without improving railroad administration or efficiency.[53] One of the most prominent railroads belonged to Nikolai Vissarionovich Nekrasov, Miliukov and Shingarev's left liberal colleague on the Kadet Central Committee. A graduate of the St. Petersburg Institute of Railroad Engineering, a founding member of the Union of Professors in Tomsk, and a well-respected professor at the Tomsk Institute of Technology, Nekrasov quickly became known for his expertise in transport matters. Elected to the Duma in 1907, he became one of its most active deputies, taking the rostrum more than one hundred times. In addition to serving in 1917 as the Provisional Government's minister of transport in its first two cabinets, he would succeed Shingarev as minister of finance after Kerensky became prime minister in July.

---

[51] *Zheleznodorozhnik* 1 (Nov. 30, 1906).
[52] Among his other important articles on the railroads, see Anthony Heywood, "Imperial Russia's Railways at War, 1914–17: Challenges, Results, Costs, and Legacy," in Read, Waldron, and Lindenmeyr, *Russia's Home Front*, 65–92.
[53] N. V. Nekrasov, "K Voprosy o chastnom zheleznodorozhnom khoziaistva," *Novyi Ekonomist* 13 (1914): 6–8; V. N. Sokolov, "Vykup chastnykh zheleznykh dorog," *Novyi Ekonomist* 11 (1914): 4–6.

Nekrasov strongly objected to the level of profits generated by Russia's private rail lines. He was also concerned about how the division between private and state-owned lines would affect the railroads' overall ability to meet the country's wartime needs. Seven private railroads dominated the network, privately financed with bonds that were guaranteed by the state.[54] He and others thought Goremykin's predecessor as prime minister, V. N. Kokovtsov, was excessively cozy with private railroad owners. They also joined the leading railroad journals in regarding Minister of Transport S. V. Rukhlov as poorly qualified for his position.[55] A former prison inspector in the Ministry of Internal Affairs, Rukhlov had gained notoriety by introducing a law on the forced labor of prisoners, ostensibly as part of his efforts to improve sanitary conditions on the railroads. He was a strong supporter of strengthening the state's role in the economy, however, and like Nekrasov, regarded Russia's seven major private lines as excessively privileged, especially in their ability to set tariffs. Of a total state debt of 4 billion rubles in 1914, 1.2 billion was in the form of loan guarantees to private lines. Rukhlov advocated their nationalization to increase state revenues and reduce inefficiencies.[56]

These inefficiencies were partly structural on both state and private lines. One set of problems centered on signals and switches, which were still largely operated by hand, as were almost all railroad crossings. Major depots lacked adequate storage and repair facilities. The number of locomotives and rolling stock was already considered inadequate in 1913 for Russia's current and future commercial needs. According to some estimates, the empire needed some three thousand miles of new line a year, an additional two thousand passenger cars, and some eighty thousand additional freight cars to keep up with demand.[57] A second set of problems concerned line administration. Both state and private railroads had developed in Russia around a strong system of district rather than centralized administration. This was true in the United States as well, although less markedly, and for similar reasons: the vast extent of Russian territory favored strong local administrations that could more closely monitor traffic, rolling stock, and local construction or repair work.[58] In 1910, a Duma commission headed by Nekrasov's Kadet colleague D. V. Shchukin found in addition that

[54] The seven largest private lines together earned profits of more than 19 million rubles in 1912, or 65 percent of the total. See N. V. Nekrasov, "K voprosu o chastnom zheleznodorozhnom khoziaistva," *Novyi Ekonomist* 3 (1914): 6–8, 31.

[55] *Zheleznodoroznoe Delo* 18 (1909); P. P. Migulin, *Vozrozhdenie Rossiia* (Kharkov: Pechatnik, 1910), 20–27.

[56] Nekrasov, "K voprosy," 6–8; D. N. Shilov, *Gosudarstvennye deiateli Rossiiskoi Imperii*, 2nd ed. (St. Petersburg, 2002), 643–45;

[57] V. Bukin, "Zheleznye dorogi v mirovuiu voinu i ikh blizhashie zadach i v podgotovke strany k oborone," *Voina i revoliutsiia* 3 (1926): 101–3, 108.

[58] *Zheleznodorozhnoe Delo* 13–14 (1915); 29–30 (1915); I. D. Mikhailov, *Evoliutsiia russkogo transporta 1913–1925* (Moscow, 1925), 20–21.

centrally located line administrations, especially those of private lines, showed no particular interest in investing resources to modernize district shops, given the already high levels of profitability they enjoyed. Many of these were built between 1860 and 1880. Some were even too small to manage properly the larger equipment that lines were now acquiring.[59]

Thus, while its forty-three thousand miles of track was the third most in the world in 1914, Imperial Russia was dead last among European powers in density per square mile as well as the quality of its technical equipment. Only 27 percent of the net was double-tracked, in contrast to the European average of from 40 to 56 percent, and most of the Russian rails were underweight, again in comparison with European lines.[60] One-quarter of Russia's twenty thousand locomotives were more than twenty years old; almost 9 percent more than forty years.[61] In contrast to the United States, where heavy equipment was typically rebuilt or replaced after twelve years or so, the useful life of an engine in Russia was considered to be twenty-five years.[62] According to a report prepared by the Ministry of Finance in 1914, just before the war began, the failure of the government to take decisive action to improve railroad transport had left Russia's lines seriously underequipped. So had the regime's inability to mediate competitive and other tensions between state and private lines. Of particular concern to Nekrasov was the fact that Russia's railroads were still largely laid out to support the state's strategic and defense needs, as we have noted, despite the rapid expansion of privately owned lines after 1907. No one in authority at the Ministry of Transport had apparently considered how this would affect the railroads' ability to support Russia's nonmilitary needs during any extended period of conflict.[63]

The outbreak of war obviously placed huge demands on railroad transport in all warring powers, but nowhere was the imbalance between need and technical capacities greater than in Russia. Two days after the start of mobilization on July 18, the Ministry of Transport issued orders suspending the transport of commercial goods already in transit and diverting rolling stock to military needs. A Special Allocational Committee in Rukhlov's ministry was also empowered to work out agreements with line administrators to meet military's needs and regulate nonmilitary traffic.[64] It was quickly apparent, however, that the committee could not cope with the problems at hand. Some sixteen thousand miles of track that was either within or in close proximity to the war zone, approximately

---

[59] Shmukker, *Ocherki finansov*, 31–32, 215–18, 274–75ff.; I. D. Mikhailov, *Osnovy voprosy transporta* (Moscow, 1918), 9–13.
[60] A. L. Sidorov, "Zheleznodorozhnyi transport," *Istoricheskie zapiski* 26 (1948): 5.
[61] N. Vasil'ev, *Transport Rossii v voine 1914–18* (Moscow: Narkomat Oboron, 1939), 64–65.
[62] Mikhailov, *Evoliutsiia*, 18–19.
[63] Ministervstvo Finansov, *Kratkii ocherk razvitiia nashei zheleznodorozhnoi sety za desiatelietie 1904–13* (St. Petersburg: Ministerstva Finansov, 1914), 43–44, 80–92.
[64] Vasil'ev, *Transport*, 65–67.

one-third of the railroad net as a whole, was then subordinated directly to the army's Office of Military Transport and Communications.[65] The rest of the net remained under the supervision of the line's individual boards, setting up a dual administrative system.[66] Lines subordinated to military control included some 60 percent of Russia's entire state railroad capacity but less than 13 percent of the capacity of private lines. The very task of shifting administrative responsibility from the Ministry of Transport to the General Staff's Office of Military Transport and its Main Quartermaster's Office was daunting at every level. Using the district administrative system in place on these lines, the army tried to assign two of its own officers and two engineers from the Ministry of Transport to supervise operations at each major junction and depot.

According to one officer involved in the process, at first there were simply not enough competent people to effectively support this "dual authority," or *dvoevlastie* as it was disparagingly labeled, anticipating the way the division of power in 1917 between the Provisional Government and the Petrograd Soviet was critically described. Military commanders armed with the power to send trains in any direction set up next to railroad dispatchers who sometimes learned about where their equipment had been sent after the fact. The result was confusion and, in some instances, complete paralysis until contradictory orders could be reconciled.[67] In the meantime, the resulting bottlenecks spread domino fashion even across the railroads closest to the front. While railroads in Germany resumed normal operations by mid-October, and in France the ban on transporting commercial goods was lifted before the end of August, restrictions on the Russian lines continued through the fall and into the winter.

Much of the public press (and some of the later historiography) still painted a rather optimistic picture of line operations in the fall of 1914, especially in terms of Russia's successful mobilization. Yet the detrimental effects of these measures on Russian commerce were immediate. Freight traffic for the second half of 1914 was some 70 percent of what it had been during the first half, measured by the number of freight car loadings. Coal shipments in November and December were down more than 20 percent; peat and other fuels, manufactured products, and foodstuffs declined comparably.[68] At a meeting just after the New Year in 1915, the leadership of the Council of Industrial Congresses composed a strong letter to the government about the growing shortage of freight cars and its effect on the supply of essential goods. The problem was highlighted in the January

---

[65] This process is well reviewed by A. H. Heywood in "The Militarization of Civilians in Russia's First World War," unpublished paper, cited with the kind permission of the author.
[66] Shmukker, *Ocherki finansov*, 45–49.
[67]
[68] Vasil'ev, *Transport*, 67–68.

and February issue of *Promyshlennost' i Torgovlia* (*Industry and Trade*) under the heading "The Destruction of Railroad Transport."[69]

Nekrasov himself was particularly agitated over the dislocation created by the division of the railroad net into lines directly subordinated to the military command and those that continued to operate outside the military's jurisdiction. In his view, the division not only created a cumbersome administrative structure; it also created particular difficulties in using the entire net efficiently, especially in terms of shipping both military and commercial goods over long distances. The reduction in the transportation of grain was particularly severe.[70]

During the winter and early spring of 1915, the situation became even worse. Both private and state lines were now feeling the effects of overused equipment and overworked personnel. There was no effective coordination between lines. Key employees continued to be drafted in large numbers. All lines needed funding for new equipment and repairs, but when the Ministry of Finance allocated new credits for the purchase of forty thousand freight cars and four hundred locomotives, Russia's own shops could not produce them and most of the orders were sent to the United States. Also of great concern was the deterioration of the roadbed. Resources in many places were no longer readily available to maintain track properly, especially with the arrival of heavy-duty locomotives from the United States through Siberia, which generally required heavier rails. Among other consequences was the rapid increase in accidents, events that were relatively rare before the war. In 1915 desperate efforts were underway to open new supply lines through ports on the Black Sea to relieve the overworked and increasingly bottled-up Trans-Siberian route, still single-tracked in many places.[71] In late April, just as the Russian Galician campaign was beginning to crumble, British and French troops landed in Gallipoli in the hopes they could seize control of the Dardanelle Straits and do just that. The awful failures in Gallipoli by the end of the fall were received in Petrograd with great apprehension. Miliukov and others were reaffirmed in their conviction that control over Constantinople and the straits was vital to Russia's long-term security as well as its future economic prosperity. In the summer of 1915 General Alekseev's staff wrote Minister Rukhlov from headquarters that some lines in the military zone had become "completely dysfunctional."[72] As the Special Commission on Transport in Russia would later complain, administrative and organizational confusion had brought near chaos in many places.[73]

---

[69] *Promyshlennost' i Torgovlia* 2 (Jan. 1915): 96; 3 (Feb. 1, 1915): 130–31; *Izvestiia Obshchestva Zavodov i Fabrikantov Moskovskogo Promyshlennogo Raiona* 3 (1915): 25.

[70] Shmukker, *Ocherki finansov*, 43; Sidorov, "Zheleznodorozhnyi transport," 21–22.

[71] Sidorov, "Zheleznodorozhnyi transport," 22–23; Mikhailov, *Evoliutsiia*, 44–46. A full discussion is in *Zheleznodorozhnoe Delo* 32 (1915): 317ff.

[72] V. Bukin, "Zheleznye dorogi," pt. 2, *Voina i revoliutsiia* 4 (1926): 88.

[73] Vasil'ev, *Transport*, 11–12.

Here, too, it is important to recognize how administrative structures and the problems of efficiency on Russia's lines tended to obscure the ways these were embedded in the social relations and cultures of its large "army" of railroad workers, as they were called, and how these substantive elements also affected line operations. Railroad workers were categorized into as many as ten different "services" (*sluzhby*) on most lines. The two largest were the traction and roadway services, the first including locomotive and train crews, the second including shop workers and ordinary laborers on repair gangs. Engine drivers in the traction service generally saw themselves as members of the railroad army's working elite and were regarded as such by others. Their long years of apprenticeship and their skills in keeping locomotives running put them at the center of a circle of relative importance. Comprising less than 4 percent of the total railroad workforce in 1914, engine drivers earned on the average more than twice the wages of the firemen who worked with them in the cabs, and almost five times the wages of those toward the bottom of the complex railroad labor hierarchy. Crews were commonly assigned to individual locomotives rather than to schedules that would require them to use different equipment. Locomotives and crews were switched at district borders. Crews then waited with their locomotives at depots for cars and wagons to take them back to their home locations. The long-held rationale here was that engine brigades knew their own equipment best; their attachment was romanticized into the notion that they would more "lovingly" maintain their "own" locomotives. In fact, the consequences for efficiency were severe. On the eve of the war, freight on Russia's railroads was transported at the slowest level in Europe, measured by the movement of wagons per verst or kilometer.[74]

Conductors and trainmen on both passenger and freight trains obviously had quite different sets of skills and authority. Conductors ruled the wagons like engine drivers ruled their cabs. Station masters and district administrators often had fancier uniforms that represented their authority in selling tickets or assembling and dispatching trains, but more modestly uniformed conductors and trainmen exercised substantial control over which passengers and consignments were actually loaded and where they were let off. Venality and other forms of corruption were long associated with their functions. Conductors were regarded as particularly notorious in this regard. Meanwhile, ordinary laborers maintaining the roadways along with unskilled shop and depot workers were at the bottom of the railroaders' social spectrum. They were often treated contemptuously by the

---

[74] The role of engine drivers in the railroad workforce elsewhere is discussed in two interesting essays: F. Caron, "Essai d'analyse historique d'une psychologie du travail: Les Mecaniciens et chauffeurs de locomotive du Nord de 1850 a 1910," *Le Mouvement Social* 50 (1965): 3–40 and Margot B. Stein, "The Meaning of Skill: The Case of the French Engine Drivers, 1837–1917," *Politics and Society* 3–4 (1978): 399–428.

officious petty "service intelligentsia" in ticket bureaus and administrative offices up and down the lines.[75]

For their part, district administrators tended to hoard freight cars in order to assure goods being loaded in their areas could be moved. Each district commonly had its own repair shops. Russia's freight yards in some districts might be filled with idle rolling stock, while others lacked enough capacity to ship their goods. In turn, the hoarding and concealing of supplies affected the practices by which railroad district administrators repaired and maintained their equipment. In many places, repairs would not be made until central line administrations provided funds to cover the work. This required elaborate paperwork and step-by-step accounting, often many hundreds of miles from where the repair work was done. It also institutionalized impediments to undertaking and completing repairs quickly.[76] The district system multiplied the number of repair shops on each line, requiring more skilled workers but using them inefficiently. Increasingly during the war it also encouraged the hoarding of repair materials in short supply. Here, however, the tasks and routines of shop workers were very much those of metallists in the major plants of Petrograd and Moscow.

There were various reasons for these disparities. To a large extent they were rooted in workplace cultures and social hierarchies as well as inadequate administrative coordination, communication, and accounting practices. They also reflected, however, a deep-rooted tendency of local railroad administrators to protect their own interests and those of others around them. Each service on Russia's railroads had its own culture and rules, and each was linked to the others in a formal and fairly rigid hierarchy of importance and command. The common laborers who maintained the tracks were largely peasants from nearby villages and had strong local and kinship ties. (Many would become illegal traders—bagmen and -women—during the Civil War, illegally selling sacks of grain to city dwellers.) Shop workers could readily take the place of their comrades in the big metal plants of Petrograd's Vyborg district. Both joined engine drivers in their often palpable disdain for what they perceived as the airs and attitudes of the "bosses," the *nachal'stvo*, who administered local districts and depots and who more closely resembled white-collar employees and other administrative elites. As Nekrasov himself would understand when he became minister of transport in 1917, confronting the problems of efficiency on the lines and the key role of the railroads in distributing urgently needed goods would require wholesale

---

[75] A. G. Rashin, *Fabrichno-zavodskie sluzhashchie v SSSR: Chislennost', Sostav, Zarabotnaia Plata* (Moscow: Voprosy Truda, 1929), 5–11; V. Rachinskii, *Zheleznodorozhnyi transport v 1913 g.* (Moscow: Transpechat, 1925), 146–50. Also see P. F. Metel'kov, *Zheleznodorozhniki v revoliutsii* (Leningrad: Lenizdat, 1970), 23–24.

[76] *Zheleznodorozhnoe Delo* 11 (1915); Vasil'ev, *Transport*, 61–63.

changes in railroad administration as well as in the entrenched social relations and cultures in which railroad operations took place.

With the dislocations of war, this "localism" became a serious problem especially in supplying wagons to depots that needed them and produced loud complaints from regional shippers, especially those in the Donbas coal region. But "localism" was increasing everywhere, including Moscow and St. Petersburg. Some observers regarded the large junctions as the railroads' "biggest mess."[77]

The Strains of State Finance

The last key fault line of economic mobilization was the state's ability to pay for the war. When Peter Bark replaced Vladimir Kokovtsov as minister of finance in March 1914, the Russian budget was in reasonable shape. Expenditures had grown significantly between 1905 and 1914, especially to build up the military, but so had state revenues, including tariffs on foreign trade and proceeds from the spirits monopoly. On the eve of the war, the treasury even had a small surplus in the "ordinary" budget, which excluded secret military costs. Overall, however, the latter did not seem problematic given Russia's substantial gold reserves. These could be used as collateral against foreign loans, as well as the expectation (again) that any war would be both short and successful and therefore likely to position Russia in an economically advantageous postwar position. The only real area of concern was again the railroads. Efforts at encouraging private railroad development in Russia had consistently ended in failure, partly because the costs were higher than the resources allocated to the lines, partly because commercial development in many places, and hence railroad traffic, did not meet expectations. State railroads, meanwhile, had been built largely to meet military needs. They were notoriously indifferent in plan and design to the demands of industry and commerce, constraining private initiative even as they increased its need. Focus here was on moving troops and equipment. Little if any consideration was given to the possibility that a large extended war would create problems in supplying population centers with adequate supplies of necessary goods.

The extension of loan guarantees to support private railroad development as the state moved to build up its military after the humiliating war with Japan was an effort to remedy this problem. In addition to expanding state lines, more than 1 billion rubles had been allocated to guarantee a 5 percent return on shares and obligations issued by private lines after 1905 to facilitate their expansion without reducing their profitability. As a result, more than half of Russia's 5.7 billion rubles of state debt before the war was related in some form to railroad

---

[77] *Zheleznodorozhnik* 283, no. 3 (1909); Mikhailov, *Evoliutsiia*, 8–22.

operations.[78] Total Russian capital expenditure on all railroad development in the ten years between 1903 and 1913 was virtually the same as for all other industrial development combined.[79] As the war began, Russia's private railroads were able to guarantee their shareholders a profit even if they operated at a loss, an arrangement fairly criticized by the economist and publicist Migulin as "fostering private initiative without private risk."[80]

Bark agreed, at least in principle, but the need to finance the unexpected scale of war after July 1914 soon forced his reservations aside. Bark's Ministry of Finance was the largest and, in the view of many, the most important ministry in the government together with the Ministry of War. Among its sprawling offices and responsibilities were those of the state bank, the treasury and the emission of money, the network of state savings institutions, revenue collection through taxes and tariffs, the state liquor monopoly, the national debt, financing state railroad development, loans to industrial firms and smaller businesses, the landlord and peasant banking network with its vital credit operations, export and import tariffs and controls, and a substantial research division that attracted some of the country's best economists. In addition to funding railroad construction, Bark's ministry maintained its own schedule of tariffs for state lines and supported a whole office concerned with the collection of railroad revenues. After those from the state liquor monopoly, which was budgeted in 1914 at 935 million rubles (or 26.5 percent of the total nonmilitary or "ordinary" budget), the second largest source of revenues was state railroad operations. The 1914 budget set these at 856 million rubles (24.3 percent of the total). An additional 87 million rubles was budgeted to come from income from state bonds for railroad construction, increases in passenger and freight tariffs, and profits from the corporate shares the ministry itself held in private railroad companies.[81]

One of only three ministers to hold his post throughout the last years of the tsarist regime, Bark has been seen by some historians as something of a sycophant, more notable for his ability to please Nicholas and the court than for his fiscal competency. A graduate in law from St. Petersburg University, his training in finance was largely through appointments in various private and state banks. Perhaps influenced by disdain for his prominent predecessor Kokovtsov, who served simultaneously as prime minister after the assassination of Stolypin, this view was partly shared by an interesting cohort of contemporary analysts, including the prominent liberal and social democratic economists M. I. Tugan-Baranovskii, S. S. Katzenellenbaum, V. G. Groman, M. N. Fridman, A. A.

---

[78] Ministervstvo Finansov, *Kratkii ocherk,* 36–41, 109.
[79] Ibid., 49–50, 58; Strumilin, "Ushcherb v proizvoditel'nosti truda," 623.
[80] Migulin, *Vozrozhdenie,* 20–21.
[81] S. G. Beliaev, *P. L. Bark i Finansovaia politika Rossii 1914–1917* (St. Petersburg: St. Petersburg University Press, 2002), 550, table 1.

Chuprov, and S. N. Prokovovich, as well as Migulin, whom Bark often looked to for advice.

Bark had come to office in early 1914 as a result of pressure to loosen the restraints imposed by Kokovtsov, a fiscal conservative. Like others of his generation, Kokovtsov had been a strict adherent of the gold standard and fiscal orthodoxy. Russia maintained a balanced budget under his direction in large part by limiting state credit and securing favorable international loans. Russia's economy expanded at a healthy rate in this period, but influential figures within and outside the government, including the former prime minister and minister of finance Count Sergei Witte, pressed for the separation of the prime minister and finance minister positions and the appointment of someone more familiar with private enterprise and more flexible about credit and deficit financing. Bark seemed to many an ideal candidate. Among other advantages were his comfortable relations with leading figures in the State Duma, to whose Financial Committee, headed by Shingarev, he was required to submit the state's ordinary budget for review and approval. Socially well connected, Bark had held various positions in the Finance Ministry and the Ministry of Trade and Industry since his graduation from the juridical faculty of St. Petersburg University in 1891 and headed the St. Petersburg office of the State Bank before being promoted to associate director.[82]

Bark was undoubtedly attractive to Nicholas because he accepted the tsar's view that as a matter of principle, the Russian treasury should not depend on intemperance to fund so much of its budget through the state liquor monopoly. Nicholas had developed strong views on this subject. When he experienced the listless response of so many of his subjects during his jubilee tour of the country in 1913, the three-hundredth anniversary of the dynasty, he conveniently attributed this to excessive drinking. In Kokovtsov's view, the liquor monopoly held this excess in check by regulating prices and supply. In Bark's view, the treasury would be much better served by a comprehensive and judicious tax structure, including a tax on income.[83] One of his intentions as minister was to effect a gradual shift to new tax revenues over a period of time sufficient to compensate for the loss from liquor sales.

With the outbreak of war, the tsar first issued a temporary halt to these sales as a way of easing the stresses of mobilization, at least for the state. Other warring powers did the same. At the one-day Duma session on July 26, 1914, Bark spoke with the confidence of one who many hoped was Russia's best hope for significant financial reform. His "first obligation" was to ensure the state could provide the massive resources the war would require and strengthen the industrial

[82] Beliaev, *P. L. Bark*, 10–51.
[83] P. L. Bark, "Vospominaniia," *Vozrozhdenie* 157 (Jan. 1965): 61–62.

sectors which produced them with new investments. What the war also required in his view was a "calm" population and industrial class, both of which "could count on assistance from the State Bank."[84] To applause and shouts of "Bravo!" he announced that the State Bank would soon issue short-term treasury notes to the extent required to meet the war's needs, that he would undertake a thorough culling of "unnecessary" expenses from the state's budget, and that he would take measures to ensure the currency markets could sustain the state's and Russian industry's need for new funding. The regime would implement these and other reforms through the use of Article 87, the "emergency" provision in the Fundamental Laws which gave it authority to issue binding laws when the Duma was not in session. The tsar's temporary prohibition on liquor sales would benefit Russia by "strengthening the people's energy, ability to work, and stamina."[85] Bark concluded by turning to the "extremely important question of the concern now weighing heavily on us, and in particular on the Ministry of Finance: the security of families whose loved ones have been called to war.... You can be completely confident that the government is ready to bear the broadest costs to meet this urgent need."[86]

In fact, the regime was woefully unprepared to finance the war. There were only two obvious ways to do so: domestic and foreign borrowing, and state revenues through taxes and tariffs. Foreign borrowing, of course, increased Russia's national debt and imposed service costs. Domestic borrowing through the issuance of new short-term state bonds also imposed service costs, draining capital that could be used to support domestic industry. If these proved insufficient, an additional possibility was simply to print money, despite its obvious inflationary implications.

On August 22, however, just before Samsonov's Second Army was destroyed during the first battle of the Mazurian Lakes and apparently to Bark's surprise, Nicholas issued his notorious order making the ban on liquor sales permanent; 328 stores and almost 26,000 shops selling more than 280 million gallons of vodka were permanently shut down.[87] Contemporaries and historians alike have long considered this one of the primary indicators of imperial incompetence at the end of the old regime. (One predictable consequence was that the stocks of these stores became attractive targets for looters, especially new recruits who had traditionally lubricated their last moments of freedom with drinking bouts.)[88]

---

[84] Gosudarstvennaia Duma, *Stenograficheskii otchety*, July 26, 1914, col. 12.
[85] Ibid., col. 14.
[86] Ibid., col. 17.
[87] A. P. Michelson, N. Apostol, and M. V. Bernatskii, *Russian Public Finance during the War* (New Haven, CT: Yale University Press, 1928), 34–35, 73–87.
[88] Joshua Sanborn, "Besporiadki sredi prizyvnikov v 1914 g. i vopros o russkoi natsii: Novyi vzgliad na problem," in *Rossiia i pervaia mirovaia voina*, ed. N. N. Smirnov (St. Petersburg: Bulanin, 1999), 202–15; Joshua Sanborn, "The Mobilization of 1914 and the Question of the Russian Nation: A Reexamination," *Slavic Review* 59, no. 2 (2000): 267–89.

Influenced no doubt by the excoriating comments of many contemporary critics—Shingarev famously said in a Duma speech that never since the dawn of human history had a single country in time of war renounced the principal source of its revenue—historians have emphasized the disastrous consequences that prohibition had on the government's wartime budget.

In fact, an equally if not more severe blow was inflicted by the disruption in the fall of 1914 of Russia's railroad operations. In principle, Bark was right. Much of the revenue loss from the monopoly sale of spirits could have been made up by new transport tariffs, especially as the quantity of freight grew to meet the army's needs, the lines functioned effectively, and the war did not last beyond the few short months almost everyone expected. Bark's ministry quickly levied a special tax on individuals, luggage, and goods traveling on passenger trains. Using Article 87 of the Fundamental Laws, he also imposed new and rather complex sets of additional tariffs on the shipment of freight without the benefit of discussion with Shingarev and the Duma's Budget Committee.

It was soon apparent, however, that even the most responsible members of Bark's expansive ministry did not have a clear idea of what was actually occurring on the railroads, especially at some distance from the capital. In fact, the piecemeal introduction of the new tariff system and an additional *ukaz* of November 12 setting a new Provisional War Tax on Goods Conveyed by Rail caused enormous confusion. For obvious reasons, shipping goods on passenger trains had always been substantially more expensive than shipping them in freight cars. In an effort to expedite priority shipments, the revised system reduced the tariffs on primary goods that had previously been more expensive than others, and raised the cost of shipments for more discretionary goods that were not going to the army. According to one analyst, the freight rate that in some cases used to be one-thirtieth to one-tenth of that for shipping the same goods in the baggage cars of passenger trains now became from one to four times more. Hence textiles and other consumer goods were soon being stacked in passenger cars on seats and in the aisles. In some places, freight cars were then refitted for transporting people. Central junctions like Moscow and Petrograd, already disrupted by the emergencies of war, found their depots packed with freight awaiting transport or unloading and overwhelmed by passengers needing to travel.[89]

Meantime the army itself clearly needed new funding to cover its rapidly escalating needs. So did major state and private enterprises working for defense. As with every other warring power, credits and other resources had to be increased to meet the lengthening war's unexpectedly high costs. From July through December 1914, military expenditures were far larger than those of the entire Russo-Japanese War, on the basis of which the current military budget had

---

[89] Michelson, Apostol, and Bernatskii, *Russian Public Finance*, 97–100; Prokopovich, *Voina*, 41–42.

been prepared. Complicating the matter was the fact that foreign commercial banking operations were now severely curtailed or suspended.[90]

Early on, consequently, Russia was forced to turn to Britain and France for financial relief.

Thanks to Kokovtsov's conservative fiscal policies, the Russian state was still creditworthy because of its gold reserves. To assure this continued, Bark imposed a temporary suspension of foreign payments in gold and on July 23 ended the convertibility of state banknotes. Loans were quickly arranged from Britain and France, but both involved encumbering the gold supply. (At Britain's insistence, three physical shipments of gold were made in great secrecy to the Bank of England, which demanded they be sent "on loan," to be "repatriated" as Russia paid down its debt after the war.) A program of domestic borrowing was also put in place that involved new issues of short-term bonds and the emission of new ruble notes as unbacked credit certificates—legal tender that increased the money supply along with the state's debt. On July 1, 1914, there were 1.6 billion ruble notes in circulation. Immediately after the war began Bark directed the State Bank to issue 1.2 billion new rubles in the form of credit notes and short-term treasury bills.[91] Meanwhile, the first series of domestic war bonds was issued in October 1914, denominated at amounts from 50 to 1,000 rubles in the hope that they would be purchased by a large cross section of the population.[92] On January 9, 1915, the Council of Ministers gave Bark permission for additional credit operations up to 9 billion rubles to cover "exceptional" war expenditures. Still, on January 19 only 213.5 million rubles remained in the treasury's State Bank account, while 400 million rubles were needed by February 15 to cover expiring bonds and interest on short-term obligations.[93] In February 1915 and again in April two new series of war bonds had to be issued, this time in denominations as large as 10,000 rubles; already by March 6, Bark again had to request authorization to initiate still more credit operations. One billion rubles of additional credit notes soon flowed into the system.[94] When it then became clear that state revenues for the first nine months of 1915 would likely be as much as 14 percent lower than for all of 1914, yet another series of bonds was sold with denominations as large as 25,000 rubles.[95]

---

[90] The figures vary in different sources, but the most reliable show expenditures of some 2.5 billion rubles between July and December 1914. See G. Dement'ev, *Gosudarstvennye dokhody i razkhody Rossii i polozhenie gosudarstvennago kaznachestva za vremia voiny s Germaniei i Avstro-vengriei do kontsa 1917 god* (Petrograd: Ministerstvo Finansov, 1917), 31; TsSU, *Rossiia v mirovoi voine 1914–1918 (v tsifrakh)* (Moscow: TsSU, 1925), 46–47; and the discussion in Sidorov, *Finansovoe polozhenie*, 115.
[91] RGIA f. 583, op. 3, d. 1134, l. 19.
[92] Michelson, Apostol, and Bernatskii, *Russian Public Finance*, 248–50; *Vestnik Finansov* 43 (1914): 9, 18; 45 (1915): 18, 45.
[93] RGIA f. 1276, op. 11, d. 195, ll. 2–9.
[94] Ibid., l. 9.
[95] RGIA f. 1276, op. 12, d. 224; f. 583, op. 3, d. 1130 and 1134.

In effect, the state's increasingly urgent need for funds signified its lack of preparedness to fund a modern war. Adhering to the gold standard, Russia had never financed its wars in this way. Taxation rates and other revenues had always been adjusted to help meet military costs. The State Bank was restricted by an 1897 law to circulating credit notes at a level greater than 300 million rubles above the sum of current gold holdings, a limit Bark and others regarded as much too restrictive for a growing economy even in peacetime. Bark himself supported higher taxes, especially on income. The Council of Ministers as a whole resisted, however, whether to avoid impeding industrial mobilization, as some believed, or more simply to defend the interests of Russia's industrial and commercial communities, as critics loudly argued. In either case, there was little if any possibility once the war crippled Russian foreign trade that increased revenues from taxation or other sources would cover the growing deficit. This would have been so even if the regime had continued to enjoy revenues from vodka sales.

All of this led other liberals and moderate socialists to press for a radical increase in luxury taxes and the profits now flowing to Russia's favored industrialists. The editors of the progressive journal *Promyshlennaia Rossiia* (*Industrial Russia*) joined them, as did others. Still, even a dramatic increase in the 3.1 billion rubles in ordinary revenue that largely balanced the state's total budget in 1913 would hardly have covered the runaway costs of the war. Although accurate information remained difficult to come by, the respected contemporary economist S. N. Prokopovich calculated in 1918 that war expenses increased by 31 percent in 1914–15, 85 percent in 1915–16, and a full 148 percent by 1917–18.[96] While more than 3.3 billion in credit notes were in circulation by April 1915, twice the figure it had been when the war began, the only way to cover a significant portion of Russia's dramatically escalating financial obligations was by printing more money.[97]

This was true to some extent in other warring countries as well. But in France and Great Britain increases in currency circulation were more readily absorbed by war bonds that a far larger proportion of the population could afford (and were willing) to buy. Major sources of revenue still remained relatively stable or grew, while widespread rationing and price controls, especially in Germany, acted as a brake on inflation, at least until 1918.[98] In Russia, moreover, the end

---

[96] Prokopovich, *Voina*, 173.
[97] RGIA f. 1276, op 11, d. 248, ll. 15, 46; f. 563, op. 2, d. 517; Michelson, Apostol, and Bernatskii, *Russian Public Finance*, 373, 379.
[98] See Stephen Broadberry and Mark Harrison, *The Economics of World War I* (Cambridge: Cambridge University Press, 2005), esp. the articles by A. Ritschl, "The Pity of Peace: Germany's Economy at War, 1914–1918 and Beyond," 59–63; Pierre-Cyrille Hautcoeur, "Was the Great War a Watershed? The Economics of World War I in France," 183–87; and Stephen Broadberry and Peter Howlett, "The United Kingdom during World War I: Business as Usual?," 215–10.

of convertibility and the influx of new money in the fall of 1914 also had several unanticipated effects that other countries largely avoided: a run on private banks by those who hoped withdrawals in convertible notes would at least preserve the value of this currency when the ban was eventually lifted; uncertainty fueled by the fear that additional kinds of restrictions would be imposed; and perhaps most serious in terms of maintaining the economy more generally, confusion in commercial circles about the future availability of credit to meet new production and shipment costs.

When a worried Minister Bark had his Chancery commission a special report together with his friend Migulin from the journal *Novyi Ekonomist* on ways to meet the growing deficit, the commission suggested new direct and indirect taxes on matches, tobacco, sugar, and other essential foodstuffs. They also proposed new and steeper increases in railroad tariffs.[99] Shingarev and other Duma deputies, on the contrary, worried that any new taxes on foodstuffs would be socially as well as fiscally problematic, insisting again on new direct taxes on enterprises to absorb war profits and the introduction of an income tax. All of this evoked strong protests from the commercial communities and public organizations. The association of publicly traded commercial banks and members of the Moscow provincial council (*zemstvo*) went so far as to warn that any such actions would threaten the entire economic life of the country and lead Russia to "catastrophe."[100]

Meanwhile, Bark and his colleagues were inundated with increasingly strident demands for direct financial assistance from both state and private defense producers. Although A. I. Putilov and other Petrograd magnates were initially apologetic, expressing their regret that new uncertainties in the credit markets as a result of the war were "forcing it to turn to the government for help, the industrial giant wanted state backing for 15 million new shares as well as guarantees for new bonds."[101] The Russko-Baltic Shipbuilding and Mechanical Works wanted 3 million rubles for new equipment, new state credits that would protect it from changing currency rates, and a large advance payment for unfulfilled orders from the Naval Ministry. Beker (Becker) Shipbuilding threatened that unless state funds were provided to cover a 21 million ruble deficit in operating funds, the firm would fall into foreign hands.[102] In March the Council of Ministers affirmed an increase in state credit operations to 1.2 billion rubles, but on April 11 Bark requested authorization to issue 200 million rubles' worth of new 5 percent notes on English and American currency markets and take 15 million pounds sterling from Britain in the form of short-term 5 percent obligations.

---

[99] RGIA f. 560, op. 26, del. 30, ll. 117–25.
[100] RGIA, f. 1278, op. 2, d. 1225, ll. 92–93.
[101] RGIA f. 1276, op. 11, d. 248, l. 4.
[102] Ibid., ll. 1–8, 31–32.

The National City Bank in New York was ready to loan Russia $10 million at the same interest rate.[103]

Surprising as it seems in retrospect, the editors of *Promyshlennost' i Torgovlia* did not see any cause for alarm: "At present, Russia is not going through any kind of economic crisis. . . . The arduous efforts of the state in the military struggle are having a very limited [*ves'ma malo*] effect on the economic well-being of the country." Setting the stage for struggles to come, the editors cautioned that "any effort of the government taken only with the aim of increasing its revenues will isolate the state from the nation and lead to a singular form of bureaucratic socialism."[104] For their part, state officials preparing a review of the economy on the basis of information provided by the State Bank did not consider their task to be urgent; concerns about Russia's economy were "greatly exaggerated." While problems existed in terms of raw materials production, the collapse of foreign trade, and especially the railroads, the regime was well enough prepared to manage them.[105] The one prominent voice of dissidence belonged to Witte, the former state official most engaged in Russia's industrial modernization during his years in the government between 1881 and 1905. His warnings fell on deaf ears. "Is Russia really threatened with a crash?" the editors of *Novyi Ekonomist* asked rhetorically. Doomsday views like Witte's were "laughable."[106]

Assessing Loss

Ironically, the most familiar illustration of Polanyi's economistic fallacy has nothing to do with economics per se. It is the way the statistical multiplication of victims from any awful event tends to dilute an understanding of their experience, as in "one death is a tragedy, six million deaths a statistic." The reasons for this are easy to understand. We comprehend the experience of others in large part by imagining consciously or unconsciously what it must have been like if that had been us. Associations of this sort can transcend time and cultural differences, even if this distorts historical actualities. When we learn about events with hundreds or thousands of victims the relatively clarity of individual associations is much more difficult. The event itself becomes the tragedy, obscuring the individual costs involved.

---

[103] RGIA f. 563, op. 2, d. 529, ll. 1–4.
[104] *Promyshlennost' i Torgovlia* 7 (Apr. 1, 1915): 340; 10 (May 15, 1915): 497.
[105] *Khoziaistvennaia zhizn' i ekonomicheskoe polozhenie naseleniia Rossii za pervye deviat' mesiatsev voiny (Iiul 1914–Aprel' 1915) po svedeniiam dostavelnnym uchrezhdenimi Gos. Banka, Gos. Dvorianskago, Zemel'nago i Krest'inskago Pozem'nago Bankov, i Inspektsiei melkago kredita* (Petrograd: Ministerstva Finansov, 1916), iv–v.
[106] *Novyi Ekonomist* 20 (May 17, 1914).

From almost the first day of the war, Russian casualties were reported in stupefying numbers: 30,000 killed or wounded in four days at Tannenberg; from 60,000 to 100,000 or more killed, wounded, or captured shortly afterward at the Mazurian Lakes. From the beginning of the war through April 1915, official statistics list almost 600,000 wounded and 123,000 killed. With 454,000 taken prisoner, total casualties in these nine months were recorded as almost 1.2 million.[107] While these figures cannot be considered fully accurate, they clearly indicate orders of magnitude that are (and were) staggering to comprehend.

Was Russia prepared for these losses? Was it even possible to prepare adequately when the near universal assumption was that the war would be short? From the beginning the army lacked adequate medical staff, field hospitals, medicines, and basic first aid items. Evacuation of the wounded to collection points was haphazard, transport of the more seriously wounded from there to hospitals hampered by long distances to rail heads, too few medical trains, and inadequate hospital space itself. In this escalating realm of suffering and human loss the question is not whether Imperial Russia was prepared, but the effect of its almost total lack of being so. How can we get some sense of human losses too large in the aggregate to readily comprehend, and what they might have portended?

As we have seen, we can do so in part by reading soldiers' letters and memoirs against the grain. These give us focused insights on the suffering of individuals that we can extrapolate from broadly with some confidence. We read in the field notes of Florence Farmborough, for example, of wounded men "with stricken faces and frightened eyes," long processions of "dirt bespattered desperate men ... calling out to us in piteous language to stop for them.... The badly crippled crawled after us, all begging, beseeching us not to abandon them in their need ... their prayers intermingled with curses ... repeated by [others] we had left to their fate."[108] Such language presents a reasonably accurate picture of the terror and mayhem of loss at the front. Many soldiers and officers were shocked at the army's inability to care for casualties.[109] Even for exhausted legions on the Northwestern and Galician Fronts, the fear of being wounded seemed more horrible than death itself. Being wounded usually brought prolonged agonies; as many as a third of estimated battle deaths in 1915 were of those already in medical care who died of their wounds.[110]

---

[107] TsSU, *Rossiia v mirovoi voine*, 30.
[108] Florence Farmborough, *Nurse at the Russian Front: A Diary 1914–1918* (London: Constable, 1974), 37–40.
[109] RGIA f. 1088, op. 2, d. 164, l. 1; f. 2067, op .1, d. 11, l. 164; RGVIA f. 2048, op. 1, d. 905, l. 269 ob.; f. 2067, op., d. 2937, l. 32.
[110] L. I. Sazonov, "Potery russkoi armii v voinu," in *Trudy komissii po sledovanniiu sanitarnykh posledstvii voiny 1914–1920 gg.*, ed. M. M. Gram (Moscow: Gosizdat, 1923), 161–63.

Those fortunate to be taken to field hospitals commonly found themselves in overwhelmed and understaffed facilities. Moments of retreat worsened matters exponentially. The situation for those who managed to reach evacuation points was often little better. Rail lines were snarled, equipment was inadequate, soldiers sometimes lay for long periods in the cold awaiting evacuation. In places where trains failed to arrive, "soldiers were transferred out in great agony, just like at the beginning of the war, in unclean freight cars just barely emptied of their goods, including cattle, without any medical equipment or personnel."[111] Many trains continued to lack any hospital facilities at all; most had too few medical personnel. At major reception and transfer points the wounded were backed up awaiting care. According to a report to the General Staff in December 1915, medical resources were totally inadequate.[112] Nor would the situation improve as the war continued. As late as the fall of 1916, the majority of Russian wounded were still dying en route to hospitals on sanitary trains, from gangrene that went untreated, the absence of medicine, and the lack of well-trained medical personnel.[113] The general in charge of evacuating casualties, Prince Boris Aleksandrovich Vasil'chikov, decried that a system thoroughly inadequate at the beginning of the war was in full disarray and rapidly growing worse. Intended to save Russia's wounded, it "was having the opposite effect": hospital trains were "destroying" them.[114]

By this time unflattering popular stories about class distinctions in treating the wounded had also gained traction. Some wrote bitterly that doctors looked only after officers and treated ordinary soldiers "like cattle."[115] Nurses, too, began to come under attack, especially those the historian Laurie Stoff has called "celebrity nurses," exemplified by the imperial family's two daughters, Ol'ga and Tatiana, and the Empress Alexandra Fedorovna. Photographs and block prints of them and other prominent figures tending the wounded in clean and carefully starched nursing garb painted a patriotic picture of competence and dedication. The reality, however, was grim. Nurses trained for a full year before the war were almost immediately in short supply once the fighting began. To meet what in weeks became an urgent need, the Russian Red Cross set up training courses of only two months in duration, and soon reduced the time to six weeks. Medical units at the front remained chronically understaffed, their limited personnel poorly trained. Triage, amputations forced on resistant soldiers, and the agony of being unable to reach the wounded or abandoning them in retreat took

---

[111] RGIA f. 651, op. 1, d. 1030, l. 4.
[112] Ibid., ll. 1–2.
[113] RGIA f. 651, op. 1, d. 1029, ll. 1–2.
[114] Ibid., ll. 2, 4–6; M. Vol'fovich and K. Medvedeva, eds., *Tsarskaia armiia v period mirovoi voiny i fevral'skoi revoliutsii* (Kazan: Tatizdat, 1932), 35–36.
[115] RGVIA f. 2067, op. 1, d. 2932, ll. 73–74 ob.; d. 2935, l. 154; d. 3853, ll. 74ff.; f. 2003, op. 1, d. 1486, l. 225; RGIA f. 651, op. 1, d. 1030, l. 4.

a devastating emotional toll.[116] Wounded soldiers wrote "with hatred at the Red Cross, which used to be a symbol of mercy, caring, and self-sacrifice." Letters complained bitterly about the nurses represented on the home front as heroes. "They go after the officers like mountain goats looking for garbage, more like prostitutes than nurses. . . . To see one, you have to go hunting with dogs since they are 30–40 versts away, always flirting with the officers."[117] As Stoff reports, the records of the Red Cross were soon filled with complaints from military officials about "improper behavior" at the front, causing scores of nurses to be expelled from Red Cross ranks.[118]

Those fortunate enough to have survived transport from the front found hospitals overflowing, especially in Petrograd and Moscow. As late as January 1916 supplies, personnel, and training remained inadequate. Reports described variations of chaos, lack of preparation, and disaster.[119] Russian military doctors themselves echoed these charges. Those competent in psychiatry identified what they called "trench psychoses": the collapse of adaptive and resistance mechanisms that led especially to manic depression and dementia. Soldiers with these conditions needed attention, yet in many units they were hardly acknowledged. And while soldiers in France on the Western Front developed similar symptoms, the physical distress of trench warfare in the East was almost certainly worse than that in France's milder climate. Bitter cold, inadequate clothing, and especially the shortage of food amplified the comparable torments of artillery bombardment and the danger for those who left the trenches. Even the relatively long periods of inaction during the winter of 1915–16 may have made matters worse in this regard, pitting brief, inconclusive fighting against long periods of boredom made more intense by great physical and emotional discomfort.

From these and similar reports we can get some sense that Russia was not prepared for the growing hostility within the ranks even among putatively stoic soldiers toward their privileged officers, especially those held responsible, fairly or not, for military incompetence and their suffering. We can also presume that the regime and the tsar's own family must have lost a good deal of luster through the losses of battle, even if outright mutinies would not occur until later in 1916. There is little question, moreover, that tens of thousands of families waited each day for word of their loved ones, rightfully fearful about their well-being, compromising the familiar notion of peasant fatalism. Soldiers commonly gave their units and locations as return addresses on their cards and letters in the hope their families could send them food and clothing. When military censors began to

---

[116] Laurie Stoff, *Russia's Sisters of Mercy and the Great War: More Than Binding Men's Wounds* (Lawrence: University Press of Kansas, 2015).
[117] RGVIA f. 2067, op. 1, d. 2932, ll. 21–36.
[118] Stoff, *Russia's Sisters*, 71.
[119] RGIA f. 651 op .1, d. 1029, ll. 1–6.

discard these in huge numbers, breaking communication with home, the army was inundated with desperate appeals for information which they were unable to handle. In response, millions of preprinted postcards and envelops were prepared with generic return addresses, which in turn diverted tons of mail sent to the soldiers.

A final dislocation from unwavering commitment to fighting for Tsar and Country may have occurred when the regime itself largely abandoned its paternal role of caring for the wounded. As early as August 1914 the All-Russian Union of Zemstvos to Aid Sick and Wounded Troops was organized under the direction of Prince G. E. L'vov, future prime minister in the first Provisional Government in 1917. It soon found itself overwhelmed and unprepared for the tasks of treating the wounded. Already by 1915 the Zemstvo Union had spent almost 200 million rubles in the effort, most of which had come from the state. It was maintaining more than 170,000 hospital beds, operating some fifty special hospital trains, staffing almost a hundred military hospitals, and deploying more than six thousand medical personnel, including twenty-three hundred physicians. A Union of Towns was organized several weeks after the Zemstvo Union for a complementary purpose, assuming the increasing burden of supporting refugees in almost two hundred municipalities.[120] Shouldering responsibilities the state was proving unable to bear, the two unions brought "responsible" publics directly into the administration of the state's welfare needs.

Not surprisingly, neither the state nor the two public organizations were prepared for the burdens of caring for the hapless flood of refugees and wounded soldiers produced by the war. According to Interior Minister Khvostov, the situation was becoming increasingly "dangerous" and liable to stir additional unrest.[121] While the Zemstvo Union managed to provide some relief in the war zone, serving some 10 million meals between June and December 1915, according to one source, there was little if any organized support further into the interior. No one knew how many were going where, or who, other than the financially strapped local zemstvo and town organizations, would provide for them. The provincial zemstvo board in Ufa, for example, telegraphed the union's headquarter in October 1915 that it was in a position to accommodate only a thousand persons a day, whereas ten thousand were arriving. "The situation is terrible," the board reported. "[W]hole trainloads are being dispatched without food."[122] Within the year, the numbers of refugees and wounded swelled to over

---

[120] B. B. Grave, ed., *K istorii klassovoi bor'by v Rossii v gody imperialisticheskoi voiny* (Moscow: Gosizdat, 1926), 254.
[121] RGIA f. 457, op. 2, d. 65, l. 6.
[122] T. I. Polner, *Russian Local Government during the War and the Union of Zemstvos* (New Haven, CT: Yale University Press, 1930), 173.

3 million, reaching all the way to Vladivostok.[123] Meanwhile, the one-time payment offered to families of the wounded or killed was no longer adequate to relieve distress. In many places it seemed to provoke more resentment than relief.[124] The role and value of the zemstvo and town public organizations grew in these ways, proportional in all likelihood to increasing disaffection within and outside the army about the regime itself. Prince L'vov reportedly told his colleagues that the government had suspended Russia over a dreadful abyss of human misery and loss.[125]

---

[123] Ibid., 162–74. Peter Gatrell gives a careful review in *A Whole Empire Walking* (Bloomington: Indiana University Press, 1999), appendix 1, 210–15.

[124] Corinne Gaudin, "Rural Echoes of World War I: War Talk in the Russian Village," *Jahrbücher für Geschichte Osteuropas* 3 (2008): 391–414.

[125] S. P. Mel'gunov, *Na putiiakh k dvortsovomu perevorotu* (Ann Arbor: University of Michigan Press, 1962), 38.

3
"Dying of Hunger"
Representations and Realities of Scarcity

The first voices of "extreme need" came as something of a shock. The word "extreme" in Russian (*chrezvychainyi*) is more powerful than its English variant, connoting both emergency as well as something extraordinary. (In Soviet Russia the feared Cheka was the Chrezvychainaia Komissiia). As we have seen, already by the middle of August 1914 Russia's armies in East Prussia found themselves lacking ammunition and essential military equipment and were poorly supplied with food. Yet Russian rifles were well made and up to European standards. There were four thousand good Maxim machine guns in the arsenals, and the basic Russian field gun was only slightly inferior to the world standard at the time. While Russian troops were less well equipped than the Germans, whose mortars and artillery would soon prove so effective in trench warfare, both Samsonov's and Rennenkampf's troops were fighting moving rather than stationary battles in August and September 1914. The problem was not so much that the quality of equipment or quantity of stores was insufficient but that the army could not adequately manage the problem of supply. Both Samsonov's and Rennenkampf's troops moved forward without adequate field kitchens, caught between pressure from headquarters to move quickly and increasingly unsustainable distances from points of supply. Soldiers were constantly hungry, at times even "starving," according to the British general Alfred Knox, who visited both armies at the front.[1]

Sustained marches away from railroad lines took Samsonov's troops into territory with few good roads, exacerbating the problem. So did poor communication, the unexpected level of casualties, rutted lanes clogged with wounded, the chaos of uncertainty, and a reluctance to retreat. Rennenkampf's troops initially fared somewhat better than Samsonov's, but problems there soon became acute as well.

---

[1] Alfred Knox, *With the Russian Army, 1914–1917*, 2 vols. (London: Hutchinson, 1921), 1: 80, 91.

Early Voices of "Extreme Need"

As a result, "scarcity" and "extreme need" soon became common tropes in communications and reporting from the front, even in Galicia, where General Aleksei Brusilov and others were managing to push back the Austrians in the fall of 1914. Urgent telegrams couched in terms of extreme need were largely dismissed by higher levels of command as misrepresentations intended to hide field commanders' own failings. Implicitly and directly they also impugned the competency of well-placed figures like General Polivanov, for many years responsible for military supply in the General Staff, and Generals Kuzmin-Karavaev and Barzukov, who headed the Main Artillery Administration (GAU) under the direction of Minister of War Sukhomlinov. The forty-nine-year-old General Aleksei Manikovskii, soon himself to become head of the GAO, blamed Sukhomlinov and Polivanov for the shortages, while Polivanov was able to get Commander in Chief Grand Duke Nikolai Nikolaevich to join him in blaming Sukhlominov, a favorite of the tsar but a man with pro-German sympathies. A concerted effort began to remove the minister of war himself from office.[2]

At the highest reaches of the army and the regime, the army's needs thus joined its military failures as part of a rancorous cycle of interdepartmental and personal recrimination. It was far easier to engage in these circular accusations of failure than it was to accept that real scarcities were the result of failures in mobilizing and distributing available goods. The belief that the East Prussian offensive would lead to a quick march on Berlin was particularly intoxicating in this regard. The more it proved illusory, the easier it was to lay blame on incompetence, especially since that was undoubtedly in good supply. Surprise and shock at the magnitude of Russia's losses confronted the outsized scale of expectation in the clashing tropes of optimism and acrimony. In 1916 a special commission would conclude that the army had suffered from an acute scarcity of shells and other munitions from the very beginning of the war, justifying the voices of need. Throughout the fall and into the winter of 1914–15, however, representations of need at the front continued to be widely rejected as exaggerations to excuse incompetence.

In this regard as well as others, letters from soldiers became a key window on actual conditions. Censorship and other restrictions severely limited public information. (In February 1915 the newspaper *Den'* [Day] was even forbidden to publish a long piece describing the "excellent morale" of French soldiers lest it give the impression that the morale of Russian troops was less so.)[3] While censors

---

[2] See the extended discussion by William C. Fuller Jr., *The Foe Within: Fantasies of Treason and the End of Imperial Russia* (Ithaca, NY: Cornell University Press, 2006), 191. The report of the Commission is in RGVIA f. 962, op. 2, d. 43.

[3] RGVIA f. 2005, op. 1, d. 70, ll. 20–21; Otdel Rukopisei State Public Library, St. Petersburg f. 11152, op. 3, d. 98, esp. ll. 12–29.

were extremely keen about stopping correspondence whose content or return address revealed military information, there appeared to be little concern about mail that reported a lack of food, shortage of arms and munitions, or the "extreme need" expressed for adequate winter clothing. Censors generally treated the new postcards on which troops wrote openly about these matters as having no military significance.[4] Fifteen percent of the letters reviewed from the Southwestern Front in the early winter of 1914–15 touched these issues, second in number only to expressions of hope that the war would soon end. Censors also did not regard these as reflecting unpatriotic sentiments or compromising soldiers' "awareness of the necessity to fulfill their duty to Tsar and Fatherland." Commanders were repeatedly told that the huge majority of soldiers was "burning with desire to destroy the enemy." Families at home learned that their sons and husbands were fighting without adequate weapons or food.[5]

Respected field generals like Anton Denikin and Aleksei Brusilov saw the situation as their soldiers did. Brusilov later complained bitterly that the exhaustion of his troops was fueled during the first winter of the war by the lack of warm clothing. In November 1914 Brusilov wrote, "[M]y army . . . was literally unclad. Their summer clothing was worn out; there were no boots; my men up to their knees in snow and enduring the most severe frost had not yet received their winter kit. I . . . considered this as nothing less than a crime on the part of the Commissariat on this front." When Brusilov ordered soldiers to purchase warm clothing on their own, he was accused of being "carried away by personal motives."[6] Soldiers' letters in the fall and winter of 1914–15 spoke as forcefully as Brusilov about these deficits. In the same issue of the newspaper *Den'* in which the morale of French troops was censored, there was a report from the Union of Cooperatives to the Ministry of Internal Affairs about the growing struggle in various localities with rising costs and scarce goods, and a plea that cooperatives and other organizations be allowed to organize a national conference to discuss the problem.[7]

The degree to which the Galician disaster in May and June 1915 was related to military shortages remains controversial in the literature. In his challenging study of the Russian origins of the war, Sean McMeekin declares without question that the "notorious (and much exaggerated) 'shell shortage'" of 1915 was in any case "brilliantly overcome."[8] In contrast, Western and Soviet historians have long accepted the vivid first-person accounts of Sir Bernard Pares and others

---

[4] RGVIA f. 2048, op. 1, d. 904, ll. 74–75; f. 2067, op. 1, d. 3853, ll. 432–34.
[5] RGVIA f. 2067, op. 1, d. 3853, ll. 72–73.
[6] A. A. Brusilov, *Moi Vospominaniia* (Moscow: Gosizdat, 1929), 96.
[7] *Den'*, Feb. 1, 1915.
[8] Sean McMeekin, *The Russian Origins of the First World War* (Cambridge, MA: Harvard University Press, 2011), 218.

about Russian troops fighting without rifles or ammunition, a view that has been accepted in Russian- and Western-language texts alike. According to Pares:

> From a neighboring height one could see an uninterrupted line of enemy fire from the heaviest guns for five miles to each side. The Russian artillery was practically silent. The elementary Russian trenches were completely wiped out and so, to all intents and purposes, was human life in that area. The Russian division stationed at this point was reduced in this and the immediately succeeding operations from a normal 16,000 to 500.... Any attack from the enemy's side ... found the troops condemned simply to sit under fire without any defense from their own guns....
>
> This was the moment of the worst disorganization as to drafts. Recruits, young or elderly, drawn from anywhere without any local cohesion, were hurried up into the line, often without a rifle, with instructions to wait for one till a neighbor was wounded.... Irmanov, when he was pressed over the frontier, had no cartridges.... I recall some of [the soldiers'] comments: "You know, sir, we have no weapon except the soldiers' breast." "This is not war, sir, it is slaughter."[9]

Archival evidence strongly supports Pares. So do accounts by thoughtful observers like the French ambassador Maurice Paleologue, who reported that General Beliaev, chief of the General Staff, was aware that in some places one-third of Russia's soldiers were without rifles.[10]

Yet in an important way, accuracy here is not the only point. Firsthand reports and anxious correspondence created anxieties about scarcity on their own, especially around the supply of food, the representations themselves carrying the weight of actuality. For many it was the constant stream of reports and letters about "extreme" and "catastrophic shortages" at the front that shaped perceptions as much as or more than objective statistics about military production and supply. Soldiers' pleas that they lacked rifles, that artillery shells were scarce or exhausted, that the management of ordnance was deficient, that they lacked adequate food or winter clothing, were all easily read as evidence of "extreme need" back in their villages and shops and especially in the spring of 1915, as the much-heralded Galician offensive became a disastrous rout.

During the long summer that followed, the supply situation improved somewhat as the army regrouped. By this time, however, complaints about inadequate clothing and food were commonplace, as survivors and new recruits alike seemed to seize hold of a familiar discourse at the front. In one instance it was reported

---

[9] Bernard Pares, *The Fall of the Russian Monarchy* (New York: Vintage Books, 1961), 231–32; Brusilov, *Vospominaniia*, 138–41.

[10] RGVIA f. 2067, op. 1, d. 3853, l. 433; Maurice Paleologue, *An Ambassador's Memoirs*, 3 vols. (New York: Doran, 1927), 2:12–13, 34–36.

that a whole unit was not sent to the trenches because its soldiers lacked adequate boots. Some urged their families to send these and other supplies directly in special parcels "to keep them alive."[11] As the war progressed, the complaints increased. Veterans in one unit wrote that they were given cloth *botinki* instead of boots, and in one report only one foot wrapping for two men! Others angrily expected that there would again be shortages of trench heaters and warm clothing as yet another winter of fighting approached.[12]

As the Brusilov offensive would demonstrate in the summer of 1916, the Russian army remained a formidable fighting force after the Great Retreat from Austrian Galicia despite its astounding losses and continued scarcities in equipment and supplies. This hardly prevented the hundreds of thousands who received letters from their loved ones at the front from seeing them as forced to fight hungry, poorly clothed, and without adequate arms—perceptions of "extreme need" that were culturally situated in ways recipients imagined, heard, and read about accounts of life at the front. Wives and mothers were especially vulnerable, Fears about the dangers of war itself compounded anxieties over their loved ones' physical well-being. As early as the winter of 1914, soldiers' mothers and wives—*soldatki* in the special Russian designation—were already a notable social force, peppering authorities with indignant letters and gendered demands for explanation. While there are obviously no measures of the anxieties all this created, and one need not reify the gendered aspects of nurturance to appreciate the concerns of wives and mothers, it seems evident that a broad field of anxiety and concern underlay the growing and well-evidenced conviction, central to both contemporary thinking and subsequent historiography, that Russia's military and civilian regimes were compromising the country's security, social well-being, and future, not to mention contributing to the enormous losses of life and their material and emotional costs.[13]

The Military Zone of Violence

Shortly before the war began, a vast area to the east of the anticipated battle lines was placed under direct military control. Commanders were given virtually unlimited power to supply their troops locally and to suppress any possible dissidence among its inhabitants.[14] Authority over civilian life was assigned to the army's division of military supply, initially headed by Generals N. A. Danilov on

---

[11] RGVIA f. 2067, op. 1, d. 2932, l. 7.
[12] RGVIA f. 2067, op. 1, d. 2932, ll. 14–16; d. 2937, l. 5; d. 2935, ll. 576–77.
[13] RGVIA f. 2053, op. 1, d. 38, ll. 38ff.; A. L. Sidorov, *Ekonomicheskoe polozhenie Rossii v gody pervoi mirovoi voiny* (Moscow: Nauka, 1973), 23–24.
[14] *Polozhenie o polevom upravlenii voisk v voennoe vremia* (St. Petersburg, 2014).

the Northwestern Front against Germany and A. F. Zabelin on the Southwestern Front against Austria. As Danilov has described, both soon had dictatorial authority over the vast area under military control.[15] After the early defeats in the North and Northwest, the zone was expanded. It soon extended in Ukraine from the western provinces to Kiev and Berdichev, where a central command for the Southwestern Front against Austria was placed more than two hundred miles from most of the fighting. To the north and northwest, the zone stretched from Poland and the Baltic provinces to Petrograd. While in the narrow sense the front was a thin and shifting line of combat, the vast territory now directly under military control soon experienced the collateral damage of violent warfare, much of it quite devastating.

This was partly because the region embraced the tsarist Pale of settlement, the provinces, and territories in which the overwhelming majority of Russia's Jews were required to live. It also included the towns and villages where some 1 million of Russia's inhabitants of German origin had settled, many as early as the eighteenth century. As Eric Lohr and Daniel Graf have described in detail, the immediate concern of the army's High Command was to contain any possibility of subversion here, as was the case on the European front as well and notoriously in the United States against Japanese Americans during World War II. In November and December 1914, German, Austrian, Hungarian, and Ottoman subjects were ordered out of Russia's Polish provinces. After the Galician disaster, additional deportations of Slovaks, Czechs, and Serbs were ordered throughout the military zone. By February 1917 those orders had added as many as 250,000 long-established inhabitants of German origin, including many with family members serving in the Russian army. Many were forcefully deported to Russian internment camps in the provinces of Kazan Simbirsk, Penza, and Viatka, adjacent inland regions on the Volga. Others were settled farther east. Despite some resistance, possibly even from Minister of War Sukhomlinov and among high-ranking Russian officers of German extraction, the army's chief of staff General N. I. Ianushkevich, a fierce nationalist, gave the expulsion his full blessing.

About expelling Jews, however, there was no discernable resistance within the army's High Command. Already in the first months of war entire Jewish communities were expelled from their homes in East Prussia, Poland, and Galicia. By 1915 more than 200,000 Russian Jews were serving in the army, possibly more. Army commanders at all levels, however, regarded them and their families as unreliable "aliens" and, more ominously, likely to engage in spying. Initially this animus found brutal expression in the confiscation of Jewish property and foodstuffs, justified in action if not in form by the army's early difficulties

---

[15] Iu. N. Danilov, "Moi Vospominaniia iz vtorogo perioda mirovoi voiny," autograph ms. with corrections, Houghton Library, Harvard University, no date, 40–41.

in supplying its troops in the field. As the Southwestern armies pressed without pause against the Austrians in Galicia during the fall of 1914, increasingly brutal expulsions were justified on the pretext of Jewish sympathies for the enemy. In fact, as Austrian citizens, Jews in Galicia enjoyed a full range of civil liberties denied their coreligionists in Russia. Jews in Russian Poland and the Baltic were also better off in this and other regards than those in other provinces of the Pale like Volhynia or Chernigov, tapping easily into the deep and ugly anti-Semitism that ran rampant through the army command and the government itself.

According to Vladimir Grabar', a renowned international lawyer attached by the Ministry of Foreign Affairs to army headquarters between July 1914 and May 1915, everyone without exception referred not to "Jews" but to "kikes." At morning tea, members of the chancelleries for diplomacy and civil affairs discussed "exterminating" the Jews in Galicia, mass expulsions to Austria, and the total confiscation of Jewish landholdings.[16] In effect, this engendered a self-fulfilling bias that made resistance to it extremely difficult. Within the Russian army, Jewish soldiers tried to hide their feelings from the censors by writing Yiddish in Cyrillic, or Russian with Yiddish letters. "More than anyone else," one censor reported, "Jewish soldiers also tried to avoid the military censors in communicating their true sentiments."[17] A November order of the High Command declared Jews to be "trustworthy allies of the enemies of Russia." After L'vov was taken, a placard was posted there and in surrounding towns warning Jews that "in cases of espionage, the punishment will be execution by hanging and for each Jew-spy two hostages will also be held accountable."[18] Shortly afterward, Ianushkevich authorized the expulsion of Jews throughout the areas of fighting, giving local commanders power to deport whole communities if any of their inhabitants were suspected of spying. In the spring and summer of 1915 the taking of hostages was officially condoned in Jewish communities still within the battle zone. Ianushkevich was replaced in September as chief of staff, but his orders remained in effect until the February revolution.[19]

---

[16] Vladimir Grabar' diary, cited by Peter Holquist, "Personality in the Occupation of Galicia and Bukovina," in *Anti-Jewish Violence: Rethinking the Pogrom in East European History*, ed. J. Dekel-Chen et al. (Bloomington: Indiana University Press, 2011). See also Eric Lohr, *Nationalizing the Russian Empire: The Campaign against Enemy Aliens during World War I* (Cambridge, MA: Harvard University Press, 2003); and Eric Lohr, "The Russian Army and the Jews: Mass Deportation, Hostages, and Violence during World War I," *Slavic Review* 60, no. 3 (July 2001): 404–19.

[17] RGVIA f. 2067, op. 1, d. 2932, ll. 73–74 ob., 144 ob.; f. 2031, op. 1, d. 1184, ll. 163–63 ob.; f. 2048, op. 1, d. 904, ll. 60–62 ob.

[18] Maxim Vinaver, "The Jewish Problem," in *S"ezdy i konferentsii konstitutsionno-demokraticheskoi partii: 1905–1920 gg.*, ed. O. V. Volobuev, 3 vols. (Moscow: Rosspen, 2000), vol. 1, pt. 1, p. 66; S. Ansky, *The Enemy at His Pleasure: A Journey through the Jewish Pale of Settlement during World War I*, ed. and trans. J. Neugroschel (New York: Henry Holt, 2002), 75–78 and passim; Eugene Avrutin and Elissa Bemporad, eds., *Pogroms: A Documentary History* (New York: Oxford University Press, 2021), 115–18.

[19] Lohr, "The Russian Army," 409.

Both as confiscation to compensate for inadequate supplies and the expulsion of "undesirables," the army's policies at the front and the adjacent military zone were a well-documented disaster even before the offensive into Galicia. Decimating Jewish towns and villages—"appropriate punishment" for their pro-Austrian sentiments—destroyed local economies along with lives. Driving out landowners of German ancestry disrupted grain distribution and practically decimated the sowing of spring crops. Requisitioning stored grain wreaked havoc in local and regional markets. As Russian supply lines were extended in 1915, moreover, and German troops began to shore up Austrian defenses, the situation rapidly became worse. All along the front and throughout the adjacent military zone, plundering by troops replaced authorized confiscations. One soldier in Austrian territory wrote of spending several days "completely drunk. We drank wine, cognac, and beer, not paying for any of it, simply stealing it. . . . The local people say that the Germans did not do as much damage in occupying the village for three weeks as we did in a single day." Another expressed "deep sympathy" for the local population that was "now suffering as much as the troops" as a result of "extremely cruel confiscation policies." (Pares wrote of these same troops that they showed "great kinship with the majority of conquered people.")[20] Military discipline broke down entirely in many places as the extended Russian armies could not maintain adequate supply lines. When the advance into the Carpathians stalled in April 1915, and then became a full-blown rout through early summer, Russian units seized everything they could in villages they passed through before burning them to the ground. Fear, panic, and often desperate need fueled the cruel chaos and depravity of the Great Retreat. Russia's field commanders operated essentially without controls.

All local populations within the front-line zone of violence suffered terribly as the war stretched out on the Eastern Front during 1914–15, but no group more so than the Jews. Russian public figures, Jewish leaders, and even some government figures were already addressing the issue by the spring of 1915. In June, Maxim Vinaver, the well-known former Duma member and a prominent Jewish figure on the Kadet Party's Central Committee, spoke in detail about the "extraordinary government repression of the entire Jewish population" at a well-attended party conference. Jewish activists were beginning systematically to gather information on attacks on Jews and their expulsions from Poland and Galicia in a new organization formed expressly for this purpose. Many of its findings were assembled as "The Black Book' of Russian Jewry," edited by the eminent historian Simon Dubnow and later published in the journal *Evreiskaia Starina* (*Jewish*

---

[20] RGVIA f. 2067, op. 1, d. 3853, ll. 75 ob.–76, 433–34, 486, 572; f. 2031, op. 1, d. 1184, ll. 1–3; M. Vol'fovich and K. Medvedeva, eds., *Tsarskaia armiia v period mirovoi voiny i fevral'skoi revoliutsii* (Kazan: Tatizdat, 1932), 26–27, 37ff.; Bernard Pares, *Day by Day with the Russian Army* (London, 1915), 26–27.

Antiquity).[21] As Vinaver insisted, it was hardly possible considering the wave of denunciations leveled everywhere against Jews that the High Command did not understand the evil it was inflicting on an entire population or its effects on thousands of Jewish soldiers. In the view of his conservative liberal colleague Vasili Maklakov, a renowned lawyer whose brother served as minister of the interior, no cases of Jewish espionage would justify what was now being done to Russia's Jewish population.[22]

In many places, of course, Jews and non-Jews suffered together, especially as they fled the violence. Indeed, the difference between those forcibly deported and those fleeing the violence was often difficult to discern. Jews were sometimes packed brutally into box cars or open gondola cars and sent to Kiev and other interior cities. In some places they became victims of a new wave of pogroms in the summer and early fall of 1915. According to Lohr, local inhabitants, soldiers, and even Cossacks sometimes protected Jews from attacks, but in many instances the pogroms were abetted by the army.[23] Refugees of all ethnic stripes clogged roads and rail lines as well, sometimes commandeering empty freight cars on their own. By the time the long Galician retreat finally ended in September 1915, several million tsarist subjects had been displaced, either by force or voluntarily. Duma leaders saw the army's cruelties toward the flow of desperate humanities as underlining the incompetence of the regime.[24]

The economic historian Peter Gatrell warns in his fine study against treating refugees as helpless and passive casualties, however much they were victims of forces beyond their control. Still, when the Russians were driven from Lodz in late 1914, Jewish and Polish refugees may have numbered more than 100,000, even if many had left the battle zone on their own volition. The army's retreat here and later in 1915 from Galicia, Warsaw, and all of East Prussia had devastating consequences for civilians of all ethnicities, but especially Jews. Without adequate food or medical help, the trek east was a manifest horror: trains and roads strewn with corpses, fouled by dysentery, and layered with physical and emotional misery. Ambassador Paleologue has this description in his diary for March 30, 1915:

> Everywhere the process of departure [from Plotsk, Kutno, Lodz, and Lublin eastward] has been marked by scenes of violence and pillage under the complacent eye of the authorities. Hundreds of thousands of these poor people have

---

[21] Vinaver, "The Jewish Problem," 52–80; "Iz 'chernoi knigi' rossiskogo evreistva: Materialy dlia istorii voiny 1914–1915," *Evreiskaia Starina* 9 (1918): 195–296.
[22] *S"ezdy i konferentsii konstitutsionno-demokraticheskoi partii*, vol. 1, pt. 1, p. 90.
[23] Lohr, "The Russian Army," 148.
[24] I. Belova, *Vynuzhdennye migranty: Bezhentsy i voennoplennye Pervoi mirovoi voiny v Rossii 1914–25* (Moscow: AIRO, 2014), 104–5, 114–15; RGVIA f. 2005, op. 1, d. 48, ll. 45–59.

been seen wandering over the snows, driven like cattle by platoons of Cossacks, abandoned in the greatest distress at the stations, camping in the open around the towns, and dying of hunger, weariness and cold. And to fortify their courage these pitiful multitudes have everywhere encountered the same feelings of hatred and scorn, the same suspicion of espionage and treason. In its long and grievous history Israel has never known more tragic migrations.[25]

Is it possible to link the rapacious behavior of Russian troops to the shocks of war they themselves experienced at the front? Did the sanctioned violence of battle also sanction wanton violence against "enemy" civilians? We know that Cossack squads took the lead in many places in ravaging Jewish and other communities that regular army units had initially left alone, and that their cruelty was then emulated when commanders let their own troops loose on the population. General Ianushkevich himself regarded pillaging (and possibly even rape) as a reward for service and a deterrent to desertion or surrender, as other military leaders have before and since. One can thus infer a broadly based cultivation of a culture of rapacious license against civilians that was directly linked from the start to the military effort. The extraordinary loss of Russia's best trained troops in the first months of the war may also have lessened more normative restraints. At least one recent study emphasizes the importance of training and drill in this regard, especially that of younger soldiers and recent recruits.[26] Yet there is little evidence beyond some soldiers' letters of how all of this was affected by the emotional dislocations and mentalities of troops involved in the carnage or its effects on those who managed to survive their time on the front.

Here we can only rely on what we know of the better-studied actualities of war in other times and places and pick out occasional clues. It is likely, for example, that what Gatrell aptly calls Russian "military paranoia" created indifference or worse toward the fate of anyone thought capable of giving support to the enemy, again especially the Jews.[27] As soldiers increasingly longed for an end to the fighting, commonly wrapping their fears and anxieties in the tropes of victory, the notion of Jewish espionage took on far-reaching personal meaning. With increasing frequency, soldiers wrote that if it were not for the "Jew-spies," the war would end quickly or already be over. Their suffering and losses were at least partly the Jews' fault. According to one censored correspondent, it was Jews, not Germans or Austrians, who were "the kind of people that we must wipe from the face of the earth."[28]

---

[25] Paleologue, *An Ambassador's Memoirs*, vol. 1, p. 315.
[26] M. Van Creveld, *Fighting Power: German and US Army Performance, 1939-1945* (Westport, CT: Greenwood, 1982).
[27] Peter Gatrell, *A Whole Empire Walking* (Bloomington: Indiana University Press, 1999), 20–22.
[28] RGVIA f. 2067, op. 1, d. 3853, l. 74 ob.

We know from subsequent studies that indifference to suffering and carnage is a common and perhaps even instinctive psychological strategy for survival for many caught up in military atrocities. At best, indifference reflects the way in which the nature of warfare itself necessarily legitimizes cruelty as a very condition of survival. At worst, indifference dissolves into unrestrained aggression, sanctioned in the one environment where shooting or bayoneting a stranger is not simply sanctioned but championed as a sign of courage and manhood. Here we can depend on well-regarded psychological literature on aggression as well as important work on the often paradoxical inhumanity of battlefield courage and its subsequent rewards.[29] As Richard Holmes has suggested, what we understand as patriotic feeling in 1914 did not long endure on the battlefield or in the trenches anywhere during the Great War. For Robert Graves's comrades in the British army, for example, it was too "remote" a sentiment, fit only for civilians or prisoners and bearing little relation to why and how soldiers did what they did.[30]

It is not, moreover, that well-trained soldiers cannot be taught to control their instinctive (or other) reactions to the traumas of war. One of the overlooked aspects of Russia's huge early losses in 1914 that may have had a bearing on the breakdown of discipline is that more than half of Russia's best-trained soldiers were lost, leaving too few officers and even fewer NCOs to effectively train new troops. In any event, what we can assume was left even to the most stoic peasant soldiers of Russian patriotic imagination was an emotional state largely stripped of whatever might once have been even minimal normative inhibitions. Depravity on the battlefield was easily transferred to the fully defenseless as if brutality itself was a means for survival.

To this must be added another dimension of scarcity and loss, that of plundered and forcefully displaced Russian citizens in the front-line zone of violence carrying the heartache of losing their homes, communities, social supports, and even their loved ones as they trekked and were carried eastward. Resettled in hundreds of towns that soon lacked adequate resources to support them, as a government survey of the problem in 1916 was to reveal, Russia's civilian victims and the flood of internal refugees were yet additional bearers of disaffection and anxiety as the challenges, costs, and dislocations of war deepened and spread more broadly.

---

[29] Konrad Lorenz, *On Aggression*, trans. Marjorie Kerr Wilson (New York: Harcourt Brace, 1966); Erich Fromm, *The Anatomy of Human Destructiveness* (New York: Holt, Rinehart, 1973); Frank Richardson, *Fighting Spirit: A Study of Psychological Factors in War* (London: Cooper, 1978); Shelford Bidwell, *Modern Warfare: A Study of Men, Weapons and Theories* (London: Allen Lane, 1973); John Keegan, *The Face of Battle* (New York: Viking, 1976); Richard Holmes, *Acts of War: The Behavior of Men in Battle* (New York: Free Press, 1986).

[30] Holmes, *Acts of War*, 274–75; Robert Graves, *Goodbye to All That* (London: Cassell, 1957).

"Dying of Hunger": Procurements, Prices, and the Rising Cost of Living

Almost from the very start of the war, the language of "extreme need" began to spread outward from the military zone. On July 29, 1914, the Ministry of War sent the Council of Ministers plans to deal with the scarcities by placing the state's defense plants under a "special regime" (*osoboe polozhenie*). A list of factories, arsenals, and shops was drawn up in which workers would be forbidden to leave their jobs and subject to severe penalties for absences or negligent work, including being sent immediately to the front. The GAO planners also prepared a list of twenty-two private weapons plants to place under the same regime. The plans were approved in principle by the Council of Ministers on August 3, but immediate implementation was considered "untimely," and for the moment they were not put into effect. Instead, industrial enterprises were to give priority to military and naval orders. They were threatened with sequester if they failed to do so.[31] When the question of a "special regime" came up again in December, the Council of Ministers again put it off, agreeing with Minister of Internal Affairs Nikolai Maklakov that its implementation might reignite labor unrest.[32] Pressed by the military command, the regime decreed instead the creation in the War Ministry of the Special Interinstitutional Conference on the Question of Militarizing Production and Assigning Workers and Administrators the Status of Military Service, although actual efforts in this direction did not get underway until the Galician rout five months later.[33]

While neglecting defense production, the regime and military both took steps to procure food and fodder for the army and its horses. New regulations and orders created a small legion of local officials empowered to procure grain and oats. Since their goal was to supply the army, they were not tasked with assessing how their purchases might otherwise affect the availability of food for local populations. Nor did they pay particular attention to transporting it. At the same time, military commanders at the front were expected to forage on their own. When purchased supplies failed to keep up with the army's needs, a decree of December 8, 1914, gave field officers expanded rights "in situations of extreme need" to requisition supplies from those under military control.[34] Not surprisingly, requisitions soon became common all along the front, even the norm, whether or not commanders thought they were urgent.

---

[31] S. O. Zagorsky, *State Control of Industry in Russia during the War* (New Haven, CT: Yale University Press, 1928), 77.
[32] Sidorov, *Ekonomicheskoe Polozhenie*, 46–49.
[33] RGIA f. 1276, op 12, d. 1800, l. 30.
[34] Ibid.

Meanwhile, overall responsibility for procuring foodstuffs and other nonmilitary goods outside the military zone was assigned to Alexander Krivoshein, the minister of agriculture, who soon mistakenly prided himself on how well the system was functioning.[35] Krivoshein was widely seen as one of the regime's more liberal and competent figures. He had close ties to Duma members like Andrei Shingarev, liberal industrialists like the freemason and Progressist Party leader Alexander Konovalov, who would become minister of trade and industry in 1917, and leaders of the Zemstvo and Town Unions like Prince Georgi L'vov, prime minister after the February revolution. Under his direction local officials of the Ministry of Agriculture were organized into a Main Administration with separate divisions for grain, meat, fish, and vegetables. They were given authority to make direct purchases on credit from local producers.[36] As two of the leading analysts of the subject have demonstrated, however, the task itself brought ministry officials onto the "front lines" of what would soon become another of Russia's major "battlegrounds": the fight to procure foodstuffs and manage their distribution. The Council of Ministers was initiating an administrative and regulatory response to the problem of food supply at odds with that of the military, and in ways that would likely complicate procurement as scarcities increased.[37]

This was so in part because both military officials and the ministry's local procurement agents were given the power to set the prices at which grain would be procured. The category "grain" covered seven different products, including wheat, rye, and oats. In September 1914, the Council of Ministers decreed that procurements for all military goods, including foodstuffs, should be on the basis of "normal prices for products and goods." "Normal," however, was now a moving target in terms of its relation to costs and varied considerably in different localities. As a consequence, the procurement prices set by army officials were frequently lower than what merchants or sellers could get from other buyers. As a result, not surprisingly, grain and other foodstuffs were increasingly secreted by traders for private sale.[38] Fixing prices, however, was dismissed as unworkable, given their variation in different localities. Already in October 1914 the High Command informed Prime Minister Goremykin that if prices were fixed by local agents of the Agriculture Ministry's Main Administration it would "greatly complicate" procurements by army commanders. Members of the High Command

---

[35] RGIA f. 456, op. 2, d. 29, ll. 104–6.
[36] RGIA, f. 582, op. 5, d. 17, l. 79.
[37] T. Kitanina, *Rossiia v pervoi mirovoi voine, 1914–1917 gg.: Ekonomika i ekonomicheskaia politika* (St. Petersburg, 2003); T. Kitanina, *Khlebnaia torgovlia Rossii v kontse XIX–nachale XX veka: Strategiia vyzhivaniia, modernizatsionnye protsessy, pravitel'stvennaia politika* (St. Petersburg: Bulanin, 2011); P. B. Struve, ed., *Food Supply in Russia during the World War* (New Haven, CT: Yale University Press 1930), 5–6.
[38] RGVIA f. 1005, op. 1, d. 67, ll. 1–3.

also expressed doubt that the growing demand for grain and the disruption of transport would even make adequate army procurements possible.[39]

While these early signs of inflationary pressures sent a worrisome message, the government was not yet ready to consider fixing prices more comprehensively. One reason, again, was that the *aggregate* estimates of grain production for 1914 and 1915 did not hint at significant scarcities. After grain exports abroad had been suspended and the summer harvest of 1914 had been completed, Agriculture Minister Krivoshein and his staff expected that military needs for a short war would be met without seriously affecting the domestic market. More than a year later he believed the food supply problem resulted primarily from deficiencies in its transport.[40]

In early January 1915, meanwhile, the Ministry of Internal Affairs received a petition from regional governors worried about increasing shortages. To assure they had enough foodstuffs for their regions they demanded their own agents also be given the right to requisition grain from speculating traders who were hiding it for resale later at higher prices. (Reports about this were prepared for publication in the press but struck out by the censors.)[41] Initially, moreover, outright requisitions instead of contracted procurements by military officials were still relatively rare away from the front lines. For recalcitrant sellers, the threat of requisition was sufficient to force them to sell. But as the supply problem continued, requisition not only became more common, but its pricing and other practices predictably became more harsh. Closer to the front, meanwhile, soldiers' immediate needs were now more frequently met by outright confiscation, as delays in shipments and transport problems forced them to find alternatives. Officially only goods abandoned by householders who had fled could be confiscated—that is, taken without compensation. In practice the line in many towns and trading centers between purchase and confiscation was very thin or completely dissolved, or at least some offended traders complained bitterly that it was. In Austrian Galicia, Russian commanders seized such large quantities of goods that some blithely reported they did not have the resources to store or pay for them. Russian commanders felt justified in this because they suspected goods were being sent illegally to Germany, "huge amounts" of foodstuffs, cotton, leather, and even raw materials like rubber, causing "colossal harm" not only to the military effort but to Russia's entire economic well-being. Their anger quickly turned on the railroad workers, who they suspected were colluding with Jewish speculators.[42]

---

[39] Ibid.
[40] RGIA f. 457, op. 1, d. 12, ll. 25–26.
[41] RGIA f. 777, op. 22, d. 6.
[42] RGVIA f. 2005, op. 1, d. 67, ll. 63–64.

It is difficult to know how widespread these tensions were already in the summer of 1915, or the degree to which throughout and beyond the military zone local officials, grain dealers, and peasants colluded to embargo shipments of grain or traded illicitly. Almost certainly, however, nests of corruption were already strengthening in many places, especially along the railroads. Some officials embargoed food shipments even to other parts of their province out of concern that their own local needs might not otherwise be met. Traders took advantage of increasing anxieties to further raise prices, even if this required special permission (read: special bribes). Forms requiring traders to certify that grain shipments were sent in specially numbered freight cars to specific destinations were simply falsified.[43] The war effort was clearly subordinated here not only to speculative greed but to an embedded resistance to policies considered disadvantageous to local interests. In this, traders and local officials in provincial grain-producing towns reflected the practices of local communities in many partly commercialized economies, funneling goods out of competitive national and regional markets into monopolistic local networks or black market channels for distribution. In the process, of course, the war effort was hindered and prices pushed higher. The emergence of black markets was hardly unique to wartime Russia, but the Russian situation was also related to the lack of plans for mobilizing industry and regulating distribution as well as the curtailment of foreign trade. Railroad bottlenecks made matters worse.

A number of contemporary industrialists and commercial figures like the Kharkov and Baltic German industrialist N. F. von Ditmar, the chairman of the Association of Mining Industrialists, regarded the situation with increasing unease. So did N. N. Kutler and other members of the industrialists' Council of Congresses (Soviet S"ezdov). Von Ditmar saw the decrease in the number of coal miners because of the war as a critical influence on the supply and cost of fuel, and hence the rising cost of most other commodities as well. His voice was echoed by leading Petrograd industrialists in the Society of Factory and Mill Owners. Already in early 1915 von Ditmar was calling for "forced labor" and other "special measures" to increase production, including bringing "yellow laborers" from China who could be paid less or even not at all. In his view, using German and Austrian prisoners of war to increase production in the mines and elsewhere was "extremely desirable."[44] Leading Moscow industrialists joined Kutler and von Ditmar in urging that skilled workers be returned from the front lines back to their benches. They also pressed the regime to address problems on the railroads and deal with inflation.

---

[43] RGIA f. 456, op. 1, d. 143.
[44] RGIA f. 244, op. 1, d. 9, ll. 8, 31 ob., 46, 63–64.

Among the most knowledgeable of those alarmed about these problems were the economists and public figures affiliated with Moscow's Chuprov Society, named in honor of one of Russia's leading statisticians. Prominent among them was a forty-one-year-old zemstvo economist with strong Menshevik sympathies, Vladimir Gustavovich Groman, who would later play important roles in both the revolutionary governments of 1917 and the Bolshevik regime. A large man of unimpeachable integrity (as his friend and fellow economist Naum Jasny later recalled), Groman believed already in 1914 that rising prices were a grave threat especially to the well-being of industrial workers and their families. But he was no less concerned about their effect on Russia's war effort and the maintenance of social order. Along with other moderates on the political left, Groman also worried that if strikes and labor protests resumed to any degree, they could easily spin out of control if wages did not keep up with costs, strengthening the Bolsheviks. With the support of A. A. Chuprov himself, Groman organized already in the fall of 1914 the Commission to Study the Current Cost of Living.

Groman's group faced formidable problems. Accurate data was difficult to come by. Prices for essential goods varied widely within and between areas labeled "consuming" or "producing"; producing areas were obviously areas of consumption as well. Market fluctuations in prices geographically and over time within these categories were difficult to translate into meaningful averages. Still, Groman and his colleagues worked assiduously to focus on what was, in effect, a continually moving target. In the first of three summary volumes issued early in 1915, he and the Commission argued that unless the rise in prices was quickly brought under control, the regime would not be able to manage its effects. Some regarded Commission members as unnecessarily alarmist. It was not until an additional report was presented to a large gathering of public figures in June 1915 that their views began to have resonance. New information, much of it published in the newspapers, showed prices on essential goods continuing to increase rapidly. Aaron Retish shows that in Viatka province the prices of essential goods were rising sharply already by the end of 1914, rye by 40 percent in some parts of the province.[45]

In these circumstances, again, voices of "extreme need" not only carried increasing weight because of the social status of those alarmed but, as with the question of military supplies, created realities of their own. Full-throated expressions of concern were widely broadcast in January 1915 during the one-day meeting of the State Duma, convened to exercise its formal responsibilities over the state budget. Knowledgeable figures like Shingarev, the now prominent voice of the Duma's Budget Commission, shared his Kadet Party colleague Paul

---

[45] Aaron Retish, *Russia's Peasants in Revolution and Civil War: Citizenship, Identity, and the Creation of the Soviet State, 1914–1922* (Cambridge: Cambridge University Press, 2008), 5.

Miliukov's belief that the regime was either "defrauding" them by concealing the actual state of affairs or did not itself understand what was going on, and was thus "organically unable" to improve things.[46] For Shingarev, who continued to chair meetings of the Duma's Budget Committee even when the Duma itself was in recess, Russia's economic situation was clearly worsening. Private commercial and industrial loans from abroad had stopped, practically eliminating short-term commercial credit. Production everywhere had been disrupted by the indiscriminate drafting of essential workers. Transport was chaotic. Peter Bark and his Ministry of Finance were being called on to advance credit directly to enterprises. The Ministries of Trade and Industry and Transport were similarly besieged. As the Council of Ministers acknowledged, the Russian press was full of discussion about the mismanagement of city administrations, the lack of railroad freight cars, and especially the "embarrassing efforts" of local officials.

What the ministers feared most, however, was that the press would "agitate the crowd." They wanted the public informed not that they were confronting the problem in any comprehensive way but that rising prices were occurring everywhere in all warring countries, and that there was nothing exceptional about this problem in Russia. The ministers' Information Bureau was instructed to prepare an official publication to this effect.[47] Rising prices well in evidence by the spring of 1915 were thus, again, less important in some ways than the discourse that described them, especially in leading establishment newspapers and journals like *Birzhevye Vedomosti* and *Novyi Ekonomist*.

The language of "extreme need" was also increasingly expressed in petitions to various ministries and institutions from people describing their "extreme" and "desperate" situations, new committees to help the "newly poor" and provide charitable relief to families of soldiers to supplement the meager state allotments. Rumors circulated about hoarding and other forms of malfeasance. In early June, the chief of staff of the Sixth Army reported that telegraph information convinced him that a "huge amount" of foodstuffs, leather, cotton, metal goods, and other materials was still being transported to Germany by Russo-German firms and other German sympathizers, creating "colossal damage" to the well-being of the provinces as well as to the capitals and the army.[48] From the front, meanwhile, soldiers wrote poignantly about their anxieties that rising prices were putting their families at risk. As the summer harvest approached, "almost every letter" spoke passionately about the wish to see their families and their homes. Many longed for the war to be over so they could do so, a sentiment frequently

---

[46] P. Miliukov, *Istoriia vtoroi russkoi revoliutsii*, 3 vols. (Sofia: Ros-Bolgarskoe izd., 1921–24), vol. 1, p. 24.
[47] RGIA f. 1276, op. 12, d. 1800, ll. 29–30.
[48] RGIA, f. 23, op. 27, d. 48, passim.

translated by military censors into an eagerness to fight under any condition to achieve victory.[49]

By the late spring and early summer of 1915, public and state agencies everywhere were also being inundated with plaintive pleas for help. "I have been left with two children 10 and 2 years old without any means of support," Nikitina Paraskeva wrote in April 1915 to a committee organized by the Ministry of Finance to help the families of soldiers two months after her husband was drafted. "I have only the most meager income from a small part of my husband's former wages and face an extremely hopeless situation as a result of the increase day by day in the cost of living." The wife of a wounded worker too weak to work or return to the army found her family in "the most difficult circumstances" as a result of living costs that "no longer allowed the purchase of medicine and even our ability to feed ourselves." Others claiming "extreme need" asked for emergency grants of as little as a hundred rubles. In mid-April 1915 Duma leaders themselves received a petition signed by twenty-four women with "no resources to cope with the rising cost of living" and who were "dying of hunger."[50]

"Extreme Need" in the Workplace

In the spring of 1915, just as Russian troops in Galicia were bearing the brunt of the Austro-German counteroffensive, the first clear signs appeared of growing agitation among Russia's industrial workforce. Already in April, an urgent (*srochno*) telegram from the Naval Ministry to Prime Minister Goremykin warned that broad "dissatisfaction and unrest" throughout the Petrograd defense industries appeared to be having a "great affect" on more "peaceful" workers, raising the dangers of disorder.[51] On the morning of May 1, more than eight hundred workers from leading Petrograd defense plants took advantage of the May Day holiday to demonstrate for higher wages. While protesters aired a range of grievances, including the demand that they be treated with dignity by their foremen and plant managers, the main cause of unrest was the rapid rise of prices on essential goods and foodstuffs. Most returned to work in the afternoon, but shortly afterward new strikes hit Novyi Lessner, Nevskii Shipbuilding, Aivaz, and other major enterprises that had received lucrative state contracts for military goods. Wages were still the workers' primary demand. The same was true in Moscow. Striking workers (and others) there also participated in violent attacks on German-owned shops, a "patriotic" action in the eyes of the police, who did

---

[49] RGVIA f. 2067, op. 1, d. 3853, ll. 433, 486, 542, 572–72 ob.
[50] RGIA, f. 268, op. 6, d. 80, ll. 260, 290, 323–30; f. 1278, op. 5, d. 1193, l. 61.
[51] RGIA f. 1276, op. 11, d. 167, ll. 3–4.

nothing to stop them. Ambassador Paleologue attributed the attacks to anger and humiliation aroused by the Galician defeats, but some of the rioters openly insulted the tsar on Red Square. Feelings clearly went deeper.[52]

Also notable about these strikes was the risks they now involved. Organizing or "agitating" for a strike was strictly illegal, even if striking against private plants was not. Strikers could be sent immediately to the front. Because of the indiscriminate drafting of workers at the beginning of the war, skilled workers were still in short supply, so the risks were calculated ones. But strikes indicated that the patriotic feelings the regime so relished when the war began were already rather thin here, and certainly more so than an "unpatriotic" anxiety about one's individual or family's well-being as opposed to the state's.

Petrograd and Moscow defense workers were not alone. Coal miners in the Don Basin began to stage a series of protests over the rising cost of living. A report to the Ministry of Trade and Industry stressed that the dissidence did not yet involve work stoppages and that Don workers were "fully patriotic," their apartments covered with portraits of the tsar and his family. Protests were being stirred by rising prices and, even among those described as "semi-literate," by newspaper and other reports of still higher prices to come. While managers succeeded in scaling back wage demands to "moderate" levels, the report urged the ministry to begin an immediate review of prices and ways to bring them under control.[53]

In Moscow, meanwhile, a secret communication on the disorders reported that workers for the first time were demanding that unpopular foremen and administrative personnel be dismissed, in some cases citing their German surnames. Equally ominous, workers were now leaving their benches to search for affordable food and other necessities and were demanding they be paid for this time away because low wages required them to do it.[54] The term for this truancy—*proguly*, from the Russian verb "to stroll around"—thus joined an expanding vocabulary of need.[55] Such truancies had long been a way for workers to avoid the penalties of strikes, as were "Italian" slowdowns, but they were no less disruptive to production. In some cases they were even more so if foremen had to shut down whole shops because skilled workers were temporarily absent. Thousands of man hours were likely being lost in this way. The argument that such absences were compelled by circumstances was difficult for authorities to

---

[52] Paleologue, *Ambassador's Memoirs*, 2:13; M. G. Fleer, ed., *Rabochee dvizhenie v gody voiny* (Moscow: Voprosy Truda, 1925), 261; Reinhard Nachtigal, "Germans in Russia during World War I," in *Russia's Home Front in War and Revolution 1914–1922*, bk. 2, ed. Adele Lindenmyer, Christopher Read, and Peter Waldron (Bloomington, IN: Slavica, 2016), 333–34.
[53] RGIA f. 40, op. 1, d. 71, ll. 169–71.
[54] RGIA f. 1276, op. 11, d. 168, ll. 1–14.
[55] *Vestnik Finansov, Promyshlennost', i Torgovlia* 31 (Aug. 2–15, 1915): 195.

refute without calling even more attention to the problems of food shortages and insecurities.

In effect, *proguly* were becoming a powerful new form of indirect protest and resistance. The demand to be paid gave a positive moral valence to the act of leaving work by implying that factory and plant administrations should shoulder responsibility for their employees' hardship. Here was thus at least some notion of the workplace as a "moral community" in which factory and plant administrators were involved not simply in supervising production but also in "patriotically" assuring the needs of its members. Although not articulated in these later conceptual terms, the notion itself found reflection as well in ways workers were also demanding to be treated with dignity by foremen and plant managers. In a secret report on the situation the minister of trade and industry Prince V. N. Shakhovskoi expressed his "grave concern" about the implications of these demands. In his view, all of this could "very seriously complicate the entire structure of factory and plant administration," issues of patriotism aside, as indeed it was soon to do.[56]

Against this background the strike movement in Russia suddenly escalated. In early June, more that six thousand textile workers left their jobs in Kostroma, near Moscow, just as the Galician retreat was at its height. Like their comrades in Moscow and Petrograd they demanded higher wages, but dignity issues were also a source of real grievance, especially for women. Throughout Russia's growing industrial sectors women were commonly victims of body searches and other sexually motivated deprivations. The random drafting of workers in other industries had already brought thousands of women into the workplace for the first time. By 1915 they dominated not only the textile sector but chemical plants making gunpowder and other explosives. Women even joined sectors in the large metalworking sector, replacing men who had been drafted.

Moreover, unlike the other warring powers, the outbreak of hostilities in Russia came after months of intensive labor conflict and strike activity between January and July 1914, as we have noted. In the short run, unrest stemmed from a broad range of unresolved grievances, amplified in 1912 by the brutal suppression of the Lena gold fields protests. More consequentially, the unrest reflected the social, economic, and political issues that underlay the massive strikes of 1905 and their repressive aftermath. Only a handful of strikes had occurred in Russia's industrial centers in the fall and winter of 1914–15. All were primarily over wages, all were peaceful, and all had been short-lived.

In contrast, the demand of both male and female Kostroma strikers to be treated with dignity added sociocultural issues to economic ones. More protests on June 5 turned into a violent confrontation with police. In the first major

---

[56] RGIA f. 1276, op. 11, d. 168, ll. 1–14.

deadly civilian violence since the beginning of the war, mounted police trying to clear the gates to the Sotovskii plant opened fire on strikers. Twelve were killed and at least forty-five were wounded. The next day, the strikers' demand for additional housing allowances were met, but at the cost of reductions in wages. The strike continued until June 10, when the government declared martial law. Those identified as "agitators" were arrested. Open conflict with tsarist authorities broke out again soon enough, however, in nearby Ivanovo. For the first time, a general strike took place throughout the city, reminiscent of 1905. Workers presented themselves as being in desperate need. They demanded higher wages and the cancelation of new taxes on foodstuffs. Plant owners responded with small wage increases and pressured traders and local authorities to lower the price of bread. Unrest then continued in Kostroma and spread broadly through the region. In early August, police again opened fire on demonstrators, killing twenty-five and wounding thirty.[57]

Despite the violence, the relative success of Kostroma's workers in increasing their wages was empowering. It gave new authority to strike leaders, demonstrating again the value of collective action and strengthening the still fresh memories of experiences in 1905–6 and the Lena gold fields massacre. These effects may be difficult to measure, but newspapers openly linked them to worker militancy in the prewar past, as did leading figures in and outside the regime. As many as twenty-five thousand participated in the second round of Ivanovo strikes. Shockingly for some, the violence of war was no longer directed only against a foreign enemy or suspect groups like the Jews. Protests were now fueled as much by anger toward the authorities for their brutality as by demands for better wages, better working conditions, and dignified treatment—legal economic strikes turning implicitly into illegal political ones. Meanwhile, the second half of July saw new strikes at some of Petrograd's largest defense plants, including Novyi Lessner, Nevskii Shipbuilding, and Erikson Electric. For the first time since the war began, the demonstrative language of "extreme need" was also expressed on signs that read "Down with the War!" and "Down with the Tsar!"[58]

Food Insecurities and the "Baba" Question

How serious were scarcities in essential goods by the summer of 1915? Certainly the early voices of "extreme need" reflected concerns that the war would not be short, anticipating the insecurities to come. Yet scarcities of foodstuffs and

---

[57] K. F. Sidorov, "Rabochee dvizhenie v Rossii v gody imperialisticheskoi voiny," in *Ocherki po istorii oktiabr'skoi revoliutsii*, 2 vols., ed. M. N. Pokrovskii (Moscow, 1927), 1:261–64, 284.
[58] Ibid.

goods in many places and rising prices almost everywhere *were* quite real. So were the increasing anxieties of everyday life for ordinary Russians, as indeed they were for Germans, Austrians, and Russia's allies, the consequences of the hitherto unimaginable scale of conflict. Some in the Russian government seem to have thought grain production would continue to be adequate after statistics showed a 20.4 percent increase between 1913 and 1914. It was clear by early 1915, however, that there was a significant drop in all grains besides wheat and rye in 1914, although production increased in 1915, according to available figures, before falling again for all grains except buckwheat in 1916.[59] In the view of Richard Pipes, the most prominent recent narrator of the liberal Great Story, higher prices were sorely felt in urban areas, but inflation positively benefited the rural population. Peasants were "swimming in money."[60]

In formalist terms, what is problematic about these measurements is the accuracy of the data. Within the Ministry of Agriculture and the Special Council on Food one of the most common frustrations was the inability to assemble accurate information on sown land and harvest yields. The reasons are obvious. Given the steady increase in the prices paid for Russia's seven principal grains and the diversion of industrial production away from manufactured commodities that might incentivize peasants to sell, significant quantities of grain were being hoarded or funneled into black markets by the so-called bagmen and -women, some of whom managed to reach villages in the deep countryside to buy or trade any surpluses or concealed supplies that could be found.

The army's voracious appetite was also not easy to calculate. Procurers for the military roamed the grain-trading points throughout the Ukrainian provinces of the huge military zone. Armed with military orders, official directives, and flexibility in setting purchase prices, they were usually able to contract for what they wanted, regardless of the needs of the local populations. In addition to the objective difficulties this presented for villages, grain extraction, whether by requisition or coercion, touched raw substantive feelings. As the pressure to produce ratcheted up, the increasingly fraught issue in many villages was securing more land to cultivate, especially that held unproductively fallow by neighboring gentry.

There was also the effect on the accessibility to food of steadily rising prices, especially in cities and towns. The increasing number of *proguly* which took workers away from their benches during work hours to look for food testifies as

---

[59] TsSU, *Statisticheskii sbornik za 1913–1917: Trudy* 7, nos. 1–2 (Moscow: TsSU, 1922), 2:60–90; TsSU, *Fabrichno-zavodskaia promyshlennost' v period 1913–1918*, vol. 26, nos. 1–3 (Moscow: TsSU, 1926), 3:22–26; Peter Gatrell, *Russia's First World War: A Social and Economic History* (London: Pearson-Longman, 2005), ch. 7; S. S. Demostenov, "Food Prices and the Market in Foodstuffs," in Struve, *Food Supply in Russia*, 307–14.

[60] Richard Pipes, *The Russian Revolution* (New York: Knopf, 1990), 236.

much to its cost as its scarcity. Here, too, statistics are of uneven reliability, but the government's own figures showed the cost of staples like rye flour rising almost 30 percent between July 1914 and March 1915, potatoes and onions some 37 and 42 percent, and comparable increases for other essential commodities.[61] New sales taxes on articles of mass consumption designed to compensate for lost liquor revenues added to the problem. So did questions about shipping priorities and simple administrative confusion. At many depots goods in transport without "special orders" were not moved or unloaded, however much they may have been needed at their destinations. At others, military procurement officers stood at odds with their civilian counterparts from the Ministry of Agriculture.[62]

Finally, in terms of "extreme need" we must emphasize again the emotional toll the losses of war were taking on peasant women who suddenly found themselves without the labor and support of their sons and husbands, however difficult it is to measure. We will take up later the increasing role of the *soldatki* wives in demanding additional food and support from the regime as the war wore on, but from the first a very large proportion of petitions and complaints like those cited in this chapter were written by women. In the gendered culture of the village the voices of the *bab'i* (womenfolk) had something of a privileged place as the righteous talk of motherhood. It is possible that on the one hand, most of the voices of extreme need were women's, and on the other, that many who heard or read them did not take them seriously for that reason.

More important, difficult changes in family lifestyles and the new burdens and responsibilities soldiers' wives had to bear may have been thought to be temporary at first, and even short term, given the near universal expectation of a rapid victory. In Viatka province, Retish tells us, mass mobilization in 1914 robbed the countryside of adult males. The number of marriages dropped by 34 percent between 1913 and 1915, while almost half of all able-bodied men of working age went into the army. So much the worse, then, for so many hundreds of thousands when their family's losses proved to be permanent. By 1917, 40 percent of the households in the province would be without a male worker.[63]

No measure can be made of the quantity of grief and deprivation women in the villages experienced. Nor can we measure the "desperate" feeling of Kostroma textile workers or the depth and quality of feeling involved even for

---

[61] RGIA, f. 40, op. 1, d. 71, ll. 174ff.
[62] A. Michelson et al., eds., *Russian Public Finance during the War* (New Haven, CT: Yale University Press, 1928), 99–100.
[63] Retish, *Russia's Peasants*, 46.

"DYING OF HUNGER" 121

presumptively stoic peasants. We can only suggest the hardships and anguish escalating losses may have forced on Russia's women peasants in particular, but women workers as well, and keep a sense of their likely anxieties in mind as we explore how these may have affected later behaviors and outlooks after the collapse of the tsarist regime.

4
Empowering "Responsible Publics" and the Emergence of War Capitalism

The magnitude of the Galician disaster and the sharp renewal of labor unrest in May and June 1915 shocked government officials and public figures alike. Early summer also saw the army driven from Russia's Polish and Lithuanian provinces. Some 115,000 square miles of territory were lost to the Germans and Austrians. As many as a million soldiers were killed, wounded, or taken prisoner. On the Southwestern Front, General Nikolai Ianushkevich, the army's chief of staff, ordered a scorched earth policy. Russian troops needed no encouragement. Meanwhile, rumors circulated freely about possible subversion by German sympathizers, a ready explanation for why soldiers were so poorly equipped. Vladimir Sukhomlinov was replaced as minister of war. Many looked askance at the tsarina herself.[1]

The liberal leader Paul Miliukov notably described the moment as one of "patriotic anxiety."[2] Another anxious voice urging new initiatives to coordinate the war effort was that of the president of the State Duma, Mikhail Rodzianko. A wealthy Ukrainian nobleman, graduate of the exclusive Corps of Pages, and member of the personal staff of Alexander II, Rodzianko had faultless credentials. Along with his Duma colleague Alexander Guchkov, he had played a leading role in organizing the loyalist Octobrist Party in 1905, supporting the regime while also pressing for the full realization of the constitutional reforms Nicholas proclaimed in his October Manifesto. After seeing firsthand the disastrous consequences of the army's shortages during visits to the Galician Front, Rodzianko spoke directly to the tsar himself when the two met in L'viv in the beginning of April, laying out a dire picture of need. "You always try to frighten me," the tsar responded, according to Rodzianko, "and tell me unpleasant things."[3]

Shortly afterward, the Duma president traveled to army headquarters to persuade Grand Duke Nikolai Nikolaevich, still the commander in chief, to

---

[1] B. I. Kolonitskii, "Slukhi ob imperatritse Aleksandre Fedorovne i massovaia kul'tura (1914–1917)," *Voprosy Istorii* 1 (2005): 362–78.

[2] William G. Rosenberg, *Liberals in the Russian Revolution* (Princeton, NJ: Princeton University Press, 1974), 38–44; State Archive of the Russian Federation [GARF] f. 523, op. 1, d. 32, ll. 170–80.

[3] M. V. Rodzianko, *The Reign of Rasputin: An Empire Collapses* (Gulf Breeze, FL: Academic International Press), 126.

organize a special council to direct the production and distribution of all military goods. Rodzianko was convinced that "responsible public figures," leading industrialists, and well-respected Duma deputies needed to be brought directly into the effort. The special council would be chaired by the minister of war and have the authority to sign contracts in the state's name. The Grand Duke was supportive. So was his chief of staff, Nikolai Yanushkevich, who "spoke with tears in his eyes," in Rodzianko's telling, as he described the "mental tortures" he was going through in not being able to obtain the necessary supplies from the Main Artillery Administration and knowing that it was in such "dishonest hands."[4]

Back in Petrograd, Rodzianko enlisted broad support for his plan. The industrialists A. I. Putilov and A. I. Vyshnegradskii both saw significant advantages for their own enterprises in such a council, as did Guchkov and other leading Duma figures, who hoped with Rodzianko that it would rationalize the whole system of military procurements. Together they worked out a detailed plan. The Grand Duke and his staff then agreed to set it in place, the tsar and his ministers as well, although without much enthusiasm. In the looming shadow of the Galician disaster, the new organization was initiated on May 14 as the Special Council on the Defense of the State—a "stark admission," in Rodzianko's view, of the failure of industry and government to properly supply the army.[5] Shortly afterward the Ministry of Transport's Committee on Fuel was also reorganized into a special council, modeled in the same way. The Duma itself then approved two additional special councils when it reconvened in August, one to manage food procurement and one for transport, with special focus on the railroads.

War Industries Committees and the Special Councils

Central to the Duma resident's effort was the involvement of representatives from public organizations, including the private organizations of industrialists and the now coordinated Unions of Cities and Zemstvos.[6] Already tasked with the responsibility of treating the wounded and assuring their welfare, the Unions by the summer had cared for more than 1.1 million soldiers as well as they could, despite their lack of preparedness. Almost 7 million ration packets had also been distributed and over 2.5 million articles of clothing.[7] As Rodzianko knew, his views were shared not only by the Zemstvo Union's Prince Georgi L'vov

---

[4] Ibid., 130–31.
[5] *Zhurnal osobykh soveshchanii po obespecheniiu deistvuiushchei armii artilleriei, glavneishimi vidamie dovol'stviia, predmetami boevogo i material'nogo snabzheniia, 11 Maia–19 Avgusta 1915* (Moscow: Inst. Istorii RAN, 1975) [henceforth *ZOSODA*] 1 (May 14, 1915): 1–2; 3 (May 23, 1915): 1–19; 4 (May 27, 1915): 31.
[6] *ZOSODA* 3 (May 23, 1915): 19.
[7] A. Michailovsky, "Russia and the War," *Russian Review* 1 (1916): 117–18.

and leading Duma figures but also by prominent members of the Council of Congresses of Representatives of Industry and Trade, the coordinating organization for local and regional producers and commercial groups. On May 26, representatives at the Council's ninth annual meeting heard an impassioned speech from the progressive Moscow textile magnate Pavel Pavlovich Riabushinskii demanding his colleagues give "everything for war!"[8]

Already in 1905 Riabushinskii and others had struggled to organize the Moscow business community behind a platform of liberalizing reforms. As the regime reneged on the promised reforms of 1905, their Progressist Party carried on the struggle. Their Duma delegates worked closely with Alexander Guchkov and his Octobrists as well as many Kadets in trying to diminish the role of industrial trusts centered in Petrograd and other impediments to entrepreneurial independence. They resented Petrograd colleagues like Putilov using ties to the capital's ministries and banks to advance their personal interests, inhibiting the consolidation of Russia's business community more broadly. As Alfred Rieber has demonstrated, no common social or political consciousness united Russia's two largest commercial and entrepreneurial communities or joined them with smaller producers and traders into a coherent and self-confident social group.[9] Indeed, as Ruth Roosa and others relate, business as usual early on in the war even earned some condemnation in the press.[10] Still, at the ninth congress of the Representatives of Industry and Trade in May, a strong effort was made to bring the industrial and commercial communities closer together in support of the war.[11]

A way to do this was already percolating among industrial and public figures. It involved organizing a nationwide network of local War Industries Committees (WICs). These would be formed out of leading industrial and commercial figures at a local level and headed by a Central War Industries Committee (CWIC) in Petrograd. Some envisioned the participation of workers themselves, whose voice they thought important to defining new production routines and pay scales (*tariffs*). For democratic socialists the advantages of workers' participation were related to a historical imagination about the course of Russia's future, since it would help organize workers, raise their awareness, and prepare them for an active political role in what the democratic socialist Great Story hoped would be Russia's democratic socialist future. Supported by the Council of Congresses (Soviet Soiuzov), the CWIC was quickly organized at the end of May.

---

[8] RGIA f. 1276, op. 11, d. 814, ll. 2–3.
[9] Alfred J. Rieber, *Merchants and Entrepreneurs in Imperial Russia* (Chapel Hill: University of North Carolina Press, 1982), 415.
[10] Ruth Roosa, "Russian Industrialists during World War I: The Interaction of Economics and Politics," in *Entrepreneurship in Imperial Russia and the Soviet Union*, ed. Fred V. Carstensen and Gregory Guroff (Princeton, NJ: Princeton University Press, 1983), 161–62.
[11] RGIA f. 1276, op. 11, d. 814, ll. 2–3.

It held its first meeting on June 2, led by the Octobrist Party leader Guchkov and the Progressive textile magnate Alexander Konovalov, both to become ministers in 1917. The new CWIC appealed immediately to trade industrial groups throughout the country to help organize local affiliates. Many did so with enthusiasm. One of the first matters the CWIC took up was a draft statute sharply limiting requisitions that it planned to submit to the new Special Council on Defense.[12]

One of the principal objectives of the CWIC was to gain the authority to issue and regulate contracts in the state's name. Working with the local committees, CWIC would coordinate the complex tasks of managing the contracts and providing state funds to finance their fulfillment. Pressed by Rodzianko, its members saw their task as nothing less than ending the scarcity of essential goods by placing this obligation in "responsible" hands like their own.[13] While tensions about all of this continued, the urgency of the moment took precedence. In early July, the army in the Southwest was still retreating from Galicia, and in the Northwest preparing to evacuate Warsaw.

On June 1, at precisely the moment tensions between workers and plant managers in the Kostroma textile plants were building into Russia's largest strike since the beginning of the war, the WIC initiative was formally accepted by the new Special Council for Defense and authorized to act as an agent of the Ministry of War in distributing of orders. A first advance of 3 million rubles went to the CWIC for the procurement of shells. The next day jubilant CWIC leaders set up office in Petrograd at 46 Liteinyi Prospekt, where the Soviet S"ezdov also had its headquarters, an easy walking distance from the offices of imperial state power. By mid-July the CWIC consisted of nineteen different departments. It was also receiving data from the Ministry of Finance on subsidies being provided to Russian producers.[14] Responsible people seemed finally to be taking charge.

Devolving Authority, Engaging the Localities

By early July 1915, as bloody labor conflicts broke out again after a year of quiescence, intense discussions were occurring at 46 Liteinyi Prospekt, which quickly became a lively gathering spot for many of the city's most prominent commercial and financial figures, a role it would continue to play well into the spring of 1918.

---

[12] *Zhurnal Zadedaniii Tsentr. Voenno-Promyshlennogo Komiteta* [*Zhurnal TsVPK*] 1 (June 3, 1915); 3 (June 9, 1915); 5 (June 16, 1915); 6 (June 23, 1915) in RGIA f. 32, op. 1, d. 1983. (TsVPK is designated in the text as CWIC, Central War Industries Committee).
[13] ZOSODA 3 (May 23, 1915); 4 (May 27, 1915); *Zhurnal Zadedanii Tsentr. Kom. Soveta S"ezdov* in RGIA f. 32, op. 2, d. 10, ll. 43–43 ob.
[14] ZOSODA 9 (June 24, 1915): 75–76.

Some were formal (and recorded in the CWIC journals), others more casual, but both reflected a rapidly growing anxiety about the ability of the government to ensure both the army and the country were adequately supplied with food and essential goods. Billions of rubles in credits were being extended with little or no knowledge about local conditions or whether the credits would be well used.[15]

The vastness of the country and the diversity of its local economies presented serious problems regarding planning, production, and especially the distribution of scarce goods. Local city and town dumas, councils of various kinds, and especially the provincial zemstvos were important elements of local administration, but neither fully developed nor prepared, as we have seen, for coping with the effects of scarcity and loss brought on by the war. Zemstvos representing both peasants and the rural gentry had never been established at the district level and functioned at an often considerable remove from much of Russia's village life, especially deep in the countryside. (The creation of elected district zemstvos would be one of the first acts of the revolutionary government in 1917.) Since the word for "council" in Russian is *soviet*, the summer of 1915 saw a growing wave of local soviet administrations and other "home-grown" groups that, as we will see, would become the institutional locus of local authority in 1917.

Local WICs organized in early July with remarkable speed, testimony to the serious problems at hand. Within a few weeks there were seventy-eight newly formed committees primarily in European Russia. In mid-July 231 delegates gathered in the capital for the first WIC national congress. The loudest voices were those of local delegates who demanded the authority to manage matters in their areas, where various socioeconomic problems confronting the country were best understood. Some members of the CWIC worried, however, that unrestrained local autonomy might compromise the commanding role of the state. Riabushinskii, Konovalov, and other Moscow figures responded that the concentration of authority in Petrograd was part of the problem: command had to be replaced by coordination. Perhaps the most important accomplishment of the Congress was thus to affirm local prerogatives and their implications for democratic practice, a view that would be fully institutionalized in the February revolution. Efforts to solve the problems Russia faced would now be shared by respected members of Russia's industrial and commercial communities "from the bottom to the top," as it was expressed at the conference, resolved by mutual efforts at the local as well as national level.[16]

---

[15] *Zhurnal TsVPK* 3 (June 9, 1915); 5 (June 16, 1915); 6 (June 23, 1915) in RGIA, f. 32, op. 1, d. 1893; *Zhurnaly mezhduvedomstvennogo soveshchaniia dlia izyskaniia sposoba finansirovaniia chastnykh metalurgichesskikh predpriatii rabotaiushii po nuzhny gosudarstvennogo oborony, Mar.–Dek. 1915* in RGIA f. 1276, op. 11, d. 248.

[16] *Zhurnal TsVPK* 6 (June 23, 1915): 31; *Trudy S"ezda Predstavitelei Voenno-Promyshlennykh Komitetov* [*Trudy S"ezda VPK*] *25–27-go iiulia 1915 goda* (Petrograd, 1915), 10.

The WIC congress also became the first public forum of the war to discuss in detail the difficulties being experienced at a local level all over Russia: inflation, declining real wages, requisitioning, work conditions, and the consequences for workers of evacuating industrial plants. While requisitioning was accepted as a necessary measure in a war zone, the issue was not one of necessity but of the damage it was inflicting on local communities. So was some deterioration in workplace conditions, if not in the treatment of workers themselves.[17] Transport problems were also a center of attention, along with questions of fuel supply. The situation differed significantly between localities. Some local WIC members, like the delegate from Ekaterinodar, drew a very different picture from those being described in Petrograd. According to his reports, Odessa, Ekaterinodar, and other southern cities lacked fuel not because of inadequate production but because the large firms were monopolizing storage facilities, hoarding railroad tank cars, and discriminating against smaller producers. The WIC's new Committee on Supply urged control over shipping goods be assigned to local WICs at all major railroad stations and depots.[18]

The most important accomplishment of the WIC congress was to affirm the broad authority of local committees to deal directly with local problems. In this connection some participants worried that the Special Council for Defense as it had just been constituted was perhaps *too* powerful, since it was not formally responsible to any other body, including the Council of Ministers and, more important for some, the Duma. Andrei Shingarev, representing the Duma's own Commission on Military Supply, also saw problems in the War Ministry's plan to concentrate all supply matters, including requisitioning, in the Special Council's hands and thus "the entire economic life of the country ... in brief, to make it an institution for a special kind of military dictatorship, to which everything and everybody would be subordinated, and which itself would not be subordinate to anyone."[19] Nikolai Astrov, a left-leaning Moscow Kadet, agreed. He and others pressed instead for broadening representation in local WICs from Zemstvo and City Union personnel as well as workers themselves, bringing "the vital forces of the country" into play and reaching beyond defense production, stirring images of 1905.[20]

The dominant impulse here was not overtly political. Throughout these busy days there was a great deal of talk about the need for more competent and responsible people in the Duma and the importance of extending the role of the Duma itself. Yet the devolution of authority downward had clear implications for reforming Russian governance. WIC delegates saw themselves representing

---

[17] *Trudy S"ezda VPK 25-27-go iiulia 1915,* 267ff.
[18] Ibid., 222-23.
[19] Ibid., 19-20.
[20] Ibid., 139.

Russian grassroots more directly than delegates to the Duma. As elected representatives to the WIC Congress, Riabushinskii emphasized, "we are not people materially interested" but "citizens of the state," able to look at matters objectively.[21]

There were two notable problems here. First, as delegates from different localities made clear in three days of intense discussion, the needs of some areas not only differed significantly from those of others, but in some cases stood in contradiction to each other. Financing local production, securing food supplies, ensuring adequate wages, and controlling requisitioning were shared problems almost everywhere. But Nizhnii Novgorod was largely a grain-exporting province whose peasants and traders could prosper from rising prices, while the inhabitants of adjacent Tambov largely relied on imports of foodstuffs and suffered greatly from rising prices. The relatively prosperous industrial northwest region was suffering particularly from its proximity to the front and the constant arrival of new officers who ordered they be given this or that with no warning or preparation. The pressing issues in Vilnius and the Baltics were evacuation, refugees, and forceful anti-Semitism. In Smolensk, it was retaining adequate grain and other foodstuffs for local needs. The Kuban production was suffering from lack of coal, while in the Donbas coal supplies were held up by a lack of adequate transport. According to the delegate representing Orenburg, Samara, Ufa, and Simbirsk provinces, this region as a whole was "much closer to the edge of disaster" than one would imagine from what other areas were reporting. Some problems in the localities could be worked through only if responsible local officials had the authority now promised by the WICs. Others, however, required central directives capable of being enforced locally with a strong hand even against the desires of local authorities. Russia in one sense was a country now diverse it its circumstances, needs, and practices. In another, Russia was a centralized, imperial, and autocratic state for whom the question of autonomous local rule was also a question of preserving the multinational empire itself. In contrast, increasingly audible voices from Ukraine and other regions with non-Russian nationalities insisted that the war was also being fought to make the world "safe for democracy," as Woodrow Wilson was to put it, and the right to self determination. While this was not yet germane to the WICs' agenda, it was beginning to loom in the background as one of the great political issues of the war and which the devolution of authority downward from Petrograd could not help but animate.[22]

This in turn touched a second difficult problem facing the WICs and Russia's "responsible publics": the fact that scarcities and losses were also attributable to

---

[21] Ibid., 143–46.
[22] Ibid., 40, 42, 49–55, 67, 71, 75.

incompetence within the regime and the army itself. Progress in support of the war and wartime society required competence in state administration and the instruments of governance. As M. S. Margulies, the well-regarded Jewish lawyer, zemstvo physician, and vice chair of the CWIC put it to his colleagues, "We know of no time in history when old wine could be put successfully into new bottles."[23]

The participation of the "public men" in its ranks and especially their aid in the formation of the WIC network were thus important steps toward engaging the public more broadly in addressing the country's needs and ensuring that competent and responsible people were involved in its governance. Indeed, the formation of WICs throughout the country was itself a radical political reform, even if not yet understood as such by those at the center. As the passionate Riabushinskii put it, Russia was in "acute danger" (*strashnaia opastnost'*). Now responsible people would be taking charge. "We will save Russia," he declared. "We will do a great thing."[24]

The Progressive Bloc and the Question of Autocratic Power

It is within this context of anxieties about scarcity, military losses, and the engagement of responsible publics at a local and national level that we should assess the best-known political episode during the anxious summer of 1915: the efforts to increase the governing role of the State Duma when it reconvened in August and the formation of more than half of its delegates into what they called the Progressive Bloc. After the brief special session at the beginning of the war Russia's legislature had been allowed to convene exactly once, for a single day in January 1915. In early July the tsar agreed under strong pressure to call the Duma into session on the first anniversary of Russia's declaration of war. Several changes in the Council of Ministers were also encouraging. The greatly unpopular minister of war Sukhomlinov was dismissed, Minister of the Interior Nikolai Maklakov resigned, and the appointments of Alexander Khvostov as minister of justice and Alexander Krivoshein as minister of agriculture seemed to create the core of what some hoped would become the cabinet's moderate wing. As its delegates reassembled, one of the Duma's first acts was to join the Council of Ministers in authorizing the formation of the three additional special councils: for transport, fuel, and food. Like the Special Council for Defense, each was structured to bring prominent public figures together with members of the government. Rodzianko himself emphasized the "close cooperation" they reflected between the regime and Russia's "social forces" (*obshchestvennye sily*).[25]

[23] Ibid., 58.
[24] Ibid., 36.
[25] ZOSODA 8 (June 20, 1915): 68.

Nicholas's disdain for the Duma, however, had hardly lessened. Partly in response to the sense of urgency created by the Galician disaster, but largely because he had felt from the start a sacred duty to join his loyal soldiers at the front, the tsar himself now took command of the army, leaving politics and the hated Duma for the moral comforts of the field. It was widely thought that the forty-seven-year-old tsar lacked both knowledge and temperament for the position. His Council of Ministers as a whole opposed it. In effect, Nicholas was tying his own fate, if not the fate of his government and the three-hundred-year-old Romanov dynasty, to his soldiers' willingness and ability to fight. The tsar left for the front on the day the Duma reconvened, demonstratively expressing his disdain. In preparation for the Duma's reconvening, meanwhile, its leading political figures struggled with how to persuade the tsar to appoint more demonstrably competent ministers. Riabushinskii, Konovalov, and both center and left Kadets joined democratic socialists in supporting a stronger role for the Duma, specifically its assumption of the responsibility to ratify ministerial appointments. This constitutional change would make the government responsible to the Duma, as in Britain.

Recognizing that the Duma's political authority was still tenuous at best, Miliukov and others on his right insisted that what was needed was not constitutional change but administrative and bureaucratic reform: an end to what the Kadet leader called the "abnormal relationship" between the regime and Russia's social forces.[26] Rather than a ministry constitutionally responsible to the Duma, Russia needed a ministry of responsible men in which the Duma, Russia's social organizations, and the country at large had confidence. Working with Rodzianko, Guchkov, and others, the Kadets assembled a Duma majority around a discrete set of progressive demands. These called for clemency and the return from exile for those charged with political or religious offenses, the end of all religious persecution, the abolition of restrictions against Jews, and the immediate drafting of a bill for Polish autonomy (all matters that would be put immediately in place with the tsar's abdication in 1917). The list of potential ministers it drew up was published in Riabushinskii's newspaper *Utro Rossii* (*Morning Russia*). Duma president Rodzianko was advanced as prime minister, Guchkov as minister of internal affairs, and Miliukov as foreign minister. Almost all of the others who would assume power in 1917 were included. As the Duma reconvened, 300 of its 430 deputies supported the Bloc's program.[27]

In effect, the Progressive Bloc was a concerted effort to reposition the tsarist state in its relation to the Duma and the country at large. In the course of events since the revolution of 1905, it represented those in and out of government

---

[26] P. Miliukov, *Taktika fraktsii narodnoi svobody vo vremia voiny* (Petrograd, 1916), 23–24.
[27] *Utro Rossii*, Aug. 13, 1915.

who saw the Russian state's future best situated in the engagement of society in addressing the dangers that social discontent and Russian radicalism seemed to forecast. Great Britain was the model here both for securing monarchal authority and for advancing the country economically and socially. In opposition stood a firm group of what David McDonald has called "official conservatives," represented most prominently by longtime interior minister Peter Durnovo, whose famous Memorandum of February 1914 urged the tsar to shed his alliance with Britain and France and join instead with Germany and Austria, Russia's closest economic partners and natural political allies in defense of autocratic power.[28] Having rejected Durnovo's argument, which was widely read in government circles, Nicholas and Goremykin understandably regarded the Progressive Bloc along with the engagement of public figures in the WICs and the special councils as weakening rather than strengthening the wartime state and risking precisely the renewal of fatal revolutionary activism forecast by Durnovo. Nonetheless, the political possibilities of the moment reflected in the Progressive Bloc were very great, as contemporaries and historians alike have recognized. The very formation of the Bloc itself testified to the willingness of its leading figures to bridge political differences. The presiding officer and leading members of the State Council, the Duma's upper house, joined them in their effort.[29] Especially in the aftermath of the Great Retreat from Austrian Galicia, many regarded this moment as the autocracy's best chance to strengthen the Russian state and avoid the upheavals many worried would otherwise lie ahead.

Were these realistic appraisals? Despite its limited powers, the Duma was still Imperial Russia's most important public forum. Its delegates represented a broad range of contending interests and outlooks whose positions had to be mediated in various committees and forums, including its important commissions on finance, trade, and defense. The very formation of the Progressive Bloc was testimony to the ability of its leading figures to bridge political differences among its liberal and conservative groupings and offer the regime a set of reforms designed in the first instance to strengthen the state. Whether the revolution was still avoidable remains an open and contentious question, but certainly the changes demanded by the Progressive Bloc would have strengthened the state's capacity to work with Russia's "responsible publics." At the very least this would have bettered the country's chances of muddling through the deepening crises. Whether it could actually resolve the growing problems of scarcity and loss as the war and its consequences intensified is another question.

---

[28] David. M. McDonald, *United Government and Foreign Policy in Russia, 1900–1914* (Cambridge, MA: Harvard University Press, 1992), ch. 8.

[29] *Rech'*, Aug. 25, 1915.

In the event, Prime Minister Goremykin, reflecting the views of Durnovo, was a fierce opponent of the Bloc's initiative. Traveling to army headquarters, he was prepared to argue forcefully that the tsar's response should be to again dismiss the Duma. Nicholas, however, needed no argument. When the prorogation decree came on September 3, many in the Duma were shocked. Some ministers only learned about it from newspapers. Some were astonished. Others thought that Goremykin and the tsar were "artificially inflaming the public."[30] Rodzianko was crestfallen. Calls were heard for the Bloc to continue meeting despite the Duma's dismissal, as delegates had done in 1906 and as the Duma leadership would do again in February 1917. Rodzianko demurred but joined an unofficial ("private") gathering of members where the Menshevik leader Nikolai Chkheidze and the prominent SR Alexander Kerensky both reportedly scolded their colleagues for not allowing them to appeal to the nation, as the Constitutional Democrats had done after the abrupt dismissal of the first Duma in the summer of 1906.[31]

The strikes and protests that followed reflected a familiar range of grievances but were now focused directly against the tsarist state. As in 1905, moreover, popular protest in the factories and streets was accompanied by formal protests from important local political leaders and their parties. Already in Moscow before the Duma had reconvened the city government passed a strongly worded resolution demanding forceful action to extend its authority. Not surprisingly, the city's civic leaders and local press also regarded the tsar's decision as an openly provocative act. At a number of protest meetings speakers urged an even more active struggle against him and his regime.

While protests mobilized the workplace, public figures, social organizations, and sixty-three local dumas and public groups around the country followed Moscow's lead in condemning the State Duma's dismissal. Resolutions call it an act "deeply against the nation's interest," one that "greatly raised anxiety about the fate of the country."[32] Ufa deputies wanted an immediate Russia-wide convocation of Zemstvo and City Union delegates to discuss the situation; in Vladivostok, a resolution stressed that a "healthy industrial life" could be created only through local management and control.[33] The duma in Tsaritsyn not only demanded new officials "in whom we can have confidence" but new "social controls" over industries and trade in order to end speculation and temper the rising cost of living, both of which were "threatening the entire internal life of the country." They urged the state itself to take control over financial and industrial enterprises, which "at this very difficult moment are either abusing the country's

---

[30] *Russkoe Slovo*, Sept. 3, 1915.
[31] *Russkoe Slovo*, Sept. 4, 1915.
[32] RGIA f. 1278, op. 5, d. 1225, ll. 42, 53.
[33] Ibid., ll. 5–6, 22–23, 42, 53–70, 92.

needs for their own profit or don't otherwise fulfill their obligations."[34] Equally strong protests came in places as distant as Vladivostok. In Petrograd, a special meeting of the city's stock exchange members voted full support for the Moscow resolutions.[35] Worried leaders of the Zemstvo and City Unions sent a joint delegation of their own to see the tsar, led by the impeccably credentialed Prince L'vov, the future head of the Provisional Government. When the tsar refused to receive the delegation, one police report declared that Russia was now "on the brink of ruin," precisely what Durnovo had predicted sixteen months earlier.[36]

Funding Production, Regulating Distribution

In one important way, the hopes and expectations placed in the Progressive Bloc were not well founded. The reaction to the Duma's dismissal clearly indicated that demands for responsible government and a dose of civil liberties were widely supported, as police accounts testified. And who could oppose the appointment of "responsible" people to high political positions if some agreement could be reached about what "responsible" meant? Yet the most pressing issues were only partly political. They also related to the realities and increasing anxieties about the supply of food and other scarce goods, especially in Petrograd and Moscow but elsewhere as well, even in villages where it was feared required deliveries would compromise local welfare. The army's needs, too, remained insatiable, and early predictions about the size of the harvest were not encouraging. The effects of Russia's huge military losses in the war were affecting the peasants' ability to manage their own needs, especially in rural areas that imported much of their food. The army's aggregate casualty statistics masked the grief and suffering of hundreds of thousands of peasant (and other) families. The level of need among diverse districts even within some provinces could not be usefully distilled into aggregate statistics or a single organic conception of Russia as a state, a society, or a people.

Perhaps because he was more aware of these problems as chair of the Duma's Defense Committee, sometime participant in both the Special Council for Defense and the CWIC, and one the Duma's most active members on matters of state finance and defense, Andrei Ivanovich Shingarev was one of the few leading liberals or moderate socialists who minimized the importance of the tsar's decision to dismiss the Duma. A physician with a degree in math and physics, provincial landowner, zemstvo figure, and Duma representative elected first from

---

[34] Ibid., ll. 22–22a.
[35] Ibid., ll. 5–6, 22–22 ob., 42, 70, 92.
[36] B. B. Grave, ed., *Burzhuaziia nakanune fevral'skoi revoliutsii* (Moscow, 1927), 39, 50–58.

provincial Voronezh and then St. Petersburg, Shingarev was one of the most active and respected members of the Duma leadership. He had become prominent in the liberal movement in the early 1890s with the publication of *The Dying Village*, a cogent (if, some thought, exaggerated) analysis of the plight of hunger and even starvation affecting large areas of the countryside that showed deep sympathy as well as understanding. While Shingarev's dedication was fueled by moral commitment, his focus was practical: how to address Russia's deepening socioeconomic and administrative problems. In his view the Progressive Bloc would likely have broken apart when it came to formulating actual policies, especially about Jews, Poland, and civil rights more broadly. Shingarev supported the Bloc's efforts as statements of principle and intent but was sure it "rested on air," unable and unlikely to secure the solid political foundation it needed to address the country's pressing needs effectively.

In Shingarev's view, the formation of the special councils and WICs was an important step in the right direction. (Some of his party colleagues disagreed, worried these initiatives would weaken the Duma itself.) Considerable initiative had passed from the Council of Ministers to these groups, which were vested as state agents for the purpose of distributing funds and monitoring contracts, and structured around cooperation between state officials, "responsible" public figures, and the owners of individual factories and mills. The September events only seemed to energize these groups. "Responsible" administration now rested largely on their shoulders. By the middle of the month, in Shingarev's view, the real work to address Russia's growing socioeconomic problems and strengthen the war effort was already underway.[37]

The most important of these problems—ensuring adequate funding for defense production—was a case in point. Working with the special councils and local WICs and tasked with the mobilization of "all industrial production" in support of the war, the CWIC focused initially on gathering information on the actual state of defense production and assessing financial needs. The most important of the seven sections and several major committees concerned finances and weapons production. From the start, however, their members found themselves handicapped by a lack of information about plant capacity, numbers of workers, and available resources. The CWIC did not even have accurate figures on the needs of the army. Some members worked their social connections to gain this information, but industrialists were less than fully enthusiastic about sharing it, especially in Petrograd. Some metals and metallurgical enterprises refused to cooperate at all. As a consequence, in October the CWIC received only 8.5 million rubles to support what may have been as much as 120 million in orders. The industrialists did little to ease the concerns of Konovalov, Guchkov, and other

---

[37] Ibid., 55.

Moscow figures about the excessive degree of self-interest among the Petrograd industrial elite.[38] Increasingly concerned about the long list of requests from different firms the CWIC estimated it would need at least 13 million rubles immediately to meet its primary needs.[39]

By this time regional and local WICs had begun to enter into their own production contracts. The most important of these was the Petrograd provincial (regional) WIC committee, chaired by Emanuel Liudvigovich Nobel' of the prominent family of oil producers, which included four provinces and the city of Petrograd. Its ten divisions included representatives from the city, province, and district Zemstvo and City Unions, the regional board of trade, the Petrograd Stock Exchange committee, the Imperial Russian Technological Society, and the trade-industrial organizations from the Northern and Baltic districts. The largest number (twelve) came from the Petrograd Society of Factory and Mill Owners, which would play a major role in assuring some stability in Petrograd after the February revolution. Its Artillery Section included twenty-eight members from different regional factories and shops. Contract agreements with these and other firms for the production of new artillery soon accounted for more than 80 percent of the Committee's contracts, worth more than 16.6 million rubles.[40] (By August 1916 this sum would reach 14,049,656 rubles.) Plants were informed that if they lagged in their deliveries, the Committee would require detailed information on the reasons.[41]

In effect, the CWIC and local committees like this one were assuming the quasi-juridical role of enforcing contracts as well as funding them because of the state's own difficulty doing so. In the process, prominent figures in Russia's wartime capitalist economy, like those in the Petrograd and Moscow Societies of Factory and Mill Owners and the Associations of Trade and Industry, acquired from the state the responsibilities and resources to increase production in support of the war, along with the profits this would return to them as owners and shareholders. Whether or not profits themselves were an issue of prime importance to those involved is open to different interpretations. What is not is the broad identification emerging between the interests of Russia's favored industrial and commercial communities and those of the imperial state itself, one that was bridging historical antagonism between them as well within the communities themselves.

---

[38] RGIA f. 32, op. 1, d. 1994, l. 32 [*Protokoly zasedanii finansovoi komissii CWIC*, Sept. 29, 1915]; RGIA f. 32, op. 1, d. 721; *Zhurnal TsVPK* (Sept. 21, 1915): passim; RGIA f, 1276, op. 11, d. 248, ll. 1-8, 31-32. A. L. Sidorov, *Ekonomicheskoe polozhenie Rossii v gody pervoi mirovoi voiny* (Moscow: Nauka, 1973), 202.
[39] RGIA f. 32, op. 1, d. 1994, ll. 1-3.
[40] RGIA f. 45, op. 1, d. 93, l. 36.
[41] Ibid., ll. 25-36, 241-57.

This identification was further strengthened as local WICs began to work on measures to control transport costs and other prices in their localities and impose order on the ways foodstuffs and goods were marketed for both the army and the civilian population. A key problem in dealing with these issues was the lack of accurate information on the actual supply of food in the localities. On October 2 the Special Council on Food sent out a questionnaire to all cities and larger towns, asking them to detail the food supplies in their areas. Two weeks later a similar questionnaire went to all provincial zemstvo boards or directly to provincial governors. In addition to the difficulties created by the lack of essential information, some on the Council saw a ministerial culture of misinformation and confusion over these questions as potentially disastrous for their efforts.[42]

Contesting Authorities: The Emissary Problem

The special councils also faced other difficulties. They lacked adequate information and statistics. They struggled with local producers and officials resistant to their efforts. And despite the constructive role played by Minister of War Aleksei Polivanov in chairing the Special Council for Defense, they faced the hostility of some in the government who resented its new authority. (Even the liberal leader Miliukov worried the councils would further weaken the Duma's authority.) After the Duma's dismissal, the Council's leadership acted in its stead to mitigate repressive conditions in defense plants and strengthen the role of local factory workers in addressing the tasks at hand. Permission was given for new factory assemblies to meet for this purpose. In early September Polivanov also formally recognized twelve regional "factory conferences" (*zavodskie soveshchaniia*) as its local organs. Each was authorized to coordinate the activities of local enterprises and the Special Council for Defense and help ensure their mutual cooperation. They were also empowered to requisition equipment and supplies in order to improve and coordinate local production, participate in setting local wage levels, and appoint their own plenipotentiaries to carry out these and other tasks at both the regional (*oblast'*) and district (*raion*) level. The notorious Ministry of Internal Affairs was particularly resistant to these initiatives, especially after some members of the Special Council for Defense vigorously objected to police interference in the newly authorized factory meetings. A particularly egregious case was the arrest of workers after visits to their plant by Rodzianko and other members of the Duma.[43]

[42] RGIA f. 457, op. 1, d. 12, ll. 25ff., 54ff.; d. 209, ll. 1–4.
[43] RGIA f. 1276, op. 11, d. 167, ll. 37–38.

The other new councils found themselves with overlapping interests. The Special Council on Fuel, for example, began appraising available supplies and investigating whether defense plants were actually inflating their demands for fuel in order to sell surpluses to third parties at a substantial profit.[44] In September the Council of Ministers decreed harsh penalties for hoarding fuel and submitting false information. Yet "hoarding" fuel was regarded by some on the Council on Defense to be prudently accumulating reserves, given the likelihood of additional scarcities over the winter. The railroads presented another case. In an effort to ensure a steady supply of essential goods to Petrograd and Moscow, the Special Council on Food issued a directive setting special norms for transport of foodstuffs: 405 freight cars every twenty-four hours for Petrograd, for example, plus an additional 120 cars for Petrograd province. For Moscow the norm was set at 480 cars.[45] Control over the use of railroad freight cars was nominally the purview of the Transport Ministry, however, and now the Special Council on Transport, both of which insisted they had priority in setting these norms. While the Council on Food was attempting to control this use of rolling stock, private and state railroads were both beseeching the Transport Council for additional funding to increase available rolling stock, to reduce the backlog of locomotives and cars waiting repair, and to stem what some regarded as the "excessive" reduction in the number of railroad employees through the military draft. (In some places, apparently, the number of skilled railroaders had been reduced by as much as 25 percent and only poorly or even untrained workers had been left to perform essential tasks.)[46] At its very first meeting members of the Transport Council determined to prepare a monthly transport plan on the basis of information they received on the 20th of each month from the other three special councils.

Not surprisingly, this soon proved to be unrealistic, but Transport Minister Sergei Rukhlov and the Transport Council moved forward in any case to craft something resembling a national plan. A special council commission on the problem soon recommended that the administration of railroads at the front be taken entirely out of the hands of military personnel.[47] By early November an authoritative new Railroad Management Committee (Razporiaditel'nyi Komitet) was in the works to supervise and control the use of locomotives and rolling stock throughout the country.[48]

---

[44] RGIA f. 457, op. 1, d. 64, ll. 34–35, 51, 64–65 ob.
[45] RGIA f. 1276, op. 12, d. 1239, ll. 1–6 ob.
[46] *Zheleznodorozhnoe Delo* 15 (1916): 131; N. Vasil'ev, *Transport Rossii v voine 1914–17* (Moscow, 1939), 191–93.
[47] Sidorov, *Ekonomicheskoe polozhenie*, 158–59.
[48] RGIA f. 457, op. 1, d. 64, ll. 20–21 ob., 51–52; f. 45, op. 1, d. 12, ll. 13–14; f. 290, op. 1, d. 1, l. 34.

In the meantime, representatives from each of the four special councils and the CWIC spread out around the country to strengthen local ties and assert their new power, some conspicuously displaying their authority by traveling first class.[49] The CWIC appointed specially designated plenipotentiaries to visit plants, to review production, and, what some thought was equally important, to check on possible misuse of its funds.[50] For the Special Council for Defense, Polivanov himself granted authority to special plenipotentiaries to requisition equipment and supplies and set local wage levels in coordination with the new regional factory conferences the Council set up as its local organs. The tsar himself personally approved the list of people appointed to these posts. The other special councils followed suit, sending their own plenipotentiaries out with officially sanctioned orders and responsibilities. Many were high-ranking military officers.[51]

The goal here was an understandable one from the standpoint of economic mobilization and administrative order. Given the lack of reliable information about actual conditions in the provinces, direct personal contact between Petrograd and the localities was the best way for the center to gain a reasonable understanding of local conditions. The newly authorized officials were formally designated *upolnomochenie*, the Russian word for "plenipotentiary," and soon colloquially as "commissars," a term that was institutionalized well before the Bolsheviks came to power. Both before and after 1917, however, the administration problem was the same. Coordination between policies and practices at the center and the localities was an essential part of ameliorating the problems of procurement and distribution for the army and the country at large.

Again, however, both the perceptions and the actualities of scarcity and inflation moved various authorities to act at cross purposes in the localities, especially on the railroads. Different understandings of urgency were at odds with different and contending conceptions of local needs and institutional interests. In some places, military authorities in and beyond the zone of military administration were in conflict with local railroad officials from the first day of the war. Military commanders armed with the power to send equipment in any direction set up next to railroad dispatchers who sometimes learned after the fact where their trains had been sent. The result in some instances was complete paralysis until contradictory orders could be reconciled. In the meantime, the resulting bottlenecks spread domino fashion, especially across the railroads closest to the front, while administrators on both private and state lines struggled to remain attentive to their civilian customers'

---

[49] RGIA f. 456, op. 1, d. 37, l. 11.
[50] RGIA f. 1276, op. 11, d. 248 ll. 46–47, 255ff.
[51] *ZOSO* 5 (Sept. 9, 1915): 257; Sidorov, *Ekonomicheskoe polozhenie*, 101–5.

needs.⁵² As Baron Maidel reported on the Transport Council's behalf to the Special Council for Defense, even where railroads were entirely under military administration it was "impossible to regulate transport when it was under the control of so many bosses."⁵³

As the new wave of plenipotentiary "commissars" reached Russia's hinterland the pejorative notion of dual authority (*dvoevlastie*) also entered Russia's political discourse. First applied to the conflicting roles of military authorities and civilian administrators on the railroads, the term soon reflected not so much dual political authority, as it would in 1917, but simply multiple and competitive authorities all empowered with formal and often contradictory documents and orders. Clashes began to occur with local officials of the Ministry of Agriculture on the storage of grain. Ministry of Transport people tried to contradict local railroad administrators on tariffs and the dispatch of freight. Regional officials from provincial governors to town officials (*gradonachal'niki*) insisted their powers and prerogatives superseded those of the special councils and WICs. The Main Administration of the Ministry of Agriculture alone now had several thousand local agents in the field, many drawn from regional zemstvos.⁵⁴ As it would prove to be 1917 and afterward, it was difficult and in many instances even impossible to sort out the hierarchy of these authorities at the local level.

While it is impossible to measure how much local friction all of this created, it especially agitated police and other officials of the Ministry of Interior. Some officials from the Ministry in the localities were not only bent on limiting the special councils' spheres of activity but even determined, in the emphatic voice of one report, to *"fully abrogate some of the orders from their Chairs."*⁵⁵ Special plenipotentiaries from the Council on Defense might have struggled less with this resistance than others, but the problem was soon widespread. When the army's procurement office failed to receive an expected shipment of grain barges in early October, for example, the vice minister of War appointed his own special emissary to intervene directly with local military and civil authorities. When a plenipotentiary from the Ministry of Finance showed up at the Putilov works to supervise the dispersal of funds allocated by the Special Council for Defense, Shingarev himself demanded to know what this person's official function was and whether it had anything to do with repaying private loans.⁵⁶ When it was discovered in some places that the Ministry of Agriculture's representatives had

---

⁵² S. A. Ronzhin, "Zheleznyia dorogi v voennoe vremia," unpublished ms., 1925, Hoover Institution Archives, Stanford, CA, 11ff; I. D. Mikhailov, *Evoliutsiia russkogo transporta* (Moscow: Ekon. Zhizn', 1925), 5–6.
⁵³ *Zhurnaly TsVPK*, Nov. 16, 1915, in RGIA f. 32, op. 1. d. 1983, l. 77.
⁵⁴ T. M. Kitanina, *Voina, khleb i revoliutsiia* (Leningrad, 1985), 186–87.
⁵⁵ RGIA f. 457, op. 1, d. 12, ll. 1 ob., 2–3. Italics in the original.
⁵⁶ RGIA f. 457, op. 1, d. 209, ll. 1–3; f. 456, op. 1, d. 37, ll. 3–27, 83–86; *ZOSO* 13 (Oct. 7, 1915): 327–28.

purchased more grain than could be shipped and was storing the surplus, other commissars tried to use their own special authority to seize it. In Petrograd and Moscow in November *upolnomochenye* from the Defense Council's regional factory conferences were given the power to requisition all foodstuffs which were not delivered promptly to their buyers, further aggravating the problem of distribution if also, at least according to one report, also increasing the timeliness of food deliveries.[57] In the fall of 1915 Russia still did not have one general law governing requisitions. As a consequence, plenipotentiaries from the special councils, the Ministries of War and Agriculture, and local army commanders all seized goods and arranged compensation on their own, creating what some involved in the process regarded as an "absolutely chaotic situation."[58]

In important ways, the "commissar problem" reflected both the successes and the hazards of mobilizing "responsible publics" in the fall of 1915, as it would again in 1917. On one hand, the proliferation of WICs and the expanded responsibilities of the Zemstvo and City Unions reflected an important devolution of authority from the center to the localities. On the other, the CWIC and the new special councils reflected the conflicted relations between the exercise of power locally, the governing institutions authorized to do so, and the indivisible authority of the state itself, presaging the struggles to come.

Militarization vs. Mediation: The "Worker Question"

Although the Moscow city duma's resolution protesting the prorogation of the State Duma fell on deaf ears, the equally strong support it garnered from other local dumas marked an important moment in the broader mobilization of "responsible publics." For the first time since the beginning of the war, legal political protest by means of formal local duma resolutions was joined by strikes and protest demonstrations that were strictly prohibited from having similar political objectives. In the process, the line between legal and illegal protests was not only blurred on the street and in the workplace but publicly set around discrete social boundaries that segregated workers from their social "betters" in the city. What was possible for Moscow's propertied elements resulted in the arrest of its workers. In a secret letter to Prime Minister Goremykin on September 3, Minister of War Polivanov himself called the arrests of workers a "provocative act" and "an enormous error" on the part of the police, "extremely undesirable in the present circumstances" and "exceptionally harmful to the operational abilities of our army." Writing as both minister of war and chair of the Special

---

[57] RGIA f. 45, op. 7, d. 12, l. 136.
[58] RGIA f. 23, op. 5, d. 86, ll. 1–2; f. 456, op. 1, d .75, l. 2.

Council on Defense, he requested that Prime Minister Goremykin take "extreme measures" to eliminate the causes of worker unrest.[59]

In this the minister of war was complementing from the position of formal state power the strong views of provincial delegates to the first WIC congress in July who sought workers' direct participation in the committees at all levels. In their view there was "no more important question" than this one confronting the WIC effort. Workers had to be seen as more than simply the "objects of mobilization," to be used and manipulated in the name of rationalizing production and supporting the war.[60] The importance the local WIC delegates attached to the issue signified a shift in the way these activists and others were now reframing the "worker question": away from social and political resistance to the larger democratic socialist issue of integrating workers' representatives in decisions relating not only to defense production but to the governance of the country itself, a key element of the democratic socialist Great Story.

Meanwhile, the "worker question" was being reframed in government and industry circles in a quite different way. Already by late spring, the question of militarizing privately owned defense plants and their workers was a subject of open discussion.[61] Sounding the first loud notes of what would later become a fundamental element of Bolshevik military production during the Civil War, industrialists demanded the mandatory introduction of three eight-hour shifts and the placement of all defense workers under military regulations and controls. As they described it, their goal was to create a "labor army." Drafted workers reassigned back to their factories would continue their military service at their benches. The regime had to recognize that the production of military supplies and equipment was "as much a task of the government as direct participation in armed conflict itself." Moreover, the goal here was not simply increasing production. A labor army would play an "enormously important" role in deterring "the real dangers" of agitation and worker unrest. Waiting to impose these measures until labor protest spread more widely would "obviously be too late."[62] Militarization would also facilitate a much wider use of German and Austrian prisoners of war, especially in coal and iron mines.[63] According to decrees issued by the State Council shortly after the war began, POWs could be used under military supervision only for purposes like cleaning up the rail lines after snowstorms.[64] Already in the spring, a committee organized by Transport

---

[59] RGIA f. 1276, op. 11, d. 167, ll. 37–38.

[60] *Trudy S"ezda VPK 25–27-go iiulia 1915*, 46–48.

[61] Ibid., 197–214; *Izvestiia obshchestva zavodchikov i fabrikantov Moskovskogo promyshlennago raiona* 7–9 (1915).

[62] RGIA f. 1276, op. 11, d. 814, ll. 2, 2 ob.

[63] RGIA f. 244, op. 1, d. 9, ll. 1–3.

[64] *Sobranie uzakonenii i rasporiazhenii pravitel'stva* (St. Petersburg: Gos. Typ, 1914–17), l.2138, Oct. 7, 1914.

Minister Rukhlov argued that "forced labor" (*prinuditel'naia rabota*) would be "extremely desirable," using either POWs or "yellow labor" from the Far East. Some now extended this argument to plants whose production was "of particular importance to the state."[65]

Worried about provoking further worker unrest, Goremykin and the Council of Ministers were still resistant to militarization in early 1915. Maklakov at the Ministry of Internal Affairs warned that militarization was likely to spark violent protests. A special commission organized by the Ministry of War to study the issue further recommended that POWs be forced to work and that they should do so under the general supervision of the War Ministry itself. Provincial governors and a specific list of state officials could request POW labor detachments, along with the Ministries of Agriculture, Transport, and Trade and Industry. Local military commands could, if they wished, assign detachments to local zemstvo boards, administrators, and even private entrepreneurs. The ostensible advantages of militarization thus got a substantial push forward.[66]

Militarization was also being discussed in the Special Council for Defense as an alternative to the military draft. Rodzianko offered the positive example of France, where military service could be satisfied in this way. Like Goremykin, many Council members believed this would provoke even more labor unrest from those working alongside their militarized comrades.[67] However, most seemed to change their mind after new strikes disrupted the important Tula arms complex south of Moscow and several major plants in the city. Early in August a detailed plan preventing defense workers from leaving their enterprises was formulated. It granted management the right to require compulsory overtime, including night work, and loosened restrictions on the hiring of women and underage workers.[68]

In the view of the Moscow Progressist and textile magnate Konovalov, a serious defect in the plan was that it would create two very different categories of workers, often within the same plant: those obligated to work (*obiazannye*) and those free to work (*neobiazannye*). This could only create new tensions and defeat any efforts to increase productivity. For Guchkov and others in the CWIC, the risk that militarization would backfire into additional social unrest was compounded by the regime's increasing use of POWs as forced labor in "militarized shops." His view was reflected in a secret report to the Council of Ministers that detailed the agitation their use was stirring up.[69] The important

---

[65] RGIA f. 244 op. 1, d. 9 [MPS, Komitet po raspredeleniiu topliva], ll. 29, 46–49.
[66] RGIA f. 1276, op. 11, d. 212, ll. 3–4 ob., 15–35, 43–53.
[67] ZOSODA 5 (June 1, 1915): 37–39.
[68] ZOSO 2 (Aug. 29, 1915): 220–30; RGIA f. 1276, op. 11, d. 212, ll. 15–35, 47–53.
[69] RGIA f. 1276, op. 11, d. 212, ll. 3, 37–38, 54; op. 22, d. 212, ll. 1–3, 26; *Osobyi Zhurnal Sovetov Ministerstva*, Mar. 14, 1915: Mar. 17, 1915; June 30, 1915, 92–97.

task was integrating "forced" and "free" labor in ways that actually increased productivity. Still, at the end of July the CWIC endorsed sending 100,000 POWs to work in the mines. Militarization of labor and production as well as the use of forced labor brigades were seeming like "solutions" to the problem of increasing industrial productivity.[70]

For many members of the WICs, especially those sympathetic to social democracy, all of this touched an even more important aspect of the "worker question": as one of the country's "vital social forces," workers had to be directly involved in resolving the problems Russia was facing, side by side with representatives of trade and industry. Worker representatives needed to sit on local WICs as well as the CWIC itself to provide a unique and extremely useful perspective on the issues of productivity, wage rates, and even the value of adding POWs to the workforce. Importantly, this would also allow at least an informal forum for the airing of grievances and possibly assist in their mediation. In a somewhat convoluted way, the prominent industrialist A. I. Putilov made a similar case to the Special Council for Defense for creating new "links" between workers and employers, "the lack of which in connection with the circumstances of the present war is having undesirable consequences." In his view, the participation of elected factory representatives would help avoid the escalation of protests that had such grave consequences for the country, as in 1905.[71] Prime Minister Goremykin was also warned to this effect. Duma president Rodzianko agreed. Granting workers the right to elect their own factory representatives would serve the broader purposes of conflict mediation and social stability.[72]

For its part, the CWIC now took up the question of workers' participation in earnest, led again by Konovalov. The Progressist Moscow industrialist was sure that militarization could not be effectively implemented in any event if workers' representatives were not directly involved in the process. Along with other CWIC members, including the liberal agrarian specialist N. N. Kutler and the engineer P. I. Pal'chinskii (who would serve in the Provisional Government and continue working in Soviet Russia until his arrest in 1928), Konovalov recognized that the question was compounded by the fact that workers had no legal organizations through which they could chose their representatives—that is, trade unions. The CWIC then issued an appeal that workers be allowed to join its ranks. As the Kharkov WIC official P. P. Kozakevich put it, part of the problem of scarcity and inflation lay in workers themselves not understanding the importance of behaving like soldiers in a "great army," willing to engage directly and constructively in the process of addressing the country's pressing needs. For him and

---

[70] *Zhurnal TsVPK* 2 (Aug. 10, 1915): 2–4.
[71] RGIA f. 1276, op. 11, d. 167, ll. 37–38.
[72] *ZOSO* 23 (Aug. 15, 1915): 196; 24 (Aug. 19, 1915): 202.

others, what Prime Minister Goremykin and the Council of Ministers were likely to resist as empowering workers politically was an essential element of Russia's national mobilization, the necessary foundation for success at the front and political stability in the country at large.[73]

This perspective crystalized in the late summer of 1915 as a key element of both the democratic liberal and democratic socialist understandings of the "worker question." Mediation, not militarization, was the effective way to move forward. By not recognizing workers' rights to elect representatives and organize strikes, the regime lacked an orderly and effective mechanism to mediate legitimate grievances, including wage issues and affronts to dignity, especially for women. The democratic socialist position on this issue added that the participation of elected workers' representatives in the network of WICs would open the way to revitalize trade unions, secure specific and recognizable gains, and thus raise the level of workers' "consciousness" about the power inherent in their class position and its importance to Russia's political and social democratic future. (As we will see, mediation would also become the basis for Provisional Government labor policies when Shingarev, Konovalov, and others on the Progressive Bloc's list of "responsible" ministerial candidates took office in 1917.)

There were two problems here, however, only one of which was easily recognized at the time. It was clear that workers were divided among themselves about whether participating in the WICs would advance or diminish their social and political interests. Support for Lenin and the Bolsheviks was clearly growing in the factories. However difficult it is to measure, an antagonistic class-based conception of capitalism and its bourgeoisie was also increasing in the workforce, especially among skilled industrial workers in Petrograd, Moscow, Kharkiv, and other centers of industrial production. In part this reflected the successes of radical social democracy in the 1905–7 revolutionary period. In part it was also an inevitable extension of the estate-based foundations of autocratic and imperial Russia, where one's social position in the processes of production still directly determined political rights. Despite the regime's promises in October 1905, the electoral law governing the new State Duma discriminated heavily against workers and peasants in favor of those who owned property or were formally members by heritage of the aristocracy and landed gentry, increasingly reduced simply to "the bourgeoisie."

Less evident in the fall of 1915 was the very way efforts to militarize the workplace linked even Russia's progressive bourgeoisie to the politics and goals of the tsarist state. If the WICs were now playing a key role in distributing state contracts and resources, they were also coming to be seen more easily as agents of a hated state system, however much they demanded its reform. Militarization

---

[73] *Trudy S"ezda VPK 25–27-go iiulia 1915*, 270.

from the shop floor had to look different than it did from the CWIC offices at 46 Liteinyi. Here, too, the absence of effective trade unions, mediation boards, and other representative institutions distinguished the "worker question" in Russia from its analogs in Britain, France, Austria, or Germany. Militarization was being imposed on workers and workplaces there as well in 1915, in various forms and ways. French, German, Austrian, and English workers were resisting in sometimes violent strikes and labor protests. Yet elsewhere among the warring powers there were still institutionalized processes of conflict mediation that limited the vulnerability of the state itself. In Russia, *all* strikes during the summer of 1915 were political in their implicit opposition to the state, however much their formal demands were specifically economic. A form of social protest generally recognized as "legitimate" elsewhere was in Russia readily proscribed and repressed as political opposition.

In retrospect it should not therefore be surprising that progressive WIC officials and others soon found themselves facing more resistance from workers themselves to participation in the committees than they did from some in the government. Workers in Petrograd metals plants were clearly divided over the merits of "collaborating" with "the bourgeoisie." Such forums as they could arrange were also increasingly sites of antiwar sentiments, if not yet full-throated protests. The careful distinction drawn by factory inspectors between "economic" and "political" strikes was increasingly difficult to draw. Guchkov, Konovalov, and other prominent members of the WIC leadership thus found themselves in the uncomfortable position of supporting the principles of mediation and urging their institutionalization, while also wary of giving a louder voice to antiwar sentiments and calls for revolutionary change. Worker delegates in the WICs risked alienating their constituents by relying on the support and influence of the WIC leadership to improve wages and conditions, especially as the cost of living continued to rise.

The story of worker resistance to joining the WICs in the fall of 1915 has been well told.[74] Despite the best efforts of CWIC members and especially those from Moscow, what some were coming to regard as one of the most important of Imperial Russia's "vital social forces" strongly resisted participating directly with the "bourgeois" WICs in the tasks of mobilizing industry. Opposition to participation continued throughout the fall. When electors from Petrograd plants were finally able to meet to select their delegates at the end of November, sixty-seven voted against doing so and quit the meeting. Many industrialists and government officials were also opposed despite strong support by *Vestnik Finansov,*

---

[74] A. I. Guchkov, *Otchety i deiatel'nosti rab. gruppy TsVIK 10 Feb. 1916–15 Feb. 1917* in RGIA f. 32, op. 1, d. 2126, ll. 17–41; Lewis Siegelbaum, "The Workers' Groups and the War-Industries Committees: Who Used Whom," *Russian Review* 2 (Apr. 1980): 150–80.

perhaps Russia's most important financial journal, and the measured arguments of Konovalov to the Special Council for Defense: "The representation of workers groups in our committees does not so much reflect their class interests as the interests of the state itself, since by participating amicably in the common effort, workers will undoubtedly come to realize the necessity of relating calmly to events and working more intensively for defense, protecting our mobilized industry from any disorders and interruptions."[75]

It was not until December 2, however, that the CWIC was finally able to welcome ten worker representatives to its ranks. Six others joined the important Petrograd Regional Committee. By this time, however, the lines of social conflict were even more sharply drawn. The mutual tasks of economic mobilization and social mediation were fixed in a context of increasing polarization that itself strengthened antagonistic social identities. The pressing tasks of mobilization and mediation had actually become more difficult. And as between meditation and militarization, many within and close to the government now regarded militarization as a much easier "solution" to the problems of production and productivity and, more important, the task of controlling dissidence and maintaining social order.[76] The Bolsheviks would later agree.

War Capitalism and Its Cultures

By the late fall of 1915, the difficulties of managing a wartime economy defined a critical weakness of the Imperial Russian state. Its government and administration were unable to ensure an adequate supply of essential goods to the army and major population centers to assuage food insecurities. The state was not able to create mechanisms to mediate immediate and longer-term grievances in the workplace. Inflation continued to undermine real wages and stimulate speculation. Losses at the front continued to grow. Meantime, enterprises and industrial sectors working for defense were increasingly dependent on the state for material and financial resources. Favored enterprises meant favored personal relations between plant managers and state officials, a well-established connection in Petrograd but one that now spread more broadly through the defense sector as a whole. Those producing textiles, paper, wood products, and processed foods whose production was not deemed necessary to defense suffered increasingly from shortages. It soon became both risky and unprofitable for many of these firms to continue production despite the fact that favored enterprises needed their output to fulfill their own military contracts. By the end of 1915 some five

[75] RGIA f. 1278, op. 5, d. 1149, ll. 3, 6–7.
[76] *Zhurnal TsVPK*, Dec. 3, 1915, 82–88.

thousand plants had closed their doors. If the war was a "godsend" for many major industrialists as well as the tsarist regime, in the words of the British ambassador Buchanan, it was equally a disaster for most others.[77] The turn to forced labor made the stresses even worse. So did the increasing availability of women workers pressed into the labor force in gendered work roles where lower wages for equal work accompanied frequent assaults on their dignity (and worse). It was not simply the rude hand of impersonal market forces that constrained many workers and employers, but the very visible arm of the state that financed private as well as state plants that were their biggest or only customer.

The Russian countryside, meanwhile, was hardly exempt from these distortions. When military authorities in local areas were given permission to requisition or embargo various products, they were also empowered to set prices for their purchases, which by the end of 1915 were close to 50 percent of all marketable grain. Commodities coming into the villages began to dry up with the closing of unfavored plants, while local and regional markets lost much of their earlier vitality. In 1916, the bellwether Nizhnii Novgorod Fair registered less than two-thirds the volume of 1913. Even the special assistance provided to soldiers' families stirred discontent. Neighboring women who did not receive assistance felt they needed it just as much. Those whose sons or husbands had avoided the draft were resented for burdening the community.[78]

The editors of *Promyshlennost' i Torgovlia* and others saw all of this as an accelerating form of state socialism. "If even before the war one could speak of the slow but inexorable growth of state socialism, the war and the economic difficulties it has created [seem to] have given the state the right to accelerate artificially this process of displacing private with state economic elements. [Many say] the realm of private interests, striving toward maximal personal advantage, must end, that a new era is at hand in which the interest of the state and society are triumphant."[79] Yet what was emerging in socioeconomic terms through the processes of state financing can more fairly be described as a form of "war capitalism" in Russia: a system of state-financed processes of production in certain private and state enterprises that linked owners and managers directly to the state's financial resources as well as its imperial goals and a well-embedded system of social values. State authorities had no interest in curbing private production or private wealth, providing it also served the tsarist order. Leading public figures in and outside the Progressive Bloc wanted political reform, but

---

[77] *Zhurnal TsVPK* 17 (Feb. 22, 1916): 4; George Buchanan, *My Mission to Russia* (Boston: Little, Brown, 1923), 213.

[78] B. H. Kerblay, *Les marchés paysans en U.R.S.S.* (Paris: Mouton, 1968), 100 L. Lih, *Bread and Authority in Russia, 1914–1921* (Berkeley: University of California Press 1990), 9–13; Kitanina, *Voina, khleb i revoliutsiia*, 70–71.

[79] *Promyshlennost i Torgovlia* 4 (1916): 85–86.

not to level socioeconomic inequalities or replace state-centered values with democratic ones. In the process, the state and the leading sectors of Russian finance, commerce, and industry further repositioned their historical relations, strengthening collaboration despite their historical antagonism and accelerating a process that was already well underway in the years immediately preceding the war.

This was true to some extent in other warring powers. What was particular about war capitalism in Russia, however, was the potential clash of its socially and culturally embedded value systems with those of its geographically concentrated industrial workforce and its still overwhelmingly peasant and partly commercialized countryside. Profits, speculation, and the role of social inequalities in the ways goods were produced and distributed tended to focus the manifest problems of scarcity and loss directly on the association between profiting industrialists, traders and market speculators, and the state itself, reinforcing the social and cultural inequalities at the base of the tsarist order. State socialism would come when these same resources were deployed to end private ownership, nationalize all production, and replace the cultures and forms of socioeconomic difference with those idealized in the name of universal social equality, however elastic its meaning. In the common terms of "class" that were permeating much of Russian public discourse by the fall of 1915, the engagement of responsible publics at the national and local levels joined a "bourgeois" industrial and commercial elite to the needs and values of an imperial autocracy as a way of strengthening the state, maintaining social order, winning the war, and preserving the promises of capitalist economic development expected in its aftermath from Russia's continued imperial reach.

Here, of course, was a dilemma for the more progressive industrialists like Riabushinskii and Konovalov who assumed leading roles in the WICs. Within Russia's responsible publics were many deeply committed to political liberalization. Cooperative efforts implicitly identified them with the regime's inadequacies. Moderate Mensheviks and other democratic socialists shied away from the close political alliances left and center Kadets desired to avoid being tainted, while Lenin's Bolsheviks found easy targets for the libel "bourgeois collaborators," sharpening the rhetorical swords which would wreak considerable havoc in 1917.

One key matter here was the maintenance of "reasonable" profits in conditions of growing scarcity and loss. A select number of private banks and enterprises reflected the ways these advantages now accrued through close relations with state officials. In addition to retailing state bonds at a substantial profit and supporting various commercial and business transactions without requiring the collateral common in European and North American transactions, directors like Putilov of the Russian-Asiatic Bank actively used their positions to channel loans toward enterprises in which they were closely involved. When Baron Maidel approached H. Fessenden Meserve, New York's National City Bank's new representative in Petrograd, about the formation of a new financial institution, the Union of Provincial Banks, he promised not only a 10 percent commission to National City but the assurance that the president of the new bank would be the editor of the government's *Financial Recorder* and that his colleague in the Finance Ministry's credit department responsible for controlling the provincial banks would be one of its directors.[80]

As scarcity and loss increased in the late fall of 1915, moreover, so as a result of state support did the profitability of major industrial enterprises and leading Russian banks. Not surprisingly, Russian stock markets responded positively to indicators of increased output and profits. Share prices for leading metals and mechanical plants like the Briansk works increased some 14 percent in the eighteen months between July 15, 1914, and December 31, 1915. Others rose even higher. The same was true for Russia's major banks and private railroads. The Russian Bank for Trade increased its dividend in 1915 by 50 percent. Russia's administratively troubled railroads also paid handsome dividends. On the Moscow-Kazan line, a 15 million ruble profit in 1915 enabled a 30 ruble per share dividend. On the Southeastern line, profits were 24 million rubles.[81] Just after the New Year, *Birzhevye Vedomosti* (*Stock Market News*) reported a "buoyant mood" among investors.[82] Meserve's National City Bank published a prospectus for investors touting Russia's underdeveloped natural resources and low tax rates, along with signs that purchasing power "was holding its own quite well." Advances and declines in the prices of various commodities were said to be due chiefly to changes in supply and demand. Meserve himself waxed eloquent in his communications with National City's president F. A. Vanderlip about the attraction especially in railroad bonds, which Finance Minister Bark personally offered National City at a rate of 7.5 percent, 2 points higher than the general issue.[83] When Russian investors learned about the battle beginning in France at Verdun, the Russian stock market jumped to its highest level of the war.[84]

More important even to the developing cultures of war capitalism were the connections between scarcities, rising prices, speculation, and black marketeering. The subjective elements of both resentment and collusion may have begun to fuel speculative behavior as much as rising prices. As with all

---

[80] RGIA f. 624, op. 1, d. 5, ll. 20–22.
[81] *Novyi Ekonomist* 16 (Apr. 16, 1916); *Birzhevye Vedomosti* 5 (Jan. 29, 1916), 9 (May 5, 1916), 11 (Nov. 12, 1916); Sidorov, *Ekonomicheskoe polozhenie*, 380ff.
[82] *Birzhevye Vedomosti*, Jan. 9, 1916.
[83] RGIA f. 624 op. 1. d. 5, ll. 35, 50, 116–17, 119. For a full description of National City's adventures in revolutionary Russia, see Hassan Malik, *Bankers and Bolsheviks: International Finance and the Russian Revolution* (Princeton, NJ: Princeton University Press, 2018).
[84] *Birzhevye Vedomosti*, Feb. 15, 1916.

subjectivities, they were also more difficult to control. In cultural terms, the very meaning of speculation in the fall of 1915 broadened out from the market activity of buying low and selling higher to the manipulation of markets themselves: taking unfair advantage of shortages for personal enrichment by controlling what was sold and where. Speculators in this sense emerged (and were condemned) in Germany, Austria, and the Entente powers in 1915. Chancellor von Bethmann Hollweg's government introduced a series of regulations on the pricing and distribution of essential goods as early as August 1914. Ceilings were set on the prices of a long list of goods. Similar practices were soon adopted in England and France. While goods were still relatively plentiful, it is hardly surprising that traders everywhere tried to accumulate large reserves of products whose prices were still relatively low, speculating on their resale at the preset maximum levels. In Russia, however, most prices were not fixed, there were few enforceable regulations on how goods were distributed, and the sheer size of the country warranted the devolution of authority that also made economic coordination inherently difficult.

The immoral connotations of speculation had special resonance in Russia, especially among peasants. "Capitalism" as a concept had never carried virtuous connotations in Imperial Russia's partly commercialized agrarian economy, nor did commercial activity in general. In Moscow, the widespread engagement of Old Believers in commerce after the seventeenth-century church schism identified commercial practices with rejected religious ones. So did the "disreputable" Jews, Armenians, and other merchants who peddled goods in Russian towns and villages, especially in places where speculators were held to set personal profit against the well-being of the village community.

The very value of commercial market exchange was brought into question here, especially in the deeper parts of the countryside. A supposed advantage of fully commercial transactions—where the buyer and seller are often at some distance from each other and trade through various kinds of brokers—is that the exchange process is "morally free." In contemporary economic theory, only "perfectively competitive" markets are thought to be fully free, morally or otherwise, since the full willingness of each side to participate in the transaction denies the possibility of one taking immoral advantage over the other.[85] This view has been challenged, but certainly the systems of market exchange in place in Russia during the war created strong feelings of unfairness rather than moral neutrality. Merchants were blamed for the constant increase in prices for

---

[85] See, e.g., Daniel M. Hausman, "Are Markets Morally Free Zones," *Philosophy and Public Affairs* 18 (Fall 1989): 317–33; William M. Dugger, "Process and Enabling Myth: The Two Faces of the Market," *Journal of Economic Issues* 23, no. 607 (June 15, 1989): 607–15; Thomas R. Dye, ed., *The Political Legitimacy of Markets and Governments* (Greenwich, CT: JAI Press, 1990), esp. pt. 1; Amitai Etzioni, *The Moral Dimension: Toward a New Economics* (New York, 1988).

foodstuffs and other goods of primary need, even after some rationing was put in place locally. When some rationed items were not available in stores but could be bought by those with means in other places, it was hard to argue that the "system" was fair. Little wonder that petitions from local authorities demanded additional emissaries be sent from the Ministry of Internal Affairs with the authority to requisition *all* goods secreted by "speculators" and forcefully "bring an end to their greed."[86] In the countryside, those who had separated from the commune and set up individual farmsteads were thought to be among them. Partial and uneven commercialization meant that many villages still relied more on personal trust and "honest" transactions in kind than those mediated by paper money of uncertain and unstable value.

Commercial transactions themselves were also sites of collusion by the end of 1915. As early as the beginning of 1915 local officials and grain dealers in some areas colluded to embargo shipments of grain and other goods out of their districts. Black markets appeared to be supported by the army when procurement officials fixed prices that were lower than those on the open market, leading to hoarding and speculation. Even away from the military zone local army commanders requisitioned scarce supplies on their own with little attention to local needs. In Tambov, southeast of Moscow, for example, the local army command requisitioned large quantities of oats for their horses for immediate delivery at a price more than 25 percent higher than that agreed to by civilian procurement officials.[87] The use of requisitioning made dealers everywhere cautious about having contracts with outdated prices. Many began concealing their supplies and refusing deliveries unless their contracts were rewritten. According to officials from the army's own procurement office, other forms of private trade in many places had virtually come to a halt.[88]

Speculation of course was now common in urban areas as well. As in all contexts of scarcity, it was relatively easy for well-connected urban traders to corner a share of the market in particular types of commodities, fueling a public discourse increasingly hostile to what was perceived as inadequate market regulation. By the end of 1915, as Taisia Kitanina has detailed, large grain-trading firms like I. Stakheev & Company had adjusted to the ban on exports by moving to dominate the internal market, swallowing up lesser firms and enjoying a disproportionate share of purchases at elevated prices from the military as a result of close relations with state and army officials. In her view, the higher the demand, the more grain was withheld and the higher the prices and profits from requisitioned goods.[89]

---

[86] *Den'*, Feb. 1, 1915.
[87] RGIA f. 456, op. 1, d. 75, ll. 3–4.
[88] Ibid., ll. 25–26; Lih, *Bread and Authority*, 21.
[89] T. M. Kitanina, *Voenno-inflatsionnye kontserny v Rossii 1914–1917gg*. (Leningrad: Nauka, 1969), 54–55;, Kitanina, *Voina, khleb i revoliutsiia*, 161–66.

In the moral and material practices of war capitalism in Russia, moreover, it was not simply that war profits seemed disloyal as they did elsewhere in Europe, but that the relatively free play of commercial market exchange seemed to work against both state and social interests. In the streets and undoubtedly in some aristocratic salons as well, "petit bourgeois" and "speculator" became the discursive equivalents of "scoundrel," especially if they were connected with "Jew." In all of this, the long-term issues of manifest social inequality in Russia could not help but be joined to immediate popular anxieties about escalating scarcity and loss and, however implicit their various expressions, a popular understanding of fairness.

In sum, the weakening state's vastly increased role in Russia's wartime economy was poorly cushioned by the substantive elements associated with well-developed commercial orders: shared attitudes about the legitimacy of wealth; internalized respect for private property; confidence in a relatively stable currency; respect for law as an institutionalized control over malfeasance; and a positive attitude toward entrepreneurial behavior in the service of individual well-being. By the end of 1915, what had culturally become a matter of state importance was the sheer visibility of social inequality at a time when sacrifice was supposedly universal. The constitutions of fairness under war capitalism were not simply about social differences rooted in tsarist Russia's traditional social system. They concerned quite visual differences in access not only to scarce foodstuffs and other essential goods but to the seemingly flaunted differences in lifestyles that could not help but signal for many as the war progressed the differential effects of its privations. When the British financier Lord Revelstoke arrived in Petrograd to attend an inter-Allied financial meeting, he professed being surprised by the city's opulence. "It is interesting to note the evident 'war prosperity,'" he wrote: "the shops brilliantly illuminated, the florists' windows full of color, and the jewelers are doing a tremendous trade. Prices have risen to a phenomenal degree [but] owing no doubt to the inflation of the currency [so have] those of bank shares and of local industrial companies. Money is being freely spent, they say, by a new class who have recently acquired fortunes."[90]

Rising Anxieties with the Coming of Winter

As the winter of 1915–16 approached, the moral and material divides in Russia almost certainly widened. A steady flow of letters and petitions were now coming to the regime and the Duma from peasants complaining about the "huge profits" being made by local grain traders, lamenting that the full costs of the war were

---

[90] Malik, *Bankers*, citing Revelstoke Petrograd Mission Diary, Jan. 29, 1917.

"being borne by 18-year-olds from the countryside." Some demanded that when the war ended "holy justice" be realized in the reallocation to them of gentry land to compensate them for their sacrifice. Some railed against local police who "not only were not contributing to the war but were prospering from it in criminal ways." One petitioner demanded that 200,000 police, gendarmes, and local Interior Ministry agents be sent immediately to the front. Even Minister of Agriculture Krivoshein identified Russia's "market problem" in the countryside with irresponsibility, confusion, speculation, corruption, and resentment.[91]

Meanwhile the early fall witnessed the largest flow of refugees yet to the Russian interior, arriving from the battle zones in Galicia and placing serious new burdens on local communities. The relief center at the Sukhinichni railroad station south of Moscow, for example, served a hot meal, bread, and tea with sugar to 33,700 persons in August and three times that number in September. Other stations in the Moscow and Kiev regions were similarly overwhelmed. In a few months the numbers of refugees and wounded would swell to over 2.8 million.[92]

There was growing cause for concern within the army as well. Soldiers' letters increasingly described the corruption scarce supplies and high prices were spawning among troops being forced to pay for their food; bribes to sergeants and others to ensure packages were delivered; letters that had obviously contained money arriving open and empty; accusations against lower-ranking officers of stealing, profiteering from the sale of military supplies, and being personally responsible for shortages of clothing, food, and munitions. Real or imagined, the belief that officers were taking widespread advantage of military shortages for personal gain was sufficient to provoke outrage. Some censors now blamed a significant lowering of the soldiers' "mood" on this behavior and the suffering it was causing. The 4 million new troops mobilized in 1915 only exacerbated the problems of inadequate equipment and supplies. Many of these soldiers must have reached the battle zone with as much apprehension and foreboding as the surviving troops they joined. Reservists stationed in Petrograd and other cities around the country openly resisted being called to the front.

Thus, soldiers continued to ask for all sorts of goods to be sent to them from home—gloves and warm clothing, underwear, tobacco, paper and envelops, tea, sugar, a whole commissary roster even though the most common worry in letters coming to the front was now the "terrible [*strashnyi*] cost of living."[93] Military censors with the Eighth Army on the Southwestern Front reported that

[91] RGIA, f. 777, op. 22, d. 6, ll. 8–11; f. 457.1.12, ll. 55–67; f. 1276, op. 11, d. 258, ll. 3–12; f. 1278, op. 5, d. 1193, passim.
[92] T. J. Polner, *Russian Local Government during the War and the Union of Zemstvos* (New Haven, CT, 1930), 173; I. Belova, *Vynuzhhdennye migrant: Bezhentsy i voennoeplennye Pervoi mirovoi voiny v Rossii 1914–25* (Moscow: AIRO, 2014), 105; Peter Gatrell, *A Whole Empire Walking: Refugees in Russia during World War I* (Bloomington: Indiana University Press, 1999), 211–15.
[93] RGVIA f. 2003, op. 1, d. 1486, ll. 7–11.

40 to 50 percent of letter writers at the end of October 1915 voiced concern for their family's well-being. While it is not easily measured, the range of anxieties accompanying all of this on the battlefield as well as the home front almost certainly became palpably stronger in the fall of 1915, especially with the approach of another winter. In turn, the soldiers' desire for an end to the war became even more urgent.[94]

In this connection, one of the most alarming tendencies noted by military censors in late 1915 was soldiers' anger over the link they drew between shortages and corruption, both at the front and in their towns and villages. Letters in December 1915 described surprise that authorities were not doing more to stop speculators "among our commercial people and other sharks," one soldier wrote, even as some returned from leaves relieved that the scarcities at home were not as severe as they had thought.[95] One bit of dark humor quoted by censors reported that Germans felt no need to attack a town because Russian generals would sell it to them.[96] Others were blamed when soldiers received parcels filled with wood and stones instead of the food and warm clothing they expected. Bribery was rampant. Sergeants were demanding three rubles for one week's leave, five rubles to decrease disciplinary measures. Larger sums were being paid to avoid more rigorous field duties or change posts, even more—420 rubles in one case—to escape military courts or to be released from service altogether. Censors allowed that the large number of letters containing evidence of this sort would "undoubtedly" have been much greater had their writers not feared they would be identified. "Thank God I have a little money," one wrote. "If you don't send money, I could die."[97]

As many military censors understood, the supply of goods to the front had improved somewhat over the summer. A case could be made that by the fall, the situation was much better in many places than it had been a year before. Yet large numbers of soldiers' letters continued to complain that food was inadequate ("How can one carry on and even survive if one cannot on occasion sit down without feeling starved"; "Sometimes you can't even look at it, dirty water and groats, with little things pieces floating around"); that other supplies were lacking even if there were fewer shortages of weapons and ammunition ("They can't send us back to the trenches because we have no shoes"; "We lie in filth . . . and go around barefoot and naked"); and that many officers were incompetent, especially younger company commanders ("The older ones are

---

[94] RGIA f. 777, op. 23, d. 3, ll. 1–2.
[95] RGVIA f. 206, op. 1, d. 2932, l. 174; f. 2048, op. 1, d. 904, ll. 39, 60; f. 2067, op. 1, d. 2932, 149–65.
[96] RGVIA f. 2067, op. 1, d. 2932, ll. 7–8, 33; f. 2003, op. 1, d. 1486, ll. 194–205; f. 2067, op. 1, d. 3853, ll. 73–75.
[97] RGVIA f. 2067, op. 1, d. 2937, ll. 156–60; d. 2932, l. 144 ob.; f. 2067, op. 1, d. 2937, ll. 157–58 ob., 47. 156–60; d. 2932, l. 144 ob.
RGVIA f. 2048, op. 1, d. 904, ll. 52–58; f. 2067, op. 1, d. 2932, ll. 111, 225.

better"; "It is laughable how little the artillery commander understands about it, and only interferes with our efforts"). Importantly for those at the front, the evacuation of wounded soldiers was still woefully inadequate. The general in charge of evacuating causalities, Prince Boris Aleksandrovich Vasil'chikov, himself decried an evacuation procedure "in full disarray" in a report to the General Staff in December 1915.[98] Despite the difficulties of measurement, the range of anxiety about all of this seemed clearly to increase as survivors of the previous winter campaigns warned about more hardships to come.[99]

In the meantime, the Ministry of Interior was also receiving reports from its provincial agents shortly before the New Year holidays about a growing "revolutionary mood" in Russia's provincial cities and towns, particularly on the part of young people.[100] Concerns were such that the tsar himself expressed his alarm from military headquarters, ordering that the problem of scarcity receive urgent attention.[101] Just before the Christmas holidays Minister of Internal Affairs A. N. Khvostov wrote a top-secret memo of his own to Prime Minister Goremykin describing the confusion and disorder in food procurements and their distribution. Russia's top policeman was adamant that Russia's need for food and fuel could only be met by strong local organizations built on the initiative and authority of town and zemstvo boards and coordinated by the state. In this, Khvostov felt it was his duty to report, "the government is doing exceedingly little."[102]

Often accused of anti-Semitism, Khvostov also reported "strong rumors" that Petrograd would witness pogroms and disorder in connection with the holidays. Everywhere in factories and on the streets, Khvostov wrote, there was angry talk about possible looting. Shortly before Christmas, two-thirds of the city's butcher shops had no meat at all to sell. Others had some, but were rumored to have too little to satisfy even their regular customers. One-third of the bakeries were closed because they lacked flour and oil; most of the remainder were open only two or three hours in the morning. According to Khvostov, there were deficits in Petrograd of matches, soap, peat, kerosene, beetroot, sugar, and other common products. More than a year before similar scenes would precipitate the fall of the three-hundred-year Romanov dynasty, police reported a crowd of some five hundred to six hundred angry women swearing and hurling insults outside one butcher shop when rumors that it was about to be supplied turned out not to be true. They went away empty-handed and, one suspects, even angrier.[103]

---

[98] RGIA f. 651, op. 1, d. 1029, ll. 1–2.
[99] RGVIA f. 2067, op. 1, d. 2932, ll. 7–8, 176–77 ob.; f. 2031, op. 1, d. 1184, ll. 1–2; f. 2003, op. 1, d. 1486, ll. 11, 25, 22 220–25.
[100] RGIA f. 1282, op. 1, d. 736.
[101] RGIA f. 457, op. 1, d. 64, l. 1.
[102] RGVIA f. 1276, op. 11, d. 167, l. 117; RGIA d. 457, op. 1, d. 209, ll. 1–3 ob.
[103] RGVIA f. 1276, op. 11, d. 167, l. 117.

What had thus become a matter of state importance as 1915 drew to a close was not how well the stock market was performing but the quite visible implications of how scarcity and loss within the broadening context of war capitalism were affecting perceptions of fairness, social sacrifice, governance, and the very purpose of the war itself. As Shingarev visualized the scene, the "disgusting [*obratitel'no*] sight" of "certain strata of society squandering and carousing in luxury during this time of national hardship requires us to struggle, for society and the state to struggle together ... to say to those people 'remember, you are citizens of Russia, remember that there is a war on, remember that people are fighting with their last drop of energy, realize how shameful it is for you to cloak yourself in silk and velvet.'"[104]

---

[104] Gosudarstvennaia Duma, *Stenograficheskii Otchet 4th sozyv*, 1916, col. 1768.

5
Seeking Solutions, Drowning in Blood

The winter holidays of 1916 were dismal ones throughout Russia for those not cloaked "in silk and velvet," as Shingarev described them, especially in Petrograd. Just as they were in Vienna, Berlin, and throughout much of Europe. Austrians were suffering through their "turnip winter"; the British blockade choking imports to Germany created equally long lines for food; and military commanders in both countries regarded food shortages as the decisive influence on the popular mood. Strikes and social protests were reflecting both need and anger in France, England, and certainly Austria and Germany, even if the numbers of incidents were considerably lower than in Russia. In France, every small advance that brought the enemy closer to Paris spread apprehension in the capital and the provinces beyond.[1]

The angry food lines in Petrograd had a different implication, one that echoed the regime crisis of 1905. In Germany, Austria, and especially France and England the meaning of the war seemed relatively clear. Their wartime governments continued to enjoy relatively broad support. Britain, France, Austria, and Germany all accommodated trade unions, which had broad popular representation in governing institutions. Mediation boards and other institutions capable of resolving social conflict were also functional, along with significantly stronger popular confidence in both government and military leaders. In France, the Socialist Party remained distant from strike actions. The Ministry of Armaments was headed by Albert Thomas, one of that party's most prominent figures. In England, the outcomes of strikes were still largely favorable to workers, as they would be throughout the war, laying the foundations for the Labour Party's future political success.[2] In Germany and Austria, inflation diminished real incomes, and growing shortages generated substantial anger toward bureaucratic mismanagement only as defeat loomed with the American entry into the war in April 1917.

---

[1] Alexander Watson, *Ring of Steel* (London: Allen Lane, 2014), 374, ch. 6; C. F. Wargelin, "The Economic Collapse of Austro-Hungarian Dualism, 1914–18," *East European Quarterly* 3 (2000): 261–88. Among a large literature, see also Belinda J. Davis, *Home Fires Burning: Food, Politics, and Everyday Life in World War I Berlin* (Chapel Hill: University of North Carolina Press, 2000); Roger Chickering, *The Great War and Urban Life in Germany: Freiburg, 1914–1918* (Cambridge: Cambridge University Press, 2007); S. Broadberry and M. Harrison, eds., *The Economics of World War I* (Cambridge: Cambridge University Press, 2005).

[2] Leopold Haimson and Giulio Sapelli, eds., *Strikes, Social Conflict, and the First World War: An International Perspective* (Milan: Feltrinelli, 1992), 25–64, 89–140, 247–322.

In some contrast, as military censors and agents of the Ministry of Interior understood, New Year celebrations in Russia as 1916 began hardly indicated support for the regime. For soldiers, a willingness to fight was now closely linked to the hope that even a modicum of success against the enemy might force Austria and Germany to leave the war. Indeed, the winter lull only increased the privations and tensions of waiting in miserable conditions. For some who wrote home pleading for supplies, even the dangers of action seemed more attractive than filthy, disease-ridden trenches and long stretches of anxious boredom interrupted by sudden bombardments. All across the front, meanwhile, soldiers felt "great anxiety about the condition of their families." In January 1916 supplies, personnel, and training were still inadequate.

On the home front supplies of essential goods were also "precarious," according to Interior Minister Khvostov, the situation "extremely dangerous."[3] In the countryside, the onetime payment offered to families of the wounded or killed was proving inadequate to relieve distress. The conservative governor of Moscow province Count N. L. Murav'ev told the interior minister that the lack of essential foodstuffs was creating "enormous unease": a wave of protests was "sweeping the province." Provincial agents of the Ministry of Interior were reporting a growing "revolutionary mood," especially on the part of young people.[4] In Kherson province, the commander of a Nikolaev railroad inspection point warned the ministry that local branches of the right-wing Union of Russian People were actively stirring up protests against Jews and "progressive elements," especially among railroad workers. Police in Tambov province warned that peasants expecting to get additional land in compensation for their military service refused to pay taxes. In Bogorodsk, townspeople joined strikers in pillaging stores. Clashes with troops called to restore order resulted in two deaths.[5] Significant disorders occurred in Perm and the Cheliabinsk region. More broke out in Moscow and elsewhere as the holidays began, just as Khvostov had predicted. When the tsar sent his imperial rescript to Goremykin in mid-December expressing his personal anxiety about the situation, he had reason to be concerned.[6] In his own memos, Khvostov warned that Petrograd and Moscow were in "urgent need." "All measures" had to be taken to ensure calm in the country. Russia was "approaching a real catastrophe."[7]

---

[3] RGIA f. 457, op. 2, d. 65, l. 6.
[4] RGIA, f. 1282, op. 1, d. 736, l. 1.
[5] RGIA f. 1276, op. 11, d. 167, ll. 167–68; Iu. I. Kirianov, "Massovye vystupleniia na pochve dorogovizny v Rossii (1914–fevral' 1917 g.)," *Otechestvennaia Istoriia* 3 (1993): 3–18; O. S. Porshneva, "Problemy voiny i mira v obshchestvennoi bor'be na urale, 1914–18," in *Pervaia Mirovaia Voina*, ed. V. L. Malkov (Moscow, 1998), 467–70.
[6] RGIA f. 457, op. 1, d. 64, l. 1.
[7] Ibid., l. 102; RGIA f. 457, op. 1, d. 209, ll. 1–3 ob.; f. 1276, op. 11, d. 167, l. 54; f. 1282, op. 1, 736, ll. 1–4.

Winter and Spring of 1916: Anxieties about Mismanagement and Malfeasance from Below

But what measures, exactly? And directed at which problems? Unlike 1905–6, when the regime set its artillery on protesting workers in Moscow and deployed troops returning from the war with Japan to pacify the countryside, massive repression was hardly an option. To manage the crisis one had to clarify its key elements and their causes. This was hardly an easy matter even for relatively well-informed officials like the minister of interior. The fault lines of economic mobilization were not readily apparent. The anxieties and stress of dislocations and dismissals as well as the effects for so many of personal loss could only be assumed. Scarcities in essential goods were more readily remedied than the anxieties and insecurities they created. There was also little question that these were related to rising prices as well as insecurities about food, a key element of popular grievance. They were far more easily expressed than the grief and hardship of loss. Fifteen months of fighting had now produced more than 3.4 million causalities, including more than forty-four thousand diagnosed cases of shell shock.[8]

In these circumstances the regime sought to identify problems where ameliorative measures might be relatively easy to apply. Just before Christmas Khvostov joined the ministers of war (Polivanov), trade and industry (Shakhovskoi), agriculture (Naumov), and transport (Trepov) in a special conference with other officials to formulate new measures. The group soon included the vice chair of the newly formed Railroad Management Committee and the military governor of Petrograd. Prime Minister Goremykin was notably absent. Soon known in high circles as the Special Council of Five (but officially the Conference on Supplying the Capital with Items of Primary Need), Khvostov and his colleagues considered first what they regarded as the urgent problem of supplying Petrograd with food. Late in December they extended their mandate to ensuring adequate supplies of food and fuel to Russia's localities more broadly, which they regarded as the key to containing social unrest. Linking the work of the four special councils around this effort, the Special Council of Five sketched an official narrative over the course of several meetings about the sources of these critical scarcities and possible solutions.[9]

The ministers' emphasis was not on hoarding, speculation, or the implications of sociocultural inequalities. Their focus instead was on the problem of distribution, specifically on inefficiencies and corruption on the railroads. Assuming from official forecasts that the fall grain harvest and the level of fuel production

---

[8] TsSU, *Rossiia v mirovoi voine 1914–1918 (v tsifrakh)* (Moscow: TsSU, 1925), 30.
[9] RGIA f. 457, op. 1, d. 64, l. 33.

were adequate, they saw the two key problems as misadministration in the use of railroad equipment and the corruption of railroad employees, what D. I. Zasiadko, master (*hofmeister*) of the tsarist court, described to his colleagues as "extremely widespread malfeasance [*zloupotreblenie*]."[10] To address the first, the Council of Five emphasized the importance of controlling the use of locomotives and rolling stock throughout the country, the task now of the newly formed Railroad Management Committee (Razporiaditel'nyi Komitet).[11] On December 21, the Council learned that plans had been worked out to regulate the use of cars and locomotives for January and that "with their strict fulfillment, the supply of essential goods to Petrograd would be guaranteed [*obespecheno*]." The committee would allocate all freight cars for civilian use on the basis of specific needs and available inventories.[12] In the meantime, the Railroad Management Committee was trying to find some six thousand freight cars to move 4 million Russian pounds of frozen meat to Petrograd from Siberia. If these could be found, 60 carloads of frozen meat were planned for arrival in the capital every twenty-four hours, along with 15 carloads of fish, 20 of sugar, and 185 of grain.[13]

Additionally, the Council of Five determined that the distribution of these and other foodstuffs within Petrograd should be the responsibility of the military governor, essentially militarizing the process of wholesale distribution. Foodstuffs already in the city would be prohibited from being sent elsewhere. Any goods not picked up in a timely way would be confiscated. Their timely delivery would then indirectly address the goals of controlling prices and fighting speculation.[14] Petrograd's military governor was more than willing to take on the task of distributing foodstuffs even if the army might then be blamed for shortages. So was the governor general of Moscow. Russia's second capital was also "in extreme need." Local authorities were bracing themselves for more trouble.[15]

Khvostov and his colleagues also addressed what they understood as two related reasons for scarcities: inadequate information about existing supplies and insufficient authority on the part of plenipotentiaries from the four special councils. To address the first, they demanded measures to better coordinate and share information. To strengthen the power of their emissaries the Council of Five demanded they be assigned "exceptional powers" to impose local remedies as they saw fit.[16] These recommendations were then discussed in the Council

[10] RGIA f. 457, op. 1, d. 65, l. 64.
[11] Ibid., d. 12, ll. 13–14.
[12] Ibid., d. 64, l. 54 ob.
[13] Ibid., l. 38; RGIA f. 290, op. 1, d. 5, ll. 2–20 [*Zhurnal zasedanii Vremennogo rasporiaditel'nogo komiteta po zheleznodorozhnym perevozkam*].
[14] RGIA f. 457, op. 1, d. 64, ll. 33–67.
[15] RGIA f. 1276, op. 11, d. 167, ll. 117–49; op. 12, d. 1239, ll. 6–6 ob.
[16] RGIA f. 457, op. 1, d. 64, ll. 4–5, 40–42.

of Ministers, which accepted them. While the needs of the home front had to take second place to those of the army, "order and calm within the country" was now essential to maintaining the army's fighting spirit.[17] Success, however, depended on rooting out railroad corruption, which required that local agents of the Ministry of Agriculture be charged with inspecting food shipments at their point of origin and given the power to take appropriate action. The flood of refugees and wounded on the railroads also had to be slowed, and the garrison, now 360,000 strong, had to be reduced, both measures the ministers considered "absolutely essential." But far more urgent was taking hold of corruption and sacking or arresting those to blame.[18]

Echoing the language of recrimination that engulfed the failures of the army's leadership in 1914, Khvostov and his colleagues ignored the structural problems underlying speculation and the rising cost of goods as well as the inadequacies of Russia's state administration. The greatest source of danger was a corrupt "enemy" from within: the sociocultural conditions of corruption and venality, against which the strongest weapons were vigilance, repression, and state control. Unannounced inspections would be conducted by the police to uncover hoarding at freight depots. The activities of anyone bypassing set priorities in the sending of goods or otherwise suspected of wrongdoing would be investigated without evidence of actual criminal activity. Corruption and mismanagement had to be fought with "extreme and decisive force."[19]

Shortly after the new year began, Nicholas himself seemingly identified an additional source of mismanagement at the top, pressured by the empress and Rasputin: the prime minister himself. The seventy-seven-year-old Goremykin was unceremoniously sacked. In his place the tsar appointed sixty-nine-year-old Boris Shturmer, a proud reactionary of questionable integrity with few if any qualifications for the position. Shturmer was soon reporting directly to Alexandra, and thus indirectly to Rasputin. At a meeting on January 24, 1916, the Council of Five, determined that the supply of food to Petrograd and Moscow was still inadequate. Essential norms had not been met, speculation had not abated, anxieties and food insecurities were even higher. Taking his place as chair, an angry Shturmer blamed the scarcities on poor planning and other deficiencies of the responsible agencies. The task of the Council was changed from issuing instructions to informing the new prime minister, who was determined to take strong action.[20] Meanwhile, none of the sixty carloads of frozen Siberian meat that were supposed to arrive every twenty-four hours had reached

---

[17] Ibid., ll. 21–22.
[18] Ibid., ll. 35–35 ob., 56–59, 177.
[19] Ibid., ll. 144–47, 163.
[20] RGIA f. 1276, op. 12, d. 1239, ll. 2–12.

the capital. According to the reports, much of the shipment had been prepared for transport but spoiled waiting for transport.[21]

Contending Anxieties: Confusion and Chaos from Above

Within the English-language literature, the most familiar Great Story is the liberals' view of high politics during the critical winter and spring of 1916, a narrative of individual and collective irrationality, mismanagement, and malfeasance. Here the narrative is not one of lowly railroad administrators and ineffectual service personnel but of the regime's own disorganization and incompetence at the very top: a legion of irresponsible "hangers on" at army headquarters and the court in Petrograd. The conservative liberal famously articulated the liberal vision at this time as a motor car with no brakes driven along a narrow mountain path by a "mad chauffeur." The Kadet leader Paul Miliukov despised the elderly Goremykin for his unremitting opposition to the Duma, a position he traced all the way back to 1905. He and the Kadet leadership also saw Minister of Justice Alexander Khvostov as well as his nephew Aleksei, the minister of interior from September 1915 to March 1916, as "protégés" of the reactionary Union of Russian People. But Shturmer, the new prime minister, was both ignorant and a fool, whose reported Germanophile sympathies made his actions either "stupidity or treason," as the Kadet leader would later describe them in his famous Duma speech the following November.[22]

The keen British observer Bernard Pares reinforced the liberal story. For him, early 1916 was a time of "atrocious mismanagement' and "complete confusion and chaos." Shturmer was shallow, dishonest, cowardly, and a liar with almost a preference for prevaricating.[23] Pares and Michael Florinsky, the distinguished liberal émigré Russian historian who was wounded and decorated four times during the war, both describe the appointment of Shturmer as a major turning point in the process of imperial collapse, the second player in a game of "ministerial leapfrog" that saw four different prime ministers in 1916. A reactionary former governor of Iaroslavl deeply hostile to the public organization whose former distinction was as *Ober Hofmeister* (master of ceremonies) at the court, Shturmer's appointment came as a shock even to many at the highest reaches of state power: "a crushing blow," according to A. N. Naumov, who replaced Krivoshein as minister of agriculture in 1915; an "utter nonentity" in Duma president Rodzianko's view; "absolutely unprincipled," according to the conservative

---

[21] RGIA f. 651, op. 1 d. 1029, l. 34.
[22] Paul Miliukov, *Istorii vtoroi russkoi revoliutsii*, 3 vols., reprint ed. (Gulf Breeze, FL: Academic Intl. Press, 1978), 1: 16–20.
[23] Bernard Pares, *Fall of the Russian Monarchy* (London: Cassell, 1988), 328.

publicist Vasili Shulgin; "two-faced" and without integrity, in the view of Minister of Interior Khvostov himself.[24]

Just before Goremykin's dismissal Rodzianko wrote him a strong letter about the current situation, with a copy for the tsar. Russia was "menaced with famine"; a stoppage in munitions production was "imminent"; "the victorious spirit of the Russian people and their faith in their own powers [were] being crushed by the inactivity of the regime"; "events, stern and inexorable, [were] drawing near, pregnant with consequences which may prove fatal to Russia's honor and dignity."[25] For Rodzianko and others in and outside the Duma, the aloof and reactionary Shturmer, backed by Rasputin, was the opposite of a government in which the country could have confidence. War Minister Polivanov later said he thought his appointment was the beginning of the end.[26] When Shturmer became interior minister as well in April, apparently at Rasputin's behest, the levers of state power were firmly in his hands and those of the empress and her "mad monk."

Much of this testimony comes from the statements Polivanov and other former tsarist officials gave to an investigating commission set up in 1917 by the Provisional Government. For Pares and others the seven large volumes of the commission were a particularly valuable source, given that official documentation was not yet available. Little in these materials is easily controverted. The director of police in the Ministry of Interior even describes how Minister Khovstov himself decided it was necessary to assassinate Rasputin after the appointment of Shturmer, providing explicit details of the plot. Yet these testimonies also serve, if not an explicitly exculpatory purpose, at least to some degree as an effort at casting blame for the regime's collapse on the perverse interference of Rasputin and the empress and the culpability of men like Shturmer, Sukhomlinov, Goremykin, and the tsar himself. In this way the commission's materials fit well with the cultures of war capitalism that understandably focused more on assigning blame to incompetent state officials than to the socioeconomic dislocations and anxieties of war capitalism itself.

The "catastrophic state of railway transport" was certainly a key problem, as Rodzianko's letter to the tsar described. Malfeasance was "everywhere," and as a result, the "Fatherland was in danger" even as the army sustained its defense.[27] There could be little doubt about either mismanagement or malfeasance on the lines, as many inside and out of the government insisted. But the problem lay

---

[24] Ibid., 317; M. V. Rodzianko, *The Reign of Rasputin* (London: Philpot, 1927), 178; V. V. Shulgin *Dni* (Belgrade: Suvorin, 1925), 79; *Padenie tsarskogo rezhima: Stenograficheskie otchety doprosov i pokazanii*, 7 vols. (Leningrad, 1924–27), 5:458.

[25] Rodzianko, *The Reign of Rasputin*, 166–68.

[26] *Padenie*, 7:77.

[27] Rodzianko, *The Reign of Rasputin*, 166–68.

deeper: in the geographic stretch of the lines in which the still largely single-tracked Trans-Siberian line was now a principal route of supply for a seemingly endless war after the disasters at Gallipoli shut off the possibility of a direct link to the Black Sea. State and private railroads by 1914 were also managed in terms of their profitability, although most had been built for defense. The years just before the war were exceedingly profitable for both the state and private owners. They created a culture of expectation for both that high levels of returns would continue despite the hostilities. State revenue projections in 1914 were based on this projection, and as we have noted, Finance Minister Bark's support for ending the sale of hard spirits was premised on the belief that additional revenues from the railroads would largely replace those lost from liquor sales. Between 1909 and 1913 the profits of private lines rose by more than 100 percent, from 147 to 307 million rubles a year. State lines returned more than 1.5 million rubles in this period, making them one of the most important sources of state income.[28] Since the war was expected to be short, the effect on the transport and distribution of foodstuffs and other goods throughout the country was at first not thought to be a great problem. Neither was the transfer of substantial numbers of locomotives and rolling stock from ordinary service elsewhere in Russia to the war zone, along with large numbers of railroaders, nor the effect the war would have on state revenues and private profits.

If the disorganization of the railroads contributed to scarcities and insecurities, however, there were other elements both material and subjective that underlay the crisis Rodzianko had spelled out. Russia's finances were stretched perilously thin, as Minister of Finance Bark tried to hold on to the gold standard. Escalating prices had to be addressed in effective ways if the great strains they were causing from the countryside to the workplace were to be resolved. And beyond the familiar problems of maintaining and supporting the army, there was the need, simply, to further bridge the gap between high politics of the well-off and local politics and practices of those who continued to supply the seemingly endless stream of recruits being chewed up at the front.

What was problematic about the narratives told with such conviction by Pares, Rodzianko, Miliukov, and others was not therefore that Russian governance was in any way adequate nor that the distribution of goods was corrupted by mismanagement and malfeasance. Missing from the liberal perspective was a complex of issues, both specific and more general: the sociocultural dynamics of commodity production and exchange in conditions of scarcity and loss; their effects on the availability of essential goods; the problem of markets in mediating disparities in access to deficit goods in both rural and urban Russia; the labor

---

[28] A. L. Siderov, "Zheleznodorozhnyi transport Rossii v pervoi mirovoi voine i obostrenie ekonomicheskogo krizisa v strane," *Istoricheskie zapiski* 26 (1948): 9.

and other protests they engendered; and, perhaps above all, the specific issues of regulating prices, controlling the rapidly rising cost of living, financing the war effort, and relieving the anxieties being felt by ordinary Russians and other nationalities across the empire during this time of increasing want and great personal and community loss.

The Vexing Problems of Rationing and Fixed Prices

Regulating prices, financing the war, and controlling the risks that a rising cost of living were certain to produce in terms of social unrest were closely related problems the imperial tsarist regime faced from the first days of the war. Finance Minister Bark recognized them in his speech to the special session of the Duma in July 1914; Andrei Shingarev and other members of the Duma Budget Committee warned of their dangers when the Duma convened briefly in January 1915; and they found increasing resonance in newspapers and journals throughout the country. While those participating in the Special Council of Five focused on lower-level corruption and malfeasance as the reasons for scarcities and high costs, especially on the railroads, more fundamental was the problem of prices itself and the way escalating currency emissions compounded the inflationary effects of hoarding and speculation. Should the state step in and fix prices for essential goods, or should these be set by commercial markets on the basis of supply and demand?

At the very moment the Special Council of Five was meeting at the end of December, two other committees were focusing on these dimensions of Russia's "approaching catastrophe," as Minister of Interior Khvostov was describing it. One was the Economic Committee of the Union of Towns, chaired by the moderate socialist Vladimir Groman from Moscow's Chuprov Society. Joining him in this effort were some of Russia's most prominent public-sector economists, including the Odessa economist and founding member of the Kadet Party Alexander Manuilov, the liberal politician and revisionist social democrat Sergei Prokopovich, and the prominent Menshevik agrarian economist Peter Maslov, who would be elected in 1929 to the Soviet Academy of Sciences. All would play important roles in 1917.[29] The other was a special commission on measures for fighting the cost of living created by the Special Council on Food. This blue-ribbon effort was chaired initially by State Comptroller and former deputy finance minister Nikolai Pokrovskii and then by G. V. Glinka, the vice minister of agriculture. One of its most notable members was the former social democrat and now right-wing liberal Peter B. Struve, formally representing the

---

[29] *Trudy Komissii po izucheniiu sovremennoi dorogovizny*, vol. 3 (Moscow, 1915).

Zemstvo Union and about to be honored by election to the Academy of Sciences. Vladimir Groman participated as a guest in this group as well.[30] For three months the Pokrovskii Committee, as it was initially known, had struggled to assess food stockpiles around the country, channel funds for their purchase, and work through plans to fix prices on certain commodities. Early on, for example, it had set a price of five rubles ten kopecks for granulated sugar in all production districts despite protests from some of its members that this was higher than the already inflated market price of four rubles seventy kopecks. By late December, some already regarded this effort as a failure.

During the first weeks of January both committees presented their findings, Groman's group to a national meeting of the Union of Cities, the Pokrovskii/Glinka commission to the Special Council on Food. Like the ministerial Council of Five, both groups stressed that shortages and rising prices were being caused by administrative confusion and overlapping authorities, rampant speculation, and especially the lack of reliable transport. In the view of Struve and the Pokrovskii Commission, however, Khvostov and the Ministry of Interior were themselves part of the problem. Khvostov had completely reneged on an initial promise not to interfere in the Special Council's activities. Ministry officials would not meet with the Council. Its local officials refused to give up their policing and supervisory roles, and its ministerial staff was ignoring the extensive help that the Special Council on Food was providing in terms of credits to local town and zemstvo organizations to facilitate purchases. The most egregious interference was in the provinces of Vitebsk, Vologda, Voronezh, Kursk, Minsk, Nizhnii Novgorod, Orel, Poltava, and Samara. In sum, speculation, inflation, and inadequate transport were not only local problems; they were encouraged by policies and behaviors at the top.[31]

The most important issue in this regard for both Groman's Economic Committee and the Pokrovskii/Glinka group was whether prices on essential goods should be fixed by local and national authorities or be set by the market. Within the Pokrovskii Commission opinions were divided. One "statist" view was that it was impossible under current circumstances in Russia to preserve anything resembling normally functioning free trade. According to the Special Council for Food's own plenipotentiaries, private trade had virtually come to a halt in some places because traders feared being undercut by lower fixed prices set by local authorities, who also had the power to prevent goods that were not purchased for the army from being shipped out of their districts.[32] The state itself

---

[30] RGIA f. 457, op. 1, d. 12. [*Obzor deiatel'nosti Osobogo Soveshchanie dlia obsuzhdeniia i obedineniia meropriatii po prodovol'stvennom delu 17 avg. 1915–17 Feb 1916*]; RGIA f. 457, op. 1, d. 256 [*Doklady komissii o merakh bor'by s dorogoviznoi. 1915–16*].

[31] RGIA f. 457, op. 1, d. 12, ll. 1–5 ob.; d. 262, ll. 103–4.

[32] RGIA f. 465, op. 1, d. 12, ll. 25–26.

therefore had to take steps to regulate prices in the localities even if this would greatly extend its role and responsibility in supplying Russia's civilian population with food.

The majority opinion, however, was that state intervention to this degree was impractical and even "dangerous," since the regime would then "bear full responsibility for the adequate and equitable supply of food to the population while there could be no confidence whatsoever in the possibility of doing this in the current circumstances."[33] The steadily increasing cost of living and the rampant speculation in essential goods simply left no effective way to set prices in the localities. Attempting to do so in conditions of great scarcity would only worsen the already critical problem of goods exchange. Prices on specific commodities had to be fixed at the national level, with extreme care not to stimulate speculation and black markets, and only for certain necessary items in exceptional circumstances. Otherwise, prices were still best set by local markets, however imperfectly.[34]

Countering this view were both Groman and Struve, despite the differences in their political positions. Groman maintained that it was precisely market conditions that were the source of the problem, underlying and compounding the lack of order in transport, the confusion created by the multiple local authorities, and the wholly predictable speculation in these circumstances on the part of traders large and small. In the localities, fixed prices were being set by various officials with no understanding of how local markets were functioning. Since fixed prices differed substantially in different markets, goods still flowed speculatively to higher bidders elsewhere regardless of local need. Hence the inadequacy of even regulated local markets in terms of equitable distribution and affordable pricing. In a phrase, prices of essential goods no longer corresponded to the purchasing power of ordinary people who needed them most. "In the nearest possible future," Groman argued, an empire-wide system of fixed prices for primary goods had to be carefully worked out.[35] The expectation at the beginning of the war that Russia's commercial markets would be adequate for the country's needs was a mistake. "We have to say frankly," he told representatives of the Union of Cities, "that at this moment, January 1916, our commercial mechanisms are broken."[36]

Struve agreed. In his view the regime was endangered not only by disorders and widespread political dissidence—he was about to resign from the Kadet

---

[33] RGIA f. 457, op. 1, d. 256, l. 9 ob.

[34] Ibid., ll. 9–11.

[35] RGIA f. 457, op. 1, d. 262, 8 ob.–9, 52; V. G. Groman, *Deiatel'nost Osobogo Soveshchaniia po Prodovol'stviiu i osnovnye zadachi ekonomicheskoi politiki* (Moscow, 1916); T. M. Kitanina, *Voina, khleb, i revoliutsii* (Leningrad: Nauka, 1985), 170–71.

[36] Vse Rossiiskii Soiuz Gorodov, *Trudy Ekonomicheskago Soveshchaniia 3-4 Jan 1916* (Moscow, 1916), 24–27.

Party for its oppositional stance—but also from pursuing policies that could not be effective. "In conditions of war," the influential economist argued, "private trade cannot be considered free." To act on such a principle could only lead to "the debauchery of speculation and to the factual strengthening of the monopolistic conditions that served exclusively private interest." Like Groman, Struve insisted that fixed prices had to go hand in hand with the strict regulation of supply. Otherwise, speculation would continue to distort both the supply and the distribution of urgent goods, discrediting in the process the very attempt at regulating prices. "If there is danger in theoretically dogmatic schemes of state interference, and in linking the question of supplying food to the broad task of governing, then no less danger, and perhaps even more, lies at the present moment in consciously and on the basis of principle for the government to refrain on its own from interfering in the economic life of the country because of a lack of confidence in its own strength."[37]

Thus Groman and Struve, a leading socialist economist and a sometime left liberal who was now a prominent economic activist on the right, came to the same conclusions: the state itself had to take a stronger role in regulating the economy, starting first with ensuring adequate deliveries of goods by close management of the railroads, and then by moving as quickly as data and administrative competence would allow to fix prices at a national level in ways that reflected real costs. As long as the variation in local costs and supplies led inevitably to local and regional variations in fixed procurement prices themselves—in the absence of "national pricing," in other words—the distribution of goods would be even more vulnerable to black and gray markets at the point of distribution because fixed procurement prices for scarce goods increased the margins of traders in these markets.

Reflecting the core element of social democratic thinking, Groman saw the question even more broadly. "The biggest mistake of all the measures we have taken both at the private level and by the state," he reported to the Union of Cities conference, "is that they all aspire to the partial regulation of separate aspects of the country's economic life, and that they do not confront the largest question of all: that of a comprehensive system of regulating production, trade, transport, distribution, and finally, demand itself."[38] Presenting the report of the Union's Economic Section, Groman stressed the enormously deleterious effect of these efforts on prices and popular demand, which had created an "absolutely insufficient" supply of goods. The basic idea that had now to guide all economic measures was the "subordination of private interests to the demands of the nation as

---

[37] RGIA f. 457, op. 1, d. 256, ll. 11–12 ob.
[38] Vse Rossiskii Soiuz Gorodov, *Trudy,* 28; Vse Rossiskii Soiuz Gorodov, *Organizatsiia narodnago khoziaistva (Materialy po V ocherednomu S'ezdu Soiuza Gorodov)* (Moscow, 1917).

a whole."[39] Rationing and fixed prices could only work at a local level if food and other essential goods could be obtained in sufficient quantities, if its transport and distribution were closely controlled, and if there were not wide variation in fixed prices across different localities, often within the same province or region. Representatives from throughout the country at the Union of Cities conference agreed, including the conference chair Nikolai Astrov, a leading Moscow Kadet and member of the party's Central Committee.[40]

In the fraught circumstances of Russia's second long winter of war, these arguments were about more than prices and the cost of goods. How Russia's markets were functioning and the deficits many Russians were experiencing in essential goods both reflected and produced social values and colored political outlooks. Local price regulations were not working to provide essential needs. Industrial workers in many places were being forced onto inadequate labor exchanges or unemployment because financial or commodity markets were failing to provide enterprises with capital goods and adequate wages. Indeed, as in other times of economic crisis, the very objectification of market relations and the corresponding distancing of political authorities from their seemingly natural effects at mediating supply and demand could only reinforce a sense of the market's own coercive power and lead to political demands for its amelioration.

Whether imperial Russia was objectively in such a crisis in the late fall of 1915 remains a subject of debate, as we have noted. There can be little doubt, however, that war capitalism and its distorted market relations were both seen as contributing to the scarcities and rising prices that many were clearly anxious about. The state's failure to guarantee lower prices or increase supplies could not help but engender feelings about its seeming indifference to popular welfare that continued to be expressed in the language of "extreme need." The same held true for rationing. Especially in urban areas where goods were most scarce and demand was highest, rationing could only equalize deprivation for those unable to access clandestine channels of supply. In short, rationing and fixed prices at a local level would work adequately in Russia's circumstances only if food and other essential goods could be obtained in sufficient quantities, if its transport and distribution were closely controlled, and if there were not wide variations in fixed prices across different localities. In the journal *Novyi Ekonomist* P. P. Migulin now called for state monopolies to replace market trading for the scarcest commodities. Writing in *Rech'* and *Russkoe Slovo* his sometime Marxist economist colleague Tugan-Baranovskii and Professor M. V. Bernatskii, the future liberal minister of finance in 1917, both concurred. The problem itself remained unresolved. Scarcities and rising prices continued unabated, as did

---

[39] Vse Rossiskii Soiuz Gorodov, *Organizatsiia*, 5.
[40] Vse Rossiskii Soiuz Gorodov, *Trudy*, 13, 31–34; RGIA f. 465, op. 1, d. 12, l. 24.

their effects on widespread anxieties. *Russkoe Slovo* reported that the cost of medicine had risen 1,000 percent since the start of the war. Meat was practically absent from markets in Ekaterinburg, Smolensk, Dvinsk, and Vitebsk. In Samara on January 11 "not a single cartload of grain" had arrived at the city's market. The editors, too, called for an all-out struggle against the "food crisis," fearing an impending "catastrophe."[41] The editors of *Birzhevye Vedomosti* asserted that the cost of living had reached "epidemic levels"; they had lost hope that effective price controls would be initiated anytime soon. In response, Petrograd censors labeled the newspaper part of the "yellow press" and briefly shut it down for publishing "subversive statements."[42]

State Finance as a "Bacchanalia of Corruption"

Since the intense discussions about markets and pricing were directly related to the ways the regime was financing the war, they were soon matched in the Duma by arguments over what many called the crisis of state finance. The tsar was compelled to reconvene the Duma in February 1916 to deal with budgetary issues, the principal prerogative assigned to it by the Fundamental Laws. The sole hope Duma president Rodzianko saw in the appointment of Prime Minister Shturmer was that he might prove more amenable than Goremykin to cooperating with Duma leaders. And indeed, it was soon announced, possibly at the instigation of Rasputin, that for the first time the tsar himself would make an appearance at the Duma, for some at least a hopeful sign.[43]

In the event, Nicholas took the smallest of possible steps toward reconciliation by greeting Duma delegates as "representatives of his people." Immediately afterward he departed for army headquarters. Pares and others who heard his address thought his it was "admirable." The British and French parliaments marked his visit with exaggerated telegrams of congratulation.[44] The delegates themselves were much more restrained across the board. Some allowed that only the tsar's presence inhibited them from hissing at Shturmer. Almost immediately thereafter the sessions erupted into an all-out confrontation between the ministers and the Duma's liberals and moderate socialists.

Shingarev took the lead as chair of the Duma's Budget Committee. In questioning Minister of Finance Bark his interpolation was forceful. In October the Council of Ministers had again used Article 87 to bypass the Duma's budgetary authority by authorizing Bark to sell an additional 5.5 billion rubles' worth

---

[41] *Russkoe Slovo*, Jan. 12, 1916.
[42] *Novyi Ekonomist* 4 (Jan. 23, 1916); *Rech'*, Jan. 12, 1916; *Birzhevye Vedomosti*, Jan. 24, 1916.
[43] Rodzianko, *The Reign of Rasputin*, 163.
[44] Pares, *Fall of the Russian Monarchy*, 308.

of bonds on the French and English markets.[45] Yet before the month was out he had sought and received permission to raise an additional 1 billion from the domestic market. Still more credits authorized in November and December had now brought the treasury's total indebtedness since the start of the war to more than 11 billion rubles, almost all of which, some 9.8 billion rubles, went to support the military. Some 100 million was allocated to the Ministry of Internal Affairs for its extensive police operations.[46] In addition to the outrage felt by Shingarev and others that the Duma's own legal responsibilities in these matters had been bypassed, the division between a largely secret military budget and the remainder of the state's expenditures made it extremely difficult for him and his colleagues to exercise the Duma's constitutional budgetary oversight.[47]

While Bark now accepted that Russia's growing deficit was of real concern, he reported that 1916 would likely see only a relatively modest increase of 370 million rubles. The reaction of many delegates was disbelief.[48] Shingarev accused Bark of a complete lack of transparency (a charge he himself would later receive when he occupied Bark's office in 1917). With a rhetorical flourish, he positioned his Duma colleagues as playing as important a role in Russia's struggle as those who "bore the honor of fighting in the trenches." In contrast to those at the front, however, the Duma was "fighting blindly," without the information needed to make responsible and effective decisions. Bark and his ministry, Shingarev argued, lacked the "confidence of the country that state finances were being used with integrity."[49]

Andrei Ivanovich was right to be alarmed. Ordinary expenditures subject to Duma approval for 1915 were 2.6 billion rubles, according to the accounts of the State Bank, including 516 million to service existing loans; "extraordinary" military and related nonmilitary expenditures were over 9.0 billion.[50] Ordinary revenues would prove to be 2.8 billion, creating an actual deficit of 8.8 billion that was formally covered through domestic and foreign loans and short-term treasury bills.[51] The accepted calculation of Russia's total national debt through

---

[45] RGIA f. 1276, op. 11, d. 195, ll. 39–42.

[46] Ibid., ll. 43–44.

[47] Gosudarstvennaia Duma, *Stenograficheskii Otchet 4th sozyv* (Petrograd, 1916), col. 1790. *Osobennaia Kantseliariia po Kreditnoi Chasti pri Ministerstva Finansov* [RGIA f. 583, op. 3, d. 1134] reports 2.9 billion credit notes in circulation on January 1, 1915, 5.6 billion on January 1, 1916, and 6.8 billion on August 1, 1916. For these same days Russia held the equivalent of 1.5, 1.6, and 1.5 billion in gold, about 11 percent in British and French repositories.

[48] Gosudarstvennaia Duma, *Stenograficheskii Otchet*, cols. 1733–51.

[49] Ibid., cols. 1751–802.

[50] A. L. Siderov, *Finansovoe polozhenie Rossii v gody pervoi mirovoi voiny 1914–1917* (Moscow: Nauka, 1960), 118, citing RGVIA f. 2003, op. 2, d. 9731, ll. 15–24; Alexander Michelson, Pavel Apostol, and Mikhail Bernatskii, *Russian Public Finance during the War* (New Haven, CT: Yale University Press, 1928), 125, 129.

[51] Michelson, *Russian Public Finance*, 124. This total included 2.9 billion from domestic loans, 2.0 billion from foreign loans, and 3.2 billion from short-term treasury bills.

1915, meanwhile, showed a rise from 8.8 billion rubles before the war to 18.8 billion.[52] In 1916 it was certain to grow much larger. Yet among other problems, as Shingarev noted, the costs of servicing this debt were not adequately calculated in the government's past and current estimates. If one did so, both the short- and longer-term dangers to Russia's fiscal stability would be clear. On January 1, 1916, there were 5.6 billion ruble notes in circulation, almost double the amount from the previous year. During 1916 the figure would almost double again. Printing money was the only way the government was able to service its foreign and domestic debt. Although Russia was still nominally on the gold standard, as much as 80 percent and possibly even more of the current and deferred costs of the war were being funded by the issuance of paper money and short-term debt rather than by revenues.[53]

What was important here was not simply the specificity of Minister Bark's facts and figures. Where was the government's plan to address the deficit, however large it proved to be? How would this effort be affected by the radical contraction of Russian defense production when the war came to an end? What would be the effect on social well-being of empty benches and closed shops in the favored defense sector, the absorption into the economy of thousands of discharged workers, and the economic and social instability that would almost certainly ensue? Shingarev was no radical. Unlike his party colleague in the Duma, Nikolai Nekrasov, he could hardly even be considered a spokesman of the liberal left. Yet in addressing both the actualities and abstractions of Russian state finance, he channeled the perspective not simply of the left Kadets and Progressists but of the moderate social democrats under increasing pressure by the Bolsheviks in factories and elsewhere. To strong applause, according to Duma transcripts, Shingarev drew a direct line between the visible signs of luxury and war profiteering.[54]

Like the contentious problems of markets and prices, the "deficit question" was not an abstract issue. It engaged the question of state revenues, taxation, and war profits. It directly linked the question of currency emissions and inflation to scarcity, hunger and insecurities over food, and social unrest. Yet like the question of markets and prices, the problem of financing the war also defied obvious solutions. Costs were proving to be immense, far more than even the most knowledgeable people anywhere had predicted. Bark and Shingarev both were now calculating the likely costs of two more years of fighting, something no one thought possible when the war began.

---

[52] Ibid., 125.
[53] Siderov, *Finansovoe polozhenie*, 132–34.
[54] Gosudarstvennaia Duma, *Stenograficheskii Otchet*, col. 1768.

The immediate question, however, was how to continue financing a war that showed no signs of abating and could conceivably bankrupt the state. Would there ever be a realistic possibility that the Russian state could service its debts, much less pay them off? While some new taxes on corporate profits and personal compensation were put into place in late November 1915 by means of Article 87 to ease the "severe strain" on the treasury, the strain had only gotten worse. Bark estimated that by January 1, 1917, the cost of servicing a state debt of more than 28 billion rubles would be annual payments of not less than 1.5 billion. Pensions and other obligations would add 430 million more.[55] Meanwhile, factory owners were complaining in their own language of "extreme need" that they could not survive if their profits were only 7.5 percent.[56] However defensive he was in the Duma debates, Bark was alarmed enough to request the Council of Ministers to appoint a special commission to study the financial and economic problems of the postwar period. He also sent broad plans for imposing new income and war profits taxes to the State Council.[57] Talks on postwar reconstruction and other matters were scheduled for May in Paris. Russia's delegation would include Shingarev and other leading Duma members.[58]

The debate about finances, prices, and revenues also necessarily engaged the "railroad problem," in this instance particularly the issue of deficits in expected railroad revenues. If Shingarev was relentless in his attack on Bark and the Ministry of Finance, so in questioning Transport Minister Alexander Trepov were his left Kadet colleague Nekrasov, the party's expert on railroads, and the liberal Progressist delegate from Perm, Alexander Bublikov, who would serve under Nekrasov in 1917 as vice minister of transport and special commissar for the railroads.

Trepov was an ambitious and combative careerist whom the tsar had unexpectedly appointed to replace S. V. Rukhlov in October. The railroads now seemed to be in shambles. As the Saratov provincial zemstvo assembly had petitioned the regime, its delegates regarded disorder on the lines as the biggest defect in the country's economic and state life, placing Russia "at this most difficult moment in a position of extreme danger."[59] Targets set by the Ministry of Transport in 1915 for the production of freight cars and rails were apparently missed by some 50 percent.[60] Winter weather had aggravated already difficult conditions. Only 51 percent of the grain procured for the army was reportedly transported on the Southeastern line in January 1916. At the moment the Duma

---

[55] RGIA f. 560, op. 26, d. 1309, l. 9.
[56] *Birzhevye Vedomosti*, Jan. 24, 1916.
[57] *Birzhevye Vedomosti*, Jan. 31, 1916; RGIA f. 1276, op. 11, d. 258, ll. 136–39.
[58] RGIA f. 1276, op. 11, d. 258.
[59] *Birzhevye Vedomosti*, Jan. 24, 1916.
[60] Siderov, *Finansovoe polozhenie*, 45.

began debating the problem, the figure fell to 38 percent. As many as thirteen thousand freight wagons were also reported snowbound.[61]

Not surprisingly, Trepov presented the Duma with an optimistic report. Stern measures being taken together with the Ministry of Interior would suppress corruption on the lines. In response, Bublikov, Nikolai Chkheidze, Groman, Kuz'ma Gvozdev, and others speaking for democratic socialists lashed out at what they regarded as the unfair condemnation by the regime of the million-strong "family of railroad workers" whose sacrifices in support of the war were being slandered by those who saw them only as corrupt colluders in bribery and malfeasance in everyday railroad operations. The regime seemed to have no clear idea what was actually occurring on the lines. "The epidemic of bribery," as Bublikov called it, existed well beyond the railroaders themselves. The very context of railroad operations was now making it extremely difficult for railroaders to carry out their tasks. Workers were being fined and imprisoned for lateness entirely beyond their control. They were demoralized not only by the debilitating struggles of everyday life but by the arbitrariness of their *nachalniki*, section administrators who ruled their parts of the line with heavy and self-interested hands. The issue was one of welfare as well as morale. Stability would not be restored by random arrests, fines, or other kinds of repression, but by the direct engagement of social organizations and the courts—only, in other words, if workers themselves felt they were being treated fairly and with dignity. Bublikov's link between welfare and dignity seemed to have particular resonance. Even *Birzhevye Vedomosti* editorialized that the regime's posture toward the nation's railroad workforce was "untenable."[62]

For his part, Nekrasov assailed Trepov for being "completely wrong" both in his optimism about railroad operations and in his confidence in the powers of repression. The future minister of transport in 1917 described a telegram "in his hands" reporting that lines to and from Moscow were restricting freight traffic at that very moment to only a handful of trains.[63] The Ministry of Trade and Industry itself had reported that the decline in capacity was creating havoc among producers, who found themselves competing intensely with each other for scarce raw materials, further fueling speculation. The routine collection of railroad tariffs was in shambles as well.[64]

With all of this, it is hard to see in retrospect how by February 1916 even a dramatic increase through higher railroad tariffs and new taxes on the 3.1

---

[61] RGIA f. 457, op. 1, d. 65, l. 20; f. 32, op. 1, d. 721, ll. 25 [*Zhurnaly rasporiaditel'nago komiteta po zheleznodorozhnym perevozkam*].
[62] *Birzhevye Vedomosti*, Mar. 22, 23, 1916.
[63] Gosudarstvennaia Duma, *Stenograficheskii Otchet*, col. 3713.
[64] RGIA f. 23, op. 15, d. 618, l. 71.

billion rubles in ordinary revenue that had largely balanced the state's total budget before the war could now cover its costs in any significant way, particularly considering the proportion of ordinary revenue that had earlier been produced by stable railroad operations (24.6 percent) and the net loss of 678 million rubles from the state's spirits monopoly (19.8 percent).[65] Even the return of the spirits monopoly would have made barely a dent in the problem. Bark and his ministerial colleagues might have leaned more in the direction of social favoritism by issuing low-cost loans to favored enterprises in 1914 and 1915 than sound fiscal policy required. And although it was not yet part of the public discussion, there was also the problem of the WICs' own discretion to provide credits backed by the state to enterprises working for defense.

The CWIC and the Petrograd regional WIC were particularly active in this regard. Already by October 1915 the seven industrial groups in which the CWIC was divided funded production with some 13 million rubles in loans, sometimes by its own admission without adequate information about the financial capacities of the firms themselves. The same was true with Shakhovskoi's Ministry of Trade and Industry, which began working with the CWIC in the summer of 1915 to provide loans to Petrograd enterprises preparing for evacuation.[66] Meantime the need for new emissions of credit notes steadily increased. Even if Bark and his ministerial colleagues aggressively pursued war profits and new tax and railroad revenues, the treasury would still have had to cover Russia's escalating costs in part by issuing more money and granting more loans, adding to the 5.6 billion rubles in credit notes already in circulation.[67] In the view of *Promyshlennaia Rossiia*, it was not only the railroads but the Russian banks that were linked in a "bacchanalia of corruption," enabled by the regime, syphoning high profits from a failing economy by retailing state loans at significant discounts and marking up other financial transactions under the pretext of scarce money. Its editors demanded the State Council undertake an investigation of the Finance Ministry's complicity.[68]

---

[65] Michelson et al., *Russian Public Finance*, 15–24, 55–72. The total ordinary revenue is listed here as 3,415 million rubles (61).
[66] RGIA, f. 32, op. 1, d. 1994, ll. 1–6, 32ff.; GARF 7327, op. 1, d. 1, l. 4. The loans were issued at 6.5 percent at not more that 75 percent of the assessed value of the enterprise for a term of fifteen years.
[67] RIGA, f. 1278, op. 5, d. 331, ll. 31–34 [Steno. Reports of Duma Budget Commission]; RGIA f. 560, op. 26. d. 30, ll. 117–25 ob. [Reports and Other Materials of the Chancellery of the Ministry of Finance]; RGIA f. 582, op. 5, d. 17, l. 184; f. 583, op. 3, d. 1134, l. 19 [Special Chancellery for Credit of Ministry of Finance].
[68] *Promyshlennaia Rossiia* 5–6 (Mar. 20, 1916): 6–7.

Political Dilemmas

In effect, the Duma debates joined the challenges of scarcity and loss brought on by the war to notions of political competence and transparency, sharpening the already contentious issues of responsible governance and the war's enormous costs. Financial issues were also about providing ordinary Russians and soldiers in the field with adequate supplies of food and other essentials, and hence the question of social stability. How to finance the war was also about the fundamental relationship between autocratic government, social inequality, and collusion between Russia's political and socioeconomic elites—war capitalism—as well as Russia's prospects in its aftermath. Shingarev's attention to the economic crises lying ahead almost certainly raised new anxieties, even assuming Germany's defeat. Historical memories in 1916 were hardly short term. In the countryside, on the railroads, and within the regime itself, the experiences of the Japanese war and revolutionary aftermath could not help but loom large, and in quite antagonistic ways. Among many democratic socialists, liberals, and members of the intelligentsia during the French revolution, 1789 also had varying degrees of resonance, corresponding to competitive historical imaginations. Not surprisingly, the verbal jousting by Duma members in their Tauride Palace chambers was widely reported in the press.

Social anxieties were increasingly evident. The opening of the Duma session precipitated a new wave of petitions from the provinces describing deficits in a range of goods and pleading for relief.[69] In the view of historian Olga Porshneva, it is impossible to exaggerate the level of conscious protest in the countryside at this time against the heavy effects of the war.[70] In the midst of the acrimonious Duma debates, two large markets and several stores in Baku were destroyed during protests over the cost of food. Restoring order required the deployment of two regiments of Cossacks. The disturbances predicted by Minister of Interior Khvostov in December were also occurring elsewhere. By the Ministry's count there were some three hundred crimes a day related to the shortages of food. In Orenburg, soldiers refused to fire into a group of protesting soldiers' wives.[71]

Agitation among industrial workers was also increasing. Especially in areas with the highest concentration of skilled industrial workers, like the Vyborg district of Petrograd, the imperial and capitalist explanations for the war pressed by Lenin and other radical social democrats seemed to be taking hold. Despite

---

[69] RGIA f. 1278, op. 5, d. 1193 and 1994.
[70] O. S. Porshneva, *Mentalitet i sotsial'noe povedenie rabochikh, krest'ian i soldat Rossii v period pervoi mirovoi voiny (1914-mart 1918)* (Ekaterinburg, 2000), 464. See also Nicos Poulantzas, "Sotsial'noe povedenie soldat russkoi armii v gody pervoi mirovoi voiny," *Sotsial'naia istoriia: Ezhegodnik* (2001–2): 355–98.
[71] RGIA f. 1276, op. 11, d. 167, ll. 143–44.

severe censorship, the popular penny press *Malenkaia Gazeta* (*Little Gazette*) and *Kopeika* (*Kopeck*) were increasingly popular, now selling as many as fifty thousand copies a day. Avoiding censorship by submitting for review only pieces on the war, the editors of *Malenkaia Gazeta* increasingly defended workers' interests, portraying workers as being exploited by "oppressive factory bosses" who were also the newspaper's "enemies." When the paper was shut down in April, the *Novaia Malenkaia Gazeta* (*New Little Gazette*) immediately appeared in its stead.[72] Perhaps partly under its influence, workers seemed to believe that the threat of sending whole shops to the front was more easily made than carried out, given its effect on defense production. Some four thousand workers at the Nikolaev defense plant were obviously undeterred when they struck for wage increases that the government said would require two years of the firm's annual profits to meet and might result in the strikers being sent to the front.[73] At the state's important weapons complex in Tula, angry workers demanded a 75 percent increase in wages, the firing of several plant managers, and improvements in working conditions. A brief illegal strike brought a promise from the regional governor to allow an elected committee of workers to present their demands to members of the factory's governing board, who were called in from Petrograd. Work again stopped briefly, this time accompanied by antiwar slogans.[74]

In Petrograd, workers at the massive Putilov works began pressing similar demands. In early February a strike broke out so quickly that the factory administration had no time even to consider concessions. Instead, retired general Meller, the factory director, sought and received approval from the Ministry of War to post a notice threatening full militarization of the plant and the immediate dispatch into the army of striking workers exempt from the draft. A number of "agitators" were seized, but tensions built even further when a contingent of German POWS arrived to replace them on February 9, the very day the Duma reconvened.[75] Shortly afterward, after months of hesitation and at the strong urging of the plant's owners, the regime formally sequestered the giant plant in order to enforce order and ensure production continued without interruption. Although Finance Minister Bark himself warned against moving further down the "slippery slope" of full state control, Shturmer assumed that worker dissidence, at least, would now be more effectively contained. Less than three weeks later, however, men and women from the Erikson and Lessner plants gathered on Sampsonievskii Prospekt in the Vyborg district and sang "The Marseillaise." When police seized one of the women, a "young man" from the crowd fired his

---

[72] RGIA f. 777, op. 23, d. 3g pt. 2, ll. 142–44 [Petrograd Komitet po delam pechati, 1916].
[73] RGIA f. 1276, op. 11, d. 167, ll. 159–159 ob.
[74] Ibid., ll. 141–42.
[75] Ibid., ll. 141–44. See also Jonathan Grant, *Big Business in Russia* (Pittsburgh, PA: University of Pittsburgh Press, 1999), ch. 5.

Browning revolver, wounding one of the officers. "That's how to save our girls!" someone shouted out from the crowd, according to the police report.[76]

These events all brought the dilemmas of political tactics to the fore. Moderate and conservative liberals in and outside the Kadet Party and the Duma were still strongly committed to a "revolution from above," but this seemed increasingly out of reach. Miliukov, chair of the Kadet Central Committee, traveled to Moscow in January to attend the Union of Cities conference and contain the more radical impulses of his left-leaning Moscow colleagues like Astrov and Mikhail Chelnokov who were demanding the entire government resign. ("Sparks that could ignite a great conflagration" and "a great threat to social stability" is what the police informant heard Miliukov arguing with his colleagues.)[77] Along with a majority of his party's Central Committee the distinguished historian-politician still believed that the sanction of the tsar himself was necessary to endow a cabinet of responsible and competent ministers with the authority required to govern effectively, and preserve in this way the possibility of Russia's historical evolution toward a full-fledged constitutional monarchy. They had a strong ally in Duma president Rodzianko.

But was the best way to achieve responsible government by collaborating in the Duma with more rightist groups in the Progressive Bloc and pressing collectively for reform? Miliukov was hopeful but cautious. In the event that the regime did not change course, he was ready for the Bloc to mobilize further, especially in the press, to expose the regime's failings. Like others, Miliukov, who would suffer lifelong guilt and grief from losing his son Nikolai in the summer of 1915 after encouraging him to enlist, was outraged that speculation and profiteering seemed practically ubiquitous in Russian commercial circles, especially the banks. He called for the most forceful measures against those found guilty, including military courts-martial for anyone from within Russia's ruling circles.[78]

In some contrast, Astrov, Nekrasov, and many Kadet liberals in provincial cities and towns now pressed even more forcefully for tactical alliances with liberal social democrats. They were not opposed to pressuring the tsar through the Progressive Bloc, but they were wary of cooperating too closely with more conservative figures and social groups who were likely to cost them broader support even among the country's intelligentsia, their natural constituency, not to mention the vast majority of workers and peasants.[79] Mensheviks and other democratic socialists were themselves under increasing pressure by Bolsheviks and Menshevik Internationalists to oppose the "imperial war" and resist

---

[76] RGIA f. 1282, op. 1, d. 737, ll. 4–5.
[77] B. B. Grave, *Burzhuaziia nakanune fevral'skoi revoliutsii* (Moscow, 1927), 88–90.
[78] Ibid., 88–90. Melissa Stockdale, *Paul Miliukov and the Quest for a Liberal Russia, 1880–1918* (Ithaca, NY: Cornell University Press, 1996), ch. 8; *Rech'*, July 25, 1915.
[79] Grave, *Burzhuaziia*, 82–83.

compromising in any way with Russia's "bourgeoisie." Chkheidze's Menshevik Duma faction may have been more open to a tactical collaboration with liberals in the current circumstances, but the public rift between workers who rejected participation in the WICs and those who supported it complicated their position. Chkheidze himself was quoted in *Promyshlennaia Rossii* as saying that Russia could now be saved from collapse only if the people themselves "take its fate into their hands."[80] To broaden the Progressive Bloc's public support, they wanted rightists excluded from its coalition. Some left liberals agreed. The tsar had to be pressured by agitational literature and the mobilization of popular resistance through boycotts, political strikes, and organized demonstrations, all of which were illegal.

When 210 delegates gathered for the sixth Kadet Party Congress in the midst of the Duma debates, left Kadets from Moscow and the provinces pressed the party toward more decisive struggle with the regime. Some were scathing in their criticism of Miliukov's moderation. The Central Committee and the Duma fraction "were on one side, the country on the other." The party leadership was not "feeling the pain" that ordinary people were experiencing, and that was evident to delegates from the provinces. The leaders were cut off from the party's rank and file as well. Even participation in the special councils was a tactical error, as Miliukov was reminded he had argued himself the previous July, since the Duma members were a small minority and their subordinate position weakened the integrity of the Duma itself.[81] Indeed, in the view of one police informant assigned to the congress, Nekrasov and others were already working behind the scenes to organize all-Russian unions for both workers and peasants, an important element in the democratic socialists' political agenda.[82]

Miliukov himself, still the chair of the Kadet Central Committee, now believed that the entire mood of the country had changed in the short time since he attended the Union of Cities conference in early January, increasing the inherent dangers of social unrest. Anxieties over actual and anticipated shortages were growing even faster than rising prices. So was what many felt was a palpable sense of popular anger in Petrograd and other industrial centers, evidenced by the mid-February protests. What this meant to the Kadet leader, however, was not that liberals should help accelerate this unrest but that they needed urgently to find some way to bring reason to the regime. No doubt in part because Shingarev stood with him, Miliukov managed to secure the majority's support. The demand for a government of "responsible" ministers was not simply a "great social struggle over words," as if "responsible was some sort of talisman," he told

---

[80] *Promyshlennaia Rossiia* 3–4 (Feb. 14, 1916).
[81] *S"ezdy i Konferentsii Konstitutsionno-Demokraticheskoi Partii*, 3 vols. (Moscow: Rosspen, 2000), 3 (pt. 1): 264, 278, 286.
[82] Grave, *Burzhuaziia*, 73, 97–98.

them. It was a rational and tactical accommodation to current political realities and the potential of the special councils. "You say 'Leave [the councils]!' But where will we go? To our own offices? To the streets? We Russians too easily retreat to the sidelines. You say that if you leave, you will not bear responsibility for what happens next. No, you will bear it whether you stay or leave. It is just not possible to refuse to work actively in the cause of defense. To leave in these circumstances would be a mistake, a crime against the army and the country!"[83]

For their part, democratic socialists faced similar dilemmas. Historical determinists like the Menshevik Duma leader Chkheidze, the head of the WIC Workers Group Gvozdev, and the members of the Menshevik Duma faction also understood that the increasing wave of protests could precipitate a massive popular uprising that lacked constructive socialist leadership and might bring massive repression. Thoughtful and knowledgeable political agency was more important than ever to steer Russia through revolutionary changes onto the longer-term path of socialist historical progress. The keys to stable and effective agency were the trade unions, whose strengthening and complete legalization were now imperative. The incompetence of the regime was not a reflection of its administrative failures alone. It reflected the absence in state administration of representatives of Russia's vital social forces, including especially its workers. The question of political tactics was thus as much an issue for Menshevik and other social democratic activists as it was for the liberals when the second Congress of the WICs convened in Petrograd at the end of February, on the very day the regime sequestered the Putilov works and fully militarized its workforce. For democratic socialists, the question was not whether they should collaborate with liberals but to what degree in and in what ways.

As we have seen, the very question of "collaborating with the bourgeoisie" in the WICs had already become extremely contentious among factory workers themselves in the fall, and consequently between moderate and more radical socialists. The workers' representatives who joined the CWIC in December after their more radical comrades refused had constituted themselves as an autonomous group within the organization, not bound by the decisions of its leadership. Gvozdev, the skilled metal worker, party organizer, and Menshevik leader of the ten-person CWIC Workers Group, was publicly excoriated as a traitor to the cause by the Bolsheviks' Petrograd committee. One police informant reported that workers at several Petrograd plants threatened to carry him and other "accommodators" off their grounds in wheelbarrows.[84]

---

[83] *S"ezdy i Konferentsii Konstitutionno-Demokraticheskoi Partii*, 3 (pt. 1): 264, 278.
[84] Iu. I. Koroblev, ed., *Rabochee dvizhenie v Petrograde, 1912–1917 gg.: Dokumenty i materialy* (Leningrad: Lenizdat, 1958), 362.

As Lewis Siegelbaum has detailed, the dilemma of the WIC Workers Group was between the struggle to gain support from their radical constituents by backing illegal strikes and protests, risking their effectiveness in the WICs, or refusing to do so and thus appearing to subordinate themselves to the interests of "capital."[85] The accommodation was that the WICs would support the convening of an All-Russian Workers Congress, something the Workers Group and Gvozdev had urged in December, and endorse "the organization of Russia's working class politically, socially, and professionally" as a fundamental principle.[86]

Gvozdev's group was only a small minority at the congress, but his arguments fit well with the views of both social democrat and liberal delegates, including the progressive industrialists Alexander Konovalov, Peter Riabushinksii, and Mikhail Tereshchenko, who still held sway in the CWIC.

Reflecting this range of views, delegates worked their way toward two quite different but complementary resolutions: one strongly supported the further organization of Russia's workforce through representative trade unions capable of harnessing constructively the power immanent in collective action; one strongly favored a ministry chosen by and politically responsible to the Duma, rejecting the position of the Progressive Bloc, which sought an appointed ministry of confidence. On these foundations the WIC Congress essentially laid out a clear and rational program for addressing the pressing socioeconomic and political problems at hand. They condemned multiple authorities (*dvoevlastie* and *mnogovlastie*) on the railroads and the "hopeless" attempt to concentrate all efforts to regulate the country's lines from Petrograd. They accepted Gvozdev's passionate appeals to address the scarcities and anxieties associated with the rising cost of living, resolving that the "only correct way out" of the crisis was through a powerful (*moshchnyi*) social organization capable of coordinating all aspects of providing for the army and the civilian population.

Most important, the congress spelled out how Russia's workers needed to be organized "politically, socially, and professionally." All administrative restrictions on the free organization of professional organizations (trade unions) had to be lifted immediately. So did those constraining rural and urban cooperatives and their unions. In addition, to ensure the labor needs of various industries and enterprises were met effectively, a network of city and rural labor exchanges had to be set up with equal representation from owners and workers. These would not be partisan institutions but places where the competition among and between plant owners and managers could be judiciously met. In the case of conflicts between workers and management over hiring matters they would maintain

---

[85] Lewis Siegelbaum, "The Workers' Groups and the War-Industries Committees: Who Used Whom," *Russian Review* 39, no. 2 (Apr. 1980): 160.

[86] *Trudy vtorogo s'ezda predstavitelei voenno-promyshlennykh komitetov 26–29 fev. 1916 g.* (Petrograd, 1916), 30–31.

"complete neutrality" and temporarily suspend their activities until the conflicts were resolved.[87] Perhaps most indicative of their understanding of the subjective as well as material aspects of Russia's deepening social unrest, the delegates also passed a strong resolution on workplace conditions that stressed first and foremost the necessity of upholding the *dignity* of workers as well as guaranteeing adequate wages that corresponded to actual conditions.

As it concluded its deliberations, the Second WIC Congress also passed a comprehensive resolution on the issue of mediating worker-management conflict, perhaps its most significant initiative to address questions of social and political stability, industrial productivity, workplace conditions, and workers' rights. Aware of the efforts Germany, France, and England were making to contain social conflict, Konovalov himself was determined to elevate labor-management relations everywhere in Russia to "European" levels. Both he and Shingarev pressed for central and local mediation boards (*primiritel'nye kamery*) not only in industrial centers but throughout the country, and for invigorating the activities of arbitration courts whose task was to adjudicate disputes that could not be worked out privately, that is, in the civil sphere.[88] The WIC delegates agreed. Their resolution demanded mediation boards organized on the basis of equal representation of workers and owners for all industrial sectors and locations.

Playing prominent roles in all of this at the WIC gathering were six men who exactly one year hence would assume leading roles in the Provisional Government: the honorary and formal congress chairs A. I. Guchkov (soon to be minister of defense) and A. I. Konovalov (minister of trade and industry); vice chairs Prince G. E. L'vov (prime minister), M. I. Tereshchenko (who would succeed Miliukov as foreign minister in the first coalition), S. N. Tretiakov (chair of its new Economic Council); and Bureau Member A. A. Bublikov (vice minister of transport). The future minister of transport Nekrasov also participated in the sessions, along with some of Russia's most prominent industrialists, including N. F. von Ditmar, Z. L. Nobel, and P. I. Pal'chinskii. Playing an important role in private discussions as well was P. P. Riabushinksii, who, according to the police, thought the regime wanted to provoke an uprising in order to crush Russia's political opposition.[89] Albeit in varying degrees, each of these scions of industry recognized the necessity of integrating organized labor into a coordinated effort to increase production and help address the critical socioeconomic problems at hand. In a similar way, they recognized that the organization of Russian workers

---

[87] Ibid., 630; Tsentral'nyi Voenno-Promyshlennyi Komitet, *Ob ucherezdenie primiritel'nykh kamerov* (Petrograd, 1916).
[88] RGIA f. 1090, op. 1, del. 91, ll. 6–7; Irakli Tsereteli, *Vospominaniia o fevral'skoi revoliutsii* (Paris, 1963), 1, 439; Heather Hogan, "Conciliation Boards in Revolutionary Petrograd: Aspects of the Crisis of Labor-Management Relations in Russia," *Russian History* 1 (1982), 49–66.
[89] Grave, *Burzhuaziia*, 14

was also necessary for effective and controlled political change, and that the key to addressing social conflict was effective mediation by representative boards supported and endorsed by the state.[90] Each would continue to play a role in these matters in 1917.

As a letter from the congress to the Duma put it on February 27, it was clear to every educated Russian their country was "hanging by a thread," that the moment was "extremely tense," and that further inattention to the needs of the people and the sacrifice of their sons would lead to the country's destruction. Yet even before the congress adjourned, the tsar publicly disparaged its efforts.[91] As a consequence, according to *Birzhevye Vedomosti*, delegates left the sessions angry and disappointed, thinking they were "spitting in the wind."[92]

Scarcity, Railroads, and the Labor Question: Militarization as Solution

One can appreciate their frustration. Prime Minister Shturmer and the Council of Ministers were already moving in quite different directions, taking steps to address scarcity by gathering more information about conditions in the countryside, increasing state financial support for industry, and tightening the state's grip on the railroads. A top priority was the militarization of industrial production and the introduction of forced labor in parts of the countryside and within the large military zone to help the army. Toward these ends Shturmer also extended his own power. He secured Khvostov's dismissal as minister of interior and assumed the post himself, becoming in addition to prime minister the country's chief policeman. In August he also took on the post of foreign minister.[93]

Scarcities in essential goods underlay all of these moves, as did a lack of comprehensive information about their distribution and extent. In April Shturmer charged a special group of ministers to ensure localities had sufficient food and fuel, but not surprisingly, the group was immediately saturated with appeals for assistance. Local officials in Kharkov insisted, for example, that the whole Donets region be exempt from requisitions of food and horses. They also wanted to bar any requisitioned foodstuffs from being shipped out of their region. Other localities complained that virtually all meat had been taken by the army, so ensuring "sufficient" food was impossible. Serious deficits were reported in available fuel for civilian use as well as skilled workers in the mines.[94]

---

[90] *Promyshlennaia Rossiia* 5–6 (Mar. 10, 2016).
[91] RGIA f. 1276, op. 5, d. 1194, l. 37.
[92] *Birzhevye Vedomosti*, Mar. 1, 1916.
[93] Draft minutes, *Osobyi Zhurnal Soviet Ministrov 3 i 6 Maia 1916*, in RGIA f. 1276, op. 12, d. 1802, not included in published volume.
[94] RGIA f. 457, op. 1, d. 65, ll. 88–124.

Already in the fall the Special Council on Food had worked up a detailed census form (*anketa*). The Ministry of Agriculture itself now undertook to extend this inquiry throughout Russia using provincial zemstvo organizations and local state authorities. The hope was not only to gain a comprehensive picture of actual conditions but to accumulate data that would allow rational implementation of fixed prices or perhaps even the formation of a state monopoly in the sales of scarce products like sugar, as some were advocating in the journal *Novyi Ekonomist*.[95]

The census had eleven specific questions. Answers were to be repeated periodically and resubmitted to the Special Council. Questions ranged from the number of inhabitants (including wounded soldiers, POWs, and displaced refugees) to the distances to railroad stations and the average quantity of each of twenty kinds of foodstuffs needed each month as well as their current prices. The forms also asked for information about a town's financial resources for purchasing goods, and whether it was desirable to organize or continue the town's own food-purchasing program. Many of the towns surveyed had fewer than seven thousand inhabitants.[96]

Even assuming the accuracy of the information tens of thousands of towns and villages were instructed to provide, one can only admire in retrospect the ambitious administrative burden Shturmer was placing on the special council and the ministries—tasks that were to be repeated each month and somehow deployed to address the challenges of supply and distribution. By the time this information was digested, local conditions were also likely to have changed, especially in the supply of food. The census form itself thus signified the magnitude of the problem more than its possible solution.

Shturmer's intervention in the area of state finance was equally problematic. Accurate data here was difficult to come by, as Shingarev and others had complained, but neither Shturmer nor the Special Council for Defense seemed particularly interested in looking closely at projected revenues and actual costs or address the deficit in any systematic way. The Council of Ministers itself continued to hand out specific sums to favored petitioners, bypassing or duplicating the work of the WICs. In March, the Finance Ministry floated a new 2 billion ruble bond issue at 5.5 percent. From all indications, new credits exceeding this amount were already disbursed by June. By July the total amount of rubles issued as notes of credit in circulation was over 6 billion. According to a later analysis, no part of the war expenditure was being met by taxation.[97]

---

[95] Ibid., d. 12, ll. 392–94; *Novyi Ekonomist* 18 (Apr. 30, 1916).
[96] RGIA f. 457, op. 1, d. 868, ll. 1–12.
[97] RGIA f. 583, op. 5, d. 17, l. 184; op. 3, d. 1134, ll. 19–20; Michelson et al., *Russian Public Finance*, 326.

Early in May Finance Minister Bark sent an urgent note to Minister of War Shuvaev urging economies in military spending. While it was impossible to continue the war "without very large and uninterrupted expenditures," he wrote, "the possibility of receiving new funding in the necessary amounts was becoming more and more difficult." Bark also suggested creating a new Special Accounting Commission (Rastsenochnyi Komitet) under the Ministry of War to act as a central purchaser (*krupneishii zakazchik*), given the urgency of funding the war as fully as possible. He gave the example of orders for the same equipment being given to three different factories at three different prices, ranging from 793,000 to 1,395,000 rubles. Inflation, meanwhile, was making the procurement of urgently needed goods even more costly. The new Accounting Commission was to be made up of representatives from the War Ministry and specialists invited from Russia's leading institutes and universities.[98]

Rather than exercise restraint, however, Shturmer and the Special Council for Defense continued to dole out credits to the CWIC, the Zemstvo and City Unions, and directly to individual enterprises and government departments without in many cases fully understanding the issues involved. In May these organizations received some 29 million rubles to distribute as credits as they thought best, plus 213,000 dollars to buy automobiles and parts from Studebaker in the United States. Two million rubles in additional funding went directly to the Kolomenskoe Locomotive and Car Shops, 30 million to the Special Committee on Metallurgy Production, and 143 million to the Main Military-Technical Administration, primarily, it turned out, for automobiles. After the special council approved 10 million rubles for the construction of an aluminum plant at a meeting on June 8, the director of the State Treasury appended a strongly worded dissent to the minutes. He castigated the council for making this expenditure without knowing whether one large or several geographically scattered smaller factories would be more productive, without resolving the question of whether bauxite or some form of clay would be used in its production, or even whether there would be a need when the construction was completed sometime in the spring of 1917. Equipment for this factory would also have to purchased abroad at a cost of more than 3 million rubles.[99] The case was thus a poster child for what *Promyshlennaia Rossiia* had described as a "bacchanalia" of profits and collusion.

Given their key roles in distributing goods, railroads were another of Shturmer's targets, one that, for the moment at least, seemed a better way to address scarcities than at the point of production itself, especially in the countryside. On a recent visit to the Northern Front, Duma president Rodzianko reported to the Special Council for Defense, he had discovered that there was

---

[98] RGIA f. 1276, op. 12, d. 1800, ll. 71–77.
[99] *ZOSO*, May 11, 18, 25, 1916; June 1, 8, 15, 1916.

absolutely no meat available for the troops. According to his friend and special council colleague from Ekaterinoslav, V. I. Karpov, only about one-third of the raw materials needed for consistent production was being provided to factories working for defense. Some 240 enterprises in Petrograd that relied on the railroads for raw materials received only 5.1 million out of the 11.1 million tons they needed for March and only 5.3 million for April.[100]

Shturmer and Minister of Transport Trepov saw a solution to these problems in expanding the responsibility of the state's Railroad Management Committee over the allocation of equipment. The Committee was now hearing regularly and in detail from different state institutions and individual enterprises about their specific needs: the shortage of cotton in the Moscow and Petrograd regions (requiring twenty-six hundred freight cars a month); an urgent communication from Perm province, where twelve grain mills had shut down and fifty-eight hundred cars had not been loaded; a demand from Petrograd for additional shipments of iron; a petition from the Kolomenskoe locomotive works for seventy-five cars of iron ingots. By March the Committee was receiving as many as forty different petitions a day. Additional demands were coming directly from the army.[101] In the Don region, coal shortages seemed to be less a question of available equipment than the failure to get it to the mine heads. For April, the Committee set specific norms for freight car loadings throughout the country as a whole.[102]

The Committee also gathered detailed information on the ways individual lines were performing. Large backlogs in shipments and traffic bottlenecks on the Trans-Siberian continued to be a major problem. Vladivostok itself was overflowing with goods waiting to be shipped. Neither the War Ministry nor the Ministry of Agriculture would tolerate any reduction in its daily allocation of equipment. The Committee wrestled with this problem for most of May, bombarded with requests from all over the country. (One such request, rejected by the Committee, came from the head of construction work in the Murmansk district asking for ten mainline [*marshrutnyi*] trains to transport Chinese workers from the Russian Far East so that the work could be quickly completed.) In response to some requests the Committee granted local authorities the power to control how freight cars were deployed within their jurisdiction. Others were given explicit and detailed orders at junctions across the country. Pressed by Shturmer, by June the Committee was meeting every two days, sometimes issuing orders about the distribution of as few as ten to twenty cars per day, sometimes dealing with thousands. Still, there was no assurance that the Committee's

---

[100] *ZOSO* 66 (Apr. 27, 1916): 244; 67 (Apr. 30, 1916): 252; RGIA f. 290, bk. 2: 130–35 ob.
[101] RGIA f. 290, bk. 1: 32, 42, 44, 49, and passim.
[102] Ibid., bk. 1: 106–7; bk. 2: 7 and passim.

directives could or would be followed. In any event they were often at odds with the decisions local authorities were still empowered to make.[103]

In these circumstances Shturmer and some members of the Special Council on Defense turned again to the question of militarizing the lines, including seven major private railroads as well as all of the state's own. The idea was not a new one. Steps had been taken in 1908 to improve discipline on the lines in this way. When Rukhlov became minister of transport in 1909 he opposed abridging the railroads' private ownership in part because it would likely have created more resistance than discipline. With the start of the war, railroaders near the front lines were given military-type uniforms to enhance their authority. Some close to the battle zone were armed. But while trains sometimes came under enemy fire, railroaders were not subject to military regimens and discipline, as militarized workers would be.[104]

Despite broad support within the special council and the Council of Ministers for militarizing the railroads, Shturmer hesitated to impose this unilaterally using Article 87, the constitutional provision that empowered the government to act on its own when the Duma was out of session, lest it precipitate another outburst of resistance. His focus in any case was now on further militarizing the Russian workforce as a whole. March witnessed a significant escalation of strikes in plants working for defense, twenty-eight in Petrograd itself involving more than forty-four thousand workers.[105] The desirability of "obligatory labor" (*trudovaia povinnost'*) was already being publicly discussed in popular journals like *Niva* as an unavoidable (and patriotic) way of overcoming scarcities, adding its voice to that of prominent industrialists like Putilov, who supported his plant's sequestration and favored the idea as an inexpensive way of increasing output.

Almost immediately after the Second WIC Congress, Prime Minister Shturmer brought together the Council of Ministers to authorize the wholesale recruitment of "yellow workers" from China, Korea, and the Russian Far East to strengthen Russia's rural and industrial workforce, especially in the mines. They would labor under the most stringent of conditions. Wages would be preset, could be altered by their employers, and were not subject to negotiation. "Yellow workers" would have no right to change jobs or return home. Shturmer also expanded the use of Austrian and German prisoners of war, who, as in the case of Putilov, were now deployed well beyond agricultural labor to some of the most important industrial plants around the country. By the end of March 1916, the total number of working prisoners had risen to more than 600,000. Shturmer's primary motivation now, however, was to address even more forcefully the

---

[103] Ibid., bk. 1: 106–7; bk. 2: 51, 62, 290.
[104] The question is the focus of an unpublished paper by A. J. Heywood, "The Militarization of Civilians in Russia's First World War."
[105] RGIA f. 23, op. 16, d. 210, l. 64 [factory inspector reports].

problem of labor shortages by repressing labor unrest, matters that were among his highest priorities.[106]

Here Shturmer was also being pressured by the army's High Command. Through early May almost half of Russia's 24 million able-bodied men had been drafted into the army. An army report characterized them as the "most capable" of the country's male workforce. The High Command now wanted a million additional workers drafted as compulsory laborers, presenting their mobilization as absolutely essential to successfully prosecuting the war. General Alekseev, who would command the army in 1917, was the only one whose objections were recorded. His concerns, however, were not primarily humanitarian. He wanted instead to use POWs and draft refugees who would not affect local economies and whose lower wages would reduce the drain on the treasury.[107]

The Council of Ministers took up the issue in secret sessions on May 3 and 6, its proceedings excluded from the published record. As Shturmer presented the question, military necessity had to override any economic or social dislocations. It was also possible that militarized worker detachments (*druzhinyi*) could be drawn from "peoples and tribes" not subject to military service, like the large Muslim populations of Central Asia and Crimea and religious sects like the Mennonites. The Council of Ministers agreed that the formation of such detachments was necessary, but also agreed with Alekseev that the first priority should be to form them from the approximately 1.3 refugees who were themselves a burden to the economy. As many as 700,000 refugees might also be drafted for field work. On May 7 a secret communication from the War Ministry to the administrative office of the Council of Ministers went even further, suggesting in addition to refugees *stariki* (the elderly) over forty-three and youth under nineteen be drafted as well.[108] Shturmer objected only that the numbers were guesswork, and called for an immediate census to determine how many refugees were actually able-bodied.[109]

Meanwhile the Special Council for Defense also took up the question. By now the council seated as many as fifty men, including representatives from the State Council and State Duma, the Ministries of War, Navy, Trade and Industry, Finance, and Transport, as well as the Zemstvo and Town Unions, and the CWIC. In mid-May a commission that had been reviewing militarization now presented that as the most effective method to struggle against increasing worker unrest. As we have seen, the question had been on the agenda of the Council of the Congresses of Trade Industrialists (Soviet S"ezdov) as early as the spring of 1915. Prominent public figures like Peter Struve publicly expressed support

---

[106] RGIA f. 1276, op. 12, d. 225, l. 248.
[107] RGVIA f. 2005, op. 1, d. 53, ll. 1, 2–6.
[108] RGIA f. 1276, op. 12, d. 1802, ll. 25–27, 89–95.
[109] Ibid., ll. 5ff.

in principle in the journal *Promyshlennost' i Torgovlia*, as had others. Concern about further aggravating labor unrest, however, now made many more cautious. Leading figures in the Ministry of Trade and Industry were opposed, and Goremykin's regime did not move forward with any comprehensive plan.

The special council's commission proposed instead that all defense plants without exception be placed on a military footing (*voennoe polozhenie*). Workers eligible for the draft would be registered as fulfilling their service at work; those not eligible would be subjected to military law. The commission also proposed that the chair of the special council, that is, the minister of war, be given the responsibility for directly regulating wages. "Severe punitive measures" would be imposed for inciting as well as participating in strikes.[110] For its part, the special council ultimately agreed to extend forced labor to seven provinces adjacent to the front and drafted a set of rules to put the program in place. All orders for the formation of compulsory labor battalions were to issue from the army's Main Supply Administration and be carried out with the assistance of local Okhrana, police detachments, and village authorities. Workdays would be ten hours long. Wages would be paid according to local conditions.[111]

With all of this, the contrast between the approaches of democratic liberals and socialists within the public organizations and the Duma to the "worker question" (as it was now being called) could not have been more clear. For State Councilor I. A. Shebeko and other conservatives on the Special Council for Defense, there was no thought of addressing worker grievances, much less involving labor organizations in any effort to improve production or mediate disputes. According to State Councilor Timashev, militarization of plants and the workplace was now "the one means for stemming the threatening increase in strikes." For his fellow State Council member, the industrialist F. N. von Ditmar, strikes and labor unrest were not about economic matters or issues of worker welfare but "political intrigue."[112] Others continued as they had earlier to "doubt the wisdom," as the protocols described it, of initiating militarization through fiat. The representative of the Union of Towns and others joined Duma president Rodzianko in arguing that decrees of this sort would aggravate rather than restrain labor protests. If militarization was to be imposed in any comprehensive way, it had to come after an open debate about it in the Duma along with an appeal to the patriotism of workers and efforts to allow them to restore calm to the factory floor themselves, that is to organize. Rodzianko's arguments proved persuasive. However reluctant some council members might have been, the decision was made to send the

---

[110] *ZOSO* 71 (May 14, 1916): 282.
[111] RGVIA f. 2005, op. 1, d. 53, ll. 137–48, 160–71.
[112] *ZOSO* 71 (May 14, 1916): 282, 285.

matter to the Duma whenever it was next convened rather than impose it unilaterally through the Constitution's Article 87.[113]

"Brusilov's Breakthrough" as Tragic Romance

Throughout the winter and spring of 1916, the subtext of these fraught discussions was the urgency of bringing the war to a victorious conclusion. The Russian High Command remained in close contact with its French and English counterparts about how victory might now be achieved. At an inter-Allied conference in Chantilly, France, in December, there was an agreement in principle to coordinate offensives in 1916, although there were serious differences about where and when.[114] More immediately important was an understanding that if the Germans launched an attack on either front, the side not attacked would launch a counteroffensive. It also seems likely that some in the High Command were eager in any case to go on the offensive again on the Southwestern Front to counter the accusations of incompetence that followed the Great Retreat in 1915.

In fact, the fall of 1915 had seen significant improvements in the army's weaponry, in both numbers and quality, especially of artillery. What still seemed like an endless pool of peasant recruits had restored Russia's armies to their designated levels and provided adequate reserves. There were now some 4 million Russian troops on the German-Austrian front, almost 1.7 million of whom were combat soldiers. Although it was difficult to be certain, the Russian High Command still assumed Russia had a significant numerical superiority over the Austrians and Germans. Under pressure, military censors continued their steady stream of optimistic reports up the chain of command. "The mood of the soldiers cannot be shaken by the hardships of their daily life or their personal misfortunes," offered one report in April. "The unanimous view of the censors for this reporting period ... [is that] the mood is first rate [*pervoskhodnoe*]." Soldiers "thirsting only for the order to attack" were ready to "go boldly on the offensive under the very threat of death [with] complete confidence in the near and final victory over the brutal enemy."[115]

When the German army in France began its massive attack at Verdun in February, the French appealed immediately for Russian assistance.[116] The initial result was the little remembered battle of Naroch Lake, near Dvinsk, a military

[113] Ibid., 286.
[114] V. K. Shatsillo, *Pervaia mirovaia voina, 1914–1918: Fakty, Dokumenty* (Moscow: Olma, 2003), 200–204.
[115] RGVIA f. 2067, op. 1, d. 2933, l. 2.
[116] A. Iu. Pavlov, "Rossiia na mezh-soiuznicheskikh konferentsiiakh v gody pervoi mirovoi voiny," *Voenno-istoricheskii zhurnal* 2 (2010): 25–31.

disaster for Russia that recalled the annihilation of Samsonov's army in the first month of the war. On the northern edge of the vast Pripet marshes, Naroch was thought to be a much safer target in the bitter February cold than it would be later in the spring when the region was largely flooded. The High Command assumed Russia had almost 2 to 1 superiority here in troop numbers. A break in the German lines would isolate the enemy in the Baltic region, forcing their withdrawal. The battle lasted a scant two weeks before Russian headquarters called a halt.[117]

Especially in its losses, but also in the ways it continued to illustrate deprivations imposed on undersupplied troops, Naroch was a preamble to the great "Brusilov offensive" which followed eight weeks later. Like most descriptions of military action, the stories of each are almost entirely told in terms of strategy and tactics, troop deployments, territorial gains and losses, and the resulting shifts in the geography of the front, as they were in the Russian press at the time. Focus has therefore been on the competency of commanders and the relationship between individual battles and the larger setting of the war. The roles and fates of soldiers are measured in aggregate and emotionally cauterizing casualty statistics, not in terms of how the prodigious bleeding of Imperial Russia's army might have weighed on the country's future.

As was the case with the Tannenberg and Masurian Lakes disasters in August and September 1914, recriminations flew in every direction after the offensive's failure. Russian commanders had failed to coordinate the First, Second, and Fifth Armies (like Rennenkampf and Samsonov at Tannenburg and the Masurian Lakes). They had failed to appreciate the difficult terrain and could not deploy their artillery in tactically effective ways. They still harbored outmoded conceptions about the effectiveness of cavalry, especially in winter. Whether or not for these reasons, Russian troops were able to advance only a few kilometers in most places before German heavy guns and dreadful weather conditions forced them to a halt. As in the Galician retreat a year earlier, there was inadequate transport for the wounded, repeating earlier agonies. By all accounts, the evacuation of casualties was a complete fiasco. In the objectivizing language of military accounting, the army (or "Russia," as newspapers usually reported it) suffered some 100,000 casualties in deaths and seriously wounded, although an accurate tally was impossible.[118]

---

[117] David R. Stone, *The Russian Army in the Great War* (Lawrence: University of Kansas Press, 2015), 235–36. For a vivid description of "eager" soldiers and their horrific losses from a commander's viewpoint, see Richard Robbins Jr., *Overtaken by the Night: One Russian's Journey through Peace, War, Revolution, and Terror* (Pittsburgh, PA: University of Pittsburgh Press, 2017), 333–54.

[118] S. G Nelipovich, *"Brusilovskii proryv": Nastuplenie Iugo-Zapadnogo fronta v kampaniiu 1916 goda* (Moscow: Tsikhgauz, 2006), 12.

In Brusilov's own telling of the story, leading Russian generals thought it unlikely that the Germans could be broken. Any further effort would cause immense additional losses without any positive result. It was best now for Russia simply to maintain a strong defensive posture on its Western border, just enough to keep the Germans from shifting troops to France.[119] Brusilov thought these views bordered on treason. French and British troops were already caught at Verdun in what would prove to be the longest and deadliest battle of the war. During an important meeting of the High Command at Mogilev in early April, General Alekseev reported on new plans for a summer offensive to relieve the pressure on France and Britain.

As Brusilov memorably described the meeting, he alone among his fellow officers expressed complete optimism about the possibilities of success, provided only that he take the lead. "I do not know the other fronts," he quoted himself in his memoirs, "so I will say nothing about them; but as for my own front I am persuaded that it not only can but should take the offensive, and that all the chances of success are on our side." Despite a warning from Alekseev that he would receive no additional troops, artillery, or supplies, Brusilov boldly declared he would attack "for the common cause" and "to lighten the work of our brothers in arms by giving them an opportunity of defeating the enemy." At the dinner that followed one senior general apparently confided to Brusilov that he would have done anything himself to avoid having to command the offensive, since "the only possible result will be that you break your neck and it won't bring you any personal gain."[120]

In narrative terms, Brusilov thus emplotted his famous offensive from the first in a romantic narrative of heroic transcendence from the mundane world of caution and the experience of failure. Contemporaries like the British military attaché in Russia General Alfred Knox followed his lead. So did much of Russia's governing elite. The very word "offensive" obscures for English speakers the initial expectations at the time. In Russian, the offensive is more accurately called the Brusilov "breakthrough" (*proryv*), connoting both the difficulty of penetrating enemy defenses and the potential significance of doing so, rather than a massive offensive that would change the course of the war. In contrast to his discouraged fellow commanders, who at best seemed ready to honor commitments to France and Britain by embarking fatalistically on a doomed adventure, Brusilov actually thought he could succeed, perhaps even "singlehandedly" driving Austria if not Germany itself out of the war. He embellished his claim by presenting what he described as a radically new offensive strategy. Instead of massing artillery and troops around a single salient to concentrate firepower and take maximum

---

[119] A. A. Brusilov, *A Soldier's Notebook* (Westport, CT: Greenwood Press, 1970), 204–17.
[120] Ibid.

advantage of superior numbers, he would open a series of narrow breakthroughs across the entire front line. The enemy would be weakened by surprise and lose its ability to transfer troops rapidly to defend a single point of attack. With reluctance the High Command, including the tsar, who apparently said nothing, accepted his proposal.[121]

Brusilov was an able and energetic commander. His success with an underequipped army on the Galician front in the fall of 1914 was one of Russia's genuine successes in the war He was attentive to the needs of his troops and a stickler for planning and precision. Before he launched his attack on May 22 (June 4 in Europe), he and his field commanders carefully drew up maps of the enemy's positions, including detailed drawings of the large defensive bunkers that proved relatively so resistant to artillery but which Brusilov thought could trap large numbers of Austrian troops during a massive Russian assault. In the eyes of Norman Stone, the acclaimed British historian of the Eastern Front, Brusilov and his aides had come up with "new ideas that made for the most brilliant victory of the war."[122] According to a more recent study, the "genius of Brusilov's offensive lay in the concrete details of its implementation" through which the bold general "demonstrated to the world, and more importantly to the Russians themselves, that they were indeed capable of victory."[123] The authoritative Soviet-era history of the war by A. M. Zaionchkovskii, republished in 2002, is more circumspect, as is the full English-language study of the episode by Timothy C. Dowling, but both dwell on Brusilov's impressive success during the first weeks on the offensive and narrate the story from this viewpoint.[124] The only notable exceptions are those of General N. N. Golovin, Brusilov's chief of staff for the Seventh Army and later author of the first comprehensive study of the army during the war, and a contemporary Russian historian-archivist who since 1991 has had unlimited access to the huge files of documents housed in the Russian State Military History Archive.[125]

In its essential outline, the heroic romance begins with the early success of Brusilov's Eighth Army against the Austrians near Lutsk, which clearly benefited from the simultaneous assaults Brusilov ordered elsewhere along the front. Austrian soldiers panicked at Lutsk, blocked in places by their own defenses. As many as fifty thousand surrendered. In the south, a numerically inferior Eleventh Army pushed the Austrians out of Sopanow and Dubno, while General

---

[121] Ibid., 216–17.
[122] Norman Stone, *The Eastern Front 1914–17* (London: Hodder and Stoughton, 1975), 229–31, 235.
[123] Stone, *The Russian Army*, 238, 249.
[124] A. I. Zaionchkovskii, *Pervaia mirovaia voina* (St. Petersburg: Poligon, 2002); Timothy C. Dowling, *The Brusilov Offensive* (Bloomington: Indiana University Press, 2008).
[125] N. N. Golovin, *The Russian Army in the World War* (New Haven, CT: Yale University Press, 1931); Nelipovich, *"Brusilovskii proryv."*

Lechitskii's Ninth Army managed to move their trenches to within thirty or forty yards of the Austrians without apparently raising the alarm. In three weeks Brusilov's troops managed to capture almost 200,000 men, 3,000 officers, and more than 800 artillery and machine guns.[126] The disintegrating Austrian defense stabilized only after Falkenhayn moved large numbers of German troops into the region, as in 1915, and integrated them into Austrian battalions. In Stone's view, "the Austrian army survived, now, by the grace of the Prussian sergeant-major."[127]

While Russian newspapers were cheering success, some strongly suggesting Brusilov was paving the way for German capitulation, the general himself was reported to have ordered a halt after all of Russia's reserves in the region were engaged and supplies again began to run short.[128] By the end of June, after only three weeks of fighting, some artillery batteries apparently had only two days' worth of shells. Brusilov appealed to headquarters for more, but true to his earlier warning General Alekseev ordered him instead to collect discarded Austrian shells from the battlefield.[129] Still, Alekseev was eager for Brusilov to continue on a full offensive. One week later, however, Brusilov was again forced to call a halt when he found himself without adequate food or sufficient reserves. In less than a month his heralded offensive had drained the blood of some 500,000 Russian soldiers, the largest number of the war. According to one count, at least another 500,000 were wounded, taken prisoner, or otherwise deserted the field of battle.[130]

Brusilov's military temperament, which he compared to Napoleon's, saw military success in terms of territory gained or an enemy in retreat. Pressed by Alekseev and after a short hiatus, he therefore prepared a second stage of the offensive, which began on July 15, when "only" 600,000 of the enemy stood against a Russian force 50 percent larger. By this time, however, Field Marshal Hindenburg had succeeded in formally subordinating all Austro-Hungarian troops from the Baltic to Galicia under his own unified command. Again Brusilov was forced to call a halt. His efforts had so far succeeded in preventing Austria from reinforcing its Italian front and Germany from replenishing losses at Verdun. This encouraged the Romanian government to enter the war on Russia's side after almost two years of indecision. By the end of July, however, these efforts had cost Brusilov's armies some 810,000 casualties, those of the

---

[126] Stone, *Eastern Front*, 224, 520, 553–54.
[127] Ibid., 254.
[128] *Ivanovskii Listok*, July 1, 1916.
[129] RGVIA f. 2067, op. 1, d. 5326, l. 30, as published in *Nastuplenie Iugo-Zapadnogo fronta v mae-iiune 1916: Sbornik dokumentov* (Moscow, 1940), 400.
[130] The details are given by Nelipovich, *"Brusilovskii proryv,"* 23ff.

Western and Northern Fronts another 480,000, most likely even more, given the difficulties of keeping track.

Yet even as the breakthrough failed to bring the hoped-for Russian victory, General Brusilov was heralded as a Russian savior. "Thou hast triumphed, Galilean," the *Ivanovskii Listok* proclaimed, "tunneling into the hearts of Hungary and Galicia!" Lauded too was the "triumphant" Russian army: "[T]he boundless courage of the Russian soldier has become a worldwide truism.... Great and Mighty Rus! So great and mighty that there is no force capable of containing it in all of its might and destiny.... Only poets can express its strength, the unity of Tsar and People."[131]

The Soldiers' Story: "Drowning in Blood"

As Samuel Hynes has argued in *The Soldiers' Tale*, the enthusiastic story has been a central element of military mobilization in every modern conflict.[132] In 1914 and throughout the war in Russia, soldiers and censors both were constantly enjoined to tell the "right" story, one that reflected and reinforced the heroic narrative of stoic and loyal subjects "prepared to give their lives for Tsar and Country, bidding farewell to their relatives not hoping to remain alive," as one censor put it.[133] Throughout the Brusilov offensive, reports from the field strengthened this narrative. The British military observer General Knox continued to romanticize the stoic fortitude of the Russian peasant-soldier. The popular illustrated biweekly *Niva* and other publications wrote enthusiastically about territories gained and enemy soldiers captured. Even recent historians have written that throughout the slaughter the mood of Russian soldiers remained good, echoing the reports of military censors. According to David Stone, the offensive had "an electrifying effect on Russian morale, and judging by Russian intelligence, a devastating effect on the Austrians."[134]

Despite its methodological difficulties, accessing the army's experience from the soldiers' perspective during the Brusilov offensive must still focus on soldiers' letters. In this respect, the nearly 100,000 casualties Russians suffered before the May offensive during the two futile weeks at Lake Naroch were far more prescriptive of what was to come than Brusilov's heroic visions. Even more so was the fact that some 12,000 of these losses were poorly supported soldiers who froze to death from exposure. Even for those who survived, the experience was

---

[131] *Ivanovskii Listok*, Aug. 28, 1916.
[132] Samuel Hynes, *The Soldiers' Tale: Bearing Witness to Modern War* (New York: Lane, 1997).
[133] RGVIA f. 2003, op. 1, d. 1486, l. 126.
[134] David Stone, *The Russian Army in the Great War* (Lawrence: University of Kansas Press, 2015), 248.

a nightmare: "All day it rained, and the next day was bitter cold. Searchlights and shells found our every corner. It was night, but you could find a needle from all the light. We had 850 men in our battalion, and by morning, half had frostbitten figures and toes. 450 left their positions, along with some of the wounded. The Germans were now killing at will. They were laughing. It was a horror."[135]

To tell the story from the trenches one must also go back to everyday life there in early 1916, even before Lake Naroch. By all evidence, January and February were an extremely difficult time at the front, as they had been a year earlier, despite some improvement in equipment and supplies. Soldiers were well aware by now that military censors carefully read their letters home, and they had become adept at using language that expressed the obligatory patriotic sentiments while also communicating more accurate information and emotions. As in 1915, the freezing trenches brought tedium and discomfort, anxiety, and dejection. Clothing was never warm enough, food never good enough; only chores were endless, and unwanted time waiting for what fate might have in store. Sanitation was primitive at best, hygiene virtually nonexistent. Perhaps most easily confused was the way these feelings also found expression in a genuine desire to end the anxious waiting by going on the offensive, especially early in March, after many weeks of relative inaction. For many, the yearning for peace that was clearly a key element in the hopes and commitments to victory also reflected the longing to return safely to their families. At the same time, it understandably fueled anger toward authorities in Petrograd as well as those who were profiting from the war, including many workers. ("At the front we struggle and fight, in the rear instead of helping us they steal and rob.") "Hang the rats!" was not an isolated expression.[136]

Easter week in 1916 also saw a remarkable degree of fraternization, especially with German troops on the relatively quiet Northern Front closest to Petrograd. "If I had not seen it with my own eyes, I would not have believed it," one soldier wrote home. "Forty or so on each side congratulating each other on the holiday. We all asked that there be no shooting. They said that they would give a three-day illustration [of what peace could be like]."[137] "Dear Mama," wrote another, "our soldiers went to the German trenches to visit, and they stuffed us with cognac, sausages, and cigarettes. Then they were also our guests, and during all that time not one person, them or us, fired a shot. Dear Mama, maybe you don't believe what I've written here but it's the real truth and I saw it myself."[138] On the Southwestern Front, "negative" feelings recorded by the military censors reached

---

[135] RGVIA f. 2031, op. 1, d. 1183, ll. 38–39.
[136] RGVIA f. 2067, op. 1, d. 3856, ll. 164ff; f. 2967, op. 1, d. 2933, ll. 27–28; f. 2067, op. 1, d. 2933, ll. 107–8.
[137] RGVIA f. 2031, op. 1, d. 1183, l. 85.
[138] Ibid., l. 176.

the highest point of the war so far. Food was still short ("they feed us like beasts of burden, as if we were horses"), weapons scarce ("we have not a single Russian machine gun, all are Austrian"), demoralization rampant ("we sit in our trenches like animals"), a near traumatized outlook about life itself ("my life is so difficult that it is difficult to describe").[139] A substantial number of letters between mid-April and mid-May called equally for "wiping out the Germans and Jews" as if both were responsible for their suffering. In the process, forecasting perhaps the atrocities to come during the Civil War in 1919, "Jew" became more than an ethnic or religious identity; it reflected all the hatred toward social "others" who were thought to the cause of such awful and extraordinary loss.[140]

According to one report after the offensive had begun to stall, the soldiers' mood was still "so indescribable, so great": "[W]ith such a mood, such a spirit in the army, we will carry the war to a brilliant victory, to a final rout of the Austrians and Germans."[141] "Joy!" another summed up: "Carpathians! Carpathians!"[142] When General Knox told Captain Bazilevich, the chief military censor of Brusilov's Eighth Army, of the soldiers' "enthusiastic patriotism" as described to him by censors at Brusilov's headquarters in Berdichev, Bazilevich laughed and said (in excellent English) that they had either been written by the censors themselves or by some ambitious officers who wanted promotion.[143] More accurate was a letter like the following: "[T]he war is having a profound effect on the psychology and worldview of the troops. Here there are almost none without religion, even former atheists, who have now started to think that if this all has no direct connection to God, then 'what is that particular force which controls the acts of man?'"[144] Certainly accurate were descriptions of the "thirst for peace" reported all along the front and the new offensive as anticipated "with impatience and nervousness."[145] When it finally began, soldiers "bade farewell to their loved ones without hope of remaining alive," once more "prepared to give their lives for Tsar and County."[146]

Very soon thereafter, military censors recorded a dramatic fall in morale. In August 1916, only 8.3 percent of letters could be classified as "cheerful" (*bodryi*).[147] Complaints about officers grew more numerous and stronger. Desertions increased; so did infractions against discipline. During the still fierce fighting in August, there was often nowhere to put the wounded. Troops

---

[139] RGVIA, f. 2067, op. 1, d. 3856, ll. 1–10, 163–64.
[140] RGVIA f. 2031, op. 1, d. 1184, l. 163 ob.
[141] RGVIA f. 2003, op. 1, d. 1486, ll. 155–56, 172.
[142] RGVIA f. 2067, op. 1, d. 3856, ll. 286–87.
[143] Alfred Knox, *With the Russian Army*, 2 vols. (London: Hutchinson, 1921), 2:464.
[144] RGVIA, f. 1067, op. 1, d. 2933, l. 107 ob.–108.
[145] RGVIA f. 2003, op 1. d. 1486, l. 79.
[146] Ibid., l. 126.
[147] RGVIA f. 2031, op. 1, d. 1184, l. 582.

in some places even needed boots. Many broke a familiar soldiers' taboo and openly expressed their fear of dying: "There is intense fighting day and night, and we wait for our death every minute."[148] When the offensive began to stall, soldiers expressed great disappointment that the enemy was still as strong as before. Many read in newspapers that Brusilov now thought Russia would be fortunate if the war ended by August 1917.[149] Still, many military censors stressed the positive, sometimes citing officers who could scarcely suppress their surprise that the army's morale was as good as officers and censors allowed. "How remarkable, really quite a miracle, for one to feel that the mood is so spirited, so militant. Our little soldiers [*soldatiki*] still conscientiously do everything they are ordered to."[150]

In fact, the Brusilov offensive was one of history's deadliest military operations. What was being narrated almost everywhere as a heroic romance was more accurately told as a tragedy. Russia's casualties may have been greater than those of the Germans, British, and French combined at Verdun, whose efforts it was intended to support. With characteristic bravado, Brusilov drove the army to exhaustion and annihilation. Writing an article titled "War and Patriotism" in *Vestnik Evropy*, Russia's leading liberal journal, G. Shtil'man argued that it was now impossible to rally the country since the Russian people (*narod*) needed clear explanations for the sacrifices and losses they were enduring, and there were none. Anxiety was now the principal emotion driving the country forward.[151]

For their part, soldiers themselves seemed desperate to think the enormous sacrifice they had made would soon prove justified. Their families must have thought so too. "Fantastic rumors" of an impending peace were being absorbed "deeper and deeper" into soldiers' thinking, "affecting the psychology of the mass of soldiers in a negative way." "There is great fatigue," one soldier wrote, "and the wish that at the end of it all peace will let us know that more than two years of drowning in blood has not been in vain for such a valiant army as ours."[152]

---

[148] RGVIA f. 2067, op. 1, d. 2935, ll. 407, 501.
[149] RGVIA f. 2003, op. 1, d. 1486.
[150] Ibid., l. 178.
[151] G. Shtil'man, "Voina i patriotism," *Vestnik Evropy* 51 (July 1916): 223–25.
[152] RGVIA f. 2003, op. 1, d. 1486, ll. 190, 222.

6
Scripting Revolution

For most of June and early July, the Brusilov breakthrough occupied the front pages of newspapers throughout Russia. Daily dispatches from army headquarters appeared in bold print or specially designated boxes. Enthusiasm for the offensive was widely reported as if the press had its hands on the national pulse. In the vital concentration of arsenals and defense plants at Tula, where defense workers in late January and February had gone on strike over scarcities and rising prices shouting antiwar slogans, the *Tul'skie Novosti* (*Tula News*) exulted that the news was "stirring all of Russia." Readers were "thirsting to know more about our brilliant new victories." A special statement from the tsar promised "the enemy will be driven from our borders." The great battle would "define Russia's fate."[1] In Ivanovo, the regional newspaper insisted that the demand for "bread and peace" in Germany would soon overcome "Deutschland Über Alles." German peace proposals were reported to have already been sent to U.S. president Woodrow Wilson.[2] "Millions of people are literally starving" in Germany and Austria, according to the leading Voronezh newspaper. Victory was clearly in sight. There were no reports of Russian casualties.[3]

It is hard to measure the disappointment when the offensive began to stall. For many it must have been severe. By the middle of July the war news was no longer on the front page. Optimism and a false sense of impending victory soon gave way in the press to renewed concerns about rising prices and the shortage of workers. On July 13 the army announced that the call-up scheduled for mid-July would be postponed for a month to provide additional manpower for the harvest. By the end of the summer accounts of the fighting had shifted from the discouraging struggle on the Romanian Front, where the frayed troops of Russia's new ally were increasing rather than alleviating Russia's burdens, to more encouraging reports of fighting in France. At the end of September *Tul'skie Novosti* published a plaintive letter from the front assuring readers that troops had not lost faith in ultimate victory. Meanwhile, the fight against scarcities and the intensifying cost of living now had to be Russia's "highest priority."[4]

---

[1] *Tul'skie Novosti*, May 27, 28, 1916.
[2] *Ivanovskii Listok*, July 7, 1916.
[3] *Voronezhskii Den'*, June 2, 1916.
[4] *Tul'skie Novosti*, Sept. 30, 1916; *Ivanovskii Listok*, Sept. 25, 1916.

"Literally Facing Starvation"

The causes of scarcity and inflation were no secret. Vladimir Groman's forceful statement to the Union of Cities conference in January that Russia's commercial mechanisms were broken had found wide resonance. Members of the state's own Financial and Economic Commission worried that Russia's commercial systems were inadequate for sustaining the war and managing the postwar transition.[5] The Petrograd Stock Exchange had been closed largely to curb speculation, but this had only driven trading into unregulated private transactions as a "feverous public interest" developed in selling shares. Between August 1 and December 15 share prices in nine of the fourteen most favored companies working for defense fell, in some cases (Parviainen and Lessner) quite sharply.[6] Adjusting for inflation, the real losses were even greater. According to *Birzhevye Vedomosti* (*Stock Market News*), Russian investors were now in a "panic." The editors thought state officials simply did not understand what was happening.[7] Articles in *Ekonomicheskoe Obozrenie* (*Economic Review*) and *Promyshlennaia Rossiia* (*Industrial Russia*) stressed that the dangers of a prolonged "goods famine" were very real. Like Groman, they argued that distribution, not production, was the key.

By now the fault lines of Russian economic mobilization were fully apparent in the localities as well as the capitals. WICs were managing to increase production in favored defense industries, but unfavored sectors and enterprises continued to languish, starved for resources. The availability of tools and goods wanted by peasants was sharply curtailed. Except for food and fuel, the consignment of goods for civilian markets lacked priority on the railroads, increasingly so as the military's needs became more urgent and railroad operations deteriorated. In these circumstances, it was not only that major marketplaces were still relatively privileged compared to provincial towns despite high prices and shortages, but that many peasants may well have lost an important incentive to produce for the market and sell their crops, as Fedor Cherevanin, a respected and longtime social democrat, wrote in *Ekonomicheskoe Obozrenie* (*Economic Review*).[8] Here was a problem that would define a major task of the Provisional Government in 1917 and structure the entire Bolshevik system of what Lenin termed "war communism" after October.

Official statistics, meanwhile, reflected the difficulty of gathering information and continued to confuse the issue. In November they showed a 14.5 percent

---

[5] RGIA f. 563, op. 2, d. 533, ll. 1–4.
[6] *Birzhevye Vedomosti*, Aug. 1 and Dec. 15, 1916.
[7] *Birzhevye Vedomosti*, Aug. 23, 1916.
[8] F. N. Cherevanin, "Khlebnyi rynok i bor'ba za tverdyia tseny," *Ekonomicheskoe Obozrenie* 1 (Oct. 1916): 159–64.

decline in the gross harvest for 1916 in comparison to 1915, but calculated "reserves" of salt, rye, wheat, oil, and other necessities might reduce the deficit entirely.[9] State revenues from direct taxes would be significantly higher than in 1915. Railroad freight traffic dubiously measured in rubles was reported to have increased in the first six months of 1916.[10] Whether or not these figures were accurate, they inspired dubious optimism at a moment when the state's short-term credit obligations had reached 7.5 billion rubles and was scheduled to go much higher. In fact, the cost of the war itself now exceeded 15 billion rubles and may have been as high as 25 billion.[11] A report of the commission to the Council of Ministers in September described a "crisis" in the circulation of paper money based on credit and the "rapid deterioration" of the gold supply underlying its value. Among other things, it stressed the urgency of additional foreign aid from Russia's allies, which a special delegation of Duma members and others to Paris had been unable to secure.[12] The government clearly needed additional resources, perhaps as much as 12 billion more rubles in Finance Minister Peter Bark's estimation. The Ministry of Finance was planning to introduce a new lottery to raise funds, and Bark also floated 3 billion rubles' worth of new short-term (ten-year) government bonds yielding 5.5 percent in denominations as small as 50 and 100 rubles in the hopes again of generating revenue from a broad range of the population.[13] As other members of the state's Finance and Economic Commission pointed out, even these additional measures would not cover the costs of servicing Russia's expanding portfolio of short- and longer-term loans.[14] Bark himself saw real danger in printing more money but thought he had no alternative.[15]

At the center of power in Petrograd even the authority mustered by the Railroad Management Committee had not managed to stem the decline in transport operations or reduce the increasing numbers of locomotives and rolling stock sidelined for repairs. Plans based on estimates of available cars were quite specific—precisely 20,887 cars assigned in October to the railroads serving Moscow and its six surrounding provinces for the transport of foodstuffs, for example—but the actual number available for use was substantially lower. Rampant corruption was still seen as a key problem despite the imposition of harsh penalties. In early October, large quantities of goods of "extremely serious

---

[9] *Statisticheskiia Svedeniia o finansovom i ekonomicheskom polozhenii Rossii: Material sostavleny k 15 Noia. 1916* (Petrograd, 1916), 3–8, 29.
[10] Ibid., 38.
[11] RGIA f. 565, op. 2, d. 555, ll. 1–2.
[12] RGIA f. 563, op. 2, d. 541, ll. 1–4; "Mezhunarodnoe finansovoe polozhenie tsarskoi Rossii vo vremia mirovoi voiny (Doklad Shingarev v Voenno-morskoi komissii Gos. dumy 20 iiunia 1916 g.)," *Krasnyi Arkhiv* 64 (1934): 3–30.
[13] *Birzhevye Vedomosti*, Sept. 20 and Oct. 18, 1916.
[14] RGIA f. 565, op. 2, d. 555, ll. 10–14.
[15] Ibid., ll. 4–5.

and immediate military importance" remained stalled in Vladivostok. Urgent requests from enterprises to move the shipments to the top of the loading lists were rejected for "administrative" reasons and because of the lack of equipment.[16]

By the fall of 1916 all of this was wreaking havoc on efforts to fix prices in the localities and continue requisitioning food and supplies for the army. Industry was affected as well as the countryside. Insisting on the need for firmer state control, the special councils and ministries sent even more special emissaries to address the problem. Far from improving matters, however, the very possibility that still more commissars might have the power to set procurement prices only raised the incentive for speculation.[17] On September 8 the Special Council on Food temporarily suspended the implementation of new fixed prices on grain purchases for the army because of objections by the Ministry of War, which worried this would remove the discretion of procurement agents. As a result, urgent telegrams reported that grain was not being sold even at a 20 percent premium to contracted prices already in place as "everyone" expected the procurement price to be even higher.[18] In mid-September, *Birzhevye Vedomosti* reported that "no one" in the country's heartland believed fixed prices were being fairly set.[19] Some in the field thought the whole system of requisitioning food for the army was faltering.[20]

On October 8, the rationing of sugar began in Petrograd. In Voronezh and elsewhere, rationing of fuel and other essential goods was also put in place. In Nizhnii Novgorod the local newspaper described the food crisis as *the* "angry topic of our day." A special meeting of zemstvo representatives resolved to spend 5 million rubles to deal with the shortages and soon set limits on the amount of flour it would distribute to bakeries. The zemstvo group also conducted a census of homeowners in preparation for additional rationing.[21]

From the first, however, the problem of assuring rationed goods would actually be available for distribution made even the Petrograd governor-general worry that rationing might cause more problems than it would resolve.[22] When the city of Saratov contemplated using ration cards to distribute sugar in July, rumors circulated that the cards were the work of the Antichrist, cleverly designed to prevent recipients from getting other essential items from city shops.[23] Nor would rationing control prices. In Ivanovo, sugar rationing was accompanied by

---

[16] RGIA f. 290, op. 1, d. 472, 100 (Oct. 5, 16); *Promyshlennost' i Torgovlia* 20 (Nov. 11, 1917): 239–45.
[17] RGIA f. 457, op. 1, d. 12, ll. 393–94.
[18] RGIA f. 456, op. 1, d. 166 ll. 3–7ff.
[19] *Birzhevye Vedomosti*, Sept. 20, 1916.
[20] RGIA f. 651, op. 1, d. 1031 (report of A. Vasil'chikov on food purchase operations of the Ministry of Agriculture).
[21] *Nizhegorodskii Listok*, Nov. 10, 1916.
[22] T. M. Kitanina, *Voina, khleb, i revoliutsii* (Leningrad: Nauka, 1985), 202–9.
[23] *Voronezhskii Den'*, July 14, 1916.

demands for the strictest possible measures—"the cruelest of punishments"—against "inhumane speculators" raising prices on rationed goods, "violating everything that is holy."[24]

Even so, by late summer rationing systems of various sorts had been put in place in some thirty-four provinces on items such as sugar, flour, and meat by cooperatives, town councils, and other local authorities without government sanction. A regional "food conference" in Ivanovo in September recognized that rising prices were difficult if not impossible to control but saw rationing and fixed prices on grain as protecting all of rural Russia against the randomness (*sluchainost'*) of the market. Controlling the cost of living required "the centralization of all authority over pricing in the hands of a single authority" (*edinovlastie*). The Ministry of Agriculture, meanwhile, was now pressed by communications about the "extreme necessity" of getting food and forage to the front. Requisitioning had completely broken down. In many places peasants were simply refusing to give up their produce.[25]

By October, the issue could no longer be avoided in Petrograd. An urgent telegram from Russia's national hero General Aleksei Brusilov threatened to order his commanders to take whatever they needed from local inhabitants without regard for the prices fixed by contracts supposedly required for all military procurements. His troops were now practically without food, "literally facing starvation."[26]

Extending Compulsory Labor: From World War to Civil War

Already in the spring, as we have seen, Prime Minister Boris Shturmer and other high-ranking tsarist officials thought the continued scarcities of food and other goods were directly linked with deficits in the supply of manpower, especially within the large military zone. When the army pressed Stiurmer to draft tens of thousands of support workers into compulsory labor brigades, as Germany was doing, he wanted to fill their ranks with refugees and from populations like Russia's Muslims who were exempt from the draft as untrustworthy, lest they be called upon to fight against their coreligionist Turks.[27] By January 1916, some 246,000 POWs had already been assigned to agricultural work under the supervision of the Ministry of Internal Affairs; 66,000 worked on the railroads and almost 140,000 in various enterprises under the supervision of the Ministry of

---

[24] *Ivanovskii Listok,* July 8 and Sept. 8, 1916.
[25] RGIA f. 457, op. 1, d. 17, l. 28.
[26] Ibid., d. 78, ll. 46–46 ob.
[27] On Germany's use of forced labor, see Robert Armeson, *Total Warfare and Compulsory Labor: A Study of the Military-Industrial Complex in Germany during World War I* (The Hague: Nijhoff, 1964).

Trade and Industry. Their presence in many places further disturbed Russia's rural order. Many who had lost loved ones resented that scarce food was being fed to German "beasts."[28] At the start of the Brusilov breakthrough Stiurmer authorized the Ministry of War to begin "requisitioning" the workers it needed even without waiting for Duma approval, as he had earlier wanted. The Ministries of War, Transport, Agriculture, and Trade and Industry then asked for more prisoners to help meet their needs. The number working in the fields had grown to 545,000, but the situation was still thought to be acute.[29] The Council of Ministers in secret sessions then extended this initiative to "peoples and tribes" not subject to military service—that is, Russia's large Muslim populations in the Crimean region and Central Asia.

Until the summer of 1916, the question of Imperial Russia's relation to its non-Russian peoples focused primarily on the Jews. The notorious pillaging of Jewish communities in Eastern Poland and Galicia in 1914 and 1915 was now known, especially through the efforts of the renowned ethnographer Shlomo Rappoport (aka S. Anskii).[30] Using newly available archival materials, Eric Lohr, Vladimir Buldakov, Tamara Leont'eva, and others have described the humanitarian consequences of ethnic-based conceptions of nationality and patriotism, especially of Jewish and German enemy aliens in the region.[31] As is well known, rank-and-file violence was fueled not only by scarcities and the shocks of war but perhaps just as much by an entrenched anti-Semitism in the Russian military command and a broader Russian national chauvinism in the war zone, especially after the occupation of the Ukrainian and Jewish areas of Galicia and the assaults on German-Russian estates and businesses. In Lohr's view, the war moved Imperial Russia away from the multiethnic understandings of empire toward a more nationalized sense of Russianness embedded in both territorial and nationalist political assumptions.

By the spring of 1916 rumors were already circulating in the fertile Fergana Valley region and Turkestan as a whole about the possible draft of Muslims given Russian losses, creating, in the words of one report, a good deal of "agitation" among the "natives" (*tuzemtsi*).[32] According to a secret report Alexander

---

[28] RIGA f. 1276, op. 12, d. 224, l. 64.

[29] RGVIA f. 2005, op. 1, d. 53, ll. 1–5, 105–6.

[30] A. Anskii, *The Enemy at His Pleasure: A Journey through the Jewish Pale of Settlement during World War I*, trans. Joachim Neugroschel (New York: Henry Holt, 2003). For other contemporary accounts, see American Jewish Committee, *The Jews in the Eastern War Zone* (New York: AJC, 1916); E. R. A. Seligman, *The War and the Jews in Russia* (New York: Workman's Committee on Human Rights, 1916); and especially the Duma speeches of Maxim Vinaver. An excellent study is Eric Lohr, *Nationalizing the Russian Empire: The Campaign against Enemy Aliens during World War I* (Cambridge, MA: Harvard University Press, 2003).

[31] Lohr, *Nationalizing*; V. P. Buldakov and T. G. Leont'eva, *Voina porodivshaia revoliutsiiu 1914–1917* (Moscow: Novyi Khronograf, 2015).

[32] RGIA f. 1292, op. 1, d. 1933, ll. 1–10.

Kerensky sent to the Ministry of War after a personal tour of the region, without any official directive impressment began by "abusive" lower-level officials who "destroyed the peaceful course of life" in what had been loyal areas.[33] In early July, mullahs in Bukhara and elsewhere were telling the faithful that the imperial regime was drafting them to fight against their Turkish coreligionists and that it was better to die fighting Russians at home than Muslims elsewhere. Soon afterward the first reports of Russian troops firing at protesters in Tashkent, Andizhan, and the Syr-Dar'inskii region began to reach Petrograd. The number of casualties was uncertain, but not their effect on local feeling. Local leaders were said to be secretly circulating pan-Islamic ideas, collecting funds to support the Turkish army, hiding goods and funds in preparation for a general strike, and otherwise preparing for civil war.[34]

Thereafter rumors, demonstrations, and armed clashes proceeded with equal intensity. According to Kerensky, the detailed regulations that were issued on September 15 "threatened the complete destruction of a regional economy that was supplying the army and the country with livestock, grain, and cotton."[35] Muslim workers on the Tashkent railroad reportedly fled to fortified villages (*auls*) deep in the steppe, creating a threatening situation all along the line. Bridges and telegraph lines were cut throughout the region. An official dispatch described the situation as "extremely serious."[36]

And indeed it was, in more ways that the regime expected. In addition to the privations the draft would produce and the ethnic issues involved, the call-up in many places was also bound to disrupt the regional harvest. In mid-July the entire region was placed under military law. General A. N. Kuropatkin, who had served as minister of war between 1898 and 1904, was reassigned from the Western Front to take command. By the end of July the Kirgiz region was in open revolt. Russian settlements were attacked, their inhabitants in some places forcefully driven into the steppe. Large rebellious bands were spreading disorder throughout the area, especially along the railroads.[37] Kuropatkin was soon engaged in an all-out battle to bring order to the region.

Russian military repression was formidable. Capital punishment, imprisonment, and sentences of hard labor were liberally meted out to those found guilty of attacks on Russians. In the meantime, the drafting of Muslims into the labor brigades proceeded without pause. By the end of the year as many as 250,000 had

---

[33] RGIA f. 1276, op. 12, d. 1806, ll. 217–18.
[34] RGIA f. 1292, op. 1, d. 1933, ll. 1–10; A. V. Piaskovskii, ed., *Vosstanie 1916 v Srednei Azii I Kazakhstane: Sbornik dokumentov* (Moscow, 1960), 59–62, 64–65. See also T. Ryskulov, *Vosstanie tuzemtsev v Sredeni Azii v 1916* (Kzyl-Orda, 1927); Edward D. Sokol, *The Revolt of 1916 in Russian Central Asia* (Baltimore, MD: Johns Hopkins University Press, 1954).
[35] RGIA f. 1276, op. 12, d. 1806, ll. 217–18.
[36] RGIA f. 1292, op. 1, d. 1933, l. 15.
[37] Ibid., ll. 258ff.

been forcibly enrolled. Dozens of villages were set ablaze, tens of thousands of cattle and other livestock confiscated, and as many as ninety thousand Russian and Muslim lives may have been lost.[38] One historian estimates that 300,000 others fled the region to the far western areas of China and Mongolia as "fire and sword" swept over the steppe, leaving it in some places completely barren.[39]

On one level, the revolt was a dramatic demonstration of the risks in the world war to the maintenance of empire. In Russia, however, it was also an indication of the dangers inherent in the militarization of dissident civilians into labor brigades and the centrifugal forces of local empowerment. Already before the practice was extended to Central Asia the Special Council for Defense had been inundated with complaints about the labor mobilization process itself. Count A. N. Tol'stoi, the governor-general for the Vilensk region, argued that brigades within the extended military zone put a disproportionate burden on local populations who were struggling more than most with the refugee problem and other effects of the fighting. Novgorod authorities found the effort to organize brigades "painful" as well as "oppressive" to the local population. In Vitebsk, Poltava, and Pskov provinces, the process was described as corrupted by people paying their way out of the obligation. Many village residents were armed and angry. Work periods were often longer than the prescribed maximum ten hours. Mobilized workers were not being paid. Fines for deserters or those who temporarily left the brigades to find food were excessive. In mid-August the governor of Lifland urged that households with one able-bodied person be exempted, that the draft be suspended entirely during the harvest weeks, and that the location of compulsory labor not be more than forty versts (forty-four kilometers) from their homes. In Vitebsk and Pskov, disorganization and corruption in the management of the brigades were raised at sessions called by the regional governors. A candid report from the Western Front stated that among the local population "the number of those voluntarily wishing to enroll in the labor brigades is zero."[40] (When the Bolsheviks re-created the system in 1920, they got the same response, as we will see.)

The Rittikh Confiscation

In the view of Peter Maslov, the respected economist and vice chair of the Chuprov Society, the root problem of Russia's scarcities in the fall of 1916 was not the lack of compulsory labor or even the decline in agricultural production.

---

[38] Tursunov, *Vosstanie 1916*, 77, 635–714.
[39] Ibid., 400–440.
[40] RGVIA f. 2005, op. 1, d. 53. ll. 8–9, 15–16, 44, 160–72, 192–97, 219–29, 233–47.

It was the fact that rampant inflation was causing traders in the market and elsewhere to hold on to their goods in the expectation of higher prices. Whether or not this speculation was an inevitable element of commercial market exchange, it was accentuating the goods famine "artificially," in Maslov's view, that is, in ways related to commercial market practices rather than the actual availability of goods. It seemed obvious that the state had to take a more active and rational role in controlling the way food in particular was being procured and delivered.[41]

In late October, many liberals and democratic socialists shared Maslov's view. Members of the Duma gathered privately to take up the question in preparation for that body's next convocation. By now the trope of extreme need permeated all levels of state and public discourse in the localities. Like Brusilov's telegram, it carried weight on its own independently of the actual material circumstances. The plenipotentiary from the Special Council on Food in Tiflis telegraphed the "extreme importance" of mitigating the food situation in the Caucasus. From Chernigov, the council's plenipotentiary used "extreme need" to describe the situation there. Similar messages came from other grain-producing areas in European Russia as well as from Siberia and Ukraine. From Ufa came a plea to clarify the ways and means by which grain should be forcibly taken from regional producers. Was this to be managed at the local level or from Petrograd?[42]

Partly in response to these pressures, the tsar replaced Stiurmer with his third prime minster for the year, Minister of Transport Alexander Trepov. (A fourth, Prince Nikolai Golitsyn, would follow in a month). Nicholas also appointed a new minister of agriculture, Aleksandr Rittikh. The fifty-four-year-old Trepov was known as a bellicose but adequate administrator and an opponent of Rasputin. His appointment in place of the hated Stiurmer was welcome. The forty-eight-year-old Rittikh was young, energetic, and thought to be reasonably competent, precisely the kind of person many in the Progressive Bloc demanded to see in the Council of Ministers. Immediately upon taking office he announced a new system for requisitioning grain across the country. His approach was to move from compulsory requisitions at prices fixed by contract to compulsory deliveries at set quantities whose price would then be assigned—a *razverstka*, or confiscatory sweep. In effect, Rittikh was making a bold effort in the inflationary conditions of late 1916 to bring order to an ever more chaotic purchasing system as both military and civilian needs outstripped supplies. Presented to the Special Council on Food, his plan was approved by a vote of twenty-three to three.

It now seemed clear that deliveries to the army of grain and other foodstuffs in 1917 would have to be almost double what they had been during 1916. Preliminary accounting of the harvest confirmed that it would be difficult if not

---

[41] *Ekonomicheskoe Obozrenie* 2 (Nov.–Dec. 1916): 58–62.
[42] RGIA f. 457, op. 1, d. 17, ll. 4–9; d. 75, ll. 1–2.

impossible to meet both military and civilian needs through the existing system. Whether or not the Agricultural Ministry's own figures were accurate—and the problem of receiving correct data from the localities in constantly changing circumstances had hardly been solved—internal reports supported these claims with characteristic if improbable exactitude. Measured in *puds* (approximately 36 pounds), between the first of September and the middle of November only 86,157,000 puds of the 208,596,000 purchased had reportedly been delivered. In the provinces closest to the Southwestern Front, deliveries of wheat, rye, and oats were less than half the amount purchased; only 30 percent of the freight cars required to transport deliveries were loaded.[43] Making matters worse was the state of railroad transport itself and an acute shortage ("with threatening consequences") of sacks to hold grain. Some 29 million sacks had been ordered but not delivered. The ministry was trying to get as many as 28 million returned from the front, but the need was still almost 40 percent higher than the projected supply from all available sources. It was also relying on the Railroad Management Committee to supply the necessary equipment and to otherwise improve conditions on the lines.[44]

On November 19 and 22, the liberals Andrei Shingarev, Nikolai Nekrasov, and some thirty-nine more members of the Duma sent written interpolations to Minister Rittikh regarding his plans. In their view the "food question" was in a state of "unacceptable disorganization and disorder."[45] Rittikh responded that he was equally concerned and committed. The young minister reiterated that sufficient amounts of grain had been purchased for the army but not delivered. He understood that "private trade had shown itself far from able to supply food to the districts demanding it," that transport problems continued unabated, and that the task of the Ministry of Agriculture and the Special Council on Food was now to supply both the army and the civilian population by direct purchases by the ministry's and council's plenipotentiaries as well as from private traders. Rittikh also recognized, moreover, that based on the information at hand the amount of grain set for purchase for the civilian population had to be increased by as much as 100 million puds and that for the army by 485 million, along with the railroad cars to transport it.[46]

Whether this was even remotely possible was unknown. Commissions to purchasing agents were being increased; those bringing requisitioned grain to railroad depots would be compensated for transport costs; prices that local zemstvo and other purchasing authorities had already fixed lower than market

---

[43] Ibid., d. 78, ll. 22–23, 79.
[44] Ibid., ll. 23–26.
[45] Ibid., l. 4 ob.; *Novoe Vremia*, Nov. 22, 1916.
[46] RGIA f. 457, op. 1, d. 78, ll. 11–14.

prices would be increased. The new minister's goal was "uniformity" in the prices of grain deliveries, an end to "the element of chance," and the creation of adequate reserves to cover any shortfalls, arguments he repeated when he addressed Shingarev, Paul Miliukov, and others now participating on the Special Council for Defense.[47]

The Rittikh *razverstka* was thus a long-delayed effort by an energetic newcomer to the cabinet to take in hand the enormous problem of grain production and distribution. As Lars Lih and Taisiia Kitanina have detailed, many traders had already built up their stocks to sell at prices higher than those fixed by procurement contracts. Grain made available for requisition by army and government agents was largely being taken from surpluses and reserves. By replacing this system with one of compulsory deliveries, Rittikh was trying to use whatever information he had about actual local conditions to secure the supply of grain available for procurement on the basis of moral obligations in support of the country and the war rather than commercial incentives reflected in prices. In other words, the *razverstka* transferred grain deliveries "from the place of commercial transactions to the place of fulfilling one's duty to the motherland, a duty obligatory of every Russian citizen in the condition of the current war."[48] If assigned deliveries were not made, the regime was prepared to seize them by force. Thus, the monthly censuses on available food supplies returned by villages throughout European Russia to the special council now made the villages vulnerable to losing their stores.

As the historian Kimitaka Matsuzato has further explained, the compulsory delivery of grain according to set quotas rather than set prices was intended to disengage procurement entirely from the processes of a broken market. It established compulsory deliveries of grain independently of market-based terms of exchange, compensating peasant producers with prices that were supposed to account for inflation but would not be subject to negotiation. The system was not intended to be managed by force. Indeed, Rittikh introduced the measure in part to *avoid* the use of force that military commanders and others had applied since the war's beginning. The *razverstka* would work through patriotism and support for the war effort.[49] The paradox of a voluntary moral obligation got little if any attention, as would be the case when the Bolsheviks made it one of the foundations of War Communism in 1918.

---

[47] Ibid., ll. 15–22; *Zhurnal Osobogo Soveshchaniia dlia obsuzhdeniia i ob"edineniia meropriiatii po oborone gosudarstvo*, Feb. 15, 1917, 219–23.
[48] Ibid., 221.
[49] K. Matsuzato, "Prodrazverstva V. A. Rittikha," *Acta Slavica Iaponica* 13 (1995): 167–83.

Subsistence Protests and the October Strikes

While the process of assigning delivery quotas was not fully in place until January 1917, the announcement of the *razverstka* coincided with an outbreak of industrial strikes and rural social protests. Some of the latter were simply by individuals engaged in what they thought were grossly unfair transactions. In her important research on the subject, the historian Barbara Engel found a revealing protest by a single pregnant woman in the volatile Kostroma textile district, where the price of a spool of thread increased 16 percent from one day to the next, if only by two kopecks. One account given to the police had the tradeswoman striking the buyer when she was caught stealing the spool. Another reported that the buyer spit on the money she was offering at the earlier price, and it was this that precipitated the fight.[50] Either way, the incident is evidence in its small way of the serious tensions that were growing over price increases, even if other issues in this case may have come into play. The question for many in provincial towns and villages was increasingly one of subsistence.

The protests have commonly been called "subsistence riots." As with scarcity itself, such riots were also taking place in other combatant states in 1916. The British naval blockade had a damaging effect on Germany in particular, where violent demonstrations over food broke out in Hamburg and other cities that precipitated military intervention. By December a rationing system was in place throughout the country. In Austria, the failure of the potato crop was equally or more devastating. Yet the Russian situation continued to be compounded by the lack of ways in which popular distress could be mediated or legally articulated. It also focused anger and other feelings on those who were thought to have the power to address scarcities in and outside the regime, reflecting a powerful undercurrent of anxiety that involved cultural perceptions of class and the unfairness of differential access to goods. In English as well as Russian, "riot" as a descriptive term connotes irrational violence and social disorder. It obscures subjective insecurities and fears as well as the implicit political objects that "protest" is against. In essence, what the food "riots" reflected in Russia in 1916 was thus a strong current of protest against the socioeconomic processes and cultural values of war capitalism itself.

Fragmentary evidence about these protests can be found in a range of sources that need to be read as carefully as censored soldiers' letters. The Russian historian Iurii Kirianov documents some 288 such protests over food prices and the cost of living in 1916, thirteen times the number he found occurred in 1915.[51]

---

[50] Barbara Engel, "Not by Bread Alone: Subsistence Riots in Russia during World War I," *Journal of Modern History* 4 (Dec. 1997): 706.

[51] Iu. I. Kirianov, "Ulichnye besporiaki i vystupleniia rabochikh in Rossii." *Istoricheskii Arkhiv* 2 (1994): 91–99, 3 (1995): 65–102.

Many of these were during the time of the Brusilov offensive. These may have involved feelings about the huge additional losses the offensive required from peasant villages. Others during the year were the result of unemployment precipitated by the state's neglect of unfavored enterprises not working for defense. By the end of June 1916, more than 300,000 Russians had filed through the small labor exchange in Moscow hungry and looking for work. As many as ten thousand were reported to have looted stores in the Kuban to protest scarcities in necessary goods, especially sugar. Workers in Samara protested "in the most forceful terms" to the State Duma when "two starving women from among the town's poor" were shot after trying to purchase meat. They expressed outrage about the "rank injustice" of such harsh measures at a time of "extreme crisis in the availability of food."[52] These and similar disorders, moreover, were not regarded by the police as "in any way dependent on revolutionary propaganda, but were the result only of the food crisis," however much revolutionary groups were trying to stimulate them.[53] A secret report in October warned that the food question, now the "single most powerful impulse in the widest possible population circles throughout our huge empire," was everywhere increasing bitterness and animosity.[54]

In the process, the stark social differences and consumptive excesses denounced by Shingarev and others became even more objectionable. When the Russian-speaking British correspondent Stephen Graham returned to Russia in the early summer of 1916, talk everywhere was of the "terribly high cost of living (*dorogovizna*)... the commonest [word] in the townsman's vocabulary." "Sadness and anxiety" were everywhere in the background. Where rationing had been introduced, "people with blue ration cards could not find grocers with goods to sell." Tuesday through Friday were declared "meatless days." Roadhouses and hotels were requesting clients not put their boots out for cleaning at night lest they be stolen. Graham noted that "everyone talked about the dearness of living and yet everyone had more money wherewith to buy."[55]

Yet "everyone" here was an unconscious language of class that clearly did not mean everyone. Police in Tver described what they called sugar riots as a crowd of mostly women, shouting that they were starving, threw rocks at shops that refused to honor their local ration cards. The rumor was that they were selling instead to "persons of means" for exaggerated prices. In Rostov, police reported almost continuous disorders over the high cost of flour and other primary goods.

---

[52] "Doklad Petrogradskogo Okhrannogo otdeleniia osobomu otdelu departamenta politsii, Oktiabr' 1916," *Krasnyi Arkhiv* 4 (1926): 24.
[53] *Krasnyi Arkhiv* 4 (1926): 28–38.
[54] Ibid., 19.
[55] Stephen Graham, *Russia in 1916* (New York: Macmillan, 1917), 36.

In Semipalatinsk, local police reportedly allowed some thirteen stores to be wrecked when, despite orders, they refused to fire on the crowd.[56]

Engel is particularly concerned with the moral assumptions that underlay protests over scarcities, and their relation to peasant values more broadly, many of which women brought into industrial centers from the countryside as they replaced workers sent to the front. She details how one of the first signal food protests over the lack of sugar in the Moscow province textile center of Bogorodsk in the fall of 1915 quickly turned into an attack on speculators, underhanded trading practices, and the merchantry in general. Despite police intervention and the fact that everyone in Bogorodsk had to know about the brutal repression of textile workers several months earlier in nearby Ivanovo and Sormovo, the ranks of demonstrators quickly increased from a handful to more than several thousand. Although the protests came to a bloody halt when a detachment of Cossacks arrived, killing two people and injuring others, unrest still spread from the street to nearby weaving mills, where several thousand workers also went on strike for higher wages, and again in Borogodsk itself, where pervasive anger precipitated a strike on October 30 by some twelve thousand women in the textile mills. The ways the social dynamics of small spontaneous demonstrations over scarcities could turn rapidly to larger protests was a harbinger of the way an uprising of anger and anxiety over the scarcity of food would soon bring down the regime itself.[57]

Protests over food in villages and towns almost certainly reflected the conflict as well between the community values of the village and the individualistic values of private ownership central to war capitalism. As Olga Porshneva has argued, hostility to Stolypin's reforms and those the government encouraged to leave the village for their own individual plots of land was about more than just land. Individual peasant landowning directly threatened the securities of communal life, however much communities were also commonly rent with their own frictions.[58] "Separator" itself became a term of derision, separation a tangible unfairness signifying the primacy of individual over collective well-being, a key cultural element of war capitalism.[59] An interesting demonstration of this emerged early in the war with the regime's decision to help support peasant families whose sons or husbands had been drafted by providing a uniform monthly stipend. "Families" included wife and children, father, mother, grandfather, grandmother, and brothers and sisters if they could persuade the authorities that they

---

[56] RGIA f. 1276, op. 11, d. 16, ll. 272, 254–55, 281, 297.
[57] Engel, "Not by Bread Alone," 696–97.
[58] Olga S. Porshneva, *Mentalitet i sotsial'noe povedenie rabochikh, krest'ian, i soldat Rossii v period pervoi mirovoi voiny (1914–mart 1918 g.)* (Ekaterinburg: UrO RAN, 2000), 82–85.
[59] Engel, "Not by Bread Alone," 706.

depended on the soldier's support. Other dependents, including wives and children from civil unions, were excluded.[60]

Engel, Sarah Badcock, and Liudmila Bulgakova have recently explored how soldiers' wives and widows—*soldatki*—felt that they were specially *entitled* to receive adequate allocations of essential goods, since their loss could be compensated only by collective support. When the real value of this support was weakened by scarcities and inflation, *soldatki* demonstrated in large numbers for redress.[61] Aaron Retish and Corinne Gaudin also show the range of conflicts and jealousies the *soldatki* payments involved, given the extra burdens placed on all village women from the loss of manpower regardless of whether they had a son or husband in the army. Equally important, in contrast to a view reinforced by postwar military and political memoirists who saw peasants as essentially ignorant about the war, both historians demonstrate that villagers were constantly engaged in discussion about it, often in connection with the letters they received from the front and the hundreds of petitions the *soldatki* and others wrote to the authorities. In their view, since the war intruded into every aspect of rural, social, cultural, and economic life, even far from the fighting, it was deeply unfair that only the losses of *soldatki* were compensated rather than their own and those of the village community as a whole.[62]

Mark Baker and Olga Porshneva have shown that mobilization of both men and livestock in the countryside was uneven across households. Some families lost their only male worker despite proscriptions against leaving families with no male support. Others lost their only horse. By 1917 in Kharkov province there were more than 80,000 households without any livestock at all and another 157,000 without any animals capable of work—35 percent of all households. The statistics may be overly precise, but the differences in welfare they indicate are not. As they hastened to prepare food and clothing packages despite their own privations, *soldatki* were well-informed from their husbands' and sons' letters about privations at the front. They also wrote themselves, as we have noted, that "injustices" were making their own lives ever more difficult. Baker provides detailed evidence for the Kharkov region, Porshneva for Cheliabinsk, Orenburg, and the Urals.[63] In Kharkov, the strong defense of community reflected by

[60] T. J. Polner, *Russian Local Government during the War and the Union of Zemtsvos* (New Haven, CT, 1930), 136.

[61] Engel, "Not by Bread Alone," 703; Sarah Badcock, "Women, Protest, and Revolution: Soldiers Wives in Russia during 1917," *International Review of Social History* 49, no. 1 (Apr. 2004): 47–70; Liudmila Bulgakova, "The Phenomenon of the Liberated Soldier's Wife," in *Russia's Home Front in War and Revolution*, 3 vols., ed. A. Lindenmeyr et al. (Bloomington, IN: Slavica, 2016), 2:301–26.

[62] Aaron B. Retish, *Russia's Peasants in Revolution and Civil War* (Cambridge University Press, 2008)), 49–54; Corinne Gaudin, "Rural Echoes of World War I: War Talk in the Russian Village," *Jahrbücher für Geschichte Osteuropas* 3 (2008): 393.

[63] Mark Baker, "Rampaging *Soldatki*, Cowering Police, Bazaar Riots and Moral Economy: The Social Impact of the Great War in Kharkiv Province," *Canadian-American Slavic Studies* 3 (2001): 137–55; Porshneva, *Mentalitet*.

"rampaging *soldatki*" was balanced by the comparable disaffection of those without special privileges, which itself created issues of fairness. Our assessment of the effect war losses had on Russian villages throughout the country has to be refracted through the lens of moral economy, which was in direct conflict with that of war capitalism.

Meanwhile, Petrograd was experiencing the largest outbreak of strikes since before the start of the war. Strikes had been occurring in the city with some regularity since early summer.[64] Now more that 138,000 workers left their benches, the majority in the city's large metalworking plants working for defense. Erikson, Russian Renault, a leading producer of mines and shells, emptied out, along with Nobel, Staryi and Novyi Lessner, Baranovskii, and others. The size of the strikes was a catalyst for protests elsewhere. By the end of the month 198 strikes throughout the country were recorded, the most by far of any month since July 1914.[65] Leopold Haimson and Eric Brian have meticulously reviewed factory inspector reports and other documents to give a full picture of industrial strike demands and especially their escalation in the fall of 1916. They argue convincingly that wage demands reflected deeper currents of unrest that stretched backward to 1905 and forward into 1917.[66]

What made the numbers of strikes and strikers in October 1916 historically significant is that they were not fundamentally about economic issues, notwithstanding a secret police report in October which described the general economic situation of the city's workers as "worse than awful."[67] Nor were they specifically political in the sense of demanding new authority for the State Duma, the singular demand of thousands of strikers in September 1915. In contrast, the outbreak of labor protests that began on October 17 carried the veneer of economic demands because strikes for wages in private enterprises were still legal (even if organizing or "instigating" them was not). Many quickly turned into overt political protests, partly in Petrograd after courts-martial of dissident sailors and soldiers in the Baltic fleet and Petrograd garrison. Protests were again concentrated in the politically active Vyborg district, where the Bolshevik underground was strongest. The strikes began when three thousand workers on the day shift at the Parviainen weapons factory did not come to work. According to reports of the Factory Inspectorate, they were soon joined in demonstrations by thousands

[64] RGIA f. 1282, op. 1, d. 740 (individual reports by province).
[65] RGIA f. 23, op. 16, d. 227, ll. 67–70; f. 1282, op. 1, d. 737, ll. 1–6; Iu. I. Kirianov, "Massovye vystupleniia na pochve dorogovizny v Rossii (1914–fevral' 1917 g.)," *Otechestvennaia Istoriia* 3 (1993): 3–18. Gvozdev's report on the activities of the CWIC Workers Group is in RGIA, f. 32, op. 1, d. 2126.
[66] Leopold Haimson and Eric Brian, "Labor Unrest in Imperial Russia during the First World War: A Quantitative Analysis and Interpretation," in *Strikes, Social Conflict, and the First World* War, ed. Leopold Haimson and Giulio Sapelli (Milan: Feltrinelli, 1992), 421–22, 445–48.
[67] "Doklad Petrogradskogo Okhrannogo otdeleniia," 10–11.

of others. They presented no formal demands. Some reportedly tried to sing "The Marseillaise" but were stopped by the police. Others broke windows. Some shots were fired. An automobile and horse tram were overturned. By October 19, some fifty-eight thousand workers were on strike throughout the city. Strike "instigators" real and imagined were arrested, sometimes brutally, escalating the unrest and a reciprocal disposition toward violence.[68]

On October 27 the administrations of three major plants poured fuel on workers' anger by announcing that all striking workers were being fired, regardless of how much they were needed to maintain production or whether they had actually joined the strikes.[69] Predictably protests here and elsewhere escalated further. However much they were encouraged by a now thoroughly radicalized social democratic underground, they were also mobilized by the unequal and repressive burdens that scarcities and the losses of an endless war were placing on them—a deep sense of social difference, inequality, and the constitution of fairness, amplified by still vivid memories of the great revolutionary strikes of September and October 1905 that had almost brought an end to the monarchy ten years before. A deepened sense of grievance now attached to a new sense of political possibility. Collective action could turn feelings into revolutionary change.

How serious this question had become was clear in mid-October when the Budget Committee of the State Duma convened a special open meeting to discuss what its members regarded as a critical issue facing the Duma. There was evidence of scarcity and food insecurity almost everywhere. According to the provincial daily *Voronezhskii Den'* (*Voronezh Day* or *Daily*), the "food question" was now "on everyone's mind . . . heading all other questions relating to our internal life . . . given the many millions in our cities, especially the huge number of our poor, who are on the threshold of cold, hunger, and sheer desperation."[70] For several days, newspapers in Petrograd and elsewhere ran full-page accounts of the Budget Committee's proceedings, detailing the remarks of leading political figures. Kerensky spoke passionately of the need to take measures to relieve "the food troubles" now being experienced by "nervous workers" forced to stand in long lines to receive even basic necessities. Nikolai Chkheidze, the Duma's leading social democrat, insisted the state remove every impediment keeping workers from "working and living calmly." His Kadet counterpart Miliukov warned of the need to pay close attention to the plight of workers' families for whom long lines made it impossible to calmly fulfill their responsibilities at work. The Budget Committee unanimously resolved to convey these statements to the

---

[68] RGIA 23, op. 16, d. 117, ll. 67–70; f. 1282, op. 1, d. 737, l. 6.
[69] RGIA f. 1282, op. 1, d. 737, ll. 1–2.
[70] *Voronezhskii Den'*, Oct. 8, 1916.

Council of Ministers. In November and December hardly a day passed without there appearing some article or analysis of the food question in newspapers around the country.[71]

None of this was lost on leading members of the State Duma. Delegates interrogating Rittikh about the food crisis on November 22 also accused the regime of disregarding Russia's public organizations or ignoring them altogether at the country's peril. They tied the now common discourse of "extreme need" directly to the issue of growing popular anxiety, clearly identifying the subjective underpinning of "catastrophe." "As a result," the deputies wrote, "the food question is close to catastrophic.... Time will not wait. We see very clearly the threatening consequences of this disorder in constant increase in the cost of food and other necessary goods and the constantly growing anxiety of the country's population, which is beginning to lose faith in a better future." Their statement was published in *Novoe Vremia* (*New Times*), one of the most influential papers of the day, with a circulation of more than 200,000. A full twelve months after Minister of Interior Khvostov warned that Russia was "approaching a real catastrophe," nothing had changed for the better.[72]

Russia's Revolutionary Situation

In these fraught circumstances the Duma reconvened in December for what would prove to be its last sitting before the revolution. The opening sessions are largely remembered as the historical moment when the Kadet leader Miliukov dramatically accused the regime of endangering the state, asking famously whether the government's ineptness was "stupidity or treason," words that would become a key part of the liberal Great Story. The Duma session's greater import, however, was the way in which speakers across the political spectrum now viewed the dysfunctionality of Russia's political economy as a whole in terms of social stability and well-being, directly tying the now common discourse of "extreme need" to the issue of growing popular anxiety and identifying clearly the subjective underpinnings of "catastrophe."

"Catastrophe," moreover, continued to have several meanings: the ineptitude of the regime itself in managing the war; the disastrous losses and meager achievements of the Brusilov breakthrough and the war; the steadily rising cost of living; the seeming lack of effective ways to support the state's burgeoning fiscal crisis; the condition and morale of the army facing another winter of hardships; the shortfall in the gross harvest of wheat, oats, and other grains that aggravated

---

[71] *Birzhevye Vedomosti*, Oct. 19, 1916.
[72] RGIA f. 457, op. 1, d. 209, l. 3 ob.; *Novoe Vremia*, Nov. 22, 1916.

speculation as well as scarcity; increasing disruptions on the railroad lifelines; and both within and outside the government the likelihood that the coming Christmas and New Year's holidays would again bring expressions of outrage, especially in the capital. Sympathy for Iulii Martov's Menshevik Internationalists, Lenin's Bolsheviks, and others firmly against the war and its imperial regimes was clearly spreading. Indeed, variations of extreme radicalism were now almost indistinguishable in many industrial plants. Bolshevism as a sentiment was by now much stronger than the Bolsheviks as a political party.

One of the more usable concepts in the Leninist political lexicon was and remains the "revolutionary situation." In 1913 the Bolshevik leader wrote that such a condition would not occur when only the lower strata of society, the *nizy*, were no longer willing to live as before, but when at the same time those at the top, the *verkhi*, could no longer manage and rule as before.[73] Even before the world war began, this notion of a simultaneous "crisis at the top" (*krizis verkhov*) and "crisis at the bottom" (*krizis nizov*) succinctly defined what he and his Bolsheviks understood as the necessary conditions for political victory. A revolutionary situation occurred when there was a break at all social levels in the belief that existing social and political structures were able to address adequately the problems at hand.

What gave the Bolsheviks political advantage in these circumstances was not so much Lenin's personal determination—his "lust" for power, as it is fairly marked in both the liberal and democratic socialist Great Stories—as an approach to social instability that explained objective realities in ways that deftly mobilized subjective feelings, linking how things seemed to how people felt. Leninism in this sense was well suited to the anxiety and even desperation that characterized individuals and social groups in the fall of 1916, as well as to the actual conditions of scarcity and loss. Imperialism, the war, and capitalism explained the anxieties of anticipated needs as well as the realities of long lines waiting for food at the risk of losing one's job, urgent new pleas from peasant soldiers at the front for warm clothing despite improvements in the army's chain of supply, the anger and even outright rage at those thought to be profiteering from constantly rising prices as well as the prices themselves. What was at stake as the last winter weeks of the tsarist regime began was not simply the need for a competent and responsible government. It was whether the conditions of scarcity and loss in all of their multiple dimensions could actually be addressed effectively while the war continued and the tsarist regime held state power.

---

[73] V. I. Lenin, *Polnoe sobranie sochinennia*, 55 vols. (Moscow: Gosizdat, 1958), 23:300. The fullest explication is in his *Left-Wing Communism: An Infantile Disorder* (New York: International Publ., 1940), written in 1920.

A key problem still related to the production and distribution of food and other scarce goods and their relation to the processes of market exchange. Some in the press reiterated Peter Struve's earlier injunction that there was "no less danger and perhaps even more" in the government refraining from moving forcefully to manage Russian economic life than there was from its leaving production and distribution to market forces alone. Maslov channeled Struve's views in the November–December 1916 issue of *Ekonomicheskoe Obozrenie* (*Economic Review*).[74] Rittikh's new plan for imposing compulsory deliveries of set quantities of grain that would then be priced was largely welcomed by liberals and moderate socialists, but while Rittikh insisted compulsion was to be based on "moral authority," the word still implied a readiness to use force, threatening the escalation of conflict. According to one count, 294 peasant protests occurred in the late spring and summer, 91 of which were forcibly suppressed.[75]

There was little likelihood that peasants shared the minister's moral principles in this regard. Before the end of 1916 there appeared to be a new surge of speculation and, in the estimation of historians who have closely examined the question, a total breakdown of the remaining commercial market in grain.[76] Moreover, as V. D. Kuz'min-Karavaev wrote in *Birzhevye Vedomosti* in early December, the whole notion of relying on personal obligation—moral compulsion—at a "critical moment in the psychology of the country" was essentially an invitation to avoid the legal markets and, by implication, to speculate in gray and black markets.[77] An inevitable side effect would be an increase in hoarding.

A significantly lower fall harvest in many places as a result, in part, of labor shortages compounded the problem, as did the difficulty of aligning the amount of available grain to the required number of railroad freight cars, still the responsibility of the central Management Committee in Petrograd.[78] By January 1917, projected deliveries were still falling short. In the Special Council for Defense, an angry Shingarev charged grain deliveries and requisitions were "only on paper" and spoke in the now equally familiar rhetoric of a "final catastrophe."[79] Just one week before the outbreak of the February revolution, a report from the Ministry of Transport to the Council of Ministers characterized deeply fatigued and poorly paid railroad employees working under the greatest of pressure and

---

[74] RGIA f. 457, op. 1, d. 256, ll. 11–12 ob.; Vserossiiskii Soiuz Gorodov, *Trudy Ekonomicheskago Soveshchaniia 3-4 ian, 1916* (Moscow, 1916), 24–27; *Ekonomicheskoe Obozrenie* 2 (Nov.–Dec. 1916): 58–59, 62.
[75] Porshneva, *Mentalitet*, 137.
[76] Lars Lih, *Bread and Authority in Russia, 1914–1921* (Berkeley: University of California Press, 1990), 42: N. D. Kondrat'ev, *Rynok khleboi i ego regulirovanie vo vremia voiny i revoliutsii* (Moscow, 1922), 106–10; Kitanina, *Voina*, 158–80.
[77] *Birzhevye Vedomosti*, Dec. 8, 1916.
[78] RGIA f. 456, op. 1, d. 166, ll. 3–7, 17.
[79] *Zhurnal Osobogo Soveshchaniia po Oborone Gosudarstva* 144 (Feb. 15, 1917): 224–25.

in the most difficult of physical conditions. Railroaders were said to deeply resent attacks on their efforts.[80]

The foremost historian of Russia's railroads in this period, Anthony Heywood, has argued that the actual state of railroad transport at the end of 1916 was less dire than was popularly believed and historically understood. In his view the railroads into Petrograd and Moscow were not the revolutionary "spark" they have sometimes been regarded as.[81] There is still ample indication, however, that shortages in the capitals were either the result of transport problems or widely perceived to be so, both of which put increasing pressure on railroad workers themselves. In November the regime declared a 10 percent bonus for railroad workers and employees across the board as an incentive to higher productivity, but wages still remained significantly lower than for industrial workers in all branches, even for skilled shop workers, and rising prices continued to cancel the gain. Paradoxically, the raises may only have increased grievance and intensified what some now regarded as an "epidemic of corruption" along the lines.[82] Supplies in Moscow and Petrograd were scarcely sufficient for meeting the needs of the population for more than several days, according to one government report for early January 1917. By one count the average turnaround time for freight cars increased by 5.4 days to 7.2 days.[83] Maintaining a supply of foodstuffs in both capitals depended not only on "how well the railroads were working," as an earlier report to the Special Council on Food maintained, but on the still rampant black marketeering in food stuffs in which railroaders continued to play a key part.[84]

An additional element of Russia's "revolutionary situation" in January 1917 was the destabilizing problem of paper credit emissions, which continued along with shortages to drive inflation and popular anxiety over rising prices. In and outside the Duma Shingarev continued his assault on Finance Minister Bark for not being honest about the huge and still escalating costs of the war. In Shingarev's view the government faced a dire financial crisis along with all the other crises.[85] While the "food crisis" and the Budget Committee discussions occupied the front pages of leading newspapers, a worried Council of Ministers authorized Minister Bark once again to issue an additional 3 billion rubles of new short-term bonds, this time at 5.5 percent interest. Bark insisted the amount and rate were not excessive given the state's precarious financial situation, but Shingarev could see no end to the need for borrowing. By January, the value of a ruble on

---

[80] I. D. Mikhailov, *Evoliutsiia Russkogo transporta 1913–1925* (Moscow, 1925), 56–57.
[81] Anthony Heywood, "Spark of Revolution? Railway Disorganization, Freight Traffic, and Tsarist Russia's War Effort July 1914–March 1917," unpublished ms. generously shared with the author.
[82] P. F. Metel'kov, *Zheleznodorozhniki v revoliutsii. Fevral' 1917–iiun' 1918* (Moscow, 1970), 15–19
[83] RGIA f. 290, op. 1, kn. 3–4.
[84] RGIA f. 457, op. 1, d. 12, ll. 190/143 ob.
[85] RGIA f. 1278, op. 1, d. 331, ll. 12ff.

the Persian exchanges had dropped to 20 kopecks.[86] As *Birzhevye Vedomosti* editorialized, the slogan "All for victory!" was now being easily translated into "Nothing for the home front!"[87] Shingarev saw the lack of subscriptions to the new loan as signaling how serious the lack of support for the regime itself had become.[88] To Maslov writing in *Ekonomicheskoe Obozrenie*, "sacrifice" was "a very easy and [fashionable] word these days," especially coming from industrialists and public figures "fully removed from the course of everyday life."[89]

Scripting the Revolution

Sir Bernard Pares, the master narrator of politics, personalities, and the liberal Great Story during the fall of the Russian monarchy, argued persuasively that the last weeks of October 1916 were a tipping point in the mentality of Russia's leading political figures. The well-connected British writer and embassy staff member described what he called the wholesale conversion of Duma members to a corporate interest in that body assuming power in some form, and the isolation in this process of Nicholas and Alexandra from even their closest friends. As a measure of alienation at the highest government levels, Pares cites the disdain in particular of the intelligent, patriotic, and thoroughly reactionary Vladimir Purishkevich, who would soon participate in the assassination of Rasputin, and his "brilliant attacks" on one of the tsar's last appointments, the fawning and ignorant A. D. Protopopov as minister of interior. From all quarters Pares heard cries for action, if not "constitutionally" through the Duma, then by way of "terrorism."[90]

After a visit to General Brusilov the tsar's cousin wrote Pares that "everyone" asks for the cabinet's replacement by a "responsible ministry" and prayed that God would help Nicholas "meet the universal wish and avert the imminent storm that is coming from the interior of Russia."[91] The Octobrist leader Alexander Guchkov, soon to be minister of war, informed Pares that even Protopopov's close friends were urging him to resign. Miliukov and Maklakov both told him they thought the new minister of interior and head of the national police was psychologically unhinged. As Semion Lyandres has detailed, a plot was hatching among high-ranking officers to take matters into their own hands.[92]

---

[86] RGIA f. 563, op. 2, d. 555, ll. 1–1 ob., 4–7; f. 457, op. 1, d. 256, ll. 11–12 ob.; Vserossiiskii Soiuz Gorodov, *Trudy*, 24–27; RGIA f. 1278, op. 1, d. 331, l. 24.
[87] *Birzhevye Vedomosti*, Oct. 16, 1916.
[88] RGIA f. 1278, op. 5, d. 331, l. 74.
[89] *Ekonomicheskoe Obozrenie* 2 (Nov.–Dec. 1916): 58–62.
[90] Bernard Pares, *Fall of the Russian Monarchy* (London: Cape, 1939), 383.
[91] Ibid., 218, quoting *Lettres des Grands-Ducs*.
[92] Ibid., 381; Semion Lyandres, *The Fall of Tsarism* (Oxford: Oxford University Press, 2013).

A secret report from the Petrograd Okhrana division confirms Pares's view of the "exceptional seriousness of the historical moment... the incalculable catastrophic miseries that might threaten the state's entire way of life in the near future." According to the report, the country would soon witness civil disorders with thousands or even tens of thousands of casualties as a result of an economic crisis that, despite increasing wages, remained untenable—"more than terrible."[93] Whether or not the document is authentic (it was published without archival citation), its arguments ring true, further amplifying Russia's revolutionary situation. So does the implication that its "very dark picture" was widely seen within as well as outside the regime.

In the historical vision of democratic socialists, the October strikes were a reenactment of the wave of protests in 1905 that forced the tsar to announce a constitutional monarchy. To Chkheidze's Mensheviks in and outside the Duma it now seemed possible that the hopes and promises of that revolutionary "rehearsal" might finally be realized. At a meeting of Progressive Bloc members before the State Duma reconvened in mid-November the question was whether Miliukov, who would lead the Bloc's challenge to the regime, would be justified in using the word "treason" to characterize its failings. Many thought the term would only strengthen defamatory rumors about the tsar and tsarina. When Miliukov used it anyway, some at the front wrote home that his and Chkheidze's comparably powerful condemnation of the regime on the Duma floor made a "huge impression."[94] In virtually all of the historical literature, Miliukov's "stupidity or treason" speech became the rhetorical tocsin signaling the start of the revolution.

But what *kind* of revolution? Ousting those deemed incompetent in the Council of Ministers and replacing them with "responsible" figures? The transfer of authority for choosing ministers to Duma members elected on the basis of a highly discriminatory franchise that privileged the landowning gentry at the expense of peasants, workers, and urban populations more broadly? The abdication of the tsar in favor of his twelve-year-old hemophiliac son, Aleksei, with executive power in the hands of an uncertain regent? As the disasters at the front early on in the war had consistently shown, the discourse of blame was the flip side of belief in the efficacy of agency. Lost battles were the fault of incompetent generals. Failures in meeting production goals could be remedied by more rational management. Controlling civil disorder required an adept and circumspect minister of the interior, precisely the opposite of Protopopov. Even Russia's dire financial circumstances could be alleviated by replacing Bark with someone more able and transparent in his actions. The rot, correspondingly, started at the

---

[93] "Doklad Petrogradskogo Okhrannogo otdeleniia," 3–35.
[94] RGVIA f. 2003, op. 1, d. 1486, ll. 252–53, 265.

top, with Nicholas, Alexandra, and a Council of Ministers headed once again by the now seventy-seven-year-old Goremykin. The mobilization of even right-wing Duma deputies like Purishkevich behind the Progressive Bloc's goal of a "responsible ministry" involved no weakening of their support for autocracy or their imperial Russian nationalism. A coup from above, contained and carefully staged, could restore the first in ways that were sure to strengthen the second.

In this Purishkevich and compatriots on the right were joined by some right and centrist liberals in and outside the Kadet Party. Following Miliukov and Shingarev, a majority of the Central Committee believed that the stability of any new government required it be legitimized as a constitutional monarchy by the tsar's appointment in terms of those constitutional provisions in the Fundamental Laws which vested executive power in the monarch. Miliukov and others were far too certain that Russia's orthodox peasants were strong supporters of the tsar and would remain so under a rationalized and more progressive regime. Sanctioned by the tsar, a new government would then have broad popular support, constraining the more rebellious and anarchic elements in the countryside and factories. When the Kadets held a two-day conference in late October, their widely circulated lead resolution stated that a successful outcome to the war was now seriously in doubt because of the "worsening of the internal mood of the country, the profound disorder in economic relations, and ineffective, incompetent policies." The responsibility for all of this lay in "a governmental system based on the alienation of power from the population, on rule by coercion, and on the systematic ignoring of the instructions of the people's representatives." The darkening national mood enhanced their fear of the anarchic dangers inherent in popular rage and threatened the possibility of rational government.[95]

By now, moreover, what rational governance was seemed indisputable. Accurate information about Russia's pressing economic problems was best gained directly at the local level. Solutions to the problems of scarcity had to be tailored to local needs by responsible local authorities working closely with responsible representatives of the regime. Throughout the Russian countryside, the devolution of authority downward had to go all the way to the district (*volost'*) level,.radical sentiments were taking hold, and there was still no popular representation through elected zemstvo or other representative bodies. In industrial areas, trade unions had again to be given legal authority to organize workers and represent their interests. Mediation boards needed to be created with equitable representation from all sides to resolve workplace conflict, their decisions binding on both management and labor. Arbitrary decisions of

---

[95] *S"ezdy i konferentsii konstitutsionno-demokraticheskoi partii 1905–1920*, 3 vols. (Moscow, 2000), vol. 3, pt. 1: 352–53.

multiple and conflicting plenipotentiaries had to be curbed, especially in food procurements and railroad management. Local policies and practices had to be responsive to the broad interests of the population rather than a reflection of special interests. At the state level excess profits had to be taxed along with incomes. In the liberal political lexicon, this meant politics, policies, and programs still had to *nadpartiinyi'* or *vseklassovyi*—above partisan or specific class interests. With peasants constituting some 80 percent of the population and with only 3 million or so industrial workers in Russia's partly commercialized economy, partisan politics could hardly allow an equitable representation of all Russian social formations and interests. Russia needed political parties that understood its pressing national and state issues and worked cooperatively to address them. Political sectarianism and the partisan class struggle were the path to continued social conflict, if not outright civil war.

In addition to maintaining Russia's military and bringing the war to a successful conclusion, Russia's most pressing problems in the liberal view were food distribution and the cost of living, fueled by speculation and currency emissions. Shingarev was now the liberals' most prominent Duma spokesman on these issues, and arguably the best informed. From his experience as chair of the Duma's Budget Committee, the physician, financial expert, and Voronezh landowner would be well prepared to assume the post of minister of agriculture or finance when these were offered in 1917. Russia's interrelated fiscal and food supply crises had to be addressed by rational and well-informed policies of fixed prices and practical procurements. Land held in long fallow had to be rationally reallocated with fair compensation to meet peasant needs and expectations as well as to increase production. The "food question" required the further engagement of public organizations, cooperatives, and local credit institutions in more energetic struggles.[96] Like Shingarev, liberals in and outside the Kadet Party also favored the rapid introduction of an income tax targeted especially at those cloaked, as Shingarev had said, "in silk and velvet." That the Southeastern Railroad reported record net profits in *Birzhevye Vedomosti* on November 12 did nothing to lessen widespread support for this initiative.[97]

What distinguished left liberals from the Kadet center and right was not their party's blueprint for how Russia needed to be governed. Nikolai Astrov, Nikolai Kishkin, Nikolai Nekrasov, and others from Moscow and the provinces who would soon take up positions in the Provisional Government focused instead on their party's political tactics. Liberals and other non-socialists had to recognize they would constitute a minority party among Russia's workers and

---

[96] Ibid., vol. 3, pt. 1: 348–55; *Protokoly Tsentral'nogo komiteta Konstitutsionno-demokraticheskoi partii 1915–1920*, 6 vols. (Moscow, 1998), 3:332–33.
[97] *Birzhevye Vedomosti*, Nov. 12, 1916.

peasants. They needed urgently to strengthen cooperation with democratic socialists not only to extend their own power and reach but because of the now widespread tendency to identify the Kadets as a party of the "bourgeoisie" and the proponents of war capitalism.

It was their colleagues' lack of full attention to the worker question, however, that troubled Nekrasov and other left liberals as much as or more than that of political tactics. In Nekrasov's view, widely shared by left liberals especially in the provinces, the Kadet Party needed to address several critical issues here: the urgency of a labor exchange to manage job placements; the importance of involving workers' representatives directly in writing new laws governing factory conditions and workers' rights; strengthening the role of workers cooperatives to alleviate shortages; creating new ministries of health and labor; and ending the now ubiquitous police surveillance of legal meetings of Russia's unions and other public organizations as well as their repressive policies. For the railroad expert Nekrasov, soon to be minister of transport, Russia's "railroad lifeline" would only be reinvigorated by endowing railroad employees who fully understood the operational problems with responsibility for managing the lines.

In these matters left Kadets on the eve of the revolution were not far from moderate democratic socialists aligned with the Mensheviks, Popular Socialists, the peasant-oriented coalition group of Trudoviks, and centrist Socialist Revolutionaries. Here the Menshevik Chkheidze and the moderate (Trudovik) socialist Kerensky were the most active spokesmen in and outside the Duma, and perhaps Russia's most popular political figures as well among workers and peasants. For all of these socialist groups and their supporters, political democracy had to be complemented with a social democracy that supported the material welfare of the *narod* (the "ordinary people"), along with their civil rights. National wealth had to be redistributed in some equitable way by taxation and the transfer especially of land held in long fallow from the gentry landlords to their region's peasants so that it could be worked. For prominent Menshevik figures like Chkheidze, Fedor Dan, Alexander Potresov, and Kuz'ma Gvozdev, the head of the Workers Group in the CWIC, dealing with the "worker question" meant not only relieving scarcities and workers' insecurities but also maintaining sufficient influence inside the factory gates to channel their justifiable anger in politically and economically effective ways. From their right, democratic liberals and socialists were confronted by strong liberal and conservative opposition to "class politics." From their left, they were pressed by Lenin's militant Bolsheviks, who urged the forceful overthrow of Russia's entire political economy and, joined by Martov and the Menshevik Internationalists, a unilateral withdrawal from the war. When Gvozdev's WIC Workers Group called on October 17 for "energetic socially organized" work, the "sole true means to keep the working class from approaching dangers," newspapers reported that speakers at workers meeting shouted that the CWIC Workers Group could go to hell.[98]

Most important for Chkheidze and the democratic socialists was to give organizational structure to the workers' radical impulses, channeling the energy of protest into effective and institutionalized social change. The model here was the Workers Council (soviet) that played a key role in leading the great strikes of September and October 1905 that forced the October Manifesto and the political reforms that were to be embedded constitutionally in the new Fundamental Laws. For the Georgian Chkheidze, leader of the Menshevik Duma faction since 1907 and soon to be chair of the Petrograd Soviet, organizing a new and effective soviet was thus the first political task of any effort to take power from the tsarist regime, one that would also involve crafting for a new "bourgeois" democratic government the socioeconomic and political policies that would best ensure the eventual transition to social democracy as well.

In analyzing the ways leading historical actors have meshed circumstances with their own conceptions of revolutionary change, the social and cultural historians Keith Baker and Dan Edelstein have utilized the notion of "scripting" in advancing a new approach to the comparative study of revolutions. In an important volume they and others have explored how leading actors in the French Revolution of 1789 fit circumstances into preformed ideas about revolutionary change, and how these "scripts" may have determined the ways their self-conscious revolutionary successors in quite different contexts structured their own approach to revolution. Revolutionary "scripts" in this sense create the frameworks for political action. They help precipitate revolution itself, define its meaning, and affect the ways revolutionary processes develop.[99]

Scripting of this sort in Russia across the principal viewpoints and groupings in the late fall of 1916 fashioned revolutionary change in somewhat different ways, all of which were at least partly informed by the French revolutionary experience.[100] The liberal script, anchored in the historical imagination of the liberal Great Story, pressured change from above to create a "legal" revolution through the Duma, one legitimized by the tsar, who would formally pass governing responsibility to a cabinet approved by its representatives, as in England. Focus here was on preserving and strengthening the state itself as the principal source of change. This, hopefully, would help maintain social order by increasing the likelihood that conservative monarchists and Russia's military leadership would accept radical political change if it was formally sanctioned by the tsar. Russia might then, again hopefully, avoid the upheavals in France and Europe after 1789

---

[98] *Mensheviki: Dokumenty i materialy 1903–17* (Moscow, 1996), 435–37; *Den'*, Oct. 23, 1916.
[99] Keith Baker and Dan Edelstein, eds., *Scripting Revolution* (Stanford, CA.: Stanford University Press, 2015), which includes an interesting chapter on Russia by Ian D. Thatcher.
[100] John Keep, "1917: The Tyranny of Paris over Petrograd," *Soviet Studies* 1 (July 1968): 22–35.

and the descent in France into terror, authoritarianism, and civil war. When the Germans were defeated, such a regime would also be positioned to lead Russia's recovery in concert with the European democracies and the United States.

In contrast, and more in the ways suggested by Baker and Edelstein, moderate Russian democratic socialists grouped largely around Menshevik party leaders scripted struggle not only against the tsar but against the very social and cultural foundations of tsarism: the regime's "irrevocable and complete removal—its full replacement by a Provisional Government passed on an organized, independent, and free people," as the CWIC Workers Group expressed it.[101] Civil liberties and a rule of law were essential foundations for Russia's development into a full-fledged democratic socialism, but it was only by harnessing the power latent in social protest that revolution would ensure lasting changes in Russia's socioeconomic as well as political order. In this element of the democratic socialist Great Story, Russia would emerge after the war as a partner with European and North American political democracies, but one that was able to reconstruct its damaged economy and develop further in a socially progressive direction through the planned regulation of production, exchange, supply and demand. Fixed rates and prices along with equitable rationing of scarce good would be introduced in places of production, on consumer markets, and on a competent system of planned transport. Industrial profits in a mixed economy of private and state enterprises would be limited. Workers would participate through their unions in establishing wages, monitoring contracts, and regulating work conditions. In the area of finance, the printing of money would be controlled by a drastic reduction in military expenditures and raising taxes on those "in silk and velvet." All of this was possible "only in conditions of political freedom and under a democratic reorganization of state power responsible to the people."[102]

Ironically, the only prominent Russian political figure who did not foresee an imminent revolution at the end of 1916 was the explainer of revolutionary situations himself. Already in the fall of 1914 Lenin called for turning the imperial war into a civil war. The Bolsheviks' *vozhd'* (leader) seemed to think it would be relatively easy for a workers' revolution to overthrow the most reactionary and barbaric government in Europe, as he frequently described it.

But good information about the tenor of resistance in Russia was difficult to come by, and in any case Lenin and other émigré Bolsheviks had little trust in what they heard. Since the actual state of Bolshevik support was never something official Soviet historiography wanted accurately explored, we can appreciate Lenin's problem. Activist workers may not have wanted the extra risk of

---

[101] "Resolution of the Workers Delegation to the Conference of Regional War Industries Committees, 12–15 Dec. 1916," in *Mensheviki: Dokumenty i materialy*, 440–48.

[102] *Mensheviki: Dokumenty i materialy*, 444–45.

identifying themselves as Bolsheviks; their more cautious comrades may not have wanted the party's often public scolding for "accommodating" the bourgeoisie. The Russian Bureau of the party's Central Committee in Petrograd under Vyacheslav Molotov and Alexander Shliapnikov had little confidence in a strike movement that was not more fully under Bolshevik control.

Holed up in Switzerland, cut off from events in Russia by distance and a lack of information, unable to gauge the radical mood of workers in Petrograd and around the country, and apparently depressed over the death of his mother in June, Vladimir Ilich bemoaned that revolution would not likely come to Russia in his lifetime. His energy and efforts were directed instead to attacks on social democratic opponents and explaining the war, whose socioeconomic and historically determined nature he defined in *Imperialism: The Last Stage of Capitalism*, a key pamphlet written between January and June 1916. Lenin had also made his views forcefully known at the international antiwar congresses in Zimmerwald and Kienthal and had prepared copies of *Sotsial Demokrat* as well as *Imperialism* to smuggle into Russia with characteristic braggadocio: it was he who would inform Russian workers about the "true" nature of their circumstances, not the other way around.

How Lenin and his supporters saw these circumstances was easily stated. Russian workers were fully situated in a capitalist system where those who owned or financed the means of production exploited them ruthlessly in order to maximize their own wealth and political power. Fighting for Tsar and Country was shedding blood to defend imperial economic and political interests, from control over Muslim Central Asia to the annexation of Constantinople and the Dardanelle Straits. Capitalism had penetrated the partly commercialized countryside sufficiently to antagonize peasants into struggle against its commercial practices and principles, including the gentry's holding of massive amounts of unused lands and their radicalizing exploitation of the peasant working poor.

Whether the Leninist Great Story remained an ideologized vision or a description of historical reality depended on whether the party as a whole and its supporters could apprehend Lenin's conviction sufficiently to advance revolutionary Russia along its historically determined path toward his own radical version of socialism—whether, in other words, Bolsheviks could harness the anxieties and power immanent in popular uprising behind his maximalist program and acquiesce to, if not actively support, his party's coming to power.

In all of this, moreover, and a principal determinant of how the revolutionary process envisioned by each of the Great Stories turned out, was the effect at the front and in the countryside of Russia's enormous military and civilian casualties, and the mood, as the military censors still labeled it, of the garrison and frontline soldiers themselves. And here, only one thing was absolutely certain: those on the front lines as well as those waiting to be moved there from Petrograd and other city garrisons wanted overwhelmingly for the war to come to an end. "Ach, my dearest, when will this horrible war come to an end?" one soldier wrote in January. "We pray to God but He doesn't hear us, and each day everything becomes more and more insufferable." "Life has become unbearable," wrote another, "and soon it will all end. . . . Everyone's nerves are shattered." "You ask when the war will end?" was now a common question in letters from the front. "When all the peasant fools are slaughtered," one soldier answered rhetorically, "and in Russia there are many."[103]

---

[103] RGVIA f. 2031, op. 1, d. 1181, ll. 139–40; d. 1184, ll. 589, 591 ob., 599.

PART II
REVOLUTIONARY IMPERATIVES

7
"Responsible Men in Whom the Country Has Confidence"
The Challenges of Revolutionary Governance

The New Year was anything but happy at the front and throughout the Russian Empire—in conflict-ridden Central Asia, the war zones of Ukraine and the Caucasus, Helsinki and the Baltic provinces, and Russia itself, the empire's imperial heart—in January 1917, an appropriate start to one of the most momentous years in modern history. Almost no one expected the three-hundred-year-old Romanov dynasty to come to an abrupt end. The murder just before New Year's Eve of Alexandra's "mad monk" Rasputin seemed to presage change, but it was hardly clear what this would entail. Other plotting was also underway.[1] The liberal leader Paul Miliukov thought the murder was disgraceful, "repulsive in its essence," an event like the Duma's prorogation the day before "that would have been impossible in the normal life of a state."[2] Even after Nicholas replaced Prime Minister Alexander Trepov with the reluctant Prince Nikolai Golitsyn in January, the tsar's antipathy toward the Duma was even greater than it had been when the Progressive Bloc was formed in the summer of 1915. The possibility that anything resembling its program would be implemented seemed remote, much less the appointment it demanded of "responsible men in whom the country had confidence." Given the anxieties over real and portending scarcities in the capital, far more likely was the possibility of even larger demonstrations more difficult to channel toward political reform than they were in 1905 because of the war and the large Petrograd garrison. When the anniversary of Bloody Sunday, the suppressed demonstration that began the revolution of 1905, was marked on January 9, it was something of a surprise that the 140,000 or so who demonstrated in the capital returned to their workplace or homes the following day.

---

[1] See, e.g., Semion Lyandres, *The Fall of Tsarism: Untold Stories of the February Revolution* (Oxford: Oxford University Press, 2013); P. N. Miliukov, *Istoriia vtoroi russkoi revoliutsii*, 3 vols. (Sofia: Ros-Bolgarskoe izd., 1921–24), 1:36.

[2] Melissa Stockdale, *Paul Miliukov and the Quest for a Liberal Russia* (Ithaca, NY: Cornell University Press, 1996), 237.

Writing the "Truth" in the Third Winter of War

The holiday was particularly dismal for the 5.57 million soldiers and 115,000 officers still "fighting with God" at the front, those beleaguered souls who remained from the 14 million mobilized since the beginning of the war. The Romanian Front was a new disaster, precipitated in part by the celebrated Brusilov offensive. General Mackensen's Germans had overwhelmed the poorly defended Romanian forces and those of their new Russian ally. In October the Russian Black Sea fleet at Constanta was forced to evacuate. By December, two-thirds of the country was occupied by the Germans. A large part of the Romanian army had disintegrated. Russia's thirty-six infantry and some dozen cavalry divisions were overextended and vulnerable. Sporadic fighting continued in the Carpathians. Russian forces were again forced back behind the Seret River near present-day Chernivtsi, giving up still more of the territory captured by Brusilov. The front now stretched from the Black Sea north to Riga, some 350 miles longer than it had been a few months earlier. It was impossible to concentrate forces. Logistics were a mess. According to Brusilov himself, the railroads in Romania were, "if possible," even worse than in Russia proper. Promised food supplies were not forthcoming. According to one report to the chief of staff, hundreds of wounded soldiers at evacuation points were again left waiting in freezing conditions because of the lack of hospital trains, some for as many as seven days. As of January 12, eighteen thousand railroad cars were reportedly needed to evacuate the wounded. Sanitary conditions were "catastrophic." It was now a given on the front that those badly wounded would not be evacuated in time to save their lives.[3]

To some Russian commanders, the Romanian disaster seemed to preclude the possibility of mounting yet another large-scale offensive, discussed at Allied meetings in Paris in November. In their view it was now unlikely victory could be forced in this way. Brusilov was again an exception. Despite having lost all faith in the tsar or any member of the Romanov family to lead Russia effectively, the self-assured national hero continued to have confidence that he, at least, could still successfully remount a new spring offensive.[4] Meanwhile, Ludendorff, Hindenburg, and the German High Command brimmed with arrogance of their own. In mid-December the German chancellor Bethmann-Hollweg used the Vatican to suggest the possibility of a negotiated settlement, given Germany's clear military strength, its territorial gains, and its demonstrated capacity to continue fighting. In mid-January a new assault was launched against Russian troops

---

[3] RGVIA f. 2003, op. 2, d. 669, ll. 119–27; Alfred Knox, *With the Russian Army,*, 2 vols. (London: Hutchinson, 1921), 2:503–4

[4] A. A. Brusilov, *A Soldier's Notebook* (Westport, CT: Greenwood Press, 1970), 310–15.

near Riga. Shortly afterward, the Germans initiated unrestricted submarine warfare, discounting the possibility of American entry into the war.

There is little doubt that morale in the imperial Russian ranks was at its lowest point in the war. By December 1916, Russia's armies had suffered 3 million casualties, 1.7 million since May alone. Another 2.7 million were formally listed as captured or "unknown," almost half again as many between May and December.[5] Unauthorized desertions were common. Duma president Mikhail Rodzianko estimated the number to be 1.5 million.[6] Some 90 percent of those formally diagnosed with shell shock by the end of 1916 had suffered their injuries since the start of the Brusilov offensive. Many being treated in medical centers refused to return to their units; they were "dissolute," according to one report, and "completely resistant to military discipline." A review of the problem in the *Voennoi-Meditsinskii Zhurnal* (*Journal of Military Medicine*) emphasized the "colossal traumatization" that soldiers were enduring, "unprecedented in its duration, variety, and its multiple specific forms."[7]

Even hastily trained newcomers to the lines were well aware of the hardships of winter. Mud, freezing rain and snow, inadequate clothing, the venality of superiors demanding payment in exchange for leave or selling off scarce supplies, the rudeness and physical brutality of commanders, constant worry about families and the rising costs of necessary goods—all of this found expression in the thousands of letters still carefully reviewed by military censors. In some places, new recruits were better equipped than those they joined, increasing the resentment of soldiers who had survived battles in foot wrappings instead of boots. On the Romanian and Southwestern Fronts letters were rife with complaints about being forced to pay for basic needs, now "all but impossible" for most. In the first two weeks of December, some wrote of going two and three weeks without rest. Troops again were "starving." During the first week of February on the Northern Front, only ninety-five of the more than three hundred freight cars carrying supplies reportedly reached their destinations. No attention was being paid to the lack of doctors and hospital trains.[8] In the aggregate, few letters openly expressed the "gloom" (*mrachnost'*) censors emphasized in their reports because, as one wrote, "one simply cannot write the truth." In

---

[5] TsSU, *Rossiia v mirovoi voine 1914–1918 (v tsifrakh)* (Moscow: TsSU, 1925), 30.

[6] Official statistics show 195,130 deserters from the beginning of the war to February 1917 (ibid., 26). Duma president Rodzianko's estimate is considered quite possible after careful recent calculations by A. B. Astashov, *Russkii front v 1914–nachale 1917 goda: Voennyi opyt i sovremennost'* (Moscow: Nov. Khronograf, 2014), 475–80 and his "Dezertirstvo i bor'ba s nim v tsarskoi armii v gody pervoi mirovoi voiny," *Rossiiskaia Istoriia* 4 (2011): 45–47. Some deserters, however, returned after visiting their families to avoid additional hardships for their villages.

[7] TsSU, *Rossiia v mirovoi voine*, 30; *Voennoi-Meditsinskii Zhurnal* 2 (Mar.–Apr. 1916): 242; RGVIA f. 2067, op. 1, d. 3853, ll. 74–75.

[8] RGVIA f. 2003, op. 2, d. 669, ll. 26–47, 102–18, 189–90; op. 1, d. 1486, ll. 234–36; f. 2067, op. 1, d. 2937, ll. 5ff., 415–28; f. 2031, op. 1, d. 1181, ll. l65ff.; d. 1184, l. 582 and passim.

some units "a full breakdown in spirit" was noticeable, a "pessimistic attitude to everything."[9] "If they order us out of our trenches," one soldier wrote, "we will go, but you can then wait for us at home."[10] "We have many Rasputins" is how an officer described to a friend why his brother had died. There was "a great gravitation towards peace."[11] After the January battles on the Northern Front as many as 20 percent of letter writers expressed themselves in ways reported as discontented (*nedovol'nye*) or depressed (*ugnetennye*). There was not one regiment in which the proportion of "cheerful" letters was higher than 10 percent.[12] Even on the Caucasian Front, where conditions were far better, officers were appealing for gifts for their troops of warm underwear, socks, boots, tobacco, flour, toilet articles, writing materials, sweets, and money.[13]

In these circumstances rumors about an impending peace were passed eagerly up and down the lines. So was blame. "Let's remind all the sharks swimming in the rear that the army knows everything, that every soldier speaks with rage about the cost of living. And if earlier there were pogroms against Jews ... it's not hard to see that after the war there will be pogroms against the traders." Why did the government not take measures to control this? Why were workers going on strike when conditions in the villages were "insufferable" and soldiers as well as their families so badly needed the goods they produced?[14] While troops on the Northern Front rallied in early January for a brief offensive in Latvia, units elsewhere refused to fight. Mutinies occurred in a number of places.[15]

The mood among garrison soldiers was not much better, especially in Petrograd. Anxiety about being cycled to the front, poor food and barracks conditions, and the indignity of having to stand on tram running boards in the cold rather than sitting inside created a toxic atmosphere. All of this was almost certainly a reflection of war weariness, as it would be in the larger and more serious mutinies soon to occur in France. Yet in France, soldiers remained in defensive positions close to their own towns and cities. The larger purpose for fighting was not in question, only the devastating "suicide" attacks that the new French commander General Pétain quickly halted. In Russia, soldiers thought and wrote about the *purpose* of the war. Defending the homeland was one thing. The reason to continue fighting in Romania and Austria or extending the war against the Turks was another, the losses the effort incurred untenable. "Everyone waits for

---

[9] RGVIA f. 2067, op. 1, d. 2937, ll. 377, 397–98; f. 2031, op. 1, d. 1181, ll. 40–42, 150–51, 582; f. 2003, op. 1, d. 1486, l. 309–10.
[10] RGVIA f. 2031, op. 1, d. 1181, ll. 30–31.
[11] RGVIA f. 2003, op. 1, d. 1486, l. 272.
[12] Ibid., ll. 309–10; RGVIA f. 2031, op. 1, d. 1181, ll. 40–42, 150–51, 582; f. 2067, op. 1, d. 2937, ll. 397–98.
[13] RGIA f. 86, op. 1, d. 31, ll. 8–9; RGVIA f. 2048, op. 1, d. 905, ll. 13–14.
[14] RGVIA f. 2067, op. 1, d. 2937, ll. 399–400.
[15] Allan Wildman, *The End of the Imperial Russian Army* (Princeton, NJ: Princeton University Press, 1980), 111–20; "Russkoe armiia nakanune revoliutsii," *Byloe* 1 (Jan. 1918): 151–76.

peace.... [W]e hear nothing in support of the war.... [E]veryone is waiting for peace, every unit."[16]

Scarcity and Anxiety on the Home Front

Russian commanders and members of the Council of Ministers were well informed about all of this. The Ministry of Interior's Okhrana agents circulated on trains carrying soldiers to and away from the front in order to write their reports, in some places at front-line encampments themselves. The same was true in the factories, particularly the large state and private complexes in Petrograd and Moscow working for defense. Almost everywhere police agents were the common point of public interaction with representatives of the regime.

In the workplace, however, as Okhrana agents reported in detail, the focus was not in the first instance on high politics but on the persistent difficulties of procuring food, wages unfairly diminished by rising prices, workplace conditions, and the hardships of factory discipline. In Moscow and Petrograd more than 800,000 men and women were now crowded into factory barracks and apartments. More than 50 percent in Petrograd were metal workers in defense plants, among the country's most militant; some 11 percent were female textile workers, many in plants side by side with the metallists. A large number were relative newcomers to the city and to its hardships, especially women, who largely continued to bear the burdens of food lines either after work or through unauthorized absences (*proguly*) that risked their jobs. Factory inspectors counted 267 strikes in January, involving more than 230,000 workers. Rancorous meetings were common after and during work shifts, when the very airing of grievances reinforced the feeling of grievance itself. Workers prepared for strikes and demonstrations on February 14, when the Duma was scheduled to reconvene.

In fact, it was hardly necessary for Okhrana agents to surveil the factories for members of the government to get a sense of the popular mood. Loud voices of "extreme need" were heard everywhere in Petrograd and Moscow, and throughout the rest of the empire as well. Reports of food shortages continued to be published in virtually every local newspaper. Russia's leading newspaper of finance warned that collecting the quantities of grain detailed for obligatory delivery by Minister of Agriculture Aleksandr Rittikh was factually impossible. *Novyi Ekonomist* (*New Economist*) published a dire warning that the Russian economy had entered a critical phase.[17] By now, moreover, it seems likely that the

---

[16] RGVIA f. 2031, op. 1, d. 1181, l. 51; f. 2067, op. 1, d. 2937, ll. 407ff.
[17] *Birzhevye Vedomosti*, Jan. 31, 1917; *Novyi Ekonomist* 4 (Jan. 21, 1917).

representations of need largely correlated with actual scarcities, again especially in Petrograd and Moscow but also in other towns and villages across the empire. January everywhere was exceptionally cold. Blizzards occurred in the South and Southwest as well as more northern areas. February was even colder, perhaps the coldest month of the entire war. Rail traffic was sporadic. In careful studies Anthony Heywood has detailed its effects, even as he discounts the argument that the railroads' failures "sparked" the revolution. In late January the Ministry of Transport held an emergency conference, detailing crisis measures for the first two weeks of February. The situation during this time did not improve.[18]

Shortly afterward, Duma president Rodzianko wrote a long letter directly to Nicholas. The situation was "not only catastrophic but deeply tragic." The army had not been defeated, but "the disintegration of the rear threatened to make pointless all of the sacrifice, all of the blood that had been spilled, all of the exceptional heroism and—even more—threatened to tilt the soldiers' cup towards the Germans." In Moscow the food situation was "critical." Instead of the expected sixty-five freight car loads of daily food, arrivals in January were barely above forty. The stores of grain reserves in Russia's second capital were about to run dry. In Petrograd only 50 percent of the most needed goods had arrived during the first two weeks of the new year. As Rodzianko described it, almost the entire country was also experiencing sharp deficits in fuel, peat, and firewood. Apartments were barely heated, disease an increasing concern. Scarcities in necessities and a currency "overstuffed" with paper credit notes were driving an unrestrained inflation. One had to expect that in three months, according to the Duma president, the food problem would become acute, "bordering on an all-Russia famine."[19]

Some historians have downplayed the extent and implications of conditions, especially in comparison to Germany and Austria. Like Miliukov and his supporters on the Kadet Central Committee, their focus has been largely on the incompetence of the regime. In relative if not absolute terms, battle casualties were higher elsewhere. Indeed, the scarcities and dissidence in Germany and Austria were a principal reason why Lenin was confident a Bolshevik regime in Russia would soon find the closest of allies in Berlin and Vienna.

---

[18] A. J. Heywood, "Spark of Revolution? Railway Disorganization, Freight Traffic and Tsarist Russia's War Effort, July 1914–March 1917" and "Frost and Snow, War and Revolution: The Impact of Winter Weather on Tsarist Russia's Railways, July 1914–March 1917," unpublished papers, cited with the author's kind permission. See also his "Climate, Weather, and Tsarist Russia's Great War, 1914–17: The Wartime Winters," in *Science, Technology, Environment, and Medicine in Russia's Great War and Revolution, 1914–22*, ed. Antony Heywood, Scott Palmer, and Aleksandrovna Laius (Bloomington, IN: Slavica Publishers, 2022), 283–331.

[19] *Ekonomicheskoe polozhenie Rossii nakanune velikoi oktiabr'skoi revoliutsii*, 3 vols. (Moscow: Nauka, 1957), 2:18–19.

Yet for Russia's leading liberal and democratic socialist figures the Russian drama remained one of historical national transformation, not simply military victory. Insofar as the Russian state was "weak," despite commanding the largest army in European history, it was because of the "irrational" domination of incompetence, blind faith over rationality, and the inability of the regime to understand the historically logical way forward. In sharp contrast to England and France, but also to Germany and Austria, whose political systems and cultures Russia's leading liberals and moderate socialists knew quite well, Imperial Russia alone in their view was fighting the world's first modern war with premodern practices, policies, and mentalities. Unrestrained state violence had left whole communities struggling anxiously with the material and emotional effects of loss and scarcity. The promise of revolution could not help but set out what was everywhere in the empire hoped would be a better future.

Uprising, Insurrection, Revolution

How, one hundred years later, should we understand the February revolution? Not simply, as the remainder of this chapter will suggest, as each of the dominant Great Stories has represented it: the liberal version, as an anticipated and surprisingly orderly transfer of power precipitated by mass demonstrations the tsarist government could not readily suppress and which opened at long last the possibility that liberal governance could win the war and lead Russia onto the path of progressive historical modernization; the democratic socialist version, as a historic opportunity brought by massive social protest to set in place a politically democratic regime able to realize in Russia the unfulfilled goals of equality through social democracy promised by its French revolutionary predecessor; or the Bolshevik version, as a mass uprising of exploited and sufficiently conscious industrial workers led by party members and sympathizers that set in place the opportunity to move Russia quickly and forcefully to a historically determined socialist order of their own conception. From the renewal again of women protesting food shortages on February 23, democratic liberals and socialists both focused on the democratic reconstruction of Russian state power, Lenin on its capture. As the demonstrations escalated and the tsar ordered the Duma dismissed lest it become the center of political revolt, their leaders in the Duma did just that, plotting the tsar's removal. The details have been thoroughly laid out by Tsuyoshi Hasegawa and Eduard Burdzhalov, the latter a Soviet historian writing under considerable duress.[20]

---

[20] An exacting description of events is Tsuyoshi Hasegawa, *The February Revolution: Petrograd 1917* (1981; Leiden: Brill, 2018). An English translation of the Russian classic written under political

Yet the revolutionary process that began on February 23 had little to do with constitutional legalities, democratic liberal or socialist values, or Russia's predetermined historical future. Precipitated in the first instance by the shortage of food and its accompanying insecurities, the protests followed those that had occurred when the Duma opened several weeks earlier. In late January, shortly after an article in *Birzhevyia Vedomosti* (*Stock Market News*) extolled the value of "social consciousness" and urged still further involvement of public organizations like the WICs in addressing Russia's crisis, police from the Ministry of Interior arrested all but three of the Petrograd Committee's Workers Group. They included its leader, Kuz'ma Gvozdev, who had warned publicly about the dangers of disorganization and "provocateurs" who could "divide and weaken us."[21] For months the workers groups in Petrograd and elsewhere had been harassed by police. Arrests occurred in Samara and Rostov. Raids in Moscow were common. The arrests were a blatant act of political folly. Public figures, Duma leaders, and many in the factories were appalled.[22]

The ostensible reason for the arrests was that the Petrograd Workers Group was organizing a mass demonstration when the Duma reconvened in February. Despite the arrests, the opening of the Duma did indeed bring some eighty thousand men and women into the streets from more than fifty enterprises, according to reports. What was most notable was that many crossing the Neva from the Vyborg district directly opposite the Winter Palace carried their protests not to the Duma at the Tauride Palace but to Nevskii Prospekt, in the heart of the city, Imperial Russia's most prominent central artery. In a portent of what was to come, the heralded space of imperial and "bourgeois" Russia, with its fancy stores and luxury hotels, was physically and demonstrably taken over, if only for one day.

As is well known, a broad wave of protests then erupted again on February 23, International Women's Day. Long lines of cold and angry women waiting at food stores were joined by others also anxious about the food shortages, including militant Putilov workers locked out of their workplace for attempting to strike. Protests soon grew larger. Again, the principal site was Nevskii Prospect. On Friday, February 24, the movement "swept over Petersburg like a great flood," according to Minister of Interior A. D. Protopopov.[23] An estimated 175,000 occupied the boulevard with placards protesting shortages ("Give us Bread!") and the

---

duress is E. N. Burdzhalov, *Russia's Second Revolution: The February Uprising in Petrograd*, ed. Donald J. Raleigh (Bloomington: Indiana University Press, 1987).

[21] *Den'*, Oct. 23, 1916.
[22] RGIA f. 32, op. 1, d. 2126, ll. 19–65.
[23] N. N. Sukhanov, *The Russian Revolution 1917*, ed. and trans. J. Carmichael (Princeton, NJ: Princeton University Press, 1984), 6.

losses of war ("Peace!"; "Down with the War!"), many again crossing the Neva with their banners in front of the Winter Palace. They also demanded a new regime ("Down with the Autocracy!"). Between February 23 and March 2, as many as 400,000 men and women from more than nine hundred enterprises reportedly participated, virtually the entire working population of the capital.

Few events in modern history have been more thoroughly described than the collapse of the tsarist regime: the "five days that shook the world," as Laura Engelstein has called it. Even the sounds and smells of the moment have been well documented.[24] Until Sunday, February 26, what Petrograd experienced was a massive popular uprising. It embraced the hope for political reform in an echo of 1905, but it was largely driven now by the anger and anxiety over food shortages, wages that did not cover rising costs, repressive workplace regimes and conditions, and, especially for women, the degradation inflicted by lecherous foremen and the multiple burdens of home and work that sapped energy, dignity, and will. In the first instance the "foot riots" on February 23 were provoked by the actualities of scarcity and food insecurities, but they now reached more broadly into the dysfunctional and repressive conditions around them, not least of which were the actualities and anxieties of a seemingly endless war and its never-ending losses.[25]

Protesting women were at the heart of the uprising, from its start in the food lines to the mobilization of mass protest when they walked out of the big textile mill in the Vyborg district, marched down Samsonievskii Prospekt, and called for support through the windows for their metalworking comrades. Many metallists were already on the street. Others needed little persuasion. Personal loss among women of husbands, sons, or brothers was intangible in these demonstrations but almost certainly a strong element underlying their shouts and placards demanding an end to the war. One can also surmise that their ranks were filled with many newcomers to the city who had taken the places of men drafted or sent punitively to the front. In the process they commonly experienced as well a sense of dislocation and social loss as they left their homes and towns and found themselves in a rough urban environment, lonely perhaps but also vulnerable to the deprivations of their workplace bosses. They may also have been even more successful than men in rallying others by evoking feelings of shame in those who stood aside.

In any event the streets were soon "seething," in Nikolai Sukhanov's eyewitness impression. Men and women from all major Petrograd plants were on the

---

[24] Laura Engelstein, *Russia in Flames* (New York: Oxford University Press, 2018); V. V. Lapin, *Peterburg: Zapakhi i svuki* (St. Petersburg: Evropeiskii Dom, 2007); Jan Plamper, "Sounds of February, Smells of October: The Russian Revolution as Sensory Experience," *American Historical Review* 1 (Mar. 2021): 140–65.

[25] RGIA f. 457, op. 1, d. 209, l. 3 ob.

streets. Some were dispersed by Cossacks and mounted police but "without energy or zeal," according again to Sukhanov.[26] The uprising swelled over the next two days, Saturday and Sunday, which were also reduced workdays, despite warnings now plastered around the city from the Petrograd military commander General Khabalov that new protests would not be tolerated. Garrison soldiers and Cossacks moved into the streets. Bridges were closed. Some troops opened fire, strewing Nevskii Prospekt with injured and dead. The brutalities of war came to the heart of the capital. The uprising seemed likely to be brought under control.[27]

By their very nature, popular uprisings pose particular problems for historians. Motivations objectified in slogans and banners often provide evidence of their purposes and goals. But just as with reading soldiers' moods, the nature and intensity of their underlying emotions are difficult to access. While historians rely largely on documentary evidence, one can reasonably deduce anger and even grief from protests against war. The violence that sometimes accompanies protest may come as well from psychologies or dispositions that are impossible to document, or even from particular cultures.[28] Anxieties and fears that beg articulation can still be linked to actual or anticipated threats or dangers.

Uprisings are thus forceful emotional expressions as well as social protests against specific circumstances and deprivations. What they are against is also frequently more coherent than what they are for. As Judith Butler has argued, there does not have to be an elaborate analysis for an uprising to occur: "It is not required that everyone reads Karl Marx.... All that is required is a sense of living within a particular regime, whether that be political or economic, requires suffering in unbearable ways, and an understanding that this should not be bearable, and that this claim is true not only for oneself but for others who are positioned in a similar situation within the field of power."[29]

From this perspective, whether or not the February uprising involved Bolshevik sympathizers adds little to our understanding. Nor is it analytically useful to think of it as a good or bad thing. As Jan Plamper has suggested, what is at stake is whether the emotional underpinning of an uprising is valorized in a positive or negative way.[30] For those on the streets, for whom the anger and passion that infused their protest was clearly related to the multiple privations of scarcity and loss, the uprising was a positive event, a risky and courageous effort to meet obvious needs and redress obvious wrongs. Desires for security fused

[26] Sukhanov, *The Russian Revolution*, 6.
[27] Ibid., 33.
[28] See the extended discussion in Carol Z. Stearns and Peter N. Stearns, *Anger: The Struggle for Emotional Control in America's History* (Chicago: University of Chicago Press, 1986).
[29] Judith Butler, "Uprising," in *Uprisings*, ed. G. Didi-Huberman (Paris, 2016), 25.
[30] See Jan Plamper, *History of Emotions* (New York: Oxford University Press, 2015), 58. I am grateful to Jan for his comments on this issue.

with less well defined needs, wishes, and expectations, reflecting what the philosopher Ernst Bloch has notably termed the "principle of hope." *Tak zhit' dal'she nel'zia! One cannot live this way any longer!* was still the Russian expression that captured these hopes, however much historians like Richard Pipes and others have devalued the uprising as "thick with that peculiar Russian air of generalized, unfocused violence—the urge to beat and destroy—for which the Russian language has coined the words *pogrom* and *razgrom*."[31] For anxious public figures and political leaders observing events from the Central War Industries offices at 46 Liteinyi or the Duma's seat nearby in the Tauride Palace, the ideas of "freedom," "liberty," and "democracy" floated as signifiers between contending meanings in relation to individual and collective wants and feelings and Russia's longer-term possibilities, projecting their own hopes on the contagion of collective emotion and anxiety in an effort to realize the uprising's larger implications.

From this perspective as well, we must incorporate another key emotional aspect of the moment into our understanding: the fear that the demonstrations would be brutally suppressed. As so often in popular memory, standing up to the authorities involved great personal and community risk. On February 25 and 26, it was likely that Cossack troops ordered to support the police would do so. The looting and assaults widely reported in the newspapers were read by many in high places as rioters run amuck. No one needed to be reminded that the government had bombarded Moscow's principal industrial district in 1905. At the very least, many of the men arrested would be sent to the front, men and women both charged with rebellion.

Hence the "unforgettable" Monday, February 27 (Sukhanov again), when workers seized weapons from the Petrograd cartridge plant, troops refused to fire on the demonstrators, and numbers of garrison soldiers left their barracks and fraternized with the crowds. At that moment the regime's monopoly on the instruments of state coercion—the very essence of its claim to legitimacy—was broken, at least in Petrograd. Everyone recognized, of course, that troops from outside the city could still be brought to bear. Indeed, plans were well underway at army headquarters to do just that. Focus in the streets as well as in the Tauride Palace thus turned to replacing the regime, the only way to avoid the lethal reprisals that suppression would undoubtedly involve. As this happened, uprising turned into armed insurrection.

Here we come to the critical point of intersection between events on Nevskii Prospekt and those that were occurring within the halls of the Duma. As the uprising grew on February 24 and 25, Duma leaders largely focused on the food scarcities. So did Petrograd newspapers. Governor-General Khabalov issued a statement insisting there was no shortage of bread in the stores. After members

---

[31] Richard Pipes, *The Russian Revolution* (New York: Knopf, 1990), 275.

of the Duma expressed doubts, Rodzianko toured the city, first by himself and then with Minister of Agriculture Rittikh. Both met with Prime Minister Golitsyn, who had kept the Council of Ministers in session on February 24 until 4:00 a.m.[32] A special conference convened in the Mariinskii Palace to address the food problem and reassure the public. Participants unanimously voted to transfer control of the city's food supply to the Petrograd City Duma. As the uprising grew on February 25, Miliukov's newspaper *Rech'* editorialized that anxiety about tomorrow's food was as important a problem as the level of today's supplies. The key question was one of confidence in the government's ability "to fight the disorganization that prevails and that constantly increases."[33]

Early the next morning Rodzianko sent his famous telegram to the tsar at army headquarters warning that the city was in a "state of anarchy." He also asked Prime Minister Golitsyn to resign. After demonstrators were killed, some suggested the entire cabinet resign as well. The tsar responded reflexively, as he had so often done before. He dismissed the Duma to prevent it becoming the center of resistance. When soldiers refused orders to fire again on demonstrators, Rodzianko disregarded the tsar's decree, just as he had done in the summer of 1915. A provisional Duma committee was formed "to restore order in the capital and establish contact with public organizations and institutions." Headed by Rodzianko, it included the prominent Duma socialists Nikolai Chkheidze and the palpably nervous Alexander Kerensky, along with Miliukov and Alexander Konovalov, the progressive Moscow industrialist (and accomplished pianist) who would soon join the Kadets. Committee members demanded the tsar replace his ministers with responsible people, as the Progressive Bloc had insisted. A list had long since been drawn up. It included Miliukov, Konovalov, and Andrei Shingarev, still chair of the Duma's Finance Committee, as well as Rodzianko, whom the tsar hated. There were still grounds for hoping a new government of respected Duma figures would finally be appointed by the tsar.

This, of course, was not to be. When garrison troops and Cossacks refused to fire on the crowd on February 27, activity within the Taurride Palace changed dramatically. The previous evening a number of socialists, including Bolsheviks, met at Kerensky's nearby apartment on Tverskaia Street to strategize the formation of a workers soviet (council), as in 1905. Early on February 27 the leader of the CWIC Workers Group was released with others from prison and made their way to the Tauride Palace. Meeting in the opposite wing of the building from the Provisional Duma Committee, they joined the Mensheviks' Duma spokesman Chkheidze and others in organizing a provisional soviet executive committee

---

[32] *Padenie tsarskogo rezhima; stenograficheskie otchety doprosov i pokazanii*, 7 vols. (Leningrad, 1924–27), 2:231–36, 364–65 (testimony of Belaev and Golitsyn).

[33] *Rech'*, Feb. 25, 1917.

(*ispolkom*). One of this group's first acts was to charge Vladimir Groman with organizing a food supply commission. On the other side of the building the Provisional Duma Committee did the same. Groman's first step was to issue a public appeal for food donations and set up a supply center in the Tauride Palace itself.

Meanwhile the first issues of *Izvestiia Komitetov Petrogradskikh Zhurnalistov* (*News of the Petrograd Committee of Journalists*) and *Izvestiia Revolutsionnoi Nedeli* (*News of the Revolutionary Week*) appeared on the streets, announcing that the soviet's first meeting would begin at 7:00 p.m. "All who have come over to the side of the People" were urged immediately to elect their delegates, one soldier from each garrison company, one worker per thousand from the factories. By midday deputies were streaming into the Tauride Palace. The possibility of receiving food packets apparently drew some workers and soldiers to the site.[34]

By late afternoon, the Tauride Palace had become the insurrection's logistical and command center. General Khabalov was arrested, as were other officers and tsarist officials. Roused from his apartment after a sleepless night and followed by a hostile crowd as he was taken to an office Kerensky had appropriated, the police chief General Alexander Kurlov later described the scene as a "dense sea of humanity, workers, and women intermingling with soldiers from the barracks and junkers from military academies, among whom I saw with sorrow even those from the Nikolaevskii Cavalier Academy."[35] Meanwhile, Miliukov and others went with officers from the House Grenadiers to the garrisons, where they called on the troops to support the new regime.

By early evening on February 27 the soviet's side of the Tauride Palace was overflowing. Chkheidze was elected the new soviet's chair. Elected as vice chairs were Kerensky and Matvei Skobelev, soon to be Russia's first ministers of justice and labor. In its first official statement, the soviet declared its foremost task to be the "organization of popular forces to fight decisively to secure political freedom and popular rule." The "entire population" of the city was called on to unite around the soviet, organize local district soviets, and to take local government into their hands. First on its list of urgent tasks was addressing the food situation. Groman warned that if troops did not assist in supplying the city, hunger "would be dire."[36] Next was setting up the soviet's own military commission. Points around the city were designated for mobilizing workers and soldiers to defend the revolution from tsarist troops marching on the city.[37]

---

[34] *Izvestiia Revoliutsionnoi Nedeli*, Feb. 27, 1917; *Izvestiia Komitetov Petrogradskikh Zhurnalistov*, Feb. 27, 1917.

[35] Alexander Kurlov, *Gibel' imperatorskoi Rossii: Vospominaniia* (Moscow: Zakharov, 2002), 220.

[36] V. P. Volobuev, ed., *Petrogradskii Sovet rabochikh i soldatskikh deputatov v 1917 (Protokoly, steno. otchety i zasedanii Ispol. Komiteta 27 Feb. 1917–25 Oct. 1915)* (Leningrad: Nauka, 1991), 27–28, 32.

[37] *Izvestiia Revoliutsionnoi Nedeli*, Feb. 28, 1917.

With the insurrection now unchecked, soldiers and officers refusing to obey orders from outside the city, and the Duma leadership defying his order to disperse, Nicholas finally agreed to accept a cabinet chosen by the Duma. Then, even more momentously, when told by his own staff that the war could not otherwise be won, he was persuaded as a patriotic act to abdicate the throne and allow his authority to fall to his son. It was now the responsibility of the Provisional Committee of the Duma itself to organize a new government. It quickly did so in cooperation with the leadership of the soviet, communicating through Chkheidze and Kerensky.[38] Some in the new regime, most notably Miliukov, hoped and expected that their revolutionary move would soon be sanctioned by Nicholas's successor, formally legitimizing its assumption of state power. The tsarist autocracy would then become a fully sanctioned constitutional monarchy, warranting support from all sectors of society. Meanwhile, Nicholas refused to appoint his twelve-year old son Aleksei to succeed him, designating his younger brother Michael instead. Miliukov and others braced for an assault by loyalist troops. When their movement was halted by militant railroad workers and garrisons in other large cities defected, the Michael refused to accept the throne. Insurrection had become revolution.

Locations and Forms of Power and Questions of Political Legitimacy

The raft of declarations and speeches greeting the moment was rapturous. "History shall forever visualize the present revolution as the eighth wonder of the world" (the liberal newspaper *Rech'*); "The inevitable has happened . . . a great and decisive moment in the life of our *rodina* has arrived" (the mainstream *Russkiia Vedomosti*); "the greatest of all historic achievements in the contemporary world!" (the Socialist Revolutionaries' *Delo Naroda*); "The long-awaited dawn of freedom . . . like a series of magic transformations. . . . But nothing is accidental in the course of historical events" (the Mensheviks' *Rabochaia Gazeta*); "The people . . . are ready for cooperative, rational actions . . . are capable of establishing order" (*Izvestiia*, now the official newspaper of the Petrograd Soviet). V. V. Zenzinov later wrote: "Over 35 years have passed, but even now I can hear every word uttered by A. F. Kerensky. We were all gripped by one feeling, one impulse. Kerensky was picked up and carried out of the hall amid wild applause. . . . [M]y face was covered with tears."[39] Even Vasili Maklakov, the right-wing Kadet

---

[38] Sukhanov, *Russian Revolution*, 34–73; *Padenie tsarskogo rezhima*, 2: 231 (testimony of Beliaev).
[39] *Rech'*, Mar. 5, 1917; *Russkiia Vedomosti*, Mar. 2, 1917; *Delo Naroda*, Mar. 15, 1917; *Rabochaia Gazeta*, Mar. 7, 1917; *Izvestiia*, Mar. 23, 1917; V. V. Zenzinov, "Fevral'skie dni," *Novyi Zhurnal* 35 (1953): 230–31.

who coined the metaphor of Russia as a driverless automobile hurtling out of control down a mountain road, soon professed the revolution was "a miracle." His and others' hopeful if cautious optimism was based, as in 1914, on the expectation that Russia's "vital social forces" could finally be constructively engaged in managing the urgent tasks at hand, that intelligent and responsible officials in whom the public had confidence could now steer revolutionary Russia in the right historical direction.[40]

Not surprisingly, this outpouring of celebration was far more tempered in the halls of the aristocratic State Council and other parts of the suddenly old regime, and even more so among those on Russia's still numerous political right. Many gentry landowners and tsarist officials and even some leading academicians may have looked on events as the nearly inevitable consequence of ineptitude in high places, but this hardly made them hopeful about the future. One of Russia's most prominent historians and a leader of Moscow's intellectual elite, Iurii Vladimirovich Got'e, labeled his diary a "lament on the downfall of the Russian land." His first entry began, "*Finis Russiae.*" The fundamental cause of this collapse was not the war but the century-long decomposition of the old regime.[41] In the chaos and confusion at the Tauride Palace, many were overcome with what V. D. Nabokov saw as the "patriotic anxiety" Miliukov first identified in the early summer of 1915. As the father of the famous writer took on the challenging task of managing the government Chancellery, his overwhelming concern was for what lay ahead. "Where is the way out?" he asked himself and others, articulating an anxiety which would continue to find expression throughout the year and those to follow. The feeling was shared by many democratic socialists, especially on the Menshevik right.[42]

Distinguishing the phases through which uprising became insurrection and revolution in rapid succession helps us understand both the exhilaration and the unease that coursed through the Tauride Palace as the Provisional Government and Petrograd Soviet both came into being. The two organs of revolutionary governance sprang from different locations and forms of power, which burdened each with their own problems of asserting their legitimacy and complicating their longer historical visions and their immediate scripts. Russia had a government of responsible men, but in the absence of a formally sanctioned change of regimes, the new ministers faced the possibility of counterrevolution from supporters of the autocracy and loyalist army commanders. Many at the moment thought counterrevolution likely. The new soviet's leaders were largely

---

[40] *Russkiia Vedomosti*, Apr. 1, 1917; *Vestnik Partii Narodnoi Svobody* 1 (Mar. 1917).
[41] Iurii Vladimirovich Got'e, *Time of Troubles: The Diary of Iurii Vladimirovich Got'e*, trans. and ed. Terence Emmons (Stanford, CA: Stanford University Press, 1988), 27.
[42] Vergil. D. Medlin and Steven. L. Parsons, eds., *V. D. Nabokov and the Russian Provisional Government, 1917* (New Haven, CT: Yale University Press, 1976), 15–24, 33–142.

experienced democratic socialist Duma deputies whose legitimacy depended on their ability to address successfully the uprising's underlying causes. Many at the moment thought this was unlikely as well. How to pursue the imperial war was another point of contention between the two groups, given the socialists' opposition to annexations and indemnities and liberals' hope that Constantinople might come under Russian control and the empire's dominions remain intact. Increasing the supply of food and lowering the costs of other essential goods was yet another. Here the peasants' demand for land came into play, as did the related issues of rights to possession and property.

For democratic liberals, the way the regime collapsed was a risk to realizing their long-term goals. In late 1916 Miliukov himself had hoped for a liberal dictatorship like Lloyd George's cabinet in London or Clemenceau's in Paris.[43] The legitimacy of the new regime now derived not from tsarist historical authority but from a historically alien concept in Russia of the sovereignty of the people, an idea not even sanctified as yet by national elections. As a worried Miliukov famously expressed the dilemma in his first public speech as minister on March 3, "I am asked, who elected you? Nobody elected us.... We have been elected by the Russian Revolution!"[44] What he did not add was that the revolution expected the satisfaction of want and need along with an end to the losses of a terrible war, and protests would surely erupt again against the self-proclaimed regime if these extremely difficult tasks were not quickly and successfully accomplished.

For many democratic socialists, the uprising and insurrection were cause for some disquiet, however much their revolutionary outcome was greeted with jubilation. The collapse of autocratic rule was sudden, untidy, and charged with uncertainty. Kerensky and others hoped the regime would be overcome, not overthrown. What had suddenly brought tsarism to its end was not the result of political strategy or organization or the mobilization of "conscious" workers in favor of coherent political and social goals, but a spontaneous uprising occasioned by the anxieties and deprivations of real and anticipated need and the material and emotional dislocations of loss. For Mensheviks, the dilemma was that Russia's workers lacked strong trade unions or other organizations that could effectively support their interests and channel passions in organized and politically constructive ways. Russia also lacked effective mechanisms to mediate workplace disputes, which portended new conflict if perceived needs were not met. The huge peasant majority in the countryside, meanwhile, had little if any organization outside the village assembly. Democratic socialists among the Socialist Revolutionary center and right wings understood that without formal

---

[43] *Rech'*, Nov. 27, 1916.
[44] *Izvestiia Revoliutsionnoi Nedeli*, Mar. 2, 1917.

restraints, peasants were historically inclined to settle grievances forcefully and meet village needs on their own.

Here, too, the claim of the Petrograd Soviet to be the legitimate voice of the popular uprising depended as well on the continued support of its constituents, as did that of the scores of similar soviets which soon organized around the country. The soviets' dilemma, like that of the government, was that their leadership rights were contingent on meeting their constituents' needs. Paradoxically, the essential democratic rights of free speech, assembly, and elections themselves subjected this question to constant interrogation, presaging the likelihood of continued contention. Elections by workers, soldiers, and peasants to everything from committees to local soviets and national congresses meant, in effect, a constant testing of those who claimed to represent their interests, a process in conditions of continued want and loss that could not help but encourage further radicalization.

These mutual insecurities in the political positions of government and soviet leaders also reflected key differences in the forms and locations of power that supported them. For the Provisional Government, bearing the formal power of the state required maintaining a monopoly on the use of force while developing policies that were likely to be controversial. It also meant repositioning the state in relation to the war, the empire, and its place in the postwar world even before the convocation of a prospective constituent (constitutional) assembly. In the volatile circumstances of insurrection and revolution, the use of force to maintain order and implement policy risked strong resistance from armed workers and peasants as well as reactionaries with deep roots in the imperial army. For the Petrograd Soviet and the burgeoning network of district and local soviets that followed its organization, the power immanent in the February uprising reflected a force that was readily susceptible to new and more radical mobilization. First and foremost, both the government and the soviet leadership had to address the underlying causes of the February events themselves: the perceptions, actualities, and anxieties of scarcity and loss—the quest for security and dignity in all their material and emotional dimensions—and give acceptable meaning to the war. In a phrase, the form of power supporting the soviet was not easily controlled, while the form of power controlled by the government was not easily applied.

In these terms we can resituate the well-known dilemma of "dual power" (*dvoevlastie*) that emerged in March, in which the overt forms of coercive state power now formally in the hands of the Provisional Government was balanced by the latent power of social protest reflected initially in the Petrograd Soviet and soon replicated around the country. Almost all variants of the three Great Stories regard dual power as the Achilles heel of the provisional regime. In this understanding a key event that weakened the revolutionary government from the start was the Petrograd Soviet's infamous Order Number 1, directing soldiers and sailors on March 1 to obey only its orders rather those of the new government or any other authority (meaning the tsarist army commanders). The order was famously complemented by a formal garrison resolution of allegiance to the new regime "only insofar as" its policies reflected the interests of ordinary workers, peasants, and soldiers.

For members of the Provisional Government, none of whom came from worker or peasant ranks, and only one of whom, Kerensky, was a socialist, the Petrograd Soviet's stance on both matters represented a crippling violation of the state's "plentitude of power," as Miliukov expressed it. Many historians and memoirists centering their stories on revolutionary politics have echoed this view. Yet while dual power facilitated polarization, it can also be thought of as reflecting something like a revolutionary form of parliamentary governance, in which different forms of power were institutionalized in two different locations. In effect, the phrase "only insofar as" made ministers (the Provisional Government) accountable to a popularly elected assembly (the Petrograd Soviet) whose continued support was essential to its ability to govern. A demonstration in some form of "no confidence" from the soviet network would precipitate a need to reshuffle the government's composition. Its legitimacy was thus contingent on its ability to function effectively enough to sustain popular support, a difficult task at best in circumstances that precipitated the February uprising itself.

In all of this, moreover, Lenin's Bolsheviks had a well-scripted advantage from the start: the Great Story of 1917 would be of a popular revolution led by a vanguard that understood how history determined it would turn out. Fully opposed to imperial war and relentless in their hostility to democratic socialists cooperating with "capitalists" and the "bourgeoisie," whom they directly blamed for its miseries, Lenin and his supporters were well positioned to harness the form of power located in insurrection itself. If democratic liberals and socialists saw the potential of anarchy in popular need and anxiety, Lenin saw food insecurities and especially the losses of war as huge opportunities for his cause. The way a "food riot" quickly became a city-wide uprising and then quickly morphed into armed insurrection and revolution demonstrated that he and his followers might accelerate history toward their own imagined future if they could capture the emotional energy of the street and link it to armed physical force, as the February uprising did with the Petrograd garrison. For Lenin there were no dilemmas of legitimacy. Legitimacy was determined by history itself. The same was true with solving Russia's great problems of scarcity and loss, which would not become the Bolsheviks' tasks until Lenin and his party seized what was left of the state and declared themselves its historically legitimated government in October.

Scarcity and Social Identity

An additional problem of revolutionary governance related to the forms and locations of power was that of social identities: the ways access to essential goods and other scarce resources sharpened one's sense of oneself in Russia's social hierarchy and valorized in positive or negative ways one's relative well-being. As historians of revolution have pointed out, the coalescence of antagonistic social groups is a common if unstable element of uprisings and rapid socioeconomic and political change. The concept of social polarization is widely deployed to describe the deepening divide during the last years of the tsarist regime between propertied elites and workers and peasants, a distancing that was already problematic in terms of Russia's longer-term social and political stability before the war.

In this sense, social identities in Imperial Russia always carried political meaning. Being a woman involved subordination to men. Being a male worker or peasant commonly meant near total subordination to factory owners, landlords, and the state. Imperial marginalization of ethnic minorities engendered a demand for political autonomy or independence among Ukrainians, Tatars, and Central Asians for political autonomy or independence. While the tsarist state and its officials were the obvious targets of the February revolution, and while the formal collapse of tsarist rule created the possibility of democratizing the state, antagonism based on the different ways individuals and groups perceived and identified themselves constituted the revolution's deeper social undercurrents.

An essential dimension of February was thus the ways social identities themselves also sharpened during these days, internalized not only in terms of their sociocultural attributes and socioeconomic positions but through experience itself. As Rosa Luxemburg wrote, the very act of going on strike generated a "mental sediment" that made the event itself a memorable experience in both individual and collective terms.[45] Not only was one's social place in the tsarist order marked in Petrograd by whether one was among the thousands of demonstrators on Nevskii Prospekt; participation inscribed social identities and positions themselves with the power of further collective action grounded in these identities rather than any higher set of principles or goals. For those watching "their" Nevskii Prospekt being overrun by "rabble," the scene almost certainly sharpened the sense of being part of a beleaguered social elite, even if it was the only common identity they may have shared.

What constituted the essence of authority both before and after February was thus not simply a network of formal political institutions. As Nicos Polantzas has pointed out, the common conceptual distinction between state and society

---

[45] Rosa Luxemburg, *The Mass Strike* (Detroit, MI: Marxian Education Society, 1920), 33.

obscures the ways real states are historically constituted.[46] Autocratic governance in Imperial Russia was embedded in an array of self-replicating and culturally legitimated social and cultural relations, ones that embodied their own forms of power and control within specific social frameworks and clearly defined sociopolitical boundaries. In the countryside, thick social and cultural networks within village communities were themselves a key location of authority and social control, structuring relations with tsarist officials and their gentry allies every bit as much as formally legislated policies of the state. In Russia's industrial centers, access to foodstuffs, housing, the opportunities of leisure and especially control over work processes and one's sense of dignity within the factory itself reflected the authority of social hierarchies, reproducing as well that of formal political institutions.

The valorization of specific social identities in the uprising and insurrection thus implied a frontal assault on the multiple forms of authority held by those on the other side of the social and rhetorically constructed barricade. At first it was not even clear if the regime's new declaration of rights applied to women. Prince G. E. L'vov, the new minister president, publicly stated that it did, but his affirmation was regarded skeptically. A huge demonstration of women on March 19 elicited an affirmation from the government concerning female suffrage and equal civil rights. Shortly afterward the All-Russian Congress of Women convened in Moscow.[47] If "worker," "peasant," "landlord," or "plant owner" defined one's place in the process of production in the sense of class, "women" signified those who were specially burdened in various ways, while "bourgeois" and "capitalist" signified those with unfettered access to necessary goods, if not outright luxury, whose original sin was wealth in a time of penury and whose practices and principles amplified the injustices of scarcity and social inequality. The revolution thus infused well established social identities with forceful new political meaning.

This was most importantly reflected in the soviet leaders' substantially different conception from that of Russia's liberals about what democracy itself now meant, published as early as February 28 in *Izvestiia Revoliutsionnoi Nedeli*. In linguistic terms, "democracy" became a "floating signifier," shifting from a description of political institutions and processes to a broad social formation defined entirely in terms of the "people" (*narod*). In terms of realizing civil liberties and abolishing all restrictions based on nationality the soviet newspaper insisted that "the *democracy* must lend its support." Soviet leaders were ready to work

---

[46] Nicos Poulantzas, *State, Power, Socialism* (London: NLB, 1978), 35–46 and passim; Nicos Poulantzas, *Political Power and Social Classes* (London: Verso, 1978).

[47] *Rabochaia Gazeta*, Mar. 16, 21 and Apr. 8, 1917. For an overview, see Rochelle Ruthchild, *Equality and Revolution: Women's Rights in the Russian Empire, 1905–1917* (Pittsburgh, PA: University of Pittsburgh Press, 2010), ch. 7.

with the new regime on the critical problems at hand. They sent their representatives to special committees in Petrograd created to deal with supply problems, transport matters, and especially scarcities of food. They also agreed to join the Labor Section of Konovalov's Ministry of Trade and Industry.[48]

But the Soviet leadership's ascription of "democracy" to a particular social category of workers, peasants, and soldiers clearly implied that a "democratic" regime embodied the particular interests of those socially identified in this way. Workers, peasants, and soldiers—*the* "democracy"—had to be supported against the privileged gentry, industrialists, and society's middle ranks, the "bourgeoisie" in the ideological reduction that homogenized Russia's traditionally dominant estates. Consistent with the democratic socialists' historical imagination, this privileging was essential to assure Russia's successful transition to a social democratic future, which would now be accelerated by the overthrow of tsarism and the creation of a bourgeois order thought to be the next chapter of the democratic socialist Great Story. If many liberals regarded the revolution as fully justified in terms of ensuring universal civil rights, the valorization of "the democracy" as a social formation thus carried with it the implicit demonization of its nondemocratic bourgeois capitalist exploiters. February, in sum, threatened a new field of potential losses well beyond those on the battlefield. From the start, all citizens of the revolutionary Russian state were not created equal.

Loss and the Meanings of War

Because officers tended to blame the government for their failures and vice versa, as we have seen, most joined their troops in welcoming the new regime, although not uniformly and in many places not necessarily for the same reasons. At headquarters, it was hoped new leadership could resolve continued problems of supply and logistics. Garrison soldiers in Petrograd and elsewhere were quick to form their own committees to redress what they considered the excesses of discipline and intolerable affronts to their dignity and welfare. They did so both before and after the Petrograd Soviet issued its notorious Order Number 1, specifying that its orders had to be obeyed, not those of the new Provisional Government. Order Number 1 was specifically directed at the Petrograd garrison troops. Despite the implication that the soviet was attempting to seize control of the army, the order was issued to ensure that any defense of the city would be directed by the soviet. It was also expected to curb excesses against officers and similar disorders that worried the soviet and the new government alike, as

---

[48] *Zhurnal Vremennogo Pravitel'stvo*, Mar. 9, 1917, in V. A. Kozlov and S. V. Mironenko, eds., *Arkhiv noveishei istorii Rossii* (Moscow: Rosspen, 2001), 3: 8–14.

it soon did among reserve troops in Moscow and other garrisons. As we know, those with German names were particularly vulnerable. In places near the front like Vitebsk and Dvinsk as well as in the Baltic fleet at Revel, there was news that commanders considered particularly offensive were being arrested, or worse.

News of the events in Petrograd spread quickly. Soldiers at the front learned what was happening from newspapers and individuals bringing reports in person. Newspapers arrived in large numbers. They soon included the Bolsheviks' *Okopnaia Pravda* (*Trench Pravda*), designed to mobilize troops behind the party. Units along the lines also began to organize their own committees and councils (soviets) and confront their officers, often at the urging of those coming from Petrograd, in some places on their own. For several days there were no clear directives from headquarters. The abdication of the tsar caused particular confusion. Hearing from his field commanders that persons claiming to represent the new government were arriving from Petrograd and addressing the troops, Chief of Staff General Alekseev ordered they be intercepted and turned away. In some places the tsar's abdication reportedly met with "wild cheering." Some soldiers donned red ribbons. One military censor described a "great holiday" at the front. On March 4, an anxious Alekseev issued an order to obey the Provisional Government and maintain strict discipline.[49]

Some tellers of the liberal Great Story have dismissively represented the army's transition in early March as chaotic, violent, and rent with the deeply rooted animosity that peasant soldiers harbored toward their officers, with little or no regard for the actualities of life and loss at the front. Pipes describes it as "the most stupendous military revolt in recorded history ... not really a military mutiny of the kind that broke out during the war in other armies ... but a typical Russian *bunt*, with powerful anarchist overtones."[50] There is ample evidence of a similar view in officers' letters and later writings. Some clearly expected the army to disintegrate.[51]

It is important, however, to set this moment in the context of the experience soldiers were still enduring at the front: the traumas of violent loss, the anxieties of anticipation, intense concerns about the well-being of their families, anger toward their commanders for a variety of reasons. So far the horrendous casualties suffered as a result of their officers' commands had not brought the war closer to an end. In these terms, it is hard to see how adding "peasant" to "soldier" explains the ways "peasant-soldiers" along the front reacted to events in Petrograd. Careful research has shown that the soldiers' committees were selective in their targets: officers whose competency they distrusted, especially

---

[49] RGVIA f. 2003, op. 1, d. 1486, ll. 310ff.
[50] Pipes, *Russian Revolution*, 281.
[51] A. L. Sidorov et al., eds., *Revoliutsionnoe dvizhenie v Rossii posle sverzheniia samoderzhaviia* (Moscow: Nauka, 1957), 229–41, 613–39.

those with German names; those they held responsible for poor tactics and unnecessary losses; sergeants and officers suspected of selling off supplies; those who inflicted harsh punishments for minor infractions; and those up and down the chain of command who demanded bribes for leaves. Peasant or not, soldiers everywhere on the front were hardly blind to the need to defend their land. Indeed, in many places soldiers' committees brought in junior field and warrant officers (*praporshshiki*), often by election, whom they trusted to replace the "incompetents" they had driven off.[52] Even as they were organizing their committees, soldiers almost everywhere maintained sufficient discipline to defend themselves and resist sporadic German attacks.

There is little doubt, however, that soldiers were keen on ending ritualized humiliations. The provisions of Order Number 1 they responded to immediately were those that abolished standing at attention and compulsory saluting when not on duty, and addressing officers with the titles "Your Excellency" and "Your Honor," a practice that reinforced a broader culture of social domination as well as military discipline. In the performance of military duties Order Number 1 demanded "the strictest military discipline." Off duty, soldiers could not "in any way be deprived of those rights all citizens now enjoy." For garrison soldiers in Petrograd, this meant, among other privileges, the right to ride inside street cars rather than outside on frozen running boards. At the front, "rudeness toward soldiers of any rank, and especially addressing them with the subordinating personal pronoun [*ty*]," was now prohibited. Soldiers were required to bring to their committees "every infraction of this rule as well as all misunderstandings between officers and enlisted men."[53] Indeed, after discussions with the soviet leadership, the new minister of war Alexander Guchkov, son of a Moscow merchant and a founder of the conservative liberal Octobrist Party, reinforced these orders with his own decree. He also announced the formation of a special commission under his tsarist predecessor Polivanov to bring all military regulations into conformity with the principles of civil liberty reflected in the new government's declarations.[54]

From various sources we know that large numbers of officers arrested by their units during these days were detained precisely for violating these sudden and dramatic shifts in military culture. Entrenched habits were hard to break. We also know that many of these men were soon released and returned to their units. Undoubtedly shaken, they then did little to prevent a wave of "security leaves" for soldiers to check on their family's welfare or to more forcefully control desertion. Guchkov himself was now deluged with petitions from villages pleading for

[52] Konstantin Tarasov, "Za predelami natsii: Krizis rossiiskoi armii v 1917 kak sledstvie transformatsii imperskoi sotsial'noi strukturi," *Ab Imperio* 2 (2020): 102–35.
[53] Volubuev, *Protokoly*, 290.
[54] *Vestnik Vremennogo Pravitel'stva*, Mar. 7, 8, 1917.

sons and husbands to be released to manage the spring planting and rescue their families from "starvation." Everywhere soldiers coming from the front jammed trains and depots, "requisitioning" food and goods along the way; often they were out of control. According to one report some one thousand soldiers a day arrived in Kiev from the Southwestern Front. Another estimated that as many as 100,000 to 150,000 may have left their posts during the month as a whole.[55] Most apparently returned to their units, satisfied that rumors of landowners burning down villages were not true and that their families were managing to get by.[56]

Thus, the Petrograd Soviet's usurpation of government authority in issuing Order Number 1 seems to have had less of an effect on how the transition occurred at the front than soldiers' anxieties and pent-up anger. Within a short time, many officers themselves saw their potential as an instrument for maintaining discipline and preparedness, as Kerensky was soon to do. One regimental officer wrote to the future head of government, "The only way to restore the army's leadership and military capacity is to have officers and other leaders enjoy the soldiers' trust, and the only way to do this is through elections, the social and political foundations on which real discipline can be created."[57] At army headquarters opposition to the committees by General Alekseev, now the army's commander in chief, also subsided, especially after Minister of War Guchkov and the Petrograd Soviet leadership appeared to be coordinating their efforts. Delegations to the front were well-received. Overwhelmingly, according to one censor's report, soldiers were "ecstatic" at the changes that were occurring, especially with respect to dignified treatment. "Things will now be different," one letter averred, "since treachery in the ranks will end and our supplies will stay with us rather than be siphoned off to the Germans." According to another censor, the new order had brought out a great desire to bring the war to an end, a feeling that soldiers, too, would gain the security and well-being the revolution promised to bring to their villages and families.[58] How, though, was this to be accomplished without further bloodshed and without giving comprehensible meaning to memorialize losses that had already occurred?

The Challenges of Revolutionary Governance

The initial tasks of the dual power regime were the easiest ones. Written in consultation with organizers of the Petrograd Soviet, the Provisional Government's

---

[55] Wildman, *End*, 235.
[56] *Zhurnal Vremennogo Pravitel'stvo*, Mar. 9, 1917, in Kozlov and Mironenko, *Arkhiv noveishei istorii Rossii*, 1:58.
[57] RGVIA f. 366, op. 1, d. 11, ll. 122–23, 155–59.
[58] RGVIA f. 2048, op. 1, d. 905, ll. 38–39 ob.

first announcements included a list of mutually supported guiding principles. In part they read as a Russian bill of rights: freedom of speech, press, assembly; the abolition of all restrictions based on class, religion, or nationality; the right to organize trade unions and conduct strikes; and full amnesty for political, religious, and agrarian offenses and military revolts. Soldiers were also granted full civil rights. In part they committed to institutionalizing democratic process: preparing for a national constituent assembly to write a constitution; replacing the hated police with a people's militia with elected officers responsible to local organs of self-government; and holding elections to these organs and the constituent assembly on the basis of universal and equal suffrage and through direct and secret ballots. For the moment, revolutionary Russia took its place among the most politically free countries of the contemporary world.

Virtually all of the cabinet's first steps had been scripted in this direction. The government and Petrograd Soviet both were determined to engage "responsible" people in addressing the tasks at hand. Prime Minister L'vov insisted on placing new people with democratic ideals in official positions across the country. The Ministry of Interior and its extensive police apparatus was essentially shut down, the task of supervising its operations given to L'vov as well. Other members of the new cabinet included "responsible" men. Shingarev became the new minister of agriculture, taking full responsibility for the food problem. His Kadet Party colleagues Miliukov (foreign affairs), Nikolai Nekrasov (transport), and Alexander Manuilov (education) also took over their assigned ministries in ways they hoped would produce immediate reforms, retaining experienced administrators. The Progressist Konovalov (trade and industry) and the Kievan industrialist Mikhail Tereshchenko (finance) did the same. The socialist Kerensky, the sole member of the Soviet Executive Committee in the cabinet, moved to sweep out the Ministry of Justice from top to bottom.[59]

In its first full meeting, which lasted until 11:00 in the evening, the new cabinet temporarily removed all provincial governors and vice governors. A new group of specially designated commissars was dispatched across the country to select suitable persons to replace them. The physician and Kadet leader Nikolai Kishkin was appointed special commissar for Moscow. Longtime Kadet Central Committee members Paul Gronskii, Vasili Maklakov, and Moisei Adzhemov became commissars for individual ministries, including importantly the Ministries of Justice and Post and Telegraph. Kadet Central Committee members Solomon Krym, Nikolai Nikolaev, and others were appointed commissars for the Tauride region, the Caucasus, and other national regions. Echoing appeals in the past,

---

[59] *Vestnik Vremennogo Pravitel'stva*, Mar. 5, 1917. Shingarev's appointment was a great disappointment to him, taken primarily for the purpose of achieving some form of political balance. He had hoped to become minister of finance, a post he secured only in May. See A. G. Khrushchev, *A. I. Shingarev* (Moscow, 1918), 89.

the Council of Ural Mining Enterprises sent an urgent request on March 4 for a special commissar for the Urals regions "with unlimited authority" to unify all government support for the work of Ural plants.[60]

Meanwhile a new oath of allegiance to the Provisional Government was made mandatory for all new or continuing government officials. Special committees were set up to investigate and address malfeasance in the fallen regime, review the organization of the court and penal systems, and coordinate new decrees with existing legislation, which was to remain in force. A special committee began to plan for elections to a constituent assembly. On instructions from the Kadets Maklakov and Adzhemov, now in the Ministry of Justice, the Bolshevik delegates to the State Duma arrested and sent to Siberia for treason in November 1914 were released. On March 12 the death penalty was abolished. New decrees soon followed on elections to municipal dumas, the creation of representative zemstvo organizations at the district (*volost'*) level, and, from Agriculture Minister Shingarev, plans to increase dramatically land sown in the spring. A representative Main Land Committee was organized along with local committees across the countryside to address the question of land usage and its potential reform.

For the time being, some leading wartime structures remained intact. The Special Council for Defense met briefly on March 6, at greater length on March 11 and 16. Fifty-three people attended the March 6 session, including a full delegation from the State Duma and State Council. Minister of War Guchkov opened the meeting by affirming that the change in regimes had in no way eased the existing military danger to the state. Continuing the war was essential, victory even more so. "Now more than ever" Russia required the united and creative work of "all vital forces." State Senator V. I. Gurko greeted Guchkov and "all those now leading Russia on a new path with all of our heart . . . [and] without any doubt in their sincere dedication to the needs of the Fatherland."[61] Throughout March and then somewhat less regularly right up until the Bolsheviks took power in October the Special Council for Defense continued its efforts to coordinate production and supply military equipment to the front.

Meanwhile, the Petrograd Soviet concentrated on managing food distribution throughout the city, organizing the Petrograd workforce, and assisting in setting up similar soviets elsewhere. Factory workers were urged to organize unions and elect their leaders. *Rabochaia Gazeta* (*Workers' Gazette*), the newspaper of the Menshevik Central Committee, detailed these efforts. "The dawn of a new life has begun," it editorialized, singling out women workers in particular. "Every one of us must unite to improve our economic situation and to achieve normal conditions in our work!"[62] Like the Provisional Government, the

---

[60] *Zhurnal Vremennogo Pravitel'stvo*, Mar. 4, 1917; RGIA f. 48, op. 1, d. 38, l. 27.
[61] *ZOSO*, Mar. 6, 1917, 237.
[62] *Rabochaia Gazeta*, Mar. 10, 1917.

Petrograd Soviet sent its own commissars out into the country. But even without their assistance, factory committees and local unions emerged practically overnight in Moscow and other major industrial centers. Many organized their own food committees and factory militias. Some tried to curb acts of violence against foremen and others, often without success.[63]

When they reached provincial cities, soviet and government emissaries found that local committees of social organizations had already been formed, bringing together representatives from public organizations, local authorities, and new local soviets to keep order. In Moscow, sixty-six well-known public figures announced that since tsarist officials and a nonrepresentative city duma were no longer capable of exercising formal authority, their Committee of Social Organizations was assuming control. Power was to be lodged in an executive committee of fifteen persons representing all sectors of Moscow's population. S. N. Prokopovich, the well-known democratic socialist and respected economist, was elected its chair. The left-leaning Moscow Kadets Nikolai Astrov and Nikolai Kishkin took on key responsibilities. More than twenty different committees and commissars were named to take charge of all aspects of Moscow city administration. When the Moscow Soviet of Workers' Deputies was formed on March 4, it sent twenty delegates to work with them.[64]

Similar groups were organized in Kiev, Odessa, Saratov, Tashkent, Tiflis, Ekaterinoslav, Voronezh, Kharkov, and a number of other cities, each with the participation of workers' representatives or newly formed soviets.[65] From newspapers and other accounts we know they assumed the tasks of local governance, focusing particularly on the crisis in food supplies and other essential goods. The Simferopol committee had some seventy-three members, twenty-three of whom represented local workers groups. In Saratov, five members of the city duma joined five soviet representatives and seven others from social organizations. In Ekaterinburg the focus was on keeping order; in Taganrog, on distributing food supplies. In Rostov and elsewhere local army garrisons placed themselves under the committee's direction. In some places the committees themselves arrested tsarist officials. Everywhere local liberals and democratic socialists played a leading part in their activities, reflecting a clearly defined sense of the cooperation Russia now needed to move forward. By the end of March

---

[63] RGIA f. 23, op. 27, d. 350, ll. 8–14; Sidorov et al., *Revoliutsionnoe dvizhenie*, 229–30; Michael Hickey, "Local Government and State Authority in the Provinces: Smolensk, February–June 1917," *Slavic Review* 55, no. 4 (Winter 1996): 863–81.

[64] *Sbornik Materialov komiteta Moskovkikh obshchestvennykh organizatsii*, 2 pts. (Moscow, 1917), 1:2–3, 2:11–24; *Utro Rossii*, Mar. 5, 1917; A. I. Grunt, *Moskva 1917: Revoliutsiia i kontrrevoliutsiia* (Moscow: Nauka, 1976), 51–56. See also the discussion by Matthew Rendle, "The Problem of the 'Local' in Revolutionary Russia: Moscow Province, 1914–1922," in *Russia's Home Front in War and Revolution*, bk. 1, ed. Sarah Badcock, Liudmila Novikova, and Aaron Retish (Bloomington, IN: Slavica, 2015), 28–29 and passim.

[65] RGVIA f. 366, op. 2, d. 31, ll. 17–18.

local soviets had been formed in more than seventy cities and towns of the central industrial region with ties to the public organizations. The first regional conference of soviets occurred in the Donbas region in mid-March. Delegates from forty-eight soviets claimed to represent 200,000 workers.[66]

For democratic liberals and socialists both, the near bloodless overthrow of the autocratic regime seemed to be a remarkable political success, creating in a matter of days the civil liberties and political goals that many had struggled a lifetime to secure. Many rightly worried that these liberties were fragile. Few failed to relish their achievement. For those who created the new government in one part of the Tauride Palace, their heartfelt obligation, in Wilsonian phrasing, was to make the Russian world safe for political democracy. "The Responsibility of Democracy" *Rech'* editorialized, was not just a political revolution but "a conscientious sense of citizenship" and "a revolution in mind."[67] For those who organized the Petrograd Soviet in another part of the Palace, the revolution was a triumph of social commitment and popular energy, a revolution in the way citizens of the empire would now relate to each other.

What neither group could yet fully comprehend was that the great challenges of revolutionary governance lay not in changing mentalities or social hierarchies and relations but in the daunting problems of assuring adequate food, managing other scarcities in essential goods, reducing food and welfare anxieties, and giving comprehensible meaning to the devastating losses of war, all of which had so far begged solution.

---

[66] William G. Rosenberg, "Les Liberaux Russes et le changement de pouvoir en mars 1917," *Cahiers du Monde russe et sovietique* 1 (1968): 46–57; E. N. Burdzhalov, *Vtoraia Russkaia revoliutsiia*, 2 vols. (Moscow: Nauka, 1971), 2: 234 and passim.

[67] *Rech'*, Mar. 10, 1917; *Izvestiia Revoliutsionnoi Nedeli*, Mar. 3, 1917; *Poslednye Novosti*, May 12, 1927; Miliukov, *Istoriia*, 1:40–43.

8
Addressing Scarcity, Confronting Loss

In the view of Russia's leading public figures as well as most historians, the members of the Provisional Government were among the most responsible and competent men the Duma committee could have chosen on February 27. All of the important posts save two were assigned to those of the "government of national unity" that the Progressive Bloc had urged the tsar to appoint in 1915. Minister of War Alexander Guchkov was the chair of the CWIC and a founder of the conservative liberal Octobrist Party. Alexander Konovalov, who became minister of trade and industry, was his deputy chair in the CWIC. Although he preferred the Ministry of Finance, Andrei Shingarev became minister of agriculture, where he took fully responsibility for the food problem. His Kadet Party colleagues Paul Miliukov (foreign affairs), Nikolai Nekrasov (transport), and Alexander Manuilov (education) took over their assigned ministries in ways the new regime hoped would produce immediate reforms, retaining experienced administrators. The Kievan industrialist Mikhail Tereshchenko (finance) did the same. One principal exception was Prince Georgi L'vov, the leader of the All-Russia Union of Zemstvos. Married to a descendent of Catherine the Great, the new minister president accepted the position with some reluctance when Duma chair Mikhail Rodizanko demurred and took on minister of interior as well. Another exception was the firebrand Alexander Kerensky, who became the government's sole socialist as minister of justice and informal liaison to the Petrograd Soviet when the Mensheviks' Duma spokesman Nikolai Chkheidze, who was originally on the list, also declined to join. Miliukov initially hesitated as well but was roused at home after five sleepless nights by a Kadet delegation that insisted he could not refuse. Even those who had resisted the Progressive Bloc's decision to accommodate the tsar's prerogative of appointing "responsible" ministers, rather than those formally approved by the Duma, were not unhappy with the choices. Public organizations like the Zemstvo and City Unions and the CWIC greeted them with "pride and joy." So did the more than two hundred committees of public organizations that had sprung up spontaneously around the country by March 5.[1]

---

[1] *Rech'*, May 24, 1917; P. N. Miliukov, *Vospominaniia 1858–1917*, 2 vols. (New York: Chekhov, 1955), 2:28; *Izvestiia tsentral'nago voenno-promyshlennago komiteta*, Mar. 13, 1917.

The government's new ministers were all well acquainted with those now leading the Petrograd Soviet. The first iteration of its Executive Committee (Ispolkom) on February 27 included two Duma colleagues, Chkheidze and Matvei Skobelev, who in May would become Russia's first minister of labor. Elected with them to the Ispolkom were Kuz'ma Gvozdev and Boris Bogdanov, the chair and secretary, respectively, of the CWIC's Workers Group. Kerensky joined the Ispolkom the next day. So did Henrykh Erlikh and Moisei Rafes, both members of the CWIC.

The first weeks of March were an exhausting time for all. The new ministers met every day in two long sessions, the second sometimes lasting well beyond midnight. Soviet leaders divided equally long hours between large and often unruly assemblies and organizational work in the factories. The offices of the CWIC and the Council of Industrial Congresses at 46 Liteinyi Prospekt were again the center of intense activity, as they had been during the first wave of industrial mobilization in 1915. For the moment at least, concerns about dual power were displaced by what the historian Ziva Galili has described as a spirit of conciliation, a desire to work cooperatively to solve Russia's most pressing problems.[2] In provincial cities, members of the new committees of public organizations worked long hours as well trying to meet local needs. Calling for close cooperation between the two sides of the dual-power divide, the Mensheviks' *Rabochaia Gazeta* (*Workers' Gazette*) argued that differences in thinking "were only useful." The "absolute imperative" that could not be postponed was "the organization of the entire population to meet the country's needs."[3]

Food Anxiety and the Grain Monopoly: Legitimacy and Function

First among these needs once the threat of counterrevolution was contained were the flashpoints of the uprising itself: the shortages of food supplies and their accompanying anxieties in Petrograd, Moscow, at the front, and around the country. Closely related were the linked questions of landholding, land usage, and grain procurement, whose reform was "the most serious socioeconomic task of the present moment," as the new government described it, as well as the transport problem, a key to distributing food and other scarce goods. Food deficits

---

[2] Ziva Galili, *Menshevik Leaders in the Russian Revolution* (Princeton, NJ: Princeton University Press, 1989), chs. 1–2.

[3] *Rabochaia. Gazeta,* Mar. 9, 18, 1917. Participating in the newspaper were all of the party's elite: Pavel Akselrod, Matvei Gvozdev, Fedor Dan, Vera Zasulich, Iurii Larin, Iulii Martov, Alexander Martynov, Peter Maslov, Potresov, Irakli Tsereteli, Fedor Cherevanin, and Nikolai Chkheidze, among others.

were immediate and pressing. Restructuring landholding and usage was essential to increasing grain production. Without immediate improvements in transport and available resources, especially in Petrograd and Moscow, new protests could be expected.

Without a clear plan to address the question of land usage, revolutionary Russia more broadly faced further peasant resistance to the procurement of grain at its source, even if the final decision on landownership was to await the convening of a democratically elected constitutional congress, the Constituent Assembly, now scheduled for September.

Following the lead of prominent contemporary figures like Peter Struve, some historians have accepted the claims of Petrograd governor-general Khabalov that supplies in Petrograd were adequate in early March to meet essential needs. Struve argued that the reassuring estimates of stored grain on which the Rittikh sequester was based in November 1916 were withheld from sale largely because the state's purchase prices were too low, even though the idea of using prices to stimulate production "remained alien to the Russian public mind."[4] There was also the ongoing question of whether scarcities were the result of the breakdown in transport rather than inadequate peasant landholdings or the admittedly poor harvest in 1916, and whether in this case the problem of food supply, at least, was almost certain to ease with warmer weather. If so, it was possible that local embargoes would end and market processes distorted by army requisitions would revive.[5]

The available government statistics, however, indicated that sown acreage was down 15 percent in the southwestern provinces and 11 percent in northwest, both encompassing the war zone. Estimates of the total amount of grain produced in 1916 were also 14.5 percent lower than in 1915 in European Russia, while the total harvest for 1917 was estimated to be barely enough to meet minimum needs, if that.[6] Everywhere there were new claims of extreme need to which the revolution's leaders now had to respond. The liberal newspapers *Birzhevyia Vedomosti (Stock Market News)* and *Russkiia Vedomosti (Russian Gazette)*, whose readers were not among those most at risk, still focused on the problem in every issue. So did the socialist papers.

Whatever the official statistics for 1916, moreover, the state at the beginning of March apparently had no significant grain reserves, if any at all. Neither for a few days did Petrograd or Moscow. Along parts of the front with hundreds of

---

[4] P. B. Struve et al., eds., *Food Supply in Russia during the World War* (New Haven, CT: Yale University Press, 1930), xv, xx.
[5] K. Matsuzato, "Interregional Conflicts and the Collapse of Tsarism: The Real Reason for the Food Crisis in Russia after the Autumn of 1916," in *Emerging Democracy in Late Imperial Russia*, ed. Mary Schaeffer Conway (Niwot: University Press of Colorado, 1998), 243–300.
[6] *Statisticheskiia Svedeniia o Finansovom i Ekonomicheskom Polozhenii Rossii: Material Sostavlenyi k 15 Nov. 1916* (Petrograd, 1916), in RGIA f. 1276, op. 1, d. 244, ll. 394–97 ob.

thousands of soldiers, reserves were adequate only for a single day. The "threatening situation" required new people and new energy. The "atmosphere of corruption" surrounding the tsarist supply committees also had to be addressed.[7] In Moscow, Nikolai Kishkin, the government's new commissar, was informed by the head of the city's administration that the food crisis was growing more acute in virtually every district of the city. Unruly garrison soldiers were cutting in line, increasing the level of agitation. During the second week of March some bakeries shut down entirely; others were open only in the morning from 9 to 11. Two weeks after the new regime took office, *Rabochaia Gazeta* warned that Russia was facing a famine.[8]

In this respect the key figures in the new Provisional Government were Shingarev and Nekrasov. Expert in both Russian agriculture and finance, as we have noted, Shingarev was ideally suited to head the Ministry of Agriculture, which now incorporated the work of the tsarist Special Council on Food. A landowner, zemstvo physician, and onetime head of the Voronezh medical district, Shingarev knew village society well. His famous early volume, *The Dying Village*, showed he was someone particularly sensitive to both the needs of the peasantry and the politically problematic inequities of the Russian countryside. More than most he understood that "countryside" itself was a convenient abstraction which obscured significant differences between villages and districts within and between different provinces. He also fully expected that the Constituent Assembly would mandate the compensated transfer of gentry land to the peasants. His immediate task, therefore, was to get more food to places where food insecurities were rampant.

In a similar way, the thirty-eight-year-old Nekrasov was well positioned to oversee the improvement of railroad operations. Trained as a transport engineer and well known as a railroad expert, the former professor at the Tomsk Engineering Institute was an influential voice of the liberal left who had served as vice chair of the Duma under Rodzianko. He immediately sought assistance from the venerable socialist Georgi Plekhanov and members of the Petrograd Soviet Ispolkom. Shingarev, meanwhile, sought the counsel of Nikolai Chaikovskii, the socialist president of the Free Economic Society who was active in organizing the all-Russian Peasants Union, and Alexander Chaianov, Russia's leading theorist on peasant economic behavior, who maintained that producing for subsistence rather than profit was one of its key cultural components and a cause of Russia's

---

[7] *Ekonomicheskoe Polozhenie Rossii nakanune velikoi oktiabr'skoi sotsialisticheskoi revoliutsii: Dokumenty i materialy*, 3 pts. (Moscow, 1957–67), 3:281; *Izvestiia po Prodovol'stvennomy Delu* 1 (1917): 60; N. D. Kondrat'ev, *Rynok khlebov i ego regulirovanie vo vremia voiny i revoliutsii* (Moscow, 1922), 111.

[8] "Prodovol'stvennoe polozhenie v Moskve v marte–iiune 1917 goda," *Krasnyi Arkhiv* 81 (1937): 128–29; *Birzhevyia Vedomosti*, Mar. 8, 1917; *Russkiia Vedomosti*, Mar. 7, 1917; *Rabochaia Gazeta*, Mar. 24, 1917.

agricultural underdevelopment. He also brought in the burly Vladimir Groman, now head of the Petrograd Soviet's Economic Commission as well as its food supply group, to work with him in the new State Committee on Food Supply, replacing the tsarist Special Council. Thus, Nekrasov and Shingarev both had representatives from the Petrograd Soviet, the State Duma, and the Zemstvo and City Unions at their tables as they charted the way forward.

In many ways Shingarev and Groman were quite different. Shingarev dressed like a statesman. Groman always wore the same suit that looked as if it had not been pressed since he bought it off the rack, according to his assistant Naum Jasny.[9] The liberal Shingarev thought broadly from the viewpoint of Russia's historical and future development along Western European lines. The Menshevik Groman was first and foremost a dedicated statistician who insisted on "facts" even as he decried the absence of reliable information. Both Shingarev and Groman were soon targets of fierce criticism, the liberal for compromising free trade by affirming the grain monopoly, the socialist for "anticipating Leninism" with his emphasis on state control.[10] From all indications, in fact, the two men pretty much agreed about what needed to be done. Both understood that grain requisitions were largely on paper. Both saw Russia faced with "a final catastrophe," as an angry Shingarev had declared in January to the Special Council on Defense.[11] Both understood that Russia's commercial markets were limited in their ability to distribute adequate supplies of grain and commodities in conditions of great scarcity. And both consequently framed the approach of the dual-power regime to solving the problem of scarcities just as it had earlier been scripted: in terms of rational planning by a strong and directive center together with the further devolution of authority to responsible local agents capable of overseeing and enforcing its effective application—precisely the approach democratic liberals and socialists had been insisting upon since shortly after the war began.

Despite his knowledge and experience, however, Shingarev found the food supply problem much more difficult to address than he had expected. Chkheidze and others writing in *Rabochaia Gazeta* tried to tell its readers that the food supply problem was enormously complex, more so than in Austria and Germany, where a principal source of hunger was the British and French blockade.[12] In the

[9] B. A. Laird and R. D. Laird, *To Live Long Enough: The Memoirs of Naum Jasny, Scientific Analyst* (Lawrence: University Press of Kansas, 1976), 21.

[10] Lars Lih gives a fair but critical assessment in his pioneering work. Nikolai Sukhanov and Naum Jasny accuse Groman of a naïve, youthful enthusiasm for state intervention. See Lars Lih, *Bread and Authority in Russia, 1914–1921* (Berkeley: University of California Press, 1990), 82–88; N. N. Sukhanov, *The Russian Revolution 1917*, ed. and trans. J. Carmichael (Princeton, NJ: Princeton University Press, 1984), 185–89; Naum Jasny, *Soviet Economists of the Twenties* (Cambridge: Cambridge University Press, 1972), 89–97.

[11] RGIA f. 1278, op. 1, d. 331, ll. 7–12; ZOSO 144 (Feb. 15, 1917): 224–25.

[12] *Rabochaia Gazeta*, Mar. 22, 1917.

Duma both Shingarev and Chkheidze had thought that food shortages and the risk of famine were due not primarily to a lack of grain but to the lack of organization, the incompetency of tsarist officials, and, as Shingarev put it, "an insufficiency of consciousness [*soznatel'nost'*]" among peasants themselves about the seriousness of the situation.

Once in the ministry, Shingarev understandably worried that he did not have a full picture. The many urgent documents and petitions of "extreme need" he found indicated that the Rittikh confiscation was strongly resisted in the countryside and likely to fail. Already in January 1917 the Special Council for Defense had heard reports that the *razverstka* was "entirely unsuccessful." Provincial zemstvo boards reported that it was condemned everywhere. In Poltava, Podolsk, Kherson, and other provinces it was rejected outright. In others the quantity of grain demanded was said to be factually impossible to procure. Nowhere was there confidence that the "fixed" procurement prices would remain fixed. The ministry's representative in Viatka, for example, reported deliveries scheduled for March would have to be postponed until July. The region simply lacked sufficient manpower.

Village assemblies were also refusing to accept how deliveries were to be apportioned between households. They persisted in the traditional moral value that the burden should be equally shared regardless of how much land each household actually worked. (According to a later report, some two-thirds of the delivery quotas set in November 1916 were not met.) In the final analysis, regional zemstvo officials reported, village assemblies therefore needed to be involved since fulfillment of the *razverstka* depended on the peasants themselves. Forced measures would only further alienate the peasantry. Some villages relatively close to railroad lines demanded, "Give us the [manufactured] goods we need at fixed prices, and we'll give you the grain in the same way."[13]

A closely related question, as Shingarev quickly learned, was whether the prices for mandatory deliveries had been set too low, encouraging peasants to find private buyers in the black markets for their grain. Groman did not think prices mattered at all. Russia's markets were essentially broken. There were few commodities for peasants to buy, and money itself in the countryside was losing its value. Struve, Shingarev, and others now thought the solution was to assure prices paid for compulsory delivery were as high as or higher than peasants could get on open or black markets. Shingarev and Groman both agreed, however, that it was necessary to establish a state grain monopoly so that prices everywhere could be controlled.[14]

---

[13] RGVIA f. 2003, op. 4, d. 2, ll. 10–11, 24–25, 135ff.; RGIA f. 456, op. 1, d. 18, ll. 115–19.
[14] RGVIA f. 2003, op. 4, d. 2, ll. 135–37, 179–80; A. I. Shingarev, *Finansovoe polozhenie Rossii* (Petrograd, 1917), 1–4; *Russkiia Vedomosti*, Mar. 7, 1917.

Already in February the new minister of agriculture had concluded that a grain monopoly was necessary if it could be properly administered. "How can we think about free trade?" Shingarev was quoted asking in *Russkiia Vedomosti*. "How can there be free trade without adequate transport, without competition, without sufficient goods for sale? To create the conditions for free trade is not within the strength of the government."[15] Even *Birzhevye Vedomosti* (*Stock Market News*) agreed. The country's experience with free trade during the war "was pitiful." Russia's needs demanded strong state intervention. The grain monopoly was "inevitable."[16] Groman, not surprisingly, was also strongly in favor of a monopoly. In his view, the revolutionary state had to embrace even further management of Russia's wartime economy, reflecting what he called the "war communism" policies of Germany. Thus the new government on March 10, supported by the Petrograd Soviet, announced its intention to introduce the monopoly as soon as legislation could be prepared. "Grains" would include beans, peas, and lentils as well as rye, wheat, buckwheat, barley, and oats and their by-products. Procurement prices would be set 60 to 70 percent higher than in the fall for seven different varieties of grain in relation to local production costs. In principle, all transactions would henceforth be controlled by the new revolutionary state, which thus took on responsibility for the monopoly's possible failure.[17]

Shingarev immediately telegraphed existing zemstvo representatives and other procurement agents around the country to begin setting new local norms for compulsory deliveries. He also ordered landowners with more than fifty dessiatins of sown land, approximate 135 acres, to turn over all their surplus grain. When legislation establishing the monopoly and temporary food supply committees to enforce it was enacted toward the end of March, almost all grain in the empire became the property of the revolutionary state. (Exceptions were made for the Caucasus region, apparently for administrative reasons, implicitly raising the question of nationality rights.) At the provincial level the food committees were required to include elected representatives from zemstvo assemblies, the city duma of the provincial capital, provincial soviets of workers' and peasants' deputies, the Peasants Union, and various other public organizations. Committees at the district level would be elected from comparable local institutions. Later, permanent committees would be popularly elected by secret ballot. Shingarev requested 3 million rubles from the treasury to purchase trucks to move their requisitions from villages to rail heads and barge-loading sites.

[15] *Russkiia Vedomosti*, Apr. 11, 1917.
[16] *Birzhevye Vedomosti*, Mar. 14, 21, 1917.
[17] *Vestnik Vremennogo Pravitel'stva*, Mar. 11, 1917. According to later analysis, the prices soon averaged 60 percent more that those paid the previous fall. See Z. Lozinskii, *Ekonomicheskaia politika Vremennogo Pravitel'stva* (Leningrad: Priboi, 1929), 137–38.

In essence, the food supply consisted of four interrelated parts: production, procurement, pricing, and distribution, although that last was now the task of Nekrasov's Transport Ministry as well as local authorities responsible for rationing. Each involved challenging problems as well as substantial risks. Calculating grain production itself was intrinsically difficult. Before February Shingarev and Groman loudly complained that the Special Council on Food did not have adequate or accurate statistics. Had grain production really declined to the extent reported by procurement agents who were unable to deliver the amounts they were assigned? How much did they account for the amounts peasants were concealing or channeling to speculators? Shingarev and Groman really did not know. Even to this day, there are no sure answers to these questions. And whether or not production had declined, there was also the possibility before the spring crop was harvested that peasants would mobilize their resistance. All those planning the monopoly could really do was assume the worst, which in any case proved closest to reality.

Production was also about property, the rights of ownership and possession, and the peasants' well-known hunger for more land, an award we have noted many soldiers and their families thought would be forthcoming from their military service. At the village level, ownership engaged the issue of peasants who had separated from their communes under the Stolypin reforms and gained ownership of their land. Resisting the reforms and in some cases reviling the "separators," many village communities continued to believe that land, like water and air, should not be owned as private property, only possessed temporarily by those who were able to work it. This was also true for those who owned large estates, like Shingarev himself, where land was either worked by hired labor or left for as many as seventeen years in long fallow. Not surprisingly, the monopoly as well as the implicit threat to landownership immediately drew opposition from landowners and industrialists who saw these measures destroying the right to property and the importance of free trade. At the first All-Russian Congress of Trade Industrialists on March 19–22, 1917, delegates from across the country spoke forcefully against anything resembling a grain monopoly. For them, free trade across the board would go much further toward alleviating the food crisis than this "dangerous plan."[18] By early April there were already reports in the liberal press of landowners mobilizing to sabotage Shingarev's efforts.[19] (Later Vladimir Groman was charged with laying the foundations of what became Lenin's War Communism after October by his strong support for state

---

[18] *Pervyi Vserossiiskii Torgovo-Promyshlennyi S"ezd v Moskve: 19–22 Marta 1917* (Petrograd, 1917), 230.
[19] *Birzhevye Vedomosti*, Apr. 12, 1917.

control. Meantime, before his murder early in 1918, Shingarev was attacked for destroying the foundation of free market trade.)

The challenges involved in actually procuring the grain from producers signaled additional risks. A key issue here was how exactly to fix procurement prices. Struve and others working with the Special Council on Food had been sure that prices to be paid for requisitioned grains were set too low. While Struve thought this was egregiously the case with the Rittikh expropriation, Gromov disagreed that pricing was the key issue. More so was the lack of industrial and consumer goods that would incentivize peasants to sell. Yet the well-known agronomist Chaianov and others argued that price incentives countered the interests of those sectors of Russia's partially commercialized countryside where peasants produced to sustain themselves rather than to accumulate wealth or improve their material condition. Many contemporary experts who disagreed with this view, including Shingarev, still recognized that without an adequate supply of manufactured goods to the countryside, higher prices in themselves were not likely to overcome the peasants' reluctance to surrender their grain, especially if production was also declining because of a lack of manpower in the countryside.[20]

For their part, Mensheviks worried that even with manufactured products suddenly available in the countryside, higher procurement prices would actually be a *disincentive* for peasants to comply fully with the monopoly because they would reasonably assume fixed prices would be set even higher as shortages continued. Still, they fully supported the monopoly, as did the liberal *Birzhevyia Vedomosti*, which called this "decisive" measure testimony to wartime Russia's "pitiful experience of free trade."[21] Shingarev himself agreed. "How can we think about free trade," he asked rhetorically to a meeting soon afterward of the Union of Cities. "How can there be free trade without adequate transport, without competition, without goods to sell? Creating the conditions necessary for free trade is simply not within the [current] powers of the state."[22]

In effect, Shingarev, Groman, and their colleagues were dealing here not just with the problem of food supply but with the very legitimacy of both the new regime and the soviet as they were initially constituted. If the greatest domestic problems were food insecurity and the real and anticipated shortages in essential goods, failure to resolve them would almost certainly engender resistance from landowners, industrialists, and commercial circles strongly opposed to the grain monopoly on the political right, and workers and others on the left. Without anything resembling a monopoly on the use of force, and without firm commitment

---

[20] *Pervyi Vserossiiskii Torgovo-Promyshlennyi S"ezd*, 230.
[21] *Birzhevyia Vedomosti*, Mar. 14, 1917.
[22] *Russkiia Vedomosti*, Apr. 11, 1917.

yet in Russia to the values and principles it professed to represent, legitimacy remained based on the new joint-power regime to function effectively in resolving the problems and assuaging the anxieties that had brought it to power. "Elected by the revolution," as Miliukov memorably declared, both the cabinet and the Petrograd Soviet leadership could readily be restructured or deposed by those who challenged its failures. Given the gravity of its problems, not to mention the ongoing challenge of war, the political future of both the regime and the soviet leadership hung by the thinnest of threads, given their claims that "responsible" democratic liberals and socialists could finally get things done.

Food Supply, Land Redistribution, and Democratic Practice

By far the greatest domestic risk in this regard, leaving aside the regime's ability to manage the questions of war and peace, was the necessity of placing responsibility for implementing the grain monopoly locally in the hands of newly formed food supply committees. Shingarev and others were encouraged by the composition of the various committees of social organizations that sprang up everywhere during the first week of March, mobilizing local expertise and resources. Like these ad hoc groups, the new local food supply committees would also have broad representation. They were organized hierarchically at the town, local, district, and regional levels, where fixed prices would be adjusted to local conditions. The predicament shared by the government and the Soviet leadership was that the dual-power regime lacked both coercive and material incentives for peasants to give up their grain. From Viatka was even a warning that unless the regime was "extremely careful" with compulsory measures, resistance was likely to produce clashes "of a very sharp nature."[23]

The food supply committees were also assigned responsibility for assuring "an equitable and uniform distribution of food" as well as adequate supplies for the army. Like "fairness" under war capitalism, however, "equitable" and "uniform" were concepts of art rather than prescription. The very composition of the food supply committees was an invitation for fierce debate and social conflict. Liberal students in Viatka province who went out to the countryside to support Shingarev's program found peasants interested in their new rights, but even more so in gaining free possession of more land, especially the untilled lands of large estates.[24] Even before the ink was dry on the new statutes rural disturbances were being reported from a number of areas. Peasants in Saratov, Chernigov, Kiev, and elsewhere were holding regional congresses. Prompted in

---

[23] RGIA f. 456, op. 1, d. 118, ll. 109–10, 118–19.
[24] *Vestnik Partiia Narodnoi Svobody* 11–13 (1917): 35.

part by local Socialist Revolutionaries, the well-established peasants' party led by Viktor Chernov, many village gatherings (shkody) were encouraging the seizure of privately owned land.[25]

Meanwhile, two other networks of local organizations were being created in the localities, along with the rapid proliferation of local, regional, and provincial soviets. One involved organizing elections to new district zemstvos as part of the new regime's commitment to bringing representative government to the countryside.[26] More important for the moment was the creation by statute on April 21 of new local and regional land committees under the direction of the Main Land Committee in Petrograd. These were charged with preparing draft legislation on the question of land use and its redistribution for presentation to the Constituent Assembly in September. The Assembly would draft a new constitution and construct a new and constitutionally legitimate regime.

With the land committees' creation in April, the questions of a grain monopoly, the role of food supply committees, peasant disturbances, and the process of distributing food and redistributing land became inextricably linked. The statute signed by Shingarev plunged the regime directly into the thorniest of all rural questions since the peasants' emancipation in 1861: Should arable land in Russia be the property of those who tilled it or those who owned it as personal property, even if unsown, by virtue of legally protected titles of ownership? In addition to assisting the Main Land Committee in preparing draft legislation, local committees were charged with the immediate tasks of "settling questions and disputes about land usage under existing statutes" and "regulating relations that might arise as a result of the arbitrary violation of anyone's rights and interests."[27] In many places, however, villagers were already taking the land from private owners as well as the church and state, assaulting landowners, stealing their equipment and livestock, and otherwise exercising the power immanent in collective action even if their activism was within their own localities. By decision of their village elders in some places, peasants were also seizing grain reserves to prevent their being shipped off. Passions throughout the countryside began to echo the February revolutionary experience in Petrograd.[28]

---

[25] *Zemlia i Volia*, Apr. 1, 15 Apr. 1917; P. P. Pershin, *Agrarnaia revoliutsii v Rossii*, 2 vols. (Moscow: Nauka, 1966), 1:296–99.

[26] T. Emmons, ed., *The Zemstvo: An Experiment in Local Government* (New York: Cambridge University Press, 1982), ch. 12; Sergei Liubichankovskii, "Revolution and the Creation of the Volost' Zemstvo in Southeastern Russia (Spring–Fall 1917)," in *Russia's Home Front in War and Revolution*, bk. 1, ed. Sarah Badcock, Liudmila Novikova, and Aaron Retish (Bloomington, IN: Slavica, 2015), 45–66.

[27] R. P. Browder and A. F. Kerensky, eds., *The Russian Provisional Government 1917*, 3 vols. (Stanford, CA: Stanford University Press, 1961), 2:528–30.

[28] RGIA f. 23, op. 1, d. 454, ll. 32, 66ff.; Mark Baker, "War and Revolution in Ukraine: Kharkov Province's Peasant Experiences of War, Revolution, and Occupation, 1914–1918," in Badcock, Novikova, and Retish, *Russia's Home Front*, 117–20; Michael Hickey, "Who Controls These Woods? Forests and *Mnogovlastie* in Smolensk in 1917," *Revolutionary Russia* 32, no. 2 (2019): 197–225.

In his pioneering study the historian Lars Lih calls Shingarev's efforts a wager on the food monopoly, evoking the "wager on the strong" that officially characterized Prime Minister Peter Stolypin's effort to separate communally held land into individual homesteads after 1906. Lih rightly suggests reasons why the food monopoly bet was not a good one. The actual size of every harvest was uncertain. The assignment of amounts for compulsory delivery was thus unlikely to correspond to actualities. The actual task of collecting the grain was itself an arduous one, fraught with tensions over concealment, illegal trade, and a socially embedded peasant hostility to officialdom in any form. Democratically representative food supply committees required cooperative efforts by representatives of often contentious groups. In organizational terms alone they were not equipped to carry out their tasks. Perhaps most important, enlisting peasant representatives on the committees implied a confidence in their desire and capacity to support the needs of the revolutionary state rather than their own collective well-being—the "insufficiency of consciousness" Shingarev himself was worried about.

But what were the alternatives at this point? It is hard not to sympathize with Shingarev in this regard. Intelligent, compassionate, and widely respected across Russia's political divides, he was the epitome of a responsible person in whom the country was to have confidence. He now found himself from that very position confronting critical problems that had no evident solutions. Procuring and distributing grain through the market proved inadequate to meet urgent needs. Markets in commercial centers were compromised by local embargoes and by requisitions of food and fodder for the army. Deeper in the countryside they provided little incentive for peasants to give up the security their grain provided or to imagine, given the losses they suffered, that this would somehow help lift them from the anxieties of simple subsistence. Rural localities throughout Russia were highly variegated, as an impressive array of recent scholarship has shown, especially with respect to available food.[29] Yet this was precisely why the specific terms of procurement and compensation in the countryside had to be set locally, just as their democratic composition was necessitated by the demands of the revolution itself.

---

[29] See e.g., Sarah Badcock, *Politics and the People in Revolutionary Russia: A Provincial History* (Cambridge: Cambridge University Press, 2007); A. Iu. Davidov, *Meshochniki i dikatura Russii 1917–1921* (St. Petersburg: Aleteiia, 2007); Peter Fraunholtz, "The Collapse and Rebuilding of Grain Procurement Authority in Civil War Russia: The Case of Penza," in *Russia's Home Front in War and Revolution*, bk. 1, ed. Sarah Badcock et al. (Bloomington: Slavica, 2015); Michael Melancon, "Trial Run for Soviet Food Requisitioning: The Expedition to Orel Province, Fall 1918," *Russian Review* 3 (July 2020): 412–37; Aaron B. Retish, *Russia's Peasants in Revolution and Civil War* (Cambridge: Cambridge University Press, 2008); A. S. Sokolov, "Prodovol'stvennoe snabzhenie i meshochnichestvo v Riazanskoi gubernii 1918–1919," *Ekonomicheskaia Istoriia* 4 (2019): 376–85.

Accused now of wanting to destroy private property and open markets, Shingarev understood the difficulties as well as anyone. Personally, he believed that individual landownership was paramount to Russia's long-term economic and social modernization. His Kadet Party's plan for agrarian reform was one of its most progressive programs. Avoiding the word "nationalization," it provided for the "forced alienation" of land not already privately owned along with compensated expropriations from large estates where significant acreage was held unsown, its gradual purchase by peasants to be subsidized by the state. The war and Russia's now critical problem of food supply clearly demanded the maximum production of grain and the minimum disruption of existing agrarian relations.[30] Yet Shingarev also understood that the peasants' demand for land and their own food insecurities were being fueled by the losses of war, while scarcities for many in the cities were partly the result of rising prices which only the wealthy could afford. In his view, unless the democratic state could ensure adequate grain deliveries and secure a monopoly on its distribution, both Russia's socioeconomic and political crises would deepen. For the moment, village interests had to give way to the state's increasing demand for more grain, at least until the land question was settled by the Constituent Assembly, while free trade in grain had to wait for a sufficient increase in supply to end deficits and assure affordable prices.

In retrospect, it may seem apparent that hopes for anything resembling a permanent improvement in Russia's food supply and material well-being while the war continued were misplaced. But who in the new government and the soviet leadership could act without hoping these essential revolutionary goals might still be met? All that the revolution's "responsible" leaders really could do was recognize the physical and emotional effects of scarcity and loss on the revolution's possible trajectory and take the risks that their reasoned "solutions" entailed.

Democratizing the Railroads and the Concept of "Statization"

The task of the food supply committees was to get sufficient quantities of grain to local railroad and barge depots for shipment around the country. The responsibility for assuring their delivery lay with the Ministry of Transport and Shingarev's left Kadet colleague Nekrasov. As we have seen, Nekrasov was well known not only for his interventions on the railroad question in the Duma,

---

[30] William G. Rosenberg, *Liberals in the Russian Revolution* (Princeton, NJ: Princeton University Press, 1974), 127–33; *S"ezdy I konferentsii konstitutsionno-demokraticheskoi partii 1915–1917*, 3 vols. (Moscow: Rosspen, 2000), 1:519–29, 604–38, 665–67.

where he served as vice president to Rodzianko, but even more so for his efforts to move democratic liberals closer to democratic socialists to secure broader popular support. While a long time Kadet Central Committee member, however, the young transport engineer from provincial Tomsk was not well liked. He would soon quit the party, staying in the government as one of Kerensky's closest allies. (Remaining in Soviet Russia after October, he was eventually arrested as part of a "Menshevik conspiracy," sentenced to ten years, and shot in 1940 as his sentence came to an end.)

Nekrasov firmly believed the railroad problem could be resolved only by informed and responsible people at the local level throughout the thirty-seven-thousand-mile system. He believed the principal causes of deficiencies on the lines were excessive administrative centralization, an archaic system of operations, and the arbitrary and capricious behavior of railroad officials. He made his views explicit at a press briefing shortly after taking office on March 9. His main tasks were administrative democratization and its broad decentralization. Toward these ends he provided the ministry's good offices as well as funds to organizers of an all-Russia railroad union and its executive committee (*Vikzhel*). They would review regulations governing railroad transport together with Duma members, representatives of the Petrograd Soviet, and workers and administrators from the lines themselves. New regulations would be drawn that gave workers representation in line administration at all levels and on all questions of railroad life.[31]

One of Nekrasov's first acts was to end the power of section administrators to level draconian sanctions for minimal infractions, demonstratively retreating from the repressive controls of his tsarist predecessors. (During one week in January 1917, for example, the notorious railroad police had jailed twenty-six workers on the Riazan-Urals line for lateness; forty others were held from one to fourteen days for "negligence on duty and failure to follow rules.")[32] Railroad work under these conditions was one of Russia's bloodiest occupations, a fact many workers tied directly to the arbitrary powers of their *nachal'niki* (bosses), whom they derisively referred to as *tsar i bog*, "Caesar and god."[33]

Support for employee participation and administrative decentralization was shared by the respected Conference of Railroad Engineers and the All-Russia Trade Industrial Congress, which passed a resolution endorsing representative "supervisory organs" on the lines. Central control was "excessive and unworkable." Even a meeting of railroad supervisors in Moscow on March 5 endorsed the idea of local committees to help unsnarl operations. So did the Soviet

---

[31] *Birzhevyia Vedomosti*, Mar. 10, 1917.
[32] *Vestnik Riazansko-Ural'skoi Zheleznoi Dorogi* 3 (Jan. 20, 1917).
[33] See William G. Rosenberg, "The Democratization of Russia's Railroads in 1917," *American Historical Review* 86, no. 5 (1981): 983–1008.

Executive Committee and its own Committee on Railroads. Repairing transport was a key to improving food supply. Sharp warnings were issued against any continued disorders on the lines. Resolutions called for one single national railroad union.[34]

Meanwhile, railroaders, like many peasant communities, were acting on their own. On March 3, the very day the Provisional Government assumed power, employees on the Nikolaev line between Moscow and Petrograd organized a temporary line committee to take over line operations. Telegrams were sent out on the national railroad telegraph calling for committees to be set up throughout the system. The next day employees of the Ekaterininskaia line serving the Don coal basin issued their own "Order Number 1," creating the Central Line Committee and convening a meeting of line workers to organize their own committees in each section and service. Other lines, both state and privately owned, quickly followed suit. In distant Vladivostok and Kharbin, large meetings elected junction committees. So did Omsk railroaders, who called for maximum efforts to increase productivity and insisted on "duty and discipline above all." (In an interesting twist, they also revealed traditional attitudes by prohibiting employees, presumably female, from bringing their children during the workday to the line's administrative center.)[35] Junction workers of the Moscow-Kazan line, meanwhile, convened their first congress on March 20, the line in its entirety shortly afterward. By early April there were nineteen separate executive committees operating on each of the line's nineteen divisions. Below them were some two hundred new local groups, the local (*mestnye*) committees. The mobilization was such that, according to one observer, there did not seem to be a single line, district, or service that remained without its committee. On April 17 the regime formalized the committee system with a comprehensive decree.[36]

This democratization of the railroads was heralded as a key element in solving Russia's wartime transport problem, unraveling local bottlenecks that the central Railroad Management Committee had been unable to effect, and taking charge of the widely abused system for allocating priority shipments. (In April the Central Management Committee was dissolved.)[37] The central (*glavnyi*) line committees were staffed by both experienced salaried employees and wage-earning line workers. In the newspapers and journals soon issued by

---

[34] *Izvestiia Sobraniia Inzhenerov Putei Soobshcheniia* 1 (1917): 11; *Volia i Dumy Zheleznodorozhnika*, May 14, 1917; *Vestnik Putei Soobsheniia* 15 (Apr. 15, 1917).

[35] *Vestnik Ekaterininskoi Zheleznoi Dorogi* 489/9-20 (Mar. 4–12, 1917): 19ff.; *Zheleznodorozhnaia Zhizn' na Dal'nom Vostoke* 10–11 (Mar. 15, 1917): 8–9; 12 (Mar. 22, 1917): 10–11; *Vestnik Omsk Zh. Doroga* 12 (Mar. 25, 1917): 1–13.

[36] *Professional'noe dvizhenie na Moskovskoi-Kazanskii Zheleznoi doroge, 1917–21* (Moscow, 1928), 8–10; *Izvestiia IPK Moskovskago Uzla Moskovsko-Kazanskoi Zheleznoi Dorogi*, June 2, 1917; RGIA f. 280, op. 1, d. 70, l. 1.

[37] RGIA f. 290, op. 1, d. 4. The last recorded session available in the archive was on April 25, 1917.

almost every line the central line committees called for "strict labor discipline" and maximum labor productivity, pledging "full support and solidarity to the Provisional Government while it fulfills its obligations to the country and works closely with the Soviet." Indeed, when railroad operations seemed to improve in April, it was easy to attribute this to the new energy and engagement committees were bringing to railroad problems all across the country. The weather, too, improved.[38]

At the same time the new government's emphasis on the vital role of railroads encouraged line committees to go beyond their formal duties and to insist that their authority along the lines was paramount, including the right to levy fines and impose harsh disciplinary sanctions. Main or central line committees also seemed to pay little attention to the rampant corruption many in Petrograd had long thought was a root evil on the lines: "the baleful effects of nests of colluding station masters and baggage masters," as *Novyi Ekonomist* had described it in January.[39] The expulsion of tsarist officials may even have enhanced the corruption. As railroad traffic improved, protests about this were brusquely turned aside. "Open your eyes," one line committee spokesman urged those in the government worried about the "syndicalism" implied in the committees' exercise of unilateral authority. "You are blind! Life has already given us the power to organize and control railroad life and you do not even see it!"[40]

Minister Nekrasov meanwhile pressed the idea that railroads and the new national railroad union that was being formed were institutions of "state significance" (*gosudarvennoe znachenie*), "the vital nerve of the whole country [as well as] the property of the whole nation." As such, they had to use their power to strengthen the revolutionary state.[41] The Socialist Revolutionaries' leader Chernov, who would replace Shingarev as minister of agriculture in May, went even further at a meeting of Petrograd railroaders in April, suggesting that the national railroad union should indeed act as the head of a transport syndicate, "a self-governing corporation of a workers' state" which administered the railroad net in its name.[42] Nekrasov's term for this was "statization." It connoted the vital importance of the entire railroad net, private and state owned, to the security of the revolutionary state itself. Private lines should not be nationalized, in his view, nor would the new railroad union shed its role of protecting railroad workers'

---

[38] *Golos Zheleznodorozhnikov*, June 4, 1917.
[39] *Novyi Ekonomist* 3 (Jan. 21, 1917): 6–8.
[40] *Volia i Dumy Zheleznodorozhnika*, Apr. 28, 1917.
[41] *Volia i Dumy Zheleznodorozhnika*, May 14, 1917.
[42] Quoted in A. Lozvoskii, "Nastoiashchee i budushchee professional-nykh soiuzov," in *Partiia i soiuzy* ed. G. Zinoviev (Peterburg: Gosizdat, 1921), 156. See also Hannu Immonen, *Mechty o novoi Rossii: Viktor Chernov (1873–1953)* (St. Petersburg: EUSP Press, 2015), ch. 12.

welfare. But their commitment would be—had to be, in Nekrasov's view—acting in the interest of the state above all.[43]

As was the case with Shingarev's new land and food supply committees, there were obvious risks in the course Nekrasov and Chernov were laying out. The already sharp differences between shop and administrative workers and the move to form trade unions within each of the railroads' primary services portended new conflicts among the country's 300,000 railroaders that were likely to disrupt transport further. Line committees were still organized on the basis of separately administered divisions along the lines, strengthening an inefficiency that required a change of crews and locomotives that were frequently unavailable. Perhaps most important, the effort to endow railroad unions with "state significance" risked empowering them in ways the government and soviet both were not intending. In sum, it was not self-evident that either procedural democracy or statization was the best way to secure a rapid improvement in the transport of grain and other necessary goods.

Among many of his conservative liberal contemporaries and in the liberal Great Story more generally, Nekrasov does not get much respect. Many in his own party thought relying on participatory committees was naïve. Railroads were not the place for political experimentation. Members on the Special Council for Transport, which still met periodically, were equally harsh. Iurii Lomonosov, one of Nekrasov's vice ministers, thought that the Main Line Committee of the Nikolaev railroad between Petrograd and Moscow had a "rapacious, malicious attitude" in its arrogation of line governance. Others were soon describing the lines as being "covered with Bolshevik propaganda" and "bent on seizing power."[44] Lomonosov also thought giving the railroad workers such power raised fears that the all-Russia union might try to replicate the railroaders' general strike of 1905, bringing the government and the country to a halt if its demands were not met.[45] For some, Nekrasov's efforts reflected precisely what was wrong with the social democratic movement itself in 1917, and why in turn the liberals' hopes for progressive revolutionary change were doomed from the outset.

Again, however, as with Shingarev's food supply committees, it is fair to ask what Nekrasov might have done better to effect the immediate improvements that were desperately needed. On one hand, it is hard to imagine he and others would have had any success in March by affirming the authority of administrators and the hated railroad police. (The Provisional Government itself eliminated the

---

[43] *Volia i Dumy Zheleznodorozhnika*, May 18, 1917.
[44] See also Anthony J. Heywood, "Liberalism, Socialism and 'Bourgeois Specialists': The Politics of Iu. V. Lomonosov to 1917," *Revolutionary Russia* 17, no. 1: (2004): 1–30.
[45] *Novaia Zhizn'*, June 3, 1917; *Mysli Zheleznodorozhnika*, July 1, 1917; report of E. V. Landsberg to the Special Council in *Ekonomicheskoe polozhenie*, 2:238–42.

special police in any case on March 13.)[46] It is also very likely that the great burst of railroad committees would have occurred anyway along the lines given the emergence of the soviet network itself and the mobilization of workers everywhere in March and April. In its first issue the *Journal of Railroad and Technical Personnel* called for fundamental reform in line administration.[47] Nekrasov and many others in the dual-power regime saw great value in the revolutionary government taking the lead in this process. Organization and mobilization were the keys to the revolution's success. As with the food supply committees, the practical question at the moment was not whether the committees should be encouraged but whether their efforts could produce the efficiencies the country so clearly needed.

Underlying all of this, moreover, were the still constant expressions of "extreme need" coming from railroaders themselves, especially underpaid track maintenance and repair workers who lived and worked close to their villages all along the enormous length of Russia's rail network. Like Shingarev, Nekrasov found a mountain of petitions describing hardship and "extreme need" when he took his ministerial position, often plaintively expressed. Recognizing this need, the young minister quickly organized a joint commission with the Petrograd Soviet to work on comprehensive wage and workplace reform. A special "war bonus" was promised to railroaders in the interim. When the commission first met in early April Georgi Plekhanov, the esteemed elder of the social democratic movement, was elected its chair.[48]

Controlling the Cost of Living: Revolutionary State Finances, War Capitalism, and the Liberty Loan

The heralded formation of the Plekhanov Commission symbolized the shared intentions of the dual-power regime to alleviate quickly the gap between industrial wages and the rising cost of living, a key pressure point of the February uprising. The commission signaled that the revolutionary government would use the state's financial resources to address the problem directly, or at least for railroad workers, and agreed that their wages were indeed inadequate to meet essential needs. Both validated popular demands even as they raised popular expectations.

The Plekhanov Commission was soon inundated with requests for relief, many with multiple signatures. Some came from lower-level state employees who bewailed their "meager salaries," lowly circumstances, and in some cases peremptory termination. (One sent initially to Rodzianko addressed the Duma

---

[46] *Vestnik Putei Soobshcheniia* 11 (Mar. 18, 1917): 49–50; *Zhurnaly Vremennogo Pravitel'stva* 17 (Mar. 13, 1917).
[47] *Izvestiia Sobraniia inzhenirov putei soobsheniia* 1 (1917): 4–14.
[48] *Vestnik Putei Soobshcheniia* 15 (Apr. 1917); *Rabochaia. Gazeta*, Apr. 13, 1917.

president as "Great Leader" [*Velikii Vozhd'*].) Line workers on the Moscow-Kursk line, for example, wanted increases that doubled or tripled their current wages: "Forgive us that you are receiving this petition from little people [*malenkie liudi*] but the cost-of-living question is critical. . . . [L]ife requires expenditure after expenditure. Our families, not to speak of ourselves, are in a critical state, all of our energies are needed just to get by. Our wages are 22 rubles but if we need to buy felt boots they cost us 18 rubles."[49] When the new government announced increases in soldiers' pay and family allowances, employees of the Finance Ministry demanded they too should get military bonuses since they were also serving their country. Meanwhile some plant managers gave out bonuses on their own in lieu of meeting wage demands, essentially admitting that real wages were inadequate.[50]

Writing on Russian finances for the Carnegie Endowment for International Peace in 1928, former Moscow University professor Alexander Michelson described the increase in state expenditure after February as "unprecedented," dwarfing the rate of increase between 1914 and 1916. In his view, reflecting an important trope of the liberal Great Story, the revolutionary regime was simply too weak to resist "unwarranted demands" being made on its resources.[51] N. N. Kutler from the CWIC told his colleague Konovalov, now minister of trade and industry, that distributing bonuses to workers like those planned for railroad workers and *soldatki* would only further drain the financial resources of firms working for defense, threatening their working capital.[52] Yet demands that were "unwarranted" from above in terms of state finance were fully "warranted" from the perspective of those feeling and expressing "extreme need" from below. *Tak zhit' dalee, nel'sia!* It is impossible to live this way any longer! Wasn't this what the revolution was supposed to bring?

But did the revolutionary state actually have sufficient resources to raise procurement prices for military goods as it was doing for grain? Not if one looks in retrospect at the exceptional costs of the war and the regime's failure to bring it to an end and has aggregate statistics that became available only later. At the moment, given the tsarist regime's lack of financial transparency that so exercised Shingarev as chair of the Duma's Finance Committee, no one could really say for sure. The Ministry of Finance and the Office of State Control had not yet managed to complete its final accounts for 1915, never mind the previous year. (It did so for 1915 only in September.)[53] The "ordinary" and "extraordinary" budgets

---

[49] GARF f. 1809, op. 1, d. 3, ll. 22–24.
[50] RGIA f. 23, op. 26, d. 83, ll. 4–5.
[51] A. Michelson, P. N. Apostol, and M. V. Bernatskii, *Russian Public Finance during the War* (New Haven, CT: Yale University Press, 1928), 191–92.
[52] RGIA f. 32, op. 1, d. 1865, ll. 1–3.
[53] G. Dement'ev, *Gosudarstvennye dokhody i razkhody i polozhenie gosudarstvennago kaznacheistva za vremia voiny* (Petrograd, 1917), 20, 31..

approved by the Duma for 1917 premised a small surplus of revenue over expenditures that, even if realized, would hardly make a dent in a projected deficit of 327.8 million rubles.[54] In addition, ordinary and extraordinary revenues (taxes, duties, and the like) were estimated to be sufficient only to cover "normal" state expenses as long as "normal" was calculated in prerevolutionary terms. The only thing absolutely certain about Russian finances was the enormous daily cost of the war. Now fueled because of scarcities by steadily rising costs and set in early March to increase even more by the higher prices the state would now pay for delivered grain, the financial burden of the war was sure to increase even further until it could be brought to an end. What in 1914 had been approximately 10 million rubles a day of exceptional war expenditures had grown to almost 40 million a day by the end of 1916, some 14 billion rubles for 1916 as a whole.[55]

Yet with France and Britain no longer willing to provide additional loans, the government's own bond offerings finding far fewer purchasers than had been hoped, and little if any possibility of substantially reducing production or transport costs, both Shingarev and the new thirty-one-year-old minister of finance Tereshchenko understood there was no viable alternative to substantial new emissions of ruble-denominated credit notes to pay the war's ever increasing expenses. Some 9 billion rubles' worth were already in circulation, according to the Central Statistical Administration's figures in 1918, an increase in 1916 alone of more than 60 percent.[56] (A somewhat lower figure was reported in *Birzheviia Vedomosti* on March 9 as well as by the eminent financial specialist and a founder of the Soviet State Bank E. S. Katzenellenbaum in 1924.)[57] By April Finance Ministry figures showed the number was more than 11 billion. The value of the ruble on the London market was now almost 50 percent what it had been in July 1914. In reality, emissions and scarcities were thus a deadly combination in terms of stabilizing prices and reducing inflation as long as the war continued. And when it finally ended, as Shingarev and others were also warning, the regime would face the huge costs of demobilization, restructuring the military economy, and servicing Russia's already enormous debt, problems that were themselves certain to bring substantial new hardships.

All of this brought enormous pressure on Minister Tereshchenko at a time when he and almost everyone else in Petrograd were still suffering from sleep deprivation and fatigue. Tereshchenko was the scion of a large landowning and sugar manufacturing family in Kiev, trained in law at Moscow University. In 1914 he had served in the Red Cross on the Southwestern Front, before taking

---

[54] GARF f. 6996, op. 1, d. 369, ll. 1–14.
[55] Dement'ev, *Gosudarstvennye dokhody*, 24; *Vestnik Finansov* 36 (1917): 307.
[56] TsSU, *Statisticheskii sbornik za 1913–1917 gg.* (Moscow, 1921), 92.
[57] E. S. Katzenellenbaum, *Denezhnoe obrashchenie Rossii 1914–1924* (Moscow: Izd. Ekon. Zhizn', 1924), 50.

a major post in the Union of Cities, chairing the WIC in Kiev, and serving as Guchkov's vice chair of the CWIC in Petrograd. In temperament, he shared Nekrasov's energy and intensity. Almost immediately at his initiative, the new government on March 4 issued 2 billion rubles more in credit notes, bringing the total value of credit notes in circulation to more than 11 billion rubles, according to the ministry's own calculations. Still more was needed. At the State Bank, officials urged a rewriting of laws governing the process to give full discretion to the ministry, although banks were already having difficulty marketing the bonds that supported them.[58] The annual cost of servicing Russia's state debt at an average of 5 percent was already 1.75 billion rubles, plus any additional obligations the new government took on in the future.[59]

Was there anything the revolutionary government could do to alleviate the potential financial crisis it had inherited besides issuing more bonds and more ruble-denominated credit notes? Was it even possible in these circumstances to curb inflation and stabilize the cost of living, so important to social and political stability? Tereshchenko, Konovalov, Shingarev, and other members of the new regime knowledgeable about financial matters had no good options. Extending fixed prices to a broader range of commodities required matching them to local costs and conditions. This was not only administratively complex; it also assured variations among provinces and even within them that would stimulate instead of reducing speculative trading.

Yet there was little question that prices on bread, meat, vegetables, and other staples were substantially higher in March in many places than they were as recently as January. According to careful work done in 1918 by the statistician Stanislav Strumilin and his colleagues in the Central Statistical Administration, for example, the average price of bread was 12 percent higher in March than in January, almost double what it had been a year earlier. For meat and vegetables, the increases were even greater. In contrast, wage increases were comparably less, especially for unskilled workers.[60] Would relying largely on markets to distribute scarce necessities be a better way to proceed? Shingarev and Groman did not think so. Nor did Groman's colleagues on the Soviet Executive Committee. They wanted the regime to bypass the market on an extended list of necessary goods, especially peat and oil, but through special purchases rather than new state monopolies. Yet Tereshchenko, Konovalov, and others worried that the direct involvement of the state in this way was a risk in and of itself, a step in the direction

---

[58] RGIA f. 560, op. 26, d. 1357, ll. 86–87; *Novyi Ekonomist* 10–11 (1917): 1–4.
[59] RGIA f. 560, op. 26, d. 1357, ll. 86–86 ob.
[60] *Statistika Truda* 1 (July 15, 1918): 10–11. Mark Harrison and Andrei Markevich calculate inflation drove prices across the board to a level in March 1917 three times that of 1913. See their "Russia's Home Front and the Economy, 1914–1922: The Economy," in *Russia's Home Front in War and Revolution, 1914–1922*, bk. 3, ed. Christopher Read, Peter Waldron, and Adele Lindenmeyr (Bloomington, IN: Slavica, 2018), 31.

of a socialized economy in which the regime would bear the direct responsibility for failures without in fact ensuring more equitable distributions.[61]

Still, something had to be done. The easiest course for the moment was to extend rationing to a range of commodities in places where scarcities were most severe and at prices set by local authorities. On March 24, consequently, bread began to be rationed at fixed prices in Petrograd, joining earlier rationing on sugar, salt, and tea. At the same time new private investments had to be encouraged in industrial and commercial firms, which meant reopening the stock market and facilitating the issuance of new company stock and commercial bonds. Taxes also had to be raised, especially on war profits, collection processes improved, and a major new issue of state bonds had to be initiated as soon as possible. The income tax that was passed by the Duma in April 1916 had come into force in January, but many of its provisions were manifestly inadequate to Russia's escalating needs. Work therefore began immediately on raising the income tax as well as preparing a new "extraordinary" levy on income and new taxes on luxury goods and profits, which had increased as much as 200 percent in 1916.[62] All of this was announced with appropriate fanfare to signal the new regime's responsiveness to widespread popular resentment. Meanwhile prices on scarce goods continued to rise throughout the country, as the Central Statistical Administration would later affirm, although it was impossible at the time in Petrograd to have an accurate assessment of the degree or extent.

What was known was that in addition to inviting a new flood of petitions demanding the revolutionary government relieve the widespread anxieties of "extreme need," the new government of "responsible men" also raised the expectations of industrialists and manufacturers themselves.

The first meetings of industrialists and commercial people in Petrograd and Moscow greeted the new regime enthusiastically as a government in which they could finally have confidence. Spokesmen from commercial banks expected that regulations on stock sales and other impediments to private investment would now be lifted. From Ural mining firms came a collective call for "removing all barriers to a flourishing of industrial life."[63] Others saw these barriers in irrational regulations that constrained production and the opportunity now to rewrite them.[64] While the stock market itself remained closed, prices seemed to be holding steady in private trading. Some enterprises were even planning to issue new stock. There seemed to be adequate demand, especially after the agreement on March 10 between workers and industrialists in Petrograd suggested that order would be restored to factories and productivity would increase.[65]

---

[61] RGIA f. 560, op. 26, d. 1357, ll. 38.
[62] Michelson, Apostol, and Bernatskii, *Russian Public Finance*, 140.
[63] *Birzhevyia Vedomosti*, Mar. 9, 1917.
[64] *Trudy Pervogo Ekon. S'ezda: Otchet o Torzhestvennom Zasedaniia Tsent. Voenno-Promyshlennogo Komitita 8 Marta 1917* (Petrograd, 1917), 72–73.
[65] *Birzhevyia Vedomosti*, Mar. 12, 1917.

It also seemed likely that the new regime would take a more generous attitude toward individual plant and factory owners than the tsarist regime had done, especially in industrial centers like Moscow, Kazan, and Kharkov, where owners had been less favored than those closer to the government in Petrograd. Representatives attending the Special Council for Defense on March 15 spoke of the "urgent measures" that were needed to supply plants away from Petrograd with working capital, either through low-interest loans or direct subsidies. A spokesman for the gentry urged low-interest state loans for seed grain.[66]

Minister of Trade and Industry Konovalov and the liberal industrialists in his Progressive Party may have been among the most hopeful in this regard. In mid-March Konovalov affirmed the responsibility of his ministry to ensure industry was adequately supplied with raw materials. On March 16 the government asked the Zemstvo and City Unions to suggest ways to expand small-scale credit by reforming local credit institutions.[67] Seeming to ignore the threats of inflation, Finance Minister Tereshchenko also responded supportively to industrial and commercial groups. Among his first steps were an expansion of industrial credits both directly and through the WICs and a directive that the WICs accelerate the distribution of new contracts for military production with higher purchasing prices. According to one report, the increase in costs of material and labor over 1916 was estimated to be around 400 percent. The additional cost to the state from contract revisions would thus be several million rubles or more. There would also be no interruption in the process of state support for defense contractors, even as the administration of these supports was reconstructed "on the basis of democratic principles."[68]

To this end, Tereshchenko formed a representative commission to review disbursements to private firms and broaden the range of enterprises eligible for state credits. As for assisting individuals, the finance minister told reporters that a state monopoly might well be introduced on sugar and tea that would increase supplies and lower their costs. Maintenance allowances for soldiers' families would also be increased, even though this would add an estimated 500 million rubles to the state's financial obligations for 1917 alone. Meanwhile his friend and colleague Konovalov organized his own commission for "military-technical" support and named vice minister P. I. Pal'chinskii, closely linked to Petrograd industrialists, bankers, and syndicates, as "special plenipotentiary" for supplying industry with metals and fuel.[69]

---

[66] ZOSO, Mar. 15 and Apr. 5, 1917.

[67] Zhurnaly Vremennogo Pravitel'stva 20 (Mar. 16, 1917): 104–05; RGIA f. 23, op. 17, d. 609, ll. 1–5.

[68] Dement'ev, Gosudarstvennye dokhody, 47–48; Michelson, Apostol, and Bernatskii, Russian Public Finance, 192.

[69] GARF f. 7327, op. 1, d. 1, ll. 1–4; Russkiia Vedomosti, Mar. 25, 1917; Izvestiia Tsentral'nago voennoe-promyshlennago komiteta, Mar. 13, 1917; Rech', Apr. 26, 1917; I. A. Garaevskaia, Petr Pal'chinskii (Moscow: Rossiia Molodaia, 1996), 63–66,

Moreover, while many industrialists vocally resisted government intervention in principle, their own dependence on the state was even greater now than it was just a few weeks earlier under the tsarist regime, given the pressure for wage relief and the ongoing problems of supply. The Trade Industrial Congress at the end of March described fuel production and supply as in "crisis," and while the powerful organization of mine owners resisted monopolization, its leader Nikolai von Ditmar still urged much stronger state intervention, calling for the government to supply new workers, provide adequate foodstuffs, and guarantee the delivery of other goods of primary need.[70] On March 28 the Executive Committee of the industrialists' Council of Congresses (Soviet S"ezdov) formed a special committee to prepare a law for the government to compulsory "military-industrial" labor (*voennoe-zavodskoi povinnost'*) for industries where it was most needed. A communication from the group on April 17 called for its application universally for both men and women.[71] By this time virtually every sector of the economy, including peasants harvesting winter crops, looked to the new democratic state for assistance. From Ivanovo, a center with Kostroma of the bloody strikes during the summer of 1915, came an urgent telegram reporting that the lack of deliveries was risking fifty thousand jobs. Returning from the Urals, Kutler reported on the "absence of legality" and the need for the state itself to pay workers in the region directly from the treasury.[72] Both Tereshchenko's Finance Ministry and Konovalov's Ministry of Trade were inundated with new requests for loans.

Each of the Great Stories of revolutionary Russia—at the time as well as afterward—emphasizes the deepening process of social polarization that this consolidation of commercial and trade industrial circles around their own interests and social identities clearly reflects. Social identities and partisan interests of both sides of Russia's class and estate divides clearly strengthened as the new dual-power regime attempted to deal with Russia's shortages in March and April, breaking the near universal support for the overthrow of the old regime into two broadly delineated and increasingly contentious social blocs. The democratic socialist and Bolshevik Great Stories speak easily in the abstractions of "bourgeois" and "worker-peasant," the latter now increasingly known (and labeled) as "*the* democracy." The democratic liberal Story favors "propertied" over "bourgeois" in identifying one side of the divide because it accurately describes a key element of increasing social antagonism as the right to ownership itself, considered by many liberals to be the foundation of progress and modern government. Polarization of this sort was well developed before 1917, of course, and was particularly sharp, as many have noted, on the eve of the war itself. What loosened its constraints after February was the opportunities for material

---

[70] *Trudy Pervyi Ekon. S"ezda*, 231–32.
[71] RGIA, f. 150, op. 1, d. 425, ll. 11–11 ob.; f. 560, op .26, d. 1406, l. 20.
[72] RGIA f. 32, op. 1, d. 1865, ll. 82–84.

betterment the revolution seemed to promise, and which in portentous ways would quickly become more contentious as scarcities continued and material betterment was not forthcoming.

What was at issue in March and early April, however, was not yet the right to property or the problem of antagonistic social interests. It was, in effect, whether the practices and values of war capitalism should be strengthened in Russia's new condition of political freedom, or whether state intervention in the economy should now move revolutionary Russia toward a more consciously defined variant of democratic socialism. If the liberal ministers understood how the scarcities and insecurities over food mandated the new grain monopoly, compromising the interests of private grain traders and their markets, why should not monopolies and the profits they could generate be extended to other essential goods as well? Indeed, this was apparently the view of, among others, Vice Minister Pal'chinskii himself, the government's new special plenipotentiary for supplying industry with metals and fuel, and Peter Migulin, the influential editor of *Novyi Ekonomist*. In Migulin's view, substantial support at the highest levels implied the need for further state expansion into economic control and regulation.

This was certainly the view of the soviet leadership as well, now strengthened by the return from Siberian exile of prominent figures in the Menshevik movement like Irakli Tsereteli. A moderate who was eager to work cooperatively with "bourgeois" elements in order to build a democratic socialist order, Tsereteli also favored the extension of the state's role in the economy but in ways that brought additional relief to workers and peasants as well as support for plant owners and respect for the rights of property. The burgeoning number of workers' soviets, however, were becoming sounding boards where voices of need were laced in strident tones with something combining demands and expectations, as were village gatherings and new peasant soviets, already inclined in some places to take matters into their own hands. In Moscow and Petrograd deputies were sent to factories to "quiet things down," as the Moscow Soviet protocols put it. In addition to helping workers organize new unions, this commonly meant reassuring them that the new government would support their wage and other demands and assuaging fears that these would lead owners to lock workers out or shut their plants down completely. "The necessary interference of the government in Russia's economic life has begun," *Rabochaia Gazeta* exulted as early as the third week in March.[73]

Meanwhile the government continued with some urgency to seek new sources of revenue. The liberal editors of *Russkiia Vedomosti* called for consideration of new taxes and a compulsory government loan. An extraordinary tax that sharply increased the amounts levied on incomes over 10,000 rubles was prepared, along with a more forceful tax on war profits. Most dramatically, just as Lenin arrived

---

[73] *Rabochaia Gazeta*, Mar. 22, 1917; GARF f. 6935, op. 6, d. 230, l. 54.

back in Russia at the Finland station after traveling by closed train through Germany, the government launched a new issue of 5 percent bonds, branded with much fanfare as a Liberty Loan to support the army and defend the revolution. Appeals for its subscription took up the front pages of Russia's leading liberal newspapers. Automobiles filled with its supporters circulated on the streets.

The bond issue was the sixth since 1914. The new offering was again set to return 5 percent over forty-nine years, denominated in small amounts to secure wide participation, just as the previous tsarist loans had been. Neither of these had proved very successful. Several major banks even held unsold allotments.[74] Government and soviet leaders both agreed with the editors of *Birzhevye Vedomosti* that in financial terms, the Liberty Loan signified that the state's situation had not changed with the overthrow of the tsarist regime. At best, even a full subscription would do little unless the rate of inflation could be curbed, which meant, among other things, increasing the supply of food and other necessary goods. At worst, it would further burden the state with interest and redemption obligations that now stretched out some fifty years, into the 1960s.[75]

One can readily understand why the new government regarded the Liberty Loan as an important symbolic gesture even if its financial benefits were almost certain to be marginal. (The largest subscription took place in April, raising 760 million rubles, enough to support the war for fifteen days.)[76] Tereshchenko, Shingarev, and their liberal colleagues intended to appeal to patriotic spirit in revolutionary Russia as much as to alleviate its dire financial straits. Yet in symbolic terms, the loan helped crystalize the still unsettled issue of the meaning and purpose of the war. For the liberal press it signified further the intention of the new government to gather the necessary resources to pursue the war to a victorious conclusion without foreign annexations or the imposition of indemnities on the defeated powers, as the government formally declared on March 28. For Bolsheviks and Menshevik Internationalists on the Ispolkom, the loan thus raised the issue directly of whether raising new funds to support the war was genuinely in the interest of workers and peasants who had overwhelmingly borne its losses. Alexandra Kollontai, a member of the Ispolkom, led the attack. One of the few Petrograd Bolsheviks who fully supported Lenin's demand that Russia pull out of the fighting, Kollontai saw any effort to strengthen the "bourgeois regime" as intrinsically harmful to proletarian interests in Russia and elsewhere. The Ispolkom was split on the question. When a vote of the whole soviet was taken, more than two thousand delegates accepted that assistance in financing

---

[74] RGIA f. 1090, op. 1, d. 170, ll. 1.

[75] *Rabochaia Gazeta*, Mar. 22, 1917; V. V. Strakhov, "Vnutrennie zaimy v Rossii v pervuiu mirovuiu voinu," *Voprosy Istorii* 9 (2003): 28–43.

[76] Michelson, Apostol, and Bernatskii, *Russian Public Finance*, 273–77. Thereafter 730 million was raised in May, 753 million in June, and 516 million in July, before falling off drastically in August and September.

the revolution was "the direct duty of the revolutionary proletariat and the army to the country as well as to the workers of the world."[77]

There was abundant reason for skepticism. Resistance to the Liberty Loan soon came from many quarters. State Bank managers from provincial towns wrote that villagers were not interested in it, influenced in some places by "all kinds of agitators, mainly soldiers returning from the front." Tereshchenko himself was told that the dismal salaries of his own ministry employees made it impossible for them to even consider subscribing. Reports from the provinces were no more encouraging. From Riga came the ominous warning that the Liberty Loan was being rejected precisely because its proceeds would continue to support an "aggressive war."[78]

Giving Meaning to Loss: Politics, Passions, and the April Crisis

Whether or not "all sorts of agitators" opposing to the Liberty Loan were Bolshevik supporters, Lenin's return and his famous April Theses clearly stimulated the war's opponents. If revolutionary Russia was hungry and nearly bankrupt as a result of the war, the logical course was simply to stop fighting. Then German and Austrian soldiers might even be encouraged to topple their own regimes. Recognizing on the contrary that Germany might in that case simply launch a new attack and drive on Petrograd with the intention of restoring the autocracy, Tsereteli guided the Petrograd Soviet to "revolutionary defensism": the purpose of the war would no longer be ultimate victory but defending the revolution itself. If past losses could not be rationalized, losses in the name of preserving the revolution would be a noble sacrifice.[79] Lenin, however, was unequivocally opposed to this view. The first point in his April Theses denounced the soviet's position. Honest workers supporting this were being deceived. There was an "inseparable connection" between capitalism and the imperialist war. Without the overthrow of capitalism itself it was *impossible*—Lenin's emphasis—to achieve a "democratic and non-oppressive peace." If necessary, world war would have to become civil war.[80]

Among many liberals and within the government itself, there was little question that the war had to continue. They agreed with Miliukov that losses in support of a military victory, including that of Miliukov's own son, were still necessary to ensure Russia's historical development as a great world power. The

---

[77] *Izvestiia*, Apr. 23, 1917; Browder and Kerensky, *Russian Provisional Government*, 488–89.

[78] *Sotsial Demokrat*, Apr. 27, 1917; RGIA f. 560, op. 26, d. 1427, 1428, and passim; d. 1406, ll. 20, 46, 71.

[79] See Ziva Galili, "The Origins of Revolutionary Defensism: I. G. Tsereteli and the 'Siberian Zimmerwaldists,'" *Slavic Review* 3 (Fall 1982): 454–76.

[80] *Pravda*, Apr. 7, 1917; Browder and Kerensky, *Russian Provisional Government*, 1205–7.

revolution notwithstanding, this still required control over Constantinople and the Dardanelles, as Miliukov had written in *Vestnik Evropy* (*Herald of Europe*) in January and February, just as for democratic France it required the reincorporation of Alsace-Lorraine and control over Germany's industrial centers in the Rhineland. For their part, democratic socialists understood that revolutionary Russia needed to protect itself from further German and Austrian attack. German victory would surely crush the revolution, and the autocracy would be restored in some form. "Revolutionary defensism" was thus as much a prescription for Russia's historical future as it was the sole legitimate reason for continuing to fight.[81] What was most important about Lenin's view of the war was not it's well-known radical internationalism, a viewpoint that was shared by many others in and outside Russia. It was that it seemed to resonate so broadly as the constraints against opposing the war dissolved.

This was especially the case at the front. Although the Bolsheviks' *Okopnaia Pravda* (*Trench Pravda*) did not begin publishing until the end of March, Bolsheviks were already bringing Lenin's views to the military zone. The evidence suggests that soldiers overwhelmingly were prepared to continue defending themselves and Russia against German and Austrian attack. Whether this included fighting until the war was won, however, was another matter. Many identified the war directly with the old regime. In their letters and among themselves, they wondered why it should be continued now. Still trying to ascertain soldiers' feelings, even more urgent now than before February, military censors reported soldiers almost everywhere saw the revolution as a giant step toward peace. The dominant "mood" was a near desperate hope that the fighting would now come to an end, even if, as one soldier wrote, the new order had brought "everywhere" among the troops a new desire to perform their tasks well in order to achieve this end.[82]

But what precisely were these tasks now that the army was no longer fighting "for Tsar and Country"? To continue to defend their positions, especially on the Austro-German Front, but also to fight for republican Russia "to the last drop of blood" and "never for dishonest gain," as Minister President L'vov composed the army's new oath?[83] In the democratic socialist vision, making the world safe for political democracy also meant making *the* democracy—the ordinary men and women, workers and peasants, who everywhere bore its losses—socially and economically secure. Whether imperialism was the last stage of capitalism, as Lenin famously wrote, or simply the logical way for capitalist political economies to extend their wealth, the war's meaning had to be forcefully redefined. About fighting to defend the new Russian order there could be no question. Yet blood could no longer be shed to extend Russia's own reach over foreign territories or secure

---

[81] *Novoe Vremia*, Mar. 12, 1917.
[82] RGVIA f. 2048, op. 1, d. 905, l. 38.
[83] "Kak_menyalsya_tekst_voennoy_prisyagi_v_rossii_v_raznoe_vremyaistoriya_nashey_voennoy_prisyagi," https://pikabu.ru/story/ kak_menyalsya_tekst_voennoy_prisyagi_v_rossii_v_raznoe_vremyaistoriya_nashey_voennoy_prisyagi_6329947

crippling reparations that would be squeezed from those whose armies were defeated. Revolutionary Russia's task was to secure "peace without annexations or indemnities" through success on the battlefield and collective negotiations.

In contrast to the Soviet position, the government itself at first stood firmly for fighting until complete victory. The formal task of describing its goals for the war was assumed by Miliukov as the new foreign minister. In his famous speech announcing that the revolution itself had "elected" the new government on March 2, the liberal leader called for new relations between officers and soldiers based on "human dignity and civic pride" that would help lead to victory. Two days later he informed Russia's allies that the new regime would fight "shoulder to shoulder" with its democratic allies to the moment of final triumph "faithful to the treaties which bind her by indissoluble ties."[84] No one familiar with Miliukov's editorials in *Rech'* or his two-part journal piece in the most recent numbers of *Vestnik Evropy* could fail to understand he thought the annexation of the Dardanelles Straits and Constantinople was essential to Russia's future well-being.[85] On March 5, however, the moderate Menshevik newspaper *Den'* declared in an editorial that Russia would "fight against all chauvinistic, nationalistic, and imperialistic words, thoughts, and deeds, whatever their source."[86] Several days later Kerensky told the English reporter Harold Williams that Russia did not need Constantinople and the Straits. A full-scale polemic then ensued between *Rech'* and *Izvestiia*. On March 14 the Soviet Executive Committee published its own statement as *Manifesto to People of All the World*, opposing "the policy of conquest of [Russia's] ruling classes." It called for a "decisive struggle against the acquisitive ambitions of governments of all countries."[87] Defense of the revolution and peace without annexations or indemnities had to be the revolution's only military goals.

The ensuing events have been told in some detail by every history of the period. Almost all focus on the political implications. Over the next ten days Miliukov and Tsereteli attempted to work these differences through. Pressed by the Soviet leadership to officially renounce any annexationist goals, Miliukov reluctantly drafted a declaration which he regarded as taking a compromise position. Evoking the blood spilled by huge numbers of Russia's sons, including his own, the liberal leader explained his view of historical progress, stressing that the Russian state itself was now in danger, the key force for its progressive development. When Minister President L'vov issued the declaration over his own name on March 27, it included at the soviet's insistence that free Russia's aim was "not domination over other nations or forcible occupation of their territories, but a stable peace based on the self-determination of peoples."[88] A fuming Miliukov

---

[84] E. A. Adamov, ed., *Constantinople et les détroits*, 2 vols. (Paris, 1930–32), 1:462–64.
[85] P. N. Miliukov, "Konstantinopol' i prolivy," *Vestnik Evropy* 1 (1917): 355–65.
[86] *Den'*, Mar. 5, 1917.
[87] *Izvestiia*, Mar. 15, 1917.
[88] *Rech'*, Mar. 28, 1917.

then took it upon himself to communicate directly to the English and French governments that this by no means renounced the securing of Russia's "vital interests" stipulated in the existing treaties. The soviet's views on the issue aside, he reported, "all the broad public circles of Russia" shared this point of view, as did the army itself.[89]

Now it was Tsereteli, Chkheidze, and their Soviet colleagues who were irate. For them, the revolution was an event of international importance precisely because it altered established notions about the war and its goals, actively spreading democratic socialist values abroad. Even moderate socialists responded angrily to what the newspaper *Delo Naroda* called a subversion of the soviet's goals. Bolshevik agitation increased; passions intensified. On April 20, huge numbers of demonstrators filled the streets as they had in February, this time denouncing the war, "Miliukov-Dardanelskii," and the "capitalist ministers." Some factory delegations were escorted by their own armed militias. Printed placards indicated substantial advance planning. Many better-off onlookers watching from apartment windows and the sidewalks saw the demonstrators as deeply unpatriotic. Especially on Nevskii Prospekt, politics were subsumed by raw emotions. Fights broke out, shots were fired. The first casualties of civil war in the capital fell in the streets. When the demonstrators dispersed in the evening, *Russkie Vedomosti* estimated that some thirty thousand supporters of the Provisional Government were still in front of the Mariinskii Palace, perhaps trying to diminish the strength of those demonstrating against the war and the government. It was not clear, however, which side had carried the day.[90]

The government and soviet leadership both called for calm. The position of garrison soldiers was of great concern. *Rech'* reported that General Alekseev, now commander in chief, thought the slogan "War without annexations" would weaken the army's morale. General Kornilov called Miliukov from his nearby encampment requesting permission to deploy his troops against the garrison soldiers.[91] In Petrograd and Moscow, large demonstrations for and against the government again filled the streets. Garrison soldiers carried banners denouncing Miliukov and Guchkov. Local soviets in a number of major cities called for Miliukov's resignation. In the name of seventy-five thousand railroad workers the Main Line Committee on the Southern Railroad demanded that the Provisional Government immediately begin peace negotiations.[92] The power imminent in mass protests had again come to the fore, this time making the war itself an existential question for Russia's revolution and its government.

---

[89] I. G. Tsereteli, *Vospominaniia fevral'skoi revoliutsii*, 2 vols. (Paris, 1963), 1, 70ff.; Adamov, *Konstantinople i prolivy*, 1:479.
[90] *Russkie Vedomosti*, Apr. 21, 1917; *Pravda*, Apr. 22–23, 1917.
[91] *Izvestiia*, Apr. 21, 1917; *Rech'*, Apr. 21, 1917.
[92] *Novaia Zhizn'*, May 2, 1917.

Trench warfare on the Russian Front was an innovative response to the deadly effects of new German long-range artillery. Initially trenches were quite primitive, without the bunkers and other structures that were subsequently built and offered more protection. Especially for new recruits, the experience in narrow and confining trenches under bombardment was terrifying.

Although they were outfitted with gas masks, which made breathing difficult and running even more so, troops were poorly prepared for the gas attacks that began in 1915. Early casualties from gas decimated whole units. This photo is from late 1915 or 1916. It may have been staged.

The difficulties of retrieving the dead in many places were second only to those of caring for the wounded, especially early in the war. Fighting in no man's zone often meant tripping over dead comrades as well as dead enemies. As this photograph from late 1914 or early 1915 shows, the dead also inhabited bunkers along with the living.

Dead Russian soldiers await collection in 1915, many without identification. As with deserters, families deluged officials for information when letters and cards stopped arriving, usually to no avail.

Laundry was the least of soldiers' everyday problems at the front, especially during warmer months, although soldiers regularly pleaded for their families to send new underwear from home. On dark winter days, soiled clothes only added to the already pungent atmosphere in the trenches.

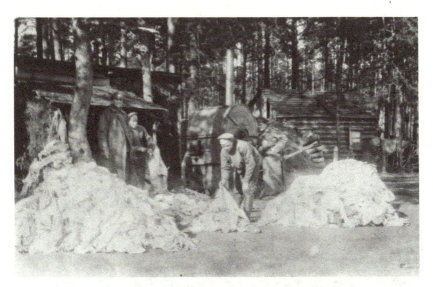

In this photo from 1915 or 1916, shortages of clean underwear were addressed by disinfecting massive quantities of used garments, many taken from the deceased.

Mobilized civilian labor brigades constructed better fortifications by 1916, when this photograph was taken. The thin line between survival and death for those under attack in large open encampments, however, was improved only marginally, if at all.

Punishment for real or alleged infractions was swift and severe on the Russian Front. Those hanged, as in this picture from the field in 1915, were commonly left on the gallows as a warning to others.

Great numbers of exhausted and hungry refugees from the active war zones complicated logistics and generally drew little sympathy from the military. Those on this overloaded train in 1915 or 1916 had the benefit of good weather, at least for the moment.

When scarce freight cars like these could be found, refugees were "fortunate" to be protected from the winter elements despite the otherwise harsh travel conditions.

As food supplies drew more problematic, local communities were often overburdened with the task of accommodating refugees who were resettled there. In this undated photograph, refugees with children wait for a bread ration.

As in other parts of Europe, Russians thirsted from the start for news from the front; this was especially true of those who had some idea where their family members might be fighting. Just after the war began in July 1914, crowds gathered daily in Petrograd at the offices of the widely read *Novoe Vremia* (*New Times*), a leading conservative newspaper published twice a day.

Long lines waited for flour, sugar, salt, and buckwheat and other grains being distributed by the Moscow office of the Society for the Struggle against the Cost of Living in 1915 or 1916.

Long lines in Petrograd early in 1917 awaiting the opening of food shops near uncollected rubble as supplies failed to reach the city and insecurity increased.

During the February insurrection, food rations were distributed to soldiers at the Tauride Palace, site of the State Duma and the Petrograd Soviet, as well as to those here at the Winter Palace.

Establishing itself as a parallel if informal authority to the new government, the Petrograd Soviet initially drew large numbers of delegates from the city's industrial plants and garrison. The body's first meeting, on , photographed here, was a rallying point for propelling insurrection into full-scale revolution.

In desperate need of funds, the provisional government attempted to mobilize Russia's wealthy population to support a Liberty Loan in April and May 1917. Here activists use a propaganda vehicle more often identified with Bolsheviks and other agitators on the political left. In the process, the dress of those in the truck clearly marked them as what workers and the political left understood as "the bourgeoisie."

After February 1917, meetings of soldiers at the front became important vehicles for maintaining a modicum of discipline as well as political mobilization. This is a seemingly orderly gathering before the Kerensky-Brusilov offensive in the spring of 1917.

Anxious depositors throughout the country attempted to retrieve their funds both before and after the Bolsheviks took control of the banks. Here, customers besiege the newly renamed "Peoples' Bank" in Moscow sometime in the fall of 1917.

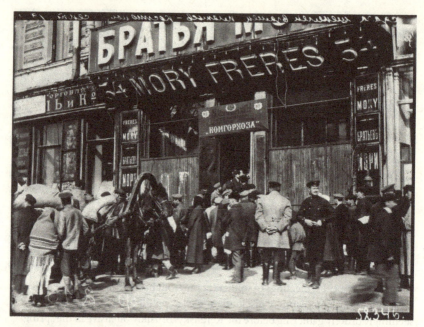

During the massive and spontaneous demobilization of the army in the fall of 1917, soldiers exchanged their coats and other clothing for manufactured products and items of primary need. Here a city's Economic Committee facilitates the process in a store seized from its previous owners, the Mory brothers.

Initially the principal means for mobilizing the Red Army, "political sections" like this one were soon attached to army units for the purpose of both civilian and military political education. From appearances, this unit drew from a diverse range of civilians as well as troops.

Railroad transport remained a key to military success as well as food distribution throughout Russia's long world war. Here the 1st Soviet Battalion poses near Samara in a heavily armed train. Note the wheeled machine guns that were an important part of its limited arsenal.

As the Civil War intensified in the northwest of Russia as well as the Don and Caucasus regions, along the Volga, and into Siberia, civilian and military casualties escalated while food and other essential supplies became even more scarce. Here a funeral for local Bolsheviks takes place in a town near the Northwestern Front in October 1918.

Funerals were political theater during the Civil War. In Petrograd a large funeral procession in June 1919 memorialized those lost defending the city.

Like tens of thousands of Jews, peasants defending themselves against the White armies were treated savagely. This photo is labeled in the archive as showing peasants killed by Kolchak's troops.

Both the Red and White armies, like the Imperial Russian army, suffered from inadequate facilities to treat or evacuate the wounded and collect the dead. These Red Army soldiers were wounded near Voronezh in 1919 or 1920.

Primitive carriages (*karetki*) drawn by horses or men were used to transport wounded Red Army soldiers in 1919. No figures exist for the mortality rates they accelerated.

Food remained a constant problem for all participants in the Civil War, whose primary means of supply was by seizure or "requisition." Here a Red Army field kitchen watched by village children prepares a meal sometime in 1919.

Whether to meet a real need or boost morale, gift boxes of various sorts were sometimes sent from cities and towns to boost morale at the Red Army Front during the winter of 1919.

The losses in the countryside during the Civil War were prodigious, if uncountable. Here peasant children orphaned by the war are gathered apparently to be photographed in Voronezh sometime in 1919.

Organized in 1917, many peasant soviets turned against the Bolsheviks in the course of the Civil War, although that is hardly apparent in the demeanor of soviet delegates posed in this photograph, taken sometime during 1918 in Samara province.

Especially deep in the countryside many village soviets and other assemblies fought savagely against food "procurement" detachments from all warring sides. The archive has identified the pile of bodies in this photograph as members of a Bolshevik procurement force "murdered by resistant peasants."

9

Social Conflict, Mediation, and the Revolutionary State

A scant seven weeks after the Provisional Government and Petrograd Soviet assumed the tasks of revolutionary governance, the April demonstrations revealed to both sides of the "dual power" divide how very difficult these tasks actually were. Bolsheviks may well have helped bring demonstrators into the streets, but only because they touched deep anxieties and rebellious feelings. On April 27, the very moment the composition of the government was in doubt, Andrei Shingarev told a large meeting of tradesmen and agriculturalists that food was the dominating issue of the moment, that responsible people could not continue to view things from a "class point of view." In many places along the front there was only a single day now of food reserves. Shingarev publicly stated that "We are living through frightening days. We find ourselves on the verge of disaster [*na kraiu propastia*]."[1]

All three Great Stories of 1917 understandably stress the political importance of the Provisional Government's reorganization at the end of April into a coalition regime. From the democratic socialist perspective as *Izvestiia* expressed it, the "bourgeois" government formed on March 3 had been based on a "juridical analysis" of state power that belied the fact that the government and the soviet both exercised authority over different and antagonistic constituencies. Shingarev's "responsible people" had to take this into account. If the government was to bring Russia successfully to a constituent assembly it had no choice but to share power with the soviet and work under its "supervision" (*kontrol'*).[2] On the same day, the Kadets' *Rech'* suggested Paul Miliukov and the party's leaders were precisely the jurists *Izvestiia* complained about. A coalition could exist only where individual ministers acted as party representatives and functioned on the basis of party coalitions and alliances. It was "irrational" to discuss a coalition for Russia since the Provisional Government was not a cabinet regime in any parliamentary sense. Its goals and policies were national, not partisan. If members of the soviet leadership entered the government, it could only be to share formally

---

[1] *Rech'*, Apr. 27, 1917; See also A. G. Khrushchev, *A. I. Shingarev* (Moscow: Kuchnerev, 1918), esp. 98–100.
[2] *Izvestiia*, Apr. 26, 1917.

the heavy responsibility of a national and nonpartisan government serving state interests rather than social ones, at least until the end of the war.[3]

What neither side could fully assess is the implication for "responsible" governance of the conflicting whirl of passions that continued to structure revolutionary power and politics: the anger and grief of households whose fathers, sons, husbands, and sometimes daughters were among the 5.8 million casualties of the war; the anxieties of those in industry and commerce whose enterprises and social positions were equally endangered; the fears of landowners like Shingarev himself whose estate near Voronezh was vulnerable to assault and who would lose his wife there in the late summer; and anxious male and female workers whose jobs and well-being were still threatened when they left work to look for food—the great swath of the Imperial Russian population, the *narod*, for whom the revolution was clearly as much about welfare and security as it was about civil liberties, and most probably more. For many liberals and supporters of the old regime, the April disorders reflected the anarchistic impulses of the *narod*. There were indeed self-proclaimed anarchists in Petrograd and elsewhere who would soon draw national attention by occupying a well-known mansion in Petrograd and raising the anarchist flag. It is difficult, of course, to tease out the emotions of this moment, as it is for all events of this kind. Still, reading the placards and descriptions by observers it is fair to say that those demonstrating against the war and the "capitalist" ministers were motivated by coherent anxieties as much as were those counterdemonstrating in support of the regime. "Down with the Provisional Government" and "End the War" were countered by those demanding "Death to the Traitors."[4] It was not clear how much the antiwar demonstrations were organized by Lenin's supporters and how much they acted spontaneously. It was even less clear which was worse. In Moscow the soviet voted eighty-nine to fifteen in opposition to further demonstrations and disavowed further calls for workers to go out on strike. Demonstrations had to be organized, not spontaneous, and only by the soviet.[5]

Politics and the First Coalition

In political terms, the April Crisis, as it came to be called in all three of the Great Stories, was the first major clash between the elemental power inherent in demonstrations and uprisings and the formal power of the state, with its claim to monopoly over all its coercive instruments. At the moment, the angry

---

[3] *Rech'*, Apr. 26, 1917.
[4] GARF f. 6935, op. 6, d. 230, l. 111.
[5] GARF f. 6536, op. 6, d. 230, l. 114.

power of the street, an effect of the losses of war and scarcities in essential goods, overwhelmed the forces of coercion. The possibility of state forces repressing the demonstrators reared its head on April 20 when General Lev Kornilov prepared to bring his troops into the city to somehow "restore order." Countermanded by the soviet, the angry general then left for army headquarters at Mogilev to regroup. Fully aware of how the French Revolution had run its course, democratic liberals and socialist leaders alike were still as wary of political counterrevolution from above as they were about the potential violence of social revolution from below.

The historian Ziva Galili has fully laid out the tensions of Menshevik leaders in the face of the April demonstrations and the increasingly hostile criticism they were receiving from more radical Socialist Revolutionaries and Bolsheviks. As she describes, a small group led by Irakli Tsereteli gathered every day to coordinate the position of the Executive Committee and to strategize on how to move forward. Fedor Dan, the Menshevik editor of *Izvestiia*, was part of this group.[6] So were the Duma delegates Nikolai Chkheidze and Matvei Skobelev, Vladimir Groman (now head the Soviet Economic Commission), and the two Socialist Revolutionaries (SRs) Nikolai Avksent'iev and Viktor Chernov, the first now chairing the newly formed Peasants Soviet, the latter just back from European exile. What shook this group as well as their comrades in Moscow and elsewhere was not only Miliukov's guileful note to the allies upholding Russia's commitment to the still secret war treaties and undermining the government's own declaration of March 27 forswearing annexations and indemnities, but the passion of demonstrators both attacking and defending the war.

Miliukov and Shingarev, meanwhile, left for army headquarters, as did Kornilov. The Kadets' trip had been scheduled well in advance, but the coincidence appeared ominous. In the aftermath of both demonstrations support grew rapidly for socialists entering the government. Some of the strongest appeals were from the committees of social organizations, which were now losing their soviet members.[7] The Soviet Executive Committee initially rejected the idea of its members joining the government, partly because they were likely to be assailed by Lenin and others as "cooperating with the class enemy."[8] For their part Miliukov and his colleagues were also shaken by events but divided about how to move forward. Miliukov was strongly opposed to coalition. Nikolai Nekrasov was in favor. Greatly concerned by reports he was receiving about violence in the countryside and the unruliness of some local food committees, Shingarev was uncertain.

---

[6] Ziva Galili, *The Menshevik Leaders in the Russian Revolution* (Princeton, NJ: Princeton University Press, 1989), chs. 3, 4.
[7] *Sbornik materialov komiteta moskovskikh obshchestvennykh organizatsii* (Moscow, 1917), 2–3.
[8] I. Tsereteli, *Vospominaniia o fevral'skoi revoliutsii*, 2 vols. (Paris, 1963), 1:87ff.

What broke the impasse was the resignation of Alexander Guchkov as minister of war and a fervent appeal by Minister President Georgi L'vov for a coalition cabinet. By May 1, the soviet leadership had worked out a set of eight demands as planks for a coalition regime. These included a reaffirmation of support for peace without annexations or indemnities; further democratization in the army; and, most important in terms of Russia's concurrent economic crisis, increased state control of industry and support in principle for the restructuring of land relations in the interests of the peasantry. With varying degrees of reluctance, its members agreed to soviet representatives joining the government on this basis. To avoid even further escalation, they did not demand Miliukov leave the cabinet, but that he give up his position as foreign minister for that of minister of education. When he and Shingarev returned to Petrograd on May 2 to find negotiations already underway in their absence, he angrily refused. Soviet demands usurped the prerogatives of the Constituent Assembly. Nonpartisanship was being sacrificed to social and political factionalism that would further weaken state power. Worst of all, democratic socialist figures entering the government were subject to the soviet's recall as if it were a parliamentary regime. Russia's very historical future was now at stake. Resigning in indignation if not full-blown rage, the country's most prominent liberal expected his Kadet ministerial colleagues to leave the government with him. To his great regret, they demurred.[9]

When the composition of a new coalition cabinet was finally settled, Shingarev moved to the Ministry of Finance, the SR leader and peasants' advocate Chernov became minister of agriculture, and the progressive Ukrainian sugar magnate Mikhail Tereshchenko took Miliukov's place as minister of foreign affairs. The tireless firebrand Alexander Kerensky replaced Guchkov as minister of war; the Soviet Executive Committee's mistakenly hoping that he would now have control over any new efforts by Kornilov or others to move forcefully against them. The moderate Menshevik Matvei Skobelev assumed the new position of Minister of Labor. Irakli Tsereteli, the informal head of the Soviet delegation, joined the cabinet as well. From this moment forward the fate of democratic liberalism and democratic socialism was inextricably linked to the fate of the Provisional Government itself. In effect, Lenin's socialist and liberal opponents had consolidated into one clearly defined political target. Unless reactionary military figures like Kornilov got there first, ousting the regime meant the Bolsheviks would come to power.

---

[9] William G. Rosenberg, *Liberals in the Russian Revolution* (Princeton, NJ: Princeton University Press, 1974), 112–16; *Rech'*, May 5, 1917.

Coalition Governance and the Weighty Actor Thesis

How much did the formation of a coalition government nine short weeks after the overthrow of the tsar reflect the weakness of the Russian state in 1917? Much of the historical writing about the fall of the monarchy and the short life of its democratic successor has been dominated by a single paradigm, clearly articulated at the time by the statist historian Miliukov: that of the instrumentalist state as a weighty actor in social organization and development, an autonomous set of functional institutions capable of defending the country against foreign enemies as well as supporting social well-being and stability within. From this perspective, the last years of tsarism and the failure of the Provisional Government in 1917 are evidence of the "weak state" syndrome that both facilitated revolution and assured the democratic revolutionary state itself would not be sustainable. Although they describe its causes in slightly different ways, each of the Great Stories—democratic liberal, democratic socialist, and Leninist—see the resulting power vacuum in the dual-power regime as the political requisite to October, the inevitable consequence of a weighty actor gone soft.[10]

That the contending Great Stories share assumptions about the state in 1917 is not surprising, given the need to condemn or legitimize October and the absence of more society-centered understandings of the ways state power is institutionalized and exercised. In the liberal telling, the growing power of the soviets came at the expense of state authority rather than reflecting distinct locations and forms of power that were both part of the process by which the nature of state power itself was changing. In a society with relatively weak civil traditions and a sense of law as decree rather than a reflection of constitutional principles, the elements of Russia's revolutionary experience that were clearly manifest at the end of April were readily tagged as simple anarchy from a state-as-weighty-actor perspective, an additional cause in and of themselves for its weakness.

Whether the revolutionary state was too weak to sustain a monopoly on the coercive use of force or to manage the effects of scarcity and loss when the first coalition government was empowered seems like an obvious question to ask in terms of its subsequent political fate. In the transition from tsarist rule to that of the revolutionary dual-power regime, the state still held control for the most part over the army at the front. State-supported violence continued to spill over to civilian areas in the military zone as the army's official procurement detachments and ordinary pillaging took what was wanted or needed by force. The havoc wreaked on Ternopil by troops retreating from Brusilov's offensive was clearly

---

[10] As is well known, the phrase "weighty actor" is Theda Skocpol's. See Peter Evans et al., *Bringing the State Back In* (Cambridge: Cambridge University Press, 1985), 3; Theda Skocpol, *States and Social Revolutions* (Cambridge: Cambridge University Press, 1979).

sanctioned by their commanders, however passively this might have been in some cases. Still, the fact that the revolutionary state after February did not have the power to use the armed force it formally commanded to contain and suppress internal violence had profound consequences for the ways that violence rapidly spread in urban areas and the countryside. Certainly, the weakness of the state in this respect had a determinant influence on the revolutionary process between February and October.

As Nicos Poulantzas has argued, however, states should also be seen as sites of negotiation where contending viewpoints and policies are presented and argued, an arena for resolving conflict within a largely autonomous cluster of offices and institutions which can strengthen social and political stability without the use of coercive power.[11] By April 1917, these locations included more than seventy state-owned industrial plants employing more than 300,000 workers who directly confronted state authority every day in the workplace. A little more than a third of these plants were clustered in and around Petrograd, the rest spread throughout the country. In Nizhnii Novgorod, the Sormovo shipbuilding and locomotive works was the largest employer in the city.[12] The majority of Russia's railroad workers were also state employees, directly involving the state in their well-being. From this perspective, the authority and power of the revolutionary state depended at least as much on its ability to mediate social conflict as to repress social disorder, its power located as much in the processes of mediation as in those of social control.

In this respect, the most important new member in the coalition ministry was not the well-known minister of war Kerensky, but Skobelev, who took charge of the newly created Ministry of Labor. As Boris Kolonitskii has written, a cult was already forming around Kerensky before he took his new post.[13] Now he turned his passion and electrifying speeches to preparing with General Brusilov the new spring offensive agreed to with Russia's allies in the hope that it would finally bring Germany to its knees. Plans were laid to attack again in the Galician region. In contrast, the thirty-one-year-old Skobelev, the youngest member of the new coalition, took charge of creating the Ministry of Labor, separating its functions from the Ministry of Trade and Industry. The son of a wealthy Baku oilman, he had joined the social democrats before the Menshevik-Bolshevik split and worked closely with Lev Trotsky when the two were in Vienna. After he was elected to the Duma as a Menshevik deputy, he was considered a rising star. He worked closely with the faction's leader, Chkheidze, and at the time of his appointment was deputy chair under Chkheidze of the Soviet Executive

---

[11] Nicos Poulantzas, *State, Power, Socialism* (London: Verso, 2014), and other works.
[12] RGIA f. 23, op. 16, d. 318, ll. 44–47.
[13] Boris I. Kolonitskii, *Tovarish Kerenskii: Antimonarkhicheskaya revoliutsiia i formirovaniye kulta "Vozhdya naroda" mart–iiun' 1917 goda* (Moscow: NLO, 2017).

Committee. The new labor minister quickly assumed a burden equally difficult as Kerensky's task of rousing the army: extending through the new Department for the Resolution of Conflict between Capital and Labor the mechanisms for resolving disputes and restoring order to industrial production. In some ways the young Skobelev was also the temperamental complement to Kerensky, someone who described himself as controlling a passionate heart with a rational mind. The ministry would work hard to mediate disputes without positioning itself in support of one side or another. Outspoken on the issues of labor and the economy, Skobelev plunged into his new tasks with determination and conviction.

With the coalition government seated on May 5, the Soviet leadership now had a vested interest in its success and a strong voice in determining its programs. The initial boundaries of dual power were thus permanently compromised. Six of the thirteen ministers were democratic socialists and subject to recall by the soviet. They headed the key ministries of war, labor, food, agriculture, justice, and communications (post and telegraph). Together with three leading members of the Kadet Central Committee, Shingarev, Nekrasov, and Alexander Manuilov, the coalition also included leading Mensheviks in Tsereteli and Skobelev and the left-centrist head of the SRs, Chernov, who became minister of agriculture after Shingarev agreed to take on the Ministry of Finance. They joined the respected zemstvo and Progressist Party figures L'vov, Tereshchenko, and Konovalov, now a Kadet, all of whom had played important roles in the WICs and the Progressive Bloc.

In terms of "responsible men" and political representation at this critical juncture it is hard to imagine a more promising configuration. In principle, coalition governance could ensure the authority of the revolutionary state until its democratic reconfiguration by the Constituent Assembly gave it clear political definition. The question was whether the restructured government was capable of effectively mediating social conflict, alleviating the actual and anticipated effects of scarcity, and moving the war successfully to a close with yet another spring offensive. Revolutionary politics may have been structured ideologically around conceptions of historical change, the role of the state, and the moralities of social welfare, but in practical terms democratic liberals and socialists shared deep concerns about the implications of social conflict.

Seeking Security and Dignity in the Spring Strike Wave

That a new wave of strikes began shortly after the coalition government was formed should have come as no surprise. The supply of food and other necessities in Petrograd and Moscow had improved somewhat, partly due to better weather, partly to the additional efforts of Nekrasov and the Plekhanov Commission to stimulate productivity on the railroads. Even nominal wages had increased in Petrograd and elsewhere as a result of the eight-hour day. Bonuses and changes in piece rates also increased wages. Overtime hours to maintain production schedules paid double, or at least they were supposed to. Rising prices, however, continued to compromise these gains.

Aggregate statistics for March compiled later in the year show steady price increases throughout the country for meat, vegetables, and dairy products, among others. In the important case of bread, the prices were about 12 percent higher in March compared to January. By May, the increase was close to 60 percent. There were variations in different localities, of course, but the trend everywhere was upward, with steep increases for commercial products like leather and linen as well.[14] Despite higher nominal wages, continued scarcities and higher prices in essential goods could only intensify anxieties about what was still to come as well as expectations that the revolutionary regime would quell them. In these circumstances it was predictable that workers everywhere would seek the gains new legislation on strikes now allowed. The efforts of democratic socialists to organize the workplace and invigorate the trade unions led logically to testing their power.

From the end of April to the beginning of July, over four hundred strikes occurred involving more than half a million workers, the largest outbreak by far since the spring of 1914. More strikes began in May than in any month of the revolutionary period. The highest concentration was in and around Moscow and Petrograd, but all major industrial regions were affected along with all major sectors of production. In Petrograd, clerks in some 120 shops in the Gostinyi Dvor and Apraksin markets went on strike. So did waiters, maids, and porters in hotels and expensive apartment houses, including for a time all the hotels and restaurants in the town of Piatagorsk, perhaps the best-known spa resort in Russia.[15]

Two thirds of all strikes demanded some form of wage relief: higher rates, changes in pay scales (*stavki*), paid sick days, housing supplements, reduced hours without reduced compensation, and overtime pay. Provinces in which real wages had steadily declined had the highest strike intensities, a strong indication that demands for higher wages were not, or not simply, the result of political agitation.[16] Workers' voices also spoke strongly through strike actions of the need to be treated with dignity in social interactions, workplace practices, and living conditions. Hours and conditions in Russian factories were notoriously

---

[14] TsSU, *Statistika Truda* 1 (July 15, 1918): 10–11; TsSU, *Statisticheskii sbornik za 1913–1917 gg.* (Moscow, 1921), 58–90.
[15] Diane P. Koenker and William G. Rosenberg, *Strikes in Russia, 1917* (Princeton, NJ: Princeton University Press, 1989), ch. 5.
[16] Ibid., 229–32.

bad, as they had been well before the revolution in comparison to Western Europe and the United States. Unsafe and unsanitary conditions prevailed. An eleven-hour day had long been the norm. So were poorly lighted and unventilated workspaces, unsafe machinery, and the extensive use of child labor that had fueled liberal reform movements before the war, as it had democratic socialist activism.[17]

Strikes in May and June thus unleashed long-term as well as immediate grievances. Workers in one Vladimir plant demanded sixty kopecks a week for the baths and a two-ruble supplement for housing.[18] In Kaluga, workers struck for monthly salaries instead of daily wages; an eight-hour workday beginning at nine with ninety minutes for midday dinner and a half-hour tea break; two weeks' vacation; three months of sick leave with one month at normal wages; two weeks' notice for any dismissals; tea service after dinner; full wages for time lost as the result of a strike with no retributive dismissals; and improved conditions for those studying to improve their positions in local institutes and schools.[19] This list and others of its kind published in *Pravda* and other newspapers sound to some historians like they were drafted by local Bolsheviks rather than workers themselves, and demonstrate not so much what workers desired as how deeply involved were Lenin's supporters in fomenting labor protest. In fact, there are more than enough examples of a similar kind to make it clear that the feelings and desires such lists indicate were broadly shared regardless of who drafted them. Given the reasonable nature of many of these demands and the expectation that they could readily be met, moreover, management resistance in May and June came as some surprise. The average length of all strikes during these weeks was twelve days, almost twice as long as before 1917.[20]

While industrial strikes by politically active metal and textile workers have gotten the most attention from historians of 1917, two of the most revealing strikes in terms of workers' identities and attitudes were in the service sector: those of the Petrograd laundry workers and service people in the city's restaurants and cafés. In each case, protests were not so much about wages as personal and collective dignity, reflected in workers' insistence, as soldiers had done, that they be addressed by the impersonal *vy* (you) instead of the personal and subordinating *ty* (thee). (In a notable 1923 essay Trotsky was to make this

---

[17] See esp. Rose L. Glickman, *Russian Factory Women: Workplace and Society 1880–1914* (Berkeley: University of California Press, 1984); Iu. I. Kir'ianov, *Zhiznennyi uroven' rabochikh Rossii* (Moscow: Nauka, 1979); Adele Lindemeyer, *Citizen Countess: Sofia Panina and the Fate of Revolutionary Russia* (Madison: University of Wisconsin Press, 2019), among other works.
[18] *Pravda*, Mar. 12, 1917.
[19] *Pravda*, June 8, 1917.
[20] Koenker and Rosenberg, *Strikes*, 200–203.

a core premise of the Bolsheviks' attempt at cultural revolution.)[21] The laundry workers strike began in Petrograd on May 1, the same day the Soviet Executive Committee voted to join a coalition government. Some fifty-five hundred women from two hundred firms left their jobs. Speaking through their new trade union they demanded an eight-hour workday, guaranteed minimum wages, pay books for accurate calculations, two weeks' notice for dismissal, improved sanitary conditions in the shops, two weeks' paid vacation, and one month's sick leave. At the top of the list was "polite address" from their employers.[22] Management responded harshly. Shop owners reportedly called their employees "vipers" and "filth." In *Pravda*'s possibly distorted account, owners chased strikers with hot irons and sought to have them thrown out of their apartments, fined, and even arrested.[23] In the face of this hostility, women workers and their male comrades from other sectors rallied in their support. Contributions to the union's strike fund poured in. Activists like Alexandra Kollontai addressed large meetings encouraging solidarity. Within a week shop owners began to meet strikers' wage and dignity demands, and the strike ended triumphantly for the women and their cause.[24]

The walkout of Petrograd waiters, waitresses, and other service people from the city's restaurants and cafés, meanwhile, began with a large march through the center of the city after the restaurant and café owners association refused to allow the conflict to be mediated. Strikers marched under banners declaring "We Insist on Respect for Waiters as Human Beings" and "Down with Tips: Waiters Are Citizens!" (A similar strike by waiters in distant Kazan demanded "Down with Slavery and Humiliation.") Again newspaper coverage was extensive. Some owners, unable to understand why tipping was felt to be a humiliating practice, initially rejected concessions. After several weeks, however, a settlement granted salaried wages, an eight-hour day, and one month's vacation—and *mirabile dictu*, an end to tipping.[25]

The laundry and restaurant strikes were notable because they were largely by women whose demands for dignity resonated throughout the workforce as a whole. Hardly popular with members of Petrograd's "boulevard society" who missed clean clothes and good restaurants, they seemed to symbolize the hopes

---

[21] See L. Trotsky, "'Thou' and 'You' in the Red Army" (1923), in *Bolshevik Visions: First Phase of the Cultural Revolution in Soviet Russia*, ed. William G. Rosenberg (Ann Arbor: University of Michigan Press, 1990), 230–33.

[22] *Rabochaia Gazeta*, May 2, 1917; *Delo Naroda*, May 10, 1917.

[23] *Pravda*, May 20, 25, 1917.

[24] *Edinstvo*, May 11, 1917; *Novaia Zhizn'*, May 12, 1917; *Rabochaia Gazeta*, May 14, 18, 1917; *Pravda*, May 25, 1917. The strike is discussed in detail by S. S. Goncharskaia, "Profsoiuz prachek v 1917 goda," in *V ogne revoliutsionykh boev (Raiony Petrograda v dvukh revoliutsiiakh 1917 goda* (Moscow: Mysl', 1968), 1:477–86.

[25] E. Grachev, ed., *Kazanskii oktiabr': Materialy i dokumenty* (Kazan: Ispartodel Tatoblastkoma VKP, 1926), 65–68.

of wage earners that the revolution would finally bring some degree of material betterment and security. In this regard the leadership of the Petrograd Soviet was in a difficult position. Many strikes ended without significant gains, despite the expectations that they would achieve their goals. *Rabochaia Gazeta* and other supportive socialist papers emphasized the need for strong trade unions. Of particular note were the hardships of disappointed strikers who went without wages and risked their jobs apparently to no avail.[26]

Factory and mill owners, however, were also in a difficult situation. For plant owners, protecting Russia's industrial order without engendering additional "class-based" perceptions and antagonisms was impossible. Trade and industry groups had to insist their own interests were also national ones, that the national well-being and the very fate of the revolution depended on a stable and productive industrial order. Some believed the way to do this was to forswear profits. Others spoke for concerted new funding by the state while also insisting, somewhat in contradiction, that there could still be "no other economic order in Russia besides capitalism."[27] Most now resisted further wage concessions, threatening their plants might have to close and cost workers their jobs.[28]

In many places around the country local soviets and workers committees pushed back. The Moscow Soviet promised to take "decisive measures" to ensure that factories in that city stayed open. It threatened to publish a blacklist of owners who locked their gates. Local soviets elsewhere did the same.[29] Some workers' committees began to add control over hiring and firing to their list of demands. Their own decisive measures against foremen, managers, and plant owners also increased, including the notorious practice of taking roughed-up managers and foremen out of their plants in wheelbarrows and, in some Petrograd incidents at least, throwing them into the canals. In some places workers' militias that had formed in February to defend against counterrevolution tried to keep factory doors open and forcibly prevent dismissals. Assaults were reported in all major industrial areas.[30]

In the process, expectations on both sides for the new coalition government clashed with social and economic realities. Higher wages gained by strikes would mean little if prices for essential goods continued to rise. Many plant owners around the country also hoped that Minister Skobelev would now rein

---

[26] Koenker and Rosenberg, *Strikes*, 159–60.
[27] *Ekonomicheskoe polozhenie Rossii nakanune velikoi oktiabr'skoi revoliutsii*, 3 vols. (Moscow: Nauka, 1957), 1:181–84.
[28] RGIA f. 150, op. 1, d. 557, ll. 105–8.
[29] GARF f. 6935, op. 6, d. 230, ll. 54–56 [*Ispolkom Mos. Soveta. Protokoly*].
[30] GARF f. 6935, op. 6, d. 230, ll. 101–6. Detailed discussions are in Rex A. Wade, *Red Guards and Workers' Militias in the Russian Revolution* (Stanford, CA: Stanford University Press, 1984) and L. S. Gaponenko and V. E. Poletaev, "K istorii rabochego dvizheniia v Rossii v period mirnogo razvitiia revoliutsii (mart–iiun' 1917 goda)," *Voprosy Istorii* 2 (1959): 21–44.

in workers' wage demands given the rising cost of materials. They looked to him to prevent "complete financial ruin." Those selling to the state wanted the government to cap wages or write new contracts to compensate them for their higher costs. Insisting they "had no right" to agree to settlements that threatened the country's economic well-being, some plant owners were already describing management-labor relations as a "dictatorship of the proletariat."[31] For their part, democratic socialists hoped state resources might now be used to secure at the least a minimum program of welfare reforms. A looming financial catastrophe could be prevented only by printing more money.[32] One of the Soviet Executive Committee's conditions for joining the government was the implementation of a new regulatory plan worked out by Groman's Economic Commission. New regulations would limit profits, guarantee a livable wage, and bring state planning into all spheres of Russia's economy, including trade and consumption as well as production and transport—all this as quickly as possible.[33] Meanwhile, Vasili Stepanov from the Ministry of Trade and Industry sent the government a draft declaration on economic policy that described "all major branches of industry undergoing a 'profound crisis' and stressing that in these conditions [he] had to state 'in unqualified terms' the impossibility of restructuring the economy in socialist terms during the war, now or in the near future."[34]

May and June thus witnessed not only a large wave of strikes but an equally large wave of firings, lockouts, and factory closings. What emerged during the spring strike wave was not simply a clash between workers demanding wage and job security and industrialists defending the existing economic order, but an explosion of workers' pent-up emotional as well as material demands, a sense of security as well as the right to dignified treatment. Employers felt increasing anxiety that the whole economic order was unstable, that workers' demands could not be realized without the economy going into free fall. Strikes and resistance to them thus became increasingly a struggle over who exercised what kind of power in the workplace, challenging the premises of equality in political democracy and intensifying the nature and forms of social polarization.

All this was reflected in the continued public demonstrations that occurred in May and June, amplifying Lenin's call to replace the coalition of "bourgeois" liberals and Menshevik "traitors" with a soviet socialist regime and end the war. Whether socioeconomic conditions were driving politics or the other way around, political solutions and state power were still understandably a primary focus of both democratic liberals and socialists. "More and more," the Kadets' *Rech'* editorialized at the end of May, "Bolshevism is becoming the question of

---

[31] RGIA f. 1090, op. 1, d. 168, ll. 1.2; *Ekonomicheskoe polozhenie* 1:165–80.
[32] RGIA f. 6935, op. 6, d. 230, l. 168.
[33] See the discussion in Galili, *Menshevik Leaders*, ch. 6.
[34] RGIA f. 23, op. 27, d. 65, ll. 8–10.

the day."³⁵ So it was with the Mensheviks when Lenin famously declared at the first All-Russia Congress of Soviets that he and his party were ready to replace the dual-power regime. When Lenin then called for a mass demonstration against the war for June 10—successfully prevented by the Ispolkom and the Petrograd Soviet, it turned out—it was not clear to many whether the real object was the war or the government itself. In the soviet's own demonstration one week later, arranged after the first All-Russia Congress of Soviets expressed its confidence in the regime, Bolshevik voices against both were fully on display. According to *Izvestiia*, almost all factory and soldiers' delegations carried antigovernment signs. Many with placards in support of the regime were attacked, their banners ripped away as in April. With what could easily be read as a sense of desperation, the Mensheviks' *Rabochaia Gazeta* blamed these excesses on "soldiers turned beasts" and the "universal bitterness among the masses of ordinary people for which the war more than anything else is responsible."³⁶

The Ministry of Labor as a Site of Mediation

For the young minister of labor Skobelev, these demonstrations only increased his already difficult tasks. In his first press interviews he stressed the importance of enacting legislation to benefit workers but was equally emphatic about the importance of workers conducting their struggles with management in an organized and orderly way. He also agreed with Georgi Plekhanov that workers might have to postpone significant new gains until the war was over, an outlook that was shared by Kuz'ma Gvozdev, who now joined him as assistant minister, as well as the many so-called Menshevik *praktiki* supporting the party's "minimum program." The needs of the moment required constructive labor organization and leadership. Conflict had to be constrained. The Ministry of Labor could protect workers' welfare only by carefully considering how the interests of labor *and* industry both related to Russia's broader needs, including the pursuit of the war.³⁷

First and foremost, this required preventing "the economic disintegration of the country," as the coalition government as a whole declared on May 5. To this end the government now pledged "the further systematic establishment of state supervision [*kontrol'*]" over the production, transportation, exchange, and distribution of commodities. Specific measures would "strengthen the regulation of food supplies and the distribution of essential consumer goods."³⁸ The formation

---

³⁵ *Rech'*, May 25, 1917.
³⁶ *Izvestiia*, June 20, 1917; *Rabochaia Gazeta*, June 22, 1917.
³⁷ See, e.g., Skobelev's speech to the Soviet on May 13, reported in *Izvestiia* on May 14; Galili, *Menshevik Leaders*, ch. 5.
³⁸ R. P. Browder and A. F. Kerensky, *The Russian Provisional Government 1917*, 3 vols. (Stanford, CA: Stanford University Press, 1961), 667–68, 1276–78.

of a new council under Shingarev "for the preparation of a general plan and urgent measures of financial reform" was also affirmed. So were new measures to strengthen the regulatory councils on fuel, transport, and defense, all holdovers from the old regime. The president of the Special Council on Fuel was given power over all sales of fuel (now the "exclusive monopoly of the state") and the right to fix prices at which the state acquired fuel from producers and sold it to consumers. In the textile and leather markets, the Central Cotton Committee and the Central Wool Committee, both created toward the end of 1916, now "practically eliminated all existing private commercial machinery," according to one observer, fixing prices at the local level for raw materials, cotton, wool, and other goods as well as finished products. Efforts to set "compulsory and fixed prices" for metals producers were begun in the Ministry of Trade and Industry, covering fifteen types of products.[39]

Skobelev's contribution to this effort was to institutionalize the mechanisms for conflict resolution within his ministry. Within days he created a special Bureau for Relations between Labor and Management (Otdel Vzaimo-otnoshchenii Truda i Kapitala). Six sections were to handle a range of different issues, each staffed with knowledgeable people. During its first weeks more than 550 separate disputes were brought to the bureau for resolution, a staggering number that created a huge administrative workload.[40]

Mediation boards were another well-scripted element of revolutionary politics. When the new government and Petrograd Soviet leadership both succeeded in pressing the Petrograd Society of Factory and Mill Owners (PSFMO) to accept workers committees and an eight-hour day in its heralded agreement on March 10, it called for mediation boards within every factory and a central board to settle appeals.[41] Central and local mediation boards were also set up in Moscow and other cities, although they were stoutly resisted by Ural mining industrialists, who rejected as well the introduction of an eight-hour day. (The Progressist A. A. Bublikov was dispatched to the Urals to pressure them, but resistance continued.)[42]

Liberals and progressive industrialists supported the boards as a way to avoid strikes and maintain order. Konovalov saw them as helping to elevate labor management relations to "European levels." Democratic socialists like Gvozdev saw

---

[39] S. O. Zagorsky, *State Control of Industry in Russia during the War* (New Haven, CT, 1928), 214–15, 224; *Sobranie Uzakonenii i rasporiazhenii pravitel'stva*, cited in Browder and Kerensky, *Russian Provisional Government*, 492, 658–59.

[40] *Ekonomicheskii Sovet. Stenograficheskii otchet*, July 4, 26, 1917, 6. Of these, some one hundred were actually mediated by late July.

[41] RGIA f. 150, op. 1, d. 557, ll. 40–41. The story of the boards is well told by Heather Hogan, "Conciliation Boards in Revolutionary Petrograd," *Russian History/Histoire Russe* 9, no. 1 (1982): 49–66.

[42] RGIA f. 6935, op. 6, d. 65, ll. 1–5; f. 48, op. 1, d. 38, ll. 41–52.

them as a way to strengthen labor organization in the factory.[43] On March 14 the PSFMO elected its designated sixteen members to the new Central Mediation Board. In the hope of gaining the industrialists' support it was to be housed at Troitskaia 26, where the PSFMO itself was headquartered. Given the incidents of factory unrest, the Central Board was to start its work immediately. When the soviet had not designated its representatives by March 21, the PSFMO sent an "insistent" request that they do so, since "urgent measures had to be taken to calm the working masses."[44]

For workers themselves, the boards were an acceptable innovation, but not one they greeted with any enthusiasm. When they began to rule in favor of reinstating management people arbitrarily dismissed by the new workers' committees, the committees simply overruled them.[45] Despite a unanimous decision of the Moscow board that women could serve as conductors on the Nikolaev railroad between Moscow and Petrograd, for example, the conductors' committee refused to allow them on passenger trains.[46] The boards functioned as they were intended largely in cases that ruled in workers' favor. In one plant the dismissal of a bookkeeper for apparent incompetence was upheld by a vote of seven to three; in another involving a female foreman, the board voted nine to one not to allow her back to work after hearing witnesses verify accusations of rudeness, excessive fines, and refusing to allow a sick worker to leave the plant.[47] In some plants antagonism was so deeply rooted in past experience and emotions as to preclude any possibility of reconciliation, as Heather Hogan noted in her examination of an astounding 160 cases at the state owned Baltic Ship Building plant. One of these involved a long-time supervisor charged with "looking upon women as playthings. . . who he could buy for ten rubles."[48] Instead, the very airing of grievances seemed to provoke more rather than less conflict. Factory committees and new trade union organizers saw the boards infringing on their own prerogatives. Owners and managers saw them encroaching on their authority.

One of the more dramatic failures of mediation during these weeks took place on the Plekhanov Commission, set up by Nekrasov's Transport Ministry to review the salaries and living conditions of railroad workers who were still responsible for maintaining Russia's "lifeline."[49] Membership on the commission included an

---

[43] Irakli Tsereteli, *Vospominaniia o fevral'skoi revoliutsii*, 2 vols. (Paris, 1963), 1:439.
[44] RGIA f. 150, op. 1, d. 511, ll. 5–6.
[45] The available documentation is hardly comprehensive on these matters, but it is sufficient to give a general picture, e.g. RGIA f. 150, op. 1, d. 560 [PSFMO, *Protokoly zasedanii primiritel'nye sudy Fev.–Iiun. 1917*].
[46] RGIA f. 6935, op. 5, d. 65, l. 27.
[47] RGIA f. 150, op. 1, d. 560, ll. 6–10, 19–20, 46.
[48] Hogan, "Conciliation Boards," 63, citing the Petersburg State Historical Archive f. 1304, op. 1, d. 3667, l. 32.
[49] *Volia i Dumy Zheleznodorozhnika* 8 (May 14, 1917).

equal number of representatives from the Soviet Executive Committee and the Ministry of Transport as well as worker representatives from the lines. The WIC labor activist Gvozdev from the soviet's labor section was also a member. When the commission announced that Russia's 300,000 railroaders would each receive a special bonus until wage rates were reset, expectations were almost certainly raised to levels beyond what the commission could secure.

With the approval of the new coalition government, the bonus structure was publicly announced on May 13. "The Plekhanov Commission has decided," the announcement began, using Plekhanov's good name to sanction the proposal, that the bonuses were "first and foremost to help the railroads' most needy workers" pending the setting of new wage norms that would correspond to the country's economic conditions. Financed by large credits from the State Bank, the bonuses were retroactive to April 1 in order "to serve the vital interests of the nation."[50]

How disappointed the commission members must have been when its decisions were immediately assailed not by soviet leaders or members of the government but by large numbers of railroad workers themselves. Why this was the case is clear from reading the railroaders' petitions. Almost all expressed in the voices of "extreme need" issues the commission had not addressed: the poverty level rates of hourly day workers, the burdens of forced overtime, inadequate stipends for housing, and the ways in which upper-level administrators on both private and state lines distributed premiums to railroaders themselves.[51] "I consider it my duty to inform you that our salaries are less than the minimum required to survive," a railroader wrote from Perm. "The situation is worsening each day. Along the line it is literally people are starving. It is literally impossible to exist and each day the situation is worsening, approaching unbearable extremes. We insist on the immediate setting of minimum salary norms, increases in other salaries according to our own accounting, and that you send the necessary sums by May."[52] Plekhanov and others recognized that these matters required carefully drafted legislation. They could not be dealt with quickly in an ad hoc way. At the same time, the bonuses themselves were seen as a sign of the inadequacy of state intervention, not its strength. While it placed a substantial new burden on the treasury, the bonuses distributed in April and May were a failure. In fact, railroaders themselves did not think they needed the Plekhanov Commission to work out their bonuses and new wage schedules. Line committees could exercise their own authority to do so.[53]

---

[50] RGIA f. 32, op. 1, d. 1871, ll. 1–3; GARF f. 1809, op. 1, d. 6, ll. 78–79.
[51] GARF f. 1809, op. 1, d. 3 and 6.
[52] Ibid., d. 6, l. 26.
[53] Ibid., ll. 3–7, 71–78.

In a precarious position between labor and capital, Skobelev continued to see his task as supporting the well-being of the revolutionary state as well as that of its revolutionary workers. This was made clear in two well-publicized disputes, one involving mining and metallurgical workers in the Donets basin, the other at the huge and privately owned Sormovo defense complex near Nizhnii Novgorod. The manifest point of conflict in both cases was wages, and in both cases, the ministry's response was that neither side could advance its class interests at the expense of the state's. The question of wage increases could not be disassociated from the issue of management profits, but neither could workers ignore the realities of rising production costs, or the danger work stoppages posed for Russia's national welfare. Unless workers and industrialists both agreed to arbitration, the Ministry of Labor could not impose settlements. Nor could the state enforce them. Both sides had "to put the needs of the country" before their own.[54]

Yet much more powerful issues than wages were involved in both disputes. In the Donets case, wage concessions had already been granted. To Don industrialists, the principal threat was the workers' effort to gain more authority over work routines, conditions in the mines, and "the complete absence of industrial discipline." All sorts of "self-appointed committees" were interfering in managerial directives. Administrative employees felt "terrorized." The "most capable" in all specialties were "trying to leave."[55] The Sormovo dispute also turned on questions of managerial authority rather than wages alone. At first, the plant's directors insisted that additional wage increases were "unthinkable," a response that stoked outrage in the workforce. A strike committee that included several of the many Bolshevik supporters at the plant immediately took the issue to the local soviet, which wired Skobelev himself for help. The situation was "extremely tense." On May 23, management agreed to increase wages if the state raised its procurement prices, workers accepted the return of management personnel expelled in early March, and the factory committee granted management complete control over production. Workers rejected these demands outright. So did their supporters in the local soviet. A strike was set for May 31. By now, reports of the Sormovo "crisis" were appearing in every major newspaper. The country waited to see whether one of its largest and most important defense plants would be shut down.[56]

On June 20, just as the Kerensky offensive was getting underway, some twenty-five thousand Sormovo workers walked off the job. Some interpreted the strike

---

[54] *Ekonomicheskoe polozhenie*, 1:170; *Izvestiia*, May 24, 1917; *Novaia Zhizn'*, May 24, 1917; Koenker and Rosenberg, *Strikes*, ch. 5.
[55] *Ekonomicheskoe polozhenie*, 1:178.
[56] *Dokumenty velikoi oktiabr'skoi sotsialisticheskoi revoliutsii v Nizhegorodskoi gubernii* (Gorkii: Obl. Gosizdat, 1945), 147–53; *Edinstvo*, July 2, 1917.

as a reflection of antiwar sentiment stimulated by the Bolsheviks as much as a genuine expression of workers' grievances.[57]

Activism in the Countryside

As the coalition cabinet was being seated on May 5, Minister President L'vov admitted that while the regime had honestly pursued a program supported by the Soviet Executive Committee, two months of governing on this basis had "brought us to the threatening situation in which we now find ourselves."[58] In its first formal declaration, the coalition stressed the urgency of ending the war, supporting to this end the democratization of the army in the hope that soldiers' committees would strengthen its resolve to defend the new order. Equally imperative was fighting "resolutely and inflexibly" against further economic disintegration. The government would strengthen its control over production, transport, market exchange, and distribution. Taxes on the wealthy would be increased. So would efforts to develop "at all possible speed" local institutions of democratic self-government, including new representative zemstvos at the district level in the countryside. The declaration concluded with the pledge to take "the most energetic measures" against "attempts at counterrevolution, anarchic, illegal, and violent acts," further confirming the "victories of the revolution." What these were precisely was not spelled out.[59]

Certainly the revolution had brought little in the way of social or economic security. Food insecurity had not abated, even if supplies in hard-pressed cities like Petrograd and Moscow had improved somewhat. On May 1 the cost of a minimum ration for ordinary workers had more than doubled since the beginning of 1916 and was more than 300 percent higher than when the war began, according to the best calculations. For women especially the dual burdens of working long hours for low wages and trying to find affordable food continued. Twice as many women between the ages of twenty-one and thirty were now in the industrial workforce compared to 1915. Relations between women workers and their foremen remained tense.[60]

The Great Stories commonly lump worker and peasant activism together as signs of increasing anarchism and political instability in May and June, locating the problem essentially in political terms. There is also a common binary between town and countryside which obscures significant differences between and within regions and provinces. Peasant activism and unrest were complicated as

---

[57] *Izvestiia*, May 24, 1917.
[58] *Volia Naroda*, May 7, 1917.
[59] *Vestnik Vremennogo Pravitel'stvo*, May 6, 1917.
[60] *Statistika Truda* 2–3 (Aug. 15–Sept. 1, 1917): 5–6; 6–7 (Oct. 15–Dec. 15, 1918): 2–3, 5.

well as more difficult than strikes to record accurately. Reports from government commissars, police, and others in the field were spotty, and Few were publicly available. With the recent work of Aaron Retish, Sarah Badcock, and others, we know that large provinces like Viatka had multiple forms of local organization, land use, and community activism, while adjacent provinces like Nizhnii Novgorod and Kazan presented quite different local pictures.[61] Almost everywhere in the spring of 1917 there was antagonism over the possession and use of land and the distribution of grain, but peasants in grain-importing areas suffered more from inadequate holdings and were understandably more prone to hoarding than those in areas with surpluses where the fear was confiscation. The distance between villages and trading centers around railroad depots or river ports complicated the picture, especially in terms of access to black and gray markets. The same was true for the effects of loss. Villages that had lost a disproportionate number of husbands and sons to the war faced particularly difficult economic and social problems. Soviet historians have given plausible estimates of more than four thousand separate rural disturbances between March and October, but even what constituted a "disturbance" had (and has) different meanings.

The importance of these differences for our purposes is not only that they suggest the losses overwhelmingly of village men to the war affected rural production and well-being; in practical terms they also greatly complicated the tasks in May and June of deploying a consistent set of measures to improve Russia's food supply. These were now divided between the Ministry of Agriculture under Chernov, which was supposed to concentrate on issues of property and land usage, and the new Ministry of Food Supply, assigned to the moderate Popular Socialist Aleksei Peshekhonov, a former village teacher and zemstvo activist in Tver, Orel, and Kaluga. Peshekhonov's ministry was created around the administrative structure of the Special Council for Food, separated now from the Ministry of Agriculture. Despite a continued lack of dependable information, what was happening generally in the countryside was well enough known to raise the anxieties of government and soviet officials alike. Both dispatched still more commissars to explain government policies, appraise local situations, and assist local governing groups like the food supply committees and local soviets. The problem of food supply and its accompanying anxieties was clearly getting worse almost everywhere, if not among the wealthier strata of traditional Russian society.

---

[61] Aaron B. Retish, *Russia's Peasants in Revolution and Civil War* (Cambridge: Cambridge University Press, 2008; Sarah Badcock, *Politics and the People in Revolutionary Russia: A Provincial History* (Cambridge: Cambridge University Press, 2007). See also Orlando Figes, *Peasant Russia, Civil War: The Volga Countryside in Revolution (1917–1921)* (Oxford: Clarendon Press, 1989).

It was also clear, moreover, that the deeper roots of this activism lay in the connections between the losses of war and the peasants' long-term need for more land. Accentuated by the war's privations and now widely assumed would be satisfied as a reward for military service, longing for land was also set within the varying contours of customary law, communal autonomy, and strongly held conceptions of equity and fairness.[62] Where the efforts of Peter Stolypin to grant private ownership to individual homesteads had made progress, they had also evoked strong antipathy and resistance. Many in the countryside resisted these measures not because they were against private ownership in principle but because separating communal holdings compromised the moral economy of the village. Communal holdings and labor ensured some modicum of fairness in the distribution of work, essential goods, obligations, and village prosperity. "Separators" often increased the hardships of those they left behind, or at least were blamed for doing so.

Despite the variety of practices in the Russian countryside, one of the first acts of many villages in 1917 was thus to attack the separators and forcefully "repatriate" them and their land to their former commune, strengthening its food security. Land forcefully seized in this way was reallocated on the basis of need and available labor, including to the separators themselves. Moreover, like air and water, land held value in peasant culture only through its use. *Private* property in land was essentially a legal abstraction that violated the principles of equity and fairness governing usage. In fertile areas where much of the best land was owned privately by large landowners, the church, and the state itself, but worked by peasants living near subsistence levels, the end of tsarism was an invitation to seize unused state land and put it under cultivation.[63] It was a short step from there to taking hold of gentry land that lay unused or in long (seventeen-year) fallow. Elsewhere peasants also went after the church's extensive holdings. As Shingarev himself had argued in *The Dying Village* twenty years earlier, the peasants' well-known hunger for land was fundamentally a demand for food security, some marginal level of well-being, and the tenets of fairness embedded in customary village law, a fair description now for the mood in most if not all of the countryside.[64]

---

[62] A full discussion is Colleen M. Moore, "Land for Service: Russian Peasant Views of a Postwar Land Settlement during World War I," in *Russia's Home Front in War and Revolution, 1914-1922*, bk. 3, ed. Christopher Read, Peter Waldron, and Adele Lindenmeyr (Bloomington, IN: Slavica, 2018), 297-320.

[63] Mark Baker takes this up in some detail for Kharkov province in "War and Revolution in Ukraine: Kharkiv Province's Peasants' Experiences of War, Revolution, and Occupation, 1914-1918," in *Russia's Home Front in War and Revolution, 1914-1922*, 3 vols., ed. Sarah Badcock, Liudmila Novikova, and Aaron Retish (Bloomington, IN: Slavica), 1:119-20.

[64] See, e.g., Richard Robbins, *Famine in Russia, 1891-92* (New York: Columbia University Press, 1975); Boris Mironov, *The Standard of Living and Revolution in Russia 1700-1917* (New York: Routledge, 2012).

The Provisional Government's decree on land committees did not directly address these questions. They were to be decided by the Constituent Assembly. But a key task explicitly assigned to local committees was to settle disputes about land usage and halt the acts of private persons that depreciated productivity, "raising before the Central Land Committee questions of removing such properties from the possession of private persons." Moreover, the Central Land Committee's first resolution stated that the basis of land reform "must be the idea that all agricultural lands be transferred to the use of the toiling rural population."[65] This was also the view of the Soviet Executive Committee, clearly expressed at the first national Peasant Congress that convened on May 4, and virtually all activists in the newly formed peasant soviets, including Chernov, the new minister of agriculture.

On May 2, *Izvestiia* headlined an editorial "All Land to the People." Land would "pass into the hands of the people without redemption" since the revolution itself "will not permit a different resolution of the land question."[66] On the same day in early May that Shingarev warned delegates from 150 local food committees that Russia's larger cities had only two to three days' supply of grain, a draft SR resolution for the Constituent Assembly was circulating that abolished all private property in land "once and forever." "Land shall not be sold, purchased, mortgaged or pawned, but each man and woman who desires to work the land with his or her own labor will be able to receive it free for their use."[67] In some places this was easily read as empowering local authorities to transfer land right away from landlords, gentry estates, and "separators" to village control.[68] Here and elsewhere, however, in places like Viatka where district and provincial land committees did not meet until midsummer, peasants acted entirely on their own or by what they were told were the new regime's "instructions."[69]

As it related to food supply in May and June, the complexity of the "land problem" thus created a great deal of confusion. So did the decentralization of authority so important to both government and soviet leaders as well as being a key part of the revolutionary script. Shingarev thought local food and land committees were necessary in part because of the chronic lack of accurate information that had beset his tsarist predecessors. The central, provincial, and district land committees were intended to collect information on local land usage and peasant needs and take necessary measures to increase production. Chernov, Shingarev's successor in the Ministry of Agriculture and de facto head of the new Union of Peasants, was an enthusiast of decentralization as well. He saw the

---

[65] Browder and Kerensky, *Russian Provisional Government*, 528–32, 541–43.
[66] *Izvestiia*, May 2, 1917.
[67] *Izvestiia Glavnogo Zemel'skogo Komiteta* 2–3 (Aug. 1–15, 1917): 30.
[68] Browder and Kerensky, *Russian Provisional Government*, 528–32.
[69] Retish, *Russia's Peasants*, 97.

committees as key to the revolutionary reconstruction of peasant life and openly championed the peasants' quest for land.[70] During May and early June, peasant congresses were held in twenty-five provincial cities. Local committees were formed in 24 provinces, 121 regions, and 481 districts. While the first session of the Central Land Committee was not until May 20, when reports of disorders were already rife, Chernov waxed eloquent about the process of realizing the peasantry's great yearning for land in lawful ways.[71]

The land question was not the only issue agitating the countryside in May and June, even if it drew the most attention. Anxieties over food continued to beset towns and villages in areas that imported grain and other foodstuffs. The processes that had corrupted commercial marketing of grain and other scarce goods for the past two years were becoming even more problematic. In many commercialized market centers and village markets not too far from the railroads or river docks, rising prices and the absence of manufactured goods agitated peasants. Deeper in the countryside where communal practices held sway, it was the quantity of grain that was set for compulsory delivery that corrupted distribution.[72] Whether areas were food exporters or importers also made a great difference, even within a single province. Although Shingarev and Groman reset fixed grain prices at a substantially higher rate, scarcities and inflation in deficit areas continued to drive market prices higher, squeezing those in producing areas between the cost of obeying the law and the profits to be made outside it. In many places "bagmen" carrying sacks of grain on their backs to needy areas were a common site.[73] According to provincial delegates at the first Congress of Peasants in May, hunger was now a "common experience" in areas where peasants lived closer to subsistence levels and where the huge losses of the war left many villages without adequate hands. In some places, POWs were seized from private estates to work on peasant land.[74]

All of this provides abundant reason for understanding the objective nature of peasant activism in May and June, even allowing for its unevenness around the country: the outright seizure of estates and their redistribution by peasants for sowing summer crops; the confiscation of cattle and hay and other kinds of fodder; the cutting of trees, especially on gentry estates, for lumber and firewood. It also shows the inherent limitations of trying to transform Russia in 1917 on the principles of political democracy. As the historian Michael Hickey has described

---

[70] Viktor Chernov, *The Great Russian Revolution* (New Haven, CT: Yale University Press, 1936), ch. 8; Khanny Immonen, *Mechty o novoi Rossii: Viktor Chernov (1873–1952)* (St. Petersburg, EUSP Press, 2015), chs. 12–13.
[71] *Izvestiia Glav. Zemel. Komiteta* 1 (July 15, 1917): 20–21; 2–3 (Aug. 1–15, 1917): 30–32.
[72] Browder and Kerensky, *Russian Provisional Government*, 589; A. L. Siderov, *Ekonomicheskoe polozhenie Rossii v gody pervoi mirovoi voiny* (Moscow: Nauka, 1973), 467.
[73] A. Iu. Davidov, *Meshochniki i diktatura v Rossii 1917–1921* (St. Petersburg: Aleteiia, 2007), 40–41.
[74] A. D. Maliavskii, *Krest'ianskoe dvizhenie v Rossii v 1917 g.* (Moscow: Nauka, 1981), 88–89.

in detail, a provincial peasant congress in Smolensk early in May rejected the authority of the provincial commissar and soviet by issuing an instruction on its own authorizing local land committees to take control of manorial meadows and woods. Not surprisingly, peasants elected to the land committees voted to go much further in many places, seizing control of private holdings.[75]

One distinguished Russian historian writing in 1994 located the origins of Soviet authoritarianism itself in peasant popular culture.[76] But the seizure of land can also be seen as corresponding to the urgent need for additional food production and security in the countryside after February and facilitated by imprecise guidelines of the decree on land committees. On one hand, imprecision was necessary to accommodate quite different local circumstances. On the other, the misuse of their authority by newly created land committees and local peasant soviets and committees was a logical consequence of authority's devolution downward from the center. The premise of devolution was the same as it had been when pressed by the public organizations in 1915: the rational exercise of authority by responsible people in whom their communities had confidence. In scripting reform before February, neither the liberal nor the democratic socialist leadership was prepared for the rapid emergence of multiple and competitive local authorities as tsarist officials were displaced. Nor were they prepared for peasants to use the power embedded in community governance to ameliorate their own material needs.

It is important to recognize that acts of dissidence in the countryside were set not so much in authoritarian elements in peasant culture but within the context of a ferocious and continuing war that was still inflicting great losses on Russia's rural population. In March, April, and May, casualty numbers increased by more than 280,000 despite a lull in the fighting. A large number were listed as taken prisoner or "lost without further information," although this also included desertions. The effects of these losses could be felt in grain-producing as well as grain-consuming areas, in remote villages far from rail lines as well as those clustered near central trading points. Trains were packed with troops moving to and from the front. Deserters and soldiers on leave could be seen in virtually every major station. Properly equipped hospital trains were still lacking for the more than forty thousand new wounded. Soldiers writing home were no less anxious about the well-being of their families now than before February, however much they cheered the revolution.

One clear indication of peasant anxieties continued to be the protests of soldiers' wives and widows, the *soldatki*. After the Provisional Government

---

[75] Michael C. Hickey, "Peasant Autonomy, Soviet Power, and Land Redistribution in Smolensk Province, November 1917–May 1918," *Revolutionary Russia* 9, no. 1 (June 1996): 19–32.
[76] Boris N. Mironov, "Peasant Popular Culture and the Origins of Soviet Authoritarianism," in *Cultures in Flux*, ed. Stephen P. Frank and Mark D. Steinberg (Princeton, NJ: Princeton University Press, 1994), ch. 3.

broadened this designation on June 22 to include foster children and stepparents, demonstrations often included other family members as well.[77] As Russia approached 15 million mobilized men in 1917, Sarah Badcock's estimate of 14 million *soldatki* seems quite reasonable.[78] *Soldatki* represented families in which the most able-bodied men had been called into service, almost half of the entire able-bodied rural population in May and June 1917. Loss thus fell especially hard on those whose sons and husbands were primary family providers.

Recent research by several first-rate historians allows us to discern the impulses driving *soldatki* protests in these weeks.[79] The most powerful was almost certainly raw anger. The "avalanche" of petitions and appeals to various authorities during these weeks, as the historian Liudmila Bulgakova describes them, continued to use the language of "extreme need" that characterized earlier appeals: unmanageable prices, ill health, dependent children, inability to work, and especially hunger and the anxieties of food insecurity. In May *soldatki* from Vladimir province wrote to Kerensky demanding new allowances "in light of hunger"; officials in provincial Eniseisk worried the rumblings of unmarried soldiers' families might threaten public order.[80] While "rampage" fairly characterized a number of protests before February, as Mark Baker has detailed, rural anger was now amplified by the unmet expectations and subsequent disappointments the revolution itself had brought to many villages along with civil liberties—indeed, the civil right to act out one's anger in confronting the new regime's local authorities.[81]

Looking at Kazan, Tambov, and Nizhnii-Novgorod provinces, Badcock shows us that *soldatki* were poorly represented on the various committees and councils formed after February, most of which were still determinedly male in their composition and most likely their outlook. Democratization left well-motivated women on the margins of institutional power. This may have been more the case with new committees and soviets than with traditional authorities like the village assembly (*shkod*), but the combination of urgency and lack of representation almost certainly inflamed emotions and weakened social restraints. Members of the Tambov

---

[77] Browder and Kerensky, *Russian Provisional Government*, 589; Siderov, *Ekonomicheskoe polozhenie*, 466–68.

[78] Sarah Badcock, "Women, Protest, and Revolution: Soldiers' Wives in Russia during 1917," *International Review of Social History* 49, no. 1 (April 2004): 47–70.

[79] In addition to Badcock, see Liudmila Bulgakova, "The Phenomenon of the Liberated Soldier's Wife," in *Russia's Home Front in War and Revolution 1914–1922*, bk. 2, ed. Adele Lindenmeyer, Christopher Read, and Peter Waldron (Bloomington, IN: Slavica, 2016), 301–26; Mark Baker, "Rampaging Soldatki, Cowering Police, Bazaar Riots and Moral Economy: The Social Impact of the Great War in Kharkiv Province," *Canadian-American Studies* 2–3 (2001): 137–55; Emily Pyle, "Peasant Strategies for Obtaining State Aid: A Study of Petitions during World War I," *Russian History/Histoire Russe* 24 (1997): 41–64.

[80] Bulgakova, "Phenomenon," 321.

[81] Baker, "Rampaging Soldatki," 137–55.

Committee of Public Organizations were assailed as "thieves" and "embezzlers." In Kazan, *soldatki* marched with banners simply demanding they be heard.[82]

This did not mean that activities like supporting the Red Cross or making bandages for the wounded did not also continue in many villages. Like others, villagers could still bend their efforts to support their soldiers without at the same time supporting the war. Still, the physical and emotional elements of deprivation and loss—the hardships as well as the anxieties that accompanied them—became even more difficult once restraints on expressing them were dissolved. One does not have to posit uniformity or authoritarianism in peasant mentalities and moral values to accept that both were deeply affected in 1917 by the emotional, material, and physical losses of the war. The resistance of villages to outside authorities was hardly assuaged by the legion of commissars and party agitators who descended on them in April and May.

Once More "on the Brink of Catastrophe"

It is easy to understand why politics rather than the problems of scarcity and loss have dominated the Great Stories of these difficult weeks, as they largely did at the time. Political questions were the focus of a rash of "all-Russia" conferences and congresses which occurred in May and June, including the first Congress of Soviets, the eighth congress of the Kadet Party, the first conference of Mensheviks, the first Petrograd city conference of factory committees, the first conference of trade unions since 1906, and a national conference of peasants. The most important of these in terms of support for the coalition regime was the first All-Russia Congress of Soviets, which met during the first three weeks of June. More than a thousand delegates representing some four hundred soviets attended, including a large number of soldiers.

Throughout, the sessions were dominated by Mensheviks and SRs supporting the war as the only effective way to defend the revolution. An Austro-German victory would almost certainly restore the autocracy. The 105 Bolshevik delegates, including Lenin, constituted little more than 12 percent of those attending. Ministers Skobelev, Chernov, Peshekhonov, and especially Tsereteli played key roles. Under Tsereteli's guidance the congress supported revolutionary defensism by a vote of 543 to 126. It condemned the anarchists' well-publicized seizure on June 10 of the Durnovo mansion and their attempt at creating a Kronstadt "republic." Delegates repeatedly expressed support for a strong coalition regime. According to Tsereteli, this was "an anxious time, a dangerous time," and it was "necessary to save the country."[83]

[82] Badcock, "Women, Protest, and Revolution," 56, 63–64.
[83] *Pervyi Vserossiiskii S"ezd Sovetov R. i S.D.*, 2 vols. (Moscow: Gozisdat, 1930–31), 2:65.

The Menshevik leader also proposed the congress expel the Bolsheviks from the community of revolutionary democracy. Fearing a possible Bolshevik move against the government, he wanted Kerensky to disarm army units that supported Lenin's call for a massive demonstration on June 10 against the war and the regime. His effort drew a fierce reaction. Bolsheviks accused the Menshevik leader of using the "fiction" of an armed revolt to disarm Petrograd workers and disband the Petrograd garrison. A major display at the congress was the irrevocable animosity between Lenin's supporters and its large majority of democratic socialists. Political battle lines on the left were drawn more sharply than those dividing democratic socialists from democratic liberals.[84]

Indeed, Tsereteli, Skobelev, and other democratic socialists sounded almost like Kadets. Skobelev's speech on Russia's economic condition might have been given by Shingarev. ("The situation, comrades, is such that the economic life of the country is more and more coming apart.")[85] When Lenin in a fiery speech posed the question "Do we go backward or forward?," Tsereteli countered that genuine socialists already *were* moving forward with measures to save the economy that would be most favorable to all sectors of the democracy. These were being worked out by Groman and the soviet's own economic commission. Miliukov and his Kadet followers saw Tsereteli's stance as the height of irresponsibility. The Menshevik ministers were unilaterally linking state authority to the satisfaction of mass demands, openly admitting they saw the soviet congress as a "revolutionary parliament" with the right to formulate state policy. At the eighth Kadet Party congress in early May, Miliukov again argued that his party had to resist further soviet-sponsored reforms and instead strengthen the Provisional Government's unitary authority. He readily admitted once again that he thought Russia's future well-being still required possession of Constantinople and the Straits. In somewhat intemperate rebuttals, Nekrasov and others described Miliukov's statist perspective as increasingly disconnected from social and economic realities. Soldiers did not want to continue the war because they failed to revere the state and saw little purpose in the conflict other than to defend their homes. Workers were focused on the urgent needs of their everyday life, with its constant anxieties and concerns. Soviet leaders had popular support because they supported popular goals. The Kadets had to spell out clearly what they thought were Russia's vital interests in *these* terms and define their goals accordingly.

All of this was accompanied by the first clear evidence that the democratic socialists had the strongest popular support in cities and towns, at least for now. When the ten city districts in Petrograd had their first duma elections on May 30, the socialist bloc of moderate Mensheviks and SRs polled 376,000 votes to

---

[84] Ibid., 1:54–67, 286–88; 2:22–23. The literature on the congress is extensive, but see esp. Galili, *Mensheviks*, 304–15; Tsereteli, *Vospominaniia*, 2:184–201.

[85] *Pervyi Vserossiiskii S"ezd Sovetov*, 1:228.

the near evenly divided Kadets (171,000) and Bolsheviks (160,000).[86] According to the future professor of Russian history at Yale, the Kadet Georgi Vernadskii, previously strong provincial party groups were becoming centers for landowners and factory owners. The party's own official journal allowed that Kadets "had to think seriously about this danger from the right."[87] Miliukov's supporters accused Nekrasov of "stabbing him in the back."[88]

Thus, while divisions sharpened between socialists in these weeks, Russian liberalism was becoming more fractured as well. At the Trade Industrial Conference that convened on June 1, calls were again heard for new forced labor battalions. Delegates also demanded far greater financial support from the regime.[89] At the Conference of Petrograd Factory Committees which met at the same time, workers themselves described Russia as hurtling toward hunger and destitution.[90] The labor section of the Moscow Soviet was estimating unemployment levels would rise to the "tens of thousands" by the end of June due to closings in resistance to wage increases and lack of raw materials.[91] Skobelev himself tried to calm anxieties. Unemployment was a problem, but there was actually a deficit of competent workers throughout the country. Increased wages were necessary, but they had to be decided in relation to the needs of all workers and the condition of the economy as a whole, rather than on a plant-by-plant basis. His audiences were quite unfriendly, especially at the All-Russia Trade Union Conference and the Conference of Factory Committees.

In mid-May, two days after the soviet's *Izvestiia* demanded the "immediate, total, and systematic" extension by the government of state control over the economy, Konovalov shocked many by resigning as minister of trade and industry. He could no longer work under current "catastrophic" conditions that "were destroying Russia's entire industrial foundation." (*Promyshlennost' i Torgovlia* editorialized that Konovalov hoped to force the creation of an all-socialist cabinet, following Miliukov's lead. A simpler explanation may have been sheer fatigue.)[92] One week later Peter Migulin echoed Konovalov on the first page of *Novyi Ekonomist*, claiming that Russia was "on the brink of collapse." What Russia needed was "immediate and decisive state intervention in industrial affairs."[93] In Shingarev's view, workers' demands were largely justified despite the further threat to state finances. Deprivation was "extreme." The sole recourse was

---

[86] *Sotsial Demokrat*, June 2, 1917; *Rech'*, June 3, 8, 9, 1917; *Novoe Vremia*, June 2, 9, 1917; *Delo Naroda*, June 1, 2, 8, 9, 16, 1917.
[87] *Vestnik Partiia Narodnoi Svobody* 6–7 (1917): 5.
[88] A. S. Izgoev, *Sotsialisty vo vtoroi russkoi revoliutsii* (Petrograd: PNS, 1917), 43. Major speeches at the congress appeared in *Rech'* and *Russkiia Vedomosti*.
[89] RGIA f. 32, op. 1, d. 63, ll. 79–84.
[90] *Pervaia Rabochaia konferentsiia fabrichno-zavodskikh komitetov* (Petrograd: Tsen. Sovet Fabzavkomov, 1917).
[91] GARF f. 6935, op. 6, d. 65, ll. 18–19.
[92] *Izvestiia*, May 17, 1917; *Novoe Vremia*, May 20, 1917; *Promyshlennost' i Torgovlia*, May 20, 1917.
[93] *Novyi Ekonomist*, 20 (May 20, 1917): 1–2.

printing more money.[94] Trade industrialists also demanded state intervention, and not only in terms of financial support. To avoid "catastrophe," the state had to take forceful measures to restore orderly production and restrain abuse.[95]

As we have seen, "catastrophe" had been a familiar trope in public discourse from the beginning of the war. Nor in May and June was it the term used by the trade industrialists alone. In Moscow, the editors of *Rabochaia Gazeta* urged factory committees to understand that "with each passing day all of Russia is moving closer and closer to economic destruction." A long editorial in *Sotsial Demokrat* described the "destruction of the economy taking on a more and more threatening character." In the near future, the paper warned alarmingly, Russians would be "threatened with hunger and cold [*golod i kholod*]."[96] Even members of the Moscow Soviet pointed to new ruble emissions and the apparent failure of the Liberty Loan in warning of economic catastrophe. In their view revolutionary Russia was also positioned "on the brink of disaster."[97]

In the midst of all these warnings, a soviet-supported demonstration took place in Petrograd on June 17, one week after the Soviet Executive Committee had managed to stall the Bolsheviks' efforts to lead a march of their own. The call was for workers to show "unity" and "maturity" in support of continuing the war and "moving the revolution through a Constituent Assembly to a democratic republic." The effort was a disaster. Many stayed away. Bolsheviks and their supporters seized the streets, turning the event into a massive antiwar and antigovernment protest. According to *Sotsial Demokrat,* as many as 400,000 people carried banners declaring, "All Power to the Soviets," "Down with the Ten Capitalist Ministers," "Long Live Control over Production and Distribution," and "Down with the Offensive." "Excesses," as the newspapers described them, occurred around the country, many reportedly by garrisoned soldiers.[98]

Two days later Kerensky and Brusilov launched their new offensive. Russian forces attacked Austro-German forces in Galicia almost exactly as Brusilov had done one year earlier. For those at the center of national governance, at least, it seemed that peace through victory was the only way to save the revolution.

---

[94] RGIA f. 560, op. 26, d. 1427, ll. 21, 53; d. 1428, ll. 21–27; A. I. Shingarev, *Finansovoe polozhenie Rossii* (Petrograd, 1917), 1–2. See also *Vestnik Vremennago Pravitel'stva,* May 31, 1917; *Birzhevyia Vedomosti,* May 30, 1917.
[95] RGIA f. 32, op. 1, d. 63, ll. 75–76.
[96] *Rabochaia Gazeta,* May 26, 1917; *Sotsial Demokrat,* June 11, 1917.
[97] GARF f. 6935, op. 6, d. 230, l. 168.
[98] *Izvestiia,* June 18, 1917; *Den',* June 20, 1917; *Rech',* June 20, 1917' *Rabochaia Gazeta,* June 22, 1917, *Sotsial Demokrat,* June 21, 1917.

10
"Slaughter" at the Front, the July Insurrection, and a "Government to Save the Revolution"

Brusilov Redux: The Kerensky Offensive

Events quickly revealed that peace through victory was "a hopeless task," as commanders at the front themselves described it.[1] To reduce casualties the offensive began with a ferocious artillery bombardment on June 16 and 17, reportedly the most intensive of the war. Russian armies on the Southwestern Front under Brusilov then engaged the Germans and Austrians, just as they had a year earlier. Supporting the effort, Kerensky expected "shock detachments," including his famous Women's Battalion of Death, to lift morale, shame reluctant troops, and once again lead an advance toward L'vov (L'viv). (The shock troops wore special red and black chevrons, but it was not clear to most troops what these meant. The Women's Battalion was intended to shame reluctant male soldiers into fighting, but there is no evidence it ever did so.)[2] The same ground had been well bloodied during the first assault on L'vov in 1914, described in all its brutality by Brusilov himself in his memoirs, as well as his offensive in 1916 that in the upper reaches of public imagination, at least, made him a national hero.

Most front-line units went on the attack when ordered to do so by their committees and officers. Some units simply refused. (According to General Knox, almost every division had one "bad regiment.")[3] When resistance stiffened and the predictable casualties mounted, they pulled back. The offensive stalled. Within days, almost all surviving troops were back in their original trenches. When the enemy then launched a counterattack they began to retreat. According to some reports, defiance and mass disobedience grew to "epidemic proportions." Large numbers of units passed resolutions against the offensive. Support units refused to engage. Mass flight occurred in units like the 6th Finnish Rifle

---

[1] RGVIA f. 366, op. 1, d. 31, l. 84.
[2] A full and sensitive analysis is Laure Stoff, *They Fought for the Motherland: Russia's Women Soldiers in World War I and the Revolution* (Lawrence: University of Kansas Press, 2006).
[3] Alfred Knox, *With the Russian Army*, 2 vols. (London: Hutchinson, 1921), 1:642.

Regiment, which suffered 50 percent casualties. When Labor Minister Skobelev arrived on July 1 to help restore order, his delegation was almost lynched by what one observer called "panicked, sobbing, leaderless troops."[4]

The story of what became known as the Kerensky offensive is a familiar one.[5] So are the explanations for mounting it. Contemporary liberals and democratic socialists understood the importance of revolutionary Russia honoring its commitments to its European allies and making one last major effort to bring the peace Russia's fledgling democracy needed to survive. So do later tellers of their Great Stories. With the formation of the first coalition, strenuous efforts were made to persuade the allies to change their war aims and to support an international conference to conclude peace. These efforts failed. Especially with the United States joining the war on April 6, the strategy again of complementary June offensives on the European and Russian Fronts seemed likely to bring results.

Members of the coalition regime also understood the urgency of additional European financial assistance, as well as for the massive needs for reconstruction afterward. Miliukov's supporters and others strongly believed that the government had to behave "honorably" in this regard to take its rightful place at a peace conference. *Izvestiia* on June 22 declared that the fact of the offensive itself was much more important than all the words that had yet been spoken about the war. It showed Russia's allies that the revolutionary state was mobilizing all its moral and material forces.[6] The question was as much one of moral obligation as of political and military strategy. Support for an offensive was shared by virtually all Russia's leading figures besides Lenin's Bolsheviks and Martov's Menshevik Internationalists.[7] The establishment papers *Russkaia Vedomosti* and *Novoe Vremia* joined *Rech'* and much of the provincial press in calling the offensive indispensable, the last best hope for defeating the Germans and preventing the autocratic restoration defeat would surely bring.[8]

The reasons for the offensive's collapse are also generally shared. Shaped by the newspapers and memoirs of the period, which both reflected and created contemporary outlooks, the liberal Great Story has emphasized the follies of "democratizing" the army. In addition to the soldiers' committees organized in March, it has stressed the Declaration of Soldiers' Rights pressed on the Petrograd Soviet by Kerensky in May. Among its provisions was the abolition of

---

[4] Allan Wildman, *The End of the Russian Imperial Army*, 2 vols. (Princeton, NJ: Princeton University Press, 1987), 2:104.

[5] See esp. Boris I. Kolonitskii, *Tovarish Kerenskii: Antimonarkhicheskaya revoliutsiia i formirovaniye kulta "Vozdya naroda" mart–iiun' 1917 goda* (Moscow: NLO, 2017).

[6] *Izvestiia*, June 22, 1917.

[7] *Izvestiia*, June 1, 20, 1917; *Novoe Vremia*, June 20, 1917.

[8] *Russkiia Vedomosti*, Apr. 30, May 17, June 20, 1917; *Novoe Vremia*, June 20, 1917; *Rech'* June 20, 21, 1917; *Penzenskaia Rech'*, June 25, 1917; *Svobodnyi Narod*, June 1, 20, 1917.

compulsory saluting and all punishments "that degrade soldiers' honor and dignity," whose vagueness could be interpreted to include punishment itself.[9] The principal reason, however, has thought to have been the relentless antiwar agitation of Lenin's Bolsheviks, manifest not only in the demonstrations of April 20 and June 18 but by the flood of Bolshevik agitators on the front and the widespread dissemination of *Okopnaia Pravda* (*Trench Pravda*).

Democratic socialists largely shared these views. They, too, saw the Bolsheviks' role in ridiculing revolutionary defensism as destructive not only to soldiers' willingness to fight but to the governing capacity of the coalition regime itself. Bolshevik radicalism seemed to have gained a lock on peasant-soldier mentalities, reinforcing their resistance to carrying the fight beyond Russia's borders and encouraging disobedience. Historians of the period have largely agreed, their analysis shaped by the memoirs and newspapers of the period.

Yet military censors and many army commanders had a different perspective. Between June 17 and July 15, some eighty censors for the Southwestern Front intercepted more than 225,000 letters and packages by official count, reading most and withholding only a few hundred from delivery.[10] After review in early March, it had been determined that military censorship did not violate the right to free speech. Censors were enjoined to select excerpts for their commands with objectivity. Views and acts that had earlier been described simply as "socialist" now had to be carefully labeled as of a "criminal, antidisciplinary, and anarchist nature." According to censors' reports, liberals and socialists were not wrong in assessing the effects at the front of Bolshevik radicalism, but the continuities in soldiers' attitudes and feelings in the weeks and months leading up to the revolution more accurately explained the "demoralization" and "war weariness" that commanders and censors alike now discerned. Already in April some front-line soldiers wrote that it was "un-Christian" to kill Germans. Others confessed that they were shooting their own officers whom they held responsible for their lack of food and supplies as well as their military incompetence. "War was the task of the old government, so why continue it now?" some asked. "The land we are fighting for can't even be plowed."[11] According to Brusilov, many soldiers now had no idea what they were fighting for since the Germans had not attacked. For many, fighting for peace without annexations or indemnities was even more incomprehensible.[12]

---

[9] *Vestnik Vremennogo Pravitel'stva*, May 14, 1917.
[10] RGVIA f. 2067, op. 1, d. 2938, ll. 1–3, 11–12.
[11] RGVIA f. 2048, op. 1, d. 905, ll. 58–59; d. 1181, ll. 357–59; See also Olga S. Porshneva, *Mentalitet i sotsial'noe povedenie rabochikh, krest'ian, i soldat Rossii v period pervoi mirovoi voiny (1914–mart 1918 g.)* (Ekaterinburg: UrO RAN, 2000), 108.
[12] Brusilov, *Vospominaniia*, 71.

Moreover, the anxieties that successive waves of recruits experienced at the front before February were basically the same after the Provisional Government came to power. Food was still scarce. The horses in some cavalry and artillery units were starving because of the lack of oats. "The huge [*gromadnyi*] factor destroying the army's spirit is the acute problem of food," one censor reported. Complaints about provisions dominate the content in every letter. Corruption and black markets still thrived. Soldiers continued to hold their officers and commissary staffs responsible. Wounded still languished for want of effective relief. Even as the offensive was being prepared, soldiers continued to leave their positions to check on their families with or without the permission of their committees or commanders. Soldiers "did not have the least desire to continue the war with their families starving and their fields unplowed."[13]

Lacking any single law on requisitioning even after three years of war, commanders still struggled with these problems on their own initiative, with often brutal effects on local populations. The third War Industries Congress in May described the situation as chaotic. The Zemstvo Union warned the Petrograd Soviet the whole procurement process for the army was in a state of collapse. Property owners close to the Southwestern Front were reportedly threatening to withhold food from the army.[14] According to the censors' reports, many officers also opposed the offensive, although commonly citing different reasons; the army committees were doing "titanic" work, one wrote as the offensive began, trying to educate soldiers about "peace through victory" and working closely with their commands. Still, discipline had become impossible: "There have been pitiful instances which I cannot bring myself to write about." The front-line army was little more than an "armed mob." The army "has completely lost its military capacity."[15] Chief of Staff General Alekseev himself spoke of the "anxiety in his heart." Russia was again "on the edge of an abyss."[16]

Evidence from soldiers' letters is again very informative, especially if one recognizes the filters deployed to avoid the censors. It strongly suggests that while front-line units were ready and capable of defending their positions, there was now little appetite for going on the attack. By 1917, almost 16 million had been brought under arms, reflecting in its total the largest military force in history. According to the best available information, between the outbreak of war and January 1, 1917, 587,357 had been killed outright or died of their wounds, 2,402,137 were wounded, and some 32,000 died or were severely incapacitated by poison gas attacks. As many as 2,720,000 others were taken prisoner

---

[13] RGVIA f. 2003, op. 4, d. 12, passim; f. 2067, op. 1, d. 2398, passim; f. 2048, op. 1, d. 905, ll. 58, 72–77; d. 908, ll. 71–74.
[14] RGIA f. 23, op. 5, d. 86, ll. 1–5; RGVIA f. 2067, op. 1, d. 2938, ll. 8–10; f. 366, op. 1, d. 2, l. 6.
[15] RGVIA f. 2048, op. 1, d. 905, ll. 80–81; RGIA f. 2048, op. 1, d. 905, ll. 72–77.
[16] *Novoe Vremia*, May 10, 1917.

or otherwise unaccounted for. Thus, almost half of the Russian army had been lost since 1914 to a cause that for most did not extend far beyond "for Tsar and Country," an average of almost 200,000 men a month. Equally ominous were the continued losses in March, April, and May, when an additional 71,100 casualties were recorded despite the lull in combat, and some 213,000 became prisoners, deserted, or were otherwise unaccounted for.[17] Censors in May and June recorded "an avalanche" of rank-and-file protests against the offensive: "They are issuing orders to attack, but we categorically refuse. We will hold the front but go on the offensive—never!"; "We don't want to fight. . . . We are spilling our blood for England and France. Down with the war. We sit starving in our trenches. There is no food. Give us peace!"; "We are the dark people, they are upset with us, but now we have begun to think for ourselves"; "Our officers are either blind or consciously destroying the country, putting the army in this situation"; "Coming out of our trenches we clearly saw they were leading us like cattle to slaughter! We refused to move."[18]

Why, then, were these and other portents of disaster given little heed, especially by Kerensky after he became minister of war in May and received sharp warnings to this effect? One reason may have been that while some censors' summaries noted that soldiers "propagandized by Leninists" were writing that notions of victory were "complete nonsense," they also continued to insist from skimming tens of thousands of letters that "the huge majority" wanted peace only after "finally crushing the enemy"; "no one" wanted peace "before the enemy is vanquished."[19] In this respect, their summaries likely reflected presumptive readings of feelings still deeply embedded in the army command's own political vocabularies.

As the historian Boris Kolonitskii has suggested, Kerensky himself was surely reinforced in these presumptions by the reception he received from soldiers' committees as he toured the front in May and early June, no doubt reassured by his own oratorical powers.[20] Even dissident soldiers knew how to perform at staged rallies of this sort when some level of discipline still prevailed. The event created the image of what it was supposed to reflect: dedicated patriotic troops willing if not eager to charge from their trenches in a heroic "last hurrah."

It also seems clear that while General Alekseev and others thought the offensive was risky from the start, pressure from government and soviet figures was difficult to resist, especially after Miliukov and Guchkov gave the government's strong support when visiting headquarters just after the April demonstrations. Brusilov's enthusiasm also played a role. According to General Knox, who was

---

[17] TsSU, *Rossiia v mirovoi voine (v tsifrakh)* (Moscow, 1925), 30.
[18] RGVIA f. 2031, op. 1, d. 1181, ll. 257–59, 357; f. 2048, op. 1, d. 905, ll. 879–80, 268–70, 358–59.
[19] RGVIA f. 366, op. 1, d. 11, ll. 122–59.
[20] Kolonitskii, *Tovarish Kerenskii*.

on the Southwestern Front at the time, Brusilov again bragged that he would "lead all the armies to victory" as he had done in 1916, while "most officers" were disdainful of his "political gymnastics."[21] Meanwhile, the coalition government did not take a formal position. An offensive inherently contradicted the notion of defending the revolution from German attack, but even within soviet circles pressure to seek a negotiated settlement unilaterally got little support.

Many historians have made a case for the role played by *Okopnaia Pravda* and other Bolshevik propaganda in spawning antiwar attitudes at the front. Others have stressed the fatalistic elements of peasant-soldier mentalities that they believe cushioned loss from the very beginning of the war.[22] Yet the desire for peace, as we have seen, was one of the most forceful emotions at the front since the end of 1914, and it is doubtful that even the most stoic peasant-soldier exemplars of Russian cultural imagination could have failed to resist further slaughter as the Brusilov breakthrough was once again enacted. Bolshevik and other antiwar agitators undoubtedly "raised consciousness" in this regard, but the emotional fields against the war were already well set and readily cultivated. Brusilov and his champions supported the revolution because they thought it would save the army and the country. Democratic socialists supported it because they wanted Russia out of the war without betraying its allies. Reinforced by Kerensky, they also hoped soldiers' committees would rein in incompetence and excess of the tsarist army that was responsible for so many deaths. Like the revolutionaries in France after 1789, they now saw their country as a democratic nation in arms against the old regimes that created it.

In the event, the offensive rekindled deep-seated grievances even in places where soldiers' committees urged their comrades to attack. The depth of feeling in soldiers' letters was an effect of scarce food, insufferable deprivations, and losses that no longer seemed necessary or worth tolerating. The disorder that soon engulfed especially the Southwestern and Western Fronts was deeply rooted in the deficits and losses of the past. In sum, wishful narratives about revolutionary Russia's appealing future occluded clear perceptions of the offensive's likelihood for success and the consequences of its failure. What Kerensky and other contemporaries failed to fully grasp was how widespread resistance was by soldiers at the front "sitting hungry in the trenches," as one wrote in a letter home. "We don't want to fight," wrote another. "[T]he English and French want war and we are spilling our blood for them."[23] In the censors' offices, "Against the Offensive" now became a new sorting category of its own. In no one, perhaps,

---

[21] Knox, *With the Russian Army*, 2:628; R. Browder and A. F. Kerensky, eds., *The Russian Provisional Government: Documents*, 3 vols. (Stanford, CA: Stanford University Press, 1961), vol. 1, 931–32.

[22] Porshneva, *Mentalitet*, 108.

[23] RGVIA f. 203, op 1, d. 1881, ll. 357ff.; f. 2048, op. 1, d. 905, ll. 79ff.; f. 2067, op. 1, d. 2938, passim.

was wishful thinking more the case than the now cult-like figure of Kerensky himself, blinded by egoism, deafened by his own rhetoric, and standing heroically in his own imagination at the very apex of "history's turning point."[24]

One week after the Germans launched their counterattack, Russian armies had retreated almost 150 miles, a staggering distance on what had recently been a relatively static front. At a conference at army headquarters chaired by Kerensky on July 16, General Denikin reported that forty-eight battalions on the Western Front had refused to go into combat. "Insurrection, robbery, and looting had swept through the units." Seventy-five hundred soldiers had wounded fingers, ten thousand other "miscellaneous" wounds.[25]

Threats to "Great Russia" and the Liberals' Retreat

As soldiers began to flee the front, many bearing the emotional scars of war along with their self-inflicted wounds, two additional well-known markers of the revolution's political trajectory occurred. On July 2, the Kadet ministers resigned from the government, precipitating a full-scale governmental crisis. Led by Miliukov, who had hoped his colleagues would follow him when he quit his post as foreign minister in May, the Kadets wanted to send a strong message about the urgency of dealing firmly with "anarchists, Bolsheviks, dissident workers and separatists," as *Rech'* described the sources of social conflict and political weakness.[26]

The immediate cause of the liberals' departure was not the unfolding disaster at the front, however much party leaders linked this to their perception of the regime's weakness. It was the acquiescence of a special delegation headed by Kerensky himself to the demand of the Ukrainian National Parliament (Rada) for autonomous control of the region. By implication, the larger question was how much independence should now extend to the various national regions of the empire. In effect, the issue was whether the great Russian state of the liberals' historical imagination, necessary in their view to assure the country's place economically and politically in the postwar world, would itself become a victim of unrestrained revolutionary impulse. In the prevailing liberal view, a strong, prosperous, and politically liberal Russia required the creation of an effective and functional federation within the old imperial boundaries, with the express

---

[24] A. F. Kerensky, *Russia at History's Turning Point* (London: Cassell, 1966).
[25] Browder and Kerensky, *Russian Provisional Government*, vol. 1, 989–1010. Official records later recorded 4,000 deaths and 14,000 seriously wounded for all of June and July, and 147,000 listed "without information," which included prisoners of war and desertions. See TsSU, *Rossiia v mirovoi voine*, 30.
[26] *Rech'*, June 24, 1917.

exception of Poland, whose independence had already been conceded. In any case, the complex issues of autonomy and federation were for the Constituent Assembly to decide.

Regional autonomy and political federation had long been thorny issues for liberals. A dominant view was that a federal structure was not practical for Russia. Significant numerical differences existed among the country's nationalities and the size of their territories. Many who lived outside these borders could not be effectively represented in nationality terms and might readily be discriminated against. Before 1917, this perspective complemented many liberals' own imperial ambitions, especially in Miliukov's case with respect to Constantinople and the Dardanelle Straits. Britain and France, after all, were great imperial powers as well as strong democracies. The United States was expanding its position in the Philippines and regarded all of Central and Latin America as under its "protection." How could Russia compete in the postwar world if its own empire fell apart?

After February, as some Kadet Central Committee members and many regional party leaders understood, this view contradicted the basic political principles of democratic self-determination. During the first weeks of the revolution it also ran counter to the determined efforts of even conservative political figures to devolve authority outward from Petrograd to address effectively the problems of scarcity, distribution, and procurement at the local level. Devolution of authority implicitly engaged the question of regional and national autonomy, and hence the question of empire. Ukrainians needed to deal with problems in Ukraine, Georgians with those in Georgia. While prominent liberals in Kiev, Rostov, Erevan, and other nationality centers supported greater regional autonomy precisely to ensure their own local needs were met, Fedor Rodichev thought they reflected a Russia "drunk with revolution."[27] Many, especially in Petrograd, agreed with him. The increasingly pessimistic Vladimir Nabokov thought that any step toward the fragmentation of "one Great Russia"—the "Fatherland"—was "unthinkable," a source among others of what he called a growing and "tormenting anxiety."[28]

For many citizens of non-Russian nationality, however, the civil liberties bestowed by the February revolution also implied the possibility of separation and the end of Great Russian imperial domination. Political autonomy in any formal way presumed the right to produce or distribute goods as local authorities and their people desired. For Ukrainians, Turks, the peoples of the Caucasus and the Baltics, it was also a claim to language and cultural change. When the issue reemerged after February, the focus was on Finland and Ukraine. Like the Poles,

---

[27] *Rech'*, June 17, 1917.
[28] *Vestnik Partii Narodnoi Svobody* 3 (May 25, 1917): 2.

a vast majority of Finns assumed the revolution would bring them full independence, as Poland had been promised. For their part, Ukrainian political leaders expected to obtain substantial autonomy over what they regarded as their own affairs, especially in view of the tsarist regime's historic repression of Ukrainian culture and any signs of a national movement. So did prominent figures in Turkestan, still reeling from the Russian state's brutal repression in 1916, as well as those in the Baltics and the Caucasus. Some democratic liberals themselves in Ukraine favored autonomy already in March.[29] In early April, the Rada convened in Kiev. In June it declared its own exclusive authority over Ukrainian affairs, including some 900,000 Ukrainian soldiers and its representation of Ukrainian interests abroad.

Many feared the movement would spread.[30] Just as the offensive began, Finnish Social Democrats informed the Soviet Executive Committee that Finland would soon go even further and declare independence unilaterally, ignoring the authority of the forthcoming Constituent Assembly. The official Kadet newspaper, *Svobodnyi Narod*, headlined the move as "dangerous" and demanded "decisive" if unspecified measures. For A. S. Izgoev the question was whether Russia would remain a "great world power or turn into a small Muscovite principality."[31] Shortly after the offensive began, Nekrasov suggested to the Council of Ministers that a special negotiating committee go immediately to Kiev to resolve the matter. The Soviet leadership agreed. On June 27 Ministers Tsereteli, Peshekhonov, Nekrasov, and Kerensky himself went to Kiev. According to Tsereteli, local Kadets in the Ukrainian capital supported their efforts to negotiate with the Rada.[32] When the delegation returned to Petrograd on July 2 with an agreement accepting the Rada's major demands, a furious Miliukov and his Central Committee supporters determined to force the government to change course, calling the agreement reached in Kiev "a criminal document."[33]

Given the centrality of a strong Great Russian state to liberal understandings of historical progress, one can understand their distress. More than ever, perhaps, the contemporary liberal Great Story centered now on the fateful consequences of the state's political weakness—the absence of *gosudarstvennost'*, or "state consciousness," in the Constitutional Democrats' well publicized lexicon—as it has in much of the historiography. Russia's revolution simply could not mean the end of the Great Russian state, "Russia One and Indivisible," as it would soon be defended by White armies during the Civil War. Nor could the breakup of

---

[29] *Poltavskii Den'*, Mar. 22, 25, 1917; *Russkiia Vedomosti*, July 9, 1917; *Narodnaia Svoboda* (Tiflis), July 5, 1917.
[30] *Vestnik Vremennago Pravitel'stva*, June 2, 1917; *Rech'* June 14, July 13, 1917; *Svobodnyi Narod* June 17, 20, 1917.
[31] *Rech'*, June 24, 30, 1917; *Svobodnyi Narod*, June 24, July 1, 1917.
[32] I. Tsereteli, *Vospominaniia o fevral'skoi revoliutsii*, 2 vols. (Paris: Mouton, 1963), 2:138.
[33] Ariadna Tyrkova in *Narodnaia Svoboda*, July 22, 1917.

the Russian Empire be a casualty of military victory. Separatism, not to mention autonomy and independence for Russia's constituent nationality regions, would do the Germans' work for them even if they were defeated, dismembering the country from within. "When a Russian historian writes the history of the revolution," Miliukov told a meeting on June 20 just after the start of the offensive, "he will linger on two critical days: 27 February and 18 June.... Today we have reached a watershed."[34] Twelve hours later the July Days insurrection began against the regime in Petrograd. Unlike February, it was started this time by soldiers, and it was the workers who joined in.

The July Insurrection

Miliukov was right about the watershed, but not for the reasons he advanced. His fixation on a Great Russian state failed to engage the material and emotional fault lines of scarcity and loss that shaped its military weakness. In this regard the predictable demand for regional or national autonomy was not simply a question of politically restructuring the empire. It reflected the desire as well for greater local control over scarce resources and had implications for how Ukrainian troops and whole units based on nationality were being supported and deployed. Indeed, partly for this reason the Kiev regional party committee considered a strong regional organ for all of Ukraine to be timely and expedient, "fully corresponding to the needs of the moment." The withdrawal of their party colleagues from the government at this difficult moment was "incomprehensible and not without its own danger for the state itself."[35]

The July Days events have been meticulously studied.[36] All three of the Great Stories focus on the role of the Bolsheviks and Lenin's own unrestrained determination to seize state power by investing "all power" in radicalized soviets. Lenin had talked about taking power for weeks, exhilarated by the rapid growth of his party's apparatus, the support for the party's positions on workers' control, transferring land to the peasants, and especially the war. The 1st Machine Gun Regiment and others in Petrograd who could certainly be described in these terms led the assault, perhaps taking Lenin's words more seriously than he yet intended. Many in the party were more cautious than their leader, concerned that the moment was not right in tactical terms. In any case, on July 3 the regiment's rebellious soldiers spread out through the Narva and Vyborg districts

---

[34] *Rech'*, June 21, 1917.
[35] *Russkiia Vedomosti*, July 8, 1917.
[36] See esp. Alexander Rabinowitch, *Prelude to Revolution* (1968; Bloomington: Indiana University Press, 1991); O. N. Znamenskii, *Iul'skii krizis* (Moscow: Nauka, 1964).

denouncing the coalition regime and calling for support. Early the next day, they were joined in the streets by huge numbers of men and women, perhaps as many as 275,000, judging by the number of factories involved. Participants represented every sector of the city's industrial and service workforce, including restaurant employees and postal workers demanding the removal of the "counterrevolutionary" Menshevik minister Tsereteli. For two days Kerensky and the rump cabinet struggled together with the Soviet Executive Committee to regain control.

The important question historically, however, is not the role the Bolsheviks played in this episode. Sooner or later Lenin and his supporters were bound to make their move. Reveling in his party's growing popular support, including unexpected success in the early municipal duma elections and the growing influence of party supporters in soviets around the country, Lenin certainly was determined to capture the state, as he had brazenly indicated in June at the All-Russia Congress of Soviets. In Petrograd, Lenin's supporters had received almost the same percentage of votes as the Kadets in district duma elections; in Moscow, as many as the Mensheviks.

In this sense politics mattered, of course. Obviously, the party's intensive agitation against the war and the "bourgeois-capitalist" regime found broad resonance among garrison soldiers and Petrograd workers, "sparking" the insurrection, in Leninist terms, even if many in the party rightly thought it was politically risky and likely to be suppressed. Yet the more significant issues underlying the insurrection had to do with the losses of war and the continued insecurities of scarcities and rising prices. If the key question disquieting Miliukov and other members of the new revolutionary government in March was "Who elected you?," the questions agitating Petrograd's garrison soldiers and the city's workforce in by early July were "Why are we fighting?" and "Why hasn't the revolution improved our well-being and social security?" The first question animated soldiers in Petrograd and elsewhere now deeply resistant to being sent to the front, as well as those already there. The Bolsheviks' condemnation of the war now found wide acceptance. The second question largely explains why some one thousand Putilov workers left their plant despite the urging of their own factory committee for restraint and marched slowly on July 4 to the city center, mobilizing thousands of others along the way.

Sequestered by the tsarist government in 1916 to contain their radicalism, as we have seen, and the largest factory contingent supporting the street protests on February 23 when they were locked out of their massive plant, the Putilovtsy reflected continuity, memory, persistent insecurities about food, and the more generalized anxieties about wages and well-being that the revolutionary regime had so far been unable to assuage. That as many as three-quarters of the city's workers may have joined them by July 4 signaled how widespread these insecurities and grievances continued to be.

In several other cities garrison soldiers also took to the streets after learning by telegraph what was happening in the capital. They, too, found ready support among local workers. In Nizhnii Novgorod soldiers were joined by militant workers from the huge Sormovo plant, where twenty-five thousand men and women had walked off their jobs just as the Kerensky offensive was getting underway and where Minister of Labor Skobelev himself had just put great efforts into temporarily resolving the dispute. Here as in Kazan, 220 miles away, the radicalism of garrison troops was augmented by a large contingent of evacuated soldiers recovering from their wounds. Face to face with the carnage, the reserve troops may have been even more resistant to being sent to the front than those in Petrograd, especially after some units had been dispatched earlier to support the offensive. As Sarah Badcock has shown, events in Nizhnii Novgorod clearly reflected the pressures underlying the July Days in the capital.[37] The same was true in Saratov, as Don Raleigh has described. An unpopular rationing system had begun there on July 1 because of food scarcities. News from Petrograd arrived by telegraph on July 3. On July 4 evacuated soldiers and garrison troops joined workers and others in a large demonstration with a distinctly Bolshevik tone.[38] In Moscow, a city-wide meeting of workers and trade unionists held just as the Kadet ministers were quitting the government demanded the regime immediately enact a living minimum wage closely indexed to prices. Bolsheviks and others in the Moscow Soviet demanded that it be funded by a complete overhaul of tax policies. "It is impossible to wait any longer," they declared in the soviet. "All peaceful paths have been exhausted."[39]

When the July insurrection broke out in Petrograd, the Moscow Soviet Executive Committee banned all demonstrations for three days.[40] With the same reluctance voiced by some in Petrograd but fearing to lose popular support, the city's Bolshevik committee acceded to its more militant members' demand that the order be defied. By all accounts, the demonstrations that then occurred were countered by a hostile crowd that jeered the participants. Meanwhile General Alexander Verkhovskii, the district military commander somewhat sympathetic to the moderate socialists, managed to maintain discipline among the city's garrison troops, who were not scheduled in any event to move to the front.[41] While Moscow thus remained relatively calm during the Petrograd insurrection,

---

[37] Sarah Badcock, *Politics and the People in Revolutionary Russia: A Provincial History* (Cambridge: Cambridge University Press, 2007), 154–57.

[38] Donald J. Raleigh, *Revolution on the Volga: 1917 in Saratov* (Ithaca, NY: Cornell University Press, 1986), 192–94.

[39] RGIA f. 626, op. 1, d. 267, ll. 68–71; *Sotsial Democrat*, July 6, 7, 1917.

[40] *Sotsial Demokrat*, July 5, 1917.

[41] Diane Koenker, *Moscow Workers and the 1917 Revolution* (Princeton, NJ: Princeton University Press, 1981), 121–22.

the underlying conjuncture of circumstances also spoke to the urgency of guaranteeing the city's supply of food and other needed goods.

It is also important in understanding the July Days to emphasize that economic, social, and cultural change always moves at a much slower pace than political change. The four short months between March and July witnessed a phenomenal *compression* of political events and political change. The problems of scarcity and its insecurities as well as other social and material circumstances underlying the overthrow of the tsar simply could not improve very much in that short period, if at all. Nor could the subjective elements fueling the massive February uprising simply dissolve in the burst of hope and expectation, however difficult, again, these elements of emotion and culture are to measure. The great hopes for political freedom and civil liberties were relatively easy for the new regime to gratify. Those based on expectations of a quick improvement in material well-being and especially the end of food insecurity were unrealistic at best, despite all the efforts of the new regime to address them. While soviet and government figures in Petrograd managed together to quell the uprising, the still urgent problems of scarcity and welfare remained to be solved. So did the effects of the war's enormous losses on the revolutionary state's ability to establish a monopoly over coercive power.

The "Real Demands of Russian Life"

If one reads carefully the documentation on the July crisis, it is not hard to understand why the Great Stories have emphasized how this sequence of events was a direct political assault on the coalition regime, a "dress rehearsal" for October, and downplay or ignore its socioeconomic and emotional underpinnings. The Kadet resignations and the July Days insurrection were both understood in just this way by the leading figures of the moment. From the perspective of Miliukov's Kadets the coalition regime was no longer a "government of responsible men in whom the country could have confidence." Nor could there be political freedom without the power of the Great Russian state to enforce it. First and foremost among the "real demands of Russian life," as Miliukov called them, was to strengthen the state by suppressing the Bolsheviks and restoring social discipline. Now more than ever the government had to be independent and nonpartisan, its ministers responsible only to their own conscience. For the purpose of saving the state, the moment also allowed for the participation of the military in politics. The only way forward was to consolidate and strengthen Russia's "healthy elements."[42]

---

[42] *Vestnik Partiia Narodnoi Svobody* 11–13 (Aug. 10, 1917): 29; *Rech'*, July 17, 18, 1917; P. N. Miliukov, *Istoriia vtoroi russkoi revoliutsii*, 3 pts. (Sofia: Ros-Bolgarskoe izd., 1921–24), 1:29–35.

For Tsereteli, Skobelev, and other democratic socialists in and outside the government, however, the primary issues were ones of practicality and possibility. The task of the moment was not simply strengthening the coercive capacities of the regime. The restoration of the death penalty "for traitors and betrayers" in the war zone being demanded by General Kornilov and others would itself be an immoral act. So were the ways Cossacks and other "loyalist" troops opened fire on protesting workers. The real issue in practical terms was how this use of coercive force would affect soldiers' and workers' willingness to defend the government. What was needed to fortify the regime's popular support was to restore confidence in the revolution itself—*deepening* the revolution, as it was expressed. This meant setting a course toward further economic and social change through a restructured "government to save the revolution."

What everyone still within this government agreed upon was that the insurrection had to be put down. On July 5 forces loyal to the government raided the offices of *Pravda* and shut the paper down. A broad effort was undertaken by *Izvestiia* and other newspapers to discredit Lenin by accusing him of receiving German money. Leading Bolsheviks were targeted for arrest. Trotsky, who famously saved Minister of Agriculture Viktor Chernov from a possible lynching by Kronstadt sailors on July 4, soon found himself with other party leaders in the notorious Kresty Prison. The militant SR leader Chernov was also accused of being in Germany's pay. Going into hiding, Lenin soon made his way to Finland, agreeing with his comrades that he was too important to the party to risk being arrested.

Strengthening the state was also taken immediately to mean a ruthless suppression of disorder and disobedience in the army, for many more the cause of the collapsing offensive than its effect. Everywhere in high places there were strident calls for discipline, especially after retreating troops ravaged the Galician town of Tarnopol' in one of the worst incidents of its kind in the entire war. Appointed now to command the Southwestern Front and charged with restoring order, General Lavr Kornilov now ordered officers to take exceptional measures, including the use of machine guns. In his unvarnished view, retreat, like the street demonstrations, was tantamount to treason. As the general's insistence, a decree soon signed by Kerensky reimposed the death penalty. New "military-revolutionary courts" consisting of soldiers and officers were to be formed to carry it out. Executions were set for a broad range of offenses, many ill-defined. When a whole regiment abandoned their positions and fled the Germans' advance toward Riga, Kornilov later reported with pride that he had issued a telegraphic order to "exterminate" the entire command.[43]

---

[43] *Gosudarstvennoe Soveshchanie: 12–15 Avg. 1917 (Stenograficheskii otchet)* (Moscow: Gosizdat, 1930), 60–61.

Tsereteli, Skobelev, and other democratic socialists saw the coalition regime in danger from both the right and the left: Bolshevik supporters among the garrison soldiers, in the workplace, and at the front, as well as the authoritarianism of tsarist generals like Kornilov and Russia's well-honed reactionary nationalists. Meeting throughout the threatening days and nights of July 3–4 and 4–5, some ninety members of the executive committees of the worker and peasant soviet congresses debated the implications of taking full state power demanded by armed workers and soldiers who pushed their way into the Tauride Palace. At one point during the night of July 3–4 the floor was taken over by fifty Putilov workers. Their spokesmen insisted they would not disperse until the ten capitalist ministers were arrested and the soviet alone held state power. Many soviet figures in the hall must have felt like the Menshevik leader Dan that the issue might literally be one of their own life or death.[44]

This acute sense of vulnerability did not come only from the demonstrators' rage. Tsereteli, Dan, and others understood that "all power to the soviets" implied a usurpation of state power that violated the premises on which the Provisional Government claimed its legitimacy. In terms of Russia's longer historical trajectory, the July insurrection only confirmed that revolutionary Russia was not ready for socialism. The task of the moment during the long night of July 3–4 was thus "to defend the unity and integrity [tsel'nost']" of the Russian Revolution itself. Tsereteli continued to think that the revolutionary government required the participation in some form of "all vital forces" of the nation. This meant representation by groups that soviet constituents around the country increasingly regarded as enemies (vragi). There was also a question about the status and potential influence of those who might join a new coalition. Unless they had the support of leading trade industrial groups, there was little hope for anything resembling broad support for efforts by an all-socialist government to implement change and defend against counterrevolution. For Tsereteli an all-socialist government might well come to power prematurely, but the decision could come only under the aegis of a fully representative body like the Constituent Assembly. It could not "be taken by bayonets."[45]

As all the Great Stories rightly describe, the Kadet resignations and the July Days together provoked a major political crisis. There was no question that the remaining democratic socialists in the government were politically vulnerable in and outside the regime, as was democratic socialism as a broad political movement. An all-socialist regime was almost certain to provoke counterrevolution. Revolutionary Petrograd might then become a sequel to the Paris commune of 1871, with all of its disastrous consequences. General Kornilov had

---

[44] *Izvestiia*, July 4, 1917.
[45] Ibid.

already chafed at the bit in April, wanting to send his troops against the antiwar demonstrators. General Brusilov believed civil war was "inevitable."[46] Indeed, as freewheeling Cossack troops overwhelmed garrison soldiers and Kronstadt sailors and fired on workers, the possibilities of civil war seemed stark. In these fraught circumstances, the soviets' exhausted leaders held firm to the political importance of maintaining the coalition.

How the broken cabinet of ministers should be reconstituted was another matter. Russia's leading industrial groups were now in no mood for accommodation. Their members, too, were struggling with loss, both actual and anticipated: in their control of their factories and plants; in their well-institutionalized and long-held social positions; in the very cultural elements of hierarchy and well-being that many of their members had achieved despite tsarist resistance. Many entrepreneurs and business owners experienced the animosity expressed by workers within and outside their plants as more than politically disturbing. It threatened their whole way of life and their livelihood, as well as whatever sense of achievement their long and arduous efforts at economic modernization may have brought them. In contrast to an accommodating position just four months earlier, in March, they now declared that all agreements with workers made under threat or force were no longer binding.[47] For leaders of the Union of Congresses and CWIC at 46 Liteinyi Prospekt, as well as Petrograd and Moscow Societies of Factory and Mill Owners, the revolution had descended into anarchy. (When Sampsonievskii plant workers threatened the director with the wheelbarrow if wage increases were not granted immediately, he reportedly sat down in the wheelbarrow himself.)[48] Though warned that the supply of shells was near exhaustion, the Guzhon metal works in Moscow, the most important of the country's three major producers, shut down in response to "administrative disorganization" and its workers incessant demands. The "sole possibility" for its reopening was to place it under direct government control.[49] After the acting minister of trade and industry Vasili Stepanov traveled to Moscow to deal with the crisis, he became convinced the struggle of workers against management had sharpened to the point of threatening the country's military defense and very survival. The country stood "on the verge of economic and financial collapse." The situation was "hopeless."[50]

Reports from the provinces were no more encouraging. The Ministry of Internal Affairs itself was being inundated with reports and petitions about

[46] N. Bukhbinder, "Na fronte v predoktiabr'skie dni," *Krasnaia Letopis* 6 (1923): 18–52; *Izvestiia*, July 9, 14, 1917; *Rech'*, July 14, 1917.
[47] *Ekonomicheskoe polozhenie Rossii nakanune velikoi oktiabr'skoi sotsialisticheskoi revoliutsii: Dokumenty I materialy*, 3 pts. (Leningrad: Nauka, 1957–67), 1:526.
[48] RGIA, f. 23, op. 1, d. 454, ll. 10–21; *Novaia Zhizn'*, July 7, 1917.
[49] ZOSO (Moscow, 1978), 3:497–509.
[50] *Birzhevye Vedomosti*, June 30, 1917.

seizures of land, woods, property, cattle, and other inventory, sometimes through violence. Local villagers menaced Andrei Shingarev's own estate in Voronezh. Orders had gone out to the regime's provincial and regional commissars "to take all measures" together with the local militia to preserve landholdings from peasant seizures, apparently to little avail. When the Main Land Committee convened its second meeting on July 1, the number of representatives from local committees was "much too small," making it "impossible" to have a full grasp of the problem in the view of its chair, the Progressist A. S. Postnikov, former head of the prestigious Free Economic Society. This did not stop him from reporting that the news from many places was "extremely alarming," that "under such deplorable conditions it was impossible to solve the land problem, one of the greatest importance."[51] In fact, peasants were "solving" the land problem on their own. The success of the coming harvest was at risk, as Tsereteli himself warned, threatening "immeasurable harm to the army, the country and the very existence of the government."[52]

The July Days insurrection was thus only the most proximate source of vulnerability facing Tsereteli, Skobelev, and other democratic socialists left with the task of forming a new cabinet. Of equal or greater consequence were the still intractable problems of food production and supply, transport, and the inflationary consequences of scarcities that still begged solutions. To move the revolutionary process forward, democratic socialists had somehow to construct a new government that was at least acceptable to Russia's industrial and propertied groups and angry generals like Kornilov, while responsive as well to the needs of workers, peasants, and soldiers that had just been so forcefully expressed.

The "Government to Save the Revolution"

In their exhausting efforts to beat down the insurrection, the remaining cabinet members and the soviet leadership had little time or energy to discuss carefully what was practical or possible, much less reach a consensus on these vital questions. The result was a hastily drafted declaration prompted by Minister President L'vov's threat that he, too, would resign unless a new coalition could be organized around a declaration of principles that promised a decisive fight against anarchists and Bolsheviks and the repudiation of all kinds of seizures. What the rump cabinet drafted instead outlined principles the remaining socialists in the government thought should guide efforts to "deepen the revolution." Future agricultural reforms would be based on "the principle of transferring land to the

---

[51] Browder and Kerensky, *Russian Provisional Government*, vol. 1, 544.
[52] *Krest'ianskoe Dvizhenie v 1917 godu* (Moscow: Gosidat, 1927), 413–14.

those who worked it." The food supply would be improved by expanding the work of land committees with well-defined legal authority to decide all local issues except the right to ownership. New legislation would be passed governing the eight-hour day, the protection of labor, and labor insurance. Traditional social estates would be abolished and civil ranks and orders eliminated. Most important, measures would be introduced to regulate and control industry. The new Main (Glavnyi) Economic Committee would immediately be charged with working "decisively" to stem the country's economic collapse. Seeking to effectively address continued scarcities in essential goods, persistent inflation, speculation, and the still pressing problems of distribution, the new council would essentially lay the foundations of a socialist political economy—what Tsereteli called a "platform of the socialist movement."

The declaration was published on July 8 just as the extent of the German breakthrough at the front was becoming clear, directly threatening Riga and possibly Petrograd as well. It threw liberals and others opposed to the socialists' agenda into an uproar. Minister President L'vov considered it an "obvious deviation from the nonparty principles toward the realization of purely partisan socialist aims" and promptly resigned.[53] The rump government seemed intent on pursuing socialist goals even before a new constitutional regime was formally reestablished. At a hastily convened evening meeting of the soviet groups that had carried the regime through the July Days, Tsereteli responded instead that the German offensive was also "a matter of life or death" for the socialists, since they would clearly be the enemy's first victims if Petrograd was seized. "The democracy"—that is, Russia's workers and peasants—now had to take a vigorous stand to defend the revolution and raise the morale of the army. "Only a single revolutionary and popular government" could save the country from this new danger. For the Menshevik Dan, the government needed to be given "the most comprehensive powers." For the SR leader Avksentiev, "everyone who is not with us is now the enemy." Speaking for the Bolsheviks, the future Commissar of Enlightenment Anatoli Lunacharskii dared to "extend our hand for a union of forces despite . . . our mutual distrust." When the meeting ended at 2:00 in the morning a resolution formally declared the still unconstituted regime the "Government to Save the Revolution."[54]

It is hard to underestimate the significance of the July 8 Declaration for liberals and others who held the socialists largely responsible for the breakdown in law and order. The implementation of its goals would preempt the Constituent Assembly. It would further undermine efforts to respect existing law or individual rights. It placed the future of the Russian state in the hands

[53] *Izvestiia*, July 9, 1917.
[54] *Izvestiia*, July 11, 1917.

of those "absolutely incapable of determining what constituted Russia's national interests."[55] The result was two weeks of fierce contention in and around the government as Kerensky was charged with making the cabinet whole. At first the Petrograd Kadets refused to join. After intense discussion they also dissuaded their left-leaning Moscow colleagues Nikolai Astrov and Nikolai Kishkin from doing so. (Shortly afterward Kishkin's brother was killed at the front.) Some demanded the resignation of SR leader and agriculture minister Chernov, whom liberals thought had condoned local land committee seizures and village gatherings running amok. When a full description of the German breakthrough appeared in the newspapers on July 18, *Izvestiia* accused the Kadets themselves of "betraying" the revolution, just as the Bolsheviks had done.

Heightening the drama, Kerensky suddenly resigned. Miliukov, too, went to a provocative extreme, demanding that an all-soviet government take power so that responsibility for Russia's impending disasters would be firmly on its shoulders.[56] Kerensky was then given full powers to negotiate a new cabinet, withdrew his resignation, and moved into the Winter Palace, insisting his regime would not budge from the July 8 Declaration.[57] When the political dust finally settled, the new regime declared itself a coalition of individuals rather than parties. Socialist ministers would not be responsible to any soviet organization, nor would the government as a whole stand officially behind the July 8 Declaration, despite Kerensky's pledge.

Russia now had its second coalition and third revolutionary government in a little more than four months, outdoing even the tsar's four "merry-go-round" governments in 1917. Tsereteli, the most influential architect of the first coalition in April, was gone. Chernov stayed on as minister of agriculture, lest his departure further ignite the peasantry. Quitting the Kadet party, Nekrasov moved from transport minister to minister of finance, a position for which he had no special competence but one that was too risky to be assigned to a socialist. The frenetic Kerensky became prime minister as well as minister of war—the only person around who still seemed to retain at least some begrudging support of the parties despite the breakdown of the front. The Winter Palace rather than the Tauride became the seat of government, symbolizing to some its continuity with the past, or at least its failure to disavow it. While the immediate political crisis came to an end, it remained to be seen whether the underlying causes of the July insurrection could now be effectively addressed.

---

[55] *Svobodnyi Narod*, July 11, 1917.
[56] *Rech'*, July 23, 1917
[57] *Russkiia Vedomosti*, *Izvestiia*, and *Novoe Vremia*, July 18, 19, 1917; Tsereteli, *Vospominaniia*, 2:375ff.

Once Again "on the Brink of Catastrophe"

Suppressing Bolsheviks was not the same, of course, as suppressing Bolshevism. While Kerensky and Kornilov laid down strict new punishments for disorder at the front, harsh new decrees were also targeted at violators of civil order. Incitement to a range of offenses, including disobedience to lawful orders of the authorities, was to be punished along with those who committed the acts, reflecting the tsarist law making the agitation to strike a crime even if strikes characterized as economic were formally still legal. In provincial cities and towns the July Days also strained political relations. The Bolsheviks were momentarily on the defensive, especially in provincial cities like Saratov, where city duma elections strengthened the democratic socialists and revolutionary defensists united as a socialist bloc. Bolshevism, if not always members of Lenin's party, continued to fuel grievances in and outside enterprises in virtually every place where wages were thought to be inadequate, essential goods were scarce, and owners threatened to shut down their factories. In cities and towns across the country as well as Petrograd and Moscow, scarcity and loss continued to stoke a sometimes lethal mix of anxiety, disappointment, and anger over the revolutionary regime's failure to realize its promises of security and well-being, even if these were also directed against a capitalist and bourgeois "enemy within." Nor was it possible to suppress these feelings with Cossack patrols.

Leading industrial figures no longer had respect for the soviets' leadership. Pavel P. Riabushinskii, a leader in the WICs who now headed Union of Trade Industrialists in Moscow, publicly described those forming the new coalition as "ignorant, nameless, unenlightened and irresponsible."[58] State factory inspectors believed that Russian industry was on the brink of disaster. Intervention was absolutely essential. Prince N. B. Shcherbatov told the State Committee on Food that the grain monopoly was a failure, that Russia was threatened with famine.[59] On July 19 a congress of district representatives in the oil sector described Russia's current fuel situation as "catastrophic."[60] The Special Council on Fuel had lost all authority; control was in the hands of radical local fuel committees and local soviets. Little besides interference came from Petrograd.[61]

Thus the crucial issue here was not the political composition of the regime. It was instead how and where the revolutionary state might effectively intervene in the economy and whether it had the power to enforce a politically acceptable set of controls capable of preventing economic and political disaster. Virtually every leading political activist wanted new economic regulations in principle.

---

[58] *Russkiia Vedomosti*, July 19, 1917.
[59] RGIA f. 23, op. 29, d. 2, ll. 11–12.
[60] RGIA f. 92, op. 1, d. 160, l. 16.
[61] RGIA f. 92, op. 1, d. 162, ll. 8–9; f. 280, op. 1, d. 70, ll. 16ff.; f. 150, op. 1, d .428, passim.

The question was, on whom and on what should regulations be imposed, and how could they be enforced?

Delegates to the second Trade Industrial Congress in early August understood "regulation" as state control over wages and state financial support to industry, key elements along with private ownership of plants of what we have called war capitalism. The state also had to set manageable nationwide wage levels that assured at lease some degree of profitability. Members of the Provisional Government's Special Commission on Restoration of Industry agreed. Its members saw "complete chaos" in the factories that could be resolved only by decisive state intervention.[62] So did representatives from the Petrograd and Moscow Societies of Factory and Mill Owners who now regretted the concessions made in March that empowered workers committees in their plants. They, too, demanded the state control workers committees by force, if necessary. No one seemed clear, however, about how this could be done without stirring up even more agitation and possibly repeating the bloody excesses of 1915.

Regulation thus meant very different things to different groups. Under the headline "Facing the Threat of Bankruptcy," the Mensheviks' *Rabochaia Gazeta* insisted that there could be no improvement in productivity until the state began seriously to control profits and "greedy entrepreneurs."[63] Former vice ministers of trade and industry V. A. Stepanov and P. I. Palchinskii believed that if wage demands prompted the closing of factories, workers had to be forced back to their benches. If management compromised production, the state had to step in there as well. If the government was "especially sharp" in denouncing the efforts of workers committees to "socialize" individual enterprises, plant owners would put their own full efforts into increasing production. Stepanov and Palchinskii rejected demands, especially from commercial bankers, to end existing regulations and return to a "completely free" economy.[64] Meanwhile, their colleague M. V. Bernatskii, soon to be appointed minister of finance, believed that "Russia's near future belonged to capitalism, not socialism."[65] When the revisionist social democrat Sergei Prokopovich, scorned by Bolsheviks for endorsing gradualism, agreed to become minister of trade and industry and chair of the state's new Main Economic Committee, the appointment was sharply criticized by industrialists in Petrograd despite his close ties to Alexander Konovalov and Moscow's liberals.[66]

---

[62] RGIA f. 32, op. 2, d. 1, ll. 151–56.
[63] *Rabochaia Gazeta*, Aug. 3, 1917.
[64] RGIA f. 23, op. 7, d. 409.
[65] A. Drezen, ed., *Burzhuaziia I pomeshhiki v 1917 godu: Chastnye soveshchaniia chlenov Gosudarvennoi Dumy* (Moscow, 1932), 68–69; M. N. Pokrovskii, ed., "Ekonomicheskoe Polozhenie Rossii pered revoliutsii," *Krasnyi Arkhiv* 10 (1925): 86–94; *Stenograficheskii otchet zasedaniia ekonomicheskogo soveta pri vremennom pravitel'stve* (Petrograd, 1917), 10–20.
[66] RGIA f. 23, op. 1, d. 27, ll. 142ff.

Within the new Economic Committee and its Executive Council, tensions between the perception and actualities of Russia's economic circumstances remained acute, as they had throughout the war. Were those forecasting economic collapse simply doomsayers, or was the country actually on the brink of economic catastrophe? Did Petrograd and Moscow reflect the economic situation in the country at large, or did proximity to a militant workforce distort understanding? Comprehensive economic data was still lacking. The lag time between its collection, assembly, and distribution was such as to make even a reasonably accurate picture problematic. There were also significant variations locally as well as conflicting reports from the small army of commissars officially charged with assessing local conditions. Still, the contours of Russia's economic crisis were sufficiently clear. Among the early presentations to the new Economic Council was a report from the Ministry of Transport that huge numbers of freight cars were now being dispatched without full loads, that freight traffic as a whole was down more than 20 percent compared to 1916, and that transport conditions on some main lines, especially the vital supply line from Vladivostok, remained as bad as or worse than before the revolution. From June 15 to July 1, the rate of locomotives requiring repair had risen some 25 percent.[67]

Council members Kutler and Struve focused attention on the collapse of productivity rather than distribution as "a grave danger" to the economy, code words for the baneful influence of workers committees and constant conflict on the shop floor. The change from piecework to daily wages was a disaster in terms of productivity. So was the eight-hour day when workers refused to work longer hours in order to meet production targets.[68] There was also a potentially "disastrous" shortage in the production and distribution of fuel, according to district plenipotentiaries of the Special Council on Fuel who met in Petrograd on July 19. Local authorities were said to be better able to cope with the situation than the Special Council in Petrograd, whose orders did not properly reflect local conditions. The efforts before and after February to devolve authority on issues of production and distribution outward from the center now seemed to be a serious impediment to state regulation.[69]

Yet Struve and council member Groman also believed there was more danger in the regime failing to regulate the economy forcefully than there was in its direct engagement. Russia's commercial markets were simply unable to distribute increasingly scarce goods effectively or contain the effects of scarcity itself on industrial and agricultural production. Rather than an efficient means of distributing scarce goods, markets had become a rich source of speculation and

---

[67] *Stenograficheskii otchet zasedaniia ekonomicheskago soveta* 5 (July 31, 1917): 2–12.
[68] Ibid., 24–28.
[69] RGIA f. 92, op. 1, d. 160, ll. 16–22; d. 162, l. 8.

were simply unable to meet the country's current needs. Echoing the position of the beleaguered socialist ministers, Struve and Groman both regarded the only way forward to be comprehensive state regulation over production, prices, and distribution, enforced by affiliated local economic committees.[70]

As in 1916, however, the same vexing financial questions remained. One was the familiar problem of fixed prices, seemingly impossible now because of the continued increases in the real costs of production. Speculation in grain and other commodities was rampant since the fixed prices of the grain monopoly varied significantly even within individual provinces. The grain monopoly itself was thus problematic in this regard as well as others, a source of increasing rural protest. With the rising costs of grain and other products on the black market, it was almost certainly encouraging hoarding and concealment as well.[71] Another continuing problem was that of consolidating food supply committees and of coordinating their work. In effect, the more active the Main Economic Committee was in this regard, the more it would become like a central state planning commission or a socialist committee of state supply, directing activities at regional and local levels with relatively little coordination with the ministries.[72]

Was planning of this sort actually feasible? Was the strict regulation of industry and the industrial workforce it implied? And could the regime actually enforce wage rates without fixing prices across a broad range of needed products and commodities despite the different costs and black-market prices in different regions? Even in state-owned factories working for defense, close control over the shop floor was hardly containing worker activism. In Petrograd, Moscow, and even distant Sormovo it seemed to only aggravate conflict. Control over distribution was theoretically easier, but while democratizing the railroads had greatly empowered myriad local line committees, they were often in conflict with each other as well as the railroaders' increasingly powerful all-Russia union, Vikzhel. Overall, railroad operations, with their huge demand for fuel, had not significantly improved.

In all of this, moreover, there was one overarching problem that would shape the contours of Russia's ongoing revolutionary experience: the absence of a regime with sufficient coercive power to regulate production, prices, and distribution and contain the different kind of power located in demonstrations, mass activism, and the increasingly militarized workers committees, many of which were now forming their own militias and Red Guards. Paradoxically, the various demands for regulating the economy could be realized only by a government informed enough to know what needed to be done and strong enough to enforce

---

[70] *Stenograficheskii otchet zasedaniia ekonomicheskago soveta* 5 (July 31, 1917): 2–12, 24–28; RGIA f. 23, op. 7, d. 739, ll. 9–30.
[71] RGIA, f. 1600, op. 1, d. 5, l. 54.
[72] RGIA f. 23, op. 7, d. 739, ll. 9–37.

its decisions. Did the government even have the coercive power to regulate production in the way the new coalition government intended? Russia may not have been "drunk on revolution," as the liberal activist Fedor Rodichev averred, but the influence and empowerment of local and district soviets, land committees, workers committees, trade industrial associations, and even newly elected city dumas put the enormous tasks of economic regulation squarely at odds with the conflicting local interests these groups reflected as well as their politically democratic foundations.

Two weeks or so after the impassioned and charismatic Kerensky assumed the role of prime minister in late July, Pavel Riabushinskii warned delegates at the second Trade Industrial Congress of the "inevitable catastrophe" of economic and financial collapse. In a soon to be prominent part of Russia's revolutionary discourse, he warned it might be avoided only if "the bony hand of hunger and national poverty grabbed the throats of the false friends of the revolution" and brought them to their senses.[73]

---

[73] *Novoe Vremia*, Aug. 10, 1917; *Vtoroi vserossiiskii torgovo-promyshlennyi s"ezd v Moskve 3–5 avg. 1917* (Moscow, 1917), 8.

11

The Collapse of War Capitalism

While the revolution's political leaders fought over the program and composition of Russia's third government in less than five months, soldiers were fleeing from the front in record numbers, and in some places as whole units. The wholesale disintegration of the army would not occur until September and October, but already the fear at army headquarters was that desertion and disorder would encourage the enemy to march on Petrograd.

Nowhere, however, was the rhetoric of discipline after the July crisis less effective than at the front. The harsh new measures ordered by Kerensky and Kornilov had relatively little effect. Mutinies on the Southwestern Front were unresolved. One attempt at disarming a whole regiment failed as soldiers ambushed the cavalry and artillerymen sent to repress them. The death penalty was restored for the army. Included in the list of offenses subject to the penalty were "incitement, instigation, or agitation to surrender" and "fleeing or failing to resist the enemy," which made penalties virtually impossible to carry out in units that were disintegrating even if higher-ranking officers were determined to do so. Only a dozen or so death sentences apparently took place. Soldiers themselves blamed the slaughter once again on officers' incompetence and corruption.

Stiff penalties did not deter desertion. While there are no reliable statistics and anything near an accurate count is hidden within the much larger number of those taken prisoner or listed as unknown (123,691 for July 1917), the official count of deserters published for July was more than thirty-seven thousand, the most for any month before the great wave after October and almost six times the monthly average before February.[1] As the Russian scholar A. B. Astashov has noted, even before the revolution at least some regimental officers recognized that "the smart ones saved themselves, the fools remained."[2] Resistance stiffened, however, especially on the Northern Front as German and Austrian troops moved into Russian territory, even as General Kornilov, who had replaced Brusilov as commander in chief, was convinced the army had been overcome "by soldiers in a nightmarish atmosphere of irrational, hideous group law, of interminable ignorance and abominable hooliganism."[3]

---

[1] TsSU, *Rossiia v mirovoi voine, 1914–1918 goda (v tsifrakh)* (Moscow, 1925), 26, 30.
[2] A. B. Astashov, "Dezertirstvo i bor'ba s nim v tsarskoi armii v gody pervoi mirovoi voiny," *Rossiiskaia Istoriia* 4 (July–Aug. 2014): 45.
[3] *Gosudarstvennoe soveshchanie* (Moscow: Gosizdat, 1930), 61.

Some fleeing the front may not have received the warm reception they expected. Family situations changed, wounded and traumatized soldiers may have created new burdens, and the war after all was not over. In some factory towns deserters demanded their old jobs back, bringing new tensions to already fraught shop floors. Here as well as in the villages deserters could still be arrested by local authorities and sent back, at least in principle. In fact, many deserters traveled home in marauding bands that terrorized railroad passengers and brought these skills to local Red Guards and both factory and village militias. More important, perhaps, was the extent to which thousands of deserting soldiers in July also carried home along with their guns the range of debilitating scars well evidenced in the literature on battle trauma: intense irritability, aggressive and reckless behavior, socially exaggerated responses to the stresses of ordinary life, nightmares, disassociation from spouses and family, avoidance of social contact, and, not least, a propensity for violence. As the new coalition government regrouped in mid-July, in other words, preoccupied now with developing a feasible plan to save the revolution, this flow of armed and bellicose men returning from the failed offensive further disturbed Russia's industrial centers, towns, and villages, preparing the ground for still more brutality to come.[4]

Yet soldiers were not the only ones experiencing the traumas of war under Kerensky's and Brusilov's commands. During its chaotic retreat in early July, Kornilov's Eighth Army wreaked enormous violence on Tarnopol's remaining residents, only the most recent of the many unspeakable brutalities inflicted on Jews and other local inhabitants in the region since 1914. Jews everywhere were still an easy "enemy" to destroy. Even the smallest stores of goods were not easy to conceal from armed soldiers. A new wave of civilian flight brought the total number driven from the war zone to as many as three million or more. Their experience was comparably traumatic to what the marauders may have experienced themselves, their horrors also deeply embedded in individual and collective consciousness and lives. Many of those newly displaced found themselves relocated in provincial cities and rural towns where they were particularly vulnerable to hostile residents who themselves bore the emotional scars of war.

Village Sovereignty

How much these kinds of loss further radicalized Russian villages in July and August is difficult to know. In her efforts to describe the mentality of workers, peasants, and soldiers throughout the course of the war, Olga Porshneva identifies "traditional" as well as "radical" outlooks and shows the increasing

---

[4] RGVIA f. 366, op. 1, d. 79, passim.

domination of the latter in the countryside in 1917, especially in terms of land and the war. Aaron Retish describes the "fractures" occurring in Viatka's villages after February but suggests that the soldiers' influence should not be overstated. Village elders were still largely in control. Still, one can surmise from reports about rural violence in the summer that the effect was substantial in other ways, such as the increasing use of force to "solve" village problems and often those within families as well, even if we can determine only the nature and objects of violence, not its causes.[5] Certainly soldiers returning home were not likely to shy away from taking out their feelings on local landowners and other gentry whom they identified with their officers, nor from using force to pillage livestock or grain for their own use or consumption. One can assume their intolerance of Jews and corruption also affected their behavior toward traders and strengthened the resistance of their communities to forced grain deliveries and other obligations. One again must be careful not to conflate those in grain surplus with those in grain deficit areas, or those whose villages were close to towns and railroads with those in the deep *glubinia*—the distant reaches of the countryside where precommercial relations and cultures were still the norm. Village life in parts of Siberia differed substantially from that in many parts of European Russia, which themselves differed from each other.

The best way to generalize what was happening in the countryside is to describe a process of villages enclosing themselves in defense of their own needs. Peasant resistance to grain requisitions was increasing in many places in anticipation of a smaller harvest. In some reports, like those in *Saratovskii Listok (Saratov Post)*, the grain situation throughout the province was considered hopeless or nearly so. Under the headline "Anxious News from the Countryside," *Novoe Vremia* reported that "every little village considers itself an independent state and dictates its own decrees." Decrees from the center were increasingly ignored.[6] In grain-exporting districts this meant refusing or resisting obligatory deliveries to the state in favor of hoarding or selling at higher prices to private traders. Commodities that might have incentivized new production remained subordinated to military production and the still massive needs of the army. In deficit districts, it meant gathering additional foodstuffs and resources in whatever way possible and making sure nothing was taken out of the village. From distant Novonikolaevsk (now Novosibirsk) the Menshevik head of the regional Consumers Cooperative wired the Ministry of Trade and Industry on July 16 that there was "absolutely no possibility" in the region to meet the demand for

---

[5] RGIA, f. 126, op. 1, d. 48, ll. 17–18; O. S. Porshneva, *Mentalitet i sotsial'noe povedenie rabochikh, kresti'ian i soldat Rossii v period pervoi mirovoi voiny (1914–mart 1918)* (Ekaterinburg: UrO RAN, 2000), ch. 6; Aaron Retish, *Russia's Peasants in Revolution and Civil War* (Cambridge: Cambridge University Press, 2008), 105–8.

[6] *Saratovskii Listok*, June 23, 24, 1917; *Novoe Vremia*, June 25, 1917.

tea, matches, paper, processed fish, leather, shoes, clothing, and other goods. Scarcities there and elsewhere pressed peasants to keep their produce off the market, ignore obligatory deliveries, and hide it from requisition. In deficit areas like Viatka, clashes occurred between peasants and soldiers sent to take compulsory deliveries.[7]

Where there were surpluses, grain and other essential goods were still locally embargoed, despite the clear needs of even nearby districts. Black markets continued to flourish. The new prices reworked after February and fixed by the grain monopoly at the insistence of Shingarev, Struve, and Groman, among others, were not working either to increase the grain supply or to reduce speculation as inflation began to reach what the Russian historian A. Iu. Davydov calls "apocalyptic" levels.[8] Sarah Badcock has shown for the province of Kazan that the new fixed price for requisitioned grain in March was already 17 percent lower than that in local markets. Although the fixed price had doubled by late August, it was now some 65 percent lower than the same grain could get illegally. Individual "bagmen" (also described as "walkers") carried sacks of grain from Kazan to adjacent Nizhegorod, the uncertain surpluses of one easily distributed by these more traditional means of trade to the meet the needs of the other. Bagmen were augmenting and even replacing more formal markets elsewhere as well as protesting against the fixed price spread.[9]

It is likely that events in Petrograd also accelerated the taking of land when its transfer to peasants was promised in the government's July 8 Declaration. Certainly the peasants' "right" to land was loudly supported by the SR leader and Minister of Agriculture Viktor Chernov, whom the liberals tried and failed to drive from the cabinet precisely for this reason.[10] In much of the countryside Chernov's SRs were very active in the new district zemstvo elections. Perhaps surprisingly, Lenin's followers put considerable effort into the elections as well, centered around the party's slogan "Land, Peace, and Bread." While more moderate parties held increasing sway in local municipal duma voting, socialists becoming the dominant party about half the time in election blocs with other democratic socialists, for many in the countryside the main enemy was no longer

---

[7] RGIA f. 23, op. 7, d. 409, l. 35; Sarah Badcock, *Politics and the People in Revolutionary Russia: A Provincial History* (Cambridge: Cambridge University Press, 2007), 181–202; Retish, *Russia's Peasants,* 91–102.

[8] A. Iu. Davydov, *Nelegal'noe snabzhenie rossiiskogo naseleniia v vlast' 1917–1921 gg.* (St. Petersburg: Nauka, 2002), 14–57.

[9] Badcock, *Politics,* 214; Lars Lih, *Bread and Authority in Russia, 1914–1921* (Berkeley: University of California Press, 1990), 77–81; Mark Baker, *Beyond the National: Peasants, Power, and Revolution in Ukraine* (Alberta: CIUS, 1999); *Ekonomicheskoe Polozhenie Rossii nakanune velikoi oktiabr'skoi sotsialisticheskoi revoliutsii: Dokumenty I materialy,* 3 pts. (Leningrad: Nauka, 1957–67), 3:200ff.

[10] Khanny Immonen, *Mechty o novoi Rossii: Viktor Chernov (1873–1952)* (St. Petersburg: EUSP Press, 2015), ch. 14.

the Germans or Austrians. It was those responsible for unmanageable increases in prices: speculators, merchants, and landowners.[11]

In all of this, villages across the country were implicitly declaring their sovereignty from the revolutionary state, adapting in this way to scarcities, requisitions, and huge losses in manpower. The summer harvest was expected to be poor. In Nizhnii Novgorod province and elsewhere, there were serious worries that the winter would bring starvation to villages without sufficient arable land.[12] Telegrams and newspaper reports warned of anarchy as peasants mobilized in defense of their own interests.

Who Owns the Workplace?

As we have seen, the socialist goals of the July 8 Declaration clearly put the Government to Save the Revolution in direct conflict with the practices and ethos of war capitalism. When the industrialists demanded stronger regulation of the economy, they assumed that the reconstructed government would still fund profitable defense production in private as well as state plants. It would also provide other kinds of assistance to ensure plants had necessary resources and could maintain the commercial marketing of essential goods not requisitioned through the grain monopoly or by other local authorities. Sequester was also a possibility. As with the huge Putilov works in 1916, the state's temporary control to keep plants in operation and suppress workplace activism was strongly advocated in some quarters. Few if any plant owners disagreed with the new minister of finance Bernadskii's statement that Russia's future had to be a capitalist one. If Kerensky and his colleagues took responsibility for funding wages indexed to rising prices, they might also address the sources of resentment and fairness so graphically illustrated by what Shingarev had described as "a certain strata" of society "cloaked in silk and velvet."[13]

Additional challenges for plant owners to war capitalism came from the sheer strain of everyday life: widespread anxieties about what was happening to them and their businesses and the deterioration in workplace relations. For some it was already time to shut their plants and think about going abroad, not necessarily in that order. What was reported now from the provinces reinforced these inclinations: uncontrolled requisitions; the hoarding of fuel and other scarce resources; continuing problems on worker-controlled railroads, including still

---

[11] A. V. Astashov, "Russkii krest'ianin na Frontakh pervoi mirovoi voiny," *Otechestvennaia Istoriia* 2 (Mar. 2003): 81–82.
[12] Badcock, *Politics*, 220–24.
[13] Gosudarstvennaia Duma, *Stenograficheskii Otchet 4th sozyv* (Moscow: Gosizdat, 1930), col. 1768.

rampant corruption; and the general breakdown of commercial market exchange in the face of black-market alternatives. Underlying all of these concerns in addition to worker activism were the actualities of inflation and the deepening crisis in state finance itself. War capitalism centered on state financing for favored private enterprises working for defense as well as state-owned plants, and the government's ability to ensure sufficient additional capital through a functional banking system for production and commerce more broadly. Textile and other plants had to pay for cotton and other resources with grants or loans before they earned income from new production. Metals and chemical plants needed guaranteed deliveries of fuel. Processes had to be in place to assure the equitable distribution elsewhere of raw materials and scarce goods. Markets distorted by speculation had somehow to be controlled. The question now was not whether Russia's near future belonged to capitalism or socialism. It was whether the Government to Save the Revolution could regulate the processes of production and distribution sufficiently at both the local and national level to achieve the needs of society as well as the state.

Many industrialists and commercial figures now doubted that it could. Shortages in many places were becoming more severe or threatening to do so. According to a report sent to the Special Council on Transport in early August, freight shipments on the railroads were off more than 244,000 cars in July compared to 1916. Twenty-five percent of the country's locomotives were out of service, more than five thousand undergoing repair. The important Russian locomotive and mechanical works in Kharkov shut down in August because management claimed it lacked the resources to meet strikers' demands. It laid off six thousand workers and did not reopen until the end of September.[14] The managers of Petrograd's metalworking plants estimated their fuel needs for August to be more than 13 million pounds, almost 175 percent higher than expected deliveries and 50 percent more than the need estimated by the Special Council for Fuel. By the end of the month even defense plants in Petrograd were seriously affected. Production there reportedly dropped more than 30 percent compared to 1916. In the chemicals industry, responsible for gunpowder and other explosives, the decline was almost 40 percent. Without fuel and funding, owners threatened massive new closings, ratcheting up already tense relations with their workers.[15]

Powerful challenges to war capitalism also came from anxious workers themselves. In some ways the intensification of workers' activism was analogous to

[14] RGIA 560.26.1358, ll. 72–73.
[15] TsSU, *Fabrichno-zavodskaia promyshlennost' v period 1913–1918*, vol. 26, no. 1 (Moscow, 1926), 394–403; N. A. Vorob'ev, "Izmeneniia v russkoi promyshlennosti v period voiny i revoliutsii," *Vestnik Statistiki* 14 (1923): 153; *Vestnik Petrogradskago Obshchestva Zavodchikov i Fabrikantov* 20 (July 15, 1917), 1. Detailed lists are in *Ekonomicheskoe Polozhenie*, 2:37–46.

that of village assemblies and peasant soviets that took it upon themselves to seize privately owned land. If peasants rejected the right of ownership in land in favor of the right of possession for those who tilled it, factory workers were increasingly facing the loss of their livelihood by plant owners who were closing their plants or suspending production with little warning and putting them on the streets. Workers in state plants and the railroads were somewhat protected in this regard, but like their private industry comrades they could also be fired with or without cause. The private ownership of factories—of the means of production, as many Marxist activists expressed it—was thus a comparable threat to workers' welfare as private landownership was to peasants. This was particularly the case with the large number of women and recent arrivals from the countryside who replaced drafted workers after 1914.

There were good reasons for workers' concerns, just as there were good reasons for the anxieties of owners. Lockouts and plant closings were both increasing. Unemployment was growing rapidly. From later compilations we know that more than twelve hundred enterprises had already shut down permanently or for some period of time between 1914 and 1916.[16] During the spring and summer of 1917 there were not yet comprehensive figures, but newspapers and other contemporary sources provided dire warnings. The greatest number of workers losing their jobs was in the textile industry (and hence largely women), while the largest number of enterprises was in the food-processing sector (also a large employer of women). Wood and wood product firms failed largely for lack of fuel and materials, or so they reported, while more than ninety metal-processing plants closed their doors for at least some period of time during June, July, and August. According to Ministry of Trade and Industry data published by the Central Statistical Administration in 1925, 560 enterprises closed down throughout the country between March and August, bringing more than 100,000 workers into the ranks of the unemployed.[17] In the aftermath of the July Days, the Ministry of Trade and Industry asked the Factory Inspectorate to inform it immediately regarding factory closings.[18]

Again, one has to be cautious about such statistics. Whatever the correct numbers actually were, however, what mattered for the moment was that reports in virtually every newspaper indicated that plant closings and unemployment were both growing at a rapid pace. Such reports alone could not help but raise workers' anxieties. As least fifty textile plants were shut down in July and August. The large textile plant in Likino stopped work because its owners said they lacked fuel, causing workers to demand that they be considered on leave rather than

[16] TsSU, *Fabrichno-zavodskaia promyshlennost'*, vol. 26, no. 2, 34–36.
[17] Ibid., no. 1, 394–403; N. Ia. Vorob'ev, "Izmeneniia v russkoi promyshlennosti v period voiny i revoliutsii," *Vestnik Statistiki* 14 (1923): 153.
[18] RGIA f. 23, op. 27, d. 357, ll. 1–2; f. 32, op. 1, d. 1885, passim.

fired.[19] The managers of Petrograd's metalworking plants threatened massive closings when their estimated fuel needs for August were almost 175 percent higher than expected deliveries and 50 percent more than the need estimated by the Special Council for Fuel.[20] Freight shipments on the railroads were off more than 244,000 cars in July compared to 1916. Closings escalated by the week. In August, both *Rabochaia Gazeta* and *Novaia Zhizn'* printed a list of almost one hundred plants that had shut down or were planning to.[21]

The anarcho-syndicalist *Golos Truda* saw shutdowns as an intentional effort of collusive plant owners and government officials to make workers hungry, hoping with Riabushinskii that this "bony hand" would help preserve order.[22] The Menshevik trade unionist L. M. Kleinbort also referenced Riabushinskii's "bony hand" when he posited in 1925 that factory closings tripled between March and July, while the number of workers losing their jobs increased eightfold. His statistics, too, may be inaccurate; the consequences he describes of losing one's job are not. In many enterprises workers lived in employee housing; in others they rented space in basement apartments or similar places. In both cases unemployment frequently meant suddenly being homeless as well and, if not reinstated, a trip back to their villages for those who still had this connection or into the ranks of the impoverished unemployed. One of the urgent concerns of Skobelev's Ministry of Labor in mid-July was putting in place an effective state labor exchange. The labor market was disorganized and chaotic, unable to meet the needs of either industry or the unemployed. The effort had the support of the Conference of Trade Unions and the first Congress of Soviets, but both insisted the service be free. The cost was estimated at 500,000 rubles, perhaps more, which neither industry nor the government was willing to bear alone.[23]

In these circumstances workers and plant owners both looked urgently again to Russia's railroads to improve deliveries of food and fuel. Just as in 1915 and 1916, the newly constituted Main Economic Committee in Petrograd once again singled out railroad workers for blame. On August 6 the Mensheviks' *Rabochaia Gazeta* described Russia's "life blood" being choked off by near disastrous operational conditions. "Comrade railroad workers," the newspaper pleaded, "save transport, save the country, save the revolution!"[24]

As we have discussed, the logistical problems for Russian transport were daunting from the very beginning of the war. Efforts to centralize the allocation of locomotives and rolling stock through the Railroad Management Committee

---

[19] GARF f. 6935, op. 6, d. 65, ll. 90–91; d. 114, ll. 1–2; *Ekonomicheskoe Polozhenie*, 1:450–55, 485–87.
[20] *Vestnik Petrogradskago Obshchestva Zavodchikov i Fabrikantov* 20 (July 15, 1917): 1.
[21] *Rabochaia Gazeta*, July 22, Aug. 3, 5, 1917; *Novaia Zhizn'*, Aug. 5, 1917.
[22] *Golos Truda*, Aug. 3, 5, 1917.
[23] GARF f. 6996, op. 1, d. 93, ll. 13–15.
[24] *Rabochaia Gazeta*, Aug. 6, 1917.

had only made matters worse. Yet Minister Nekrasov's efforts at democratizing the railroads to improve operations underestimated the divisions of expertise and authority between different railroad services, such as locomotive brigades, line repair workers, and those who labored in Russia's many railroad shops. The division of lines into sections still delimited by length and now administered by committees compounded the need for central line coordination, as it did in the United States and elsewhere. So did the tendency of engine drivers to personalize their locomotives and resist or prevent others from driving them. The more authority local committees organized by service and sector gained in Russia after February, the more difficult the problem of coordination became. Already in May Nekrasov himself had issued a special order (Circular 6321) setting restraints on committees' autonomous powers and demanding "strict revolutionary discipline." While it officially sanctioned "democratic" railroad committees up and down the lines, these were ostensibly to become local units under the supervision and control of a new All-Russia National Railroad Union and its All-Russia Executive Committee, Vikzhel.

In some ways local railroad committees represented an alternative model of ownership. They had the power to hire and fire, to set priorities for transport, and to administer operations in their sectors. Nekrasov's intention was to centralize these activities through the all-Russia union, situating it as a union of "state significance." As constituent parts of a single national union, local committees would facilitate subordinating the particular interests of its constituent professions to the service of the state, since all railroads themselves were now "the vital nerve of the whole country [as well as] the property of the whole nation," as one major railroad newspaper described them.[25] (As we will see, Lev Trotsky as transport commissar in 1920 would try to do the same with his creation of Tsektran, a central trade union committee charged with reorganizing and controlling the lines.)

The "statization" of Russia's railroad workers in this way distinguished them both as an alternative (some critics said "socialist") model of ownership and of the role of trade unions themselves. When the All-Russia Railroad Union convened its constituent congress in Moscow in the middle of July, the six hundred delegates from every railroad around the country met for forty days debating the core issues of the moment. With some 300,000 railroaders working along six thousand miles of track in quite different professions, the very task of creating an all-Russia union was a daunting one. Whether the union organized by the congress would be a "professional-state" organization or a "purely professional" one was tied directly by congress leaders to the question of whether revolutionary Russia itself would become a broad-based democratic republic founded on the principles of territorial federation and self-government. In the

[25] *Volia i Dumy Zheleznodorozhnika*, May 14, 1917.

expectation that the realities of Russian political life were all pointing in this direction, some thought an all-Russia railroad union should become a constituent part of the federation itself, a "railroad republic." The liberal press saw this as anarcho-syndicalism. The democratic socialist majority at the congress saw it as a possible step toward bringing discipline to the lines and averting the economic catastrophe that was now a key trope in public discourse. At the national level union leaders would work closely with the central government, at the local level with the local organs of self-government. Under the leadership of its executive committee Vikzhel, the railroad republic would effectively put ownership of Russia's "lifeline" in the hands of workers and their union leaders.[26]

Summer Strikes

Among the many achievements of the February revolution were the full legalization of strikes and trade unions, the right of workers to organize and negotiate their needs within their plants, and the freedom of assembly, including the right to public demonstrations that had played a key role in toppling the tsarist regime. The new government deemed it "its sacred duty and responsibility to fulfill the people's hopes and lead the country onto the bright path of free civil organization... executing the will of the people in its honest efforts to ensure the happiness of Russia."[27] When the government and Petrograd Soviet together created a network of mediation boards based on the principles of equal representation and impartial adjudication, there was hope this further institutional achievement would help resolve legal strikes and adjudicate legitimate interests. As we have seen, this effort was strengthened in May when the first coalition's new Ministry of Labor created its special Department for the Resolution of Disputes between Capital and Labor.

The events of early July confused the already tenuous distinction between "legal" and "legitimate." Strictly speaking the demonstrations on July 4 were not illegal. Even garrison soldiers had the right to protest publicly, fully earned, some thought, by their leading role in the February insurrection. Until the demonstrators tried forcefully to replace the existing government with a soviet one, there was also nothing clearly illegitimate about pressing for another change of regime, as in April, especially with the departure of the liberals. What hopelessly blurred the line was the way Bolshevik sailors and workers now asserted the power of collective action, personally endangering cabinet members, bringing

---

[26] GARF f. 6939, op. 6, d. 230, ll. 59–60; *Biulleten' Vseross. Zheleznodorozhnogo Kongressa* 5 (Aug. 1917), covering sessions on July 18, 19, and 20, 1917.
[27] *Vestnik Vremennogo Pravitel'stva*, Mar. 7, 1917.

government momentarily to a halt, and rampaging in the streets. The unproven allegation that German money was at work at the height of the July campaign further tainted legal protest with treason. The intervention of Cossacks and other ostensibly loyal troops that so worried the revolutionaries of February and April was now also legitimized in the new Government to Save the Revolution.

The reactions of industrial and commercial circles blurred the distinction even further. The difference between strikes and other labor actions appropriate to Russia's "bourgeois-democratic" order and "unacceptable" forms of activism disappeared in tainted assumptions about worker radicalism. The struggle for power reflected in strikes was readily understood in terms of Russia's future political and economic order, even its very existence, given the ways in which it accentuated the implications of collapse at the front. The metals section of the Petrograd Society of Factory and Mill Owners saw only anarchy in the July uprising, with no legitimate political or social goals. At the height of the insurrection it seized the moment on these grounds to declare that "all promises, written or oral, given to workers under threat or force are not binding for the enterprise."[28] Riabushinskii expressed the view of even moderate and progressive industrialists when he told an audience of plant owners that "the present revolution is a bourgeois revolution, and this is recognized by all groups on the left. A bourgeois order at the present time is inevitable, and since inevitable, should lead to a completely logical conclusion: those who rule the country must think and act in a bourgeois manner."[29] This meant private owners should have full control of their plants and were entitled to whatever profits they could squeeze out of wartime production. To them, workers' militance simply reflected illegitimate force.

In many places, consequently, workers now found their new demands for wages and improved conditions summarily turned away. Managers of the Vulkan machine works reportedly took pleasure in announcing they were "forced" to cut in half the wages of factory committee members and those elected to other representative organs. Restaurant and tavern owners reneged on concessions they had granted weeks earlier. Leather manufacturers refused to accept a compromise proposed by the Minister of Labor after three weeks of negotiation. Workers felt compelled to resume work when they learned of the owners' refusal.[30] In Moscow coopers were told their wage demands were simply unacceptable. Print shop owners refused to consider any new agreement about wages that would be effective on August 1. Deploring the "aggressive" posture of the Petrograd and Moscow Societies of Factory and Mill Owners, the

---

[28] *Ekonomicheskoe polozhenie*, 1:526, citing TsGA MO f. 186, op. 1, d. 61a, ll. 7–7 ob.
[29] Ibid., 1:200–201, 526.
[30] *Golos kozhevnika* 4–5 (1917); *Ekonomicheskoe Polozhenie*, 1:528; *Rabochaia Gazeta* July 12, Aug. 1, 1917.

metalworkers union concluded that peaceful agreements with its members were now "impossible." It rejected calls to strike because its leaders doubted it would be effective. Plant owners were locking their gates "simply to provoke workers." Militants were playing into their hands.[31] Especially strikes by individual plants were more likely to lead to their closing than to gains for their workers.[32] The same was true in industrial and commercial centers around the county. Donald Raleigh has shown that production in some plants in Saratov fell by 50 percent because of a lack of fuel and materials. Fifteen hundred food-processing workers lost their jobs. Mill workers went on strike only because owners were preparing layoffs, hoping to assure full employment. When the administration of one plant announced it would close because of rising labor costs, among other reasons, the best its workers' committee was able to do was to demand to see the company's financial records. It was not successful.[33]

The weeks between the July Days and the end of the month thus saw a sharp reduction in this key legal form of protest around the country. Between July 7 and July 28, the average number of new strikes fell to 2.4 a day, with an average of fewer than 450 participants, the lowest number of the revolutionary period. Across the country workers' attention through the summer focused almost as much on factory control (40 percent) and other challenges to managerial authority (47 percent) as on wages, something direct actions could do little to resolve. Textile workers in the Moscow region accounted for most of those actually going out on strike, while other regions of Russia now experienced even more strikes over factory issues than the capitals. A strike of Singer sewing machine employees over work conditions spread around the country, and the number of multi-enterprise strikes increased. Workers and their unions sought relative strength in numbers. Some 110,000 Moscow leather workers, for example, demanding a grace period for tardiness and the right to participate in hiring and firing, brought that industry to a brief halt but failed to gain their objectives. Almost one-third of all workers on strike between July 29 and August 28 also sought the right to participate in hiring and firing, reflecting an increasing worry about losing their jobs.[34]

The most important element in this summer cluster was the decreasing effectiveness of strikes. In contrast to the successes of April and May, two-thirds of all strikes in these weeks had failed or compromised outcomes. As conflicts continued in their aftermath, the government issued new legislation on mediation

[31] *Ekonomicheskoe Polozhenie*, 1:528.

[32] Z. V. Stepanov, *Rabochie Petrograd v period podgotovki i provedeniia oktiabr'skogo vooruzhennogo vostaniia* (Moscow: Nauka,1965), 148ff.

[33] Donald J. Raleigh, *Revolution on the Volga: 1917 in Saratov* (Ithaca, NY: Cornell University Press, 1986), 208–9.

[34] Diane P. Koenker and William G. Rosenberg, *Strikes in Russia 1917* (Princeton, NJ: Princeton University Press, 1989) 92–93, 245–52.

boards, designed to encourage their use to prevent or settle further disputes.[35] Many if not most continued to decide in favor of workers. But this was met by increased resistance of factory owners and managers to implementing these decisions, especially after strikes ended without their having to make any concessions. Losing confidence in the boards, workers turned to the state's Factory Inspectorate for help.[36]

At the same time, newspapers in Petrograd and Moscow reported an increase in street actions of various sorts, an indirect result perhaps of the diminishing effectiveness of strikes. The papers' focus seems to have changed from comparable events in the spring. During May and June newspapers commonly reported on crowds attacking thieves and burglars, often beating them without mercy. After the July Days, attacks of this sort still occurred but far less frequently than reports of food protests, attacks on suspected hoarders, even warehouse break-ins by those in search of food and other goods. The reduction in late August in Moscow of the daily bread ration to one-half pound (*funt*) touched off a series of street actions. *Russkoe Slovo* (*Russian Word*) described a crowd in the central district calling authorities to search a building where hoarding was suspected. Elsewhere crowds stopped pushcarts and broke into houses looking for food.[37] When shops ran out of bread in a district just outside the city, demonstrators reportedly threatened to beat officials from the local food supply office and ransacked a nearby meat store.[38] Similar events occurred in these weeks in provincial cities and towns where food insecurity now was also at high levels, although for some, proximity to grain-producing areas might have tempered their extent.

Beleaguered Ministries: Labor, Trade and Industry, and Finance

While the Great Stories largely focus on the political importance of the July Days and the arrest of Lenin, these were not the matters that preoccupied those in the government most concerned with averting Russia's socioeconomic collapse. In addition to its pledge to expand the number of land committees and that agrarian reform would be based on transferring land to those who worked it, the programmatic declaration of July 7 ordered the Main Economic Committee and its Economic Council to start working immediately on a general plan

---

[35] R. Browder and A. F. Kerensky, eds., *The Russian Provisional Government: Documents*, 3 vols. (Stanford, CA: Stanford University Press, 1961), 2:843–43.
[36] RGIA f. 23, op. 29, d. 1, ll. 78–79.
[37] *Russkoe Slovo*, Aug. 26, Sept. 2, 1917.
[38] *Russkoe Slovo*, Aug. 26, 1917; *Trudovaia Kopeika*, Sept. 6, 1917.

to "regulate economic life and the control of industry."[39] Almost immediately petitions and complaints about the lack of food and fuel began to flood into the Ministries of Labor, Trade and Industry, and Finance, demanding some sort of relief. (The work of the Ministry of Transport, now headed by the Moscow Kadet Peter Iurenev, was largely dominated by the six weeklong meetings of the All-Russia Railroad Congress.) The Ministries of Food and Agriculture received new complaints about "extreme need" in urban areas as well as excesses of landowners in the countryside, but the heaviest burdens fell on the Ministries of Labor, Trade and Industry, and Finance. And the most pressure fell on Mikhail Skobelev, still the minister of labor.

As we have seen, Skobelev's energy in May and June had been devoted overwhelmingly to mediating labor-management conflict. More than 550 separate disputes had been brought to the ministry's Section on Mutual Relations between Labor and Capital. Liberal newspapers like Moscow's *Russkiia Vedomosti* hoped the ministry would secure "an armistice in class warfare," while "the interests of workers, until recently the weakest group in society, will now be protected in appropriate fashion."[40] After the July Days, mediation became especially difficult. When the young minister initiated discussions about refining strike legislation and invited industrialists to approach the question "from the point [of view] of the state, having in mind the interests of Russian industry as a whole," participants from the Council of Industrial Congresses demanded that legislation governing the workers' right to strike should give employers the right to strike as well, "on the principle of equal rights for both sides."[41]

Skobelev along with the soviet's Executive Committee member Kuz'ma Gvozdev, who had headed the workers' section of the CWIC, were particularly embattled as they pressed for peaceful settlements. A common complaint from workers in July and August was that employers were failing to honor their contracts and refusing to submit the issue to mediation boards. In some instances individual firms refused to accept broader agreements entered into by owner associations. Other firms tried to tie compliance to labor productivity despite shortages of fuel and materials. Workers at the large Treugol'nik rubber plant demanded the right to stop work on the day before all holidays. Their plant soon shut down along with eleven others, due, management said, to lack of fuel, materials, and financing.[42] When strikes threatened defense production in Kharkov and Kiev, Skobelev and Gvozdev, who would become minister of labor in September, intervened with local soviets to secure agreements.

---

[39] *Vestnik Vremmenago Pravitel'stva*, July 8, 1917, translated in Browder and Kerensky, *Russian Provisional Government*, 3:1386–87.
[40] *Russkiia Vedomosti*, May 11, 1917.
[41] GARF f. 4100, op. 2, d. 12, l. 11.
[42] RGIA f. 150, op. 2, d. 50, ll. 9, 14; op. 1, d. 567, ll. 5–6.

Their efforts failed. In Kiev the enterprises in question closed, encouraging directors of the important Kharkov locomotive works to hold firm in their refusal to yield to wage demands. When their workers then seized the plant (and some of its administrators) in an effort to continue working, the industrialists' association appealed directly to Kerensky to take "decisive measures."[43] At the end of July, Skobelev traveled to the Volga region to avert a shipping strike, and to Baku at the oil firm's request to head off a major war with Caspian oil workers. Skobelev thought he had brokered a settlement, but as soon as he left the firms demanded that the state itself pick up their new wage costs, and the agreement collapsed.[44] Toward the end of August the harried minister took it upon himself to declare that only plant owners and their staffs could hire and fire their employees, undermining what many local unions and factory committees regarded as their most important weapon against layoffs. He also proposed the introduction of labor books (*razchetnye knigi*) that would effectively keep track of individual workers' employment and regulate relations with their employers.[45]

Labor activism also prompted a deluge of complaints to the Ministry of Trade and Industry, now headed for the first time by a social democrat, Sergei Prokopovich. An early critic of Bolshevism, Prokopovich was well known for opposing Lenin's views about the inevitability of social conflict and its progressive historical role. From the industrialists' perspective, not having the Moscow industrialist Konovalov as minister was itself a source of alienation. The Conference of Representatives of Trade and Industry had pressed for the appointment of S. N. Tretiakov, president of the Moscow Stock Exchange, as minister of trade and industry. (When Prokopovich was appointed instead, Tretiakov became chair of the Main Economic Committee and its Economic Council.) The key issues here were still the dire scarcity of fuel, what they regarded as unreasonable wage demands, the interference of committees in hiring and firing, and especially workers' demand for access to financial records in order to confirm whether their plants truly lacked adequate financial resources.

The dominant anxiety, as it was expressed at large gatherings of trade industrialists in July and August, was that the revolution was "spiraling out of control," beyond the ability of Russia's economically powerful groups to contain it. Representatives from owners' associations employing almost a million workers in some two thousand firms and fourteen major industrial centers joined their Petrograd and Moscow colleagues in stressing the urgent need for financing, fuel, and workplace control. From Kiev came a demand for an end to the government's "improvisational" methods; from Ekaterinoslav, help in

---

[43] *Ekonomicheskoe Polozhenie*, 1:490–91; Koenker and Rosenberg, *Strikes*, 253–54.
[44] *Bakinskii Rabochii*, Aug. 6, 1917.
[45] RGIA f. 560, op. 26, d. 1358, ll. 183–91.

resisting workers' demands for a 100 percent increase in wages; from Revel, despair over the absence of raw materials and fuel; from Petrograd, Moscow, Kharkov, Kazan, and elsewhere, the need to unify and coordinate financing and the distribution of materials and supplies. The Petrograd Society of Factory and Mill Owners demanded that the Ministry of Trade and Industry intervene directly in talks with the city's metallists. First and foremost was the necessity of "strong measures" for maintaining factory discipline and "regulating relations between labor and capital."[46] The Petrograd Society of Factory and Mill Owners, now representing almost eighty enterprises, reported a number of fires and demanded military force to protect their plants.[47]

New wage demands were a special concern. A long report to the Ministry of Trade and Industry prepared by N. N. Kutler for the Council of Industrial Congresses (Soviet S"ezdov) detailed his view that workers' wage demands threatened not only profits but firms' entire capital, including current accounts and working capital. According to his calculations, the average increase for one worker, including women and youth, had already reached 2,600 rubles, whereas the annual average wage for one worker in 1914 was 500 rubles and as recently as February had reached only 1,000. In three weeks' time, he warned, enterprises would be closing one after another. In Kutler's view, the question for plant owners was not one of profits, although private enterprise could not survive very long without them. It was whether the state could protect the foundations of industry from destruction.[48] In distant Omsk a regional board forbade the export of any manufactured goods out of the region because of a torrent of "requisitions."[49]

Thus Nekrasov, now minister of finance as well as Kerensky's deputy president, was also inundated with appeals from businesses, most demanding that the reconstructed government provide funds to pay wage demands, buy raw materials, secure fuel, and stay open. The directors of Bromley and Dinamo in Moscow, Langenzippen and Lessner in Petrograd, and the Donets iron fabricating plant all pressured for direct assistance. In the case of Bromley, the directors' decision to shut down in July was reversed only by a direct grant of 2 million rubles. Sormovo's administrators said they could not stay open with less than 10 million rubles.[50] The most pressing cases were urgent appeals by plant owners and factory committees for direct financial assistance to keep enterprises open and adequately supplied. In some cases workers demanded their plants be nationalized, assuming the state would then meet their needs.[51]

[46] RGIA f. 150, op. 1, d. 428, ll. 12–29ff.; d. 557, l. 206; f. 4100, op. 1, d. 63, ll. 1–28.
[47] RGIA f. 150, op. 1, d. 7, ll. 2–6.
[48] RGIA, f. 32, op. 1, d. 1865, ll. 1–5.
[49] RGIA, f. 23, op. 7, d. 731, ll. 8–10.
[50] *Ekonomicheskoe Polozhenie*, 1:392, 597.
[51] RGIA, f. 150, op. 1, d. 557, ll. 105–8; GARF f. 4100, op. 1, d. 16, ll. 1–2, and passim; d. 18, l. 9, passim.

Meanwhile the Ministry of Finance through the State Bank was now riding on a "flood of money," as *Russkiia Vedomosti* described it on August 1. Nekrasov's Ministry of Finance reported a huge shortfall in government revenues through the first seven months of 1917.[52] During the interregnum between the July uprising and the formation of the new government the legal limit on currency emissions was increased by another 2 billion rubles. The U.S. consul in Petrograd had written already in June about a "ruble panic," but one problem among many, according to the Ministry of Foreign Affairs, now seeking additional loans from Paris, London, and Washington, was that the additional emissions could not be printed in such enormous amounts.[53] On August 3 the Mensheviks' leading newspaper *Rabochaia Gazeta* jointed the liberal press in warning that Russia itself was faced with bankruptcy.[54]

War Capitalism and the Revolutionary State

Every warring power shared some elements of war capitalism in their pursuit of a victory in the Great War: state financing of defense industries through purchases or direct grants; war profits for owners in favored sectors and contraction for most of the rest; constraints on labor along with labor protests; and scarcities as well as rationing of foodstuffs. Austrians suffered the threat of famine as well as its actualities. The British blockade constricted trade and productivity, while the centralization of economic planning in Germany and elsewhere was a model to some for the special councils created in 1915. What distinguished Russia before the February revolution were insufficient internal revenues and foreign loans to fund the war, an inadequate railroad lifeline that covered the empire's huge territory and whose line from Moscow to Vladivostok became its principal supply route, a partly commercialized countryside with value systems that still privileged collective possession of land over individual ownership, and the absence of any effective mechanism to resolve labor-management disputes or other social conflicts. Whether war capitalism would have been sufficient to carry the tsarist government through the war or whether the internal problems it faced were intractable is a moot question whose possible answers require too many counterfactuals to be analytically useful. After February, however, it is clear that these problems increased exponentially as the new managers of the revolutionary state pressed to meet the social interests and welfare interests of Russia's population at large: peasants in their quest for land, workers in their quest for dignity

---

[52] RGIA, f. 560, op. 26, d. 1359, l. 120; *Ekonomicheskoe Polozhenie*, 2:382–87.
[53] *Ekonomicheskoe Polozhenie*, 2:377.
[54] *Rabochaia Gazeta*, Aug. 3, 1917.

and the means to meet the challenges of scarcity and inflation, and a diverse propertied stratum which found itself struggling with a widening social and cultural divide in which its own welfare was rapidly subordinated to that of increasingly antagonistic adversaries. The purpose of the war itself in these circumstances had to be reformulated in ways that justified its horrific losses, something that set revolutionary Russia clearly apart from its allies and enemies alike.

One of the striking characteristics of Russia's sudden transition from tsarist autocracy to democratic republicanism was how symptoms of economic and social distress had deteriorated so quickly in a few short months—an acceleration of time and compression of events that must have exhausted activists on all side. After the failure of Kerensky's and Brusilov's offensives and the July Days crisis, the revolutionary state was managed by the antithesis of ministers in whom the country had confidence. Contending with the power located in demonstrations and local collective actions of all sorts, the revised coalition government was pressed even further to resolve Russia's socioeconomic problems and the cultural polarizations they reflected, as the torrent of petitions to its ministries demonstrated.

In this important respect the endorsement by the rump government after the July demonstrations were repressed of key socialist positions in the July 8 Declaration shifted it away from nonpartisanship into overt support for the "democratic" interests of workers and peasants, now broadly understood in social rather than political terms: workers in their demands for higher wages and greater factory control, peasants in their efforts to possess communally the individual property of Russia's rural landowners and to control the grains and other foodstuffs they produced. While the Declaration blocked the formation of a new cabinet for two weeks and was formally walked back, its effect was not only to further mobilize factory owners in defense of their own interests but to mobilize them behind the notion that theirs were also the interests of state and society at large.

Meanwhile, appeals to the state for relief that now came to the government from all sides taxed its role in mediating disputes, its regulatory powers, and its resources. Skobelev's mediation efforts in the Ministry of Labor were compromised by demands from all sides that state resources be applied directly to meet their own "extreme needs." This meant restoring public order, controlling factory and village violence, financing production and ensuring its timely delivery, and especially relieving scarcities in food and other essential goods compromised the values of political democracy that the revolutionary state itself ostensibly represented. In the spring Transport Minister Nekrasov had used the concept of "statization" to describe how he intended a national railroad union to position its economic and political goals in support of the interests of the state, of which they were declared a component part. For many workers what statization came to mean by August was that the government itself should take on the full responsibility for keeping their factories open and paying their wages.

From all sides as well came new demands for state funding, significantly beyond the levels supporting war capitalism before February. Since March all government contracts had been revised upward to cover an estimated 400 percent increase over 1916 in the costs of materials and labor. According to estimates presented to the new Economic Council by G. D. Dement'ev from the Ministry of Finance, the additional drain on the state treasury was likely to be several billion rubles. War expenditures had increased even more, as much as 10 billion rubles during the first six months of 1917. Estimates for the whole year were now three times as high, partly because of support for the flood of refugees escaping the new offensive, partly because requisitions in the war zone were further affecting production, and partly because of increased allowances to soldiers' families, which were now likely to reach 11 billion rubles by January 1918.[55] Somewhat less of a draw was estimated to support the state's grain monopoly, but this was also likely to be more than a billion rubles. When the estimate of a total deficit of some 31 billion rubles was compared to projected income and state reserves, there was a gap of 13 billion. The sum seemed impossible to cover, given the disappointing returns from the Liberty Loan and the likely economic and political consequences of additional taxation. When it was added to Russia's total state debt, that figure would rise to 60 billion rubles or more, a sum requiring 3 billion rubles simply to service. "What is the chance," the Economic Council was asked, "that the state could find this amount for 1917, much less the still unknown billions that will be needed for 1918?"[56] Some on the Economic Council questioned the estimates. Finding accurate data was still a great problem. As late as July neither the Ministry of Finance nor the State Comptroller's Office had accurate final income and expense figures for 1915.[57]

Within and outside the Finance Ministry and the Economic Council some continued to press for maximum taxation: a revision upward of the new war profits tax enacted in early June; an extraordinary income tax; indirect sales taxes; even an "obligatory loan" imposed on those with high incomes that the state would eventually repay. In the Economic Council as well as the press, these were all rejected. The nonpayment of existing taxes was already substantial, and the accuracy of tax and income audits could hardly be assured. Measures like these were only likely to cause even more plant closings and social conflict. Instead, pressured by some localities that reported insufficient currency

---

[55] G. D. Dement'ev, *Gosudarstvennye dokhody i razkhody i polozhenie gosudarstvennago kaznacheistva za vremia voiny* (Petrograd, 1917), 28, 32.
[56] Ibid., 33; K. Shmelev, "1914–1918 gg. i financy Rossii," *Vestnik Finansov* 8 (Aug. 1924): 6–24.
[57] RGIA, f. 1276, op. 12, d. 224, passim; 32, op. 1, d. 1855, ll. 1–23; A. Michelson et al., *Russian Public Finance during the War* (New Haven, CT: Yale University Press, 1928), 192–94.

even to conduct most normal transactions, the Ministry of Finance was left with what was still regarded as its least worst remedy: to issue still more currency denominated as credit notes.[58] Some 2 billion rubles were added to those in circulation, increasing by six times the amount at the beginning of the war. As *Russkiia Vedomosti* described it, the country was being inundated by a flood of paper money that the state printing press simply could not supply fast enough. One immediate result was the effect of this on both fixed and unfixed prices, lowering the value of the first and raising the level of the second, further weakening the processes of commercial market exchange. Another was its effect on the ruble in the international currency market. In a single week it dropped some 25 percent against the English pound.[59] The American consul in Petrograd, who earlier had enthused with City Bank's H. F. Meserve about Russian investment opportunities, now described a "ruble panic" in his cable to Washington.[60]

Accurate data or not, by midsummer there was no question that state support for an economy still based in principle on investment capital and market exchange—a key element of war capitalism—was tenuous at best. Even the most generous allocations would likely not stimulate new private investment or prevent many plants from closing. Not surprisingly, people of wealth were already transferring their assets to safer havens abroad, making contingency plans for their families. Requisitions and confiscations were above all interactions between people. So were the engagements on shop floors or retail stores that owners felt were likely to destroy their own livelihoods as well as those of their clients or employees. Where factory committees suspected owners of selling off materials and preparing to close, owners were denied control of their plant. No goods were permitted for shipment without the committees' permission. Workers militias were expanding in part to enforce committee decrees to the point that many industrialists thought they were impossible to disband. Some twenty-four hundred workers at the Geiferikh Sade plant in Kharkov, for example, drove out its entire administrative staff when the factory's owners threatened to close, selling off movable property themselves to pay wages while their factory committee audaciously appealed for loans from a local credit society and the Moscow Narodnyi Bank.[61]

Among other results was panic selling by commercial traders and others to avoid having their goods confiscated.[62] In Kursk, during a "special investigation" of their business, the owners of Chernov and Sons trading company were

---

[58] RGIA, f. 23, op. 7, d. 738, ll. 25–31.
[59] *Russkiia Vedomosti*, Aug. 1, 1917.
[60] Browder and Kerensky, *Russian Provisional Government*, 2:510.
[61] RGIA f. 23, op. 27, d. 357, l. 6. On the guards and militias, see esp. Rex Wade, *Red Guards and Workers' Militias in the Russian Revolution* (Stanford, CA: Stanford University Press, 1984).
[62] RGIA f. 23, op. 7, d. 409, ll. 35–46 and passim; d. 731, ll. 1–10.

humiliated by long interrogations, forbidden to enter their firm, and threatened with being hanged, echoing Lenin's call at the June Congress of Soviets for aggressive action.[63] The sense of unfairness which the cultures of war capitalism had engendered in broad swaths of the rural and urban population was now finding its expression in getting one's "due" by whatever means were available. It is likely that popular anger over the gap between privilege and need was growing even faster than the difference itself. States of anxiety loomed as heavily over Russia's propertied groups as it did over the workplace and the village.

While this emotional distress cannot be measured, what was being lost here was not only profits, property, and workplace livelihoods but the whole system of war capitalism, with all of its attendant social, economic, and cultural deformations. This was not, as one observer put it, because proprietors were evil, as many were being told: "On the contrary, it was in their interests to do everything to save the situation. It was instead a natural death caused by an extreme lack of economic blood."[64] G. D. Dement'ev from the Ministry of Finance now agreed with *Rabochaia Gazeta*: the revolutionary state faced bankruptcy.[65] Like the industrialist Riabushinskii, the Menshevik stalwart Tsereteli now hoped "anxiety and fear about the fate of the revolution" might "stir the people to save it," but there was no indication whatsoever that the "bony hand of hunger," as Riabushinskii had put it, was bringing the "false friends of the revolution to their senses," or anyone else for that matter.[66]

Meanwhile, programs for the nationalization of production were formulated in various places. The Central Committee of the Metal Workers Union adopted a program in mid-July that, among other things, called for the compulsory amalgamation of industrial enterprises into state-controlled trusts, state control over banks and the processes of capitalizing production, and the compulsory transfer under state control of production resources from branches and plants with surpluses to those with deficits.[67] Workers at the Franco-Russian Fel'zer and Co. in Nizhnii Novgorod appealed for their plant to be nationalized as the only way to guarantee their living.[68] They wanted the state to take it over because the plant could not meet workers' demands. Production had fallen by some 50 percent since February.[69] Rather than calling on industrialists for "sacrifice, sacrifice, sacrifice," as liberals like Shingarev had insisted, industrialists and others in

---

[63] RGIA f. 23, op. 7, d. 408, ll. 4–28; d. 731, ll. 1–10.
[64] RGIA f. 32, op. 1, d. 1885, l. 8.
[65] *Stenograficheskii otchet zasedaniia ekonomicheskago soveta* 5 (July 31, 1917): 2–12.
[66] *Rabochaia Gazeta*, July 28, 1916; *Vtoroi vserossiiskii torgovo-promyshlennyi s"ezd v Moskve 3–5 avg. 1917* (Moscow, 1917), 8.
[67] GARF f. 5469, op. 1, d. 4, ll. 7–8.
[68] RGIA f. 23, op. 7, d. 408, ll. 4–15.
[69] *Vestnik Petrogradskago Obshchestva Zavodchikov i Fabrikantov* 3 (June 6, 1917).

commerce around the country demanded that the state align itself firmly with them and the "stronger" elements of society, their military allies.

At the same time, reports continued to come from all quarters about the interference of state and soviet officials locally in the requisitioning of scarce goods and their continued disregard for directives from the center. First among those accused by plant owners and traders were local soviets, food committees, and "legions" of newly appointed commissars from Petrograd and Moscow: issuing orders, confiscating goods, interfering in individual enterprises, even setting local prices sometimes in cooperation with local soviets and other groups, sometimes on their own. A long report from the Kursk Trade Industrial Union on July 29 described the "critical and absolutely intolerable situation" of the local soviet executive committee implementing economic "economic reform energetically... without any consideration of the interests of the state or law and justice, not to mention science."[70]

Shortages of goods also continued to be "solved" by requisitions and outright confiscation, sometimes assisted by soldiers returning from the front. Local soviets were seizing scarce consumer goods illegally. Requisitions in one region reportedly paralyzed the activities of all branches of trade. Demanding lower fixed prices, higher wage levels, and control over distribution from the government, local soviet authorities proceeded to enact these changes on their own.[71] Those most often accused by provincial workers and peasants were the agents of the state itself. Sometimes accompanied by soldiers, government commissars seized stores and set fixed prices on their own. They carried an air of authority more like their tsarist predecessors, some of whom were among their number, than agents of revolutionary change and material well-being.[72]

By August the political implications of all this seemed clear. The July Days had thrown down a gauntlet before the revolutionary regime. For democratic socialists, the conceptual framework of a bourgeois revolution as a necessary stage toward a fully socialist order was breaking down. For democratic liberals, a commitment to democratic norms was being shaken. For many, even the hope that elections to the Constituent Assembly, now postponed until November, would produce a constitution that embodied the basic norms of a rule of law, created a strong democratic state, and embodied liberal norms and values seemed rather naïve.

On July 12, as Kerensky and the remaining ministers were struggling to reconstitute the coalition government, they decided to convene an All-Russia State Conference in Moscow from August 12 to 14. Representatives of all major

---

[70] RGIA f. 560, op. 26, d. 1358, ll. 97–98, 138; f. 23, op. 7, d. 408, ll. 1–22.
[71] RGIA f. 23, op. 7, d. 732, ll. 8ff.
[72] Ibid., ll. 408–9; d. 739, ll. 9ff.

political, public, industrial, commercial, and nationality groups were invited to attend. Special invitations were sent to the army's leadership, chairs of the four State Dumas, and soviet leaders. The Central Soviet Executive Committee agreed its members would participate. Fearing political conflict would only be further exacerbated, the liberals were opposed but willing to attend. The Bolshevik Central Committee saw the meeting as a step toward consolidating the forces of counterrevolution and refused. Fearing a repeat of the July Days, the commander of the Moscow military district General Verkhovskii ordered troops deployed in support of the Moscow Soviet's proscription against "unorganized protests and demonstrations." When the delegates began arriving at the Bolshoi Theater, they passed through a cordon of troops.[73]

They also had to walk. Instead of demonstrating, tens of thousands of Moscow workers went on a one-day protest strike to focus attention on their circumstances. Trams stopped running. Cafés and restaurants closed. Cab drivers, leather workers, metallists, and those from the city power station stopped work, along with members of virtually every other industrial and commercial sector. Well over 100,000 apparently took part. Comparable protest strikes occurred in Kiev, Tsaritsyn, Samara, Petrograd, Kostroma, and other places around the country, many encouraged if not organized by local Bolsheviks. The message Lenin's supporters wanted to send to the conference was that the coercive state power of counterrevolution would be met by the massive power of popular protest. *Tak zhit' dalee, nel'zia!* The message striking workers hoped the state conference would heed was that the Government to Save the Revolution must attend to their pressing needs.

At this very moment German troops were advancing toward Riga on the road to Petrograd, threatening the very existence of the revolutionary state.

---

[73] *Vestnik Vremennago Pravitel'stva*, July 13, 1917; *Rech'*, Aug. 12, 1917; *Izvestiia*, Aug. 13, 1917; *Russkie Vedomosti*, Aug. 12, 1917.

12
Democratic Predicaments and the Bolshevik Coup

Scarcity, Loss, and Politics at the Moscow State Conference

Perhaps no event better illustrates the disconnect in 1917 between the pace of political and socioeconomic change than the Moscow State Conference. During the July Days the divide was reflected implicitly in the unrestrained passions of the street. At the State Conference, it was articulated clearly in the focus of speakers on the imperatives of law and order.

By invitation, the presidents of each of the four state Dumas between 1906 and 1917 were present, along with Generals Kornilov, Alekseev, and Brusilov from the High Command. Soviet leaders, political parties, religious and university organizations, and prominent trade industrial organizations were also asked to send representatives. Peasants and workers were represented by leaders of their national associations and trade unions as well as soviets. Among the parties, only the Bolsheviks were absent. All four tiers of the Bolshoi Theater were filled to overflowing.

The formal purpose of the conference was informational: to "hide nothing" about the "breakdown, disintegration, and potential ruin of our Motherland," as Kerensky put it in his opening address. Its goal was to rally the country in support of the army and General Kornilov's efforts to restore discipline, and to reaffirm the premises on which the Provisional Government had initially assumed state power. The situation was "very grave," a time of "deadly danger." The army was proving unable to stop the German advance toward Riga and Petrograd, weakened by "those who have once already attempted to raise their armed hand against the people's government." Finnish and Ukrainian nationalism could "spell ruin." The details of economic life showed "a picture of great collapse."[1] What made the greatest impression on many participants, however, as it has later on historians, was not any reassertion of the values of nonpartisanship on which the government had originally been formed but the fiery speeches of Kerensky,

---

[1] *Gosudarstvennoe Soveshchenie* (Moscow: Gosizdat, 1930), 3–16; excerpts in Robt. Browder and Alexander Kerensky, eds., *The Russian Provisional Government 1917: Documents*, 3 vols. (Stanford, CA: Stanford University Press, 1961), 3: 1451–522.

Supreme Commander Kornilov, and Cossack ataman General Kaledin, insisting in the strongest terms on a "ruthless struggle against anarchy," one that Kornilov himself was attempting to implement at the front.

Kornilov disparaged the soldiers under his command in particularly harsh words considering the causalities endured during the June offensive. Some soldiers had "become animals," attacking their commanders in a "nightmarish atmosphere of irrational, hideous tribalism, of interminable ignorance and abominable hooliganism."[2] Kaledin's Cossacks, on the other hand, who were well known in the military zone for their brutalities against Jews and other civilians, were "fulfilling their historic mission of serving the Motherland with arms in hand, both on the battlefield and inside the country in the struggle against treason and betrayal." To "tempestuous applause," according to the transcript, Kerensky himself warned any new insurrections against the government "will be stopped with iron and blood." Along with this bravado he also appealed for sacrifice and patriotism, echoing the famous State Duma session at the start of the war. Instead of sacrifice "for Tsar and Fatherland," which had brought tens of thousands to their knees three years and 4.5 million casualties earlier, Kerensky called for the patriotic will to "fulfill one's duty" in defense of law, order, and the revolutionary state. When General Kornilov then promised the state would engage a "ruthless struggle against anarchy" and Kaledin declared that the "usurpation of state power" by committees and soviets "must be ended immediately" and labor conscription begun, no one in the hall or reading the newspaper transcripts could have missed the threats of martial law and military dictatorship.[3]

The only speaker to offer a sustained look at the longer arc of combat and frontline conditions since 1914 was Grigori Dmitrievich Kuchin, who represented army and front-line committees and whose very appearance at the rostrum on the last day of the conference caused an uproar. A graduate in economics from the juridical faculty of St. Petersburg University and a Menshevik activist, three times arrested before 1917, Kuchin was an artillery officer and delegate to the first Congress of Soviets. (He would later serve in the Red Army before being arrested for the second time in 1935 and shot.) Fresh from the fighting near Riga, Kuchin confronted directly the issues of demoralization and resistance at the front: the effects of scarce supplies on soldiers' morale; the impact of Minister of War Sukhomlinov's arrest for treason; incompetent commanders; and especially the feeling among soldiers that huge losses, brutal combat, and the traumas they had suffered since the beginning of the war were in vain. The revolution had promised peace and the end to senseless bloody offensives. In this crucial sense, the June offensive was more than a profound disappointment for both soldiers

---

[2] *Gosudarstvennoe Soveshchenie*, 61–62.
[3] Ibid., 74–76.

and their families. In Kuchin's view, soldiers' committees were the only way the rank and file had regained some confidence in their officers after February. Suppressing the committees would only compound soldiers' disaffection. The soldiers might appear to be submissive; silent submission had long been a key element of soldiers' lives at the front. But this would hardly make the army more healthy. Even more soldiers would simply desert. The effects of suffering and loss at the front had less to do with a lack of patriotism or willingness to sacrifice than it did with incompetence, corruption, concern about the well-being of families, and the failure of both the tsarist and revolutionary regimes to justify the war's horrific human costs even in defense of Russia's lands and peoples. Here was where the real danger lay for Russia's future.[4]

According to the transcripts, Kuchin's speech was received with jeers and cries of "Shame!" from the right, applause and "Bravo!" from the left. (It was not included by Kerensky and Browder in their translated excerpts of the conference proceedings.) In contrast, most other spokesmen at the meeting complemented Kerensky's and Kornilov's emphasis on law and order. Conservative liberals like Guchkov and Maklakov were emphatic in denying that their or the government's efforts were in defense of partisan class interests. Russia's leaders had shouldered the "historic responsibility" of suppressing their "personal and class interests to save the Fatherland" (Nabokov); this responsibility also lay heavily "on the people without power" (Guchkov), and the only way forward was through "rational governance, without utopia, sins, and mistakes" (Maklakov). In terms of the larger Great Story narratives, however, the two most interesting speeches were those of Iraklii Tsereteli and Paul Miliukov, the leading democratic socialist and democratic liberal, and the out-of-order polemic between them that followed Miliukov's presentation (also omitted in the English-language transcripts). Each saw Russia's current crisis through longer-term historical lenses, laying out competing narratives structured ideologically by their party programs and deeply set historical imaginations.

Speaking in the name of all soviet organizations, Tsereteli first refuted the liberal argument that the task of the government was to act independently of the social forces which had so far supported it and the revolutionary state. February demonstrated clearly the power imminent in popular protest, which brought down the monarchy and imbued the government with its legitimacy and authority. The revolutionary task was to organize and channel this power in support of a great free people, Russia's promised future (*budushchnost'*). The revolution saved the country in February. "Only the consciousness and power of the organized popular masses" in support of the provisional regime could save it now. Advancing a core Menshevik position, Tsereteli also accepted that the revolution

---

[4] Ibid., 212–18.

was historically premature, brought on by the war rather than the evolutionary processes of state and social development. Tsereteli understood, however, how difficult it actually was to maintain this support. Ordinary people had made great sacrifices, experienced grave losses. They had taken up the heaviest burdens in the struggle to defend the revolution and its freedoms. In return, the government and Russia's propertied elements had to complete the revolution's essential tasks by supporting the platform of revolutionary democracy. The well-being of the people and the task of saving the country from collapse were one and the same, "synonyms inseparable from each other."[5]

Miliukov's focus continued to be on the state and its institutional power, the key instrument of historical progress in the liberal imagination. He disparaged "so-called" revolutionary democracy in this respect (provoking laughter from the left, according to the transcript). The revolution owed its victory not to the popular masses but to the State Duma, "which united the whole people." Organizing the democracy, as Tsereteli had put it, could not save the revolution from the "disastrous consequences of its own mistakes." Parties and partisanship, the "seeds of all that has happened," were "sown from the start before the formation of the first coalition, when parties organized to fight for partisan gains." The army itself had capitulated to this destructive process.

As in 1914 and often afterward, a key question was who was to blame. First and foremost Miliukov asserted it was the Bolsheviks and others with a "Zimmerwald mindset," one that wanted to turn a foreign war into a civil war like Lenin and the radical wing of anti-war socialists gathered at the Swiss town in 1915. The Petrograd Soviet's Declaration of Soldiers' Rights and other such manifestos aided and abetted their efforts. Now the responsibility of the revolutionary state was to ensure law and order. In a dramatic turnaround from his opposition to the Soviet's use of the concept in March, Miliukov declared that the Kadet Party would support the current coalition government only "insofar as" it does not compromise "bourgeois" interests. The authority of the government was not divisible. The strength of the Russian state depended not on the government's implementing this or that partisan program but on its readiness to maintain order and subordinate to itself not only an internal sense of moral conviction but the external means of coercion as well.

In an impromptu rejoinder, Tsereteli forcefully disagreed. The army itself could not be mobilized any longer around Miliukov's idea of a strong state, only around goals that soldiers considered revolutionary. Support for popular welfare and political democracy was not partisanship, but the declared goal now of the war itself. To restore "rational discipline" in the army and elsewhere, democratic organs had to preserve their influence and set a clear example. Democratic

---

[5] Ibid., 118–27.

socialists well understood the dangers from the left as well as the right: "I say to you: the revolution was not experienced in the struggle with anarchy coming from the left [stormy applause] but as soon as that danger became a real threat and the first lessons were learned, the revolution did not resist any measures to secure freedom and the country from this danger." Still, "irresponsible action" from the right—from Kornilov and Kaledin, in other words—is where the "real danger" lay.[6]

What is notable here is not simply the implicit translation by Tsereteli and Miliukov of this perilous moment in Russia's revolutionary development into broader narratives of Russian historical progress. The two political leaders also set out how and why later tellings of the revolution's Great Stories focused on the politics of political conspiracy as the forces standing in the way of revolutionary Russia's democratic fulfillment—the "only forces," in Kerensky's own later telling. Even more notable was the failure in both Tsereteli's and Miliukov's presentations to contextualize the moment in terms of the still unresolved problems of scarcity and loss that directly underlay the overthrow of tsarism: the effects of shortages in food and other essential goods; the further unraveling of the economy; the accompanying anxieties about the disintegration of social and political order; the effects on peasant households of the war; the plight of refugees who had been pillaged, raped, and displaced, and were now seen in some places as a burden to the communities where they resettled; and the assault, finally, on educated and propertied Russians that created the suffering of social and cultural dislocation that complemented in a way the more literal shell shock experienced at the front. Vladimir Nabokov, the great writer's father, declared it was the government's historic responsibility to lead Russia out of this "terrible blind alley."[7]

But what *were* the solutions to these problems in midsummer of 1917? More pointedly, were there any workable solutions at all? Of the eighty-five speakers at the Moscow Conference, a handful spoke directly to the material and emotional dimensions of scarcity that were affecting social and political order top to bottom, even fewer to the emotional scars borne by deserting soldiers and desperate refugees. There were detailed descriptions of confiscations by local committees and other authorities, the assaults on landowners and their property, the failure of local courts to maintain order, and the consequences for industry and the country at large of the indiscriminate tarring of the "bourgeoisie"— "the brains and will of the country," according to one speaker—as "enemies of the revolution. The weaponizing of language, mastered by the Bolsheviks, was clearly intensifying the nature of social identities and social conflict. Among the themes that ran through many of the presentations was the call for a universal

---

[6] Ibid., 128–34.
[7] Ibid., 46.

compulsory labor obligation, the militarization in effect of Russia's entire workforce that would essentially nationalize labor by making work analogous to service in the army. Russia's railroad lifeline was especially singled out for this requirement., which would replace the committee structure Transport Minister Nekrasov had sanctioned in the spring with a more "lawful administration." One speaker suggested that compulsory service also be required of the "capitalists," whose plants would then be forced to operate twenty-four hours a day and whose profits would be limited to the percentage return on the Liberty Loan. Another suggested the "laboring intelligentsia" be immediately drafted into state service in the same way.[8]

The only comprehensive efforts to address the economic crisis in its own terms were made by Nikolai Chkheidze and Nikolai Kondrat'ev, the well-respected twenty-five-year-old socialist economist who focused with unusual sensitivity on the peasants. Kondrat'ev derided the tendency of Russia's upper social classes to look on peasants as coarse and ignorant. Their disproportionate responsibility for both defending and feeding the country over the past three years had taken a heavy toll. Russia's military situation was now extremely difficult, but it was hardly the peasants' fault. The current harvest was inadequate, villages in and out of the war zone had been pillaged of cattle and horses, the rural workforce had been decimated, and villages lacked essential commodities and industrial equipment. The actual burdens on Russia's peasants were now heavier than ever. They would not be lifted by additional confiscations of grain or more fixed prices, given the "fearful" fall in the value of money. Political leaders had to recognize the sacrifices peasants had made and understand that peasants, too, were not indifferent to the fate of the Russian state—turn their face to the village, in other words, as Kondrat'ev and Trotsky would argue again in the 1920s. The issues of property in land could not be resolved at this moment of crisis through repressive force. The only solutions lay in an increase in the flow of commodities to the village, compulsory labor obligations, state regulation of industry, and a drastic reduction of military spending. It was not food supply committees or other local organizations who were to be blamed for Russia's possible bankruptcy, as some had suggested. It was the war, pure and simple.[9]

The fifty-three-year-old Chkheidze complemented Kondrat'ev's youth with his long and arduous service leading the social democratic faction in the Duma and his role as chair of the Petrograd Soviet. Like Kondrat'ev, Chkheidze introduced his remarks with an unvarnished description: the army was retreating, the nation's finances were not secure, railroads were in a state of complete disorganization, and industry was being destroyed. Starvation was imminent in towns

[8] Ibid., 146, 148, 160–61, 173–76.
[9] Ibid., 91–94.

across the country. Corruption continued in the army. Outbreaks of anarchism testified to the frustration of a people worn out from suffering "unbearable burdens." The government had to recognize that the regulation of economic life was required for national defense. Urgent measures toward this end as described in the government's July 8 Declaration had to be implemented immediately, even before the convocation of the Constituent Assembly. The grain monopoly and fixed prices had to be maintained despite their hardships on the peasantry. Any extension of free trade and fluctuating prices would be disastrous under present conditions. At the same time, as he and others had argued well before February, fixed prices had to be set on basic commodities and wages had to be regulated to assure some degree of balance between countryside and city. Private commerce was desirable to maximize food distribution, but only under the "exceptionally strict control" of food supply organs to quell speculation. In the area of trade and industry, government control over production had to increase, along with the organization of new state syndicates, trusts, and monopolies. Control over industry was "the principal condition for increasing its productive capacity." More tax reforms and the emergency imposition of an "exceptionally high" capital levy had to be imposed on propertied classes to strengthen state finances, along with sales taxes on articles of mass consumption and compulsory subscription to additional state loans by Russia's banks.

None of these proposals differed in any great degree from comparable measures deployed by Germany, England, and France during the war. Nor could they have come as any great surprise to conference participants. The problem was not only resistance from the trade industrial community to these proposals but the sheer difficulty of implementing them. However strong the declarations of support for Kerensky and his regime were from many at the conference, the state administration was ill prepared to enact even emergency measures without strong trade industrial support. Even then, it was one thing to declare a monopoly on scarce commodities and another to guarantee their fair and effective distribution.

Chkheidze's program also relied on the quickest possible elections of city and town dumas and district zemstvos. These new bodies would carry the legitimizing imprimatur of universal suffrage and hopefully bring all the "vital forces" of local communities to bear in implementing the government's programs and decrees. But here, as Chkheidze undoubtedly recognized, it was one thing to demand that these new governing bodies should not be opposed by other local organs, and another to enforce it. Chkheidze took the bold step of insisting that as soon as organs of local self-government were democratically elected, the authority of other officials and local organizations would cease to have force.

In sum, the detailed program Chkheidze presented on behalf of the soviet leadership at the Moscow Conference touched all of the key socioeconomic problems facing revolutionary Russia in August. It also positioned the bloc of democratic socialist parties that were consistently winning local duma elections to dominate the proceedings of the Constituent Assembly, now promised for January. Its great flaw was in the difficulties of its implementation. It relied on the agreement and cooperation of all Russia's "vital" social forces rather than on the instruments of coercive state power. That this would actually happen in the current fraught conditions was improbable at best.

A similar improbability clouded the remaining sections of Chkheidze's program: that prior to the Constituent Assembly all seizures of any other person's land, either by individuals or groups, would be repudiated; that the army command immediately remove all officers who had revealed themselves to be counterrevolutionaries and confirm the rights of soldiers committees; and that the Provisional Government had to declare that all nationalities had the right to self-determination, but only by means of a covenant concluded by the Constituent Assembly. If the strength of a democratic state depended on its ability to institutionalize the peaceful resolution of social conflict rather than, or even in addition to, its monopoly on coercive force, Russia's revolutionary government was ill prepared five months after taking state power to use it to solve the critical problems of scarcity and loss that the war and the tsarist regime had bequeathed it and ensure the great hopes of February could still be realized. Received as he finished with a "stormy" ovation from "the left and part of the center," according to the transcripts, a visibly tired Chkheidze concluded his long address with a strong call to the government to find the energy and strength needed to enact the measures he had laid out, "ruthlessly" suppress anarchy and counterrevolution, and make the "popular masses" know that it would not tolerate "the least encroachment on their revolutionary goals."[10]

A little after 1:00 a.m. on August 14 Kerensky brought the State Conference to a close. Reportedly, those remaining in the Bolshoi Theater responded with a standing ovation and cries of "Long Live the Revolution!," "Long Live the Russia Republic!," and "Long Live Kerensky!"[11]

Kornilov, the Front, and the Countryside

Given the dire assessments and bellicose language offered at the Moscow State Conference, how surprising could it have been that the army's new commander in chief, General Lavr Kornilov, attempted two weeks later to march on Petrograd, suppress the soviets, and establish a military dictatorship? Avatar of punitive military discipline, the death penalty, and using machine guns against soldiers

[10] Ibid., 77–86.
[11] Ibid., 306–9.

running from the front, Kornilov had hoped to repress the April demonstrations and was instrumental in mobilizing Cossacks to put down the July insurrection. On the night of August 19, Russian troops evacuated Riga. It was widely expected that the enemy would soon march on Petrograd. The next day, elections were held in the capital for a new city duma. Despite a high degree of absenteeism, socialists together received almost 80 percent of the vote, the Bolsheviks alone some 33 percent, only a few percentage points behind Chernov's Socialist Revolutionaries. Kadet leaders in both Moscow and Petrograd now felt certain it was necessary to replace Kerensky, Nekrasov, Tereshchenko, and especially Chernov with more capable leaders. Russia again needed a ministry in which the country could have confidence. On August 23 factory committee and trade union leaders met to help organize Petrograd's defense. According to the Kadet Central Committee, Petrograd was "in great danger." The leading Menshevik newspaper warned the city not to panic.[12] Bolsheviks, too, helped prepare for its defense.

Widely discussed in the historical literature, the immediate impact of Kornilov's adventure was easy to predict. Apparently in a state of high anxiety (versions about this differ), Kerensky and soviet leaders called on the workers' militias being organized against the Germans to defend the soviets and the government from Kornilov. Newly formed Red Guards received arms. Leading Bolsheviks under arrest were released to help ensure a united effort. Kornilov and Kerensky famously engaged in an ambiguous exchange of telegrams in which Kerensky seemed to be asking Kornilov for assistance. As minister of war, Kerensky clearly needed the commander in chief to help organize the city's defense against the Germans. As minister president, he was not averse to having his help in bringing social order to the city. What is not ambiguous is the immediate mobilization of railroad workers to stop Kornilov's trains, the wholesale arming of the city against "counterrevolution," and the general's ignominious dismissal and arrest. As events would turn out, however, he would soon be released to help organize armed resistance to Lenin's seizure of power.

In the compressed sequence of events signaling revolutionary Russia's transition from the promises of democratic governance in February to the relative lack of resistance to Lenin's promised authoritarianism in October, the Kornilov mutiny was a notable moment. Kerensky's second coalition collapsed, but in the minister president's mind there was no question about his continuing to lead what was left of the government. State power now fell to a truncated third coalition that included the progressive Moscow Kadet Nikolai Kishkin (who was

---

[12] *Novaia Zhizn'*, Aug. 23, 1917; *Rabochaia Gazeta*, Aug. 26, 1917; William G. Rosenberg, *Liberals in the Russian Revolution* (Princeton, NJ: Princeton University Press, 1974), 196–233, which includes detailed election results.

appalled by Kerensky's arrogance), the former Progressist (and now Kadet) Alexander Konovalov, and General Alexander Verkhovskii, the new minister of war, who had suppressed garrison soldiers in Nizhnii Novgorod during the July Days. Unable to consolidate support for a full coalition, Kerensky was soon governing with a small directorate rather than a policymaking cabinet. Hoping to secure additional support from the left, he unilaterally declared Russia a republic, usurping the prerogative of the Constituent Assembly. He also declared his intention to fix prices on basic goods; regulate relations between capital and labor, including wages and hours of work; and introduce special legislation to allow the state to interfere actively in the management of enterprises. Within days the Bolsheviks repudiated his new regime by securing hostile majorities in the Petrograd and Moscow Soviets.

Partly in response, partly simply to pull themselves together and regroup, Menshevik leaders then convened a large democratic conference. Its purpose was to gather "all forces of the country" to bolster socialist unity and further organize the revolution's defense. Having lost virtually all political credibility with the socialists who accused them of support for Kornilov, if not outright collusion, Miliukov and the liberal leadership were not invited to attend.

At the front and in the countryside the aftermath of Kornilov was also disastrous for political and social stability. In the northwest, Russian troops continued to defend against the German thrust beyond Riga which began on September 1, but a communication from army headquarters described "disorganized masses of soldiers in an uncontrollable stream pouring down the Pskov highway." The influence of soldiers' committees on the troops they represented greatly declined. Kornilov's failure also stimulated the army's further unraveling on the southwestern Galician and Rumanian Fronts.[13] And just as they had been since the beginning of the war, what happened at the front and in the village was closely linked in ways that directly affected Russia's economic circumstances. Concern about families and a longing to be home continued to be the most prevalent sentiment expressed in the huge number of soldiers' letters that continued to pass through the hands of military censors. (On the Western Front alone in September some 2.4 million pieces of correspondence were recorded.)[14] Some reports on the soldiers' mood from the Northern and Western Fronts spoke of a new understanding that stronger discipline was necessary if the German advance was to be halted. For battered units in the Southwest, Kornilov's defeat and arrest were almost uniformly a disaster, at least for officers: "You live like on top of a volcano, with your revolver under your pillow and constantly waiting for that time when the [muffled] drum will beat for you."[15] A report from the Tenth

[13] RGVIA f. 2003, op. 4, d. 31, ll. 78–78 ob.
[14] RGVIA f. 2048, op. 1, d. 905, ll. 262, 291.
[15] Ibid., ll. 268–73.

Army on the Western Front described its soldiers as "absolutely indifferent to the fate of the Fatherland ... if only it will take them out of the chaos around them and give them their homes, bread, and clothing."[16]

Garrison troops in more than twenty cities around the country grew even more restless, together with their officers, although both groups reportedly still supported the government.[17] Soldiers stationed near Kishinev, the site of a notorious pogrom in 1903, witnessed "daily killings, forceful violations of person and property" that destroyed any possibility of the regional population "fulfilling its civic duty" by providing the state and the army with food. "Drunken excesses, murders, beatings, theft, and the destruction of homes were reported in Smolensk, Podolsk, and the Bessarabian region as a whole. The "dominant feeling everywhere" among the troops was "peace whatever it costs."[18] More and more soldiers clutching their weapons headed for home, their officers and committees unable or unwilling to stop them. The historian Allan Wildman describes a virtual tidal wave of self-assertion by soldiers that by the first of October engulfed the entire front. The message was clear: peace had to be obtained before the winter set in or not a soldier would be left in the trenches.[19]

Wildman calls this a soldiers' plebiscite for peace. Although the actual number of desertions in September and October is unclear, official data likely reflects the desire of many staff members to downplay its extent.[20] Certainly the revolt at the front left the Provisional Government without a functional army to defend it, normally the principal coercive instrument monopolized by the state. Soldiers "voted with their feet," inundating committees and commanders with demands about "family emergencies" that needed tending to. Even without formal authorization they left their positions in droves, sometimes in whole units led by their committees. More so now than earlier they seized railroad cars, plundered along the lines, and terrorized civilian passengers.[21] For officers, these weeks were among the most difficult of the war. September was normally the time for reprovisioning for winter. Soldiers expected warmer clothing and winter boots. That a revolutionary regime serving the people could not do better was readily perceived as the result of bourgeois venality, as loudly claimed in the Bolshevik newspaper *Okopnaia Pravda* (*Trench Pravda*). Certainly Kornilov's fall carried

---

[16] RGVIA f. 2003, op. 4, d. 31, l. 19.
[17] RGVIA f. 366, op. 1, d. 132, l. 64.
[18] Ibid., d. 79, l. 107; f. 2003, op. 4, d. 31, ll. 19, 38.
[19] Allan Wildman, *The End of the Russian Imperial Army*, 2 vols. (Princeton, NJ: Princeton University Press, 1987), 2:225.
[20] Ibid., 2:231; M. Frenkin, *Russkaia armiia i revoliutsiia 1917–1918* (Munich: Logos, 1978), 313. The official figures are given in TsSU, *Rossiia v mirovoi voine, 1914–1918 goda (v tsifrakh)* (Moscow, 1925), 20.
[21] RGVIA f. 366, op. 1, d. 79, l. 107.

with it the personal safety of those responsible for inflicting the harsh penalties the former commander in chief so strongly supported.

If village life was churning well before Kornilov, thousands of new arrivals coming home from the front in September and October unsettled the countryside even more. Hardened and embittered soldiers arriving home with their rifles further radicalized their villages. Many were accustomed to seizing the foodstuffs they needed as well as the violence that accompanied it. The plundering of Ternopol' by Brusilov's troops fleeing battle in July, one of the most destructive incidents of its kind in the entire war, was a sign of soldiers' rage and indifference to suffering civilians. Certainly the thin boundaries between the army's institutionalized requisition practices and outright plunder largely dissolved in the countryside after Kornilov's revolt, reinforcing whatever tendencies might have been rooted in Russian rural culture.

However much this was the case, the historian Olga Porshneva's work suggests that the fear of hunger also constantly affected peasant mentalities more generally, developing for revolutionary Russia the anthropologist James Scott's argument that a moral as well as a material economy governed peasant behavior. In her view the traumas and dislocations of war could not help but strengthen those elements in the peasants' moral system that justified the use of force, compromised the value of human life, and even the affected nature of their religious faith.[22] Menshevik newspapers like *Rabochaia Gazeta* cultivated these associations as well by running long lists of provincial unrest in September under the headline "Bunty" ("Riots"). Boris Nikolaevskii, the archivist historian whose later work in emigration helped structure the democratic socialist Great Story, now wrote anxiously in the paper of a rising rural anarchist wave, referring to the list of pogroms, murders, and other horrors the newspaper detailed almost daily.[23] During the first week of September peasants sacked the country estate of Andrei Shingarev, killing his domestic animals, plundering stores, and terrorizing his wife. She died shortly afterward.

Hewing to the Leninist Great Soviet Story, Soviet Russian historians were assiduous before 1989 in massing evidence to show the extent of social unrest after Kornilov, deploying at some points nearly a legion of researchers to chart every incident recorded in every newspaper as well as the police reports received by the Ministry of Interior. Thus we find in one compilation covering forty-eight provinces and twenty-nine regions some 180 instances of seizure or destruction of estates in August recorded almost equally as "organized" and "unorganized," along with 69 seizures of harvests and 115 of meadows and hayfields. For

---

[22] Olga S. Porshneva,, *Mentalitet i sotsial'noe povedenie robochikh, krest'ian, i soldat Rossii v period pervoi mirovoi voiny (1914–mart 1918 g.* (Ekaterinburg: UrO RAN, 2000), 87–91, 141.
[23] *Rabochaia Gazeta*, Oct. 4, 1917; see also Sept. 30 and Oct. 1, 2, 1917.

September, the figures were 186 estates seized or totally destroyed, 57 seizures of harvested crops, and 63 of meadows and hayfields. The largest numbers reportedly occurred in Kazan, Penza, Riazan, and Tambov provinces, but incidents were recorded throughout the country, even in Arkhangelsk.[24]

Although these figures aggregate a range of actions across different provinces, post-Soviet historians have generally accepted their order of magnitude, emphasizing that many if not most took place under the aegis of village authorities themselves, disempowering the agents of state administration and both local and regional soviets. Orlando Figes, for example, describes peasant committees and village gatherings as essentially autonomous governments by the fall of 1917, with their own militias. At indications in the Volga region that the harvest would again fail to meet expectations, as in 1916, there were new worries that the winter would bring starvation to many villages. At the end of September a number of towns and villages witnessed raids on shops and warehouses along with a wave of pogroms.[25] In reports to the government seizures by local state authorities were described as requisitions, those by peasants as arbitrary abuses of power (*proizvol*), plundering, and robbery.[26] In this environment even the most carefully drawn system of extracting grain by obligatory requisitions was bound to fail. In many places village assemblies had become "radical dictatorships," as Figes has labeled them, taking full control of village life and adjacent private estates.[27]

"Radical Dictatorships," Autonomous Nationalities

What was crucial about peasant activism in September was not only the ways the spread of radical village dictatorships further affected revolutionary politics in the countryside. It was also the way these events and incidents thoroughly disrupted the already precarious supplies of wheat, rye, oats, and other products formally designated for requisition. If obligatory requisitions at fixed prices were spotty at best in August, the grain monopoly collapsed entirely by September. Advancing the democratic liberal Great Story, P. B. Struve and K. I. Zaitsev, who had both played important roles in the Special Council on Food, still supported the monopoly as a "moderate and careful policy of collection." Its failure only

---

[24] M. N. Pokrovskii and Ia. A. Iakovlev, eds., *Krest'ianskoe dvizhenie v 1917 godu* (Moscow: Gosizdat, 1927), 409–11, 417–19. See also P. P. Pershin, *Agrarnaia revoliutsii v Rossii*, 2 vols. (Moscow: Nauka, 1966), 1:392–420.

[25] Sarah Badcock, *Politics and the People in Revolutionary Russia: A Provincial History* (Cambridge: Cambridge University Press, 2007), 220, 224.

[26] RGIA f. 23, op. 7, d. 739, passim.

[27] Orlando Figes, *Peasant Russia, Civil War: The Volga Countryside in Revolution 1917–1921* (Oxford: Oxford University Press, 1989), 241.

testified to the impossibility of taking grain from peasant producers by force and was due to the changes introduced by Rittikh, as the tsar's last minister of agriculture, and especially Shingarev, the Provisional Government's first. Wage earners, too, were clearly more anxious about scarcities now, especially of food, with its continually rising costs. Kornilov's mutiny radicalized their anxieties even further. So, too, were plant owners vilified as Kornilov's supporters, if not so much about food, which could still be bought through illegal markets, as about their social position, wealth, property, and person, not necessarily in that order. Meanwhile leading Bolsheviks arrested after the July uprising were released. Seizing the opportunity Kornilov had provided, the Germans moved through Riga toward a Petrograd, now engulfed in the "Riga panic." Plans to evacuate key industries and people were accelerated. Across socioeconomic positions and ever more sharply drawn class lines, the present seemed frightfully unstable to workers and property owners alike, the future even more so.

Kornilov's move also further mobilized workers' militias and Red Guards. As Rex Wade has detailed, militias and Guards had sprung up early in the revolutionary process, but Kornilov managed to validate their importance throughout the industrial sector as well as with socialist leaders and the Bolsheviks.[28] To defend against the mutiny and "save the revolution" once again, the government itself distributed arms. When Kornilov's efforts collapsed, the weapons could not be recalled. Armed factory guards became even more important as a means of securing workers' goals by force.[29] An overarching need of workers themselves was now to keep their factories in operation—the only way, if at all, to support themselves. Judging by newspaper accounts and the *Bulletin of the Ministry of Labor*, September and October saw a surge in unemployment as more and more enterprises were shut down. By October some fifty thousand workers were reportedly unemployed in Moscow alone.[30] September also saw an increase in strikes, but whispers of strikes also greatly increased. Just the threat of a strike was itself enough for increasing numbers of owners to shut down.

The weeks after Kornilov saw a further move on the part of local government officials, soviets, and other authorities in the localities to intervene in their own local economies and establish their own "radical dictatorships." Government officials and soviet commissars were a particular problem because they regularly carried documents giving them "exceptional authority" to take any actions they thought necessary. A telegram to the Ministry of Finance from Odessa warned that this was making a "complete mess" in the city, confusing people as to whom they should obey. It demanded that the title "commissar" be given only

---

[28] Rex Wade, *Red Guards and Workers' Militias in the Russian Revolution* (Stanford, CA: Stanford University Press, 1984), 134–38, 223–29, 252–56.
[29] RGIA f. 23, op. 27, d. 329, ll. 46–47; f. 150, op. 1, d. 7, l. 31.
[30] For example, *Biulletin Min. Truda* 23 (Oct. 7, 1917).

to those actually occupying government positions.[31] By October the situation was even worse. To bring order to the regions the Main Economic Committee proposed that specially designated commissars be given the authority to use garrison troops to enforce their decisions and maintain order.[32] In fact, in many places this was already too late. In one report from Kursk, for example, the local economy was described as totally distorted by arbitrarily fixed prices, controls over goods distribution, panic selling, and sanctioned confiscations. Capitalism had collapsed, but replacing it was a "half pregnant socialism" created by the unrestrained authority of local officials and threatening further economic disaster.[33]

This was certainly the view of Andrei Bachmanov, still chair of the Petrograd Society of Factory and Mill Owners. At large meetings of the society's council on September 5 and 12, he and others affirmed that in fact Russia had "never been so far from socialism" as it was then. Socialism required a government in which the individual was subordinated to the goals and ideals of the state. In Russia, the idea of the state itself had lost importance. It needed to be resurrected, which required first and foremost the restoration at the local level of administrative competence. Workers would not even support evacuation, Bachmanov warned, since they "did not understand that industry needed saving."[34] On October 3, the council approved a draft statute drastically limiting the competency of factory committees and sent it to the Ministry of Labor.[35]

One strong press in this direction was the demand again for obligatory labor service (*trudovaia povinnost'*) along with the introduction of new "labor books" that all workers would have to obtain within seven days of hire. Obligatory labor service would apply across the board, matching unemployed workers with available positions. The labor books would state clearly the nature of work required, wages and the basis on which they were calculated, and the rules of internal factory order, including the obligations and responsibilities of both worker and employer. Both obligatory service and the labor books were also being advanced within government circles, the old regime's idea of obligatory service having been raised as a possibility in the Ministry of Finance as early as the spring.[36] The industrialists applauded these initiatives as a step toward strengthening their own physical and administrative control over their plants.

So did members of the Main Economic Committee, now desperately seeking ways as well to prevent further economic collapse. Here Vladimir Groman and Andrei Shingarev again found common ground, as they had in 1916. As chair of

---

[31] RGIA f. 560, op. 26, d. 1359, ll. 94–94 ob.
[32] Ibid., d. 1361, ll. 284–85.
[33] RGIA f. 23, op. 7, d. 408, ll. 15–18.
[34] RGIA f. 150, op. 1, d. 7, ll. 31–32.
[35] Ibid., ll. 67–68.
[36] RGIA f. 560, op. 26, d. 1358, ll. 183–91; d. 1406, ll. 20–21.

the Petrograd Supply Committee Groman pressed for a far stronger role of the state as an "indirect proprietor" in the economy. Catastrophe could be avoided only if the state began to act like one.[37] Shingarev urged more comprehensive intervention by the state through "the broad application of the principle of state monopolization in all areas of the economy," as had been "brilliantly applied in France and England" and which would prevent "every local committee [from] deciding questions about production." The former Duma statesman and minister of agriculture and finance called this the "statization of industry," a logical corollary to the ways labor-management conflict was also being "statized" under the purview of the Ministry of Labor.[38]

The views of Groman and Shingarev found wide support in the Main Economic Committee and its executive Economic Council. New legislation was needed to unify economic leadership around the committee itself, which would "regulate the entire economic life of the country."[39] It was soon being drafted. District supply committees around the country would now be restructured to act under its direction. Among other responsibilities, they would have "full competency to clarify and articulate all needs and demands of their districts," formulate plans for the distribution of orders to local enterprises after determining their production capacities, and set up and manage the local redistribution of workers on the basis of compulsory labor obligations (*trudovaia povinnost'*). Necessary measures would be taken "to ensure the most complete utilization of local productive forces."[40] When the legislation was released on October 12, it proposed dividing the country into twelve districts managed by regional economic committees subordinated to the committee in Petrograd. They would be headed by special commissars with the "exceptional" authority, again, to deploy troops.[41]

Was there really any possibility that such an ambitious plan could be realized by the Provisional Government, now barely managed by Kerensky and his Directorate? The regime not only lacked the coercive power necessary to bring it to fruition; it lacked the necessary financial and commodity resources to support it. By the middle of September the Petrograd Society of Factory and Mill Owners saw the country in a credit crisis. So did the Council of Ministers at its meeting on September 21. One week later the unauthorized transfer of any form of Russian money or valuables abroad was prohibited.[42] In October, M. I. Fridman from the

---

[37] RGIA f. 23, op. 7, d. 739, ll. 9–12.
[38] *Rech'*, July 26, 1917; *S"ezdy i konferentsii konstituionno-demokraticheskoi partii*, 3 vols. (Moscow: Rosspen, 2000), 3:684.
[39] RGIA f. 23, op. 7, d. 739, ll. 9–37.
[40] GARF f. 6, op. 2, d. 560, l. 30; RGIA f, 23, op. 1, d. 739, ll. 1–9.
[41] RGIA f. 560, op. 26, d. 1360, l. 138; d. 1361, ll. 284–85; GARF f. 1779, op. 2, d. 569, l. 30.
[42] RGIA f. 563, op. 4, d. 552, ll. 1–3; f. 583, op. 3, d. 1133, l. 14; f. 560, op. 26, d. 1360, l. 1; f. 150, op. 1, d. 428, passim; *Zhurnaly Zasedaniia Vremennogo Pravitel'stva* 175 (Sept. 21, 1917). A long report by Nekrasov on the government's financial situation appeared in *Novaia Zhizn'*, Aug. 6, 1917.

Ministry of Finance described a drained treasury to members of the Economic Council. Early in August Nekrasov and Bernatskii from the Ministry of Finance had signed off on new short-term treasury obligations of up to 3 billion rubles. Shortly afterward another 100 million in credit notes was put into circulation.[43] In fact there was no real possibility now of providing industry with the financial resources the Main Economic Committee's plan would require. The best the Finance Ministry could propose was the introduction of state monopolies of a range of popular but less urgent commodities like matches, tobacco, coffee, and tea. A monopoly on sugar was imposed on September 14. Vice Minister of Trade and Industry L. B. Kafengaus doubted the government could manage even this. The current monopolies on grain, bread, and leather were all doing "very poorly."[44] In his view, a better way to proceed was to create new industry-by-industry syndicates, a commercial unification of enterprises that would promote mutual regulation of trade, the supply of raw materials, and the forced distribution of production between different regions along with set regional prices—in effect an economic dictatorship under the supervision of the state that would reach into every region of the country.[45]

Given the press for autonomy by Ukrainian leaders that precipitated the dissolution of the first coalition government just before the July Days, it is hardly surprising that such a proposal spurred Ukraine and other nationalities to strengthen their own local power. While the national question was to be decided by the Constituent Assembly, like the peasants' right to land, the first All-Russia Congress of Soviets had endorsed the right of self-determination for all nationality groups already in June. The Kadets' position was quite different. Political autonomy, much less self-determination based on territorial units, would not only undermine Great Russian unity. It would stimulate a drive for independence for which Ukrainians and others were not prepared. The issue caused fissures in part because the party acknowledged the right of Poland and Finland to independence, in part because Ukrainian Kadets supported it. A special party commission in July was charged with determining whether Ukraine was another "special case."[46] A commission working on proposals for the new constitution the Constituent Assembly would decree stated unequivocally that the Russian state would be "one and indivisible."[47]

In early August, the Ukrainian Rada resolved that the Provisional Government was "imbued with imperialist tendencies of the Russian bourgeoisie toward

---

[43] RGIA f. 23, op. 29, d. 5, l. 18; f. 560, op. 26, d. 1358, l. 246.
[44] RGIA f. 560, op. 26, d. 1362, ll. 119–24; f. 23, op. 1, d. 487, ll. 62–67.
[45] RGIA f. 23, op. 1, d. 487, ll. 72–74.
[46] *Vestnik Partii Narodnoi Svobody* 4–5 (June 8, 1917): 7–8; 11–13 (Aug. 10, 1917): 1–10.
[47] N. Rubinshtein, "Vremennoe pravitel'stvo i Uchreditel'noe Sobranie," *Krasnyi Arkhiv* 28 (1928): 131.

Ukraine." National assemblies in Estonia and Latvia were insisting on full autonomy within a federated Russia. Lithuania's Sejm resolved that ethnographic Lithuania had to become a neutral independent state. The Second All-Russia Moslem Congress opted for broad national and cultural autonomy, but with the form of government for Turkestan, Kirghizia, the Caucasus, and Tatar Crimea left to local populations.[48] The questions of autonomy and independence still depended, however, on whether the Constituent Assembly restructured itself on socialist or nonsocialist principles and the degree to which it embraced federalism. But the issue in the fall was hardly the rights of nationalities alone. Russia's broad central industrial region was largely dependent on grain from Ukraine and Siberia. Political autonomy itself posed the problem of food procurement as well as its export outside these regions, whether through the food monopoly directed from Petrograd or at the discretion of local dictatorial regimes. In either case, they would have to find some way to resolve the food "crisis," as it was now described in the newspaper of the Provisional Government.[49] In every area of the empire, meanwhile, including Siberia, Central Asia, and the Caucasus as well as Ukraine, autonomous local and regional authorities were already dictating measures they thought were essential to supporting their localities and which they presumed in any case would be the foundation of a new Russian federal order.

The Railroad Republic

By September plant owners in Ukraine and other areas as well as Russia proper all spoke loudly about workers' committees pushing the country toward economic bankruptcy. This view was not entirely wrong, even if their motivation was to keep their plants open, but it was also related to their management's strong resistance to doing so on other than their own terms. The broader patterns of social and cultural polarization which had been intensifying politically since February had now extended to industrial production as a whole. If the weapons of workers after Kornilov increasingly included taking physical control of their plants, those of employers included lockouts and closures. Both sides, moreover, demanded financial and resource support from the state to pay wages and purchase materials in order to maintain production under their direction.

It is difficult to say which weapons were those of the weak, to deploy Scott's useful conceptualization: the inherently self-destructive acts of workers' ill prepared to assume supervisory or physical control of their workplaces, or those of private owners and state managers trying to save their plants by locking workers

---

[48] Browder and Kerensky, *Russian Provisional Government*, 1: 404–16.
[49] *Vestnik Vremennogo Pravitel'stva*, Sept. 19, 1917.

out or shutting plants down temporarily or for good.[50] After Kornilov, neither side paid much attention to the other's concerns as they vied for state support. Seventy-seven plant owners and managers at a meeting in Petrograd were adamant, for example, about not releasing their workers to attend a city-wide meeting of factory committees on September 12. Though threatened with the loss of their jobs or of military deferments, the workers went anyway. They also demanded to be paid for the time. Both factory seizures and lockouts met equally strong resistance in many places from Menshevik trade union figures and other democratic socialists who pressed for order and organization. The party's newspaper *Rabochaia Gazeta* editorialized at the end of August against the "social parasitism" reflected in workers' demands that the government itself provide wage increases.[51] In contrast, workers were encouraged (or even led) by the growing number of Bolshevik supporters in their midst, including radicalized soldiers back from the front. Workers also found support from district and city soviets after Bolsheviks secured 23 percent of the vote in Petrograd and 51 percent in Moscow in the August and September local elections. In these circumstances, members of the Society of Factory and Mill Owners sought as much help from the state as they could. Bachmanov, still the head of the Petrograd branch of the society, thought there were really no other practical measures that could be taken given Russia's already "catastrophic" economic problems.[52]

While demands for the "statization" of conflict only widened after Kornilov, the Ministries of Labor and Finance found themselves politically and materially unable to meet the urgent demands for assistance now coming at them from all sides. In a few cases the Ministry of Labor was still able to serve as a neutral arbitrator, a place of contention rather than a contending party, and get worker and management representatives to accept a judgment from new arbitration courts. These instances, however, were now the exception. Meanwhile a new wave of strikes broke out and spread geographically as well as across industrial sectors. Wood industry and textile workers were now much more inclined to initiate work stoppages than they had been earlier, joining the more strike-prone metallists. Less-skilled workers were participating in strikes for the first time, largely because the price index had tripled since August. More than 80 percent of all strikes demanded increased wages, many also demanding control over hiring and firing even as this was no longer amenable to mediation in the way Skobelev and other democratic socialists had hoped would advance the revolution's goals.[53] While

---

[50] James Scott, *Weapons of the Weak: Everyday Forms of Peasant Resistance* (New Haven, CT: Yale University Press, 1985).

[51] *Rabochaia Gazeta*, Aug. 31, 1917.

[52] *Rabochaia Gazeta*, July 26, 1917; RGIA f. 150, op. 1, d. 7, ll. 14–15; d. 428, ll. 29–31.

[53] Diane P. Koenker and William G. Rosenberg, *Strikes in Russia 1917* (Princeton, NJ: Princeton University Press, 1989), 268–76.

the Ministry of Labor continued to try to settle these disputes in September and October, particularly in defense plants, by September almost every case involved an appeal for state financial assistance, intervention on key issues of factory administration, and demands like the one from Trainin plant workers that the state "take whatever steps necessary" to keep their plant open.[54] Factory-based conciliation boards everywhere no longer held their earlier authority. Owners' associations were indifferent. Even the Central Conciliation Board in Petrograd virtually ceased functioning because employers refused to send their representatives to meetings.[55]

A dramatic reflection of the failure of mediation was the national strike of railroad workers on September 23–24. The formation of the "railroad republic" at the long national congress in July and August gave Vikzhel, the national union's executive committee dominated by internationalist left SRs, authority to coordinate all aspects of railroad administration, from hiring and firing to local operations. At the national level union leaders were supposed to work closely with the central government, at the local level with the local organs of self-government. The idea was that this would rein in the excessive and competitive powers of existing railroad committees organized on the basis of professional service while also defending railroaders against the increasing acts of violence along the lines that railroad newspapers were regularly reporting. Nekrasov himself was disappointed with the actions of many local committees. Democratization and "statization" presumed common efforts and support for the welfare of the revolutionary state as a whole, not the strengthening of a disruptive localism. Above all, positioning the all-Russia union as one of "state significance" was intended to ensure that the railroaders would not use their ability to shut down the lines as they had done in 1905 in pursuit of their own economic and political demands.

The September strike was thus at once the result of the Plekhanov Commission's earlier inability to satisfy railroaders' wage demands; the increasing violence along the lines, especially in areas where local food supply committees prohibited taking grain out of their districts; and the unforeseen consequences of efforts to democratize line administration in the spring, one of the many unsuccessful efforts to devolve authority downward from the center. Supported by engine brigades on the major lines leading into Moscow and Petrograd, the brigades' union threatened to begin a nationwide strike on August 20. The issue was not simply one of wages but also of recognizing the vital roles played by engine drivers and their assistants, the hazards they faced, and their elite position in the social hierarchy of railroad labor. Vikzhel and the national railroad union were simply not

---

[54] GARF f. 4100, op. 1, d. 18, l. 9.
[55] N. Dmitriev, "Primiritel'nye kamery v 1917 godu," in *Professional'noe dvizhenie v Petrograde v 1917 godu*, ed. A. Anskii (Leningrad, 1928), 907–97.

strong enough to restrain them from asserting their particular interests even at this critical moment.

When Kerensky and Vikzhel both mobilized railroaders to halt Kornilov's advance on Petrograd on August 27 and 28, the engine drivers again decided not to go forward, at least for the moment.[56] Meanwhile the proposed wage increases for shop workers and other railroad trades worked out by the railroad congress required additional funding from the state and had not yet materialized. On September 7 the demands for relief coming to Vikzhel were such that its members requested help from the soviets' Executive Committee. After deliberation, the committee decided that wage levels set at the congress should be lowered, but turned the matter over to yet another commission, this time headed by the vice minister of labor and former head of the Workers' Group in the CWIC, Kuz'ma Gvozdev.[57]

Whether or not Gvozdev recognized the irony of his position, the revolution had now brought him squarely back to the dilemmas he faced in 1915 and 1916 as he struggled to bring workers into the WICs as a way of advancing their interests and mediating their grievances. Like his Menshevik comrade Skobelev, Gvozdev had worked tirelessly and to increasingly less avail since February at settling major labor disputes across the country. Two years after facing strong resistance by more militant workers to joining the CWIC Workers' Group, he now faced the possibility that militant railroaders would contest the revolutionary regime by shutting the country down with a nationwide strike. The matter was being pressed, moreover, not primarily by militant Bolsheviks who had relatively little presence among SR-dominated track workers working near their villages but by engine drivers and those in other services who saw themselves as long-suffering subjects of state and public abuse. Few reading about the strike threat would fail to remember the railroaders' national strike twelve years earlier that brought a still powerful tsarist regime to its knees in 1905.

Gvozdev bent every effort to come up with a new schedule of wages for all Russia's 300,000 railroaders. The wage schedules his commission presented to Kerensky set rates higher than those developed by Vikzhel itself. Vikzhel members expected a settlement, but Kerensky and his regime rejected the wages as too costly, deciding instead that because of the railroad union's "state importance," the matter was properly one for the Constituent Assembly, despite worsening material conditions. Faced with this resistance and the likelihood that railroaders would otherwise begin the strike on their own, weakening Vikzhel's

---

[56] *Russkiia Vedomosti*, Aug. 30, 1917; *Rabochaia Gazeta*, Aug. 19, 20, 24 and Sept. 5, 1917; *Golos Zheleznodorozhnikov*, Aug. 30, 1917; *Vestnik Vremennago Pravitel'stva*, Sept. 8, 1917.
[57] *Rabochaia Gazeta*, Sept. 8, 1917.

authority, the all-Russia union's leaders agreed to a national strike beginning on September 23.

In the event and in contrast to 1905, the walkout was short-lived. Having failed to mediate the dispute, Kerensky and his cabinet essentially capitulated. Within two days, they arranged for railroaders to get food and clothing at low fixed prices from line commissaries and agreed to temporary wage increases across the services pending their ratification by the Constituent Assembly. Vikzhel then called off the strike, although many line workers rejected these concessions as inadequate.[58] If need be, their "republic" would act again in the future. When Lenin and the Bolsheviks seized what was left of state power four weeks later, Lenin would regard Vikzhel's power as a more serious threat, perhaps even more so than the meager forces mobilizing against him. Yielding state power to that of worker activism, at least for the moment, he would bring three left SRs into his government, as we will see, in part to keep the railroads running rather than have his Bolsheviks do all the work.

The Anxieties and Predicaments of October

For almost everyone in the former tsarist empire, including some of Lenin's closest comrades, September and October were undoubtedly the most anxious months in Russia's short-lived period of civil liberties and democratic freedoms. Liberals saw the government functioning on inertia. *Novoe Vremia* ran three whole pages of apartments for rent. The Ministry of Interior pleaded for the organization of local "committees to save the revolution," since only local organs could hope to exercise authority. The Ministry of Labor called for compulsory arbitration. Shingarev and Nabokov spoke out in favor of restoring capital punishment.[59] Meanwhile, worker and peasant activism continued unabated. Scattered railroad strikes continued to affect Petrograd and Moscow. The restraints of legal protest were now as weak as those protecting private property in the countryside. State workers at the Peter the Great Arsenal forcefully prevented the evacuation of equipment and took over the plant. In the midst of an industry-wide strike that was one of the revolutionary period's longest and most contentious, armed workers at the Skorokhod leather plant took the firm's directors hostage to secure higher wages. Cities and industrial towns everywhere witnessed similar events.[60]

---

[58] *Izvestiia Glav. Ispolkom Moskovskoi-Kazanskoi Zh.D.*, Oct. 13, 1917; *Vestnik Riazan-Ural'skoi Zh.D.*, Oct. 13, 1917; V. Gur'evich, *"Madzhel": Soiuz mladshikh agentov dvizheniia zheleznykh dorog 1917–1919 gg.* (Moscow, 1925), 16–20.

[59] *Rech'*, Sept. 4, 1917; *Novoe Vremia*, Aug. 30, Sept. 17, 1917; *Izvestiia Min. Vnutrennogo Dela* 4 (Sept. 23, 1917); *Zhurnal Petrogradskoi gorodskoi dumy* 75 (Sept. 4, 1917); RGIA f. 23, op. 1, d. 487, l. 74.

[60] Koenker and Rosenberg, *Strikes*, 286–87.

On October 19, the all-Russia textile union issued its own Order Number 1, emulating the Petrograd Soviet in March. The order set in motion one of the largest strikes of the revolutionary period, spreading out from the textile mills in the Ivanovo-Kineshma district, the site of bloody repression in 1915. The largely female workforce stayed out until mid-November.[61]

In political terms, events in the eight short weeks between Kornilov and the Bolshevik coup continued to move with dazzling rapidity. They centered on configuring party representation in yet another coalition, the fourth government since February. To this end, socialist leaders convened a large democratic conference early in September. Its primary purpose was to decide how best to take the revolution successfully forward to the Constituent Assembly, and in what form. Kadets and other liberals were refused entry. The Bolsheviks soon walked out. With Lenin now secretly back in the capital, his followers in the Petrograd Soviet secured a majority vote in favor of a revolutionary government of workers and peasants, that is, a Bolshevik regime. As much of the country soon knew, Lenin himself now pressed forcefully for his party leadership to seize power on its own. Lev Trotsky, released from prison on September 4, immediately began organizing the Military Revolutionary Committee to lead the assault.

Against this intimidating background, democratic socialists like Tsereteli and Skobelev favored reconstituting a governing coalition. A meeting of Menshevik leaders in Skobelev's apartment buried the idea of an all-socialist government in ten minutes, but a majority of the Democratic Conference delegates remained opposed to including Kadet party figures in any coalition. The arguments Kerensky and Tsereteli both advanced in favor of a coalition that included Kadets were familiar: the regime needed the support of the army, and counterrevolution from the right as well as the left was best defended by "bourgeois" representation in the cabinet. Despite their flirtation with Kornilov, the Kadets were the only bourgeois party of significance. Even more, the government needed to have broad popular support to ward off another uprising, which many rightly feared would come from the Bolsheviks, whose delegates had demonstratively walked out. This required the rapid implementation of the socioeconomic program worked through during the July Days and which Chkheidze had presented in sharper form to the Moscow State Conference. Days and nights of rancorous discussion, however, failed to produce more than a half-hearted elaboration of the directorate Kerensky had cobbled together in early September. It included

---

[61] S. K. Klimokhin, ed., *Kratkaia Istoriia stachki tekstil'shchikov Ivanono-Kineshemskoi promyshlennoi oblasti* (Kineshma, 1918); G. Korolev, *Ivanovo-Kineshemskie tekstil'shchiki v 1917 godu* (Moscow, 1927). The strike and subsequent story of the textile workers is well told by William B. Husband, "Local Industry in Upheaval: The Ivanovo-Kineshma Textile Strike of 1917," *Slavic Review* 3 (1988): 448–63 and his *Revolution in the Factory: The Birth of the Soviet Textile Industry 1917–1920* (New York: Oxford University Press, 1990).

the Moscow Kadet and physician Nikolai Kishkin and Aleksandr Konovalov, along with Kuz'ma Gvozdev, who capped his long efforts on behalf of workers by becoming the provisional regime's last minister of labor.

For their part Russia's leading liberals and trade industrialists feared the only real question was whether the Bolsheviks would make their move before, during, or after the Constituent Assembly. Miliukov thought Kerensky needed a psychiatrist. His supporters were adamant against further cooperation with the left. Shingarev thought the railroad strike reflected the psychopathology of anarcho-syndicalism. The politics of "state consciousness" was futile. At the Kadets' tenth and last Party Congress in October, anxious delegates detailed a barrage of hostile public assaults. One of the party's prominent advocates of working with democratic socialists was attacked and killed at a railroad station near Voronezh. Without any confidence in its value, Kadets agreed to participate in a new convocation, the Council of the Republic, invented by the Democratic Conference to get support for yet another broad coalition. The council was envisioned as a "pre-parliament" to which the new members of the cabinet would give frequent reports and be formally responsible in the parliamentary sense. Many now assumed the Constituent Assembly would adopt this model as Russia's constitutional form. Alluding to the difficulties of democratic socialists in getting the Democratic Conference to endorse another coalition, Nabokov wrote openly that Bolshevism was again on stage, triumphant and smug.[62]

The predicament of democratic politics in the fall of 1917, however, was not whether one or another combination of parties could better withstand the anticipated Bolshevik onslaught or another Kornilovshchina from the right. At the state level, it was instead the democratic necessity from the very beginning for any revolutionary government to be both responsive and responsible to its constituent *narod*—the workers, soldiers, and peasants in whose interests it supposedly acted, whether or not it also tried to protect the basic interests of Russia's propertied class.

As in 1915, the question for liberals focused on the state was still whether it would be stronger with a government of responsible people acting authoritatively without the threat of recall or a government constitutionally responsible to a duma with the power of a no-confidence vote, as the pre-parliament was now situated. The conception of a state in the first sense was what Miliukov thought liberals were creating in the Provisional Government, "elected," as he famously put it, by the revolution itself.

As a matter of practice, however, as we have seen, the government that democratic socialists ensured came into being in March was supported only with the soviet's equally famous commitment to support it "only insofar as" it reflected the

---

[62] *Vestnik Partii Narodnoi Svobody* 19 (Sept. 21, 1917): 1–3, 19–27; Rosenberg, *Liberals*, 231–33.

needs of *the* democracy. In effect, as we have suggested, this had created a crude form of representative government in the parliamentary sense. The Provisional Government was reshuffled first when it lost an implicit vote of confidence in the April demonstrations, and then explicitly in the decision to add soviet leaders to the cabinet. In early July, the liberals then voted "no confidence" themselves by resigning over the Ukrainian and nationalities question, while September found Kerensky's rump cabinet hanging on without the confidence of either the democratic liberals or the democratic socialists, not to mention the Bolsheviks or the country at large. The tsarist regime had been overthrown to make way for both political liberty and social well-being, as well as a successful end in some way to the war. But how, in circumstances where there were very different understandings of political liberty and social well-being, could a government even implicitly responsible to its contentious constituents maintain political stability even until the convocation of a constituent assembly, or afterward for that matter?

Political democracy, moreover, required the direct affirmation of government through popular elections. Given the "extreme needs" which were still felt acutely and which much of the population had expressed in one way or another since 1914 and the sheer difficulties now of mitigating them, it is hard to see how any newly democratic regime could maintain the support of those who had "elected" it and from the very start demanded urgent relief. Even the heavy dose of repressive force that Kornilov hoped to use in April and again in August could hardly have been invoked by a revolutionary regime against restless garrisons and armed workers committees without precipitating an uprising like the July Days. In short, the politically democratic rights of free speech and assembly invariably empower those in opposition to a regime more than its supporters. Conditions of scarcity and loss favor those outside the government who claim they can run things better.

The congruent predicament of democratic social welfare efforts was of an equally difficult sort, and almost certainly beyond the capacities of even the most "responsible men in whom the country had confidence," whether democratic liberals or democratic socialists. The great expectations for relief from food insecurity and the anxieties over shortages in steadily more costly essential goods had to be resolved to pull Russia back from the "brink of catastrophe," as Interior Minister Khvostov had described already at the end of 1915.[63] The sheer geographic breadth of the multinational empire engendered socioeconomic and cultural diversity that mitigated the effectiveness of uniform policies imposed from Petrograd. The devolution of authority downward from the center was broadly regarded as a key way to implement social and economic policies effectively, one

[63] RGIA f. 1276, op. 11, d. 167, l. 117.

shared by the government and the soviets as a logical complement to the democratization of local dumas, zemstvos, and local committees of all sorts. Yet everywhere these organizations and institutions largely went their own way. Understandably, given the material and social deprivations they struggled with, they focused as much or more on local needs than on those of the state. Miliukov and other liberals decried the lack of "state consciousness" (*gosudarstvennost'*) this reflected, but how could they expect even more sacrifice to the needs of the state by a population that anxiously experienced food insecurities or social and cultural dislocations at every level that needed relief? Everywhere the constant stream of new commissars and special emissaries with "special authority" only made matters worse.

The dual-power regime's efforts to control inflation with fixed prices and a grain monopoly involved an equally or even more difficult social predicament created by wide variations in local prices and costs, and the speculative gains from moving goods from lower to higher price districts, sometimes even to those close by. When local authorities tried to prevent grain and other goods from being shipped from their areas, the processes of free market exchange were corrupted, increasing local deficits in grain-importing districts and fueling additional speculation. None of this could be readily suppressed by force even if the democratic state was able to bring it to bear. The same was true of the integrity of transport operations, a bane on successive regimes from the beginning of the war throughout 1917 and, as we will see, especially beyond.

Underlying all this, of course, were the huge and unprecedented casualties of the war as well as its steady escalation. This was the case with all warring powers, of course, but especially so in material terms in Russia after the Ministry of Finance reached its limits on gold exports and was forced to cover costs by printing money, as Germany would be forced to do after its defeat. Issuing state bonds helped, but returns were increasingly insecure as the credibility of the government itself declined. Inflation in all of these circumstances was inevitable. So was the increasing level of material want and social discontent. Bankruptcy threatened as the size of state debt escalated along with the costs of servicing it. Successive ministers of finance all struggled unsuccessfully with this problem, whose lack of resolution affected relations with those internally seeking relief. All of these matters confounded public leaders and state officials well before February 1917. It is no surprise that they continued to do so afterward.

In assessing the effects of scarcity in 1917, however, perhaps the most significant related to the subjectivities of expectations rather than material actualities, however severe these frequently were. The war itself was also responsible for both. Hopes for relief were particularly high among the demonstrators and insurrectionists who took to the streets in Petrograd, Moscow, and other cities in February and again in April and July. The mutual efforts of the regime and the soviet leadership to empower workers' committees, organize trade unions, and fully legalize strikes clearly raised hopes even higher. So did the conciliatory positions initially taken by industrialists in the expectation that workers could be constructively engaged in addressing production problems if mutual grievances were mediated. A similar optimism underlay the mobilization of peasants into local land and food supply committees.

With hindsight, these predicaments seem obvious enough. They also became clear to many contemporaries as various shades of radicalism increasingly took hold: the sheer difficulty of overcoming scarcities rapidly enough to satisfy both expectations and needs; the difficulty of being able to do so by increasing production and distribution; and the consequent turn of workers and factory owners to the state itself to solve their problems and keep their plants in operation. In these circumstances, the limitations of strikes and other formal kinds of protest logically led to the "statization" of social conflict itself, as we have described, further weakening in an incredibly compressed period of time its actual and moral authority. The constant critical drumbeat in newspapers and journals of all political viewpoints undoubtedly played a large role as well, just as they had in the summer and fall of 1916.

In this, of course, Lenin and the Bolsheviks before October were past masters. Accompanying unrealistic expectations was an increasingly strident language of explanation, centering again on who was "guilty," a time-honored question in Russian political culture. From the start, losses like those at Tannenberg raised questions about who in high places was responsible and why, but they extended easily to incompetent officers, Jews, landowners, and a facile demonization of all things German. Killing strangers at war necessitates at least a degree of dehumanization that weakens moral restraints. Ordinary enemy soldiers personify their vilified countries as if they were personally responsible for the brutal and lethal mayhem. Rational understandings of cause and effect are readily blurred, making killing for most more acceptable. Almost always and everywhere, moreover, an evil enemy on the battlefield spawns an effort to identify enemies within.[64]

In an increasingly fraught environment of scarcity and loss, these feelings in the world war were easily grafted onto long-smoldering animosities reflected more in Russia than elsewhere in a highly politicized language of social difference. Enterprises and businesses were readily stigmatized as places of exploitation and immoral profiteering. External significations of wealth strengthened deeply held social animosities toward those literally and figuratively "cloaked

---

[64] William C. Fuller Jr., *The Foe Within: Fantasies of Treason and the End of Imperial Russia* (Ithaca, NY: Cornell University Press, 2006).

in silk and velvet," as Shingarev himself dramatically warned. Within all major powers at the time, "workers," the "bourgeoisie," and "capitalists" were reified into historically antagonistic classes with contending moral economies. Village communities rejected individualism in favor of collectivity. Arable land, like water, was rightly the possession of those who used it, not individual owners. The unequal distribution of wealth was itself inherently unfair, along with the gains of speculation. Those involved in commerce and industry were certain individual ownership and private property were essential to social as well as personal well-being, as the "modernization" of Europe seemed to testify. Russia's relative failure in these regards—its partly commercialized countryside and the tsarist state's hostility to enterprise and business—was in many minds a primary reason for its relative lack of success in the war.

In both urban and rural Russia, moreover, the ascription of class identities in discourse and documents undoubtedly reinforced their subjective elements, defining more sharply in 1917 the battle lines of emotional antagonism and political struggle. All of the Great Stories of war and revolution in Russia rightly emphasize the role Bolshevism and Lenin himself played in mobilizing these enmities, an effort that started as we know well before 1914. What gave Bolshevism particular purchase was not only its militant opposition to the war itself but the way Lenin from his first day of return in April managed so quickly to capture popular political discourse by explaining the complexities of scarcity and loss in simple and believable terms.

This was especially the case in urban areas but affected rural localities as well. Eighty percent of those mobilized in the slaughter of war came from Russia's villages. They became the overwhelming number of casualties.[65] That peasants were neither militantly against the war nor especially sympathetic to the Bolsheviks is understandable given the general hostility of villagers to outside "agitators," even if difficult to evidence. As in all wars, it could not have been easy for even the most religious and fatalist to accept that their loved ones died or suffered without good earthly reason. Peasants' patriotism, moreover, was centered on defense of their land and their right to possess it. If there was meaning and logic in these terms to repelling invaders, there was much less of either to carry the battle outside the country's borders, especially without adequate arms, food, or other necessary resources. Even before Bolshevik militants and *Trench Pravda* descended on the front in 1917 to energize soldiers' committees, the

---

[65] Among a number of different calculations, see esp. Frank Lorimer, *The Population of the Soviet Union* (Geneva, 1946), 40; Alexandre Sumpf, *War Losses (Russian Empire)*, in *1914-1918 Online: International Encyclopedia of the First World War*, ed. Ute Daniel, Peter Gatrell, Oliver Janz, Heather Jones, Jennifer Keene, Alan Kramer, and Bill Nasson, https://encyclopedia.1914-1918-online.net/article/war_losses_russian_empire.

feelings of soldiers and their families about the war were expressed overwhelmingly as a longing for peace, an emotion distinct from the denunciation of war itself.

The complex emotional fields on which Bolsheviks came to power thus centered around the brutalities and losses of a war in search of understandable meaning, the anxieties about food and scarce necessities, and desires for material betterment and social security. It was Lenin's political genius to reduce these complexities into "Land, Peace, and Bread," the party's deceptively militant slogan in 1917 that fit so easily on demonstrators' banners. As leaders of Russia's major parties and groups began to discuss the policies of Kerensky's last cabinet at the pre-parliament, working to prepare legislation for the Constituent Assembly in November, some apparently wrestled with the idea that the forthcoming All-Russia Congress of Soviets might itself replace Kerensky's weak collation unilaterally with an all-socialist "soviet" regime.

Since returning through Germany and Finland, as we know, Lenin had other thoughts. Cajoling and berating his more cautious comrades, he virtually demanded that the Bolsheviks seize power themselves. Whether this was the result of ideological commitment, a singular lust for power, or the personal realization of a goal that had lodged someplace in his head and heart ever since his twenty-one-year-old brother was hanged for plotting to assassinate the tsar in 1887, Bolsheviks at his direction forced their way into the Winter Palace on October 24 and 25. No popular uprising prompted their insurrection, nor was the event properly understood, much less celebrated, as a "revolution." At the moment, moreover, the question was not why they did so, but how they might use state power to address the problems that brought revolutionary Russia to this point and whether, in fact, the state could be used effectively to this end at all.

PART III
FROM WORLD WAR TO TOTAL WAR
Scarcity, Loss, and Dysfunctional Dictatorships after October

PART III

13
Circumstance, Ideology, and Bolshevik Power

The brief moment of historical time between General Kornilov's effort to replace Kerensky and the Petrograd Soviet with some form of military dictatorship and the "ten days that shook the world" in October have been thoroughly narrated by the Great Stories as a seminal political moment in world history. So has the equally brief period between October and early January 1918 when Bolshevik efforts were almost entirely concentrated on retaining state power. Central here is a focus on the national elections to the Constituent Assembly in November, where left and center Socialist Revolutionaries—the "peasants' party"—received a resounding 54 percent of the vote, and January 5, when the duly elected Assembly sat for a single long day before impatient Bolshevik guards shut it down. With the signing of the Brest-Litovsk Treaty in March bringing the Ukrainian "breadbasket" under German occupation, the regime was reasonably safe from being overthrown from without. Civil war from within was another matter. None of its major contenders, however, fought for a return to the kind of political democracy the revolution had brought in 1917. Capturing the revolution as well as the state during the horrific Civil War, Lenin's and his supporters were determined to set Russia's and the world's historical trajectory on a radically different course. If the February revolution "elected" the Provisional Government, as Miliukov declared in March, it was history itself that "elected" and legitimized Lenin's regime in October.

Participants and historians telling the Great Liberal Story have been divided on whether ideology or Lenin's singular quest for power mattered more here. Those who imagined revolutionary Russia might finally complete the French revolutionary task by creating politically democratic socialism have divided over whether Soviet Russia might still have evolved in this historically determined direction had Lenin not seized the state and created his aberrant form of socialism "prematurely." Kerensky put both liberal and socialist stories most succinctly: "Only conspiracy and treacherous armed struggle broke up the provisional regime and stopped the establishment of a democratic system."[1] Among

---

[1] A. F. Kerensky, "The Policy of the Provisional Government of 1917," *Slavonic and East European Review* 31 (1932): 19, and his *Crucifixion of Liberty* (New York: John Day, 1934).

tellers of the Bolshevik Great Story, meanwhile, one that conditioned historical thinking in the new Soviet Empire for the next sixty years, the only significant differences had to do with how much popular support Lenin actually had among Russia's workers and peasants, and how much the Great October Revolution was made by a god-like Leader's political will.

All three Great Stories thus privilege ideology, individual agency, and quite different conceptions of progressive historical change. Their focus is also largely on Petrograd and Moscow, the center of state power, and understandably so, given the way the Soviet Great Story required a monopoly on information and full control over who used the archives, which Lenin personally ordered nationalized in early 1918. In democratic liberal and socialist tellings, the result was a great human tragedy that could have been avoided; in the Soviet version, October carried revolutionary Russia from its "bourgeois" phase into its penultimate socialist form, the necessary precondition for the eventual emergence of a communist Russian and world order.

In all of this, the role of circumstance—the material, socioeconomic, and psychological conditions that created the environments of ideological interpretation and political action—were generally avoided by historians, at least until the Soviet Union collapsed. Happily, there are now a number of notable exceptions, many referenced throughout this volume. Yet even here the circumstantial effects of scarcity and loss have not generally been seen as *problems* that the new Bolshevik regime, like those before it, had in some way to resolve. In terms of the circumstances subsumed in the slogan "Peace, Land, and Bread" that had brought revolutionary Russia "to the brink of catastrophe." Lenin's regime now had to find solutions of its own to avoid a similar fate, assuming solutions could actually be found. Whether they could or could not may therefore have shaped this formative moment of modern world history as thoroughly and painfully as ideological belief and raw power.

Rhetoric, Realities, and the Limits of Bolshevik Power

Lenin was a master of political rhetoric. Well before the Bolsheviks seized the state, he was able to capture the most powerful elements in the revolution's political discourse and link them to his cause. The demonizing of bourgeois capitalists was an easy explanation for scarcities and easily understood. The human costs of a war that had produced some 8 million casualties by the summer of 1917 were convincingly explained as the last imperial stage of a historically doomed capitalism. Private property in land was as morally wrong as private ownership of water or air, and comparably destructive to human well-being. From the moment he returned to Petrograd in April Lenin led his party in embracing "Peace, Land,

and Bread" as the signifiers of popular strivings, rhetorical condensations that captured deeply felt and even desperate hopes. Like all such slogans, however, "Peace, Land, and Bread" also belied the immense difficulties in achieving them.

Seizing what remained of state power in October, the Bolsheviks were better armed rhetorically than they were with workable programs. Like the February revolution, October was well scripted. Details of Lenin's plans were printed in all major newspapers. Kerensky thought the Bolsheviks would again be repressed, as in July. Behind the overthrow of the tsar, however, it was a far-reaching program of reform scripted around Russia's public organizations, the devolution of authority downward to the localities, and the engagement everywhere of responsible publics. The actual politics came as a surprise.

October was just the reverse. Taking power, the Bolsheviks had no real plans to address the complex issues reflected in their slogans. The party recognized at its sixth congress in August that Russia had "already fallen into the abyss of final economic collapse and destruction." The only way to restore it was to reset Russia onto the path of rational historical development: ending the war, controlling production, eliminating scarcities, freeing workers and poor peasants from exploitation, and expropriating the bourgeoisie. This would require scientific planning. It also implied workers' control in industrial enterprises, a radical reorganization of state finances and the processes of funding production, and a "correct" exchange of goods between city and country. Young enthusiasts like the twenty-nine-year-old Nikolai Bukharin and twenty-seven-year-old Lev Kritsman were eager to move the revolution "forward" in these ways. A key was the end of controlling capitalist myths and values, including their religious and social supports, and the full application of scientific rationality. Some even imagined an end to inflation and scarcity through the elimination of paper money and its replacement with the exchange of goods in kind.[2] Those on the party's right were skeptical of such "utopian" ideas. They were also anxious about Lenin's desire for power. Except with regard to seizing the state, Lenin himself was also somewhat cautious. We will learn from experience, he wrote in early October. Nationalize the banks and syndicates, "and then we will see."[3]

Indeed, the Bolsheviks' self-assigned task of creating a fully socialist economy had no precedent, never mind the difficulties of trying to do so during wartime in the midst of great scarcity and loss. Russia's nearly bankrupt economy could not be managed by radical slogans. "Expropriating the bourgeoisie" belied the actual difficulties of liquidating ownership, redistributing property, and financing production. Nor could the hopes and expectations of those the Bolsheviks most

---

[2] The intricacies of state finance after October are expertly told by Ekaterina Pravilova in *The Ruble: A Political History* (New York: Oxford University Press, 2023), ch. 11.

[3] *Shestoi s"ezd RSDRP(b)* (Moscow 1934), 241–43; V. I. Lenin, *Collected Works* (Moscow: 1977), 26:172.

depended on for support be realized without securing an end to the war, finding new stores of grain, containing black markets and inflation, and enlisting the technical and administrative expertise that all of these daunting efforts required. In September, Lenin's *State and Revolution* articulated an idealized notion of the state and its powers with little more attention to the problems of production and distribution than the cancelation of debts, the "expropriation of the expropriators," and the revitalization of the economy "from below." His left-wing Menshevik critic the Soviet Executive Committee member Nikolai Sukhanov thought his views reflected a utopian replacement of Marxist concepts with anarchist ones, ideas that were disproportionately few in comparison with the immensity of the tasks.[4]

Seizing and holding state power in Petrograd were Lenin's main priorities. In the capital, power and authority (*vlast'*) were formally proclaimed to be in the hands of the Executive Committee elected by the Second Congress of Soviets after the Bolsheviks' opponents had walked out. Under Lenin's direction the Council of People's Commissars (Sovnarkom) was quickly created to run the government. Throughout the country, *vlast'* was declared to be in the hands of local soviets of workers', soldiers', and peasant deputies, many now growing in their ability to use force with the arrival of armed deserters from the front.[5]

Responses to the Bolshevik takeover varied around the country, but even where events in Petrograd and Moscow were greeted hopefully, concerns focused on addressing local problems. A huge net of soviets and other local committees continued to exercise their often overlapping authorities. One of the Bolsheviks' first decrees abolished landed estates and formally transferred all land to the peasants. Villages across the country acted immediately to carry it out. Almost everything else seemed uncertain pending the convocation of the Constituent Assembly. As newspapers everywhere reported on events in the capitals, parties prepared locally for the elections in November. In the process, the efforts over the past two years to empower the localities reached an unanticipated outcome. Provincial authorities in urban and rural communities were largely on their own. The new revolutionary regime in Petrograd thus faced from the start the daunting task of securing control over policies and practices at a local level, something neither the tsarist regime nor the Provisional Government had been able to do. In terms of the pressing problems of "Peace, Land, and Bread" which had brought Russia "to the brink of catastrophe," Lenin's regime now had to come up with solutions of its own.

---

[4] N. N. Sukhanov, *The Russian Revolution 1917,* ed. and trans. J. Carmichael (Princeton, NJ: Princeton University Press, 1984), 420–21, 570–71.
[5] *Dekrety Sovetskoi Vlasti* (Moscow: Gosizdat, 1957), 1:1–5.

While the political story after October centers on the effectiveness of Bolshevik state-building in Petrograd and Moscow, where Lenin moved the government in March, what the Bolsheviks seized in October was thus not the monopoly on coercive force normally associated with state power but the daunting task of assuring its effective use in the provinces and countryside to meet the hopes and needs of those in whose name the new government ruled. "Peace, Land and Bread" was the simplest of slogans that engaged the most difficult of problems.

Illusions of Peace

It is something of a paradox that having urged his supporters in and outside of Russia to turn the world war into revolutionary civil wars, the beginning of civil war and the continuation of world war were precisely what Lenin's regime struggled to avoid in the weeks after the Bolsheviks seized the state's institutions. It was hard to say which was the greater danger.

The rumblings of civil war were fully apparent in the Kornilov rebellion and its aftermath, which saw worker and peasant violence virtually everywhere. In September 1917 in *State and Revolution* Lenin called for smashing the "bourgeois" state and expropriating the "bourgeoisie." On the day the party took power, the stocks of grain in Petrograd fell below the level needed to meet a single day's meager ration of half a pound of bread. Major railroad lines were described at the Council of the Republic as on the verge of collapse.[6] The number of grain cars arriving in the city dropped precipitously during the next weeks and through the fall. The Nikolaev line between Moscow and Petrograd was now managed entirely by workers' committees.[7] At Trotsky's direction "flying squads" from the Military Revolutionary Committee were sent to nearby countryside to seize food. Hungry railroad workers demanded special rations. Similar conditions existed in all food-importing districts, especially those far from commercial areas, as well in many provincial towns.[8] In Moscow province and elsewhere the massive strike of textile workers continued, one of the largest of the year. A hundred or more plants were shut down. The textile union itself estimated that over 100,000 were out of work, mostly women who retreated to their villages. Food insecurity was now endemic there as well, as it was in major cities. The summer harvest was producing far less grain than expected.[9]

---

[6] GARF f. 1779, op. 2, d. 558, passim.
[7] GARF f. 130, op. 2, d. 71, ll. 18–25.
[8] GARF f. 1779, op. 2, d. 558, passim.
[9] *Protokoly 1-go Vseross. s"ezd tekstil'shchikov i fabrichnykh komitetov* (Moscow: Izd. VR Sov. Prof. Soiuzov Tekstil'shchikov, 1918), 67–69.

In these circumstances the forms of power immanent in strikes and mass protests were potentially much stronger than that exercised by the Bolsheviks' still motley forces. No popular insurrection precipitated the change of regimes or served to protect those now trying to rule from Bolshevik party headquarters in the Smolnyi Institute. October 25–26 was nowhere celebrated as the Great October Revolution it was to become. Nor was there any assurance that if the "railroad republic" shut down the lines as its leaders had threatened to do in September, if the Bolsheviks' political opponents were able to mobilize resistance from within the soviets, if Kerensky could muster General Krasnov's loyalist troops stationed outside of Petrograd, the Bolsheviks' effort to take over the state would again be defeated, as in July. The coalition of socialist parties envisioned on the eve of the Second Congress of Soviets would likely have taken its place.

None of this happened, of course. ("What kind of government is it," a liberal member of Kerensky's last coalition lamented, "that cannot even muster 300 men to defend it?")[10] The reasons were many: a belief in Bolshevik explanations for the war and Russia's economic collapse; the degree of force Bolsheviks could bring to bear through military revolutionary committees and the Red Guards; the belief that Lenin's new cabinet was confirmed and supported by the Second Congress of Soviets; and, probably not least, fatigue with Kerensky and his ineffective cabinets that compounded the physical and emotional exhaustion felt everywhere after more than three awful years of war. In the event, with the exception of some protests and fighting in Moscow (rather less than the vicious resistance that has sometimes been described), the Bolshevik transition was relatively peaceful. The Bolsheviks quickly sent emissaries to major soviets around the country to strengthen their position. The Committee for the Salvation of the Revolution was organized around the Petrograd City Duma representing all democratic liberal and socialist factions but lacked the force (and perhaps also the will) to move aggressively to restore Kerensky.[11] The same was true with the efforts of some to get Vikzhel to lead a national railroad strike. Kerensky famously fled in disguise, symbolizing for some the posturing that betrayed his political and personal weakness.

Still, the dangers of forcible opposition to their seizure of power remained at the top of Bolshevik concerns, Lenin's rhetoric notwithstanding. In the following days, as Vikzhel directed railroad committees to prepare for a general strike, Lenin took steps to reduce them. After a number of vituperative meetings, the leaders of a divided Vikzhel were pacified when a handful of left SRs were persuaded to join the new government, making it a coalition at least in form. The

---

[10] P. N. Miliukov, *Istoriia vtoroi russkoi revoliutsii*, 3 vols. (Sofia: Ros-Bolgarskoe izd., 1921–24), 3:232.
[11] *Zhurnal Petrogradskoi Gorodskoi Dumy* 93 (Oct. 25, 1917) and 94 (Oct. 26, 1917); *Vestnik Gorodskogo Samopravleniia* 15 (Oct. 29, 1917).

elections to the Constituent Assembly were confirmed for November. Private property in urban housing was formally abolished, but no official steps were taken as yet to displace occupants other than those by unrestrained workers and demobilized soldiers. Newspapers continued to be published or were published under new names. The nationalization of industry was postponed, an implicit if not acknowledged reflection of the need for the skills of private ownership and management keep plants in operation. (An exception was the family textile firm of Alexander Konovalov, the Provisional Government's initial minister of trade and industry and the first private firm to be taken involuntarily, perhaps for symbolic reasons.) Existing ministries, now renamed "commissariats," were purged of experienced and long-serving administrators suspected of not being fully loyal to the new communist regime.

Meanwhile the offices of the WIC and Council of Industrial Congresses at 46 Liteinyi remained a busy place even as armed Bolshevik detachments patrolled the street. Perhaps it was possible to work with the new regime to define the types of control owners might accept as a way of maintaining production.[12] The illusion of civil peace was also briefly strengthened by the electoral campaign for the Constituent Assembly, still thought to be the constitutional convention which would formalize a new government. In the event, elections in November proved to be relatively free and open. Some 40 million votes were tallied. What was somewhat surprising about the outcome given Russia's vast peasant majority was that the Bolsheviks actually gained 24 percent of the delegates, compared to 54 percent for the SRs and 6 percent for their more radical left SR comrades. Constitutional Democrats and Menshevik democratic socialists, the two key political groupings in each of the Provisional Government cabinets, each secured less than 3 percent nationally.

What was important to Lenin about these elections, however, was the democratic liberal and socialist strength in Petrograd and Moscow. Here the Kadets managed to win 26 and 34 percent of the vote, respectively, second only to the Bolsheviks' 45 percent in Petrograd and 48 percent in Moscow. While still a clear minority, the liberals displayed a stronger base of popular support in Russia's two capitals than they had during city duma elections in the spring and summer. While showing clearly the country's political polarization, the elections were as much or more a struggle to mobilize political opposition to the Bolsheviks as a referendum on the competing approaches to addressing Russia's crisis.[13]

---

[12] RGIA f. 126, op. 1, d. 8, l. 1.
[13] William G. Rosenberg, *Liberals in the Russian Revolution* (Princeton, NJ: Princeton University Press, 1974), 273–77; *Russkie Vedomosti*, June 28 Sept. 27–29, 1917; O. H. Radkey, *The Elections to the Constituent Assembly 1917* (Cambridge, MA: Harvard University Press), appendix; *Vestnik Partiia Narodnoi Svobody* 26–27 (Nov. 25, 1917): 4.

Lenin took note. Repressions against the liberals and democratic socialists were increased in both cities. Armed sailors appeared at the apartments of Miliukov, Tsereteli, Avksent'iev, and other Assembly delegates. Most leading figures managed to escape into hiding, but others were seized, including Andrei Shingarev, who had struggled all his life to improve popular welfare, and Fedor Kokoshkin, who had chaired the commission that drafted the electoral law. Days later the governing Sovnarkom announced the formation of the All-Russia Extraordinary Commission for Combatting Counterrevolution and Subversion, the notorious Cheka. Shortly after that Kadet Central Committee members Shingarev and Kokoshkin were murdered by Bolshevik sailors.

Like the tsar's worry about the State Duma, Lenin feared the Constituent Assembly would only galvanize his opposition. Some in the party felt it was even a mistake to allow the delegates to convene at all. During its one marathon session many of the revolution's most prominent figures gave impassioned speeches in support of political democracy. A number of demonstrations in support of the Assembly broke out almost immediately in some of the city's most important industrial plants, reportedly including some five thousand at the Semianovskii works and eight thousand at the Obukhov works. The Franco-Russian and Admiralteiskii shipbuilding yards served as a mobilizing center. Several dozen on the streets were shot, maybe more. Large meetings at the Aleksandrovsk locomotive plant and Nikolaev railroad shops condemned the Sovnarkom, promised material aid to the victims, and demanded the Assembly be reconvened. There was agitation as well at the Tula works and other plants around the country, including by hungry and unpaid workers at the huge Sormovo plant in Nizhnii Novgorod who had given Minister of Labor Skobelev such trouble in 1917 and where the Bolsheviks' left SR allies had recently gained majorities in local soviets. Rations previously available had stopped. Wages weren't being paid because, as Lenin was told, "there is no money in the bank."[14]

With its dispersal, meanwhile, Assembly delegates themselves fled east and south, some soon forming the Committee of the Constituent Assembly in the hopes of organizing a new regime in the Volga-Kama region, others heading south toward the Don region to join Generals Kornilov and Alekseev in their efforts to organize a volunteer anti-Bolshevik army. Several pockets of resistance were also organized in Moscow, including the so-called National and Republican Centers, whose members leaned toward creating a military dictatorship with the help of the Germans, and the Union for the Regeneration of Russia, with a broader and more politically democratic outlook.[15] Both groups soon established contacts with the rudiments of the anti-Bolshevik volunteer army being

---

[14] Russian State Archive of Sociopolitical History [RGASPI] f. 5, op. 1, d. 844, ll. 1–2; d. 2884, l. 2.
[15] RGASPI f. 191, op. 1, d. 5, ll. 4–10.

formed around Generals Kornilov, Alekseev, and Denikin, and whose activities were now being reported in detail by the Petrograd newspaper *Novyi Vechernyi Chas* [*New Evening Hour*].[16] All of this, of course, galvanized the new Cheka, which quickly picked up the long and notorious tradition of the tsarist secret police. The institutional groundwork was soon set for all-out internal warfare against real and imagined "enemies," with all of its atrocious violence and deformations.

In these circumstances, reaching a separate peace with the Germans became urgent. At the front, where new decrees revoked capital punishment and gave soldiers authority to "control weaponry," the Bolsheviks' commitment to initiating a separate peace flung the doors of desertion wide open. Reports to the General Staff in early November describe the Bolshevik coup as having a "catastrophic" effect on the army's capacities, ending any reason for continuing to fight. Even soldiers' committees in many places lost their ability to influence their troops. "Life was more important even than land and freedom" for the 7 million men still in the army, as one military censor described it, which in any case could now be had only at home. If Lenin didn't produce peace, "the tsar should take over and do it." "Demands to stay at the front, to carry out one's duty . . . have lost any meaning." Assuming the Bolsheviks would soon end the war, soldiers on all fronts, including the Caucasus, left their positions, failed to obey orders, struck out at their officers. In Smolensk, Podolsk, and Bessarabia drunken soldiers rampaged through homes and shops, robbing and murdering inhabitants. On the Northern Front soldiers still at their posts fraternized and traded with Germans troops and waited for peace.[17] The fronts were still being manned, and the German offensive paused as large numbers of German troops prepared to be transferred to France, but by November the Russian army was no longer an effective military deterrent.

Lenin's peace initiative represented the desire of an overwhelming majority of soldiers, but it also greatly increased the vulnerability of the new regime should the Germans renew their offensive. In a well-known gesture, Trotsky attempted to keep the Germans in place by telling them Soviet Russia would not capitulate to their peace terms, which included generous transfers of the Baltic lands and the right to occupy Ukraine. But neither would Russia go on the offensive. "No war, no peace" seemed to be a clever and radical idea, but almost immediately the Germans began to launch their troops toward Petrograd. Lenin now thought he had no choice but to accept their own nonnegotiable demands. In early March the decision was ratified at the Seventh Party Congress by a vote of twenty-nine to nine, despite vociferous opposition from Bukharin and others who regarded

---

[16] *Novyi Vechernyi Chas* 20 (Jan. 24–27, 1918).
[17] RGVIA f. 2003, op. 4, d. 31, ll. 38, 77–80, 138–51; d. 40, ll. 80–82.

the treaty as a betrayal of workers and poor peasants in Germany and Austria and potentially fatal to their help in building socialism in Russia. For the party's increasingly vociferous left, a socialist Germany was the only way Soviet Russia could get the material and financial support it urgently needed to survive.

Already beforehand Trotsky had been directed to mobilize Russia's own revolutionary workforce into a new Red Army. Given the number of demobilizing soldiers with strong Bolshevik sympathies, the task was difficult, but for many readers of *Trench Pravda*, defending the new revolutionary regime seemed the only way to prevent Russia's enemies from restoring tsarism. (For some it also promised rations that would otherwise have been difficult to obtain.) The effort accelerated as it became clear that the Germans meant business. Somewhat to Trotsky's and others' surprise, there was still sufficient revolutionary enthusiasm among metallists and other more radical groups in Petrograd and Moscow for him to form quickly the rudiments of the new Red Army. By the end of spring, it units were ready for combat with Alekseev's and Denikin's growing White forces in the Don. (General Kornilov was killed by a stray artillery shot in April.) Obligatory mobilization was announced by decree for those born in 1888 and 1889. The stage was being set instead for full-fledged civil war.

Land and Bread as Metaphors of Hope

Land and bread were closely related, of course, especially since the Russian *khleb* means both "bread" and "grain." Both were also metaphors of expectation as well as goods of existential importance. How land was used and who should possess it remained a defining question of the revolutionary period. The production of grain and availability of bread threatened for many to be a question of life and death. The hopes embedded in these two simple words reflected a primary meaning for many of the revolution itself: the security of physical and emotional well-being. "Land" and "bread" signified the end of want in the same way that "peace" signified the end of loss.

The immediate problems to be solved here were practical ones: increasing the output from grain-producing land and assuring its distribution. The first seemed to be the less problematic. Appropriating the platform of the SRs, among the first decrees of the new regime were those officially abolishing gentry property rights without compensation and ordering the "immediate transfer" of this land to peasant communities, along with that held by the clergy and the state. In many places the process was already well underway. Both were eagerly received. During the following weeks peasant communities all over Russia implemented them according to village traditions, as they saw fit. In many places new allotments were added to holdings of returning soldiers and their families. In a few places even nonpeasants working their own small estates were allowed to continue doing so. Disputes were common but largely settled by the existing local land committees, peasant councils, or local courts.[18]

These and other new laws-by-fiat were apparently produced from drafts Lenin wrote himself without much (or even any) consultation. Like the decision affirming elections to the Constituent Assembly, they were more a reflection of his eagerness to dampen armed popular opposition than clearly thought-out policies. In any event, the efforts over the past two years to empower the localities very quickly reached an unanticipated outcome. Assigning *vlast'* to local soviets formally empowered thousands of would-be authorities in town and village communities. The key questions were therefore not who possessed land, but how those who possessed it would distribute its production and how grain requisitioned by the regime could be distributed effectively to those who needed it most.

Meanwhile, the Bolsheviks' seizure of the state did nothing to reduce scarcities or to contain what for many was a lethal inflation, sending the costs of essential goods beyond the means available to procure them. While the new regime reinforced the grain and trade monopolies, black and gray markets continued to undermine both. As much as 60 percent of all grain may have been distributed illegally between October and December by individual traders, official exhortation and "the most strict and severe penalties" for black marketeering notwithstanding.[19] Poor harvests resulting from past expropriation and the peasants' own consumption of seed corn threatened future deliveries. Assuring adequate supplies of *khleb* ("bread," or simply "food")—now as much as a metaphor of hope and want as a physical description—remained a huge problem. Party ideologists may have believed its root lay in the residual ideas of private or communal possession as well as the institutions and traditions of commercial market exchange. But as we know, Russia's partly commercialized rural economy strengthened in practical terms the autarchic tendencies of grain-producing villages deep in the countryside and far from major towns and railroad centers. Unlike "land," moreover, "bread" was not only a problem still waiting to be solved in terms of material needs and emotional insecurities. It also threatened the reemergence of food riots of the sort that differentiated the February revolution in 1917 from the Bolsheviks' seizure of state power in October.

In any event, the promise of bread in provincial centers like Nizhnii Novgorod increasingly rang hollow. From all accounts, the situation in other major cities

---

[18] Orlando Figes, *Peasant Russia, Civil War: The Volga Countryside in Revolution 1917–1921* (Oxford: Oxford University Press, 1989), 132–35; Michael C. Hickey, "Peasant Autonomy, Soviet Power, and Land Redistribution in Smolensk Province, November 1917–May 1918," *Revolutionary Russia* 1 (June 1996): 19–32.

[19] *Vestnik Statistiki* 1–4 (1920): 56.

also became increasingly dire during the first winter of Bolshevik rule. Stocks of grain in Moscow and Petrograd fell far below the level needed to meet a single day's meager ration of half a pound of bread. Distribution was severely affected by the continued crisis of railroad transport. What the new regime imagined it could do in the fall of 1917 was to reinforce the grain and trade monopolies. New decrees reaffirmed that private trade was to remain illegal. Only the regime could direct how requisitioned or confiscated grain could be distributed. In some places all owners of private food shops were required to turn in their keys; elsewhere, they continued to operate. Over the winter the porous nature of both monopolies only worsened as villagers got their hands on new supplies. Illegal private trade expanded. Prices soared.[20]

Nationalization from Below, Refinancing Production from Above, Repudiating Debt

Taking state power, the Bolsheviks also assumed responsibility for assuring state-owned industrial plants continued to function and stemming the closures of privately owned plants whose production was also essential to national well-being. This necessarily involved assuming control over how the State Bank dispensed its funds. It also meant deciding what the role would now be of private banks directly involved in capitalizing industrial production.

On October 25, Petrograd banks began to close around noon. They stayed shut on the 26th and announced the next day that they would open only during the hours the State Bank itself was open. Withdrawals were limited to 10,000 rubles. On October 30, they closed again, this time because of disorder and shooting on the streets. Checks drawn on the State Bank were being refused. Withdrawals were reduced to 3,000 rubles a day for each private client. Many demands could not be paid. During the following days and into November banks in most places had scattered openings and processed only urgent transactions. Restrictions on withdrawals left industrial and commercial clients without funds to meet their needs. Russia's commercial circles were now extremely anxious, if not in a state of panic. Currency around the country was itself in increasingly short supply. In November Odessa and a few other cities began printing their own. In effect, the banks themselves were giving the Bolsheviks little choice but to confront the difficult task of reorganizing state finances, despite a lack of planning or even a clear understanding of how to do so.[21] Bolshevik rhetoric complicated matters

---

[20] *Raboche-Krestianskii Nizhegorodskii Listok*, Feb. 10–23, 1918.
[21] A. N. Zak, *Denezhnoe obrashchenie i emissionaia operatsiia v Rossii 1917–1918 gg.* (Petrograd: Svoboda, 1918), 33–34; M. V. Khodiakov, *Den'gi revoliutsii i grazhdanskoi voiny 1917–1920 gody* (St. Petersburg: Izd. SPb State University, 2019), esp. chs. 3–7; Steven G. Marks, "The

further. Despite the absence of any popular insurrection, the Declaration of the Rights of the People of Russia situated the "October Revolution of Workers and Peasants" under the "banner of emancipation" according to "class": peasants from the oppressive gentry, soldiers from autocratic officers, peasants from "kulaks" and landlords; and most important in regard to state finance, workers from the "caprice and arbitrariness [*kapriz i proizvol*] of capitalists."[22]

The expropriation of these "capricious and arbitrary capitalists" through class warfare was, of course, part of the Bolsheviks' ideological DNA. Yet there were obvious reasons why Lenin's preoccupation with securing state power made it prudent to move slowly beyond demonizing language. For the moment there was no administrative body or staff capable of managing the huge task of nationalization, never mind the ways the "expropriation" of current owners, managers, and propertied investors would further damage an economy already on the verge of collapse. Tarring owners and managers as "bourgeois" assumed their inherent exploitative biases were more salient than their technical and managerial experience. It was easier to imagine that any cook could run the government, Lenin reportedly suggested, than it was to imagine any cook could manage a modern industrial enterprise.

The same fatuous division of peasants into rigid categories of "poor," "middle," and "rich" (*kulak*) comparably distorted the social realities of the village commune. Income and wealth obviously varied in the village, but as Teodor Shanin has shown, the distribution of wealth within Russia's "awkward class" was constantly changing.[23] Marriage, children, the departure of villagers to cities and towns affected individual as well as collective prosperity. Many "kulaks" were at one time poor or middle peasants. "Middle" peasants in grain-importing districts might be comparable to those "poor peasants" in grain-surplus areas. In any event, making accurate "class" identifications was guesswork unless one had access to village records; even then, there was no way of accurately determining whether ascribed status correlated to social values. As a matter of policy, the very act of rigid social classification read specific moralities into ideologically derived social types. The same was true with "capricious and arbitrary" capitalists. In industrial areas, at least some "capricious" exploiters shared an interest with their workers in keeping their plants in operation. In sum, the ascription of class

---

Russian Experience with Money, 1914-24," in *Russian Culture in War and Revolution, 1914-22*, vol. 1, ed. Murray Frame, Boris Kolonitskii, Steven Marks, and Melissa Stockdale (Bloomington, IN: Slavica, 2014), bk. 1, 128-40.

[22] *Vestnik Statistiki* 1-4 (1920): 39-40.
[23] Teodor Shanin, *The Awkward Class: Political Sociology of Peasantry in a Developing Society: Russia 1910-1925* (Oxford: Clarendon Press, 1972).

identities was more an inaccurate explanation for Russia's economic crisis than it was a politically useful reading of social difference.

Many if not most industrialists and plant owners, of course, regarded the Bolsheviks with scorn. Lenin's taking power dissolved whatever reluctance they still had to shutting their plants down. Others, however, saw the issue in the larger terms of Russian national welfare. There was still a real possibility that the Bolsheviks' hold on power would be short-lived. Members of the WIC and Union of Industrial Congresses continued to gather at 46 Liteinyi to discuss ways they might cooperate with the new regime to keep plants open. In December the Moscow Society of Factory and Mill Owners met with representatives from nineteen cities to discuss this and related issues.[24]

In these circumstances Lenin's regime took three additional steps that some historians consider the epitome of ideologically driven folly.[25] It decreed the universal establishment of workers' control in all industrial enterprises employing more than five persons; it nationalized the state bank, and followed up with the nationalization of all private banks around the country; and on January 21 it repudiated state debt of any kind, including state guarantees on all domestic loans like the Provisional Government's Liberty Bonds, and those of foreign governments. These measures were part of a broader economic policy laid out by two energetic thirty-one-year-olds: the economist and left Bolshevik Nikolai Osinskii (Obolenskii), a lawyer and statistician from a landowning family, and Vladimir Smirnov, who soon became commissar of trade and industry.

Osinski and Smirnov both seemed to recognize the enormity of the economic problems at hand. They stressed the need for pragmatism in order to prevent further economic collapse. The necessary measures were not those one would expect in a "normal" transition to socialism.[26] In effect, defaulting on Russia's huge national debt was admitting that the country was financially bankrupt, the rhetoric of 1917 becoming reality. Yet like a defaulting capitalist corporation, bankruptcy essentially cleared the field so that economic reconstruction could proceed unimpeded by the financial burdens incurred by previous regimes. Exactly how this would happen remained to be seen.

For its part, the decree requiring workers' control was partly intended to strengthen the party's political support, but its bigger purpose was to prevent owners from stripping assets from their plants and selling them off.

Within a few weeks workers had reportedly organized new committees in more than twenty-one hundred major enterprises, including two-thirds of those

---

[24] RGIA f. 32, op. 2, d. 1, ll. 1–17ff; f. 126, op. 1, d. 8, ll. 1–5; d. 19, ll. 162, 322.
[25] S. McKeekin, *History's Greatest Heist: The Looting of Russia by the Bolsheviks* (New Haven, CT: Yale University Press, 2008), 11–13; Richard Pipes, *The Russian Revolution* (New York: Knopf, 1990), 601–2, 672–73.
[26] GARF f. 130, op. 1, d. 36, ll. 5–7.

with more than two hundred workers. Almost fifty central councils of uncertain political composition also sprang up in industrial areas to coordinate them.[27] An additional expectation was that factory committees could now gain access to all resources still controlled by owners, especially financial ones, and use them to stay in operation. In fact, the funds needed to finance private production were commonly provided by bank loans, generally secured by collateral in the form of bonds or stock. Without the banks' cooperation, the only source of funding was the state.

Already in July, as we have seen, workers themselves in plants threatening to close their doors pressed for nationalization as the only way to preserve their jobs. Now scores of these same committees declared their plants "nationalized" unilaterally, sometimes, as in Saratov, with the support of local soviets, sometimes simply "from below." In either case the expectation was that as newly declared state enterprises they could now secure the funds they needed.[28] While the printing press was readily at hand, there were obvious dangers here, just as there were when money was issued in the form of credit notes. The Sovnarkom itself urged "extreme caution." All technical and financial issues regarded as state support for enterprises "nationalized from below" had to be carefully worked out beforehand.[29]

In the meantime, the State Bank itself refused to disperse its funds to the new Sovnarkom, some of its employees beginning a well-publicized strike to help ensure this did not happen. Lenin may have presumed it would be a relatively simple matter to use the Bank's funds as he directed, including the issuance of new credit to support production. The Bank's unwillingness to cooperate thus presented a major threat to industrial production. Representatives from regional banks began to warn that local credit markets were essentially shutting down. In Kazan, Rostov, Tula, Odessa, and other cities, local banks began issuing new loans in their own currency, its value, like the rubles now being printed in Petrograd, relating only to its acceptance as a medium of exchange.[30]

All of these issues were openly confronted in early December at a large congress of representatives from the Moscow industrial region. A Bolshevik contingent led by Stanislav Kossior from Petrograd and Evgenii Alperovich from the Economic Department of the Moscow Soviet heard direct testimony about the collapsing economy from an array of regional figures. The discussion reportedly

[27] M. L. Itkin, "Tsentry fabrichno-zavodsikh komitetov Rossii v 1917 godu," *Voprosy istorii* 2 (1974): 21–35.
[28] V. D. Drobizhev, *Glavnyi shtab sotsialisticheskoi promyshlennosti* (Moscow: Nauka, 1966), 48–50; *Natsionalizatsiia promyshlennosti v SSSR: Sbornik dokumentov i materialov, 1917–1920 gg,.* ed. I. A. Gladkov (Moscow: Gosizdat Pol. Lit., 1954), 107.
[29] V. Venediktov, *Organizatsiia gosudarstvennoi promyshlennosti v SSSR,* 2 vols. (Leningrad: Lenizdat, 1957), 1:178–80.
[30] Khodiakov, *Den'gi revoliutsii,* chs. 4–7.

had a "funereal tone." One after another participant again spoke in the now commonplace language of "looming catastrophe." On the eve of an expected separate peace with Germany Russia had no plan to manage massive demobilization. Adequate capital was not available nor likely to be forthcoming. ("From whom?" one delegate shouted.) The ruble was in free fall, and while the regime had just decreed the "so-called" nationalization of all banks, as the Menshevik economist Lev Kafengauz described it, what it had really done was seize control of bank deposits and capital reserves, not introduce a new system of capital formation or plans for its distribution.

Lacking financing and resources, enterprises everywhere continued to shut down. Food was scarce, workers' control "chaotic," speculation out of control, and essential workers were leaving the cities "so as not to be without a scrap of bread." With no help possible from abroad and no possibility of raising adequate revenues through taxation or expropriation, the printing press was set to put out 3 billion rubles a month, maybe more if it had the capacity. Even Kossior thought the situation was dire, blaming it on the deliberate efforts of owners to create "industrial anarchy."[31]

Thus, the "so-called" nationalization of banks was not a planned step to assume full control over all Russian financial transactions but a move to help finance enterprises self-nationalized from below and to prevent resources being paid out to the regime's opponents.[32] Between November and the following February, some eight hundred enterprises were nationalized, as many as six hundred "from below" by factory committees. In some cases, the nationalization was ordered (or agreed to) by local soviets, legitimizing workers' actions and in some places enabling loans or credit. At the same time, once those involved in taking over the State Bank better understood the ways finances were managed, it was a relatively short step to repudiating international and state loans, reorganizing the banking system to finance production through state credits, and moving banks to pass through resources generated by the printing press.[33]

Meanwhile, the new All-Russia Council for the Economy (Sovnarkhoz) convened on December 8, soon commonly referred to by its initials, VSNKh, or Vesenkha. The first meeting of its governing board was chaired by the thirty-one-year-old left Bolshevik N. Osinskii, who had just been elected to the Constituent Assembly from the Riazan-Voronezh district. Its major item of business was whether the Workers Group of the CWIC should leave that organization or take

[31] *Trudy 1-go Vserossiiskogo s"ezda sovetov narodnogo khoziaistva 25 maia–4 iiunia 1918. Stenograficheskii Otchet* (Moscow, 1918), 5–7.
[32] A good recent study is Hassan Malik, *Bankers and Bolsheviks* (Princeton, NJ: Princeton University Press, 2018), chs. 4, 5.
[33] V. Z. Drobizhev, "Sotsialisticheskoe obshchestvlenie promyshlennosti v SSSR," *Voprosy Istorii* 6 (June 1964): 63.

it over. (The decision was that it should remain in the CWIC in order to provide useful information.)[34] The candidacy of Vladimir Groman for membership to the presidium was rejected over the protest of his economist colleague, the former Menshevik Iurii Larin M. A. Lur'e), who objected "in the strongest terms" to using the category of class or political affiliation to reject the best people if they were willing to work with the new regime. Groman took a position instead in the new Commissariat for Food.[35]

In these fraught circumstances private banks throughout the country were officially nationalized at the end of December into branches of the Peoples' (Narodnyi) Bank of the Russian Republic. In theory, state credit operations could now be rapidly expanded. When Russia's enormous state debt was annulled shortly afterward, relieving the regime of its huge service obligations, holders of state bonds were promised protection for up to 10,000 rubles as a way of mitigating their losses. Measures were also initiated to pay some dividends on the shares of the largest joint stock companies, again as an incentive to keep owners from closing their plants and to protect foreign interests, especially German.[36] In fact, the material and emotional losses of the moment were incalculable. So were their likely effects on Russia's future.

Meanwhile the emission of credit bills continued unabated. Contemporary accounts indicate that the nominal value of credit notes and the Provisional Government's "Kerenki" circulating in January 1918 was approximately 30 billion rubles, of which more than 24 billion were now in unbacked credit notes, two and a half times as much as a year earlier.[37] As freshly minted currency was pressed into circulation backed only by the hope, again, that it would continue to be trusted for payments and exchanges of various sorts, left Bolsheviks contemplated accelerating "socialism" by moving to a system of wages in kind that would have discernible value. In the meantime, enterprises would operate on the basis of credits and money wages linked to estimates of costs (*po smetam*).

"Still Starving" Workers and Increasingly Hungry Peasants

One of the salient aspects of Russia's revolutionary experience was that nothing changed for the better in the first winter of Bolshevik rule. Each of the new

---

[34] *Protokoly Presidiuma vysshego soveta narodnogo khoziaistva, Dekabr' 1917–1918* (Moscow: Nauka, 1991), 25–26.

[35] Other members of the board were Bukharin, Lomov (Georgy Oppokov), Miliutin, Sokol'nikov, Vasili Shmidt, and Vladimir Smirnov.

[36] Venedictov, *Organizatsii*, 181; Silvana Malle, *The Economic Organization of War Communism* (Cambridge: Cambridge University Press, 1985), 158; Narodnyi Komissariat Finansov, *Obzor finansovogo zakonodatel'stva 1917–1921* (Petrograd: NKF, 1921), 10–12.

[37] G. Sokol'nikov, "Denezhnyi Krizis," *Narodnoe Khoziaistvo* 2 (Apr. 1918): 2–4.

regime's major decrees brought disruption and dislocation. If anything, anxieties over food only increased when the 1917 summer harvest fell to the lowest amount in three years. In many places there was now a large deficit of seed for the spring crop. In Riazan the amount of sown land may have decreased by more than 1.4 million acres. The differences in hunger and food anxiety between provinces was also more acute. Voronezh was relatively secure, but adjacent Riazan suffered. Local authorities officially proscribed potatoes from being sent to Moscow, but the number of bagmen and -women overwhelmed efforts to restrain them. Many railroaders were relying on these black-market sources to get by themselves, creating anxieties on all sides about the future state of the lines and the likelihood of more industrial enterprises shutting down.[38]

Among the effects of the decree on workers' control was the further disruption of production in major industrial plants, additional closings, and an acceleration of out-migration from industrial centers, especially Petrograd and Moscow. Meanwhile, factory committees desperately sought new orders for goods in November and December, struggled to find fuel and other supplies, and ran out of funds to pay workers. They also struggled with administrative issues, seeking the help of technicians and managers in order to keep their plants running, and in some plants giving them protected seats on the committees themselves. At the Franco-Russian, Petrograd Metalworking, Skorokhod leather, and other plants in Petrograd, elected committees became "worker directors" with all managerial rights, from deciding which orders to accept and fill to purchasing raw materials, setting new wage levels, and controlling all financial operations.

The fourth New Year since the beginning of the war was thus once again a dismal one. According to the newspaper of the shop employees union, shop owners everywhere were secreting their goods, stealing receipts, and preparing to shut down. In Petrograd, the supply of foodstuffs and other goods coming into the city dropped precipitously in almost every category. While crowds again waited in long cold lines for their rationed portions of bread, now down to a half-pound, the Petrograd shop employees union demanded the government move immediately to take full control over trade.[39] The situation in parts of the countryside was also grim. Orlando Figes's research suggests the imminent possibility of starvation in Samara province and elsewhere in the normally productive mid-Volga region. T. V. Osipova's exploration shows SRs and others in rural soviets desperate for relaxation on the trade monopoly, while many in industrial towns insisted it be strictly enforced. In both places black markets and local bagmen

---

[38] A. S. Sokolov, "Prodovol'stvennoe snabzhenie i meshochnichestvo v Riazanskoi gubernii 1918–1919," *Ekonomicheskaia istoriia* 4 (2019): 376–85.

[39] N. Uglanov, "Iz praktiki natsionalizatsii torgovli v Petrograde," *Bor'ba* 17 (Dec. 1918): 1–2; *Bor'ba* 6–7 (Jan. 1918): 5–7; 8 (Feb. 1918): 1–2; Mary McAuley, *Bread and Justice: Society and State in Petrograd* (Oxford: Clarendon Press, 1991), 283.

continued to be the primary source of food for many people. In rural Saratov, grain was being stolen by armed gangs beefed up by returning soldiers.[40]

In the following weeks, as a high-level Bolshevik delegation led by Trotsky pursued peace talks near Brest-Litovsk, the consequences of demobilization also loomed heavily over industrial production. In Petrograd 80 percent of the industrial workforce was still in defense-related occupations. The Sovnarkom itself ordered military production to cease entirely for artillery shells and other weaponry that was no longer expected to have much use. According to the decree, factory committees and unions were "to take the most decisive measures" to find work for displaced workers, "sending delegations to the Urals and other places to work out the necessary arrangements."[41]

The exodus from Moscow, Petrograd, and other major cities thus began to swell during these weeks. The dissolution of the Constituent Assembly and changing political circumstances obviously played a role here, but the exodus was mostly an effect of scarcities and insecurities: over food, fuel for heat as well as production, jobs, vulnerability to a German offensive, and gloomy perspectives about immediate and more distant futures. At the end of December 45,000 fewer men and women were reportedly at work in Petrograd than at the start of the year. Within three months the figure would grow to 221,000. The figures are not likely precise, but it is still fair to assume that nearly 60 percent of the pre-October workforce was no longer employed. The greatest declines in Petrograd were in reportedly in metals and chemicals, two of the country's most-favored industrial sectors: 79 percent and 74 percent, respectively, by April 1918, according to contemporary statistics. The outflow from Moscow was similar, from provincial cities less so but still substantial.[42] As Diane Koenker and Daniel Brower have suggested, scarcities long blamed on the propertied "bourgeoisie" may also have had a contrary effect on politicized class identities, at least to some degree. The rigid class distinctions ascribed convincingly before October as explanations for scarcities may have begun to weaken as the recent rich found themselves selling their goods on the street together with the habitual poor, and want and deprivation spread rapidly across social divides. Street trading became common despite prohibitions; black markets expanded everywhere.[43] The Cheka's notorious efforts at Moscow's train stations to stop bagmen and -women from bringing their sacks of grain to trade were testimony to how urgently their efforts were needed. All of this would increase greatly in the following months,

---

[40] Figes, *Peasant Russia*, 88ff.; T. V. Osipova, *Rossiiskoe krestian'stvo v revoliutsii grazhdanskoi voine* (Moscow: Izd. Strelets, 2001), 80–83.

[41] *Dekrety Sovetskoi Vlasti*, 1: 196–98.

[42] *Statistika truda* 2–3 (Aug. 15, 1918), 8–14, 22–26.

[43] On these issues, see esp. the essays by Diane Koenker and Daniel Brower in Diane Koenker et al., eds., *Party, State, and Society in the Russian Civil War* (Bloomington: Indiana University Press, 1989).

as both Petrograd and Moscow saw the near dissolution of the best paid, most numerous, and politically most radical component of the workforce, the social foundation of Bolshevik political support.

Nothing in Marxist-Leninist ideology directed how these circumstances might be addressed. For some, the simple idea that workers in a workers' state should control industry and solve these problems themselves was an ideologically attractive way to avoid an urgent set of problems, at least for the moment. Even Bukharin, who would soon emerge as one of the party's leading theorists on developing a socialist economy, had not given the matter any real thought before October. He and the emerging group of "Left Communists" were captured by the idea that revolution in Russia would precipitate revolution elsewhere, especially in Germany. Bolshevik Russia had to do everything possible to ensure that happened. Europe's advanced economies would then come to Russia's aid. Thus while the Cheka expanded its efforts to root out "subversion and counterrevolution," some members of Vesenkha supported further nationalization as a way to control the shop floor, some for punitive reasons against prominent industrialists, while others pressed the candidacies of Bolshevik loyalists for election to factory and trade union committees..[44]

Indeed, many factory committees now were unruly organizations. Angry complaints were heard about their hiring and firing workers at random, bypassing the labor exchanges and setting their own wage levels. Workers' control in many places was now understood to mean the committees seizing plant administrations and running factories on their own: control in the physical sense rather than *kontrol'* in the sense of supervision and accountability. If committees managed with managerial and technical personnel to secure funding and resources, production could continue, at least for a while. More commonly, however, committees struggled to meet their workers' needs and became themselves the object of their wrath. Well into the spring trade union newspapers reported, "[C]omrades elect their factory committees and within a week the grumbling begins." New meetings are held, new instructions issued, and soon "the cycle begins again."[45] At the Moscow Mechanical plant, workers demanded that the factory committee hand the plant back to its former administrators and director. Invited to address the workers, the director used the opportunity to turn them down. Elsewhere, protests to the Cheka about the activities of the committees brought harsh reprisals, in one case the arrest and conviction of forty-five committee members This in turn led to hostility by some enthusiastic committee members toward their own rank and file, accompanied by charges of laziness

---

[44] M. L. Itkin, "Tsentry fabrichno-zavodsikh komitetov Rossii v 1917 godu," *Voprosy istorii* 2 (1974): 21–35.

[45] *Rabochii khimik* 4–5 (Aug. 1918): 28; *Tekstil'shchik* (Moscow) 7–8 (Oct. 1918).

and irresponsibility by their "politically unconscious" comrades that echoed long-term Menshevik and Bolshevik concerns. Over the years, both parties had worked to create effective trade unions that could lead workers in their own political directions. Their efforts now seemed in vain.[46]

Two of the most contentious political issues inherited by Lenin's regime centered on the proper nature and form of workers' *kontrol'* itself and the position of trade unions in a socialist economy moving toward full nationalization. As we have seen, contested meanings of "control" aggravated management-labor relations from the moment the Provisional Government authorized factory committees in April 1917. As the understanding of *kontrol'* shifted from the original meaning of "supervision" to workers' engagement in management, some plants that would otherwise have closed managed to stay open in the late summer and fall of 1917. The Sovnarkom's decree of November 11 seemed to many to affirm this understanding, but its language was imprecise. It formally authorized workers' control in all enterprises, banks, cooperatives, and similar institutions. It also created new city, provincial, and regional workers' control soviets as organs of corresponding to workers', peasants', and soldiers' soviets to adjudicate disputes. The wording of the degree, however, obscured the degree of their authority as well as that of committees in individual enterprises. Organs of workers' control had the right to "supervise" production, establish minimum wages, and take measures to increase production. Their decisions were "obligatory" for enterprise owners or managers, but they had three days to appeal to the higher-level bodies and could be modified by their decision. The tasks of drawing clearer lines between supervision and management in various enterprises, banks, trading companies, cooperatives, and other such bodies would be the responsibility of the "All-Russia Soviet of Workers' Control."[47] How all of this would come about without further disruption was unclear.

Not surprisingly, the results of this decree were quite mixed. In one Petrograd industrial district some nineteen firms shut down immediately afterward. In others, like Petrograd Metalworking, committee members became "worker directors" with all managerial rights. At Skorokhod leather a newly elected committee informed management that it hoped "you will come to accept our control and that on all questions . . . will be responsive, and in any case not go against our will, which is based on the juridical authority given us by the revolutionary nation [*narod*]."[48] Even at Petrograd Metals, a hotbed of Bolshevik activism, new "worker directors" explained that while they were taking control over production, "control" did not mean "direct active participation in the administration

---

[46] Central State Archive for the Moscow Region f. 146, op. 1, d. 4, passim; f. 4612, op. 1, d. 37, ll. 6–7; d. 340, passim; f. 4613, op. 1, d. 64, passim.
[47] NKT, *Sobranie zakonov, 26 okt.–17 dek. 1917* (Petrograd: Gos. tip., 1917), 16–18.
[48] RGIA f. 150, op. 2, d. 15, ll. 82–84.

of production and the plant itself." Their tasks would focus on fulfilling orders, improving work conditions, procuring raw materials and fuel, and exercising supervision and leadership in all factory departments.[49] In many provincial cities as well as the capitals a form of collegial management alone developed simply because it seemed the most effective way to keep an enterprise open. When these efforts failed and funds dried up, workers' delegations from some plants were sent to the countryside to exchange plant machinery and resources for food and other goods, a move easily misunderstood (and later commonly characterized) as self-destructive anarchism.

How widespread this more moderate form of workers' control was throughout Russia's flailing industries over the winter of 1918 is unclear. In December and January, however, it was enough of an accommodation to the mutual interests of management and labor to prompt members of the still functioning Petrograd Society of Factory and Mill Owners to enter into direct talks with the new commissar of labor, the metal worker Alexander Shliapnikov, over what they called the "control crisis" and try to work with him to ensure control as supervision rather than plant management became the recognized norm.[50] The thirty-one-year-old Shliapnikov would soon become known as a leader of the Bolsheviks' "left opposition," but he regarded this form of cooperation important for the moment to keep plants in operation. Shliapnikov had joined the Bolsheviks in 1903 at the ripe age of eighteen. Arrested several times, he had returned to Russia in 1916 from Europe, taking an active role in the party's Petrograd organization and joining the Soviet Executive Committee in March, where he worked closely with Chkheidze, Groman, Skobelev, and others. Shliapnikov's credentials for commissar of labor were thin, but his working-class pedigree, his known concern for the underprivileged, and his role in the politically important metalworkers union were enough to warrant his appointment. Among his other steps to preserve some semblance of factory order was to try to continue the mediating efforts of the Bureau for the Resolution of Disputes between Capital and Labor initiated by Minister of Labor Skobelev in the spring of 1917. These continued to meet along with trade union conflict commissions on questions like pay for workers on strike and malfeasance on the part of administrative personnel. Most decisions, not surprisingly, favored workers.[51]

Shliapnikov and others also saw trade unions as a potentially important ally in this struggle. as long as Bolsheviks could replace the unions' largely Menshevik leadership or new Bolshevik unions replaced old Menshevik ones. Here the electoral process served the party well, as it had the radicalization of factory

---

[49] Ibid., l. 41.
[50] Ibid., ll. 35–36, 101.
[51] GARF f. 382, op. 2, d. 94, ll. 19–32.

committees and local soviets in 1917. When the first All-Russia Congress of Trade Unions, representing 162 local and 19 national unions, convened with a Bolshevik majority in January, it took the position that workers' control did not mean the full transfer of enterprises into its hands nor give factory committees the right to make "definitive decisions" that related to the very existence of enterprises. Management still rested with their state or private owners.[52]

While the roles of factory committees and trade unions were being argued, material circumstances continued to worsen, especially in Petrograd and Moscow but elsewhere as well. State authority in provincial Russia was now largely claimed by commissars appointed from the center, ostensibly linking regional, provincial, and local economic and political soviets to the new departments (*glavki*) of Sovnarkhoz in Moscow. But food supplies almost everywhere remained meager, discrediting the power they represented. Many in provincial cities and towns suffered in ways comparable to before October, and in many places were increasingly worse off. In Nizhnii Novgorod the food situation was described already in January as "disastrous." The lack of seed now threatened spring planting. Armed detachments of demobilized soldiers were called on to guard the railroad depots—the foxes, as it were, to the chicken coop.[53] In Iaroslavl the food situation was "desperate." Starvation in Tula and elsewhere was described as a literal threat. In Novgorod the provincial soviet newspaper described food conditions as "dreadful." Armed civilian militias (*druzhinye*) were needed to protect goods trains. Mining firms in the Urals were in desperate need of workers and engineers. Conditions were "difficult, frightful filth everywhere." Technicians and other specialists were being driven off and abandoned apartments ransacked by unruly soldiers and armed workers. Financial operations remained chaotic despite (or partly because) banks were officially nationalized.[54]

Like members of the tsarist regime and the Provisional Government, Viktor Nogin and others in the Sovnarkom decried the lack of detailed information: "Without statistics we work blindly, which has a terribly serious [*strashno*] effect on our activities."[55] A large gathering of regional commissars of labor in early March 1918, chaired by Nogin, helped fill out the picture. In the localities the many decrees and laws coming from the center were frequently ignored or applied in "chaotic" fashion, in part because so many contradicted each other. The mandated eight-hour workday norm was not being implemented in some

---

[52] *Pervyi Vserossiiskii s"ezd professional'nykh soiuzov 7–14 Ianvaria 1918 g.* (Moscow, 1918) 199–232, 365–71.
[53] *Nizhegorodskaia Kommuna*, Jan. 5, 9, 1918.
[54] *Nizhegorodskaia Kommuna*, Jan. 6, 8, 1918; RGASPI f. 5, op. 1, d. 2887, ll. 1–2; d. 2531, ll. 3–17; op. 2, d. 2880, ll. 5–5 ob.; *Statistika truda* 6–7 (Oct 15 and Nov. 15, 1918): 20–23; *Novaia Vechernyi Chas*, Feb. 22, 1918. See also Malle, *Economic Organization*, 338–95.
[55] *Vtoroi S"ezd Komissarov Truda i Predstavitelei Birzh Truda Moskovskoi Oblasti, 10–13 Mar. 1918* (Moscow, 1918), 5–6.

80 percent of working enterprises, even in Moscow. In Kostroma, Smolensk, and other provinces, unemployment exchanges were not functioning or functioning poorly. Where they were open, factory committees were defrauding them with false lists in an effort to secure additional wage funds. A new legion of specially authorized agents sent out from Moscow with their own armed detachments only made matters worse. In some places local food committees were arrested, charged with corruption. Clashes occurred in every province and perhaps in every district. Reports sent to Moscow suggest that arbitrariness and despotism (*proizvol*) were everywhere more a rule than an exception. The central offices of the Commissariat of Transport were almost entirely cut off from local committees. Telegraph and telephone communications worked badly or not at all.[56] One common feeling among provincial anti-Bolsheviks was that "proletarian dictatorship" was another term for anarchy.[57]

While actual scarcities of food and other goods varied considerably in provincial areas, the effects of scarcity were similar almost everywhere. One of the most serious problems was the rapid rise in prices and the fall in real wages, which were estimated at an average to be least one-third less than the steady rise in the cost of living. In Moscow the prices of flour and bread had risen 300 percent between January and April, according to official statistics published one year later. Increases elsewhere were comparable despite efforts at enforcing fixed prices.[58]

A compounding problem was the lack of paper money, although again, the situation varied widely. In February private bank owners in Nizhnii Novgorod were given two weeks to bring their holdings to the city office of the new national People's Bank. Elsewhere the transfer of banknotes was forbidden but not suppressed. In some provincial cities workers committees returned from banks to their factories empty-handed and embittered. Demobilized soldiers compounded these problems, demanding their jobs back at gunpoint as well as full wages even in places where the actual workday was five hours or less. Women as always were particularly vulnerable, often pushed aside in food lines by angry and impatient soldiers and maltreated on the railroads. In Briansk, Tver, Aleksandrov, and other places women members of labor exchanges worked "not without danger to their own lives.... All of this leads to a huge fall in the productivity of enterprises and the final exhaustion of their financial resources staff."[59]

Fuel, too, remained in short supply, and the number of industrial workers still employed continued to decline. The greatest losses by far were in Russia's

---

[56] Russian State Archive of the Economy f. 3429, op. 1, d. 369, ll. 116, 146, and passim; RGIA f. 32, op. 2, d. 71 [*Biulleteni Soveta S'ezdov* 2 and 3 (Jan. 1–7, 7–23, 18)]; RGASPI f. 5, op. 1 d. 2887, ll. 1–13.
[57] *Pischebumazhnik* 1 (May 14, 1918); M. Philips Price, *My Reminiscences of the Russian Revolution* (London, 1923), 86ff.
[58] *Statistika truda* 1–4 (Jan.– Feb. 1919): 40–45.
[59] Ibid., 19–21; *Raboche-Krestianskii Nizhegorodskii Listok,* Feb. 7–20, 1918; *Gruzoborot* 2–3 (Apr. 12, 1918), 25.

previously favored metalworking and chemical plants: 79 percent and 74 percent, respectively, by April 1918 relative to January 1918. Leather workers were similarly affected. As factory militias tightened control at plant gates, employment documents with their claim for wages came to matter as much as ration cards.[60] Vesenkha's own journal, *Narodnoe Khoziaistvo*, acknowledged that panic gripped many during February, no doubt fearful as well of a renewed German offensive.[61]

Distributing additional food and fuel were the most immediate ways to relieve some of these problems, but factory committees, trade unions, or local soviets could not do very much about increasing workers' rations. One of the most important efforts to meet these needs was consequently directed toward the railroaders and their "statized" national union. Bolshevik supporters were prevalent in major railroad shops and depots and in local shop unions, the SRs dominant among the huge numbers of track and line workers, many of whom worked in close proximity to their villages, and in the union's executive committee Vikzhel. The unresolved conflicts between workers in different railroad services that emerged in 1917 now began to play out to the Bolsheviks' advantage. The "all-Russia" railroad union was quite fragmented. In November the union's journal and other railroad publications strongly opposed identification with any political party. Railroad workers in Saratov and elsewhere were sharply critical of Vikzhel for being too close to the Bolsheviks. Some Vikzhel members also reacted angrily to "the system of terror" applied against the Kadets elected to the Constituent Assembly, vowing another nationwide strike if rumors that it would be dissolved proved to be true. In contrast, Bolsheviks were strong on the important Nikolaev line between Petrograd and Moscow. Toward the end of November new railroad soviets were organized in both junctions to work closely with the Sovnarkom.[62]

Scarcities in most cities were still easily attributed to the railroads, as they had been since the beginning of the war, again for good reason. At the Council of the Republic just before Lenin seized power, the number of sidelined locomotives was reported to have increased from nine thousand to twenty-one thousand since mid-September alone. Major lines were constantly threatened with interruptions. The former minister of transport P. P. Iurenev himself warned that railroad movement around the country was close to coming to a halt. Railroad workers in Kharkov placed the blame on hungry shop and track workers who

---

[60] *Statistika truda* 2–3 (Aug. 1918): 8–14, 22–26; *Vestnik Glavnago Komiteta Kozh.* 8 (May 1918): 36–38; *Russkie vedomosti* Jan. 31, Feb. 23, and Mar. 9, 1918; *Vestnik otdela upravleniia NKVD* 4 (Jan. 23, 1918); *Novaia Zhizn'*, Jan. 18, 1918; *Vestnik narodnogo komissariata truda* 2–3 (Feb. 1918): 21ff.

[61] *Narodnoe khoziaistvo* 6 (Mar. 1919).

[62] GARF f. 1779, op. 2, d. 558, passim; *Zhizn' Zheleznodorozhnikov* 6–7 (Nov. 1, 1917); *Mysli Zheleznodorozhnikov*, Dec. 15, 1917; *Vestnik Riazan-Uralskii Zh. D.* 3–4 (Feb. 1919): 41–42.

left their posts to look for food and a spate of resulting dismissals that further disrupted line operations. Fuel was so short that from November 1 freight traffic nationally reportedly fell by some 50 percent. Passenger trains ran sporadically. An urgent telegram to Trotsky from railroaders on the Southern line warned of anarchy and asked for help.[63]

From all accounts the railroad situation was indeed "catastrophic," as *Novaia Zhizn'* characterized it already in December. So was water transport, described by one knowledgeable person as "in a state of catastrophic decline."[64] But transport workers themselves were also suffering and being blamed for situations that were out of their control. Military trains were being held up if local military revolutionary committees were not convinced their soldiers accepted the Bolshevik regime. Passengers were searched for the same reason. So were goods trains, which were then commonly switched to new destinations. Soldiers reacted violently, "requisitioning" goods and food and forcing engine drivers to move on. Unruly throngs jammed stations trying to leave Petrograd and Moscow, demanding trains and threatening railroad personnel. Along the line, material conditions also worsened. Many railroaders were not being paid. Others stopped goods trains themselves and made off with food supplies and other marketable freight "in order not to die from hunger." Under Vikzhel's leadership, the newspaper complained, the railroads had fallen under a multipower (*mnogovlastie*) regime, with conflicting and contradictory orders and a complete failure of responsible administration. In these circumstances it is hardly surprising that an emergency congress in the Aleksandrovsk railroad shops strongly condemned Vikzhel for its neutrality. *Vikzhelit'* had become a verb meaning "to vacillate."[65]

In late January 1918, the three largest railroad unions organized by professions began to form a rival to Vikzhel's all-Russia union. Toward the end of February a delegation of "starving" railroad workers met with Trotsky to demand the right to receive grain themselves directly from the grain monopoly. Otherwise, they would halt trains carrying food by standing on the tracks and "requisitioning" cargo for their own needs. Others wrote directly to Lenin, complaining that Sovnarkom decrees were making matters worse.[66] Voices of "extreme need" again echoed up and down the lines. Commissar of Transport V. I. Nevskii found Moscow's depots in a state of "chaos" when he conducted a personal inspection in March, with some nine hundred freight cars with goods and foodstuffs for the military waiting for the proper ordered to be unloaded, as *Prodput'*, the journal

---

[63] GARF f. 1779, op. 2, d. 558; *Vestnik Iuzhnoi Zhelez. Dorogi* 44 (Oct. 30, 1917); *Zhizn' Zheleznodorozhnikov* 6–7 (Nov. 1, 1917); *Russkiia Vedomosti*, Oct. 24, 1917.

[64] *Novaia Zhizn'*, Dec. 6, 1917; I. D. Mikhailov, *Osnovy voprosy transporta 1910–1925* (Moscow, 1918), 64.

[65] *Vestnik NKVD* 4 (Jan. 24, 1918): 8.

[66] *Petrogradskoe Ekho*, Feb. 18, 1918; RGASPI f. 5., op. 1, d. 2739, l. 7; *Novaia Zhizn'*, May 12, 1918; *Prodput'*, Apr. 2, 1918.

of the Central Food Bureau of the All-Russia Railroad Union, described the state of transport around the country in its first issue in March. Commissar Nevskii now blamed much of the disorder on railroad worker committees "unable or unwilling to take decisive and energetic measures."[67] "There are no collegial administrations anywhere in the world like ours," a prominent Bolshevik railroad expert agreed, "where the majority of members are switchmen, engineers, and rank-and-file employees."[68] From Ivanovo-Voznesensk workers describing themselves as "conscious and patiently starving revolutionaries" telegraphed, "We must protest against the Center's policies. Everything is taken from us, nothing is provided.... We have not a pound of reserves."[69]

In these circumstances Lenin and his supporters felt even more pressed to accept the Germans' draconian terms for a separate peace at Brest-Litovsk. In early March the signing was ratified at the Seventh Party Congress. Among its other familiar provisions was the surrender of the Ukrainian "breadbasket" to German occupation, significantly aggravating Russia's already urgent food supply crisis and stimulating what Boris Chernev has called a "Ukrainized" foreign policy in Kiev itself.[70] Bukharin and the Bolshevik left were appalled. So were the left SRs. The newspaper *Petrogradskoe Ekho* reported that the treaty seemed "treasonous" even to state workers at the Tula armament works, "destructive to the international proletarian movement and deeply harmful to the interests of Russian workers ... and the Russian economy in general."[71] The revolutionary potential of German workers, so important to Soviet Russia's own future, was now likely to be crushed as troops moved back through Germany to the European Front. Internationalist ideology seemed to have fallen under the threat of German guns.

Dictatorship as the Primary Task of Soviet Power

Just after the Brest-Litovsk Treaty was signed, Lenin defined what he called the immediate tasks of the Soviet government now that Russia had finally withdrawn from the war. The most urgent of these was "organizing *administration* in Russia," by which Lenin meant the task of governing effectively and bringing order to the country.[72]

---

[67] RGASPI f. 5, op. 1, d. 2740, ll. 1–32; *Prodput'* 1 (Mar. 1918).
[68] I. D. Mikhailov, *Osnovy voprosy transporta* (Moscow, 1918), 140.
[69] *Ekonomicheskaia Zhizn'*, Nov. 16, 1918.
[70] Boris Chernev, "Ukrainization and Its Contradictions in the Context of the Brest-Litovsk System," in *The Empire and Nationalism at War*, ed. Eric Lohr et al. (Bloomington, IN: Slavica, 2014), 163–88.
[71] *Petrogradskoe Ekho*, Mar. 30, 1918.
[72] V. I. Lenin, *Collected Works*, 5th ed. (Moscow: Progress, 1974), 27:242–43, Lenin's emphasis.

Current circumstances required several "adaptations" that some in the party resisted. The first was to rely on experts in the various fields of knowledge, technology, and experience. The second was the organization of the "strictest accounting and control of production and distribution of goods." Factory committees could not themselves take on these tasks. Workers' control meant the right to oversee experienced managers, not replace them. Third and most important was the creation of effective industrial management and "harmonious organization," as the emergency Congress of Soviets that ratified the Brest-Litovsk Treaty had just put it. Paradoxically, although Lenin did not mention the contradiction, "harmonious organization" also called for coercion—"coercion precisely in the form of dictatorship." Indeed, it was "extremely stupid and absurdly utopian to assume that the transition from capitalism to socialism is possible without coercion and without dictatorship." This meant "iron rule," a government that was "bold, swift, and ruthless in a revolutionary way in suppressing both exploiters and hooligans." In his view, the "excessively mild" current Soviet administration resembled "jelly more than iron."[73]

Lest there be any confusion about what Lenin had in mind, he elaborated further: courts were also to become instruments for inculcating discipline; piecework had to be brought back to increase industrial productivity; wages had to be based solely on total amount of goods produced or work performed. The Russian worker in whose name the Bolsheviks had seized state power was actually "a bad worker" in comparison to people in "advanced countries." And while the Taylor system regimenting work time and routines was "an example of the refined brutality of bourgeois exploitation," it was also, "like all capitalist progress," one of the "greatest scientific achievements" in the field of analyzing work processes and the "elaboration of correct work methods." In sum, coercive dictatorship—the "*unquestioning subordination*" and "*unquestioning obedience*" to the "*single will of the leaders of labor*"—was now absolutely essential for the transition from Russian capitalism to Soviet socialism.[74] Here in the clearest form were the ideologically hollow methods Lenin now thought necessary to overcome the deprivations and anxieties of scarcity, the agonies of loss and dislocation, that the experiences of world war and revolutionary expectation had brought to the peoples of the former Russian Empire.

From April into early June, discussions in the Sovnarkom and among central and regional Sovnarkhoz officials focused on four familiar and closely related problems, with Lenin's new strictures in mind. First, of course, remained the scarcity of food and the anxieties of insecurity now being felt almost everywhere throughout Soviet territory, including the countryside. The food procurement

---

[73] Ibid., 27:263.
[74] Ibid., 27:269–71, Lenin's emphasis.

committees were a failure. So, in practice, were the monopolies on grain and trade, however much these were still required. Even in provinces like Tambov, where the summer harvest was expected to be reasonably good, concealment, corruption, and the ubiquitous network of illegal private traders required a radical change in the way grain was requisitioned and distributed. Iron rule had to extract a larger "surplus." Traders had to be stopped in the villages, not only at railway stations.

Closely related were the continued struggles around industrial production, including declining productivity, factory closings, and what was described as "rampant unemployment" that was overwhelming the labor exchanges and the continued role of private ownership of many key enterprises, which some now thought might still induce forceful intervention on Germany's part to protect the holdings of German investors. Central here was the issue of nationalization. More than eight hundred plants around the country had been nationalized, sequestered, or municipalized between November and April by local soviets, regional Sovnarkhozy, trade unions, and workers themselves. These included almost half of the mining enterprises in the Donbas region and as many as 80 percent of those in the Urals. Although the statistics vary, not more than 10 percent of these were nationalized by Sovnarkhoz or the Sovnarkom. A formal decree that was supposed to govern their administration was issued only in March.[75] Authorities at all levels continued to be beseeched by new appeals for nationalization. In mid-May the eighteen thousand workers at the important Treugol'nik rubber factory formally requested nationalization. They were turned down.

The costs and responsibilities this was laying on the Bolshevik state were enormous. So were the practical problems of further nationalization. In May and June, a variety of plans and ideas on organizing the economy were sent from various party figures directly to Lenin. V. P. Miliutin, chair of Sovnarkhoz for a short time in March and April, believed the best way forward was for the state to consolidate its efforts and extend nationalization gradually. The government in Moscow also needed to have stronger control over regional soviets that acted on their own.[76] Reeling from the territorial and population losses of Brest-Litovsk, left Bolsheviks strongly rejected Miliutin's gradualism. Enthusiasts on the factory committees supported them. Only rapid nationalization across the industrial spectrum could allow a rational allocation of resources and assure the full engagement of workers themselves. Osinskii and others insisted that the continuation of private ownership created both economic and political problems: economic in terms of controlling how private capital was being used, and to whose

---

[75] *Narodnoe Khoziaistvo* 2 (Apr. 1918): 45–47.
[76] *Narodnoe Khoziaistvo* 5 (July 1918): 5–7.

benefit; political in terms of compromising the regime's energetic moves toward full socialization.[77]

A third problem concerned the loss and dislocation that underlay the violence and disorder associated with tens of thousands of demobilized soldiers, some 5 million of whom had by now flooded cities and villages all over the country. In many places soldiers had been enlisted into the irregular guards and policing forces of local soviets or had been received back into their old workplaces to bolster factory committees. In some accounts, returning soldiers faced a mixed reception in village communities, entitled to their share of redistributed land but also, as is always the case in wartime, disrupting new personal and family relationships developed with or without their knowledge while they were away. As recent soldiers with shared experiences they also formed marauding gangs in many places that terrorized railroad workers and others and sought some way of reintegrating into their changing local environments by linking with local soviets, various committees, and local armed gangs.

Intense discussion of these matters took place at various levels, including in the press, throughout the spring. A resolution adopted at the first Sovnarkhoz congress at the end of May on raising labor productivity described the problem more as the inability of workers to get food and other goods sufficient to support their capacity for work. Echoing the past, it emphasized the effects of the financial crisis and the absence of fuel and raw materials that had turned working conditions sharply for the worse and led to the great increase in the numbers of unemployed. Importantly, the Sovnarkhoz delegates specifically underlined the relationship between the workers' "moods" (*nastroenie*) and their real wages. In the first instance "the greatest possibility for increasing labor productivity [was] through the increase in real wages, not in the quantity of paper rubles they receive but in the possibility of using them to satisfy their real needs." This meant above all increasing the availability of food. As the Menshevik activist and later Soviet foreign minister I. M. Maiskii put it, "disciplinary measures ... appealed not to the best but to the worst side of human nature, not to revolutionary enthusiasm but to direct self-interest." Petrograd was going hungry (*golodaet*). Moscow was out of bread. So were "a whole list of towns and provinces in the most actual sense of the word."[78] Some estimates suggested there might still be enough grain reserves in different parts of the country to get Russia to the next harvest in August, but they were not being procured or delivered.[79] In political terms, as members of the left communist faction emphasized, a greater risk was that a

---

[77] *Trudy 1-go s"ezda*; RGASPI f. 5, op. 1, d. 2861, passim; *Oktiabr'skii perevorot i diktatura proletariata: Sbornik statei* (Moscow: Gosizdat, 1919), 87–101; V. P. Miliutin, *Sovremennoe Ekonomicheskoe razvitie Rossii i diktatura proletariat (1914–1918)* (Moscow: Izd. Ispolkom, 1918).

[78] *Rabochii mir* 3 (Apr. 28, 1918).

[79] *Trudy 1-go s"ezda*, 1–6, 15–16, 47–50.

dictatorial regime that failed to address the core issues of scarcity and dislocation might amplify the feelings of betrayal around Brest-Litovsk, shouldering directly the burden of popular discontent. Now, however, the "bourgeoisie" could no longer easily be blamed.

The strategy Lenin and the Sovnarkom put in place between mid-April and early June attempted to address these issues. Although it was not laid out in these terms, it had four key elements. The first was a radical change in grain procurement practices by applying class categories to the task. "Poor peasants" would be mobilized into "committees of the poor" (*kombedy*) to focus on taking grain from rich peasants (kulaks), in the process attending the needs of the large group of "middle peasants" situated between them. Involved here as well was a reaffirmation in May 1918 strongly supported by Groman of the need for strict application of the grain monopoly and regionally fixed prices to lessen the appeal of selling into the black markets. A special Vesenkha commission partly under Groman's direction soon afterward further proposed a program to fix prices across the board in agreement with local workers' groups, regional circumstances, and coefficients based on the five-year period 1909–13. (The issue was still being discussed almost a year later.)[80]

First and foremost, the committees of the poor would enforce the compulsory norms set by the *razverstka* by seizing undelivered surpluses. In June and July hastily formed detachments, many including demobilized soldiers, spread out across the grain-exporting districts still under Bolshevik control. The conflicts of 1917 between peasants and landowners were pushed into ideologically inspired "class" conflict within the village. It remained to be seen how the so-called kulaks would react.

Second was the enlistment of demobilized soldiers into these efforts to provide local *kombedy* with the force necessary to generate accurate estimates of community production, set targets for procurement, and deliver procured grain to collection points. This would be accompanied by a significant expansion of mobilization into the new Red Army, going beyond the motley assemblage of Red Guards and Bolshevik workers to mobilization in the countryside more broadly, according to manpower estimates generated by the *kombedy* as well as other local authorities. The ground here was thus further set toward the creation of a traditional military force, one with a familiar hierarchy of officers and soldiers recruited and drafted in large numbers from the former tsarist army.

Third were the decisions to nationalize all foreign trade but to reject the request by the Treugol'nik plant to be nationalized and not to move in this direction beyond the regime's resources and administrative capacities, maintaining

---

[80] *Dekrety Sovetskoi vlasti* (Moscow: Gosizdat, 1958), 2:261–64; *Narodnoe Khoziaistvo* 8–9 (Sept. 1918): 34–39; 11–12 (July 1919): 11–21.

in effect the policy of the Sovnarkhoz since December. Rejecting the demand of left Bolsheviks to move quickly toward full socialism in this way meant continuing to proceed on a case-by-case basis and not risk aggravating German and other foreign interests by fully eliminating private ownership, at least for the time being. This meant no retreat in principle from Lenin's "iron fist." It was only an unstated recognition that the complexities of socialist transformation required it be used with deliberation as well as force to achieve the party's goals.

Finally, there was the formal establishment of dictatorial "one-man" management of the railroads, abruptly terminating Nikolai Nekrasov's 1917 experiment in democratizing the administration of what continued to be Russia's most important and maligned economic lifeline. Here the problem of scarcities was again addressed, as it was in 1915 and 1916, by focusing on the uncertain and corrupt processes of goods distribution by the railroads as well as those surrounding its production and procurement. The "obvious" reason was to "end any further breakdown on the lines at a moment when hunger [*golod*] was already affecting so many regions." The lines also had to be ready for military purposes. The Sovnarkom therefore assigned "dictatorial powers" to the commissar of transport and to a new group of individual commissars he would now appoint for each line. The complex network of railroad committees currently managing the lines was to be replaced by experienced and reliable individuals invested with full dictatorial authority and responsible for each district or regional railroad division. In addition, new military revolutionary committees were to be formed to act against anyone on elected main and sector line committees who opposed this effort and engaged in "secret sabotage" against it. A new railroad Cheka with its own troops would combat any and all malfeasance along the lines. Those who refused to accept the full terms of the decree would be punished by immediate arrest and, in the case of armed opposition, "turned over to revolutionary tribunals." With the publication and transmission of the decree by telegraph, all local railroad commissars, emissaries, and agents were relieved of their duties until and unless they were reappointed by the commissariat.[81]

The wholesale purge as means of revitalizing railroad operations and administration by rehiring or appointing only those who could persuade commissariat officials that they deserved their positions thus emerged as a key element in the Bolsheviks' technology of rule. As the formal power of the new Bolshevik state collided with the power embedded in local practices, values, and sociopolitical institutions like the village gathering (*shkod*), dictatorship would involve a range of forms and practices, all designed to solve Russia's pressing problems by force.

---

[81] *Narodnoe Khoziaistvo* 11–12 (July 1919): 12–20.

14

"Our Lives Have Become Unbearable!"

Dictatorships in the "Fight against Hunger"

Extreme Need as Counterrevolution

Predictably, Lenin's "Tasks" were angrily rejected by railroad committee members and workers along the lines. Special meetings were called around the country. A special conference on one Moscow line declared one-man dictatorial rule extremely harmful to operations and "inconsistent with any democratic principles." In Ekaterinburg, a regional meeting elected its own committee to administer the junction. Perm railroaders demanded an explanation in person. Zinoviev, Volodarskii, and other high-level party members in Moscow and Petrograd who went to some of these meetings were greeted with hostility. On the Riga-Orlov line, Red Guards angrily demanded "in the strongest possible terms" that the regime take action against the counterrevolutionary provocateurs. After arrests were made, some committees publicly accepted the new decree. Peter Kobozev, a determined supporter of dictatorship and Special Sovnarkom Commissar for Turkestan, replaced Vladimir Nevskii, one of the authors of the decree, as commissar of transport, but the protests escalated when railroaders' access to food through their own procurement committees was cut off in places like Riazan ("taking their last *pud* of flour").[1]

Kobozev was soon accused of picking "the most reactionary figures" to head the lines, completely ignoring workers organizations and setting in place "typical exploiters and archetypical bureaucrats." Railroad workers were being forced to give up the empowerment 1917 had brought them, further crippling Russia's still vital "lifeline." Railroad Cheka agents in their new gray uniforms with green stripes and distinctive Railroad Cheka badges were particularly reviled. In some places there were short protest strikes and slowdowns, as committees in different services along the lines displayed their local power.[2]

Faulty equipment and the demands of railroad Chekists that it be used anyway led to more breakdowns, accidents, and accusations of sabotage. Engine drivers

---

[1] RGASPI, f. 5, op. 1, d. 2740, ll. 130–31.
[2] Russian State Archive of the Economy [RGAE] f. 1884, op. 3, d. 20, l. 17; RGASPI f. 5, op. 1, d. 2739, ll. 14–18; d. 2740, ll. 1–2, 12–46, 104.

and other needed personnel were summarily arrested. Protests multiplied, along, no doubt, with passive resistance. An ostensibly secret report to Lenin himself in the fall of 1918 asserted that "starving" railroad workers "hated the Red Army and all communists," a formulation for constant antagonism and conflict. Another to the Political Administration of the Commissariat of Transport stated that party members themselves saw railroaders as "authentic Black Hundreds," referring to the notorious proto-fascist organization under tsarism.[3] In response, "political education" along the lines was soon being handled by a new political section (*politotdel*) in the Commissariat of Transport, Glavpolitput'. Not surprisingly, its efforts at raising railroaders' "consciousness" only increased resentment. As special railroad Cheka units were strengthened in response, engineering and technical personnel were especially singled out for arrest for alleged malfeasance or "sympathizing with the Whites." Dictatorship on the important Moscow-Riazan line was extended to martial law.[4]

Whether industrial workers in major cities were sympathetic to the railroaders is unclear. Many blamed them for shortages of food and urgent supplies. Both in and outside their factory committees, however, similar protests erupted as well, focusing especially on unemployment and food—far and away their biggest concerns, as a meeting of workers from some forty-five enterprises expressed it in early May. Their opposition became significantly more visible in April and May, organized in part around the new Conference of Factory Representatives (Sobranie Upolnomochennykh).[5] The Conference was formed after the Bolsheviks shut down the Constituent Assembly led by Mensheviks determined to build a new representative workers movement "from below," shedding any formal party affiliation. In the midst of protests and confusion after Brest-Litovsk over the possible evacuation of Petrograd, a special meeting convened at the Putilov works on March 13. Delegates from at least fifteen other metalworking plants attended, as did others. Reports about the meeting appeared in *Den'*, *Novaia Zaria*, *Novaia Zhizn'*, and other newspapers soon to be shut down. By mid-April there were apparently Sobranie delegates in more than forty Petrograd plants, ostensibly representing fifty-five thousand or more workers.[6] Mid-April also witnessed serious unrest in Moscow over lack of food and

---

[3] RGASPI f. 111, op. 22, d. 1, ll. 66–67.
[4] *Prodput'* 2 (Apr. 1918): 83–84; *Den'*, Apr. 2, 1918; *Volia i Duma Zheleznodorozhnikov*, Apr. 13, May 12, June 8, 1918; *Znamia Truda*, Apr. 6, May 14, 29, June 12, 1918; *Znamia Bor'by*, June 5, 1918; *Petrogradskoe Ekho*, May 10, 1918. RGASPI f. 111, op. 22, d. 91, l. 223; d. 10, 14, 16, 25; and GARF f. 130, op. 2, d. 625, all deal with the struggle against counterrevolutionary speculation and crime.
[5] *Sobranie upolnomochennykh i piterskie rabochie v 1918 godu: Dokumenty i materialy* (St. Petersburg: St. Petersburg University Press, 2006). The story is told in some detail by Alexander Rabinowitch, *The Bolsheviks in Power* (Bloomington: Indiana University Press, 2007), 223–36.
[6] *Den'*, Apr. 2, 1918; *Novyi Den'*, Apr. 4, 13, 1917; *Novaia Zaria* 2 (May 1, 1918): 60–62; M. S. Bernshtam, ed., *Nezavisimoe rabochee dvizhenie v 1918 godu: Dokumenty i materialy* (Paris: YMCA Press, 1981), 204–7.

other deprivations, headlined in the newspaper *Chas* as "Battle on the Streets." According to reports at least forty people were killed. Banners declared "Down with the Government" and "Workers Have to Save Themselves." "Anarchists" were said to be responsible, but subsequent reports accused marauding soldiers and petty thieves.[7]

Meanwhile, the food situation in Petrograd and Moscow became increasingly dire. Some fifty thousand ration cards intended for people who had already left the city were rumored to be "traveling" through a lively black market that siphoned off much of the supply. During Easter week angry women and men protesting the lack of food in the Petrograd industrial suburb of Kolpino were fired on in front of the local soviet, wounding several and killing one. More casualties were soon reported. Those arrested were sentenced immediately to one year in prison. Work then stopped at a number of Petrograd plants, including Putilov and Obukhov. Twenty-one plants sent delegations to the victims' funeral.

Between the end of May and the beginning of July, archival documents and newspaper reports list more than seventy such incidents in Petrograd alone. All protested shootings, arrests, and other forms of repression. In Nizhnii Novgorod demonstrations provoked martial law. In Kharkov, a large pogrom took place against the Jews as popular anger and frustration found a familiar target now associated in some minds with Bolshevik leadership itself.[8] Clashes between Lenin's supporters and left SRs occurred in Stavropol, Voronezh, Kaluga, and Iaroslavl, where left SRs walked out of the city soviet. The Volga region and the Urals were similarly in turmoil. By one count more than 120 hunger protests occurred between March and June in grain-deficit areas.[9] "Starving" railroaders at a number of stations demanded an end to *all* restrictions on the free trade of foodstuffs, in effect an end to the grain monopoly. The food situation was termed "catastrophic" in Vladimir, Tula, Nizhnii Novgorod, and Kursk, as it was elsewhere across a Soviet republic that no longer included Ukraine.[10]

Resistance along the railroads strengthened in May and early June. Local and central railroad committees said they felt "betrayed" by the imposition of "dictatorship," echoing the anxieties and resentments many already shared concerning Brest-Litovsk.[11] Delegates at a congress of the important Moscow-Kursk line sharply condemned dictatorship. Three thousand workers on the Moscow-Petrograd Nikolaev line joined them. So did protesters and demonstrators mounting coordinated one-day strikes in Moscow and at several other

---

[7] *Chas*, Apr. 12–17, 1917.

[8] *Novyi Den'*, May 15 and 16, 1918.

[9] T. V. Osipova, *Rossiiskoe krest'ianstvo v revoliutsii grazhdanskoi voine* (Moscow: Izd. Strelets, 2001), citing RGVIA f. 25883, op. 1, d. 29, l. 138 and GARF f. 393, op. 1. d. 72, ll. 40–41.

[10] *Petrogradskoe Ekho*, May 10, 1918; *Volia i Dumy Zheleznodorozhnika*, June 8, 1918.

[11] *Novaia Zhizn'*, Mar. 27, 1918; *Znamia Bor'ba*, May 14 and 24, 1918; *Petrogradskoe Ekho*, May 10, 1918; *Volia i Dumy Zheleznodorozhnika* 29 (May 17, 1918).

important junctions on May 23–25 in the important Orel and Tula shops, and again at the huge Sormovo plant in Nizhnii. (In response, the Sormovo plant was nationalized.) The Nizhnii Novgorod Soviet sent Lenin an urgent message in mid-May that workers had not been paid because there was no money in the firm's accounts. The new commissar for transport Kobosev was publicly denounced as a "saboteur."[12] In an effort to organize the protests more effectively the Menshevik leadership of the Conference of Factory Representatives asked workers to postpone further actions "until a more favorable moment" when better organization might lead to a city-wide or even nation-wide general strike. Many, however, were clearly out of patience.[13]

By this time there were also reports of demonstrations by angry peasants in various rural localities, influenced perhaps by local SRs. Hunger and food anxiety were also a primary cause here, especially in deficit areas like parts of Viatka, Novgorod, Tver, Tambov, Orlov, Kursk, Riazan, and Samara. On May 17 a huge "starving" crowd from the environs around Makar'ev in Kostroma province directly threatened the district soviet, according to recent research. Local dependency on the bagmen and -women to supply food had effectively destroyed the grain and trade monopolies. More than 40 percent of the rural population of Kaluga was looking for food.[14]

The situation escalated further on June 20. The regime had called for new local soviet elections in Moscow and Petrograd to strengthen party control in both cities. V. Volodarskii (aka Moishe Markovich Goldshtein), a talented Bolshevik publicist and member of the Soviet Executive Committee, was assassinated on his way to a factory meeting in this connection. More angry gatherings ensued, some now involving Baltic fleet sailors thought to be staunch Bolshevik supporters. Obukhov workers and others pressured the Conference of Factory Representatives to declare a general strike. Local Bolshevik authorities responded by invading the Obukhov district and shutting it down.[15] The Conference of Workers' Representatives then convened in yet another "emergency session." The word was that out of some 150,000 workers still in Petrograd, as many as two-thirds supported the Conference. With little concern for its accuracy, the Conference set a one-day general strike for July 2. Railroad workers indicated they were ready to join.[16]

In these circumstances the Sovnarkom on June 28 formally nationalized a long list of joint-stock industrial enterprises, adding substantially to the almost

[12] GARF f. 130, op. 2, d. 223, ll. 9–10, 13–14, 22; *Znamia Truda*, May 14, 1918; *Znamia Bor'ba*, June 5, 1918.
[13] Central State Archive of St. Petersburg [TsGA SPb] f. 3390, op. 1, d. 13, ll. 116, 140–42, 158–72; RGASPI f. 5, op. 1, d. 2550, l. 1; f. 7034, op. 1, d. 1, ll. 2–3.
[14] Osipova, *Rossiiskoe krest'ianstvo*, 87,–94.
[15] *Novyi Vechernyi Chas*, June 20, 1918; *Novaia Zhizn'*, June 16, 21, 1918.
[16] TsGA SPb f. 3390, op .1, d. 13, ll. 222, 225.

three hundred enterprises already under state control. In both timing and intent, the irony was that the decree finally implemented what many workers had long demanded well before October. Now, however, it was the party's rather than the workers' need for security that was paramount. By July 1, key sectors of proletarian Russia seemed poised to rise up against the regime. The eminent Italian economic historian Sylvana Malle and others have emphasized that this timing was a political act, having largely to do with Berlin's insistence that German owners of firms in Russia nationalized before July 1 could be compensated with German redemption funds.[17] Yet in the fraught atmosphere between April and July twice as many enterprises had been nationalized by local soviets and *sovnarkhozy* than were by the decree of June 28.[18] (A few weeks later housing was also officially nationalized, apparently accompanied by cheers of "Mansions to the workers, basements to the bourgeoisie.")[19]

Preparations for a massive protest strike on July 2 included shutting down the railroads. The official slogans were "Down with Capital Punishment!"; "Down with Shootings and Civil War!"; "Long Live Freedom of Speech, Assembly, and the Right to Strike!"; and "Long Live the Constituent Assembly!" Tula workers added "The Right to Organize in Defense of Our Own Interests."[20] The powerful undercurrent of feeling, however, was better expressed by a delegate at a Conference meeting: "Our lives has become unbearable. Factories are empty. There is no bread. Our children are dying of hunger. Tens of thousands are forced to rely on soup kitchens. They give small coins to the hungry instead of bread. All who speak about it are called enemies of the people. There is no freedom to speak. We are being ruled by people who are out of control, who we did not elect, who do not know legality or honesty and who only love power."[21]

Not surprisingly, Lenin and the regime were now determined to suppress this resistance by any means available. The voices of need were heard as a chorus of counterrevolution. The dictatorship had to be even more forcefully armed.

Once Again, "the Revolution Is in Danger!"

Given the demands widely posted during these weeks in Menshevik and SR newspapers, it is obvious why memoirists and historians have seen late June

---

[17] Sylvana Malle, *The Organization of War Communism 1918-1921* (Cambridge, Cambridge University Press, 1985), 57–68.
[18] V. Z. Drobizhev, "Sotsialisticheskoe obobshchestvlenie promyshlennosti v SSSR," *Voprosy Istorii* 6 (1964): 62–63.
[19] *Dekrety Sovetskoi vlasti*, 15 vols. (Moscow: Nauka, 1957–89), 3:159; E. G. Gimpel'son, *Sovetskii rabochii klass* (Moscow: Nauka, 1974), 276.
[20] RGASPI f. 5, op. 1, d. 2885, ll. 1–4.
[21] *Novaia Zhizn'*, May 30, 1918.

and early July 1918 as evidence of intense political opposition to the Soviet regime by workers and "housewives," as some liberal historians have described women activists, and why a prominent democratic socialist observer became convinced that by June 1918 "a committed opposition... [had] gained the upper hand."[22] Protestors called for the reconvening of the Constituent Assembly. They demanded independent trade unions, the end of shootings and lynch law, and the civil liberties promised in 1917. In these circumstances, it is likely that the collective class inscriptions "worker" and "peasant" and perhaps even "bourgeois" no longer carried quite the same political freight as they had a year earlier, however much they still centered Bolshevik ideology and Soviet official discourse. The miseries of scarcity and loss were now broadly shared, especially in the cities. Perhaps the same was true with gender and the emancipatory hopes brought with the fall of the tsar. Prominent activists in the new regime like Alexandra Kollontai kept women's rights in the foreground. *Soldatki* continued to have a loud collective voice in many provincial towns and villages. Radical changes were being made in marriage laws and other repressive practices championed particularly by the progressive *intelligentki*. Yet the traditional heavy loads and personal risks of women in the workplace and village were almost certainly heavier now, however difficult they are to measure.

It is clear that many who had demonstrated so recently against the Provisional Government did not identify with an increasingly repressive Bolshevik regime. "The dictatorship of the proletariat has steadily become a dictatorship over the proletariat, agitating the masses who are the most dangerous allies of our enemies," an important journal of the railroad workers editorialized on June 1.[23] But neither did the demand for reconvening the Constituent Assembly necessarily mean that many thought a politically democratic regime could more easily solve their problems, much less control the arbitrary violence that so many demobilized soldiers were accelerating as they left the ranks. Almost four years of war had brought Russians to physical and emotional exhaustion, the deprivations of loss, dislocation, and material ruin. War capitalism had collapsed in 1917 amid calls from many quarters for a strong dictatorial regime of various orientations. Bolshevik authorities now had ample physical power, but they could not produce food, secure its adequate distribution, or even keep nationalized plants in operation. One can imagine that a significant part of the wave of protests that emerged was not a demand for the political structures of democratic socialism like those supported by the Menshevik Congress of Factory Representatives, but a strong socialist regime able to remedy the effects of scarcity and loss, restore social order

---

[22] G. Aronson, "Ouvriers russes contre le bolchevisme," *Le Contrat Social* 4 (July–Aug. 1966): 202.
[23] *Volia i dumia Zheleznodorozhnika* 33 (June 1, 1918): 1.

without excessive force, suppress random violence on the part of the authorities, and avert still more anxiety and social dislocation.

Again, in these circumstances, none of this made any difference to Lenin's government as it calibrated its response. "The Revolution Is in Danger" meant Bolshevik rule was in danger. At the Fifth Congress of Soviets in the Bolshoi Theater on July 5, 353 left SR delegates openly declared their lack of confidence in the Bolshevik regime. The next day, two of the party's leaders entered the German embassy with the help of a sympathetic Chekist and murdered Ambassador Wilhelm von Mirbach. They hoped to rekindle the war with Germany to advance the revolutionary cause. The fiery Maria Spiridonova, reflecting the party's long acceptance of terrorism as an appropriate political weapon, proudly claimed responsibility. Armed clashes occurred around the city. SR-dominated soviets and other organizations in a number of cities and districts pushed resistance as well in what was labeled then and afterward the "SR uprising."[24] The Secretariat of the Sovnarkom felt the "fully understandable nervousness" coming from the Kremlin.[25] While these protests were quickly subdued, murderous feelings persisted. In Petrograd, Moisei Uritskii, head of the Cheka, was assassinated by a former army cadet. A few weeks later, a third assassination attempt left Lenin himself gravely wounded. Meanwhile, encouraged by these events and by Russia's former allies Britain and France, the first significant anti-Bolshevik forces were falling into place in the Don region following the decision of Czech forces stranded by the Brest-Litovsk Treaty to attack Bolshevik troops hindering their way out through Siberia. The revolution was in danger from within and without.

Once Again, Mobilizing "Solutions"

Consciously identifying with the French Revolution, the Bolshevik regime in response sanctioned the most notorious "solution" for the political threats it was experiencing by officially decreeing the "Red Terror": a campaign of arrests and rapid executions of real and imagined internal enemies intended to suppress SR terrorists and other opponents through fear as well as ruthlessness. In prerevolutionary Russia's fraught political history, Bolsheviks, like other social democratic rationalists, eschewed the tactics of terrorist acts developed by Russian populists in the 1870s, which led to the assassination of the Tsar Emancipator Alexander II and a number of other high officials. The strong

---

[24] RGASPI op. 5, op. 1, d. 2450, ll. 4–10; Orlando Figes, *Peasant Russia, Civil War: The Volga Countryside in Revolution 1917–1921* (Oxford: Oxford University Press, 1989), 132ff.; Oliver H. Radkey, *The Sickle under the Hammer* (New York: Columbia University Press, 1963), 386ff.

[25] RGASPI f. 5, op. 1, d. 2450, l. 10.

left wing of the SR party that formed as the populists' successor, however, continued to support terrorism as a valid weapon of the weak. Responding to the SR assassinations with Red Terror was thus at once an admission of Bolshevik weakness and a major retreat from even the Bolsheviks' social democratic principles.

Three other "solutions" were also either introduced or expanded at this time, each of which would be affected by the legitimization of terror: a concerted effort to strengthen the Bolsheviks' control of regional and local soviets; the further mobilization of the committees of the poor (*kombedy*) to procure grain from peasant communes; and the first formal mobilizations of young men and soldiers who not been formally discharged into Trotsky's new Red Army. A plan was already underway by the end of April to expand the army to one million men. Obligatory military service had been decreed in late April, but many rural soviets simply refused to supply troops.[26]

The struggle to control local soviets and to greatly increase the procurement of grain were closely related.[27] By this time there were more than thirty-five hundred districts (*volosti*) in European Russia, many newly formed in 1917 in preparation for *volost* zemstvo elections. In many places the newly elected zemstvos simply renamed themselves "soviets" after October, but their members included all strata of the local peasantry. The transition to soviet rule locally was thus not a direct transition to Bolshevik rule, a reflection of the devolution downward after February of political authority. Periodic and specially called elections in the spring of 1918 managed to change the rural soviets' complexion to some degree, but this effort was far more successful in cities and towns where ties to the Bolshevik center were much stronger.

The deteriorating food situation and the formation of the committees of the poor seemed to offer an easy solution: many rural soviets were simply designated as *kombedy*, their ranks now purged of the better-off and less reliable. A lengthy appeal to "workers and starving peasants" on the fight against hunger declared that great stocks of grain still lay "in the hands of rural kulaks and the wealthy rural bourgeoisie." War was declared against the "kulaks."[28] Lenin and others were so uncertain how exactly to do this, however, that in August the Sovnarkom sent an extraordinary delegation under Commissar of Food Alexander Tsirupa to study the question in provincial Elets.[29] Meanwhile the *kombedy* themselves quickly institutionalized the Bolsheviks' "poor," "middle," and "kulak" social

---

[26] Figes, *Peasant Russia*, 308–10; Osipova, *Rossiiskoe krest'ianstvo*, 88–89.

[27] The issue is thoroughly explored for Penza province by Peter Fraunholtz, "The Collapse and Rebuilding of Grain Procurement Authority in Civil War Russia: The Case of Penza," in *Russia's Home Front in War and Revolution*, bk. 1, ed. Sarah Badcock, Liudmila Novikova, and Aaron Retish (Bloomington, IN: Slavica, 2015), 67–86.

[28] *Dekrety Sovetskoi vlasti*, 2:348–54.

[29] Michael Melancon, "Trial Run for Soviet Food Requisitioning: The Expedition to Orel Province, Fall 1918," *Russian Review* 3 (July 1910): 412–37.

classifications on the basis of local perspectives, assumptions, and biases as much as or more than objective indications of relative prosperity, further destabilizing the tumultuous rural scene.

In a similar way the *kombedy* were also enlisted to mobilize local men and returning soldiers into the Red Army to fight the Czech legion advancing in the Volga region, the anti-Bolshevik Don Cossack units from the old army, and their potential ally in the nascent Armed Forces of South Russia (AFSR) now being formed after Kornilov's death under General Anton Denikin. In early June the Czechs occupied Samara. Ufa and Simbirsk were taken in July, and Kazan fell on August 6. Resistance to the April mobilization decree left the Red Army essentially a poorly coordinated assemblage of unstable volunteer brigades. An additional conscription order for men between twenty-one and twenty-five in June was ineffective as well, the results in Viatka and elsewhere "pathetic." Now quotas were assigned to *kombedy* in many places listing the numbers they needed to enlist along with the amounts of grain they were to deliver. In some cases, maybe even most, it was returned soldiers active in the *kombedy* who took on this part of their responsibility.[30]

The most notorious of these "solutions" in the summer of 1918, the Red Terror itself, would soon prove to have serious flaws precisely in terms of the control it was supposed to ensure. Supposedly a new weapon of the Cheka, terror was in fact already part of Cheka practice, as we have seen, especially (but not only) in the form of random arrests and harsh penalties along the railroads. In this and as the protest wave of May and June suggested, the Red Terror had likely raised more opposition than it repressed. It also finally closed off any real hope of possible cooperation with experienced individuals on complex matters like industrial productivity, finance, statistics, and other "nonpartisan" subjects, as well as groups like the Council of Industrial Congresses (Soviet Soiuzov) and the WICs, many of whose members still hoped to be able to offer some assistance to the manifestly hostile regime "in Russia's name." Their offices at 46 Liteinyi finally closed for good in the late summer.[31]

Of more immediate importance, the formal inauguration of the Red Terror in August implicitly gave license to party officials at all levels and positions to use terrorist tactics "in the name of the revolution" itself, as they were often described. Leather jackets became a dress code of both enthusiasts and party thugs, whether they were Chekisty or not and whether or not terror was practiced against real or imagined enemies. Reports of senseless brutality by local Cheka agents found their way to the highest levels of the party, like one from

---

[30] Stephen M. Berk, "The 'Class-Tragedy' of Izhevsk: Working-Class Opposition to Bolshevism in 1918," *Russian Review* 2 (1975): 176–90.
[31] RGIA f. 126, op. 1, d. 19.

a Novgorod woman whose husband and brother were summarily executed as speculators without any investigation.[32]

Finally, of course, as a formative part of the Bolsheviks' civil war experience, terror seemed to leach into the party's DNA as its forms were nourished especially by its past master Comrade Stalin. Whatever additional harm to the greater social democratic project the Bolsheviks did during the Civil War, the embrace of political terror in the long run was among the most lethal and long lasting.

It remained to be seen if the other solutions initiated in the tense summer of 1918 would prove equally "successful."

Scarcity and the Anti-Bolshevik Dictatorships

The political and military histories of the Committee of Members of the All-Russia Constituent Assembly (Komuch) in Ufa and the anti-Bolshevik regimes in Siberia and South Russia have been well told. When the Czech legion facilitated the Komuch declaring its authority in June, and then supported its claim of provisional state power from Ufa over parts of western Siberia, it represented at least the possibility of a moderate socialist all-Russia regime legitimized by Russia's only democratic national election. Its SR leadership and ninety-seven members declared the commitment to a democratic federal republic. Russia's national minorities in Siberia and elsewhere would have their right to cultural autonomy. How the Komuch was then overthrown in a coup by those supporting Admiral Kolchak in Omsk, and how Kolchak, who had been relieved of his command in June 1917, when he proved unable to control the raucous Black Sea sailors, then became "Supreme Leader" of the anti-Bolshevik cause, are familiar and important stories of the internal and international politics of the period. British, French, and American intervention played a key and well-documented role here, one that had lasting consequences in terms of subsequent Soviet insecurity in an increasingly hostile anticommunist world.

The politics of liberal Constitutional Democrats in both Kolchak's and Denikin's administrations is another interesting part of the story, as well as a controversial chapter in the ways variants of the liberal Great Story were subsequently told. When Victor Pepeliaev, a former Kadet Duma member from Tomsk and commissar for Kronstadt, in 1917 became interior minister in Kolchak's "all-Russia" administration, he called unequivocally for military dictatorship. A Kadet conference in Omsk strongly condemned "unrealizable" democratic slogans and ambitions. The remnant Constituent Assembly was illegal. "Anti-state socialist elements" had to be repressed. Members of the Komuch's

---

[32] TsGA SPb f. 6276, op. 4, d. 52, ll. 41–41 ob.

Directorate were arrested. A Primary Statute drawn by Pepeliaev and his Kadet Party colleagues in Omsk gave "legal" foundation to the Supreme Ruler's right to take "extraordinary measures," whatever these might be. They were especially suspicious of the region's large Tatar communities.[33]

In South Russia resistance to the Bolsheviks was organized by the Don Cossacks in Novocherkassk under Peter Krasnov, who was elected ataman in May, as well as a still small force of former tsarist officers and troops under Generals Kornilov and Alekseev. Cossack status in the Don was granted to all men who joined the fight. As Peter Holquist has detailed, many of those who refused lost their status and were expelled from Cossack ranks. Courts-martial regarded deserters and Soviet agitators as traitors.[34] After Alekseev and Kornilov were killed in separate incidents, the growing volunteer army under General Denikin succeeded in forcing Bolsheviks out of the Kuban region and secured its capital, Ekaterinodar. For most in the city, its liberation was welcome. Bolshevik rule had been exceedingly harsh. All Cossacks were presumed to be anti-Bolsheviks. They and others caught wearing tsarist army uniforms were reportedly shot as counterrevolutionaries without much in the way of a trial. Whether these excesses were extensive or episodic made little difference to those who heard and read about them. Support for the White cause rapidly increased. Although the Kuban Parliament (Rada) continued to exercise local authority, Ekaterinodar quickly became a lively anti-Bolshevik center with national pretensions.

By the time Paul Miliukov made his way from German-occupied Kiev to Denikin's headquarters in South Russia, the Kadet leader was convinced that the anti-Bolsheviks should seek help from Russia's former enemy. (German rifles could be washed clean of their sins in the Don River, he intimated, and thus cleansed serve the noble cause of restoring the Great Russian state.) His position startled fellow liberals. Leading members of his party had already helped draft a statute that subordinated all areas occupied by Denikin's troops to direct military control. A special council organized to guide the movement's civil affairs "officially" gave the army command dictatorial authority. Two of its leading figures, Kadet Central Committee members Vasili Stepanov and Konstantin Sokolov, were adamant in their insistence that a single authoritative dictatorship was essential to defeating the Bolsheviks and restoring Russia as a great European power.

[33] V. V. Maksakov and A. Turunov, "Vremennoe pravitel'stvo avtonomnoi Sibiri," *Krasnyi Arkhiv* 29 (1928): 86–138; G. Telberg, "Notes on Kolchak," misc. materials in Telberg Papers, box 3, Library of Congress, Washington, DC [Telberg was Kolchak's minister of justice]; Daniel E. Schafer, "Bashkir Loyalists and the Question of Autonomy," in Badcock, Novikova, and Retish, *Russia's Home Front*, 1:226–30.

[34] Peter Holquist, *Making War, Forging Revolution* (Cambridge, MA: Harvard University Press, 2002), 158–62.

Securing alliances in the fall with the autonomous Don and Kuban Cossack regimes, Denikin's volunteer army reorganized into the Armed Forces of South Russia. Kuban Cossacks were attached as separate units, as Ukrainians and other nationalities had been in the tsarist army. Reflecting the liberals' overarching emphasis on the key historical importance of the state, those forming the heart of the AFSR's civilian governance had no doubt that the welfare of Great Russia had to take precedence over the immediate welfare of its people, even as many officers thought the Kadet influence in the special council was "noxious." There was no question, however, that the goal of Denikin's army and its founding principle was "Russia, One and Indivisible!"[35]

In sum, the political story of the anti-Bolshevik regimes during the Civil War, including the White forces in Murmansk and northwest Russia under General Iudenich aided by the Michigan National Guard, is one of forceful efforts to restore prewar cultural values and institutions, leavened perhaps by some of the gains pressed by Russia's "responsible men" before and during 1917. Peasants would keep the land they had taken. Former owners would be compensated. Imperial Russia would slowly pull itself together, and perhaps even include control over Constantinople and the Dardanelle Straits if victory over the Bolsheviks came before peace settlements were agreed upon. In the meantime, Kolchak and Denikin prepared with the help of Russia's former allies and the fervent prayers of the church to move on Moscow and rid Great Russia of the blasphemy of Bolshevism.

How in these circumstances did the anti-Bolshevik dictatorships confront the problems of scarcity that so affected Lenin's regime? In both Siberia and South Russia, the problems of scarcity and food insecurity were far less acute that in the Soviet zones. Both regions had access to more substantial local grain production, the Komuch and Kolchak regimes in terms of the relatively better off regions of the eastern districts of the central Volga and those of western Siberia, the AFSR in terms of Cossack reserves and those of the northern Caucasus, where much of the earliest fighting against the Bolsheviks took place. Both Kolchak's and Denikin's forces also had better control of relatively undamaged Trans-Siberian and South Russian railroad lines, and thus to international aid through ports on the Pacific and the Black Sea. The United States in particular was in the process of shipping locomotives ordered by the tsarist and Provisional Government regimes for use on the Trans-Siberian. In addition, the suspension of grain shipments westward to what was now Soviet Russia eased shortages considerably for a time in parts of the region away from its rapacious armies. In August Kolchak declared that land should "go to the peasantry," but the statement had

---

[35] K. N. Sokolov, *Pravlenie genereala Denikina* (Sofia, 1921), 126–27; V. A. Obolenskii, *Krym pri Vrangele* (Moscow: Gosizdat, 1928), 5.

no practical meaning. Kolchak's official informational *Biulleten'* described the Civil War in Siberia as essentially a fight over Siberian food supplies. ("They need our grain, they need our reserves, our cattle, our people.")[36] Most other matters would await the Bolsheviks' defeat.

Both regimes also rejected grain monopolies, the infringement of property rights within a program for the redistribution of land, and both, not surprisingly, supported private ownership, free trade, and efforts within a market system to control rising prices. Some in Kolchak's regime even wanted to increase peasant holdings in the region since most Siberians owned and worked their own land, especially farther east. Kadets resisted this initiative, fearful of alienating large regional landowners. The Supreme Ruler's government then left the problem of food procurement and distribution to local market exchanges, but this only marginally reduced the scope of Kolchak's dictatorial authority. Local commanders set fixed prices on food and scarce goods but tried to make these elastic enough to compete with private traders. Hoarding or otherwise hiding foodstuffs was categorically prohibited for both buyer and seller. The program of Denikin's government was not substantially different. On the key issue of land reform, his special council had no official policy besides the right of those whose lands had been seized to be compensated and private property elsewhere restored to its legal owners.

Siberia and South Russia were hardly devoid of confiscations of foodstuffs and other supplies when the armies there were on the move. In both areas White forces lived off the supplies of towns and villages that came under their control, while Cossack bands lived rapaciously off the land once they were outside Cossack territories. Semenov's and Kalmykov's legions in Siberia also siphoned goods intended for Kolchak's troops from large stretches of the Trans-Siberian Railroad they managed to control, terrorizing railroad workers and generally causing havoc even as they fell nominally under Kolchak's command. Largely made up of ex-convicts and renegade Cossacks, both were soon responsible for some of the worst barbarism of the Civil War.

Meanwhile in Omsk, the Kadet paper *Sibirskaia Rech'* insisted that Kolchak and his supporters were acting only in the interest of Great Russia as whole. Privately, they boasted that after months of "playing with coalition" they had finally taken charge of a "firm state authority destined to resurrect all of Russia."[37] As Kolchak's Siberian army prepared to go on the offensive in the winter of 1919, followed by Denikin's South Russian forces in late summer, right-wing Kadets and other political figures in their governments gave little if any thought to restoring political democracy, much less its social democratic extensions.

---

[36] *Biulleten' Osvedomitel'nyi Otdel Shtaba Verkhovnago Glavnokomanduiushchago*, July 1919.
[37] *Sibirskaia Rech'*, Dec. 10, 16, 1918; Telberg, "Notes on Kolchak."

Scarcities seemed manageable with help from abroad and traditional military requisitions. Dictatorial command and military victory were the orders of the day.

The Bolsheviks' "Fight against Hunger"

The loss of grain from Ukraine after Brest-Litovsk was compounded by fighting in the middle Volga, but the situation was dire even before, when the summer harvest again fell below what was hoped, if not expected. When Tukhachevskii's newly formed First Red Army retook the region assisted by soon-to-be-legendary partisans under Vasili Chapaev, peasant resistance to being drafted was recorded in fifty-one local districts in the region despite (or perhaps because of) severe punishments, including summary execution and the confiscation of property.[38]

By then the excesses of the *kombedy* in extracting grain from village "kulaks" were familiar events in the countryside well away from the growing Civil War. Many of these were composed of workers retreating to the countryside from Moscow and other cities, as well as former soldiers who found their former jobs had disappeared. Orlando Figes has suggested that if the Komuch regime in places like Samara had been able to hold on, perhaps the Civil War would have turned out differently.[39] Yet it is quite likely that food shortages and persistent military requisitions underlay the Volga peasants' disaffection from the regime more than political considerations, as it was for those being drafted by the Bolsheviks. Food was so scarce in neighboring Saratov province that a politically diverse provincial soviet requested Moscow reclassify it as a grain-deficit province. A strict "food dictatorship" was instituted locally in August. Barricades to halt grain shipments were set up in the city of Saratov itself, as well as further up the Volga.[40] By the time the region was fully under Soviet control, many in the countryside were not celebrating. Drafting peasants interfered with field work, an even higher priority. New efforts in nearly Tambov province were even more strongly resisted, a harbinger of the Antonov brothers' full-fledged "Green" revolt to come.

Moreover, the rhetorical "fight against hunger," as it was now called in many local newspapers, was increasingly a literal fight for grain. As was the case with the tsarist and Provisional Government regimes, the Bolshevik regime lacked accurate assessments of grain production around the country at the district level. One

---

[38] Osipova, *Rossiiskoe krestian'stvo*, 124; Lars Lih, *Bread and Authority in Russia 1914–1921* (Berkeley: University of California, 1990, chs. 6–7.
[39] Figes, *Peasant Russia*, 182–83.
[40] Donald J. Raleigh, *Experiencing Russia's Civil War* (Princeton, NJ: Princeton University Press, 2002), 284–85; *Vestnik Moskva-Kiev-Voronezh Zheleznodoroga*, Oct. 21, 1918.

provincial food committee later estimated that 99 percent of misunderstandings with the peasantry during the 1918-19 campaign were based on an incorrect accounting of the 1918 harvest.[41] While there are various sets of official figures on the state's procurements in late 1918 and 1919 that were generally accepted by Soviet historians, aggregate statistics again convey an improbable certainty and obscure the diverse and unequal local hardships of everyday life.

The use of *kombedy* to confiscate undelivered grain complicated the problem. What the committees regarded as "surplus" was now what villages and individual peasants were saving for their own use. While Lenin insisted in May 1918 that the Bolsheviks would "not take one step away from the grain monopoly," fixed prices at the local level were doubled and tripled to little avail. In late fall the monopoly essentially fell apart. Locally, workers were allowed to trade for small per person amounts. The legion of bagmen and -women expanded exponentially, again inflating currencies that were still accepted solely on faith and whose circulation continued to be fueled by the printing press.[42] An effort begun in July to set up new quotas for obligatory deliveries at fixed prices became in January the foundation of food procurement—the Rittikh *razverstka* now in its Soviet guise. Armed food procurement committees replaced the committees of the poor. Lars Lih has suggested this essentially "rehabilitated" Rittikh in some Bolsheviks' eyes, even if "taking the surplus" remained an administrative fiction and scarcities made a full state monopoly impossible. Even purportedly accurate statistics show a drastic declines in procurements throughout the spring and summer of 1919 in comparison to previous years.[43]

The new compulsory deliveries extended to all principal foods: dairy products, vegetables, meat, and other items which fueled the activity of the bag people. A major change that reverted back to the tsarist levy was the setting of delivery quotas from the center rather than on the basis of local estimates. Failure to deliver also resulted in a tax on the village as a whole on the basis of the principle of collective responsibility (*krugovaia porukha*) that extended back to before the serfs' emancipation in 1861. As in the summer and fall of 1918, food army brigades were designated to make the collections. Since most of their members had been taken into the Red Army itself when the fighting began during the summer, the brigades were reconstituted with people who would show no mercy, as many as ten thousand new recruits, according to the Commissariat of Food. In Saratov alone some one hundred collection points were set up at railroad depots and along the Volga. "In order to take grain from those who have it," Vice Commissar for Food Nikolai Briukhanov declared at the All-Russia Food Conference at the

---

[41] Figes, *Peasant Russia*, 251.

[42] A. Iu. Davydov, *Meshochniki i diktatura Rossii 1917-1921* (St. Petersburg: Aleteiia, 2007), 199-210.

[43] Lih, *Bread and Authority*, ch. 7; *Narodnoe Khoziaistvo* 10 (Aug. 1919): 99-103.

end of December 1918, "we must start anew in the formation of our Food Army, which is its absolutely necessary and unavoidable support. Without it, we could not possibly manage to take food from those who don't care an ounce about those who are starving and who want only to speculate on their hunger."[44] With this the Soviet stage was essentially set for the all-out struggle for food that would tear Soviet towns and villages apart over the next two years.

How dire was hunger and the anxieties of food insecurity in Soviet Russia by the winter of 1919? And how can we evidence its accompanying anxieties? Contradictory answers to the first question are suggested by the contrast between aggregate statistics and written descriptions, some for the changing area under Soviet control as a whole, some by specific province and district. Determined to gather the information needed to make "rational" policy decisions, the regime organized the Central Statistical Administration in mid-1918, gathering zemstvo statisticians and others throughout the country into Soviet employ. As a result of what the economic historian Stephen Wheatcroft calls "unprecedented" statistical activity, they and others sent calculations to Moscow about grain production and other matters in deceptively precise terms. In the black earth region, for example, winter wheat production was reported as falling from 44.6 puds (40 pounds) per desiatin (2.7 acres) in 1918 to 20.2 in 1920. In Samara winter rye production from 58.0 puds to 13.1, Cheliabinsk from 61.1 to 23.3.[45] In 1918 mandatory deliveries were reportedly over fulfilling their targets as if the Soviet regime had scarcity reasonably well in hand. The difficulty was initially understood as a procurement crisis, one to be met by the mobilization of "poor" peasants into armed procurement "brigades." By the beginning of 1919, in contrast, there were reportedly only sixty seven million *puds* available for procurement of the two hundred million needed. Still, procurement detachments themselves in some places reported amounts equivalent to sixty to seventy percent of all grain produced, which may have been as much about reporting "success" as it was about actually grain acquisition. In places that under fulfilled their quota the reason commonly given was the lack of detachments themselves and the perfidy of the kulaks, not the disruption, even decimation in many grain producing areas, of production. In deficit provinces, *volost* and rural soviets were also said to be stacked with kulaks, an explanation that both created and reinforced Bolshevik historically ideologized mentalities.[46]

---

[44] Iu. K. Strizhkov, *Prodovol'stvennye otriady v gody grazhdanskoi voiny i inostrannoi interventsii 1917–1921 gg.* (Moscow 1973), 151–52;; Figes, *Peasant Russia*, 260–65.

[45] Stephen Wheatcroft, "Famine and Epidemic Crises in Russia, 1918–1922: The Case of Saratov," *Annales de démographie historique* (1931): 332; TsSU, *Statisticheskii Ezhegodnik 1918–1920* (Moscow: TsSU, 1921), bk. 1: 244–45.

[46] Strizhkov, *Prodovol'stvennye otriady*, 165–74, 180–95, and passim. See also; P. I. Popov, *Proizvodstvo khleba v RSFSR i federiruiushchikhsia s neiu respublikakh (khlebnaia produktiia)*, (Moscow, 1921); *Tri goda bor'by s golodom: Kratkii otchet o deiatel'nosti Narodnogo Komissariata po Prodovol'stviiu za 1919–20* (Moscow: Narkomprod, 1920).

One prominent Western economic historian believes figures show the regime exaggerated the food crisis in wintertime, particularly in Moscow and Petrograd. A key problem, in her view, was that the formal abolition of free trade was not compensated by a successful policy of distribution. Politics, in other words, was responsible for shortages, rather than the other way around.[47] Clearly politics and state policies mattered then as they had in the area of procurement and distribution since the beginning of the war. It is also possible, of course, that some Bolsheviks exaggerated the crisis in order better to mobilize the struggle against it. But it would be hard to persuade those standing in long lines through successive regimes that the crisis was not real. Scarcities themselves produced the dysfunctional interventions of requisition and confiscation in a cyclical process that made scarcities worse, along with rampant speculation, corruption, and radical social differences in access, all of which had consequential political effects on very different successive local regimes.

But how, in fact, could those in Moscow rely on the most objectivized data in a period of such turmoil? The same was the case with inventories the *kombedy* were now charged to take of "available" grain. In many places there was simply little or none before September, when the summer harvest came in, or barely enough to meet local needs. Still, the *kombedy* had quotas, and amounts were somehow duly reported, as we have seen. Calculations based on grain production per *desiatin* were averages that disguised the significant variations with regions and hence the degree of suffering even in many grain producing areas. Rarely was Polanyi's "economistic fallacy" more likely to compromise socioeconomic understanding by reifying statistics and occluding their underlying social and economic complexities.

Many newspaper accounts and images recorded in the local press told a very different story. In provincial towns like Saratov and Poltava long lines of people were described lining up for bread as early as 5:00 a.m. Both in the city and deeper into the province local officials again relaxed the ban on free trade.[48] Workers organizations and cooperatives were permitted to purchase certain food products beyond those formally included in the grain monopoly. For a brief time the ongoing discussion about the value of free trade and market relations was also taken up in Menshevik and SR newspapers when the regime allowed them to be republished. "The very fact that the Bolshevik regime itself is seeking a path for its own transformation is extra evidence of the fact that not all has yet been lost for the Russian revolution," Russia's most prominent Menshevik, Iulii Martov, wrote, leaning firmly on the democratic socialist Great Story that there

---

[47] Malle, *Organization of War Communism*, 375–80.
[48] Raleigh, *Experiencing Russia's Civil War*, 298.

"might still be a way out besides suffocation in a utopian kingdom and capitulation to nationalist and global counterrevolution."[49]

Again, anxiety and the language of extreme need continued to carry their own weight, stimulating hoarding if goods were to be found, pushing migrations of hungry people from one district to another, fueling disorder and violence. Already in January 1918 the *Nizhegorodskaia Kommuna* was describing the food situation in its grain-exporting province as "dreadful." To ease the crisis, transport and market sales of food products would be "absolutely free." No Cheka or other authorities would have the right to interfere. Citizen patrols were needed to protect goods trains and prevent grain from leaving the city. Famine was "approaching." When the provincial Commissariat of Food was charged with solving the problem, it found the situation "catastrophic." There was no possibility of fulfilling orders coming from Moscow. During the first four months of 1919, the number of empty freight cars may have exceeded sixteen thousand. One year later the renamed newspaper was still reporting that no bread would be available between January 7 and 9, in the midst of the New Year's holiday. A "food chronicle" column listing possible arrivals of grain became a regular feature, no doubt driving crowds to the transport depots. Later in the month an urgent request to Moscow for help was categorically rejected. The region would have to feed itself. By March 1919 the situation in the province as a whole was described as "critical." All local forces had to be mobilized to stave off starvation.[50]

In the meantime, the numbers of bagmen and -women and their flourishing black-market trade in collusion with the railroaders increased. The great writer Isaac Babel created one scene in *Red Cavalry*:

> Our honored cavalry train stopped . . . it would not pull out on account of the black-market traders, those vicious enemies, among whom were also a countless number of the female sex, acting in an insolent manner with the railroad authorities. Fearlessly they grabbed hold of the handrails, those wicked enemies, scooted over the roofs, romping around, and stirring up trouble, and in each and every hand you could see the not-unfamiliar salt, sacks of up to five *poods*. But not for long did the capitalist triumph of the black-market traders last. The soldiers clambered out of the wagon. They put some of the women in the wagon, and some they didn't. [One pitiful woman with a baby begged to be allowed on.] "Let her on" the lads shouted, "after she's had us she won't want her husband." . . . Trembling, I walked over to her, took the "baby" from her arms, tore the swaddling off, and saw instead a good little *pood* of salt. . . .

---

[49] Z. Galili and A. Nenarokov, eds., *Mensheviki v 1919-1920* (Moscow: Rosspen, 2000), 24–31.
[50] *Narodnoe Khoziaistvo* 6 (July 1919): 114–15; *Raboche-Krest'ianskii Nizhegorodskii Listok*, Jan. 25, 1919.

"Forgive me kind Cossacks, it was not I that deceived you, it was my trouble that deceived you." She said to me "I have been deprived of salt. I'm not frightened of the truth. You don't care about Russia, you're just saving the Yids Lenin and Trotsky. . . ." I threw her off, down beside the rails. . . . Taking my trusty rifle I wiped that infamy from the face of the working land and the Republic.[51]

In sum, as Aaron Retish has deftly described it, Civil War developed in "a long season of hunger."[52] Statistics are virtually irrelevant here to understanding the human circumstances. In European Russia drought and crop failures in 1919–20 aggravated the crisis, along with the struggles for food that accompanied them. In 1920, spring crops in some areas were destroyed by frost. Poltava was racked with disease, drought, and "many months of hunger." One resident's diary called the 1891–92 famine "a joke" in comparison. In the Viatka region researched by Retish the production of grain in one district in 1921 may have been less than 8 percent of what was harvested in 1916.[53]

Wholesale famine did not sweep the region until later in 1920 and after the Civil War ended in 1921.[54] But 1919 it was already a "naked year" of dire hunger, deprivation, and anxiety throughout most of Soviet Russia. Another great writer, Boris Pilnyak, wrote shortly afterward, "Both the newspapers from the province on brown paper and the newspapers from Moscow on blue paper . . . were full of bitterness and confusion. There was no bread. There was no iron. There was hunger, death, lies, horror, and terror—it was the year 'nineteen.'"[55]

The Normalization of Concealment

Scarcities also afflicted provincial cities and towns during those awful months, of course, albeit in different ways and to different degrees. Just as earlier, industrial towns and former trading centers outside grain-producing areas depended largely on the railroads or river traffic to deliver needed goods. The situation of those deeper in the countryside depended on the conditions in the villages and, to some extent, the authorities responsible for its local distribution. The summer's unrest in Petrograd, the Moscow region, Tula, Sormovo, and other

---

[51] Isaac Babel, "Salt" (1926), in *Red Cavalry*, trans. D. McDuff (London, 1994), 163–67 (quotation abridged).

[52] Aaron B. Retish, *Russia's Peasants in Revolution and Civil War* (Cambridge: Cambridge University Press, 2008). 239.

[53] Mark Conliffe, "Poltava in Revolution and Civil War: From the Diaries of Vladimir Korolenko and Aleksandr Nesvitskii," in *Russia's Home Front in War and Revolution 1914–22*, bk. 2, ed. Adele Lindenmeyr, Christopher Read, and Peter Waldron (Bloomington, IN: Slavica, 2016), 467.

[54] x

[55] Boris Pilnyak, *The Naked Year*, trans. A. R. Tulloch (New York: Ardis, 1975), 80.

industrial centers concerned Bolshevik leaders as much as or more than the struggles in the countryside. In this fifth summer of anxiety and instability since the beginning of the world war, Kossior, Nogin, and other of Sovnarkhoz's leaders saw a change occurring in "the workers' mood." Their only concern had become "meeting their own real needs" since the Bolshevik regime seemed incapable of improving their situation.[56] Political Commissar B. I. Brover reported from Voronezh that counterrevolutionary publications had become so frequent as to assume a "chronic character."[57] The regime's legitimacy was being linked directly to the supply of food.

The problems at hand, however, turned on more than food insecurities. The scarcities of fuel, production materials, and other essential goods continued to threaten workers' livelihoods. So did the need for funds to support production and pay wages. It was imperative for Moscow to gain firmer control over cities and towns, especially where dissidence was still threatening or already widespread. The further mobilization of the Cheka and Red Terror after August 1918 was intended to do just that. Large numbers of Cheka enthusiasts sent into the provinces targeted local Mensheviks and manipulated local soviet elections to secure favorable outcomes one way or another. On one hand, it was impossible for Cheka agents to be effective locally without the cooperation of local authorities. On the other, their behavior made it difficult for local authorities to cooperate with them. In the deeper countryside, meanwhile, some Chekists reported that their own actions against kulaks and others seemed to encourage poor peasants and local peasant soviets toward their own form of "economic banditry": confiscating supplies that had already been requisitioned and acting without restraint.[58]

Yet even Bolshevik-dominated regional soviets exercised power largely in terms of local conditions, seeking their own ways to cope with the scarcities and dislocations that were affecting them most. As Donald Raleigh has put it, drawing nicely on the work of the anthropologist James Scott, officials in Saratov and other provincial cities were not "seeing like a state," putting their own immediate needs and interests above those in the Moscow regime.[59] Decrees and pronouncements flooding down from above were commonly ignored. Sovnarkhoz chairman Rykov himself sent out hundreds of telegrams regarding local matters large and small, with little apparent effect, from the "catastrophic" fuel situation in Nizhnii Novgorod to the "illegal confiscation" of money and goods by a district food committee in Tambov. Local *sovnarkhozy* took responsibility for addressing industrial breakdowns, replicating the large number of

---

[56] RGAE f. 3429, op. 1, d. 16, l. 3; RGASPI f. 5, op. 1, d. 2560, ll. 7, 7 ob.
[57] RGASPI f. 5, op. 1, d. 2560, l. 5; GARF f. 382, op. 4, d. 125a, ll. 104–6.
[58] RGASPI f. 5, op. 1, d. 2560, ll. 7, 93–97.
[59] Raleigh, *Experiencing Russia's Civil War*, ch. 9.

departments (*glavki*) in Moscow. Plants continued to be nationalized locally under its authority. In Rostov workers refused to take over their factory because operating capital had disappeared and there was little or no cash to pay wages. In Smolensk, local authorities assigned wage scales as much as 25 to 30 percent higher than those mandated from Moscow in a futile effort to maintain local production. Prices fixed locally to control inflation had little meaning without goods to attach them to. In Saratov province the lack of rationed bread prompted the provincial soviet to suspend the ban on free trade. Scarcities at the end of the summer led to another massive departure of workers. Those who did not leave swelled the ranks of the destitute unemployed. Those who did added to the tensions in their villages. Some localities even styled themselves "republics." The Soviet of Peoples' Commissars of the Kaluga People's Republic "nationalized" the local river boats with its own official stamp to ensure "the correct development of trade and industry in the Kaluga Republic." The question of naturalizing wages by means of ration packets or increasing productivity by restoring piece rates was discussed in the highest circles.[60]

In contrast to the local focus of regional authorities, the regime in Moscow saw all of this very much like the state it aspired to be. The Soviet state had to increase its direct engagement in all aspects of socioeconomic and political life—in effect, to create a fully socialist political economy. In variations of the liberal Great Story, the very effort to create a socialist economy was utopian, whatever "socialist" was taken to mean at the time. Richard Pipes, for example, has dismissed the entire enterprise as being the result of incapable and ignorant dreamers captivated by the illusions of power. To longtime Kadet Central Committee member Ariadna Tyrkova, the Soviets gathered around them the most malicious criminal elements: "The universal hegemony of Western democracy is fraud, which politicians have foisted upon us. We must have the courage to look directly into the eye of the wild beast—which is called the people."[61] The dominant trope in the democratic socialist literature is the Bolsheviks' resistance to market exchange. Even left-leaning Mensheviks like Martov were outspoken on this issue throughout 1918, while Bolsheviks argued, as their tsarist and Provisional Government predecessors had done, whether the confiscatory steps being taken by their regime even went far enough. Some argued for ending "Shingarev's grain monopoly," maintaining that "broad circles of the urban proletariat" saw it as a key way to fight hunger. Others thought any relaxation of grain and trade monopolies would likely strengthen class enemies in the countryside without

---

[60] GARF f. 328, op. 2, d. 333, ll. 19–32ff.; RGAE f. 3429, op. 1 d. 369, ll. 116, 146, and passim; RGASPI f. 5, op. 1, d. 2887, ll. 1–13; *Narodnoe Khoziaistvo* 12 (Dec. 1918) and 3 (March 1919).
[61] Protocols of the Kadet Conference in Kharkov, Nov. 3–6, 1919, packet 3, f. 34, Panina Archive, Bakhmeteff Archive of Russian and East European Culture, Columbia University; A. Tyrkova-Williams, *From Liberty to Brest Litovsk* (London, 1919), 453.

increasing the grain available for requisition or solving the fundamental problem of its distribution to deficit areas. Instead, left Bolsheviks like Iurii Larin, Nikolai Bukharin, and Lev Kritsman imagined these problems made the moment right for a "heroic" transition away from money itself to an entire system of goods exchange.[62] How this might be successfully effected given the scarcities of essential goods themselves was unclear.

It is hard to say how much the attraction of building a new socialist economy emerged from ideologized visions and how much was because of the sheer difficulties of administering effectively a broken economic system. Well-known efforts at cultural revolution during these first years attracted a brilliant cohort of avant-garde artists, writers, and social dreamers. The most progressive concepts of European jurisprudence were being discussed in the Commissariat of Justice, of education in the Commissariat of the Enlightenment.[63] The key problem was how effectively to administer and *control* a broken economy from above. Dictatorship called for rational assessment, planning, and carefully calibrated intervention, not arbitrary seizures. Yet the very conditions of scarcity and the subjectivities of "extreme need" made dictatorial controls extremely difficult if not impossible to apply effectively. Almost everywhere there was the arbitrary behavior (*proizvol*) of local officials. Every town and city experienced increases in criminality, attacks against those thought to be shielding wealth and theft of their belongings. In Samara, Kharkov, and elsewhere there were major pogroms against Jews, by both those who supported the Bolsheviks and those who saw the party dominated by so many like Lev Bronshtein-Trotsky and Hirsch Apfelbaum-Zinoviev with formal Jewish identities and cultural backgrounds. In these circumstances dictatorship could not simply be *declared* with a realistic expectation that terror and draconian sanctions would compel obedience.

The new legion of special plenitentiaries sent out once again from Moscow only made matters worse, just as they had in 1917 and before. Cheka teams in trademark leather jackets were the most notorious, imperiously commandeering trains and running roughshod over anyone in their way. ("There is not a single Commissar sent on the railroad who does not demand his separate car, special train, and the right to set up living quarters in an empty freight car," the head of the Transport Commissariat complained to Lenin. Red Army commanders "behaved the same way.")[64] Large numbers of complaints charged Chekists themselves with a variety of offenses: arresting people randomly or "on demand,"

---

[62] *Vestnik NKTiP* 3–4 (July 1918); *Biulleten' VSNKh* 1 (Apr. 1918): 38–40; Malle, *Organization of War Communism*, 165–66.

[63] See, e.g., the documents and discussion in William G. Rosenberg, ed., *Bolshevik Visions: The First Phase of the Cultural Revolution in Soviet Russia*, 2 vols. (Ann Arbor: University of Michigan Press, 1990).

[64] RGASPI f. 5, op. 1, d, 2749, ll. 17 104–28.

meting out immediate and severe punishments, colluding with the nests of bagmen and -women they were supposed to control. The Cheka itself later reported that at least 25 percent and maybe as many as 50 percent of those arrested in July and August 1918 were being held without cause. "Not one communist would deny the necessity of applying terror in this very difficult period ... but the horror everywhere is that the work of local Cheka units is absolutely without any control from the center," one anxious report stated. A huge number of petitions urged Lenin himself to become more involved, just as they had appealed to previous regimes.[65]

In the hope of dealing more effectively with corruption and as part of its expanding surveillance, the regime ordered special complaint boxes (*iashchki zhalob*) to be set up in all Soviet institutions. Ordinary citizens could submit their complaints against comrades and officials in confidence and vent their anger. In effect, the boxes were actually set up as "eyes" of the regime. (They could still be found in post offices and other institutions when the USSR collapsed in 1991, having performed their anonymous surveillance, for better or worse, over more than seventy years.) The predictable result was a new flood of written complaints ranging the gamut from petty personal disputes to accusations of wholesale criminality. In the Ivanovo textile region incompetent managers left ventilation systems broken; there was dust everywhere, and no systematic cleaning had been done "for months." Leather workers were forced to work on pelts that had not been sterilized because all the disinfectant had been sold off. Munitions factories were "simply ruinous for health." Little effort was being made to cope with disease. In Moscow and other places trash had not been collected for weeks, the streets awash with filth that some saw as symbolizing the false promises of October. Leading party members in the Perm region were accused of "large-scale" abuse of their offices. There were even complaints about "mass use of cocaine in Moscow which was being sold in the back rooms of pharmacies and coffee shops.[66] By May 1919 complaint bureaus were operating in twenty-three provincial areas. One report collating a month of complaints to provincial bureaus listed 97 protesting arrests, 420 protesting irregular confiscations and requisitions, 181 protesting "disorder in soviet institutions," and 155 "abuse of power."[67]

Soviet Russia's unique form of state financing also stirred suspicions, undoubtedly for good reason. Already by the summer of 1918 provincial and local *sovnarkhozy* themselves were complaining about the use and distribution

---

[65] Ibid., d. 2740, l. 232.
[66] GARF f. 130, op. 2, d. 66, l. 179; f. 4085, op. 16, d. 2385, ll. 10ff. See also Pavel Vasiliev, "War, Revolution and Drugs: The 'Democratization' of Drug Abuse and the Evolution of Drug Policy in Russia, 1914–24," in Lindenmeyr, Read, and Waldron, *Russia's Home Front*, 424–28.
[67] GARF f. 4085, op. 25, d. 2, l. 5.

of funds. Local soviets and their commissars held on to taxes that were still being paid even after a decree ordered that *all* local confiscations were to be sent to the state treasury.[68] "Credits" were being issued at the local level ostensibly correlated to local bank holdings, but in fact not backed by actual funds. In Nizhnii Novgorod, the provincial *sovnarkhoz* allocated a credit of 1 million rubles to the executive committee of the city soviet to finance sequestered and nationalized plants. (The city's officials got 20,000 rubles of this for their own use). At the same time, the provincial soviet ordered the withdrawal from circulation of all paper money held by local soviets and other institutions. All monetary transactions between local government institutions and enterprises would henceforth have to be done not by paper money transactions but by bookkeeping transfers from the account of one institution to that of another.[69]

In other places local soviets also continued to print currency of their own, adding to the huge number of tsarist bills and 1917 "Kerenkis" still in use. Twelve billion of these new old notes were issued in the first five months of 1918, even more in the late summer and fall to meet military needs. Using exact figures to convey their accuracy, the financial accounts office of the Sovnarkhoz reported in January 1919 that credits of 5,901,069,981 rubles and 48 kopecks had been issued in 1918. According to one contemporary estimate, a deficit of income over expenditures for the first six months of 1919 was 3.3 trillion rubles. The nominal paper value of money in circulation by 1921 would be 16.3 trillion rubles, 100,000 rubles equivalent to 1 prewar ruble.[70]

Again, however, like their predecessors, for those now confronting the financial crisis there seemed to be no real alternative to using the printing press in this way. The functional problem instead was control over who and what received the grants and credits the emissions allowed. There were as yet no consistent rules for financing nationalized enterprises, much less those still privately owned, despite the pressing need to increase industrial and defense production and stem the growth in unemployment.[71] According to those in the Sovnarkhoz in charge of issuing grants, recipients were showing up for the money the same day their accounting offices got their payment authorizations.

The Sovnarkom and individual commissariats were also issuing grants and credits on their own. The official newspaper *Ekonomicheskaia Zhizn'* (*Economic Life*) went so far as to accuse Moscow of being "uninformed" about the siphoning of money and other forms of malfeasance at a local level where criminal groups

---

[68] RGAE f. 3429, op. 2, d. 22, ll. 25, 30.

[69] *Nizhegorodskaia Kommuna*, May 3, 1919.

[70] RGAE f. 3429, op. 1, d. 808, ll. 34–35; GARF f. 130, op. 3, d. 259, ll. 32–36; K. F. Shmelev, "Soviet Policy in Public Finance," *Soviet Policy in Public Finance 1917–1928*, ed. G. Y. Sokonikov et al. (Stanford, CA: Stanford University Press, 1931), 110; K. F. Shmelev, "Financy sovetskoi vlasti," *Financy i Ekonomika* 1 (June. 1922): 28–33.

[71] RGAE f. 3429, op. 1, d. 251, l. 16.

became autonomous financial authorities representing no one but themselves.[72] The falsification of financial and other statistics was a particularly troublesome part of what had essentially become the normalization of concealment: the propensity in conditions of great scarcity and need to conceal from hostile authorities any information about use of state funds or the availability of goods that might jeopardize local well-being.

What is particularly interesting about the difficulties of holding officials and others to account is the mistaken belief that denunciations from below would act as a form of popular surveillance and increase internal security. Rather, it reflected a political culture comparable to the one we have seen taking hold at the very beginning of the war, and even before. A key assumption in all of this was that some person or persons had to be "guilty" of ineptitude or worse if scarcities and other failures were to be properly explained. "Treason" as an accusation was easy enough to signal through the complaint boxes and other reports, just as it colored the accusations surrounding Russia's great military failures early in the war, although now it was even easier to lodge a complaint. In the Bolshevik political dialect, a more forceful label than "traitor" was "counterrevolutionary," a term which signaled urgency even as it covered a wide variety of offenses. "Who was to blame?" was again a common trope, as it was almost from the moment the war began in 1914.

Here we can discern a set of related processes and behaviors that together constitute one of the more consequential effects of scarcity in Soviet Russia during the difficult winter of 1918–19, 1919–20, and afterward, and which link back to the first months of the world war. Well before the February revolution concealment in and outside the huge war zone developed as an obvious defense against requisitioning. By the fall of 1918, concealment extended well beyond the actualities and hoarding in the countryside to scarce goods held by legal and illegal traders and distributors in virtually every Soviet city and town. So did the suspicion that it was occurring, whether or not there was any firm evidence.

One has to be cautious about overgeneralizing on the basis of limited evidence, but archival documents are very suggestive. Thus we find secret reports to the Sovnarkom from Vologda, Voronezh, Tula, Tver, Tambov, Samara, and other provinces not only of the "anxious" mood of towns like Kostroma, Kaluga, Tver, and Mstislavl that were placed under martial law in the late summer and fall of 1918, but of undisciplined Red Army troops pillaging villages rightly or wrongly suspected of hiding food and agitated in either case at having to fight in their defense.[73] Retish details one of the most notorious instances involving the 1st Moscow Food Brigade Regiment in Viatka, commanded by Anatoli Stepanov,

---

[72] *Ekon. Zhizn'*, Sept. 25, 1919; RGAE f. 3429, op. 1, d. 289, ll. 31ff.
[73] RGASPI f. 5, op. 1, d. 2531, ll. 3ff.

a former tsarist army captain. Facing strong resistance by peasants unwilling to give up their grain, his brigades turned into marauders, forcefully seizing and selling grain on their own, brewing and peddling vodka, and soon rebelling outright against the Soviet regime, declaring a military dictatorship, and neutralizing nearby units of the Red Army.[74] Retish also shows that one of the largest uprisings against Bolshevik power in the Izhevsk region was empowered by soldiers returned from the front who briefly suppressed local Red Guards and held the Red Army at bay, but fueled in the late summer of 1918 by peasants enraged by new grain requisitions. In places they were joined by workers and others in the region's towns anxious as well about their compromised economic conditions more generally.[75] "Adequate" food reserves were reported being concealed in Iaroslavl province because the purchase price was too low and because there were too few members of the *kombedy* determined to force them out. A secret report indicated an additional ongoing problem: the proliferation of confiscations by different agencies, just as before and during the revolution. A new branch of the Cheka with unrestricted dictatorial power in the area of food and transport was proposed to control them and fight criminality and concealment.[76]

Losing the "Hunger War"

Still, the crisis continued. The "fight against hunger" was described in local newspapers as no less urgent than the fight against Kolchak and Denikin. When a delegation went down the Volga to be sure food shipments designated for Nizhegorodskaia were not diverted, "starving workers and their children" were reportedly waiting anxiously for its results.[77] Concessions intended to encourage peasants to increase their plantings only brought more hunger. The mobilization of additional armed detachments to secure "surpluses" also brought meager results. When the first tallies of the harvest in Nizhnii Novgorod showed that the amounts called for in the provincial *razverstka* had not been delivered, provincial authorities ordered another tally, insisting on the "absolute need" for correct figures.[78]

---

[74] Retish, *Russia's Peasants*, 176; D. N. Kazakov, "Slovo o 'Stepanovskom' miatezhe," *Idnakar* 1 (2014): 1–13 at https://cyberleninka.ru/article/n/slovo-o-stepanovskom-myatezhe.
[75] Aaron Retish, "The Izhevsk Revolt of 1918: The Fateful Clash of Revolutionary Coalitions, Paramilitarism, and Bolshevik Power," in Badcock, Novikova, and Retish, *Russia's Home Front*, 1:299–322.
[76] RGASPI f. 5, op. 1, d. 2560, ll. 14–18.
[77] *Raboche-Krestianskii Nizhegorodskii Listok*, Jan. 5, 11, 17, 26, 1918; Mar. 7, 20, May 11, 14, 1919.
[78] *Nizhegoroskaia Kommuna*, Mar. 7, 1919.

Reports from other places painted equally dismal pictures. A telegram to the Sovnarkhoz from the Urals in May 1919 warned that the fulfillment of production goals in local metal and metallurgical plants was very doubtful as a result of the "increase in starving workers."[79] In Samara a regular newspaper column on food supply appeared, describing in one account "kulaks hiding grain in the forest." "We are living on another planet here," a commentator wrote. "We constantly hear that there is none of this, none of that . . . without end and every day. . . . The heart of the Russian revolution has practically stopped beating from hunger."[80] Meanwhile peasant communities were described as hostile and ignorant. One report described White Guards being turned back by district soviet members waving an icon they took from the wall of their building.[81] In Chernigov province wealthier "kulaks" in the villages blamed Jews for their problems. Long-suffering peasant women, hundreds of thousands of whom had lost husbands or sons, were "extremely backward," the force of their "murderous ignorance fundamentally counterrevolutionary."[82]

Everywhere, moreover, women were bearing the brunt of the crisis, tending to families while working in cities and towns or working their own relatively meager land allocations in the deep countryside. In Moscow the city soviet counted almost 60,000 women still working in factories and plants in the spring of 1919, 30,000 in stores. Some 41,000 who had not left the city were listed as unemployed. There were also 376,000 children in the city, many without parents or homes. Material support for them as well as other displaced women and their families throughout the Soviet region had largely come to an end.[83] Failure to distribute permits needed to leave the Chernigov region was described by a local newspaper as a "death sentence."[84] Here, too, the *razverstka* was a disaster, as it was again in 1920 when many areas of the province were still described as "starving." Viatka province was tortured by crop failures, disease, mass hunger, and in some villages famine, a prelude to what the middle Volga region was to endure in 1921. As Retish has further suggested, hunger here in political terms for villages relatively close to provincial towns may now have become a two-edged sword, pushing peasants away from the regime's agents to protect their meager food supplies, but also toward those authorities that might be able to offer some relief.[85]

---

[79] RGAE f. 3429; op. 1, d. 226 l. 541.
[80] *Kommuna* (Samara), Feb. 2, 1919.
[81] *Kommuna* (Samara), Mar. 4, 8, 23, 1919.
[82] *Znamia Sovetov* (Chernigov), Apr. 17, June 6, 1919.
[83] Mos. Soviet, *Steno. otchety,* 3 (Apr. 20, 1919) and Supplement *Otchet otdela sotsial'nogo obespecheniia* in 18 (July 15, 1919).
[84] *Znamia Sovetov* (Chernigov), Oct. 5, 1920; RGASPI f. 5 op. 1, d. 2534, passim.
[85] Retish, *Russia's Peasants,* 164–75.

Deeper into the countryside it was a different matter. Here we can discern the baneful consequence of tsarist Russia's partial commercialization and rural underdevelopment that characterized the country's agrarian economy when war began in 1914. In the countryside, as we have discussed, "partial commercialization" had created a "market problem": how to assure the distribution of scarce foodstuffs, commodities, and resources in ways that met basic local needs as well as those in cities and towns while also satisfying the army's never-ending demands. The production of commercial crops like flax that had slowed dramatically in 1917 now ceased almost entirely.[86] When rural production failed to ward off growing scarcities, villages in the deep countryside away from trading towns and railroads fell back on ensuring their own well-being, even survival, in any way they could. The official journal of the Sovnarkhoz itself complained about the failure of its own local committees to carry out the government's economic program, decrying, as officials had done in 1915 and 1916, their lack of control over what their own committees were doing in the provinces.[87]

By the late winter of 1919 many of those furthest from towns retreated into a primitive autarchy, as Figes has described for the middle Volga region, completing a process of withdrawal that had begun with the collapse of war capitalism in 1917 and even before.[88] Many also had overcome whatever conflicts had earlier divided them and, like settlements on a hostile frontier, forcefully defended themselves against marauders of all stripes, perhaps especially those wearing red stars. Inscribed in this formative Civil War experience for uncountable numbers of peasants was hostility against Soviet state authority, one that carried well past the Civil War through the whole Soviet period.

Just as the dismal winter of 1919 turned into an anxious spring, a poem appeared on the front page of the provincial soviet newspaper in Nizhnii Novgorod entitled "To the Battle with Hunger." "Oh no!" it began. "I cannot be silent when the all-powerful, all-mighty Hunger, like a tsar-vampire, an impudent thief, turns the city into a tomb." "This tsar is getting even bolder," it continued, "and the wounds ever more painful." "Close ranks, people," its author, who used the name "Proletarian," concluded, "strike back and defeat the tsar-tyrant." Next to the poem was a long article, "Food Crisis in Nizhnii Novgorod Province," demanding immediate measures "to save the province from starvation." The head of the Grain Foraging Committee had just returned from Moscow. The authorities had again refused to have the official label "starving province" moved from the list of grain-producing provinces to those now experiencing deficits, just as it had earlier with Saratov. Despite an abundance of testimony to the contrary, the

---

[86] *Za Piat' Let* (Moscow, 1922), 224; S. N. Prokopovich, *The Economic Condition of Soviet Russia* (London, 1924), 78–79.
[87] *Narodnoe Khoziaistvo* 10 (Oct. 1918): 72–66.
[88] Figes, *Peasant Russia*, 257–58.

Commissariat of Food categorically insisted the province was capable of feeding itself.[89] With the harvest of a dismal winter crop, procurements became a violent battle for survival.

Thus, the more familiar political processes of Soviet state-building were occurring in the worst possible and less easily documented circumstances of scarcity and anxiety, paralleling in their ways the impossible conditions in 1917 for political democracy and a liberal republican state order. And while the consequences for the Provisional Government were almost immediately apparent in 1917, the anxieties of hunger, social dislocation, and the continuing effects of human loss and material deprivation in this formative period of Soviet rule would prove to be long lasting.

---

[89] *Raboche-Krestianskii Nizhegorodskii Listok*, Mar. 7, 1919.

15
Violence, Loss, and the Collapse of War Communism

In liberal and democratic socialist tellings of the Great Story, violence was deeply embedded in Russia's prewar social and political structures. Violence especially in the form of social protest was an element of the empire's "premodern" stage of development that had to be overcome by reform if Russia was to advance progressively as a modern European power. Violence, in a word, was inherent in Russia's "backwardness." The objective institutionalization of controls and the state's monopoly of force were necessary to stable and effective governance. The subjective internalization of restraints collectively and by individuals was foundational to civil rights and a modern social order.

In both these respects, Imperial Russia's last decades were problematic. The upheavals of 1905–6 reflected unresolved pressures in the countryside for land and sustainable well-being in an increasingly commercialized order that disadvantaged small peasant holdings in favor of large and more productive landed estates. Violence, social dislocation, and personal misery also characterized Russia's burgeoning industrial slums. Improvements could not keep pace with the expansion of industry itself. Accompanying this was the long-term pattern of violent political and cultural confrontation on the empire's colonial periphery, more problematic for Russia than with other imperial powers because its colonies were geographically contiguous and their borders largely porous. Building a modern nation in all these respects was almost certain to have its violent moments, as it had in the United States and elsewhere.

"Vectors of Social Violence"

In their prodigious studies of the revolutionary period, the Russian historians Vladimir Buldakov and Tatiana Leont'eva have brought the question of social violence to the foreground. Along with several other scholars liberated from the constraints of Soviet historiography, Buldakov and Leont'eva have reached into the most difficult areas of revolutionary understanding: individual and group psychology, mentality, and the origins and effects of the wanton brutality that turned hopes and expectations into "life in catastrophe," as Igor Narskii has notably described it. In the process, they have exposed the myths and dogmas of the Soviet Great Story itself.

Three untranslatable concepts mark their approach: *bunt, stikhiia,* and *smuta.* (There is good reason why Vladimir Nabokov believed that the essential features of national cultures lie in their untranslatable words.)[1] *Bunt* (etymologically "pack" or "bundle") joins together the mixed meanings of "riot" and "rebellion," as in women's riots over food or other matters (*bab'i bunty*) or peasant revolts. *Stikhiia* connotes "element," as in the basic elements of nature but also their destructive and uncontrolled release, as in "mayhem" or "chaos." *Smuta* absorbs both *bunt* and *stikhiia* into a range of physical and emotional horrors: a time of great trouble, hardship, dislocation, gloom, and death: the sociopolitical crisis (*smutnoe vremia*) in Moscovy at the turn of the seventeenth century or the *Krasnaia* (Red) *Smuta* brought on by the revolution, as Buldakov titled his important explorations in 1997 and 2010.[2]

Buldakov lays out the social-psychological underpinnings of *stikhiia* and the *Red Smuta* by identifying four "vectors of social violence" in the revolutionary period: radicalized workers "whipped into non-rational and destructive *stikhiia*" by inflammatory rhetoric; peasants raging over the possession and use of land; soldiers acting out the contradictions of a "bloody path to peace"; and the "us against them" animosities of the empire's "ethnic stepsons." In examining each vector—a term also used by the British historians Robert Gerwarth and John Horne[3]—Buldakov explores the destabilizations of social change and the important roles of revolutionary institutions like factory committees and traditional institutions like the village commune in channeling anger in specific social directions. These were partly defined, as we have seen, by revolutionary rhetoric itself: the "bourgeoisie" as an enemy class; workers' "revolutionary right" to set the terms and conditions of industrial production; tsarist officers harboring "counterrevolutionary" biases and inclinations; and the historically rooted antagonisms against Jews, "little Russians," and the darker Muslim peoples of the Caucasus and Central Asia forcefully subordinated to Moscow. In that last case, the bloody revolt of Muslims in Central Asia against being drafted into military labor battalions in the summer and fall of 1916 was a harbinger of the ways the ethnic ascriptions of disloyalty (Jews as "spies," Muslims as loyal to the Turks) or the desires for political independence (Poland, Ukraine, the Caucasus) fueled

---

[1] Vladimir Nabokov, "The Art of Translation," *New Republic,* Aug. 4, 1941.
[2] V. P. Buldakov, *Krasnaia Smuta* (Moscow: Rosspen, 2010), ch. 2. See also V. P. Buldakov and T. G. Leont'eva, *Voina porodivshaia revoliutsiiu* (Moscow: Novyi Khronograf, 2015).
[3] Robert Gerwarth and John Horne, "Vectors of Violence: Paramilitarism in Europe after the Great War," *Journal of Modern History* 38, no. 3 (2011): 489–512. See also Peter Holquist on violence as political culture in *Making War, Forging Revolution* (Cambridge, MA: Harvard University Press, 2002), 202–5 and passim, and "Violent Russia, Deadly Marxism? Russia in the Epoch of Violence, 1905–21," *Kritika* 3 (Summer 2003): 627–52.

violence for reasons besides those of revolutionary politics. In Soviet Nizhnii Novgorod and elsewhere a reified conception of class and class enemies played the same role. In January 1919 the penalty announced there for full nonpayment of a new "extraordinary" tax levied on the "bourgeoisie" was death by firing squad. Those found guilty of "secret speculation" and "kulak tendencies" were to be sentenced to long terms of forced labor.[4]

In his discussion of worker violence, Buldakov pays particular attention to the large proportion of women and youth who brought their own anxieties into the workforce during the war. Brutal attacks on hated foremen and factory managers were not only the result of a breakdown in policing but a reflection of repressed emotions of humiliation and the abuses of subordination. As he suggests, anger and hatred long simmered in the industrial slums and workplaces. Workers' control was sought for this reason as well as more practical ones like higher wages and pressed on them by soviet figures and other self-proclaimed defenders of their interests. Buldakov asks good questions, some of which vexed democratic liberals and socialists themselves after February: To what extent could Russia's diverse workforce master the "civilized" forms of struggle with factory owners postulated by the full legalization of trade unions and strikes? Did not this depend in part on the state's ability and willingness to control workers' violent excesses and nurture their political and cultural "maturity"?

The vector of social violence in the countryside was of a different sort. Here the issue in 1917 was the pressure not only on the village to deliver more grain but on the reconsolidation of the village commune in opposition to the tsarist regime's efforts to separate peasants into individual homesteads. For both Buldakov and Leont'eva, the idea of individual homesteads as well as the process of forcefully reincorporating those who had separated during the Stolypin reforms back into the commune was a challenge to the peasant soldiers' dominant psychology and morality. So were discharged peasants who returned home having confronted "modernity" head-on at the front, and the hardships of soldiers' wives and widows. In these circumstances the peasants' decades-long demand for additional land became more urgent and justified by their service in the war as well as in terms of challenges to the moral economy of the village. The often brutal seizures of landed estates and the peasants' increasing disregard for local authorities was part of a "communal revolution" made possible by the revolutionary regime, one that easily escalated into a struggle against outsiders as a whole—a "virus" of antipathy to aliens in Buldakov's language of social pathology that snared hapless revolutionaries and others. Although Buldakov and Leont'eva acknowledge the considerable differences that existed in various localities, a common connection, in their view, was the desire of peasant

---

[4] *Raboche-Krestianskii Nizhegorodskii Listok*, Jan. 29, 1919.

communities to rule their own worlds. In these circumstances the more traditional "weapons of the weak" were also readily deployed: concealment, withholding rent and taxes, feigned unawareness of orders and decrees from above.

In the vector of ethnic violence, the horrific massacres of Jews are in a category of their own—by Cossacks and soldiers during the world war, by Nestor Makhno's anarchists and other peasant bands after 1917, by the brutal Cossack legions in South Russia and Siberia before and after the Whites' defeat, and by those mobilized willingly or not in the organized armies on both sides of the Civil War. As Denikin's forces moved north through Ukraine toward Moscow in the fall of 1919, tsarist officers, Cossacks, and anti-Semitic peasants in and outside of his army constituted a lethal mix. Even accounting for some imprecision in the number of Jewish murders, there may have been as many as 200,000, with around the same number of mutilations, rapes, and other tortures, many vicious acts of unrestrained sadism. More than thirteen hundred defenseless "Bolshevik" Jewish villages in Ukraine were razed in paroxysms of violent rage.[5] In Chernigov the newspaper of the provincial soviet described anti-Semitism growing "across the board" in 1920, the "kulaks infected with the disease."[6] Local soviet officials linked it directly to sharpening "counterrevolutionary" elements. As the civil wars finally came to an end in 1921, gaining control over ethnonationalist violence became part of the regime's struggle to make the Russian Soviet republic into the multinational Soviet Union, extending the Civil War in this way even beyond the USSR's formal creation in 1922. An excellent recent study of Russia's civil wars runs from 1916 to 1926.[7]

It is not necessary to rehearse all of the horrors Buldakov details in his discussion of the vectors of social violence during the greater revolutionary period. What deserves to be emphasized instead is that the world war brought unprecedented levels of violence to all the warring countries, sanctioned and cultivated by modernizing states governed in the main by educated and cultured individuals who brooked no limit to its scale or scope. After the Bolsheviks seized state power, the brutality of Russia's civil wars carried sanctioned violence across all of the tsarist empire's social, cultural, and national boundaries. Everywhere in territories Red, White, Green, Black, and several shades in between it was

---

[5] See the important essay by Peter Kenez, "Pogroms and White Ideology in the Russian Civil war," in *Pogroms: Anti-Jewish Violence in Modern Russian History*, ed. John Klier and Shlomo Lambroza (Cambridge: Cambridge University Press, 2004), 293–312. Within a wide literature, see also N. I. Shtif, "Dobrovol'tsy i evreiskie pogromy," in *Revoliutsiia i grazhdanskaia voina v opisaniakh belogvardeitsev: Denikin, Iudenich, Vrangel* (Moscow, 1991);Eugene M. Avrutin and Elissa Bemporad, eds., *Pogroms: A Documentary History* (New York: Oxford University Press, 2021), chs. 6–8.

[6] *Izvestiia Gub. Ispolkom Sovetov Rabochikh, Selianskikh i Krasnoarmeiskikh Deputatov Chernigovshchiny*, June 6, 1920.

[7] Jonathan D. Smele, *The "Russian" Civil Wars, 1916–1926* (Oxford: Oxford University Press, 2015).

unimaginably brutal, merciless, devoid of normative moral restraints, and atrocious in the fundamental meaning of "atrocity."

Scarcity, Loss, and the Trauma Question

Buldakov and Leont'eva do not emphasize them, but the two consistent threads connecting much of the brutality Buldakov's vectors encompass are the actualities and insecurities of scarcity and the multiple dimensions of loss. While recognizing the awful effects of sadism and unrestrained rage, we must understand as well that virtually everyone swept up in the war and revolutionary maelstroms experienced the deprivations of loss, the insecurities of hunger, and, for hundreds of thousands in 1921 and 1922, the anguish of actual starvation, especially within families. In one way or another, primary bearers of scarcity and loss were uncountable numbers of men and women who bore the harsh tasks of war itself: killing and maiming those dressed and perceived as their enemies while bearing them individually little or no malice, or forced through widowhood to assume in addition to the arduous work of maintaining their family parcels that of managing their households and keeping their families fed.

The effects of loss on soldiers' families can only be postulated, and cautiously at that. Certainly some, like the liberal leader Paul Miliukov who lost his son, contained their feelings through the rationalizations of sacrifice for the greater good of the Great Russian state. It is possible that in many villages grief was also suppressed by fatalism and stoic values, as many have argued. Still, "for Tsar and Country" and "Fighting with God" proved inadequate explanations for loss and its hardships, which could be rationalized by many only in terms of defending their land from foreign invasion. And even this was rather easily countered in 1917 by imperial and class-based explanations that presumed the revolution would bring peace. There were no Bloody Sundays in 1917 like the massacre of protesters in 1905 in the midst of the Russo-Japanese War, although the July Days came close. What there was instead was rapid expansion of the civil disorders whose angry forms can be presumptively linked to the broader context of loss, scarcity, and urgent need, just as after October we can presume that these effects of need and loss spread quickly beyond the formal Red and White armies until the lines between military, paramilitary, and nonmilitary violence essentially dissolved.

A consistent social element in all this brutality was those who fought at the front and carried their experiences in some way as they deserted or took leave to return to their families, and then as lucky survivors left the front in massive numbers in the late summer and fall of 1917. The historian Dietrich Beyrau is undoubtedly right to argue that one cannot easily reconstruct the linkages between the violent fronts during the world war and the violence of revolution and revolutionaries themselves.[8] Cultures of state and social violence had also long existed in Russia, evidenced most recently during 1905 and the aftermath of the Russo-Japanese War. Yet both the state-sponsored violence demanded of Russian troops after 1914 and the explosive incidents of violent acts against their own commanders and others after February 1917 almost certainly interacted to make Russia's revolutionary soldiers a volatile group, as many in the army itself feared and warned about. On the Southwestern Front, those who had survived the 1916 Brusilov breakthrough may have suffered even more during the June offensive in 1917 from reencountering the risks and horrors of its familiar no man's lands. We can say with some confidence that some significant number of the 5 million or so men demobilized from the army after the Bolsheviks took hold of the state must have brought with them the residue of their own deprivation both before and after the failed Kerensky-Brusilov offensive, as well as the emotions, mindset, and especially biases against Jews and other "aliens" that played such a large role in the brutal destabilization of the Western war zone and the Caucasus Front between 1914 and 1917. There is no evidence that the overthrow of the tsarist regime softened this lethal prejudice. Nor did it diminish the feelings amply displayed in soldiers' letters about corrupt and incompetent officers, the humiliations of subordination, and the sometimes blatantly unfair punishments of field courts-martial, including hanging, whose swift execution allowed no appeal.

Some put their fighting skills to use in support of the Bolsheviks and the new Red Army. Others, largely officers and Cossacks, gravitated to the White forces in South Russia, the Murmansk region, and Siberia. By far the largest number, however, came back to their towns and villages carrying the brutal practices and experiences from the front in some way, terrorizing railroad passengers and workers on the way and often running amok even as they reached what was or used to be home. The dangers presented by demobilized soldiers forming their own gangs without any disciplinary restraints and unable to return to stable social environments is well known to military psychologists. In the countryside, former soldiers could be seen among the *kombedy* and other militarized food procurement groups as well as among armed defenders of villages and various committees. In industrial towns they merged easily with formal or self-described Red Guards and were commonly seen "patrolling" the streets. What legions of these former defenders of the Fatherland had in common were their weapons and their aggressiveness, not the forgotten commonalities of tsarist or revolutionary patriotism or military discipline. What those who encountered them

---

[8] Dietrich Beyrau, "Brutalization Revisited: The Case of Russia," *Journal of Contemporary History* 50 (2015): 15–37.

shared was a fear that is almost palpable decades later as one reads accounts of unrestrained violence in newspapers, memoirs, and the archives.

Thus, unrestrained military, paramilitary, and civilian violence emerged in all of its fury after the Bolsheviks took power, reflecting the interactions between experience, belief systems and their political uses, mentalities, pain, and, not least, an often sadistic fury that had resonance especially among Cossacks and others with military traditions. Within the vast literature on revolutionary Russia these possible relationships between loss, violence, and individual trauma still warrant scholarly attention. We have long known about the effects of shell shock that at least some of the troops making their way back from the front clearly experienced, if we are to judge by the official (though admittedly scanty) numbers. These show psychological diagnoses of some 45,000 cases in 1914–15, 53,000 in 1916, and 29,000 from January through November 1917, including 4,100 in September alone.[9] Not included in these figures are the far more widespread traumas of violent displacement, rape, confiscation, and random acts of brutality that were experienced by large numbers of the population at large, including children, particularly but not only in the war zones. Unrecorded as well are the horrific experiences of the approximately 5 million wounded, only half of whom were listed as treated at field hospitals, or the experiences of the 3.6 million Russian prisoners of war, thousands of whom managed after 1918 to escape from the hunger and anxieties of German and Austrian camps only to experience these deprivations again in their villages.[10]

We can fairly surmise, however, that for hungry peasants, bagmen and -women, refugees, rape victims, homeless children who had witnessed their parents' murder, fired or locked-out workers turned beggars, and the whole stratum of those now condemned by their social origins as "bourgeois" social enemies, experience overwhelmed the psychological defenses that normally manage stressful events even in conditions of severe deprivation. In the fall of 1917 an unprecedented number of agitated, hungry, and in some cases traumatized warriors returned to a society rent by the material and emotional effects of scarcity and now seeking politically to repurpose Russia's extraordinary losses into securing new revolutionary goals. To this must be added extraordinary numbers of deserters from the Red Army itself in 1919 and 1920, as well as from the misbegotten labor armies, as we will see. Even without further research it is more than probable that a meaningful number of those who lived through the tumultuous Civil War years experienced some form of mind-changing trauma like that of shell-shocked soldiers.

---

[9] TsSU, *Rossiia v mirovoi voine 1914–1918 (v tsifrakh)* (Moscow: TsSU, 1925), 4, 30.
[10] Ibid., 4–5, 30; Kim Friedlander, "Neskol'ko aspektov *shelshok*'a v Rossii, 1914–16," in *Rossiia i pervaia mirovaia voina*, ed. N. N. Smirnov (St. Petersburg, 1999), 325–26.

Moreover, with the emergence of neuropsychology as a distinct field of medicine in the 1990s we now have some grasp of what these mind changes are like. Breakthroughs in imaging technology have identified particular parts of the brain that are physiologically changed as a result of trauma, and what kinds of behaviors these changes induce. In addition to feelings of shame or guilt which often make it impossible for soldiers to talk about what they have seen or done, we now understand that images and sounds can stimulate that part of the brain that releases defensive hormones that trigger instinctive reactions to danger even when no danger is present. As the neuropsychiatrist Bessel van der Kolk described in his acclaimed book on the subject in 2014, "[T]rauma results in a fundamental reorganization of the way mind and brain manage perceptions. It changes not only how we think and what we think about but our very capacity to think.... The act of telling the story doesn't necessarily alter the automatic physical and hormonal responses of bodies that remain hyper vigilant, prepared to be assaulted or violated at any time. For real change to take place the body needs to learn that the danger has passed and to live in the reality of the present."[11] The psychiatrist and psychoanalyst Dori Laub, a specialist in trauma, states that there are never enough words or listening to verbalize a story that cannot be fully captured in thought, memory, and speech. In many cases the "impossibility of telling" inhibits the very imperative to relate somehow "what happened." The toxic consequence may be its articulation in violent behaviors.[12]

These new understandings of trauma provide interesting clues to some posttraumatic stress behaviors. The reflexive impulse to return from a place of great stress to a place of internalized security, for example, helps explain why tens of thousands of soldiers during these years left their posts even for short periods to go home and "look after their families," as the military censors described it. In terms of trauma, research shows that the "safe" place of home (or the relative comfort of one's "nest") is vital to managing what is otherwise unbearable, an alternative, in other words, to immobilization in the face of bombardment or attacks that constituted passive suicide. Imaging has also shown that trauma may deactivate that part of the brain which organizes experience into logical sequences and gives it meaning by translating suppressed feelings or perceptions into words. When this occurs, people who have been traumatized in the past feel like the traumatic event is happening in the present. In short, the emotional side of the brain immobilizes its rational side. They become just as enraged, terrified,

---

[11] Bessel van der Kolk, *The Body Keeps Score: Brain, Mind, and Body in the Healing of Trauma* (New York: Penguin, 2014), 21.

[12] Dori Laub, "An Event without a Witness: Truth, Testimony and Survival," in *Testimony: Crises of Witnessing in Literature, Psychoanalysis, and History*, ed. Shoshana Felman and Dori Laub (New York: Routledge, 1992), 78–85. See also Alexander Etkind, *Warped Mourning: Stories of the Undead in the Land of the Unburied* (Stanford, CA: Stanford University Press, 2018), 17–18.

violent, or passive as they were initially, and may act correspondingly. At the root of most persistent traumas is thus an inability to act in ways healthy people might think is "natural": submitting repeatedly to abuse, for example, or "accepting" by participating or not resisting violent behaviors that replicate in some way the initiating trauma itself.

All of this lay at the core of the syndrome of violence that constituted a common element of experience between 1918 and 1921, and even beyond. "We are living in the Middle Ages," a member of the White movement wrote publicly, "an epoch of horrors and madness.... We are covered in blood and there is no hope.... Blood! Everywhere blood. This is our fate!"[13]

Losing Great Russia: Paramilitary Violence and the Defeat of the Whites

While the Bolshevik regime was struggling with the effects of scarcity and loss throughout 1919, the Red Army fought to defend Soviet Russia. Trotsky insisted on the traditional principles of military discipline without the social and cultural effects of hierarchy. He also took advantage of a military ration to attract volunteers, especially from among the unemployed. A draft was instituted as Kolchak and then Denikin mobilized their forces. What the British military historian Jonathan Smele has called "the triumphal march of reaction" took Kolchak's unruly army past Perm in western Siberia toward Orenburg and Samara in the early spring of 1919. For Kolchak's chief of staff, this portended the reunification of imperial Russia, including the occupation of Constantinople.[14] The offensive was spearheaded by the semi-autonomous armies of General Gajda and Ataman Dutov. Both longed for the glory they expected capturing Moscow would bring.

The better-organized and more capable South Russian and Northwestern armies of Generals Denikin and Iudenich began their offensives in the summer and fall. Denikin now commanded more than 100,000 infantry and 50,000 cavalry. He also had aircraft, armored trains, and a small Black Sea fleet and managed to assemble a substantial amount of ordnance from various military depots as well as from the British. Led by former tsarist generals Wrangel, Shkuro, and Pokrovskii, the Don Cossacks had brutally secured a base in the north Caucasus in the late winter. (According to one account, their punitive organs may have sentenced as many as twenty-five thousand to death; according to another, the Cossacks themselves suffered similar casualties.)[15] While Kolchak was advancing

---

[13] *Biulleten' Osvedomitel'nyi otdel Shtaba Verkhovnago Glavnokomanduiushchago*, Sept. 20, 1919.
[14] Smele, *"Russian" Civil Wars*, 89.
[15] Ibid., 120; Holquist, *Making War*, 164.

in April, Russian and Ukrainian Red Army units captured Rostov. Stirred by earlier reports of mass executions of Cossacks by the Cheka after the Bolsheviks declared "merciless mass terror" against them, the whole male Cossack population between eighteen and fifty was mobilized for compulsory service or public work. One was "either for us, or for the Reds."[16] By June much of southern and southeastern Ukraine was also under nominal White control. Ekaterinoslav was taken by the thirty-two-year-old General Shkuro's fearsome Kuban Cossacks, who boasted their ferocity by calling themselves "White Wolves." In early July Denikin issued his spirited Moscow Instruction after his troops took Voronezh, ordering the capture of Moscow with its "forty plus forty cathedrals and the resurrection of Russia, One and Indivisible." Disagreements over the separatist ambitions of his Don and Kuban Cossack allies forced him to delay the offensive since their alliance remained central to his hopes for success. Iudenich, meanwhile, commanded fewer than twenty thousand troops but raised panic in Petrograd when it looked like he might occupy the city in October. Trotsky rushed back to coordinate its defense.

Much attention has been paid to the failure of the three generals to coordinate their offensives. The best explanation, supported by Smele in his 2015 study, is probably that offered by Baron A. P. Budberg: that Admiral Kolchak's influential but inexperienced advisors simply did not think coordination was necessary, and the admiral himself lacked the expertise in land warfare to override them.[17] Yet the evidence seems clear that even the coordination of the Siberian and South Russian forces would not have brought Russia back under an anti-Bolshevik military dictatorship. As Kolchak's and Denikin's troops left their bases in western Siberia and the Don, peasants in central Russia and Ukraine saw them as forces of the landed gentry and social counterrevolution, even if some came over to the White side as hungry refugees with awful tales to tell. (Local newspapers and Denikin's own propaganda apparatus circulated these accounts with enthusiasm, but they hardly reflect the prevailing view.) Especially in the economically and strategically important middle Volga and black earth regions, Reds and Whites were both marauders who caused havoc, especially when towns and villages repeatedly changed hands.

There was also little doubt that the result of a White victory would be a military dictatorship. As Peter Kenez has detailed, the leadership of the Whites was socially diverse. The tsarist generals who led the AFSR included many from peasant backgrounds who had taken advantage of the opportunities and social mobility the tsarist army had offered after the military reforms of the 1860s. The

---

[16] The story is well told by Holquist, *Making War*.
[17] A. P. von Budberg, "Dnevnik," *Arkhiv Russkoi revoliutsii* 14 (1924): 225–38; Smele, *"Russian" Civil Wars*, 10–18.

fathers of General Denikin and Alekseev were serfs, that of General Kornilov a poor Cossack. Military schools shaped an outlook that, like that of many liberals, placed them above politics. Their dedication was to the Russian state, which naturally made them conservative under the autocracy but initially more flexible in 1917.[18]

In this sense as well as others, the revolutionary governments of 1917 were a profound disappointment, as was the collapse of the Kerensky-Brusilov offensive. General Kornilov was perhaps the most outspoken among high-ranking officers about the need for authoritarian rule, but there was no doubt that others gathering around Kolchak and Denikin felt the same way. In Omsk Kadets and other civilians strongly supported Kolchak's bloody overthrow of the Komuch's Directory in November 1918 and were instrumental in its planning. At Kadet conferences in Omsk and Ekaterinodar, the loudest voices were reactionary. "[We] oppose the idea of a legislative or consultative organ," the Kadets resolved in Omsk, "for this will weaken, not strengthen, dictatorship. Our viewpoint is that it is necessary only to increase the powers of the Supreme Ruler."[19] In South Russia, too, Denikin's Kadet advisors strongly resisted the efforts of Nikolai Astrov and other party moderates to bend his regime in the direction of reform. The only issue that got serious attention was the land question. At a formal party gathering in Kharkov in early November 1919, when it was already apparent the drive on Moscow would fail, Central Committee members still focused on the tasks of extending military dictatorship. "The universal hegemony of Western democracy is a fraud," Ariadna Tyrkova insisted to her colleagues. "[W]e must have the courage to look directly into the eye of the wild beast—which is called the people."[20]

Whether or not many in the anti-Bolshevik armies agreed with Tyrkova, they certainly acted as if they did. Some of the worst military violence against civilians since 1914 was committed by Cossacks and other troops nominally under Denikin's command as they left the Don and Kuban regions. Every form of "Bolshevism" was the cause of the current catastrophe. The occupation of "Bolshevik" villages and towns was often accompanied by paroxysms of violent rage. Again, it was Jewish communities that were among the most brutalized, not this time because they were spies for the Austrians and Germans but because they had necessarily to be sympathetic to their Jewish "brethren" in Moscow. By all accounts there were awful scenes of murder and rape, children cut down, and men and women butchered, as others had been earlier in the war. In some in-

---

[18] Peter Kenez, "Russian Officer Corps before the Revolution: The Military Mind," *Russian Review* 31, no. 3 (July 1972): 226-36.

[19] *Russkoe Delo* (Omsk), Oct. 8, 1919.

[20] Protocols of the Kadet Conference, Nov. 3-6, 1919, Box 4, packet 3, Panina Collection, Bakhmetev Archive, Columbia University, New York. (my italics).

these towns, in fact, some of the million or so refugees had been resettled earlier from Galicia and Poland and were now forced to experience again the traumas they may have tried to repress. Stunningly, given the party's formal values, the Kadet newspaper *Svobodnaia Rech'* in Ekaterinodar actually suggested that given traditional Russian prejudice, anti-Semitism might be a means of increasing peasant support, "a creative force" for "national reunification."[21]

As Kolchak's and Denikin's forces moved forward, moreover, they also lived increasingly off the land through requisitions and confiscations, just as tsarist troops had in the military zone after 1914. Local zemstvos and soviets were treated with suspicion or worse. One Siberian commission officially determined they were almost all being run by "revolutionary demagogues."[22] Indeed, when Kolchak came to lead the Whites in Siberia after overthrowing remnants of the Komuch regime, as many as twenty-five hundred were summarily executed in Omsk itself. Bloody purges also occurred elsewhere as Kolchak's "all-Russia" regime formally endorsed similar executions. Kolchak's loyalists, including local Kadets, supported confiscating property, condoned mass floggings, and accepted as necessary other violent forms of repression in the name of crushing "Bolshevik criminality."[23] By all accounts, military and paramilitary units pillaged freely, especially the fierce Siberian Cossack bands that formed part of Kolchak's army, even as they brutally mobilized local populations into their ranks.

The military occupation policies of the Siberian forces were equally hair-raising. Western Siberia and the immense Siberian expanse as a whole that Kolchak claimed as his dominion was now a vast area of autonomous local authorities, many of which strongly resented the pretensions of "stinking outsiders." What Siberia lacked in Jewish villages to massacre was made up for in the hundreds of autonomous towns and self-sustaining villages from which Kolchak's troops and those of their ferocious Siberian Cossack allies confiscated food, stole supplies and personal goods, brutalized the population, and generally wreaked havoc. Local authorities of all political persuasions or even none at all were executed. So were members of local soviets where they existed and other elected local authorities considered everywhere to be Bolsheviks. The two atamans alone were responsible for some of the worst barbarism of the entire Civil War. They also controlled much of the Trans-Siberian railroad that connected Omsk with the far east, and where graft and corruption reached epic proportions.

---

[21] *Svobodnaia Rech'*, Oct. 9, 1919.
[22] Eastern Kadet Central Committee, MS report, packet 3, suppl. 2, Panina Archive.
[23] William G. Rosenberg, *Liberals in the Russian Revolution* (Princeton, NJ: Princeton University Press, 1974), ch. 13; V. Zh. Tsvetkov, *Beloe delo v Rossii, 1917–1918* (Moscow: Iauza, 2008); A. Litvin, *Krasnyi i belyi terror, 1918–1922* (Moscow: Iauza, 2004).

Some of this mayhem was pure sadism. Some may have been the result of Cossack military traditions where ferocity was honed as part of a historical responsibility for protecting Imperial Russia's porous borderlands. But especially for ex-tsarist officers, some of it must also have been related to the effects of loss and especially the traumas experienced on the battlefield before and during 1917, even if this cannot be clearly evidenced. At least in part, the overdetermined effects of loss and trauma acted to increase the intensity and scale of the cruelty, and perhaps gave some form of legitimacy to otherwise atrocious behaviors that group action tended to normalize. Neither Kolchak's nor Denikin's troops took many prisoners. Punitive expeditions in response to partisan attacks involved the retaliatory shooting of large numbers of innocent civilians. "Counterintelligence" activities often involved criminality and looting.

It is certainly the case that many, if not most, of the former tsarist officers and soldiers gathering in Siberia and South Russia experienced loss of different kinds as well. One was the sheer effect of fighting more than three years "for Tsar and Country" only to have the terrible carnage lead to Bolshevik rule, if not the revolution itself. For Lenin's supporters, as we have reviewed, the material and emotional losses of world war were explainable in terms of class domination, capitalism, and imperialism. This served to mobilize soldiers against these causes already in 1917, but even more so after October, when the Bolshevik regime declared war on all three. In contrast, it is also possible that among the Whites, the losses of the world war could be redeemed only by the restoration of the imperial state they had sworn and struggled to defend. It's impossible to say how much this may have facilitated voluntary mobilization on either side, but not, perhaps, to posit that it may have played some significant role, just as it may have given new purpose to Civil War deaths. Between 1918 and 1920, according to data compiled by the Central Statistical Administration in 1925, more than 250,000 Red Army soldiers were killed in battle or died during medical evacuations. According to recent studies by V. A. Isupov and Stephen Wheatcroft, more than 800,000 deaths from wounds that were not treated medically may have been added to the nearly 600,000 estimated between 1914 and 1917.[24]

Among the Whites at least, there was one additional and very powerful form of loss. For those of gentry and aristocratic backgrounds, gone was social order, security, and a whole way of life, at least, they fervently hoped, for the moment. Of outright reactionaries among this group, there were plenty in and outside of the army. What moderates like Denikin himself shared with them was a deep

---

[24] V. A. Isupov, *Demograficheskie katastrofy i krizisy v Rossii v pervoi polovine XX veka* (Novosibirsk, 2000), 62–64; S. G. Wheatcroft, "Famine and Epidemic Crises in Russia 1918–1922: The Case of Saratov," *Annales de démographie historique* (1983): 329. See also Frank Lorimer, *The Population of the Soviet Union: History and Prospects* (Geneva, 1946).

anger at Bolsheviks and Bolshevism as well as other radicals who deliberately sought to destroy their socioeconomic worlds, their very way of life. As many as 2 million emigrated in this modern Time of Troubles, carrying their anxieties and uncertainties along with their baggage. As Nabokov insightfully described it, Bolshevism took away their childhood.[25]

Such feelings can be read in many memoirs as well as some of the best literature of the period, like Bulgakov's *Flight (Beg)* and *White Guard*.[26] In many ways the feelings of "losing" a past era were also hardly unique to Russia or to the Civil War period. Now, however, they also had strong visual representations which may have made the conflicts more acute. Demeanor and dress now signified political orientation as well social status. Officers again wore the epaulettes that many soldiers' committees had earlier forced them to discard. Enlisted men were addressed with the diminishing "thou" instead of the respectful "you." Newspapers still carried the dates of the old calendar that the Soviet regime had discarded. Astrov recorded his Kadet Party colleague exclaiming as they stepped off their train after a hazardous flight from Moscow, "Look! Look! There are our gendarmes, yes indeed our old pre-revolutionary gendarmes!"[27]

None of these feelings could become more than nostalgia as the White cause became increasingly tenuous in the course of 1919. Restoration after large-scale sociopolitical revolutions is historically rare in any case, and the further the White armies and dictatorships were extended, the more it became clear how badly they lacked broad popular support. Villages cheering one day stole the army's supplies the next. Merchants and others hid their goods. Soldiers deserting in increasing numbers found safe haven in "conquered" villages. By the summer of 1919 the South Russian army numbered between 120,000 and 150,000 men. As it moved toward Moscow, members of the Kadet Central Committee meeting in Ekaterinodar suggested that Russia's "salvation" lay in patriotism, military valor, and self-sacrifice, not in issues like the civil rights of Jews. Resistance *behind* the army's lines, however, was arguably as serious as Bolshevik opposition at the front.[28] Peasants saw landlords returning as their precious stocks of grain were pillaged. Trade-unionists in local industrial towns were murdered and arrested. The labor press was shut down, strikes forbidden. Elementary civil rights were everywhere abused.[29] Astrov, the moderate Moscow Kadet and founding member of the Union of Cities, described the "complete horror" reigning in local

---

[25] Vladimir Nabokov, *Speak Memory* (New York: Grosset and Dunlap, 1966).
[26] See, most recently, Richard Robbins Jr., *Overtaken by the Night: One Russian's Journey through Peace, War, Revolution, and Terror* (Pittsburgh, PA: University of Pittsburgh Press, 2017). A well-known example is Terence Emmons, trans., *Time of Troubles, the Diary of Iurii Vladimirovich Got'e: Moscow, July 8, 1917 to July 23, 1922* (Princeton, NJ: Princeton University Press, 1988).
[27] N. Astrov, *Vospominaniia* (Paris, 1941), 29.
[28] K. N. Sokolov, *Pravlenie generala Denikina* (Sofia: Rossiisko-bolgarskoe kn-vo, 1921), 162ff.
[29] G. Pokrovskii, *Denikinshchina* (Berlin, 1923), 146ff.

areas. "The unrestrained pillage of the rural population ... the debauchery of the troops in the countryside, the propensity of authorities to take bribes, the overt criminality of counterintelligence agents in Bolshevik areas—all this compels the population on whom our army is supposed to be based to say: No! This is not a government capable of saving the country or resurrecting Russia."[30]

As the White armies fell back, large numbers of soldiers deserted. Individual battles were said to have been won or lost depending on which side ran away first. Siberians seemed more willing to fight against any outsiders rather than for Great Russia. Siberian peasants may have had a reputation for hardiness and resilience, but neither Reds nor Whites held the promise of a more secure future. Some deserters from Kolchak's forces joined Siberian gangs as they pillaged, murdered, and raped their way to temporary safety along the railroads and into the hinterlands. Already by the fall of 1918, as Narskii describes it, the Siberian region was "on the edge of death." During 1919 the areas around Simbirsk, Ufa, Omsk, Perm, and Cheliabinsk witnessed the worst possible aspects of "life in catastrophe," where the issue was as much the absence of authority as too many authorities. Local zemstvos and town councils struggled with what one newspaper called an insane increase in prices for primary goods, "understandable" in terms of economic circumstances but lethal in its effects. "Obligatory measures" against speculators were demanded. Local gangs were happy to comply.[31] In towns and settlements across the region people left home in the morning to seek food with no assurance they would ever return.

Some joined local bands with no political goals other than protecting themselves and driving away the "outsiders." Siberia became a sea of anarchy, desperation, cruelty, violence, and death where ordinary life could no longer be pressed into larger meaning through political ideologies or viable institutions. Women as always were especially vulnerable. Rape was common, prostitution a survival tactic. Everyday life in towns involved forced labor, terror, unending confiscations, and in some places war against those who dared to trade confiscated food and other scarce goods. All this brought indescribable anxiety to everyday life, along with desperation, "submissive passivity, and a resigned acceptance of death," as Narskii has detailed.[32]

What unfolded in South and Central Russia after Kolchak's retreat was somewhat different in form but only slightly less intense in the further losses it inflicted. Ukrainian and Russian peasants were pressed into Denikin's armies

---

[30] Kadet Central Committee Protocols, Oct. 5, Nov. 10, 1919, in *Protokoly tsentral'nogo komiteta Konstitutsionnoi Demokraticheskoi Partii 1915-1920gg.*, ed. D. B. Pavlov, 6 vols. (Moscow: Rosspen, 1998), 3:513–14, 521–22; N. Astrov "Grazhdanskaia voina" and "Neskol'ko spravok," unpublished manuscripts, Panina Archive.

[31] *Vestnik Zeminogorsk*, June 29, 1919.

[32] Igor Narskii, *Zhizn' v katastrofe: Budni naseleniia Urala v 1917-1922* (Moscow: Rosspen, 2001), 225ff., 366, 485–97.

here in much larger numbers. In many cases they joined to save their families or their villages from the consequences of refusing. In others it may have been the promise of rations or simply monetary bonuses like those paid out to many Cossacks. With their brutal expropriation of grain reserves the Bolsheviks by now held scant attraction, but neither did dying in support of the Great Russian cause. "Russia, One and Indivisible!" carried little weight. "Peace" in Russian (*mir*) was also the term for the village community itself, which privileged its autonomy even as the war and the forceful confiscation of grain intensified on both sides of the fluid Civil War front. The farther the South Russian armies moved away from the villages of their recruits, the larger the number who deserted for home. Draconian penalties failed to stop them, just as they had failed after the Kerensky offensive. As the army's leading units approached Tula, a hundred miles south of Moscow, their ranks melted away as drafted soldiers abandoned their positions and the White cause in huge numbers. By the first of the year it was half its former size, even allowing for the replacement of casualties. The ensuing retreat and Denikin's ultimate defeat were inflicted as much from within as from the Whites' enemies in Moscow, and probably even more so.

In their final departure from the Crimea in 1920, 150,000 White survivors left behind what they had valued most. Parts of Constantinople, Prague, Paris, and Berlin soon became centers of Great Russian memory, recrimination, and violence. Nabokov's Kadet father who headed the Provisional Government's Chancellery in 1917 was assassinated in Berlin by a rightist aiming for Miliukov. In Paris, the Ukrainian partisan Simon Petliura was hunted down, killed, and buried in Montparnasse Cemetery. For some, Hitler's virulent anti-Semitism and dictatorial power became increasingly attractive, as did the Nazis' Vlasov divisions of anti-Soviet Russians in World War II. Their loss may have taken its ultimate toll.

The Fight against Desertion

While the collapse of Denikin's offensive brought some measure of political security to the Bolsheviks at the end of 1919, the persistence of hunger and its insecurities could not but intensify the anxieties that were also felt everywhere in this time of "horrors and madness," as it was described in one of Denikin's official bulletins.[33] The fighting was also not over. The forty-one-year-old General Peter Wrangel, less tolerant of his soldiers' excesses, was regrouping the remnants of the AFSR. In Siberia there was another armed uprising in the making by left SRs, and in the Tambov region the Antonov brothers were gathering support for what

---

[33] *Biulleten' Osvedomitel'nyj otdel Shtaba Verkhovnago Glavnokomanduiushchago*, Sept. 20, 1919.

would emerge in 1921 as the largest peasant uprising of the Civil War. An alliance in July 1920 with a sympathetic Lithuanian government against the Poles would set the stage for Lenin's government to reject demonstrably the Curzon line being proposed at Versailles as the new Soviet-Polish border. Led by the new military heroes Tukhashevskii and Budennyi, the Red Army and its Cossack allies were soon fighting to extend Soviet control to Warsaw, their lack of success later described in brutal detail by Isaac Babel in *Red Cavalry*. At stake was not so much the reincorporation of former provinces back within Imperial Russian boundaries as the installation of a friendly Polish regime that would provide Soviet Russia with food and other needed resources and conceivably open the way to supporting revolution in Germany.

Despite the defeat of Kolchak, Iudenich, and Denikin, Soviet Russia therefore remained at war. Internal resistance to the Bolsheviks continued in the Urals region and other parts of Siberia after Kolchak's defeat. In South Russia, General Wrangel's effort was short-lived. He and the remainder of the AFSR evacuated from the Crimea in November 1920. In Tambov, however, the huge peasant rebellion led by the Antonov brothers—the Antonovshchina, as it came to be called—preoccupied the Red Army through 1921 and even beyond. At the rebellion's height the longtime SR activists may have had as many as thirty thousand peasant partisans under their command. The uprising was first and foremost an armed protest against excessive Bolshevik grain requisitions in a region where the harvest was too low to support even the minimal needs of the peasants. Hunger was rampant, starvation feared, especially in the regions of Tambov, Kherson, and Borosogleb. Lacking a clear program and crystallizing deep rural resentments in the long tradition of peasant rebellion, the Antonovshchina had no chance of dislodging its Bolshevik foes. Neither did Makhno's "Black" anarchist movement in Ukraine. Both movements essentially reflected the condensation of diverse bands into large anti-Bolshevik armed rebellions, without any functional regimes or achievable political ambitions.

Symptomatically, they reflected the deep and grievous suffering of peasants on both sides of the Red/White divide and the still unsolved problems of scarcity throughout the former empire. Archival documents made available after 1991 confirm that the Tambov uprising began in response to excessive requisitioning by both Reds and Whites, as Oliver Radkey detailed in his pioneering study of the movement.[34] Peasants reportedly felt mobilization was like a penal sentence. In Smolensk province and elsewhere, voluntary mobilization was reported a complete failure.[35] Antonov's supporters clearly saw Bolsheviks and the Red Army as their primary enemy, however little they had supported

---

[34] Oliver Radkey, *The Unknown Civil War in Russia* (Stanford, CA: Hoover Institution Press, 1976).
[35] RGASPI f. 17, op. 84, d. 26, ll. 2–4.

Denikin. Tukhashevskii's thirty-seven thousand troops were particularly brutal in suppressing the revolt, shooting on sight peasants with or without weapons, taking families hostage or sending them to newly constructed concentration camps (*kontsentratsionnye lageria*). Both revolts were crushed, but not the desperation, anger, and anxiety that underlay their resistance. The Antonovshchina's violent suppression by Tukhachevskii's troops was every bit as horrific as the brutalities that had accompanied both the offensives and defeats of the Whites.[36]

It was certainly not only the White movements that were rent with dissension, resistance, and desertion. With unstable supply lines, a lack of adequate winter clothing, and the deep longing for peace that 5 million men brought back to their villages and factories when the army collapsed in 1917, it was difficult in the extreme for Trotsky to keep his own forces intact while Kolchak's and Denikin's armies melted away. The various units of the Red Army had far larger contingents of workers than the armies of South Russia and Siberia, and thus presumably a much stronger base of political support than their opponents, at least among rank-and-file soldiers. Yet the army's social foundation was still unavoidably the same vast Russian reserve of young peasant men, many of whom had filled the tsarist army's seemingly limitless needs between 1914 and 1917. Among Red Army recruits there could not help being deep reservoirs of ill will among those who continued to struggle against the Bolsheviks' confiscation of village grain reserves. The only restraints on this animosity were that the Whites were worse, and their dictatorship would restore the old order.

Trotsky and others were well aware of the dangers of peasant resistance to mobilization. Desertion was prevalent from the start. To combat it the Central Committee for the Fight against Desertion was organized as early as December 1918. Similar committees were set up locally even earlier, during the preceding summer. The new Central Committee gave them wide latitude in their efforts. Field committees were also set up at a divisional level within the army itself under the supervision of the Revolutionary Military Council.[37] In May and June 1919 a massive public campaign was begun to enlist broad support for the "Fight against Desertion," as it was called. Special weeks were set aside to raise public awareness. Dozens of lectures and other public events took place. These were coordinated with raids and roundups aimed especially at deserters categorized as "malicious" (*zlostnyi*). In places close to the front like Saratov, Simbirsk, and Samara, the results were reported as "especially strong." In some areas Cheka and army units went after deserters hiding in the forests, fighting them into submission. Not far from Moscow, in Tver, an "uprising" of deserters was characterized

---

[36] V. Danilov and T. Shanin, eds., *Krest'ianskoe vosstanie v Tambovskoĭ gubernii v 1919–1921 gg.*, "*Antonovshchina*": *Dokumenty i materialy* (Tambov: Red. Izd. Otdel, 1994), passim.

[37] A. V. Dolgova, *Neizvestnyi front grazhdanskoi voiny: Konflikt mezhdu vlast'iu bol'shevikov I krest'ianskoi massoi v Permskoi gubernii* (Moscow: Maska, 2019).

as entirely by "rich peasants" (kulaks). In Voronezh and Tambov army deserters were reportedly joined by Cossack deserters from the Whites, and likely moved deeper into the countryside to join the first groups of Greens assembling under Antonov. In the western military region around Gomel and Vitebsk, armed bands of deserters were reported in every district. Deserters' families lost their special military rations, families and individuals were fined, livestock and property were confiscated. In December, sixty families in Saratov province were fined 475,000 rubles; in Riazan 579,000 from nineteen villages; in Petrograd province, 458,146 reportedly taken from forty-one families, although the large amounts seem more like warnings than realistic penalties, and in many places the inability to pay resulted in more repressive sanctions.[38]

For all this, and for all their likely inaccuracies, the numbers of deserters from the Red Army during 1919 are still astonishing: almost 270,000 for July alone, according to figures collected at the time (and sent directly to Lenin and the Sovnarkom); almost 300,000 during the harvest weeks of August; and another 131,000 in the last two weeks of September. There seemed to be little letup in 1920, when more than 214,000 desertions were reported for May, 228,000 for just the second half of June, almost 300,000 for August, and 211,110 for September.[39] Orlando Figes has compiled a total from official records for the thirteen months between June 1919 and the beginning of July 1920 of 2,638,000, approximately half of the entire tsarist army in October 1917.[40]

As earlier, many deserted while being sent to various fronts, others from the fighting itself, still more during the summer harvest weeks. Local and other studies published after Soviet archives were opened detail how the waves of mobilization and desertion in 1919 and 1920 further aggravated social tensions in towns and villages, feeding the rampant violence and collective anxieties which now characterized everyday life under Bolshevik and anti-Bolshevik regimes alike. Soldiers were often drunk. Looting occurred everywhere, often as "requisitions." So did small-scale mutinies. One telegram to the Sovnarkom from Voronezh complained that the actions of the procurement detachments, special plenipotentiaries, corrupt officials, and rampaging soldiers produced more anxiety and agitation than the lack of any new supplies of food.[41]

The "Fight against Desertion" soon expanded to include the industrial workforce. A publication of Sovnarkhoz in 1923 calculated that in 1919 workers failed to appear for work a startling 65 percent of the time, even when the aggregate

---

[38] GARF f. 130, op. 3, d. 198, ll. 1–11ff.; op. 4, d. 281, ll. 1–6.

[39] GARF f. 130, op. 4, d. 281, ll. 24, 30, 34, 43, 57, 60, 72; op. 3, d. 282 ll. 54–60; RGASPI f. 5, op. 1, d. 2452, ll. 10–15 and passim.

[40] Orlando Figes, "The Red Army and Mass Mobilization during the Russian Civil War, 1918–1920," *Past and Present* 129 (1990): 200.

[41] RGASPI f. 5, op. 1, d. 2814, ll. 2–3.

number of workdays for all plants was only around half of what it had been in 1913. The Briansk locomotive works and other plants reported a 40 percent absentee rate. The productive work time of paper workers was estimated as 19.6 days out of 30. According to a survey of Moscow and five provinces in the Central Industrial Region, workers on the whole were recorded as absent between September and December 1919 one day for every three they worked. Among railroad workers, absences by the spring of 1920 had reached "massive" proportions, according to the leading railroad trade union publication.[42]

By now instructions to district committees from the Central Committee for the Fight against Desertion had expanded the definition of a deserter to "anyone who voluntarily leaves a military unit, factory, or institution whose employees have been mobilized, or who has taken any sort of leave and not shown up for mobilization." In addition, a separate category was created for all those who knowingly aided or abetted deserters from factories and enterprises, including those "most guilty" of such acts, such as heads of households, close neighbors, and those responsible for enterprises or holding leadership positions in local soviets.[43] In effect, *proguly* and other unauthorized absences from work were now elevated as offenses to the category of desertion and subject to punishment with startling harshness.

Workers who quit their jobs to go elsewhere or back to the countryside could also be charged with desertion and taken directly into the army if their documents did not pass the inspections that were now occurring frequently in key enterprises as well as on the railroads. Many textile workers, for example, who failed to return to their factories after being granted leave to work the harvests of 1919 and 1920 were subject to the charge. So were track repair workers and other railroaders who left in droves to dig peat and cut wood for the winter or because food rations along the line had stopped.[44] In the late winter of 1920 the now sprawling network of antidesertion commissions struggled to control the flow. In many places, ironically, the detachments sent to round up deserters themselves faced critical shortages of food. Forced to undertake their own unplanned requisitions, they reportedly created as much dissidence as they were sent to put down. Some deserters regarded impressment by these "gangs" as equivalent to a death sentence.[45]

Illness was an increasing reason for absenteeism of course, but comparisons at the time show the overwhelming cause was the need to search for food. This in

---

[42] *Gudok*, May 13, 1920; *Ekonomicheskaia Zhizn'*, Mar. 7, 1919; S. Iosevich, "Rabota i proguly na pischebumazhnykh fabrikakh," in *Materialy po Statistike Truda* (Moscow: TsSU, 1921), 9:52–56; *Biulleten' Tsent. Pravleniiai Tiazheloi Industrii Iuga Rossii* 2 (Dec.–Feb. 1920–21): 2–3.
[43] GARF f. 130, op. 3, d. 198, ll. 44ff., 108–108 ob., 118.
[44] GARF f. 4085, op. 16, d. 337, ll. 50, 68–69.
[45] RGASPI f. 111, op. 22, d. 702, 703, 704, passim; GARF f. 130, op. 4, d. 200, ll. 5–9.

turn indicates that a great deal of time and energy was still being spent standing in lines and hoping the wait would prove worthwhile. One can imagine, too, the added anxieties brought on by the colder temperatures in the fall and winter of 1919–20, perhaps especially for women who continued to bear so much of the burden. The newspaper *Bednota* (*The Poor*) repeatedly pointed to the harsh effect on children and families from compulsory labor for women; for example, more than twenty-six thousand women were mobilized in Moscow for compulsory Saturday work, a day needed for domestic chores; local peasant women were mobilized for railroad line repair work in difficult winter conditions when male workers exempt from military service were hauled into the army as deserters. A plaintive communication to the commissar of health warned of the resulting large number of miscarriages and other issues that begged for protection and relief.[46]

Still, unlike Denikin and Kolchak, who tended to see all desertions as betrayals demanding the most severe punishments, the Bolsheviks faced a difficult choice between repression or remobilization especially for poor peasants and others whose desertion was not categorized as "malicious." The Red Army needed as many peasant soldiers as it could muster. Dissidence in the village was already at a high level from grain requisitions. Bolsheviks believed peasants lacked "consciousness," and the risks of further alienating the countryside were as great or greater than those presented by young men who left to care for their families. Many saw the problem of desertion not primarily in terms of political loyalties but as the complex set of problems it reflected: soldiers again longing for peace; a pressing concern for the welfare of their families with regard to food and other necessities; and, as the contemporary Russian historian Dolgova has suggested, the range of emotions that we have seen so widely expressed in soldiers' correspondence before and during 1917: fear, the traumas of combat, fatigue, discomfort, and their own struggles with hunger, supplies, and the physical agonies of service at the front.[47]

In many places, consequently, special short-term amnesties were declared. A surprisingly small number of deserters were shot (fewer than seven hundred from mid-June through mid-December, according to figures compiled by the Central Committee for the Fight against Desertion). A much larger number seem to have rejoined the ranks.[48] In effect, the persistence of unauthorized absences at a time when harsh measures could be applied as punishment testifies to how difficult life had become and how relentless were its anxieties. A deserter from the important Moscow weapons plant explained that he lived twenty-three

---

[46] RGASPI f. 5, op. 1, d. 2452, l. 26; f. 111, op. 22, d. 702, ll. 205, 215 ob.; *Bednota*, June 5, Sept. 25, Oct. 10, 1920.

[47] Dolgova, *Neizvestnyi front*.

[48] GARF f. 130, op. 1, d. 198, ll. 118ff.; op. 4, d. 281, ll. 26–33; d. 282, ll. 54, 57, 60.

kilometers from the plant, left home at 6:00 in the morning, returned cold and hungry at 11:00 p.m. or later to a home with frozen water and without heat, and begged that his wife not be sent to a disciplinary camp when he could not be found.[49]

In Nizhnii Novgorod the provincial Soviet newspaper even gave a "former deserter" his public voice on its front page, detaching the act of desertion itself from political betrayal and setting it instead within the broader context of physical and emotional misery:

> We deserters are covered with shame. We deserve it. Who might think that a person could leave his comrades at the most dangerous time, when they are threatened with death from all sides. Who saves himself, transferring all the burdens onto the shoulders of his brother.... Yes, he is a coward and a betrayer of comradeship.
>
> But think about us, citizens and comrades, when we find ourselves mobilized. We roam around for a long time in all sorts of places, in any kind of weather, in the cold and slush, dripping from the rain, freezing from the snow. Even the most tender soul becomes despondent. And what awaits us in the barracks? Cold, filth, nothing that could make life easier, no kettle to boil water, every place on the sleeping planks taken so that one cannot lie down next to someone but must sleep on the filthy greasy floor. The evening is gloomy. There is no light.... Hunger, cold and again anxiety about what is happening at home. This is why I became a deserter. I am aware that I acted in a base manner. Others could bear it and I could not. And the calamity is that the village and all its domestic coziness remains in front of your eyes and waves to you, and a dark mind sees nothing good in the new life and experiences only its awfulness.[50]

Rabkrin and the Obligation to Work

An important additional element in the struggle against desertion was the burgeoning practice of surveillance, as Peter Holquist has detailed. As with the tsarist military censorship, surveillance results were broken into several fixed categories. Judgments about where they belonged were made on the basis of overheard conversations, hearsay, and personal impressions more than hard evidence. Just as after 1914, first among these again was "mood." Others included counterrevolutionary activities, activities of political parties, crimes and

---

[49] GARF f. 130, op. 4, d. 233, l. 22.
[50] *Raboche-Krestianskii Nizhegorodskii Listok*, July 3, 1919.

corruption, speculation, theft, and "banditry," which was sometimes linked to deserters.[51]

A report from the front in April 1920, for example, described the situation as "more or less stable" when commanders (*nachalniki*) were honest and energetic; when corrupt, disaffection was rampant and "inevitable." Another from July falsely reported a "massive" movement of peasants in Riazan toward Siberia, rumors in Nizhnii Novgorod that the Bolshevik regime had been overthrown, brief strikes in Moscow province (for food), Kaluga (for food), Riazan (for items of primary need), Petrograd (seeking attention for grievances), Kursk (at the appearance of grain-procurement agents), and other places for similar reasons. In Ekaterinburg, White agitation was said to be stirring up the city. In Nizhnii Novgorod a hostile mood was blamed on the failure of Soviet authorities to control drunkenness, bribery, and crime.[52] In September a report from Pskov indicated that the Bolsheviks were "weak": deserters had won elections to the local soviets and cooperative associations. Many ordinary people were "tired and disinterested in politics." In Kiev, speculation was rampant in sugar, salt, and currency. Soviet bills were not being accepted for payment by many organizations and firms. In Siversk a school demanded tuition payments in 1917 "Kerenki."[53]

Overwhelmingly in the summer and fall of 1919 and into 1920 reports made clear that dissidence everywhere was related to anxieties about food: in Petrozavodsk and Olonets province northwest of Petrograd; in Tambov along the Volga; in Moscow and Penza, where groups of "revolutionary communists" held meetings about the regime's failure to deal adequately with the problem; and throughout Tomsk province and western Siberia, where the food situation was "critical," the population practically without grain, and "many workers" were not receiving their promised food rations. A trade union report from Vladimir province in July warned that ninety thousand people were "literally starving." In Kostroma, the food situation was "catastrophic." In Saratov, Samara, Vologda, Cheliabinsk, and Ufa, scarcity led to strong denunciations of the regime's "come what may" procurement policies when there was no grain to procure. In April, arms workers at the vital Tula works demanded an army food ration and the right to buy potatoes. A manifesto of the strike committee described Russia's working class suffering from hunger, unemployment, and the fear that conditions were worsening.[54]

Similar strikes and protests were reported in Moscow, Kaluga, Riazan, Kharkov, Ekaterinburg, and elsewhere around the country. In the Ivanovo-Voznesensk

---

[51] Peter Holquist, "'Information Is the Alpha and Omega of Our Work': Bolshevik Surveillance in Its Pan-European Context," *Journal of Modern History* 69, no. 3 (Sept. 1997): 425–50.
[52] GARF f. 130, op. 3, d. 414, ll. 19–20.
[53] GARF f. 130, op. 4, d. 233, l. 20; op. 3, d. 414, ll. 69–85.
[54] GARF f. 5451, op. 3, d. 460, ll. 10, 23–26, 38, 409.

region, armed bandits were "terrorizing" the population. The main reason for the "counterrevolutionary mood" in Uralsk and Riazan was the shortage of food. In a village community in Kursk province, a hostile crowd of more than a thousand formed when a food procurement detachment appeared to requisition its "surplus."[55] In Petrograd in June, trade union leaders applauded the description of workers' protests there as "pitiful," "criminal," and clearly led by ignorant "enemies of the workers" who did not understand that it was impossible to meet their demands.[56] Throughout 1920, in fact, top-secret surveillance summaries (*svodki*) describing similar protests and linking food insecurities around the country to dissident "moods" and behaviors were delivered to Lenin personally as well as other top Soviet officials. At best, the reports described popular moods in some places as "not uniformly bad," "passive," or "satisfactory," some even claiming people were "in good spirits" (*bodryi*), taking a descriptive leaf from the way military censors frequently characterized soldiers before 1917.[57] Yet even a cursory reading of the secret reports by those at the highest levels in Moscow could not fail to give the impression that on the verge of complete victory over the Whites, the population of Soviet Russia was riddled everywhere with anxieties over food, the scourge of malnutrition and disease, the fears and insecurities of everyday life, and for many at all social levels and states of political consciousness, a sense of desperation about the future.

There is thus little question that among other daunting problems Soviet Russia faced as Denikin's army retreated, the "Fight against Hunger" remained first and foremost, as Lenin himself described it at the Seventh Congress of Soviets in December 1919. It was followed on his list by the struggle against the privations of winter and the need to rekindle some degree of revolutionary enthusiasm in a hungry and anxious Soviet population.[58] (A special delegation seeking fuel in the Donbas for Moscow found the near total absence of both food and revolutionary class consciousness, and wondered which was worse.)[59] In this and other ways the Bolshevik capital found itself in "crisis" conditions, as the *Narodnoe Khoziaistvo* announced.[60] Typhus and other diseases were taking a horrific toll, adding to the other miseries affecting daily life for ordinary people. Then there was "dictatorial chaos" at all levels, as it was described in a petition to Sovnarkhoz, a continued lack of communication between local and state officials, a bane of state

---

[55] GARF f. 130, op. 3, d. 414, ll. 10, 21–23, 28, 31–34, 46, 55, 74–75, and passim; d. 415, ll. 18–22, 87–88, and passim; RGASPI f. 5, op. 1, d. 2885, ll. 52–56.
[56] TsGA SPb. f. 6276, op. 5, d. 41, ll. 67–68.
[57] GARF f. 130, op. 3, d. 414, ll. 11–12, 55.
[58] *Ekonomicheskaia Zhizn'*, Nov. 23, Dec. 7, 1919.
[59] *Ekonomicheskaia Zhizn'*, Sept. 9, 1919.
[60] *Narodnoe Khoziaistvo* 5 (May 1919): 86.

administration since the start of the world war, and a system of state financing that was largely "operating in the dark."[61]

At the Seventh Congress of Soviets Lenin linked the problem of food shortages directly to industrial production. He now asserted that many peasants were withholding grain from compulsory deliveries because they were being compensated with paper money when there were no commodities to buy. Industrial production had to be expanded to include commodities the peasants wanted.[62] The core of the problem was still the scarcity of food and its accompanying anxieties that were constantly affecting the stability of the workforce and none of which had lessened to any significant degree despite successes at the front. But "decisive measures" were also being demanded from provincial cities like Ekaterinburg, where an industrial "catastrophe" was blamed on the workers' lack of food. Even in places where restrictions on trading certain foodstuffs had been relaxed, including those on grain, meat, salt, sugar, tea, and eggs, scarcities were hardly reduced for those unable to pay the prices demanded.[63]

In fact, throughout 1919 the requirements of the Civil War had again created strong demand in favored industries and plants working for defense. In a dramatic turnaround from a year before, most enterprises still in operation were now in need of additional workers. One measure of this was the number of absences from work. The rate of *proguly* at the Sormovo plant in Nizhnii Novgorod, for example, reportedly ranged between 20 and 30 percent of all workers between July and December 1919; at the Briansk locomotive and machine shops, one of the largest defense plants in the country, it was reported to be 40 percent in January 1920.[64] There were other reasons for this besides the search for food, among them illness, unauthorized days off before and after holidays, and absences for various semi-official reasons like trade union meetings. Unhappiness over wages was another. The widespread use of piecework and bonuses for performance were constant sources of tension. In Moscow by 1920 the amounts paid as regular wages and as bonuses or premiums were roughly equivalent. For the recipients of both, however, the scarcity of goods and high prices on the black market only reduced real wages. More and more workers were now demanding payments in kind.[65] Scarcities also stimulated a flow of petitions to the highest government levels describing the "appalling bureaucracy" involved in requests for orders, funding, and resources, while excoriating the arbitrary behavior of

---

[61] GARF f. 30, op. 3, d. 161, 162, 163; RGAE f. 3429, op. 2, d. 3046, passim; d. 278, l. 25.
[62] *Ekonomicheskaia Zhizn'*, Nov. 23, Dec. 7, 1919.
[63] *Ekonomicheskaia Zhizn'*, Oct. 28, 29, Nov. 5, Dec. 5, 1919; RGAE f. 3429, op. 1, d. 1005, ll. 51–60; *Znamia Sovetov* (Chernigov), Oct. 5, 1920.
[64] *Izvestiia VSNKh* 8–9 (1920): 13–19.
[65] F. Markuzon, "Zarabotnaia plata fabricho-zavodskikh rabochikh v gorodu Moskvy v 1920 g.," *Materialy po Statistike Truda* (Moscow, 1921), 10:13–21.

Sovnarkhoz-appointed managers who forcefully restored one-man dictatorial control over workers' committees.[66]

Another measure of new industrial demand was the large increase in requests for financing. Here, however, was another problem: the government's burgeoning bureaucracy. Most nationalized enterprises were now submitting requests for funding based on unverified estimates of their additional need for workers and resources because it was impossible to calculate real costs accurately in advance. These generally went through Sovnarkhoz or directly to one of its 104 departments (*glavki*), each linked to a separate area of production. By January 1920, according to commissariat documents, the amount of credits issued by the Soviet banking network had grown from 1.5 billion rubles in December 1918 to 21.1 billion. Estimates submitted to Sovnarkhoz called for some 14,000 additional skilled metal workers, 5,000 new construction workers, and 79,000 "specialists"—approximately 100,000 new hires in total. Some four hundred requests for additional food to support new hires were also being received every day.[67]

Most important to Sovnarkhoz's own inadequate cadre of inspectors were the numerous and obvious illegalities in the funding process: the distribution without proper controls of sums and credits without any instructions; outright theft and the absence of adequate accounting procedures.[68] In broader administrative terms, there were overlapping responsibilities in the supervision of industrial production and a seemingly unlimited flow of requests that often received contradictory replies or none at all. One member of Sovnarkhoz complained that even the effort required to respond might itself bring the entire accounting process to a halt.[69] Meanwhile the network of complaint boxes was producing its own wide range of accusations of malfeasance and financial corruption, a steady river of complaints through what was now a kind of one-way postal system of state surveillance based on rumors and vendettas as well as unsupported accusations. More than five thousand letters of protest were received by party authorities in the course of 1919, according to official records, even from such loyal groups as the Central Committee of the Metallists' Union.[70] The call for "extreme means" came from below as well as from above.

In response to all of this, the regime took two decisive steps in early 1920: the concentration of responsibility for ferreting out malfeasance and corruption in a new agency, the Workers' and Peasants' Inspectorate (Rabkrin), formed out of the Commissariat of State Control; and the introduction of a universal obligation

---

[66] GARF f. 130, op. 3, d. 15, ll. 139, 161–63.
[67] RGAE f. 3429, op. 1, d. 1481, ll. 1, 59; d. 1508, l. 5.
[68] RGAE f. 3429, op. 1, d. 232, ll. 477–78; GARF f. 4085, op. 2, d. 26, ll. 1–8.
[69] RGAE f. 3429, op. 1, d. 1598, l. 5.
[70] *Ekonomicheskaia Zhizn'*, Jan. 1, Apr. 12, 13, 1919.

to work—*trudovaia povinnost'*—that was intended to end unemployment under that part of the Marxist maxim that demanded "from each according to their abilities" and ensure industrial enterprises had the workforce they needed.

The idea of obligatory labor was not new. As we have seen, in 1916 Prime Minister Boris Stiurmer and the tsarist government regarded it as an unavoidable way of supporting the army. Forcibly mobilized peasants were organized into local work battalions in the extended war zone. The idea was advanced especially by the economist and former Menshevik Iurii Larin in a widely read 1918 treatise linking the obligation to work to workers' control. It was formally invoked by a decree in October of that year for the removal of snow from railroad lines and roads. In the winter of 1918 thousands were drafted again for this purpose.

Already in June 1919 Trotsky had written to Lenin that the army needed punitive labor brigades for engineering and construction, "one of the most important tasks at the front." They were to be made up largely of deserters. (At the time, the problem was that when the detachments arrived, they could not be fed, and almost all deserted again.)[71] The obligation in principle was also affirmed in Article 18 of the first Soviet Constitution, reaffirmed in the Soviet Code of Labor Laws, and then taken up in late December 1919 by the Committee for Supplying Workers to Military Industries, chaired by Trotsky.[72] It was also widely discussed in the press.[73]

No one therefore could really have been surprised by the issuance in January 1920 of the Decree on Universal Obligatory Labor or the creation by another Central Committee decree for the Implementation of the Universal Labor Obligation.[74] According to the detailed instructions drawn up to implement the obligation, it was to apply to all able-bodied men between sixteen and fifty, women between sixteen and forty, and did not carry any obligation on the state's part to provide food or other provisions. The requirement to work was to be applied with special force against *proguly*, against employed men and women refusing to work, and against those refusing to join compulsory work on Saturdays (*subbotnkiki*) or Sundays (*voskresenniki*). Adjudication of disputes would be through the courts.[75]

Rabkrin, meanwhile, was intended to consolidate the supervision of enterprise financial and production processes into a single powerful agency, trimming the overstaffed Sovnarkhoz departments and limiting the independent supervisory responsibilities of the trade unions. Officials at the Commissariat

---

[71] GARF f. 130, op. 3, d. 580, l. 12; op. 4, d. 200, passim.
[72] RGAE f. 3420, op. 1, d. 1527, ll. 1–18.
[73] For example, *Ekonomicheskaia Zhizn'*, Apr. 11, 23, 1919; Jan. 21, 1920.
[74] RGAE f. 3429, op. 1, d. 1527, ll. 1–5, 18–23; *Dekrety Sovetskoi Vlasti.*, 15 vols. (Moscow: Nauka, 1957–89), vol. 7, 175–77; *Ekonomicheskaia Zhizn'*, Mar. 2, 1920.
[75] Central State Archive for the Moscow Region [TsGA MO] f. 146, op. 1, d. 40, ll. 16–40.

of State Control were enthusiastic. They urged a rapid shift to universal obligatory labor to accompany the new administrative changes under Rabkrin.[76] Not surprisingly, trade union activists objected. So did regional and local soviets, who wanted to maintain their own supervisory functions, and the staffs of various Sovnarkhoz *glavki* who members of the Rabkrin commissariat complained were issuing contrary circulars and orders without their sanction.[77] Supervising production through the unions institutionalized to some degree the concept of workers supervising themselves, although class identity here was totally subordinated to political affiliation. Regional and local supervision through elected soviets supported the concept of democratic practice within the boundaries of Bolshevik party and state control. A "workers' opposition" within the Bolshevik party soon began to form around the first concept, a "democratic centralist" group around the second. How the universal work obligation would be enforced and sustained was not clear. What was obvious was that both would inject additional elements of state-sanctioned coercion onto Soviet Russia's beleaguered workforce.

The Sovnarkom gave control of Rabkrin to Stalin, who had been the titular head of the Commissariat for State Control since April 1919. The future general secretary soon had twenty-five departments and more than eighteen hundred people working for him in Moscow, some five thousand in thirty-two provincial branches, and more than four thousand in various special divisions, including the railroads—a small army of inspectors whose range of actions was soon notorious.[78] This was partly because of a new "rapid response" system of "flying inspections" (*letuchei revizii*): inspectors with "extraordinary authority" (*chrezvychainyi,* as in *che-ka*) dispatched unannounced to investigate serious cases of suspected wrongdoing. Characteristically, the first flying inspections were not well organized nor staffed with competent people. They were more successful in instilling fear than correcting defects, especially when hoards of goods were not discovered, as was most often the case. There followed a soon-to-be-familiar charge by Stalin against the "formalism" of the inspections and a demand that they be more "effective." Each flying detachment was then given a detailed plan for each mission, listing its tasks and the expected results that had to be recorded, whether or not they were realistic.

Thereafter the detachments' own "productivity" was said to improve.[79] An inspection in Penza uncovered "extreme neglect." One in Tver province discovered that a local military revolutionary committee was stealing from and "terrorizing" the local population. In Kaluga, local authorities initially prevented an inspection

---

[76] GARF f. 4085, op. 16, d. 89, ll. 1–4.
[77] RGAE f. 3429, op. 1, d. 1529, l. 26.
[78] *Izvestiia Gosudarstvennogo Kontrolia* 10 (May 15, 1919).
[79] RGASPI f. 5, op. 1, d. 2660, ll. 40–41.

by arresting one of its members, but with the help of the Cheka they were themselves soon accused of drunkenness, illegal confiscations of property and arrests, and violations relating to salaries, pensions, and "uncontrolled" outlays of state funds with no accounting, discoveries that were well publicized.[80] Rabkrin's agents were widely feared. Accusation was generally enough for removal or arrest. In Penza province, agents uncovered "extreme neglect" by bookkeepers, untimely distribution of currency, negligence in relation to duties, and a slipshod (*nebrezhnoe*) relation to state property. In Tver, there was "stealing, embezzlement, and illegal activity by local authorities." In Kaluga, it was drunkenness, illegal interference by the local Military Revolutionary Committee, refusal to allow inspections, illegal confiscation of property, improper arrest, and confiscated property divided among those who took it.[81] Yet warehouses were commonly empty (just as they were in 1989 and 1990, when flying raids to warehouses rarely discovered significant hoarding as the late Soviet economy was on the verge of collapse). The chaos that often accompanied the inspections made it difficult for agents to find the evidence they were certain was there.[82] As the work of the flying detachments increased, so did the complaints about their own arbitrariness. In early 1921 Trotsky himself initiated an inquiry about them.[83]

But how *could* Rabkrin's agents accurately assess whether scarce funds were properly used or whether an effort to accumulate resources needed for production was hoarding or concealment? And if goods of any sort were stored because railroad freight cars were not available, should that be considered hoarding? Even more problematic, how could they fairly measure "productivity" when output depended on having sufficient fuel and food or complicated machinery in working order? The search for food during working hours was still a matter of sustaining workers' ability to work, even if their managers could not tell shirking from hunger or anxiety. It was also not obvious in early 1920 that obligatory labor and the formation of Rabkrin would improve its supply.

There is little question that concealment, falsification, malfeasance, hoarding, profiteering, and low productivity had by now become embedded social aspects of Soviet economic exchange, just as a comparable range of behaviors and values became embedded in what we have called war capitalism before and during 1917. Scarcities again turned each of these terms into ones of perilous elasticity. Measuring productivity was the most elusive, unless all that mattered was the quantity of goods produced. The introduction of the universal labor obligation made useful measurements of this sort even more problematic. Still, as Thomas Remington has argued, Rabkrin under Stalin soon became a key element of

---

[80] Ibid., l. 51.
[81] Ibid., l. 50.
[82] Ibid., ll. 5–54; RGASPI f. 5, op. 1, d. 2662, ll. 10–22.
[83] RGASPI f. 5, op. 1, d. 2662, ll. 10–20, 22.

Soviet state-building.[84] As it spread its authority and power in all directions the Soviet state began to "rise up," as the great nineteenth-century Russian historian Vasili Kliuchevskii wrote about the reforms of Peter the Great, while the people shrank. In the process, an inability to accurately measure productivity and control the distortions and concealments involved in the effort soon became the rickety foundation of the Soviet planned economy.

"All for Transport!" Tsektran and the Labor Armies

Just as with the idea of dictatorship in late March 1918, a key focus of the obligation to work was the railroads. By early 1920, it became obvious that the shift in procurement from confiscation to compulsory deliveries and even the relaxed measures regarding trade were not significantly reducing food shortages. The government journal *Vestnik Statistiki* estimated that as much as 60 percent of procured grain, almost 1.5 million tons, was still being distributed on the black market.[85] One typical telegram from Voronezh to Lenin insisted that the actions of the procurement detachments and special plenipotentiaries and the lawlessness of the food committees were producing only anxiety and agitation.[86] Attention now shifted to an all-out effort to address the problem of how grain taken from the peasants was shipped (or not) to its various destinations.

There is no doubt that the railroad situation was "catastrophic" in January 1920, as a report to the party's Central Committee by Pavel Vompe, vice chair of the Cheka's transport section and leading railroad trade unionist, described it, echoing his tsarist and Provisional Government predecessors.[87] At the beginning of 1920 railroad operations were immeasurably worse than at any time since the beginning of the war in 1914. According to Commissariat of Transport statistics, the total amount of goods shipped over lines under Soviet control had decreased by almost 75 percent. Only 3.2 million tons of grain were carried, compared to 20 million in 1913, 14 percent of coal, and less than 10 percent of wood and wood products. More than half of the operating locomotives in 1916 were now out of commission and even more freight cars. According to statistics gathered by the Commissariat of Transport, fewer than seven thousand locomotives were still in operation, in contrast to the more than twenty thousand in 1913. Another calculation assessed the percentage increase in locomotives out for repairs from 16.5 to 60.7. The number of working freight cars was also

---

[84] Thomas Remington, "Institution Building in Bolshevik Russia: The Case of 'State *Kontrol*,'" *Slavic Review* 1 (Spring 1982): 91–103.
[85] *Vestnik Statistika* 1–4 (1920): 20.
[86] RGASPI f. 5, op. 1, d. 2814, l. 4.
[87] RGASPI f. 17, op. 84, d. 133, ll. 1–2.

reported to be more than 50 percent less than just before the revolution. Only 129 new freight cars would be produced during all of 1920, and not a single new locomotive. Delays in repairing locomotives on the important Nikolaev line between Moscow and Petrograd averaged 150 days. Between 25 and 30 percent of the labor force was absent from railroad shops each month. Without funds (and even when some financial resources could be found), wages in many places were in kind, commonly in the form of goods purloined from freight trains themselves. Sovnarkhoz's official journal, *Narodnoe Khoziaistvo*, reported that at the end of February 1919 more than 22 million puds of grain were lying in depots because the twenty-three hundred freight cars needed to ship them to "starving" provinces were simply not available. The situation with regard to deficits in sugar, meat, and other food products was comparable.[88]

A range of anxieties among railroaders continued to underlie these conditions. The journal of the railroad union acknowledged that meeting production plans set from above depended not merely on the availability of rolling stock but on a change in the railroad workers' psychology, without, however, differentiating the mindsets of skilled engine drivers, shop workers, and the tens of thousands of worker-peasants engaged in maintaining the lines. The key to the railroaders' outlook across these divisions was a shared anxiety about food, just as the main barrier to the improvement in food supplies was the devastating state of transport itself.[89] In the provinces, seizures by local officials, bandit gangs, railroad Chekists, and the imperiousness of those arriving every day with "special mandates" continued to make the lines unmanageable.[90]

These pressures in turn reinforced the adaptations that had characterized the behaviors of local railroaders and their committees well before 1920. As a special commission of the Komissariat of State Control (Goskontrol) reported, local railroad authorities defended themselves from directives and plenipotentiaries by exercising their own dictatorial "revolutionary authority," as many regional and district soviets were doing, "officially" sanctioned by their own collection of stamped orders and directives.[91] Special commissions like Goskontrol's were literally shunted aside as their trains took unexpected detours. The legion of commissars and inspectors—*naznachentsy*, the "appointed ones," as they were called, which connoted both arrogance and ignorance—were described in railroad journals as part of the "disease of parallelism." Trains were often stalled by red signals, but since engine drivers could not know if this was because of

---

[88] *Narodnoe Khoziaistvo* 8 (Aug. 1919): 99–103 and 5–6 (Mar. 1920): 5–6; RGASPI f. 17, op. 84, d. 133, ll. 2–6; A. I. Golopolosov, *Obzor zheleznodorozhnogo transporta (po dannym chrezvychainoi revisii 1919 g.)* (Moscow, 1920), 29; *Zheleznodorozhnik* 20 (July 14, 1920); *Sovetskii transport 1917–1927* (Moscow: Izd. NKPS, 1927), 37–40, 114–15.
[89] *Izvestiia Gos. Kontrolia* 2 (Jan. 15, 1919).
[90] *Gudok*, July 1, 1920.
[91] RGASPI f. 111, op. 22, d. 39, l. 19; *Zheleznodorozhnik* 15–16 (Apr. 28, 1920).

malfunctioning equipment, dereliction by signalmen, or actual traffic on the line ahead, the safest course was simply to wait for the signal to change, however long it took. Idle engines under steam obviously wasted precious coal or oil, but if drivers shut them down and walked away, they could either be punished for leaving their posts or risk even harsher sanctions if the equipment was suddenly needed and not ready to run. It was simply safer to burn fuel.[92] While railroad Cheka units operated ruthlessly throughout 1918 and 1919, railroad employees at all levels continued to conceal information, hide equipment, reroute trains, and engage in a lively black market in stolen goods. If unloading goods meant risking a battle between different authorities fighting for the consignments, better to send the goods elsewhere and arrange for their disposal by railroaders themselves. Disputes that could not be mediated were often "settled with revolvers."[93]

All this, of course, led to charges of sabotage, as well, no doubt, to sabotage itself. It also reinforced something of a "siege mentality" among railroaders along the lines, judging by railroad newspapers and journals. It seems clear that a sense of abuse as the long regarded "pariahs" of the Russian labor force had by now become a deeply embedded element of many railroaders' emotional states, insinuations and accusations that Commissar of Transport Vladimir Nevskii suggested were either "betrayal [predatel'stvo] or stupidity," echoing Miliukov's famous criticism of the tsarist regime in late 1916. So great were the abuses that in July 1919 Leonid Krasin, Nevskii's successor, ordered full wages to be paid to all railroad personnel who were improperly or falsely arrested. It was precisely this abusive disrespect and wanton repression that was "destroying Soviet transport."[94] Indeed, one summary of Rabkrin inspections admitted that while there was an enormous amount of malfeasance, one had to distinguish three sorts: that which was "essentially made necessary by scarcity," like lack of rations, spare parts, or money for wages; that which was necessary to make the lines work, like improperly repaired locomotives or the undocumented release of freight cars; and that which was "essentially venal," like the criminal use of funds or falsifying the books. Those breaking rules because they were hungry should not be included with those deliberately committing crimes.[95]

Trotsky's approach to solving these problems when he became commissar of transport in March 1920, while remaining commissar of military affairs, was to apply a military model of administration and performance, rationalizing railroad administration itself. Doing this required changing radically the role of the All-Russia Railroad Union, from setting wages and managing welfare concerns

---

[92] *Izvestiia Gos. Kontrolia* 17 (1919): 1–2; B. Fain, "Tsektran," in *Partiia i soiuzy*, ed. G. Zinoviev (Petrograd: Gosizdat, 1921), 123–27.
[93] *Zheleznodorozhnik* 18 (1919): 1–3; *Ekonomicheskaia Zhizn'*, May 13, 1920.
[94] *Ekonomicheskaia Zhizn'*, Nov. 23, 1918.
[95] GARF f. 4085, op. 16, d. 337, l. 100.

to actively managing railroad operations under the direction of the Transport Commissariat. Trotsky's first steps were to mobilize reliable party members into the commissariat's political section, Glavpolitput', and transform it from essentially a propaganda office managing railroad "agitation kiosks"—*agitpunkty*—into a "fighting party and soviet organ." Its members were now invested with an "extraordinary" authority that officially superseded all others on the lines. Soon yet another wave of special plenipotentiaries was traveling with military escorts, replacing local officials, arresting others, and issuing all sorts of new orders and instructions under Trotsky's direction.[96]

Trotsky himself saw his efforts leading to the "complete statization [*ogosudarstvlennie*]" of the railroad union, amplifying the left liberal Nekrasov's idea when he was minister of transport in 1917. But while the Nekrasov imagined statization to mean politically part of the governing regime but autonomous in terms of controlling railroad operations, Trotsky's idea was to make the union an administrative agency of the state itself by transferring the entire administration of transport into its hands. In doing so, Trotsky hoped to implement immediately the principle formulated at the Ninth Party Congress at the end of March, where the "weakness" of the railroad union was formally denounced as a "fundamental impediment" to improving transport. Trade unions would emerge "more and more as the fundamental base of the Soviet economic apparatus," functioning as "auxiliary organs of the state" to ensure discipline and increase productivity.[97]

Trotsky set all these changes in motion soon after the Ninth Party Congress with the promulgation of Order 1042, soon to be notorious, laying out his own five-year plan for transport's complete restoration. All rail and water unions were now to be merged into a single organization subordinated in a military-like hierarchy to a new all-powerful Central Committee for Transport, or Tsektran. Tsektran would join the principal figures of the railroad union and the Transport Commissariat's political arm in a disciplined group resembling a military general staff. Military-style discipline would be rigorously imposed. Lower-level administrators would be strictly and personally responsible to those above them. While vocal opponents to Trotsky's plan argued that a "staticized" union would likely run the railroads "like Jonah ran the whale," the new militarized system was largely in place by early August 1920. The arbitrary use of state power—"categorically forbidden" earlier in the year by a circular letter of the Central

---

[96] RGASPI f. 5, op. 1, d. 2747, ll. 1–26.
[97] RGAE f. 1884, op. 40, d. 7; *Otchet Tsektrana* (Moscow, 1920), 10–12; *Deviatyi s"ezd RKP(b): Protokoly* (Moscow, 1960), 418, 533–39. See also William G. Rosenberg, "The Social Background to Tsektran," in *Party, State, and Society in the Russian Civil War*, ed. Diane Koenker, William Rosenberg, and Ronald Suny (Bloomington: Indiana University Press, 1989), 349–73.

Committee—would now be used as if the railroad workers were an army capable of solving a transport crisis that even Trotsky's opponents regarded as urgent.[98]

Rabkrin's agents were soon hard at work as well, supported by Order 1042. On the key Moscow-Kursk and Moscow-Kiev lines they found breakdowns in the telegraph system, illegal purchases and sales of scarce goods, bribery, theft, and high levels of absenteeism. In the Tula locomotive shops, engines beyond repair continued to occupy shop space, perishable parts were left outside to rust, and there was little attention to printed regulations and instructions. Even the introduction of a premium system based on productivity seemed to produce expectations of still higher payments rather than an increase in output. Out of 1,312 workers listed on the roster of one construction brigade, only 286 were actually working; 314 were simply unaccounted for.[99] Meanwhile, a steady stream of dismissals and arrests produced a passive as well as active hostility to Rabkrin's inspectors. In some places it was taking from fifteen to forty days for the demands of the Inspectorate to be answered.[100]

Trotsky's approach to the railroads ran parallel to his efforts as commissar of war to convert unneeded army units in western Siberia and the Caucasus into labor armies instead of demobilizing them, and to create additional labor armies by means of a full-scale draft of able-bodied men on the basis of the universal obligation to work. In mid-January the Third Red Army in western Siberia became the First Labor Army, centered in Ekaterinburg. Its mission was to restore the economy of the region through militarization on the principles of dictatorial rule, a military command system, and rational planning for all regional branches of industries.

Not surprisingly, things did not go well from the start. Appalled representatives of Vesenkha and the Commissariat of Labor rejected these ambitions as unworkable. Their first two meetings with the Labor Army commanders nearly turned into a brawl. Reports described the early efforts of the Labor Army's 166,000 men and women, some 69,000 of them mobilized civilians, as "highly unsatisfactory."[101] By March its commanders could report the repair of ninety-seven locomotives, extensive snow cleaning and track repairs, and a range of other accomplishments, but by April they were tangling with Cheka detachments they described in their reports as demagogues and charlatans. Weekly reports for May described struggles with receiving supplies and the need for more skilled workers. Rivalries and tensions accelerated. Those commanding the Labor Army

---

[98] S. A. Lozovskii, *Partiia i soiuzy* (Moscow, 1920), 170; S. V. Kossior, *Nashi raznoglasiia (o roli i zadachakh profsoiuzov)* (Moscow: Gosizdat, 1921); GARF f. 5451, op. 4, d. 41, l. 134; *Otchet tsektran*, 14, 20–21; *Deviatyi S"ezd*, 533–39; *Zheleznodorozhnik* 15–16 (1920).

[99] GARF f. 4085, op. 16, d. 337, ll. 11–13, 31–32, 45–70.

[100] Ibid., l. 68.

[101] RGASPI f. 5, op. 1, d. 2552, ll. 3–4.

and officials from the Commissariat of Labor and the regional Sovnarkhoz strongly resisted what they saw as a military takeover of industrial production. The situation in some places was one of "complete disorganization in the tasks of distributed labor and technical forces."[102]

For its part, the Second Labor Army sent to repair the Southeastern railroad and other lines of the region was only marginally more successful. It, too, was hindered by administrative disorganization, problematic supply lines, and a lack of competent technical personnel. An obvious problem here and in the broader Ekaterinburg region was that the labor armies themselves had to procure and forage for food for their own use, as well as buy firewood and other essential goods needed for enterprises and institutions in their region. Confiscation and often violent confrontation with those who resisted these efforts was an everyday occurrence, just as it had been in the military zone after 1914.[103] Another problem was the well-worn pattern of multiple local authorities. Both the army's command and regional Sovnarkhozy officials believed their orders were paramount.[104] In Groznyi, a Labor Army for the Caucasus ran into immediate difficulties with local officials by setting its own fixed prices for requisitioned foodstuffs. Supplies were so scarce that the local Military Revolutionary Committee was soon paying market prices of 2,000 to 2,500 rubles to avoid conflict with the local populace, a figure far higher than the Labor Army's resources allowed. When the need for additional food and other supplies (including uniforms and underwear) became urgent in the fall of 1920, the Caucasus Labor Army discharged most of those who had been drafted into its service.[105]

The overwhelming problem in all of the labor armies, however, was desertion, just as it had been for the Red and White armies. The primary causes, again, were the lack of adequate rations and anxiety about the well-being of families. Thousands took advantage of lax security while traveling to assigned localities to drop from trains and head home. Even more seem to have found ways to leave the labor armies once they had set up base. Women caught up in the mobilization drive had a particularly difficult time. A plaintive but forceful communication to Commissar of Health Semashko warned of the large number of miscarriages and other issues that begged for relief.[106] Still, as the regime confronted a serious shortage of industrial workers and the threat of economic collapse, Trotsky and others pushed an all-out effort to militarize the Soviet workforce as a whole. Skilled workers were to be recalled from the army and other state institutions.

---

[102] Ibid., ll. 1–4, 11–15; RGAE f. 3429, op. 1, d. 1529, passim.
[103] RGASPI f. 5, op. 1, d. 2550, passim.
[104] RGAE f. 3429, op. 1, d. 1529, ll. 189ff.; RGASPI f. 5, op. 1, d. 2554, ll. 7–8; James Bunyan, *The Origins of Forced Labor in the Soviet State 1917-1921* (Baltimore, MD: Johns Hopkins University Press, 1967), 147–50.
[105] RGASPI f. 5, op. 1, d. 2556, ll. 5–9, 18–33.
[106] RGASPI f. 5, op. 1, d. 2452, l. 26; f. 111, op. 22, d. 702, ll. 2–5 ob.

The unskilled would be sent to haul wood, clear roads, load and unload freight, and help rebuild bridges and buildings.

Partly as a result of Trotsky's pressure, the whole process of labor mobilization and distributing workers to places that needed them was now given to an interdepartmental Central Committee on Universal Obligatory Labor chaired by Cheka chief Felix Dzerzhinskii.[107] While small teams of "shock workers" were mobilized for specific tasks, plans were initiated to conduct a wholesale military-style draft of the unemployed who were born between 1886 and 1888. By the fall of 1920 the process was being openly discussed as a *razverstka* of people rather than grain: a confiscation of the "surplus" of those not working "each according to his ability" and their forceful distribution to enterprises around the country. Local branches of the Committee for the Distribution of Labor within the Commissariat of Labor distributed detailed forms to enterprises that needed workers. (Among its questions was whether food would be provided.)[108] In effect, the earlier forced labor practices of the tsarist and Provisional Government regimes were now being writ large as part of the Bolsheviks' desperate efforts to revive industry.[109] The mobilizing slogan "All for Transport"—equally a warning of the danger of even deeper socioeconomic catastrophe and an index of political desperation in the face of near universal material need—had become the rhetorical keystone to Trotsky's larger ambitions. Before the year was out, hunger and its effects may have claimed more than 100,000 additional lives.[110]

Yet also as before, the coherent schemes of the center became confused and contradictory practices in the localities, even within (and perhaps especially within) the myriad local committees, soviets, and Bolshevik party organizations themselves. A telegram sent directly to Lenin by M. Kalinin, now head of Sovnarkhoz, reported that regardless of whether or not it was sensible to appoint a Special Commissar to supervise coal production near Moscow, the fight between him and the government's Coal Bureau had created "complete chaos" in the administration of the pits, had left unresolved all major questions of reorganizing the mines, and had created "great practical bitterness around urgent practical questions."[111] The party-state in Moscow may have had a formal monopoly on the use of force, but power still came out of the barrels of weapons that were now being used everywhere by "official" committees, gangs, and individuals to secure what was needed or wanted. And while the party's leadership had some idea of who could rightly claim to be a Bolshevik, Bolshevism to many was as much a

---

[107] RGAE f. 3429, op. 1, f. 1527, ll. 181–89; *Bor'ba s trudovym dezertirstvom: Sbornik ofitsial'nykh polozhenie* (Moscow: Izd. Glavkomtruda, 1920), 7–8; Bunyan, *Origin*, 110–14; *Deviatyi s"ezd.*, 371–81.
[108] GARF f. 382, op. 4, d. 350, ll. 11–15; d. 406, ll. 95ff.
[109] GARF f. 382, op. 4, d. 406, ll. 60–76, 93–100.
[110] RGASPI f. 17, op. 84, d. 133, ll. 2–6.
[111] RGAE f. 3429, op. 1, d. 1002, l. 161.

descriptor of coercion and extraction as a coherent political outlook, especially in the deeper countryside and the war-torn and hungry central Volga provinces and Siberia.

The Collapse of War Communism: "Bolshevism without the Bolsheviks!"

Ironically, the "extreme means" taken by the Soviet regime between 1918 and 1920 to fight scarcity, address pressing welfare needs, and stave off economic collapse became known as "war communism" in the Great Soviet Story only when its failures were finally acknowledged at the Tenth Party Congress in March 1921. The term had occasionally been used earlier to link an all-powerful centralized dictatorship to a radiant future. Its embrace as a description of Bolshevik Civil War rule essentially rationalized three years of scarcity, loss, and administrative dysfunction into the temporary elements of a developed communist order made necessary by the existential threat to that order itself. It was not the policies of militarization, confiscation, and unbridled dictatorial force at every level that produced or aggravated the shortages, hunger, loss, dislocation, and unremitting anxiety within Soviet Russia during these months. The chaos and anxiety themselves demanded the "extraordinary" militaristic interventions that constituted an admittedly premature communist dictatorship. With the total disintegration of Russia's "bourgeois" stage of historical evolution, this would ensure communism would emerge as history intended: through the reconstruction of consciousness by means of universal education, broad-based technological competence, and the accumulation by the state of the capital resources necessary to rationally plan and construct a prosperous modern and industrialized communist order. The victory of "war communism" over the imperial bourgeois forces that fought to destroy it validated its policies and efforts retroactively. What legitimized Bolshevik rule, however, was not its formal constitution, its representations of popular proletarian sovereignty, or even its victory over the Whites. It was the process of history itself. Lenin's Russia was moving forward as history predestined. Among the three competing Great Stories about what revolution would bring to Russia, the Great Soviet Story by 1921 was the one left standing within Soviet Russia itself.

In the Western literature the political dimensions of War Communism's collapse were thoroughly rehearsed even before the party's archives were opened in 1989. Public statements, conference resolutions, and competing political platforms structured the moment. In his pathbreaking study of the "conscience" of the Bolshevik party in 1965, Robert Daniels first traced the political fractures reflected in the emergence of the "left" or "workers' opposition," who wanted a return to participatory factory administration; the "democratic centralists," who believed in participatory decision-making at all levels along with strict dictatorial administration of the decisions themselves; and the powerful group of trade unionists who took on Trotsky and Tsektran and insisted the role of unions should be to defend and protect workers' well-being even as they worked in close cooperation with the party and the state. Trotsky's "statization" plans, like his advocacy of militarizing industrial production and the railroads, again deprived workers of their ability to control their circumstances as well as their dignity, just as before 1917. Leonard Schapiro described War Communism as "determined dictatorship": the smashing of the existing machinery of the state as Lenin had demanded in *State and Revolution* as a key step to a monolithic party and its logical Stalinist variant.[112] These descriptions reflected the arguments of leading party members themselves toward the end of 1920.[113] What contemporary and subsequent publications were not able adequately to assess was the exhaustive degree of material need and anxiety that characterized so much of Soviet Russia's populace by 1921, and which was amply reflected in secret Cheka reports and other secret archival documents. As Sergei Yarov has detailed in an important and neglected volume, the tropes of "extreme need" remained constant throughout the Civil War years, especially regarding the scarcities of food.[114]

These fundamental and unsolved problems of scarcity and social dislocation got relatively scant public reference as a devastated country prepared for its seventh dismal New Year since war began in 1914, lest popular animosities and discontent be amplified, as some in Moscow warned. Even the airing of significant differences regarding the role of trade unions, militarization, and party governance was "very dangerous" for communism itself.[115] Subject to accusations of disloyalty or worse, party-controlled newspapers like *Golos Rabotnika* (*Voice of the Worker*) complained about anti-Bolshevik "yellow" trade unionists, labor desertion, and the Tsektran controversy. In the last ten days of December *Izvestiia* was almost entirely focused on the Eighth Congress of Soviets.[116]

There was little doubt, however, that militarization and compulsory labor had failed to bring significant improvements, if any at all, as a leading figure involved in the process reported to the Sovnarkom. The labor *razverstka* set for October by Dzerzhinskii's Central Committee on Universal Obligatory Labor was supposed to be implemented in thirty-seven provinces. All citizens born between

---

[112] Leonard Schapiro, *The Origins of the Communist Autocracy* (Cambridge, MA: Harvard University Press, 1966), 211, 217, 273. See also Robert Daniels, *The Conscience of the Revolution* (Cambridge, MA: Harvard University Press, 1965), ch. 4.
[113] As reflected in publications like *Partiia i Soiuzy*, Kollontai's *Workers' Opposition*, Bukharin's *ABC of Communism*, and Kritsman's enthusiastic *Geroicheskii period russkoi revoliutsiia*.
[114] S. V. Yarov, *Gorozhanin kak politik* (St. Petersburg: Bulanin, 1999), 63–95.
[115] RGASPI f. 17, op. 84, d. 73, ll. 1–4.
[116] *Golos Rabotnika*, Dec. 20, 1920; *Gudok*, Dec. 12, 14, 18–21, 1920; *Izvestiia*, Dec. 25–30, 1920.

1886 and 1888 were to report on September 18 to local offices for distribution into the labor force. Housing would be needed for some fifteen thousand men and women being sent to work on the railroads and ten thousand assigned to food-procurement organs.

When the actual deployment began on October 15 everywhere except Arkhangelsk province, it was anarchic. Many of those mobilized were detained en route because of transport problems, document errors, or absent leadership. Accounting for and matching the demand and supply of workers was chaotic. There were predictable disagreements between officials all along the way. Many of those drafted were incapable of the physical labor they were assigned, up to 80 percent reportedly in Tver province. Red Army units in Pskov would not accept their allotment of workers because they had no food to share, other organizations and enterprises because they had no housing. In some places the mobilization brought only a handful of people to the mustering point. Simbirsk and Tambov provinces were a "complete disaster." In eleven provinces the mobilization did not even occur because so many of those supposedly eligible for the labor draft had long since been taken into the army. A statement by staff members in the Commissariat of Labor drawn up "in response to the public furor" over the whole process saw it as a "cardinal question" for the Tenth Party Congress set for March 1921, since many comrades were uninformed or not clearly informed about the nature of the labor mobilization underway, nor about the methods now being used.[117]

Even Trotsky had to admit by early November that the Tsektran experiment was failing. He acknowledged the work of the "huge number of energetic and experienced organizers" who were involved in the task, but in fact it was these organizers themselves who created the most resistance among experienced railroad workers and strengthened their union's opposition. A report from the head of the Western railroad Cheka demanded a "radical purge from top to bottom." Railroad food committees were acting with total independence, "not subordinate to anyone," and creating a "pitiful situation . . . requiring complete reorganization."[118] The mix of participatory committees, repression, rival agencies, and commissars was simply not able to secure needed equipment and supplies, nor make the lines run more efficiently. Some shop and depot elections were now returning Menshevik majorities to local soviet committees. "All our work is paralyzed by failure to receive food rations and shoes," Syzran-Viazemskii line officials reported. "Our workers are threatened with starvation." The Moscow-Kursk and Moscow-Kiev lines were still struggling with hunger, cold, illness, and the frequent absences of key personnel. Bribes and corruption had not declined.

[117] GARF f. 382, op. 4, d. 406, ll. 79–80, 94–98; d. 413, ll. 2–4; d. 434, ll. 3–29; d. 405; ll. 152–54.
[118] RGAE f. 184, op. 3, d. 20, ll. 2, 10–12, 30–31.

Orders and instructions from Trotsky himself were not being followed. On the Nikolaev railroad between Moscow and Petrograd the situation remained "absolutely catastrophic." Archive files on Rabkrin's inspections of the lines are riddled with the tension and uncertainty the Tsektran "reform" had created.[119]

"Catastrophe" was also a term of choice in the mass of reports and telegrams Sovnarkhoz and its forty-two separate sections continued to receive during the winter months of 1919 and 1920, strengthening concerns about the possibility of economic collapse. "The whole idea of a food ration was a *myth*!" one report from the Urals declared. "It simply doesn't exist."[120] In October 1920 the mood of delegates at one district meeting in Moscow was so "dangerous" for those involved in political and soviet work that a new meeting had to be convened along with a "severe investigation" of all "dirt, slander, and lies" that were told.[121] In November and December the protests against Tsektran from Bolshevik trade unionists came to a head. Each member of the Central Trade Union Council presidium, the ostensible leadership organization for all trade unions, thought Tsektran was ruinous (*gibel'no*).[122] Not denying our successes, Trotsky telegraphed his colleagues, it was clear that it was not only trade union leaders who were demanding it be terminated, but the mass of railroaders themselves that Tsektran had not succeeded in mobilizing behind the effort.[123]

As is well known, late 1920 also saw a number of short strikes and other labor protests, most taken independently of Bolshevized trade unions that ostensibly represented worker interests. In the main, these were easily put down, the embarrassment they might have caused at least some supporters of the proletarian dictatorship quickly dissolved in the language of sabotage and counterrevolution.[124] It is possible that protests were also offset to some degree by the huge investment Anatoly Lunacharskii of the Commissariat for Enlightenment was trying to make to strengthen "proletarian" values among industrial workers, especially those assumed to be less "conscious" of Marxist laws of history due to lack of education or lowly profession. The efforts to develop mass participatory theater and publishing materials like "What a Communist Ought to Be Like," as Lenin's wife, Nadezhda Krupskaia, titled a famous essay, almost certainly tempered feelings to some degree by reminding workers and others what "their" regime ostensibly stood for. In art, literature, and posters the first efforts at "cultural revolution" clearly had resonance, especially in Moscow and Petrograd.[125] Scarcities and the

---

[119] GARF f. 4085, op. 16, d. 337, ll. 45–72; RGAE f. 1884, op. 3, d. 20, ll. 51–52, 296–99; *Ekonomicheskaia Zhizn'*, Nov. 5, 6, 14, 1920.
[120] RGAE f. 3429, op. 1, d. 1002, 1005, 1387, 1417; *Zheleznodorozhnik* 10–22 (Nov. 15, 1919).
[121] RGASPI f. 111, op. 22, d. 452b; d. 702, ll. 17–22; f. 634, op. 1, d. 7, ll. 3–4, 59.
[122] RGASPI f. 17, op. 84, d. 109, ll. 60, 103.
[123] RGASPI f. 111, op. 22, d. 447, ll. 49–50.
[124] Iu. Kirianov, ed., *Trudovye konflikty v sovetskoi Rossii 1918–1929* (Moscow: Izd. URSS, 1998).
[125] Among other works, see esp. Richard Stites, *Revolutionary Dreams: Utopian Visions and Experimental Life in the Russian Revolution* (New York: Oxford University Press, 1989).

tens of thousands of new losses inflicted by the Civil War were even easier to blame on counterrevolutionary movements and reactionary cultures than the world war was on capitalists and the bourgeoisie.

None of this, however, could make the New Year's holiday in Petrograd any more joyful than in previous years. Fuel supplies were at their lowest point since 1917, anxieties over food near their highest. One can assume this was not only because of the dark and cold, the hunger and worry, but also because the victories over the anti-Bolshevik armies in South Russia and Siberia implicitly promised something better. How much expectation and disappointment worsened the city's "mood" is impossible to say, but the agitated feelings of workers in the city's major industrial plants soon found expression in a new wave of strikes and protests. Trade union leaders in Petrograd had applauded the description of workers' protests there in June as "pitiful," "criminal," and clearly led by ignorant "enemies of the workers" who did not understand that it was impossible to meet their demands.[126] By New Year's 1921, the upheaval seemed to bring out all the frustrations workers in Petrograd had experienced over the past three years, marking at once the political limitations of Bolshevik dictatorship and the agonies of War Communism. For all of its forceful efforts, Lenin's government, like those of its predecessors, had failed to manage the impossible problems of scarcity and loss, even as it successfully defied the international and domestic anti-Bolshevik forces aligned against it.[127]

The agitation broke into open conflict toward the end of January with meetings and strikes. ("What have the communists given us?!"; "We will never see communism!") Much of the strike activity was passive. Fearing the loss of their jobs, workers stayed away from Baltic Shipbuilding, Lessner, and other plants to avoid arrest, effectively shutting them down but avoiding clashes with the authorities. By the middle of February leaders of the Union of Metallists met with their workers to try to mitigate the protest, explaining just how difficult their problems were to solve. In response, the workers declared their intention to reelect the Petrograd Soviet and even to arrest Chekists and hold them to account.[128]

Thereafter the agitation intensified, supported by Menshevik figures still in the city. On February 27 the party's Petrograd committee circulated an open proclamation to the city's workers praising their courage during the "unbearable suffering" of the past three years and warning that the economic collapse would inevitably continue without a fundamental change in the regime's policies, if not the regime itself: "Comrades, organize and emphatically demand the release of all

---

[126] TsGA SPb. f. 6276, op. 5, d. 41, ll. 67–68.
[127] S. V. Yarov, *Chelovek pered litsom vlasti 1917–1920 gg.* (Moscow: Rosspen, 2014), 359.
[128] V. Iu. Cherniaev, ed., *Piterskie rabochie i "diktatura proletariat" oktiabr' 1917–1929: Sbornik dokumentov* (St. Petersburg: Izd. BLITs 2000), 239–63 (documents from TsGA SPb fonds 4, 33, 1000, 4591, 6255, 6276, and 8672).

arrested socialists and non-party workers, the end of martial law, and freedom of speech, press, and assembly for all workers. Convene meetings, pass resolutions, and send delegates to the governing organs who will secure your demands."[129]

In the meantime, unrest was spreading to the nearby Kronstadt naval base, greatly worrying Zinoviev and other Petrograd party figures as they prepared for the Tenth Party Congress, and for good reason.[130] Sailors were soon in a full-fledged mutiny, demanding civil liberties and food and venting their rage at their commanders and the Bolsheviks more broadly. The ensuing story has been frequently told. After hearing about the unrest in Petrograd, sailors from the iced-in battleships *Petropavlovsk* and *Sevastopol* in Kronstadt harbor sent delegations to the city to link up with protesting workers. A meeting of some sixteen thousand two days later took up the slogans "Power to the Soviets, not the Party!," "Down with the Food *Razverstka*!," "Give Us Free Trade!," and "Bolshevism without the Bolsheviks!" As the fortress moved into full revolt, its commanders were arrested. Branding the sailors counterrevolutionaries and puppets of the Whites, Lenin sent Trotsky and Tukhashevskii to suppress them. As many as forty-five thousand Red Army troops were mobilized to the attack the fortress, assaulting it from three directions across the ice. Casualties were severe; intense fighting occurred both within the fortress and in its adjacent town. By March 17 the mutiny was over. More than twenty-one hundred were sentenced to be shot, another sixty-four hundred trucked off to prison. Eight thousand or so, including the mutiny's Revolutionary Committee and its chair, Stepan Petrichenko, managed to flee to Finland.[131]

Throughout this tense time the 1,135 delegates were meeting at the Bolsheviks' Tenth Party Congress in Moscow for what was hoped to be a celebration of their "gigantic victory in the struggle to create the conditions for the construction of world socialism," as the Congress protocols announced. Instead, the gathering became a tense effort to address the mutiny and other the pressing issues. Some delegates went off to help suppress Kronstadt, or at least to be able to say they did. Whether they and others regarded the events themselves or their underlying causes as more important is unclear, but both got full attention under the firm guidance of Lenin and the Central Committee. Among the most notable decisions was replacing the forceful confiscation of supposedly surplus grain with a simple tax in kind, leaving peasant producers free to dispose of the balance as they wished—the New Economic Policy formally liberating rural production

---

[129] *Mensheviki v 1921–1922 gg.* (Moscow: Rosspen, 2002), 113–14.

[130] TsGA SPb f. 1000, op. 5, d. 4, ll. 15–28, 50–51; Yarov, *Gorozhanin*, 139–78.

[131] Paul Avrich, *Kronstadt* (Princeton, NJ: Princeton University Press, 1970); I. Getzler, *Kronstadt 1917–1921* (Cambridge: Cambridge University Press, 2002); S. N. Semanov, *Kronshtadtskii miatezh* (Moscow: IKSMO, 2003); *Kronshtadtskaia tragediia 1921 goda: Dokumenty,* 2 vols. (Moscow: Rosspen, 1999).

and the countryside more broadly from direct party control. This necessarily meant the end of restrictions on private trade. Although a huge peasant uprising developing against the party in the Tambov region was yet to be suppressed—Tukhashevskii's next assignment after Kronstadt was to do so—a much smaller Red Army would also be expected to improve the food supply, provided the transport situation improved.

All of this was reflected in Lenin's view regarding the urgency of establishing "normal" relations with the peasants' vast "middle ranks." Through the New Economic Policy a recovering industry would begin to provide the products needed to improve peasant life, enabling the emergence, in Lenin's words, of a "normal socialist society."[132] To this end Trotsky's effort to make the railroad and other trade unions agents of the state was also terminated, at least for the moment, implicitly acknowledging that Tsektran was both an administrative failure and a lightning rod for resistance. Efforts of members of a self-styled "workers' opposition" within the party to expand and consolidate the unions' role in economic administration found little support. Trade unions henceforth would revert to their traditional role of supporting workers' interests by acting, Lenin said, as "schools of communism." Here by implication was also the acknowledgment of the need for managerial competence and the suspension of the party's struggle against "bourgeois specialists."

Finally, but not least in terms of its future importance as the Congress ended its eighteen-day meeting, was the need for the party to move forward with absolute unity. What would prove to be a notorious decision was the resolution "On the Unity of the Party," formally based on the premise that "all conscious workers clearly recognized the inadmissibility of any kind of factionalism." To realize "strict discipline within the party in all aspects of soviet work" the Congress gave the Central Committee power to expel from the party "all those who engaged in violations of party discipline or the revival or acceptance of factionalism."[133]

As War Communism came to an end and the New Economic Policy seemed to promise material betterment and an end to the anxieties of scarcity and loss, a sure path was also set toward Stalinism and their devastating reemergence.

[132] *Deviatyi S"ezd*, 550.
[133] Ibid., 571–73.

Epilogue: Scarcity, Loss, and Soviet History

While there was irony in the Bolsheviks celebrating victory at the Tenth Party Congress in the midst of the Kronstadt uprising and the Tambov peasant revolt that followed, both events had long-lasting effects on Soviet development. These were anything but paradoxical. The mutiny of formerly loyal Kronstadt sailors was the largest military revolt in Russian history, dwarfing in its scale the better remembered *Potemkin* mutiny in 1905. No Eisenstein film depicted the Kronstadters as heroic, their uprising a desperate failure to bring a change in Soviet governance. The Antonovshchina in Tambov shortly afterward signified the deep animosity of large numbers of peasants, most likely a majority, toward the confiscatory policies and the material and emotional deprivations of what Lenin and others now somewhat proudly called the heroic period of War Communism. As we have noted, the months following the Bolsheviks' seizure of state power also witnessed an impressive array of art and propaganda depicting Soviet Russia's intended military, political, and cultural transformation. There were equally impressive efforts at promoting progressive European legal and educational theories, introducing civil marriage, and advancing gender equality, although the connection between these efforts and the countryside were initially limited to the Bolsheviks' famous propaganda trains. None of these admirable initiatives, moreover, could have significantly decreased the deprivations, anxieties, losses—the collective and individual catastrophes—that constituted the essence of most Russians' experience between 1918 and 1922.

Soviet Russia's Long Civil War

As the last foreign armies withdrew from all but the very Far East, Russia's long world war came to an end. The year 1921 became a marker for most statistical calculations of its costs and losses as well as for historical periodization. Yet in ways central to the subsequent development of the Soviet state, Russia's civil wars continued in the conflicts between Russian peasants and communists, the ongoing discontents of industrial workers reflected in the Petrograd strikes in 1921, and the forceful struggles to subdue the independence national minorities' had briefly enjoyed. In an important book, Jonathan Smele studies the "Russian" civil wars, "Russian" to connote that the fighting did not always engage Russians, "wars" as a plural to connote that the struggles were of different kinds and forms.

Smele's chronology is the period 1916–26. This allows him to give attention to continued conflict around Vladivostok, the engagements between the Red Army and Siberian insurgents in 1922–23, and intense fighting around Bukhara, whose origins were in the uprisings of 1916 against the mobilization of labor battalions. For Smele, an appropriate marker to the end of the civil wars was the closing of the Turkestan Front in 1926 and its replacement by peacetime operations of the Central Asian Military District.[1]

The longer-term implications and effects of the Kronstadt uprising, however, have never been fully explored, in part because of the sheer difficulty of doing so. With several notable exceptions, the same can be said about the longer-term effects of the Tambov insurrection, as well as the continued animosities between peasants' villages and Soviet authorities, especially deep in the countryside.[2] To what extent did the revolt at the very end of Russia's long world war reinforce the need for surveillance and censorship imposed at its start on peasant soldiers "fighting with God" and assure the party's still diverse leadership of the need to permanently institutionalize the Cheka in the OGPU and its successors? The party's dependence on the Red Army was unquestionable in 1921 and beyond as Bolshevik rule spread forcibly throughout the former tsarist empire. And if Trotsky was Stalin's strongest rival to succeed the physically weakening Lenin as head of the party and state, Stalin soon regarded other party leaders and leading military figures like Tukhashevskii as potential rivals for this position, leading to their brutal trials and executions in 1936–37 and the massive purge of field grade officers that followed. Even Marshall Zhukov was marginalized after victory again against the foreign invader in 1945, his equestrian statue erected in Red Square only in 1995.

The long-term effects of the massive Tambov rebellion are more apparent. With fields and crops devastated by warfare in the region and the unrestrained confiscations (*razverstki*) from all sides, Tambov, the middle Volga region, and the contiguous grain-producing regions of western Siberia no longer had the means to feed themselves in the summer and fall of 1921. The great famine that swept across the region in 1921 and 1922 was by far the largest in modern Russian history, if not Russian history as a whole. As many as 5 million are estimated to have died, many from cholera and other diseases that preyed on the starving, others from the agonies of starvation itself. The International Committee for Russian Relief and Herbert Hoover's efforts may have alleviated some of the suffering. Its horrors also encouraged the Soviet regime to open trade with capitalist Europe, including Germany, through the Treaty of Rapallo in the spring of

---

[1] Jonathan Smele, *The "Russian" Civil Wars, 1916–1926* (New York: Oxford University Press), ch. 6.
[2] Among the most notable is Andrea Graziosi, *The Great Soviet Peasant War: Bolsheviks and Peasants, 1917–1933* (Cambridge, MA: Harvard University Ukrainian Institute, 1996).

1922. If the region's physical recovery by the end of that year was underway, however, the material as well as emotional residues of the famine carried well into the 1920s and beyond.

So, too, we can safely assume, did those of the massive losses suffered more broadly since 1914. While the statistics are uncertain, as many as 30 million people may have been lost in Russia between 1914 and 1923 from all causes, 9 to 10 million between July 1914 and the end of December 1917. Some 15 million had been drafted into the tsarist army. As many as 2 million "of the most valued men in full bloom of life and health," as the contemporary statistician Strumilin called them in 1920, had been wounded.[3] The Civil War years claimed another 800,000 military deaths, and possibly as many as 14 million civilian, including those who starved in the 1921–22 famine among the 23 million who were officially classified as affected by it.[4] Again, whatever their accuracy, these abstract statistics camouflage a brutal reality: virtually every one of these deaths was a violent one, man-made in a paroxysm of masculine fantasies and political rationalizations, even if the proximate causes in many cases were malnutrition and disease. To assess their impact on anything that might be called a collective social psyche, one has to try to grasp the existential pain and suffering these losses reflected and the emotional as well as social havoc this period evoked.

The intense debates that characterized the years of the New Economic Policy (NEP) between 1921 and 1929 are well known in terms of the political rivalries and policy differences they reflected. The concentration in the literature on the political machinations of Stalin and others as Lenin's health worsened is rightly on key aspects of the party-state's development in the 1920s and the consolidation of Stalin's own dictatorial power. At the same time, the policy issues were as much about the implicit dangers of scarcity and the residues of loss as they were about competing understandings of "what a communist ought to be like," as Krupskaia put it, if not forcefully expressed in these terms.[5] The ruble was now stabilized after a critical reform that again backed it with gold, and a limited market system in the procurement and distribution of grain legitimized to a degree the "Nepmen" traders who now took up the practices of the reviled bagmen and -women between 1918 and 1921. (Many, undoubtedly, were the same people.) The return of some foreign investment was also encouraging in

---

[3] Frank Lorimer, *The Population of the Soviet Union* (Geneva: League of Nations, 1946), esp. 39; S. Strumilin, "Trudovye poteri Rossii v voine," *Narodnoe khoziaistvo* 23–24 (Dec. 1920): 104–6. See also E. Z. Volkov, *Dinamika narodonaseleniia SSSR* (Moscow, 1930); L. Lubny-Gertsyk, *Dvizhenie naseleniia na territorii SSSR za vremia mirovoi voiny i revoliutsii* (Moscow: Planovoe khoziaistvo, 1926).

[4] S. G. Wheatcroft, "Famine and Epidemic Crises in Russia, 1918–1922: The Case of Saratov," *Annales de démographie historique* (1983): 329, 330.

[5] N. Krupskaia, "What a Communist Ought to Be Like," in *Bolshevik Visions: The First Phase of the Cultural Revolution in Soviet Russia*, 2 vols., ed. William G. Rosenberg (Ann Arbor: University of Michigan Press, 1990), 1:26–29.

the early 1920s, although some in the party's leadership worried about its longer-term implications.

In these still fraught circumstances, the regime's domestic policies were once again centered on increasing peasant productivity, strengthening industrial production, and monitoring dissidence, in other words, solving the same fundamental problems that had beset successive regimes since July 1914. A familiar dispute that emerged already in 1923 when market prices for industrial and consumer goods soared because of their scarcity in comparison to the falling cost of grain as the harvest recovered centered these questions again on the proper economic role of the state. Bukharin and others suggested these tasks were best accomplished by the party "turning its face to the village," incentivizing grain production and providing commodities peasants would want to buy. An opposing view was that the best course was to again extract grain from the "kulak exploiters" by taxation paid by compulsory deliveries and reinforce efforts to organize more efficient large-scale state and collective farms.

Advocates of both of these approaches, however, failed to appreciate fully the residual anxieties about food supply. They also failed to take full account of the cultures underlying the political economy of many villages in which production was still limited by a primary need to ensure their own security rather than accumulating surpluses for the state or to purchase consumer goods of uncertain local value. Since the partial commercialization of Russia's countryside had scarcely advanced during the war, the attraction of consumer goods was almost certainly stronger for those closest to Russia's railroad lines than the countryside as a whole. Without tractors and other modern equipment, rural labor remained arduous, especially for the legion of war widows. Bukharin and other moderates argued that, yes, the party should turn its face to the village, but its face in this respect had to be commodities that would incentivize grain production and encourage peasants, famously, to "get rich!"

Yet for harder-liners in the party, an increase in available commodities would only enrich the still cursed kulaks, the rural stratum even moderate party leaders wanted to erase. It is also hard to imagine that the diverse stratum of the now Soviet countryside—well-off "kulaks" insofar as they could be distinguished from their "middle" and "poor" village comrades and everyone else—could have forgotten the privations and anxieties of a very recent past. One can reasonably presume that this was especially the case for peasant war widows, as the later *babi bunty*—"women's' protests"—suggest. One can also reasonably assume that in some sense peasant sensibilities *had* to be defensive against any semblance of their recurrence from a still deeply antagonistic regime. Social tensions and sensibilities could hardly have healed a scant three or four years after the brutal experiences of 1918–22.

When incentives to villagers to join new and more efficient state and collective farms were resisted, and higher procurement prices and additional commodities failed to increase food supplies, the celebration of the Bolshevik Revolution's tenth anniversary was clouded by the need again for rationing. Trotsky now tried to take advantage of Moscow workers' anxieties to mobilize them against Stalin, violating the Tenth Party Congress strictures against "factionalism." In the view of many, whether or not they were active supporters of Stalin, the party's political position seemed increasingly unstable. When it was clear in late 1927 that grain exports for the year would only be some 200,000 tons compared to 9 million tons in 1913, it seemed obvious to leading party figures like Aleksei Rykov, the chair of the Sovnarkom, that the NEP was not working and that something had to be done. At the same time, it also seemed obvious that ending NEP would be a socioeconomic and political disaster.

A year later there was an even deeper concern that (Soviet) Russia was again "on the brink of catastrophe." As rationing was finally introduced, some feared discontent in the cities. Others worried about the possibility once more of a large peasant uprising as militant confiscations of grain were imposed again. As the "procurement crisis" worsened in 1929, *Pravda* called for "extreme" (*chrezvychainye*) measures, evoking the need for more force and stirring up the still robust memories of struggles less than ten years earlier.[6] Apparently believing strongly in the efficacy of class war as a necessary means to construct Soviet socialism, Stalin marked the anniversary of November 7, 1929, by announcing the "Great Turn": a massive effort to create state and collective farms that would bring all of agrarian production under party control. The "kulaks" would be "liquidated as a class," even if many labeled in this way were those who had worked especially hard to prosper in response to the party's own injunctions. The rallying cry of 'To the Grain Front!' soon mobilized the brigade of the "Twenty Five Thousanders," as it was called, and many thousands more: workers who joined the OGPU forces in surrounding and attacking villages, driving "kulaks" out, and seizing total control of agrarian production. Again, as between 1916 and 1921, the "solution" to insecurities over grain and other foodstuffs was their forceful confiscation, this time augmented by a full-throated declaration of war ostensibly on the "kulaks" but in effect on the peasantry as a whole. By late 1929 the final phase of Soviet Russia's long Civil War had begun.

Stalin's Assaults and Soviet "Redemption"

The three years or so after the initiation of "forced draft" collectivization and industrialization were again tumultuous. They were also deadly for much of the

---

[6] *Pravda*, Feb. 3, 1929.

countryside and especially for Ukraine and parts of Kazakhstan, as Lynne Viola and others have described in frightening detail.[7] So destructive was the "war against the kulaks," as it was described, that Stalin tried at one point to contain it by warning against enthusiasts becoming "dizzy with success" as they quickly exceeded the initial 25 percent target for collective farms. On the "Grain Front," however, the "troops" could not be contained. On orders from Moscow the cities and other parts of Ukraine were soon sealed off. So were sections of Kazakhstan. So much grain was confiscated that both regions in 1932 experienced horrific man-made famines. No relief efforts were allowed. The resulting scenes were as terrible as those in 1920-21, if not more so. Careful estimates suggest that at least 1.2 million peasants died in Kazakhstan, some 29 percent of the population. The figures for Ukraine were substantially higher, possibly as many as 5 million. Peasants themselves destroyed their entire holdings of pigs, cows, and other livestock so the party-state would not get them.

As with the description of earlier traumas, they require literary gifts like those of Vasili Grossman and V. F. Tendriakov to evoke the suffering and despair, the physical and emotional losses Stalin and his supporters had inflicted:

> The "grasping kulaks" did not have enough possessions to fill them so they went off in half-empty carts. The kulaks from our village, on the other hand, were sent out on foot. They took only what they could carry on their own backs—blankets and clothing. The mud was so deep it kept sucking their boots off their feet. It was a terrible sight. There was a whole column of them, and they kept looking around at their huts [where] they had been born. And what did we care. We were—activists. We could just as easily [have] been driving a flock of geese down the road. . . . Soon they were taken to the station where empty freight wagons were waiting. . . . People whispered "there go the kulaks." It was as if they were talking about wolves. Some even shouted out curses at them but the prisoners were no longer weeping, their faces were like stone.[8]

And then, inevitably, after seeds were eaten, planting disrupted, and the countryside as a whole in turmoil, the agonies of starvation again, especially in Kazakhstan and Ukraine (the *Holodomor*), this time the direct result not of war and revolution but of Stalinist state policy:

---

[7] Lynne Viola, *Peasant Rebels under Stalin: Collectivization and the Culture of Peasant Resistance* (New York: Oxford University Press, 1996) and *Best Sons of the Fatherland: Workers in the Vanguard of Soviet Collectivization* (New York: Oxford University Press, 1987) and her edited volume *The War against the Peasantry 1927-1940: The Tragedy of the Soviet Countryside*, trans. Steven Shabad (New Haven, CT: Yale University Press, 2005); Anne Applebaum, *Red Famine: Stalin's War on Ukraine* (London: Allen Lane, 2017).

[8] Vasili Grossman, *Vse techet* (Frankfurt, 1970), 119-20, translated as *Everything Flows* by Robert Chandler and Elizabet Chandler (New York; NLRB, 2009), 120-21.

In the area around Petrovskaia, cattle were not fed and died, people ate bread made from nettles, *kolobashki* [small rolls] made from weeds.... And not only around Petrovskaia. Hunger spread throughout the whole country—nineteen thirty three. Near the station in Vokhrovo, the district center, peasants from the Ukraine cast out as kulaks lay down and died. One got used to seeing their bodies there in the morning.... Not all died. Many wandered through the dusty little streets dragging their bloodless, swollen blue legs, begging each passer-by with doglike eyes. In Vokhrovo they got nothing.[9]

Unlike the world war and first phases of the Civil War, however, the enormous losses and dislocations inflicted on the peasants now found what many in and outside the party thought to be a tenable rationalization: the Soviet Union was still encircled by hostile powers. If the carnage inflicted on Russian workers and peasants between 1914 and 1918 was due to the exploitative tsarist state's own "backwardness," forced draft industrialization—the "five year plan in four years" and total state control over production—was historically necessary if Soviet Russia was not again to be "beaten for its backwardness," as Stalin put it in a famous speech in 1931, arguing against those in the party leadership who thought the pace needed to be slowed.

Whether this rhetorical flourish carried much weight as the Soviet countryside was turned upside down is unclear. (It certainly did not quiet an increasingly active opposition to Stalin or garner him the most leadership votes at the party congress in 1934.) And if the pace could not be slackened, neither could the peasants' fury: "In two nights the [number of] cattle in our village was reduced by half.... 'Kill, it's not ours now! Kill! They'll take [it] from you if you don't.' Kill! You'll never taste meat in the collective farm!" The response was equally forceful: "They are slaughtering the livestock, those bastards. They'll choke themselves on meat rather than hand them over to the collective farm. I say we must hold a meeting, pass a resolution, and ask permission to shoot them.... Shoot them I say! Whose permission do we need? We must act with utmost severity."[10]

Increasingly, however, as Hitler consolidated his power, began to populate new concentration camps first with German communists and then with Jews— an overlapping category, in his view—and then thumbed his nose at France and Britain by sending his troops to reoccupy the demilitarized Rhineland, the danger of Russia again being "beaten for backwardness" was evident. In this respect, the most persuasive if utterly false justification for the great purge trials in 1936–37 was that virtually all of the accused were part of a German-run

---

[9] V. F. Tendriakov, "*Konchina*" (Death), in *Collected Works*, 4 vols. (Moscow: Khudozhestvennaia Lit., 1980), 4:61–62.
[10] Mikhail Sholokov, *Virgin Soil Upturned*, trans. R. Daglish (Moscow: Foreign Lang. Publ.), 167.

anti-Soviet bloc. The execution of the Civil War hero Tukhashevskii in 1938 was the apogee of the "Great Terror," the personal suspicions of the Best Friend of the People augmented by a now paranoiac fear of enemies and rivals. Yet after the Munich Pact and Germany's seizure of the Sudetenland from Czechoslovakia, it was hard to deny that Soviet Russia was in real danger, as Hitler had outlined in detail in *Mein Kampf*. For hard-core Stalinists, at least, this may have translated into a belief that only the Great Leader's foresight in demanding full-throttle industrialization created at least the possibility that Soviet Russia could withstand a German onslaught. In the process, the enormous material and individual losses of both the earlier and the last stages of Soviet Russia's civil wars were for them, at least, officially redeemed. Certainly after Hitler invaded in June 1941, the large industrial complexes constructed during the first five-year plans came to play a vital role in securing the Soviets' key victories: at the gates of Moscow, in the harrowing success at Stalingrad, and in the stunning defeat of German armor by Stalin T34 tanks at Kursk. Repressions within the army of failed officers and unreliable soldiers continued unabated, but from this point forward in 1943 the Kremlin sounded victory chimes with each successive advance, up to and including the Red Army's capture of Berlin in 1945 before it could be taken by British and American troops. With victory, Stalin and Stalinism became the sole heirs of the European totalitarian impulses spawned at least in some ways by revolutionary Russia itself.

Loss and Scarcity after the "Great Patriotic Struggle"

While their effects are still under researched, it is hard to imagine that the horrors and anxieties of scarcity and the traumas and sufferings of loss were not dominant emotional fields as well in the aftermath of the USSR's Great Patriotic War for the Fatherland. As in 1914, the terminology itself signified universal patriotism, whatever the actualities. The "Hero Cities" Leningrad and Stalingrad were now places of nightmarish memory and the traumas of survival as well as official monuments to resilience and sacrifice. According to the best approximations, Soviet Russia suffered more than twice as many soldiers killed in battle or who died from their wounds (10+ million) than all the other combatants combined, including Germany and Japan. Civilian deaths are estimated to have been around 7 million, compared to 800,000 in Germany and 700,000 in Japan. The actual figures may well be higher.[11]

---

[11] "Costs of the War," Britannica, accessed June 26, 2023, https://www.britannica.com/event/World-War-II/Costs-of-the-war.

EPILOGUE: SCARCITY, LOSS, AND SOVIET HISTORY

These losses could be rationalized, of course, as the necessary costs of defeating the Nazi invader, however many were the result of Stalin's and his commanders' wanton disregard for casualties. They officially validated in victory the party-state's institutions and Stalinist policies. Victory and survival, doubtful to many in 1941 after the decimations and dislocations of 1930, hardly were reason to change the Soviet Union's historical course. By the summer of 1943, almost a year before the D-Day landings, victory chimes sounded from the Kremlin after every reported success and broadcast across the country even as massive losses continued.

How stunning it must have been for so many—if "stunning" is even an adequate descriptor—that the euphoria of victory was so quickly buried by continued hunger, deprivation, goods deficits, and ferocious repression. Reconstruction was a herculean task. Material scarcities and their insecurities were both consequences now of the costs of victory as well as (or more so) the inherent difficulties of efficient economic planning. Personal accounts also detail the shock and grief for soldiers and their families when many were sent to "rehabilitation" camps for the crime of having been prisoners of war, being too friendly toward the Soviet Union's allies, or otherwise "unreliable." Less than twenty-five years since the enormous losses and deprivations of Russia's long world war and a scant ten years from the end of the long Civil War, a now deeply embedded culture of surveillance, denunciation, and nearly absolute dictatorship swept tens of thousands of Soviet innocents to the privations and traumas of NKVD camps. Confiscation, repression, and violence continued to center the technologies of Soviet rule.

Studies focusing primarily on the politics of the mad years before Stalin's death in 1953 understandably describe his and his regime's concerns about the disparity the U.S. atomic bomb created in the Soviet Union's military strength in a still confrontational world order. An essential part of this dismal moment in Soviet history was the well-known repression of artists, scholars, and intellectuals like Alexander Solzhenitsyn and Dmitri Shostakovich as well as those like Foreign Minister Molotov's wife, Polina Zhemchuzhina. Part of the political story is the regime's move once again against the peasantry as a whole, now incorporated by force into the collective and state farm system and bound to them as prisoners are bound to their jailers. Scarcities and food insecurity were everywhere in the aftermath of the war. Famine ran again through the countryside, now fully subordinated to the rigorous control of state and collective farms. When the regime devalued the ruble by a ratio of 1 to 10 in 1948 while holding prices steady, whatever savings anyone may have been able to accumulate in case of need were suddenly wiped out. Again, we have no clear measurements, but it is safe to say that when Stalin died on March 5, 1953, the actualities, anxieties, insecurities, and traumas of loss and scarcity were again the dominant elements of Soviet subjective life.

Challenges and Adaptations: Reform, Stability, and Stagnation

Whether or not this weighed on Georgy Malenkov, Nikita Khrushchev, and other members of the Politburo in terms of popular welfare, the party's political security, or (most likely) both, it is not surprising in retrospect that after the "cold summer of '53" and the arrest and quick execution of Lavrenti Beria, the party leadership swung toward relieving scarcities and relaxing the lethal grasp Beria's NKVD had on Soviet society. By now its apparatus reached into every corner of Soviet life. It reflected the worst of Stalinist excesses in its brutal rule over the Gulag of forced labor camps as well as its midnight raids and sadistic torture in the name of domestic security. Surveillance and denunciation remained the norm inside the party and out. "The party is always right," Trotsky himself had averred at the Thirteenth Party Congress in 1924 in his famous affirmation of the Bolshevik and now Soviet Great Story, "because the party is the single historical instrument given to the proletariat for the solution of its fundamental problems. . . . I know that one must not be right against the party. One can be right only with the party, and through the party, for history has created no other road for the realization of what is right."[12] For those subscribing to this belief, ideological conviction continued to defend against social, economic, and especially psychological dislocations.

In the event, the processes of improving social welfare and relaxing repression began immediately after Stalin's death: the decree on amnesty (March 27); the cut in retail prices (April 1), and the release of the doctors denounced by Dr. Lydia Tymashuk and arrested for plotting Stalin's murder. (Tymashuk even had to return the Order of Lenin awarded for her service as an accuser.) In May wheat flour was placed on daily sale in state markets for the first time since the war. Less than three months later the Council of Ministers announced revisions to the current Five-Year Plan. Production of clothing would be increased 240 percent, of meat and butter, 230 percent and 180 percent, among other dramatic changes. A year later Khrushchev opened with equal fanfare the "virgin lands" in Kazakhstan to new grain production, offering incentives especially to younger agricultural workers to "go east."

Meanwhile, the gates of the Gulag were opened for the legions of those falsely accused or brutally incarcerated in the labor death camps, soon vividly described for Soviet readers by Solzhenitsyn in *One Day in the Life of Ivan Denisovich*. While the Gulag persisted, many who were executed or died the slow death of the camps were rehabilitated, a form of "redemption" that scarcely alleviated the deep residues of anxiety, hostility, and trauma. Uncountable numbers of those

---

[12] *XIII S"ezd rossiiskoi kommunisticheskoi partii: Stenograficheskii otchet* (Moscow, 1924), 166–67.

who survived were given small sums of money and left to find their way back to their former homes and families. The agonies of this process have been brilliantly described again by Grossman in *Everything Flows* (*Vse Techet*): the failure of family members or former friends to recognize those incarcerated many years earlier, or those released to recognize their families; the realization that wives, husbands, or loved ones who had stopped writing had found other partners rather than died; the incomprehension and disorientation that made new freedoms, so longed for during so many years, difficult to manage emotionally as well as in material terms. In his impressive study *Warped Mourning* Alexander Etkind describes this as mutual misrecognition.[13] Among its other tragic attributes was a complex combination of loss, mourning, longing, and regret that likely still characterized the emotional life of many in the immediate post-Stalin generation, now perhaps also encouraged at last by hope for material betterment and the possibility of some degree of personal security.

Khrushchev is rightly remembered for his remarkable political reforms. His denunciation of Stalin in his famous "Secret Speech" was an act of global importance. Transforming the terrorizing NKVD into a more palatable Committee on State Security (KGB) responsible to the Council of Ministers was a forceful political act designed to eliminate everyday fears in and outside the party. While surveillance and labor camps were still a brutal means of political control, the effort in 1957 and 1958 to engage broad publics in discussion of state policies and potential reforms signified an effort to incorporate some sort of political "democratization" within the party. And hardly least, the cultural thaw and the embrace of "peaceful coexistence" with the United States and other noncommunist states moved the world politically away from the possibility of thermonuclear war. By 1959, after his famous "Kitchen Debate" with Richard Nixon and the launch of the world's first orbiting satellite, Khrushchev announced with great fanfare the USSR's first Seven-Year Plan. Based, among other things, on the expected output from Kazakhstan, it was designed to overtake and "bury" the United States and the West in the production of butter, wheat, meat, and other foodstuffs. Scarcities and their anxieties would finally come to an end, the material well-being of the Soviet Great Story finally realized.

For his efforts, however, which dissolved the reputations of Stalinist loyalists and whose new promises seemed unrealistic to many charged with carrying them out, Khrushchev also faced strong opposition. Stalinists who formed an "anti-party bloc" with Molotov (now officially reunited with his wife) were perhaps undone more by the truth-telling of their own involvement in the pains of collectivization, their support and participation in Stalin's vicious and irrational

[13] Alexander Etkind, *Warped Mourning: Stories of the Undead in the Land of the Unburied* (Stanford, CA: Stanford University Press, 2018).

purges, and the desacralization of Stalin's and his paramount role in World War II as by the loss of their own authority. There were also the challenges of Hungarians and Poles to oust their own Stalinist leaderships in 1956, and by those there and elsewhere wary of more internal dissidence. Indeed, Khrushchev's political skills, his reforms, his willingness to crush the insipient revolutions in the Soviet satellites, and the popular support for his insistent promises of material betterment kept him in power far longer than any of his comrades might have expected in 1953.

What greatly undermined Khrushchev, at least before the Cuban missile crisis in 1963, was the near total failure of the Seven-Year Plan, and the consequent step backward toward an all too familiar austerity. The plan was based largely on assumptions about the continued productivity of the Virgin Lands. It was also supported by the relatively successful turn to plastics and consumer goods in the preceding Five-Year Plan and encouraged by Khrushchev's personal belief in the real possibility of "overtaking the West." As events turned out, the plan was introduced on the eve of a major drought in the Kazakhstan-Altai region, the second since the Virgin Lands were first sown in 1954. Lives of the settlers were disrupted; many left the region. After poor harvests in 1961 and 1962, the harvests of 1963 were a disaster. Almost overnight, Soviet Russia became a major importer of grain, reversing the country's long-term historical position.

Already in 1962 higher prices for meat, butter, and other commodities along with a deep cut in wages prompted a bloody protest by industrial workers in Novocherkassk. When the local party headquarters was attacked, Khrushchev joined those who insisted on its quick and forceful repression. (Solzhenitsyn later claimed the incident was "a major turning point in Soviet history.")[14] At that very moment Soviet planners were flirting with the hitherto counterrevolutionary idea of introducing measurements of profit as a basis for allocating state finances and other resources. (The Kharkiv economist Evsei Liberman even graced the cover of *Time* magazine as an advocate of this radical change, a harbinger of a return to markets and the possible demise of the whole command economy system.)[15]

As we know, the Cuban missile crisis shortly thereafter sealed Khrushchev's political fate. Aleksei Kosygin as premier and Leonid Brezhnev as the party's general secretary replaced him at first as relative equals politically, but after the military intervention to suppress Alexander Dubcek's "socialism with a human face" during the Prague Spring of 1968, Brezhnev became ascendant. Holding

---

[14] Aleksandr Solzhenitsyn, *The Gulag Archipelago*, 3 vols., trans. T. P. Whitney (New York: Harper & Row, 1978), 3:507.
[15] "The Communist Flirtation with Profits," *Time*, Feb. 12, 1965.

power for eighteen years, the "man of peace," as recent historians have called him, presided over increasing economic stagnation, the period of the *zastoi*: marginal growth, consumer products of poor quality in high demand, a measurably inferior economy to that even of reform-minded Hungary, and, through the now inevitable contacts with the prosperous West, a clear sense especially among the new postwar generation of the obvious inferiority of Soviet socialism in securing the material well-being and security still centering the communist historical imagination. Although vastly better than the Stalinist years, limited choice and scarcities, stagnation (*zastoi*) and insecurities remained embedded in the Soviet economy. So did their emotional states. Together with the unredeemed losses of Stalin's uncountable victims, they shaped the remaining years of the Soviet system.

Archiving the Soviet Great Story

As we have described, all three of what we have called the Great Stories of revolutionary Russia were founded on the teleological idea that history moved in a progressive direction, that socioeconomic progress was best achieved through the rational application of state policies. The liberal and moderate social democratic stories also linked rational progress to the recognition of basic civil rights championed by the French and American revolutions, at least for white men. The inscription of these ideas and rights in constitutional forms were a guideline to constructing institutions that ensured a progressive future of individual and collective well-being. Progress toward that future in both these Great Stories was contingent. Any number of natural or man-made events could throw history off course if they presented social or economic problems that rational policies were unable to resolve, or alternative historical imaginations that defined a radiant future in different terms.

In its essence, the Soviet Great Story was this alternative. It embraced progress and rationality but attached them teleologically to the notion of historical inevitability. Rational policies *could* resolve fundamental social and economic problems, even as "rational" here embraced the use of violent force against exploitative institutions and social groups that allowed those with power and relative wealth to dominate those who produced it, expropriating their labor and its products. There was no question in the minds of Lenin and his supporters that this was history's determined course. It formed the core of Leninist-Bolshevik ideology. So did the idea that only a rational and politically conscious party could ensure history moved properly in its foreordained direction. The conceptual trap Trotsky and others found themselves in as Stalin consolidated his dictatorial hold was not only that history "knew no other path for the realization of the right," but that one could not therefore admit that history's chosen instrument, the party, could be wrong.

What distinguished the Great Soviet Story, in other words, was that history itself legitimized the party, rather than (or some would say in addition to) its concepts, institutions, or beliefs. The affirmation of legitimacy thus required its constant retelling and popular internalization regardless of current actualities: the material well-being and collective security promised by an inevitable radiant future. Even at the height of the purges in 1936 Stalin could declare, "Life has become more joyous, comrades," and foster an elaborate constitution whose institutions, rights, and assertions of social well-being were putatively tied to the eventual achievement of communism.

As irrefutably correct, the Great Soviet Story also had to be protected from those who might document its falsifications. If history (or History) was the fundamental basis of the Communist Party's political legitimacy and hence its right to power, alternative narratives in and of themselves were seditious. After the well-publicized trials of historians in the late 1920s, the party's message was crystal clear. Historical scholarship in its formal sense could be practiced only on the prerevolutionary period, and even then on various "exploiters" and institutions of "exploitation," even if they were identified as such only in introductions and conclusions along with the obligatory citations to Lenin.[16]

One can posit that the "party is always right" component of the Great Soviet Story was dealt a fatal blow with Khrushchev's "Secret Speech" and that the processes of de-Stalinization in the 1960s were further blown open by the brilliant interventions of Solzhenitsyn, Roy and Zhores Medvedev, and other well-known dissidents. Yet the continued deprivations of "stagnation"—the perpetual material shortages and their accompanying anxieties—increasingly eroded the party-state's legitimizing claims that it was leading citizens of the Soviet Empire to the securities of material abundance, that the arrival of communism as history's final stage would bring what generations had hoped for before and after 1917. As with each successive regime after 1914, loss and scarcity proved problems Soviet governance also could not solve. Loss justified in the name of defending the possibilities of a radiant future carried less and less weight, especially after the invasion of Afghanistan. The great Soviet locomotive was *not* pulling the new empire toward material and emotional well-being.

Politics and ideology obviously mattered greatly to the ways great events between 1914 and 1922 developed, as well as to their aftermath. Politics and ideologies are readily documented. They are convincing in part because their particular narratives give coherent meaning to experience. Experience here is best understood not in the ways many historians tend to essentialize it as some

---

[16] *Akademicheskoe Delo, 1929–1931 gg.*, 2 vols. (St. Petersburg: Nauka, 1993–98).

rock-bottom foundation of historical "reality"—"I lived through that, so I know what it was about"—but as that range of emotions, perceptions, and feelings that are inherently difficult to understand and describe, lack clear evidence, or even in the case of great (traumatic) loss are literally *indescribable*.

What this volume has hoped to show is that in addition to politics and ideologies, central to understanding Russia's revolutions and their legacies are the social and economic contexts and practices through which the event of "revolution" was also constituted: degrees and effects of scarcity and urgent material need; institutionalized as well as informal violence; social dislocation and the inscription of positive and negative social identities; and the deprivations and insecurities of loss in all of its various (and uniformly awful) dimensions. By 1922, when the USSR was formally constituted on December 30, the sense of insecurity and grief this experience involved may fairly be said to have been virtually universal throughout the new Soviet Empire. It also gained official meaning through its telling and retelling, the quest of many for explanation and coherence. With its core trope of a radiant future, it also linked individual and collective experience to political, social, and ideological values, a social process of accessing and connecting—of "re-membering" in the literal sense of putting together the disjointed incoherencies of what had happened and creating a prescriptive Soviet social memory.

In all these respects archives became vital to how the story was told, both as figurative repositories of uncovered individual memories, as Jacques Derrida has described in *Archive Fever*, and as the physical repositories where historical artifacts were processed into historical truths by appraisal, selection, categorization, and restrictive access.[17] As history itself ostensibly legitimized Bolshevik and Soviet power, the role of archives became central to ensuring the validity of the Great Soviet Story itself. Lenin himself understood this very well. On June 1, 1918, he personally signed a decree establishing the Central Soviet Archival Administration. All documentary materials from all public and private institutions immediately became the property of the state, their administration subject to party-state control. Independent institutional archives were formally abolished and thenceforth illegal. So was the unauthorized destruction of documentary records. These decisions could be made only by state-appointed "scientific managers" who knew what history was really about. The training of new archivists was to begin immediately. A modern, Soviet Russia was to have a modern, total archive, totally controlled. The training school in Moscow was soon producing hundreds of archivists, growing their number to the largest in the world.

---

[17] Jacques Derrida, *Mal d'archive* (Paris: Galilée, 1995).

The production of an "authentic" and historically "legitimating" revolutionary story was thus molded from the start. As we know, the Soviet National Archive became the Central State Archive of the October Revolution, signifying by archival definition that the nation's future as well as its past would be a narrative of the "unfolding" of the revolution itself. (In the United States, by contrast, a national archive designed to hold "the nation's memory" was not established until 1934.) Only trustworthy, scientific researchers would be allowed in to reference, if not explore more fully, its documentary residues. As Stalin consolidated his power, any materials that mentioned him or Lenin were labeled "top secret" or "especially valuable." Repositories also validated the Great Soviet Story by the very way documents were ordered and catalogued by the categories the Story itself provided, verifying its truth claims by abundant and precise citations that could not be confirmed. In a great paradox of Soviet "historical science" (*istoricheskaia nauka*), the "authentically" documented Great Soviet narrative could only be accepted on faith.

At least until Gorbachev came to power in 1985 and Russia's second great twentieth-century revolution began. While there were many reasons for his heroic efforts—the last chapter of the Great Soviet Story—they began as the narrative itself became an increasingly unconvincing depiction of both the really lived past and a historically determined future. In essence, *perestroika* might be considered the final legacy of Russia's long world war and Revolution: the acknowledgment that something had gone fundamentally wrong—not in the ways the Bolsheviks coming to power had engaged deep hopes of an end to material and emotional deprivation or the eventual redemption of loss in Soviet abundance and security, but in the legitimization of the entire Soviet project by history itself, and *only* by history itself. In increasingly clear comparisons with the capitalist and imperialist West, the monopoly of Soviet power seemed to betray the way history actually worked, undermining the legitimating elements of its formal historical logic. The scarcities, anxieties, and traumatic losses experienced by the Soviet people did not immediately have to do with the pervasive crisis of the 1914–22 period and the institutionalization of dictatorial power. They rapidly led in that direction, however, as Soviet structures were reexamined in relation to those of the "decadent" but increasingly obvious material abundance and relative personal security of the West.

By the time Gorbachev brought the dissident physicist Andrei Sakharov back to Moscow the connections were unbreakable. The overwhelming mood (*nastroenie*) of the population—of such importance to tsarist and Soviet authorities—was once again one of great hope and expectation. In cities like Moscow and Leningrad, locals experienced the promise of "revolutionary democracy" both metaphysically and literally by access to a Big Mac in a friendly place with the cleanest bathrooms in the country, where one could sit and talk freely at least for a little while. In these heady conditions, it was only a matter of time before access to the archives opened as well. Soviet rule had gotten history entirely wrong. The great October revolutionary narrative needed a scholarly *perestroika* of its own.

Why and how things soon went terribly wrong again are reasonably well known. ("Everything was forever until it was no more," as Alexei Yurchak has described the experience of the last Soviet generation.)[18] In the first years of post-Soviet Russia, there was really no possibility that the material well-being envisioned by the dissolution of the command economy could be quickly produced by a market system. Nor could viable democratic political institutions be readily constructed in ways that controlled the corrupt sell-off of Soviet industries, the wealth of the Soviet state, or rampant corruption. The Western liberal belief that markets would regulate prices fairly and the absence of enforceable laws and administrative regulations increasingly nourished resistance. Markets are notoriously inequitable ways of distributing goods and services in conditions of great scarcity and social inequality. The mediating qualities that might adequately manage the distribution of goods in times of prosperity simply do not work in ways commonly perceived as equitable when needed goods are held back until prices rise or are otherwise beyond ordinary reach. Thus, while post-Soviet deficits in foodstuffs and other essential goods began to disappear, "shock therapy" affected different sectors of the population in very different ways. For many, if not most, it came with great costs, some soon obvious, some more subtle and with their own long-term consequences.

Obvious enough was the effect of scarcities and unrestrained markets on prices, just as between 1914 and 1917, especially for the elderly, the poor, and the unemployed or unemployable. Health and welfare again suffered as support from the new politically democratic state declined. Many respected professions were suddenly less attractive. Youngsters were soon earning far more working in kiosks and new luxury stores than their parents were earning as engineers and scholars. All over the territories officially liberated from economic exploitation, the privatization of property was rightly perceived as a form of theft. Homeless people—"persons without an official place to live," or *bomzhi*—soon occupied city sidewalks and underground passages.

The very generation of wealth itself bred criminality and self-styled mafia gangs. By the end of the 1990s, life expectancy in Russia ranked 135th in the world. Only 25 percent of all children were born healthy; 85 percent of the population was unable to pay for adequate medical care. Again, in the historian Kliuchevskii's words, those with access to state power and wealth "rose up" while the people "shrank." As

---

[18] Alexei D. Yurchak, *Everything Was Forever, Until It Was No More* (Princeton, NJ: Princeton University Press, 2005).

Vladimir Putin succeeded Boris Yeltsin in 2000, between 40 and 50 percent of the country was living below the national poverty line, officially set at $36 per month. Seven out of ten considered themselves impoverished. The average monthly wage was $63, including those months that payments weren't made. The average pension was $21, well below the level of subsistence.[19] "Democratic" access to social security and material well-being was far beyond the reach of the vast majority.

Were scarcity and loss then also embedded in Putin's post-Soviet state and political economy? Were the aspirations for civil liberties and democratic practices of the revolutionary period now also locked up in a figurative sense in the archives, along with their documentation? To begin to answer such questions, answers which can only be hinted at here, one needs first to disaggregate "Russia" into its principal component socioeconomic parts. The experience of the younger generation coming to age in the late 1980s and 1990s was radically different from their parents'. The group DDT sang "Prosvitela" ([A Girl Comes] Whistling By) and "Svoboda" (Freedom) together with thousands of ecstatic swaying youth and Boris Gribenchikov's "Aquarium" went the equivalent of viral with their video of the Soviet locomotive leading Russia to catastrophe "as they told us lies about the future."[20]

Here we can identify the younger generation's embrace of civil liberties and freedoms that contrast with the dislocation and loss many of their parents experienced when the values of their own lifetimes suddenly disappeared. In this loss, compounded now by the dead and wounded from what many saw as the meaningless war in Afghanistan, one can understand what Serguei Oushakine has deftly called the "patriotism of despair": an attachment to an increasingly venal and autocratic state that promised stability and order.[21] The nostalgia here was most likely for the familiar world of Brezhnev's orderly stagnation and the feelings of purpose that the late Soviet system still embraced. Their loss for many of the older generations was real and significant, however the party dictatorship circumscribed individual freedom, and must certainly have been amplified by the scarcities and deprivations of the 1990s, with its own pervasive anxieties. For many who managed to make it through these years, the promises reflected in "democracy" of material betterment and personal security remained largely or entirely unrealized.

---

[19] Murray Feshbach, "Russia's Population Meltdown," *Wilson Quarterly* 25 (Winter 2000): 15–21; *Profil* No. 7, 2000 as cited in Johnson's Russian List #4170 (Mar. 15, 2000) at https://russialist.org/archives/.

[20] Concert videos can be seen using these URLs: *Prosvitela*, https://www.youtube.com/watch?v=L4_LCUhO7Yw; *Svoboda*, https://www.youtube.com/watch?v=IQudzsWbgy4; *Locomotive in the Fire*, https://youtu.be/v3RQ6x9qD8w.

[21] Serguei Oushakine, *The Politics of Despair: Nation, War, and Loss in Russia* (Ithaca, NY: Cornell University Press, 2009).

It was logical in these conditions that Putin, trained and nurtured in the KGB, should cultivate a new oligarchic autocracy from the start. Formally described as a restoration of law and order, the Putin state demanded loyalty in return for legitimizing the theft that made oligarchs fantastically rich. It may still have been a surprise to them and many others when Putin occupied Ukraine and annexed Crimea, even a shock when his army invaded Ukraine itself in 2022. Yet too much was now at stake for both his oligarchic loyalists and those patriots of despair described by Oushakine to risk the repressions of protest or the possible dislocations of regime change. Labor camps still functioned, if not the torture camps of high Stalinism. The experience of scarcities before and after the Soviet Union collapsed restrained any inclination to reject Putin's efforts to overcome "the greatest geopolitical catastrophe of the twentieth century," as he called the collapse of the Soviet Union and set his goals with Imperial Russia as his model.

In the process, loved ones were being sacrificed for the ambitions of the Putin state rather than any internalized values or the needs of defense. Determining whether and how the traumas of loss from the invasions of Ukraine affected the Russian Federation's future remains a critical historical task. So does understanding the effect of scarcities engendered by isolation and the country's new international status as a pariah. The same must be said by the great exodus of thousands of the country's well-educated and talented younger generations who, like the deserting soldiers in the First World War, could only vote with their feet. The tragic devastation the Putin state inflicted on Ukraine, like that of Stalin's state on Soviet peasants, again demands explication and redemption.

In 2022, however, there was no promise of a radiant future that rationalized the pain, nor any external military threat to be countered lest Russia once again be beaten for its backwardness. Increasingly, the memory of Russia's revolutionary past, with its conflicting hopes and agonies, was again locked up in the archives, not so much in terms of access (although this again was restricted as Putin rewrote its past) but what historians in the Academy of Science institutes were able to research and publish without discrimination. A careful examination of the collaborationist Vlasov and Soviet POWs fighting with the Germans cost a young historian his position. Key elements of the Great Soviet Story like Stalin's victories in World War II were resurrected along with tsarist imperial ambitions, now, however, devoid of the ideological cores of either.

We should not exaggerate the effects of scarcity and loss in the transition from Gorbachev's *perestroika* to Putin's authoritarianism. Nor should we underestimate the role of politics and ideologies during these turbulent years or during the whole revolutionary period and its Soviet aftermath. Yet just as earlier, scarcity and loss clearly affected the counterrevolutions in political and cultural thinking and practice that marked successive authoritarian regimes during and after revolutionary Russia and its Soviet aftermath. By 2022, again just as earlier, they also underlay the vicious efforts of a dictatorship's own historical imagination and its new Great Story to drastically reconstruct Russia's politics, economy, and culture, this time to restore the tsarist and Soviet imperial empires and again through violent force, atrocity, and indescribable suffering somehow make Great Russia great again.

Bibliography

Archives

Central State Archive for the Moscow Region (TsGA MO)

f. 146 Labor Section of the Moscow Soviet 1918–20.
f. 180 Moscow Provincial Soviet of Trade Unions 1917–19.
f. 4612 Moscow Province Revolutionary Tribunal 1918.
f. 4613 Moscow Revolutionary Tribunal 1917–18.

Central State Archive of St. Petersburg (TsGA SPb)

f. 101 Executive Committee of Petrograd District Soviet, Oct. 1917–Apr. 1918. Protocols and Correspondence.
f. 143 Cheka (ChK) Jan.–July 1918; Committee for the Fight against Counterrevolution and Speculation Apr.–July 1918.
f. 1000 Stenograms and other accounts of meetings with soldiers working in factories. 1918.
f. 1446 Sormovo. Reports, correspondence. 1917–18.
f. 2995 Protocols and materials of the Cheka 1920–21.
f. 3390 Sobranie Upolnomochennykh. Protocols, ankety, enterprise lists. 1918.
f. 4591 Leningrad Committee of Trade 1917–21.
f. 8098 Cheka. Union of Communists of the Northern Region 1919–21.
f. 9618 Materials on Counterrevolution in Petrograd July 30–Dec. 28 1918.

Central State Historical Archive for Leningrad Oblast (TsGIA-LO)

f. 87 Strikes and Protests by Workers in Petrograd 1921.
f. 457 Bolshevik faction, Petrograd Province, Soviet of Trade Unions 1919–20.
f. 1264 Mechanical Plant Vulcan. 1917–18.
f. 1296 Peter the Great Arsenal. 1917–18.
f. 1440 Franko-Russian Plant 1918.
f. 1446 Sormovo Plant Materials 1918.
f. 1488 Hartman Machine Construction Plant 1918.

Russian State Archive of the Economy (RGAE)

f. 1884 Peoples Commissariat of Transport (NKPS). 1920–21.
f. 3429 All-Russia Soviet for the Economy (VSNKh).

Russian State Archive of Sociopolitical History (RGASPI)

f. 5 Secretariat, Soviet of Peoples Commissars (SNK) and the Soviet of Labor and Defense (STO). 1918–21.

f. 17 Central Committee RKP(b). Informotdel and materials sent to the committee. 1918–26.

f. 95 Fraction of the RKP(b) in the All-Russian Soviet of Trade Unions. 1920–21.

f. 97 Fraction of the RKP(b) in the Central Committee of the All-Russian Soviet of Communication Workers. 1918–24.

f. 111 Political Section of the NKPS Administration 1920 (Glavpolitput). 1918–21.

f. 634 Main Political Administration of the NKPS of the Russian Soviet Federated Socialist Republic [RSFSR]. 1919–20.

Russian State Historical Archive (RGIA)

f. 6 Chancellery of the Provisional Government. 1917.

f. 20 Council of Ministers. 1914–17.

f. 23 Ministry of Trade and Industry (MTiP). 1915–17.

f. 27 Committee for the Restoration of Industry of the MTiP. 1917.

f. 31 Committee for the Affairs of the Metallurgical Industry. 1915–18.

f. 32 Council of Congresses of Representatives of Industry and Trade (Soviet S"ezdov). 1915–18.

f. 45 Petrograd Regional War Industry Committee (WIC). 1915–18.

f. 48 Council of Congresses of Ural Region Mining Firms. 1917.

f. 92 Special Council for Fuel of the Ministry of the MTiP (Osotop) 1915–17.

f. 126 All-Russian Union of Factory and Plant Owners. 1917–18.

f. 150 Petrograd Society of Factory and Mill Owners (PSFMO). 1917–18.

f. 244 Committee for the Distribution of Fuel of the Ministry of Transport (MPS). 1915–16.

f. 273 MPS Administration. 1915–17.

f. 280 Central Committee for the Regulation of Transport of the MPS. 1915–17.

f. 290 Management Committee for Railroad Transport. 1915–17.

f. 456 Chancellery of the Main Authority for the Purchase of Grain for the Army. 1915–17.

f. 457 Special Council on Food. 1915–17.

f. 560 General Chancellery of the Ministry of Finance. 1914–18. Protocols of the sessions of its Mediation Committee Feb.–June 1917.

f. 563 State Committee on Finance 1915–17.

f. 565 State Treasury: Journals and Materials. 1915–17.

f. 582 Administration for Short-Term Credit of the State Bank. 1916.

f. 583 Chancellery for Credit of the State Bank. 1913–17.

f. 587 State Bank. 1916–17.

f. 616 Ministry of Finance correspondence and other materials, Mar.–Dec. 1917.

f. 624 Letters on Russia's economy to Citibank, New York, from their representative G. F. Meserve. 1915–17.

f. 626 Petrograd International Bank 1917.
f. 634 Russian Trade Industrial Bank. 1916-17.
f. 651 Papers of Prince Boris Aleksandrovich Vasil'chikov (On the administration of transport for Russian wounded). 1915-16.
f. 777 Petrograd Committee of Press Affairs: Correspondence with the Military Censor. 1914-17.
f. 1063 Papers of Baron M. A. Taube. Diary, 1914.
f. 1088 Papers of S. D. Sheremet'ev (Regarding the state of the army) 1915-16.
f. 1090 Papers of A. I. Shingarev.
f. 1182 Resolutions of "Starving Workers" Aug. 1918.
f. 1235 Protocols and reports on strikes July 1918.
f. 1276 Council of Ministers.
f. 1278 State Duma: Stenographic reports of sessions of the Budget Committee and other materials. 1914-17.
f. 1282 Chancellery of the Ministry of Internal Affairs. 1915-16.
f. 1289 Main Administration of the Ministry of Post and Telegraph. 1915-16.
f. 1292 Main Administration for Matters relating to Obligatory Military Service. 1914-16.
f. 1297 Protocols of Workers Meetings and other materials June 1918.
f. 1405 Ministry of Justice: Reports and accounts. 1914-16.
f. 1571 Papers of A. V. Krivoshein. 1915-16.
f. 1600 Ministry of Labor 1917.
f. 6991 Chancellery of the Ministry of Finance May-Oct 1917.

Russian State Military History Archive (RGVIA)

f. 366 Office of Political Administration, Ministry of War 1917.
f. 369 Special Council for the Unification of Measures to Increase Military Production. Material on labor requisition, labor transport, and other matters. 1915-Feb. 1918.
f. 2003 Staff of the Supreme Military Administration (Stavka) 1916-17. Summaries and citations by military censors Oct. 1915-Feb. 1917; political influence of the Bolsheviks; correspondence relating to transporting wounded.
f. 2004 Administration of the Railroads at Army Headquarters (Stavka) 1917-19. Plekhanov Commission; correspondence on overthrow of provisional government.
f. 2005 Chancellery for Military-Political and Civil Management at Stavka 1914-18. Principal liaison with highest Russian civil institutions after Oct. 1914.
f. 2031 Summaries, excerpts, and observations by military censors 1916.
f. 2048 Summaries, excerpts, and observations by military censors, Nov. 1915-Jan. 1917.
f. 2067 Summaries, excerpts, and observations by military censors, Jan. 1916-Dec. 1917.

State Archive of the Russian Federation (GARF)

f. 6 Chancellery of the Provisional Government. Journals of the Main Economic Committee; correspondence. Mar.–Oct. 1917.

f. 102 Survey of Special Department of Military Censorship 1916.

f. 130 Sovnarkom. Complaints and correspondence 1918; Activities of Glavpolitput; Desertion. 1918–20.

f. 382 Peoples' Commissariat of Labor (NKT). Instructions for accounting and distribution of the workforce; Main Committee for the Introduction of Obligatory Labor [Protocols] 1917–21.

f. 523 Constitutional Democratic Party. 1907–17.

f. 1809 Plekhanov Commission. Materials from the localities Mar.–June 1917.

f. 4085 Peoples' Commissariat of State Control (RKI). Reports from localities; protocols of members of the "Flying Commissions"; fight against absenteeism 1919–21.

f. 4100 Material from various factories and enterprises 1917.

f. 5451 All-Russian Central Council of Trade Unions 1917–21.

f. 5457 Materials of the Trade Union of Textile Workers in Moscow Region 1917–20.

f. 5474 Materials from the Central Committee of Railroad Workers 1919–20.

f. 5498 Plekhanov Commission journals Apr.–Sept. 1917.

f. 5504 Central Committee on Transport (Tsektran) 1920–21.

f. 6751 Council of Labor and Defense (STO) 1920.

f. 6875 Union of Administrative Workers, Moscow district 1917–19.

f. 6935 Committee for the Study of the History of Trade Unions in Russia, All-Russian Central Council of Trade Unions (VTsSPS) 1917–18.

f. 6941 Special Commission on Transport of the STO 1920–21.

f. 6991 Chancellery of the Ministry of Finance, May–Oct. 1917.

f. 6996 Ministry of Finance of the Provisional Government. 1917.

f. 7274 Central Committee of the Struggle with Labor Desertion Feb. 1920–Mar. 1921.

f. 7275 Main Committee for the Implementation of Universal Labor Obligation (GlavKomTrud) 1920.

f. 7327 Committee on the Restoration of Industry Jan. 1916–Nov. 1917.

f. 7952 Materials for the History of the Factories Project 1917–21.

Manuscript Division, State Public Library (SPb)

f. 11152 Fond of K. A. Voenskii. Materials on Central Military Postal Control and other materials. 1914–17.

Bakhmeteff Archive of Russian and East European Culture, Columbia University

Panina File. Kadet Party documents and related materials. 1918–21.

Hoover Collections and Nikolaevskii Archive

Box 8. N. A. DeBasily notes on prewar financial regulation. 1916.
Box 11. S. P. Mel'gunov materials on Bolsheviks in Tsaritsyn and Rostov 1919.
Box 15. F. Golder correspondence on 1922 famine; Kropotkin ms. "In Search of Daily Bread."
Box 217. Materials on Vikzhel, Dec. 1917.
Box 663. Materials relating to the Sobranie Upolnomochennykh 1918; Menshevik meetings.
Box 692. G. Aronson ms. "On the Fate of Russian Trade Unions, 1917-20."
Box 693. Commissar for Transport for Petrograd Naglovskii notes and materials 1918-19; ms. "The Railway Workers in the Russian Revolution" 1943.
Box 779. G. Aronson ms. "On Fate of the Union of Employees, 1997-1920"; ms. S. Shvartz, "Politika zarabotnoi platy v Sov. Rossiii v gody Voenno-Kommunizma."
Ronzhin, S. A. "Zheleznye dorogi v voennoe vremia," Unpubl. ms. 1925.

Newspapers and Journals

Bednota (Moscow), 1918-20.
Biulleten' Ministerstva Truda (Petrograd), 1917.
Biulleten' Narodnogo Komissariata Putei Soobshcheniia (Moscow), 1919-20.
Biulleten' Narodnogo Komissariata Truda (Petrograd-Moscow), 1918.
Birzhevye Vedomosti (Petrograd), 1914-17.
Biulleten' Otdela Statistiki Truda (Petrograd), 1919-20.
Biulleten' Osvedomitel'nyi Otdela Shtaba Verkhovnago Glavnokomanduiushchago (Omsk), 1919.
Biulleten' Vseross: Zheleznodorozhnogo Kongressa (Moscow), 1917.
Bor'ba (Moscow), 1918.
Byloe (Petrograd), 1918.
Delo Naroda (Petrograd), 1917.
Den' (Petrograd), 1915-17.
Ekonomicheskoe Obozrenie. (Moscow), 1916-17.
Ekonomicheskaia Zhizn' (Moscow), 1918-20.
Golos Kozhevnika (Petrograd-Moscow), 1917-18.
Golos Metallista (Kharkov), 1918-19.
Golos Rabotnika (Moscow), 1920.
Golos Zheleznodorozhnika (Moscow), 1917.
Gudok (Moscow), 1920.
Ivanovskii Listok (Ivanovo-Voznesensk), 1916-17.
Izvestiia Glavnogo Ispolniktel'nogo komiteta Moskovsko-Kazanskoi Zh.D. (Moscow), 1917.
Izvestiia Glavnogo Zemel'skogo Komiteta (Petrograd), 1917.
Izvestiia Gosudarstvennogo Kontrolia (Moscow), 1918-19.
Izvestiia Gub. Ispolkom Sovetov Rabochikh, Selianskikh i Krasnoarmeiskikh Deputatov Chernigovshchiny (Chernigov), 1919.

Izvestiia Komitetov Petrogradskikh Zhurnalistov (*Izvestiia Revolutsionnoi Nedeli*) (Petrograd), 1917.
Izvestiia Obshchestva Zavodchikov i Fabrikantov Moskovskogo promyshlennago raiona (Moscow), 1914–17.
Izvestiia Petrogradskogo Soveta Rabochikh i Soldatskikh Deputatov (Petrograd), 1917.
Izvestiia Tsentral'nago Voennoe-promyshlennago Komiteta, 1916–17.
Izvestiia Vysshesgo Soveta Narodnogo Khoziaistva (Moscow), 1918.
Izvestiia Sobraniia Inzhenerov Putei Soobshcheniia. 1917.
Kievskaia Mysl' (Kiev), 1917–18.
Kommuna (Saratov), 1919.
Krasnyi Arkhiv (Moscow).
Krasnyi Put' Zheleznodorozhnika (Moscow), 1918–20.
Moskovskiia Vedomosti (Moscow), 1915–17.
Mysli Zheleznodorozhnika (Petrograd), 1917–18.
Nash Vek (Petrograd), 1917–18.
Nizhegorodskaia Kommuna (Nizhnii-Novgorod), 1918–19.
Nizhegorodskii Listok (Nizhnii-Novgorod), 1917–18.
Narodnoe Khoziaistvo (Moscow), 1918–21.
Narodnaia Svoboda (Baku), 1917.
Novaia Zhizn' Gazeta (Petrograd), 1917–18.
Novaia Zhizn' Zhurnal (Moscow), 1914–16.
Novoe Vremia (Petrograd), 1914–17.
Novyi Ekonomist, 1914–17.
Novyi Vechernyi Chas (Petrograd), 1917–18.
Odesskii Listok (Odessa), 1914–17.
Okopnaia Pravda (Riga), 1917.
Osobyi Zhurnal Sovetov Ministerstrov (Petrograd), 1914–17.
Penzenskaia Rech' (Penza), 1917.
Poltavskii Den' (Poltava), 1917.
Pravda (Petrograd), 1917.
Prodput' (Moscow), 1918.
Promyshlennaia Rossiia, 1916.
Promyshlennost' i Torgovlia (Petrograd), 1914–17.
Rabochaia Gazeta (Petrograd), 1917.
Rabochii Khimik (Moscow), 1917–18.
Rech' (Petrograd), 1914–17.
Russkiia Vedomosti (Moscow), 1914–17.
Russkoe Slovo (Moscow), 1915–17.
Saratovskii Listok (Saratov), 1917–18.
Serp i Molot (Chernigov), 1919.
Sinii Zhurnal (Petrograd), 1914–16.
Statistika Truda (Moscow), 1918–19.
Svobodnyi Krai (Irkutsk), 1918–19.
Svobodnyi Narod (Petrograd), 1917.
Tekstil'shchik (Ivanovo), 1918–21.
Transport i Zhizn' (Moscow), 1918–19.

Trudovaia Kopeika (Moscow), 1916–17.
Tul'skie Novosti (Tula), 1915–17.
Utro Rossii (Moscow), 1915–17.
Vestnik Aleksandrovskoi Zheleznoi Dorogi (Moscow), 1917–18.
Vestnik Ekaterininskoi Zheleznoi Dorogi (Ekaterinoslav), 1916–17.
Vestnik Evropy (Petrograd), 1914–17.
Vestnik Finansov, Promyshlennost' i Torgovlia (Petrograd), 1915–17.
Vestnik Moskovsko-Kievo-Voronezhskoi Zheleznoi Dorogi (Moscow), 1918–19.
Vestnik Narodnogo Komissariata Torgovli i Promyshlennosti (NKTiP) (Moscow), 1918.
Vestnik Omsk Zheleznoi. Dorogi (Omsk), 1917.
Vestnik Partii Narodnoi Svobody (Petrograd), 1917.
Vestnik Petrogradskoi Grazhdanskoi Dumy (Petrograd), 1917.
Vestnik Petrogradskago Obshchestva Zavodchikov i Fabrikantov (Petrograd), 1917–18.
Vestnik Putei Soobshcheniia (Petrograd), 1915–17.
Vestnik Riazano-Ural'skoi Zheleznoi Dorogi (Saratov), 1916–17.
Vestnik Statistiki (Moscow), 1918–19.
Vestnik Tobolskogo Uezda (Tobol'sk), 1918–19.
Vestnik Vremennogo Pravitel'stva (Petrograd), 1917.
Vestnik Zabaikal'ia (Chita), 1919.
Vestnik Zmeinogorska (Zmeinogorsk), 1919.
Voenno-meditsinskii Zhurnal (Petrograd), 1915–16.
Volia i Dumy Zheleznodorozhnika (Moscow), 1917–18.
Voronezhskii Den' (Voronezh), 1916–17.
Zemlia i Volia (Petrograd), 1917.
Zheleznodorozhnik (Petrograd), 1906–7.
Zheleznodorozhnoe Delo (Petrograd), 1914–17.
Zhurnal Zasedanii Vremennago Pravitel'stva (Moscow: Rosspen), 2001.
Zhurnal Osobykh Soveshchanii po obespecheniiu deistvuiushchei armii artilleriei, glavneishimi vidamidovol'stviia, predmetami boevogo i material'nogo snabzheniia, 11 Maia–19 Avgusta 1915 (Moscow: Inst. Istorii RAN), 1975.
Zhurnal Petrogradskoi Gorodskoi Dumy (Petrograd), 1917.
Zhurnaly Osobogo Soveshchaniia po Oborone Gosudarstva (Petrograd), 1915–17.
Zhurnaly Zasedanii Tsentral'nogo Voenno-Promyshlennogo Komitita (Petrograd), 1915–16.
Zhurnal Zasedanii Vremennogo Rasporiaditel'nogo Komiteta po Zheleznodorozhnym Perevozkam (Petrograd), 1916.
Znamia Sovetov (Chernigov), 1920.

Primary Sources

Akademicheskoe Delo, 1929–1931 gg., 2 vols. St. Petersburg: Nauka, 1993–98.
Ansky, S. *The Enemy at His Pleasure: A Journal through the Jewish Pale of Settlement during World War I*. Edited and translated by J. Neugroschel. New York: Holt, 2002.

Astrov, N. I. "Grazhdanskaia voina." Unpublished ms., 1920. Bakhmeteff Arkhive, Columbia University.
Astrov, N. I. "Neskol'ko spravok." Unpublished ms., 1919. Bakhmeteff Arkhive, Columbia University.
Astrov, N. I. *Vospominaniia*. Paris: YMCA Press, 1940.
Avrutin, Eugene, and Elissa Bemporad, eds. *Pogroms: A Documentary History*. New York: Oxford University Press, 2021.
Bark, P. L. *Vospominaniia poslednego ministra finansov Rossiia 1914–17*. Moscow: Kuchnoe Pole, 2017.
Bernshtam, M. S., ed. *Nezavisimoe rabochee dvizhenie v 1918 godu: Dokumenty i materialy*. Paris: YMCA Press, 1981.
Bor'ba s trudovym dezertirstvom: Sbornik offitsial'nykh polozhenie. Moscow: Glavkomtruda, 1920.
Browder, R., and A. F. Kerensky, eds. *The Russian Provisional Government: Documents*. 3 vols. Stanford, CA: Stanford University Press, 1961.
Brusilov, A. A. *A Soldier's Notebook*. 1930. Westport, CT: Greenwood Press, 1970.
Buchanan, George. *My Mission to Russia and Other Diplomatic Memories*. Boston: Little, Brown, 1923.
Budberg, A. P. von. "Dnevnik." *Arkhiv Russkoi revoliutsii* 14 (1924): 225–38.
Bukhbinder, N. "Na fronte v predoktiabr'skie dni." *Krasnaia Letopis* 6 (1923): 18–52.
Cherniaev, V. I., ed. *Piterskie rabochie i "diktatura proletariata oktiabr" 1917–1929: Sbornik dokumentov*. St. Petersburg: Izd. BLITs, 2000.
Chernov, V. *The Great Russian Revolution*. Translated by P. Mosely. New Haven, CT: Yale University Press, 1936.
Chislennost' i sostav rabotnikov zheleznodorozhnogo transporta k kontsu 1920 g. Moscow: Gosizdat, 1921.
Danilov, Iu. N. "Moi vospominaniia iz vtorogo perioda mirovoi voiny." Autograph ms. with corrections, Houghton Library, Harvard University, n.d.
Danilov, V. P., and T. Shanin, eds. *Krest'ianskoe vosstanie v Tambovskoi gubernii v 1920–1921 gg. Antonovshchina: Dokumenty, materialy, i vospominaniia*. Tambov: Uprav. kul'tury, 1994.
Deiatel'nost' Osobogo soveshchaniia po prodovol'stviiu i osnovnye zadachi ekonomicheskoi politika: Doklad V. G. Gromana na s"ezde vserossiiskogo soiuza gorodov. Moscow: Gor. Typ., 1916.
Dement'ev, G. *Gosudarstennye dokhody i raskhody Rossii i polozhenie gosudarstvennago kaznachestva za vremia voiny s Germaniei i Avstro-vengriei do kontsa 1917 god*. Petrograd: Min. Finansov, 1917.
Dokumenty velikoi oktiabr'skoi sotsialisticheskoi revoliutsii v Nizhegorodskoi gubernii. Gorki: Obl. Gosizdat', 1945.
Ekonomicheskoe polozhenie Rossii nakanune velikoi oktiabr'skoi sotsialisticheskoi revoliutsii: Dokumenty I materialy. 3 pts. Leningrad: Nauka, 1957–67.
Ekonomicheskii Sovet: Stenograficheskii otchet. Petrograd: Min. Finansov, 1917.
Farmborough, Florence. *Nurse at the Russian Front: A Diary 1914–1918*. London: Constable, 1974.
Fleer, M. G. ed. *Rabochee dvizhenie v gody voiny*. Moscow: Vopr. Trudy, 1925.
Galili, Z., and A. Nenarokov, eds. *Mensheviki v 1919–1920*. Moscow: Rosspen, 2000.
Golopolosov, A. I. *Obzor zheleznodorozhnogo transporta (po dannym chrezvychainoi revisii 1919 g.)*. Moscow: Tip. SNKh, 1920.

Golovin, N. N. *The Russian Army in the World War.* New Haven, CT: Yale University Press, 1931.
Gosudarstvennoe Soveshchanie. Moscow: Gosizdat, 1930.
Gosudarstvennaia Duma. Stenograficheskii Otchet 4th sozyv. Moscow: Gosizdat, 1930.
Got'e, Iurii Vladimirovich. *Time of Troubles: The Diary of Iurii Vladimirovich Got'e.* Translated and edited by Terence Emmons. Stanford, CA: Stanford University Press, 1988.
Graham, Stephen. *Russia in 1916.* New York: Macmillan, 1917.
Groman, V. G. *Deiatel'nost Osobogo Soveshchaniia po Prodovol'stviiu i osnovnye zadachi ekonomicheskoi politiki.* Moscow: Soiuz Gorodov, 1916.
Groman, V. G., ed. *Dinamika rossiiskoi i sovetskoi promyshlennosti.* 2 vols. Moscow: Gosizdat, 1929–30.
Grossman, Vasili. *Everything Flows.* Translated by Robert Chandler and Elizabet Chandler. New York: NLRB, 2009.
Grave, B. B., ed. *Burzhuaziia nakanune fevral'skoi revoliutsii.* Moscow: Gosizdat, 1927.
Izgoev, A. S. *Sotsialisty vo vtoroi russkoi revoliutsii.* Petrograd: PNS, 1917.
Jenkins, A. "'Substantivism' as a Comparative Theory of Economic Forms." In *Sociological Theories of the Economy,* edited by Barry Hindess, 66–91. London: Palgrave Macmillan, 1977.
Grachev, G. *Kazanskii oktiabr': Materialy i dokumenty.* Kazan: Ispartotdel, 1926.
Kerensky, A. F. *Crucifixion of Liberty.* New York: John Day, 1934.
Kerensky, A. F. "The Policy of the Provisional Government of 1917." *Slavonic and East European Review* 31 (1932): 1–19.
Kerensky, F. *Russia and History's Turning Point.* New York: Duell, 1965.
Kirianov, Iu., ed. *Trudovye konflikty v sovetskoi Rossii 1918–1929.* Moscow: Izd. URSS, 1998.
Knox, Alfred. *With the Russian Army.* 2 vols. London: Hutchinson, 1921.
Koroblev, Iu. I., ed. *Rabochee dvizhenie v Petrograde, 1912–1917 gg.: Dokumenty i materialy.* Leningrad: Lenizdat, 1958.
Kossior, S. V. *Nashi raznoglasiia (o roli i zadachakh profsoiuzov).* Moscow: Gosizdat, 1921.
Krest'ianskoe dvizhenie v 1917 godu. Moscow: Gosizdat, 1927.
Kronshtadtskaia tragediia 1921 goda: Dokumenty, 2 vols. Moscow: Rosspen, 1999.
Krupskaia, N. "What a Communist Ought to Be Like." In *Bolshevik Visions: The First Phase of the Cultural Revolution in Soviet Russia,* 2 vols., edited by William G. Rosenberg, 1:26–29. Ann Arbor: University of Michigan Press, 1990.
Kurlov, Alexander. *Gibel' imperatorskoi Rossii: Vospominaniia.* Moscow: Zakharov 2002.
Lenin V. I. *Left-Wing Communism: An Infantile Disorder.* New York: International Publ., 1940 (written in 1920).
Lenin, V. I. *Polnoe sobranie sochinennia,* 55 vols. Moscow: Gosizdat, 1958.
Leninskie dekrety 1917–1922. Moscow: Izvestiia, 1974.
Lobanov-Rostovsky, A. *The Grinding Mill: Reminscences of War and Revolution in Russia.* New York: Macmillan, 1935.
Lorimer, Frank. *The Population of the Soviet Union.* Geneva: League of Nations, 1946.
Lozvoskii, A. "Nastoiashchee i budushchee professionalnykh soiuzov." In *Partiia i Soiuzy,* edited by G. Zinoviev, 139–75. Peterburg: Gosizdat, 1921.
Lubny-Gertsyk, L. *Dvizhenie naseleniia na territorii SSSR za vremia mirovoi voiny i revoliutsii.* Moscow: Planovoe khoziaistvo, 1926.
Luxemburg, Rosa. *The Mass Strike.* Detroit, MI: Marxian Education Society, 1920.

Markuzon, F. "Zarabotnaia plata fabricho-zavodskikh rabochikh v gorodu Moskvy v 1920 g." *Materialy po Statistike Truda* 10 (1921): 13–21.
Materialy po obzoru deiatel'nosti Osobogo Soveshchaniia po Toplivu za pervyi god ego sushchestvovaniia. 2 vols. Petrograd: Uprav. delami O.S., 1917.
Medlin, V. D., and S. L. Parsons, eds. *V. D. Nabokov and the Russian Provisional Government, 1917*. New Haven, CT: Yale University Press, 1976.
Michailovsky, A. "Russia and the War." *Russian Review* 1 (1916): 118–20.
Migulin, P. P. *Vozrozhdenie Russiia*. Kharkov: Pechatnik, 1910.
Mikhailov, I. D. *Evoliutsiia russkogo transporta*. Moscow: Ekon. Zhizn', 1925.
Mikhailov, I. D. *Transport. Ego sovremennoe sostianie*. Moscow: Zheludkovskoi, 1919.
Miliukov P. *Istoriia vtoroi russkoi revoliutsii*. 3 vols. Sofia: Ros-Bolgarskoe izd., 1921–24.
Miliukov P. *Taktika, fraktsii narodnoi svobody vo vremia voiny*. Petrograd: PNS, 1916.
Miliutin, V. P. *Sovremennoe Ekonomicheskoe razvitie Rossii i diktatura proletariat (1914–1918)*. Moscow: Izd. Ispolkom, 1918.
Ministervstvo Finansov. *Kratkii ocherk razvitiia nashei zheleznodorozhnoi sety za desiatiletie 1904–13*. St. Petersburg: Min. Fin., 1914.
Nabokov, Vladimir. *Speak Memory*. Rev. ed. New York: Putnam, 1966.
Narodnyi Komissariat Finansov, *Obzor finansovogo zakonodatel'stva 1917–1921*. Petrograd: Narodnyi Komissariat Finansov, 1921.
Obolenskii, V. A. *Krym pri Vrangele*. Moscow: Gosizdat, 1928.
Oktiabr'skii perevorot i diktatura proletariata: Sbornik statei. Moscow: Gosizdat, 1919.
Os'kin, D. P. *Zapiski soldata*. Moscow: Federatsii, 1929.
Otchet o torzhestvennom zasedaniia tsent: Voenno-promyshlennogo komitita 8 Marta 1917. Petrograd: Tsen. Voenno-Promyshlennyi Komitet, 1917.
Otchet Tsektrana k VR Soveshchanie Rabotnikov Soiuza. Moscow: Narodnyi komissariat transporta, 1920.
Padenie tsarskogo rezhima: Stenograficheskie otchety doprosov i pokazanii. 7 vols. Moscow: Gosizdat, 1924–27.
Paleologue, Maurice. An *Ambassador's Memoirs*. New York: Doran, 1927.
Pares, Bernard. *Day by Day with the Russian Army*. London: Constable, 1915.
Pares, Bernard. *Fall of the Russian Monarchy*. New York: Knopf, 1939.
Pervaia mirovaia voina 1914–1918 gg. v dnevnikakh i vospominaniiakh ofitserov Russkoi imperatorskoi armii: Sbornik Dokumentov. Moscow: Polit. Entsik., 2016.
Pervyi Vserossiiskii s"ezd professional'nykh soiuzov 7–14 ianvaria 1918 g. Moscow: VTsSPS, 1918.
Pervyi Vserossiiskii S"ezd Sovetov Rabochikh i Soldatskikh Deputatov. 2 vols. Moscow: Gosizdat, 1930–31.
Pervyi Vserossiiskii Torgovo-Promyshlennyi S"ezd v Moskve 19–22 Marta 1917. Moscow: Riabushinskii, 1917.
Piaskovskii, A. V., ed. *Vosstanie 1916 v Srednei Azii i Kazakhstane: Sbornik dokumentov*. Moscow: Nauka, 1960.
Popov, P. I. *Proizvodstvo khleba v RSFSR i federiruiushchikhsia s neiu respublikakh (khlebnaia produktiia)*. Moscow: Gosudarstevnnoe Izdatel'stvo, 1921.
Professional'noe dvizhenie na Mosksko-Kazanskii zheleznoi doroge, 1917–21. Moscow: Transpechatnyi Otdel, Narodnyi Komissariat Putei Soobshchenie, 1928.
Protokoly 1-go Vseross. s"ezd tekstil'shchikov i fabrichnykh komitetov. Moscow: Izd. VR Sov. Prof. Soiuzov Tekstil'shchikov, 1918.

Protokoly Presidiuma Vysshego Soveta Narodnogo Khoziaistva, Dekabr' 1917-1918. Moscow: Nauka, 1991.
Protokoly Tsentral'nogo Komiteta Konstitutsionno-Demokraticheskoi Partii 1915-1920 gg. 6 vols. Moscow: Rosspen, 1998.
PSFMO. *Protokoly zasedanii primiritel'nye sudy Fev.-Iiun.* Petrograd: Izd. Petrograd Society of Factory and Mill Owners, 1917.
Revoliutsionnoe dvizhenie posle sverzheniia samoderzhaviia. Moscow: Nauka, 1957.
Revoliutsionnoe dvizhenie soldatskikh mass na zapadnom fronte. Minsk: Nauka i tekhnika, 1981.
Robbins, Richard, Jr. *Overtaken by the Night: One Russian's Journey through Peace, War, Revolution and Terror.* Pittsburgh, PA: University of Pittsburgh Press, 2017.
Rodzianko, M. V. *The Reign of Rasputin.* Translated by E. Svegntsova. London: Philpot, 1927.
RKP. *XIII S"ezd Rossiiskoi kommunisticheskoi partii: Stenograficheskii otchet.* Moscow: Gosizdat, 1924.
Rossiia 1917 v ego-dokumentakh. Pis'ma. Moscow: Nauchno-politicheskaia kniga, 2019.
Rubinshtein, N. "Vremennoe pravitel'stvo i uchreditel'noe Sobranie." *Krasnyi Arkhiv* 28 (1928): 107-41.
Sazonov, L. I. "Potery russkoi armii v voinu." In *Trudy komissii po sledovanniiu sanitarnykh posledstvii voiny 1914-1920 gg.*, edited by M. M. Gran, 153-78. Moscow: Gosizdat, 1923.
Sbornik materialov komiteta moskovskikh obshchestvennykh organizatsii. Moscow: Tip. Rabushinskikh, 1917.
S"ezdy i konferentsii konstitutionno-demokraticheskoi partii 1905-1920. 3 vols. Moscow: Rosspen, 2000.
Shelokhaev, V. V., ed. *Mensheviki, dokumenty i materialy 1903-17.* Moscow: Rosspen, 1996.
Shingarev, A. I. *Finansovoe polozhenie Rossii.* Petrograd: Ministerstvo finansov, 1917.
Shtif, N. I. "Dobrovol'tsy i evreiskie pogromy." In *Revoliutsiia i grazhdanskaia voina v opisaniakh belogvardeitsev: Denikin, Iudenich, Vrangel,* edited by S. A. Alekseev, 138-58. Moscow: Otechestvo, 1991.
Shtil'man, G. "Voina i patriotism." *Vestnik Evropy* 51 (July 1916): 116-29.
Shulgin, V. V. *Dni.* Belgrade: Suvorin, 1925.
Sobranie upolnomochennykh i piterskie rabochie v 1918 godu: Dokumenty i materialy. St. Petersburg: Spb. University Press, 2006.
Sobranie uzakonenii i rasporizhenii pravitel'stva izdavaemoe pri pravitel'stvuiushchem senate. St. Petersburg: Gos. Typ., 1914-17.
Sokolov, K. N. *Pravlenie generala Denikina.* Sofia: Rossiisko-bolgarskoe knigoizdatel'stvo, 1921.
Statisticheskie svedeniia o finansovom i ekonomicheskom polozhenii Rossii. sost. Kantseliariei Soveta Ministrov. Petrograd: Gos. Tip., 1916.
Steinberg, Mark. *Voices of Revolution 1917.* New Haven, CT: Yale University Press, 2001.
Stenograficheskii otchet zasedaniia ekonomicheskogo soveta pri vremennom pravitel'stve. Petrograd: Gosudarstvennaia tipografiia, 1917.
Strumilin, S. "Trudovye poteri Rossii v voine." *Narodnoe khoziaistvo* 23-24 (Dec. 1920): 104-06.
Struve, P. B. ed. *Food Supply in Russia during the World War.* New Haven, CT: Yale University Press, 1930.
Sukhanov, N. N. *Zapiski o revoliutsii.* 7 vols. Berlin: Z.I. Grzhebin, 1922-23.

Sukhanov, N. N. *The Russian Revolution 1917*. Edited and translated by J. Carmichael. Princeton, NJ: Princeton University Press, 1984.

Time of Troubles: The Diary of Iurii Vladimirovich Got'e. Translated and edited by Terence Emmons. Stanford: Stanford University Press, 1988.

Tri goda bor'by s golodom: Kratkii otchet o deiatel'nosti Narodnogo Komissariata po Prodovol'stviiu za 1919–20. Moscow: Narkomprod, 1920.

Trudy Ekonomicheskago Soveshchaniia 3–4 ian. 1916. Moscow: Vserossiiskii Soiuz Gorodov, 1916.

Trudy Kommissii po izucheniiu sovremennoi dorogovizny. Vol. 3. Moscow: Gorodskaia Tipografiia, 1915.

Trudy Pervago ekonomicheskago s"ezda Moskovskago promyshlennago raiona. Moscow: Izd. Mos. Raion Ekon. Komitet, 1918.

Trudy Pervogo s"ezda Sovetov Narodnago Khoziaistva 25 maia–4 iiunia 1918. Moscow: S"ezd, 1918.

Trudy S"ezda predstavitelei voenno-promyshlennykh komitetov 25–27-go iiulia 1915 goda. Petrograd: Gershunina, 1915.

Tsentral'nyi Voenno-Promyshennyi Komitet. *Ob ucherezdenie primiritel'nykh kamerov*. Petrograd, Tsentral'nyi Voenno-promyshlennyi komitet, 1916.

Tsereteli, I. *Vospominaniia o fevral'skoi revoliutsii*. 2 vols. Paris: Mouton, 1963.

Tsentral'noe Statisticheskoe Upravlenie. *Fabrichno-zavodskaia promyshlennost' v period 1913–1918*. Vol. 26, no. 1. Moscow: Tsentral'noe Statisticheskoe Upravlenie, 1926.

Tsentral'noe Statisticheskoe Upravlenie. *Rossiia v mirovoi voine 1914–1918 (v tsifrakh)*. Moscow: Tsentral'noe Statisticheskoe Upravlenie, 1926.

Tsentral'noe Statisticheskoe Upravlenie. *Statisticheskii Sbornik 1913–1917*. 2 vols. Moscow: Tsentral'noe Statisticheskoe Upravlenie, 1921–22.

Tsentral'noe Statisticheskoe Upravlenie. *Statisticheskii ezhegodnik 1918–1920 gg.* Moscow: Tsentral'noe Statisticheskoe Upravlenie, 1921.

Vol'fovich, M., and K. Medvedeva, eds. *Tsarskaia armiia v period mirovoi voiny i fevral'skoi revoliutsii*. Kazan: Tatizdat, 1932.

Volobuev, P. V., ed. *Petrogradskii Sovet rabochikh i soldatskikh deputatov v 1917: Protokoly, steno. otchety i zasedanii Ispol. Kom 27 fev. 1917–25 okt. 1915*. Leningrad: Nauka, 1991.

Vorob'ev, N. A. "Izmeneniia v Russkoi promyshlennosti v period voiny i revoliutsii." *Vestnik Statistiki* 14 (1923): 115–54.

Vserossiiskii Soiuz Gorodov. *Organizatsiia narodnogo khoziaistva: Materialy po V ocherednomu s"ezdu Soiuza Gorodov*. Moscow: Soiuz gorodov, 1917.

Vserossiiskii Soiuz Gorodov. *Trudy Ekonomicheskago Soveshchaniia 3–4 ian. 1916*. Moscow: Soiuz gorodov, 1916.

Vtoroi Vserossiiskii Torgovo-Promyshlennyi S"ezd v Moskve 3–5 avg. 1917. Moscow: Gorod. Typ., 1917.

Washburn, Stanley. *Field Notes from the Russian Front*. London: Andrew Melrose, 1915.

Washburn, Stanley. *The Russian Advance*. New York: Doubleday, 1917.

Washburn, Stanley. *The Russian Campaign*. London: Melrose, 1915.

Secondary Sources

Abrosimova, T. A., ed. *Malen'kii chekovek i bol'shaia voina v istorii Rossii*. St. Petersburg, Bulanin, 2014.

Anfimov, A. M. *Rossiiskaia derevnia v gody pervoi mirovoi voiny (1914-1917)*. Moscow: Izdatel'stvo Sotsial'noi i Politicheskoi Literatury, 1962.
Anskii, A., ed. *Professional'noe dvizhenie v Petrograde v 1917 godu*. Leningrad: Izdatel'stvo Leningradskogo oblastnogo soviet professional'nykh, 1928.
Antsiferov, A. N., A. Bilimoviich, M. O. Osipovich, and D. N. Ivantsov. *Russian Agriculture during the War*. New Haven, CT: Yale University Press, 1930.
Applebaum, Anne. *Red Famine: Stalin's War on Ukraine*. London: Allen Lane, 2017.
Arendt, Hannah. *On Revolution*. New York: Viking Press, 1965.
Arkhipov, Igor. "Patriotizm v period krizisa 1914-1917 godov." *Zvezda* 9 (2009): 177-204.
Armeson, Robert. *Total Warfare and Compulsory Labor: A Study of the Military-Industrial Complex in Germany during World War I*. The Hague: Nijhoff, 1964.
Aronson, G. "Ouvriers russes contre le bolchevisme." *Le Contrat Social* 4 (July-Aug. 1966): 14-26.
Ashworth, Tony. *Trench Warfare, 1914-1918: The Live and Let Live System*. New York: Holmes and Meier, 1980.
Astashov, A. B. "Dezertirstvo i bor'ba s nim v tsarskoi armii v gody pervoi mirovoi voiny." *Rossiiskaia Istoriia* 4 (2011): 44-52.
Astashov, A. B. "Russkii krest'ianin na frontakh pervoi mirovoi voiny." *Otechestvennaia Istoriia* 2 (Mar. 2003): 72-86.
Avrich, Paul. *Kronstadt*. Princeton, NJ: Princeton University Press, 1970.
Badcock, Sarah. *Politics and the People in Revolutionary Russia: A Provincial History*. Cambridge: Cambridge University Press, 2007.
Badcock, Sarah. "Women, Protest, and Revolution: Soldiers' Wives in Russia during 1917." *International Review of Social History* 1 (April 2004): 47-70.
Badcock, Sarah, Liudmila Novikova, and Aaron Retish, eds. *Russia's Home Front in War and Revolution*. Bk. 1. Bloomington, IN: Slavica, 2015.
Baker, Keith, and Dan Edelstein, eds. *Scripting Revolution*. Stanford, CA: Stanford University Press, 2015.
Baker, Mark. "Rampaging *Soldatki*, Cowering Police, Bazaar Riots and Moral Economy: The Social Impact of the Great War in Kharkiv Province." *Canadian-American Slavic Studies* 2-3 (2001): 137-55.
Baker, Mark. "War and Revolution in Ukraine: Kharkov Province's Peasant Experiences of War, Revolution, and Occupation, 1914-1918." In *Russia's Home Front in War and Revolution*, bk. 1, edited by Sarah Badcock, Liudmila Novikova, and Aaron Retish, 111-41. Bloomington, IN: Slavica, 2015.
Beloborodova, A. A. "Zashchita gosudarstvennoi tainy v rossiiskoi imperii: Deiatel'nost' voennoi tsenzury v 1914-17." *Voenno-istoricheskii Zhurnal* 6 (2011). http: istory.milpor tal.ru/zashhita-gosudarstvennoj-tajny-v-rossijskoj-imperii-deyatelnost-voennoj-cenz ury-v-1914-1917-gg/.
Beliaev, S. G. *P. L. Bark i finansovaia politika Rossii 1914-17*. St. Petersburg: St. Petersburg University Press, 2002.
Belova, I. *Vynuzhhdennye migrant: Bezhentsy i voennoplennye pervoi mirovoi voiny v Rossii 1914-25*. Moscow: AIRO, 2014.
Berk, Stephen M. "The 'Class-Tragedy' of Izhevsk: Working-Class Opposition to Bolshevism in 1918." *Russian Review* 2 (1975): 176-90.
Berkhofer, Robert F. *Beyond the Great Story: History as Text and Discourse*. Cambridge, MA: Harvard University Press, 1996.

Beyrau, Dietrich. "Brutalization Revisited: The Case of Russia." *Journal of Contemporary History* 50 (2015): 15–37.
Bidwell, Shelford. *Modern Warfare: A Study of Men, Weapons and Theories.* London: Allen Lane, 1973.
Blouin, Francis X., and William G. Rosenberg, eds. *Archives, Documentation, and Institutions of Social Memory.* Ann Arbor: University of Michigan Press, 2006.
Blouin, Francis X., and William G. Rosenberg. *Processing the Past: Contesting Authority in History and the Archives.* New York: Oxford University Press, 2011.
Bondarev, N. I. "Zatrudeniia voiskogo vracha v sluchaiakh psikiatricheskoi diagnostiki." *Voenno-Meditsinskii Zhurnal* 5–6 (1931).
Broadberry, Stephen, and Mark Harrison, eds. *The Economics of World War I.* Cambridge: Cambridge University Press, 2005.
Brooks, Jeffrey. *When Russia Learned to Read: Literacy and Popular Literature 1861–1917.* Princeton, NJ: Princeton University Press, 1985.
Brooks, R. *The Stress of Combat, the Combat of Stress.* Brighton: Alpha Press, 1999.
Buldakov, V. P. *Krasnaia Smuta.* Moscow: Rosspen, 2010.
Buldakov, V. P. "Revolution and Emotions: Toward a Reinterpretation of the Political Events of 1914–1917." *Russian History* 45, no. 2–3 (2018): 196–230.
Buldakov, V. P., and T. G. Leont'eva. *Voina porodivshaia revoliutsiiu.* Moscow: Novyi Khronograf, 2015.
Bulgakova, Liudmila. "The Phenomenon of the Liberated Soldier's Wife." In *Russia's Home Front in War and Revolution 1914–1922*, bk. 2, edited by Adele Lindenmyer, Christopher Read, and Peter Waldron, 301–26. Bloomington, IN: Slavica. 2016.
Bunyan, James. *The Origins of Forced Labor in the Soviet State 1917–1921.* Baltimore, MD: Johns Hopkins University Press, 1967.
Burdzhalov, E. N. *Russia's Second Revolution: The February Uprising in Petrograd.* Edited and translated by Donald J. Raleigh. Bloomington: Indiana University Press, 1987.
Bushnell, John. *Mutiny amid Repression: Russian Soldiers in the Revolution of 1905–1906.* Bloomington: Indiana University Press, 1985.
Butler, Judith. "Uprising." In *Uprisings*, edited by G. Didi-Huberman, 23–36. Paris, 2016.
Caron, F. "Essai d'analyse historique d'une psychologie du travail: Les Mecaniciens et chauffeurs de locomotive du Nord de 1850 a 1910." *Le Mouvement Social* 50 (1965): 3–40.
Chernev, Boris. "Ukrainization and Its Contradictions in the Context of the Brest-Litovsk System." In *The Empire and Nationalism at War*, edited by Eric Lohr, Vera Tolz, Alexander Semyonov, and Mark von Hagen, 163–88. Bloomington, IN: Slavica, 2014.
Chickering, Roger, and Stig Förster. *Great War, Total War: Combat and Mobilization on the Western Front, 1914–1918.* Cambridge: Cambridge University Press, 2000.
Cohen, Aaron J. *Imagining the Unimaginable: World War, Modern Art, and the Politics of Culture in Russia, 1914–1917.* Lincoln: University of Nebraska Press, 2008.
Conliffe, Mark. "Poltava in Revolution and Civil War: From the Diaries of Vladimir Korolenko and Aleksandr Nesvitskii." In *Russia's Home Front in War and Revolution 1914–22*, bk. 2, edited by Adele Lindenmyer, Christopher Read, and Peter Waldron, 455–75. Bloomington, IN: Slavica, 2016.
Copp, T., and B. McAndrew. *Battle Exhaustion.* Montreal: McGill-Queen's University Press, 1990.
Corney, Fred. *Telling October: Memory and the Making of the Bolshevik Revolution.* Ithaca, NY: Cornell University Press, 2004.

Daly, Jonathan. *The Watchful State: Security Police and Opposition in Russia, 1906–1917*. DeKalb, IL: Northern Illinois University Press, 2004.

Daniels, Robert. *The Conscience of the Revolution*. Cambridge, MA: Harvard University Press, 1965.

Davidjan, I. "Voennaia tsenzura v Rossii v gody grazhdanskoi voiny." *Cahiers du Monde Russe et Sovetique* 1–2 (1997): 117–25.

Davidov, A. Iu. *Meshochniki i diktatura v Rossii 1917–1921*. St. Petersburg: Izd. Aleteiia, 2007.

Davidov, A. Iu. *Nelegal'noe snabzhenie rossiiskogo naseleniia i vlast' 1917–1921 gg*. St. Petersburg: Nauka, 2002.

Dekel-Chen, J., David Gaunt, Natan Meir, and Israel Bartal, eds. *Anti-Jewish Violence: Rethinking the Pogrom in East European History*. Bloomington: Indiana University Press, 2011.

Denisov, B. *Voina i lubok*. Petrograd: Izd. Nov. Zhurnala, 1916.

Derida, Jacques. *Mal d'archive*. Paris: Galilee, 1995.

Diakin V. S., ed. *Krizis samoderzhaviia v Rossii, 1895–1017*. Leningrad: Nauka, 1984.

Diakin V. S., ed. *Russkaia burzhuaziia i tsarizm v gody pervoi mirovoi voiny, 1914–1917*. Leningrad: Nauka, 1967.

Dmitriev, N. "Primiritel'nye kamery v 1917 godu." In *Professional'noe dvizhenie v Petrograde v 1917 godu*, edited by A. Anskii, 907–97. Leningrad: Izd. Leningradskogo oblastnogo soveta professional'nykh soiuzov, 1928.

Dolgova, A. V. *Neizvestnyi front grazhdanskoi voiny: Konflikt mezhdu vlast'iu bol'shevikov i krest'ianskoi massoi v Permskoi gubernii*. Moscow: Maska, 2019.

Doob, Leonard. *Patriotism and Nationalism: Their Psychological Foundations*. New Haven, CT: Yale University Press, 1964.

Dowling, Timothy C. *The Brusilov Offensive*. Bloomington: Indiana University Press, 2008.

Drobizhev, V. D. *Glavnyi shtab sotsialisticheskoi promyshlennosti*. Moscow: Nauka, 1966.

Drobizhev, V. D. "Sotsialisticheskoe obobshchestvlenie promyshlennosti v SSSR." *Voprosy Istorii* 6 (1964): 43–64.

Dugger, William M. "Instituted Process and Enabling Myth: The Two Faces of the Market." *Journal of Economic Issues* 607 (June 15, 1989): 607–15.

Dye, T., ed. *The Political Legitimacy of Markets and Governments*. Greenwich, CT: JAI Press, 1990.

Emmons, T., ed. *The Zemstvo: An Experiment in Local Government*. New York: Cambridge University Press, 1982.

Engel, Barbara. "Not by Bread Alone: Subsistence Riots in Russia during World War I." *Journal of Modern History* 4 (Dec. 1997): 692–721.

Etkind, Alexander. *Warped Mourning: Stories of the Undead in the Land of the Unburied*. Stanford, CA: Stanford University Press, 2018.

Etzioni, A. *The Moral Dimension: Toward a New Economics*. New York: Free Press, 1988.

Feshbach, Murray. "Russia's Population Meltdown." *Wilson Quarterly* 1 (Winter 2001): 15–21.

Figes, Orlando. *Peasant Russia, Civil War: The Volga Countryside in Revolution 1917–1921*. Oxford: Oxford University Press, 1989.

Figes, Orlando. "The Red Army and Mass Mobilization during the Russian Civil War, 1918–1920." *Past and Present* 129 (1990): 168–211.

Fraunholtz, Peter. "The Collapse and Rebuilding of Grain Procurement Authority in Civil War Russia: The Case of Penza." In *Russia's Home Front in War and Revolution*, bk. 1, edited by Sarah Badcock, Liudmila Novikova, and Aaron Retish, 67–86. Bloomington, IN: Slavica, 2015.

Frenkin, M. *Russkaia armiia i revoliutsiia 1917–1918*. Munich: Logos, 1978.

Friedlander, Kim. "Neskol'ko aspektov *shellshok'a* v Rossii 1914–1916." In *Rossiia i pervaia mirovaia voina*, edited by N. N. Smirnov, 315–25. St. Petersburg: Bulanin, 1999.

Fromm, Erich. *The Anatomy of Human Destructiveness*. New York: Holt, Rinehart, 1973.

Fukuyama, Francis. *The End of History and the Last Man*. New York: Free Press, 1992.

Fuller, William C., Jr. *The Foe Within: Fantasies of Treason and the End of Imperial Russia*. Ithaca, NY: Cornell University Press, 2006.

Furet, François. *Interpreting the French Revolution*. Cambridge: Cambridge University Press, 1981.

Furet, François. *The Passing of an Illusion: The Idea of Communism in the Twentieth Century*. Chicago: University of Chicago Press, 1999.

Furet, François, and Ernst Nolte. *Fascism and Communism*. Translated by K. Golsan. Lincoln: University of Nebraska Press, 2001.

Galili, Ziva. "Archives and Historical Writing: The Case of the Menshevik Party in 1917." In *Archives, Documentation, and Institutions of Social Memory*, edited by F. X. Blouin and William G. Rosenberg, 443–50. Ann Arbor: University of Michigan Press, 2006.

Galili, Ziva. *The Menshevik Leaders in the Russian Revolution*. Princeton, NJ: Princeton University Press, 1989.

Galili, Ziva. "The Origins of Revolutionary Defensism: I. G. Tsereteli and the 'Siberian Zimmerwaldists.'" *Slavic Review* 3 (Fall 1982): 454–76.

Gaponenko L. S., and V. E. Poletaev. "K istorii rabochego dvizheniia v Rossii v period mirnogo razvitiia revoliutsii (mart-iiun' 1917 goda)." *Voprosy Istorii* 2 (1959): 21–44.

Gatrell, Peter. *Government, Industry, and Rearmament in Russia, 1900–1914*. Cambridge: Cambridge University Press, 1994.

Gatrell, Peter. *Russia's First World War: A Social and Economic History*. New York: Longman, 2005.

Gatrell, Peter. *A Whole Empire Walking*. Bloomington: Indiana University Press, 1999.

Gatrell, Peter, and Mark Harrison. "The Russian and Soviet Economies in Two World Wars: A Comparative View." *Economic History Review* 3 (1993): 439–40.

Gaudin, Corinne. "Rural Echoes of World War I: War Talk in the Russian Village." *Jahrbücher für Geschichte Osteuropas* 3 (2008): 391–414.

Gerwarth, Robert, and John Horne. "Vectors of Violence: Paramilitarism in Europe after the Great War." *Journal of Modern History* 3 (2011): 489–512.

Getzler, I. *Kronstadt 1917–1921*. Cambridge: Cambridge University Press, 2002.

Giddens, Anthony. *Modernity and Self-Identity: Self and Society in the Late Modern Age*. Cambridge, UK: Polity Press, 1991.

Gimpel'son, E. G. *Sovetskii rabochii klass*. Moscow: Nauka, 1974.

Glickman, Rose. *Russian Factory Women: Workplace and Society 1880–1914*. Berkeley: University of California Press, 1984.

Golopolosov, A. I. *Obzor zheleznodorozhnogo transporta (po dannym chrezvychainoi revisii 1919 g.)*. Moscow: Narodnyi Komissariat Rabkrina, 1920.

Goncharskaia, S. S. "Profsoiuz prachek v 1917 goda." In *V ogne revoliutsionykh boev (Raiony Petrograda v dvukh revoliutsiiakh 1917 goda*, vol. 1, 477–86. Moscow: Mysl', 1968.

Grafton, Anthony. *The Footnote: A Curious History*. Cambridge, MA: Harvard University Press, 1999.

Granovetter, Mark. "Economic Action and Social Structure: The Problem of Embeddedness." *American Journal of Sociology* 3 (1985): 481–510.

Grant, Jonathan. *Big Business in Russia*. Pittsburgh, PA: University of Pittsburgh Press, 1999.

Graves, Robert. *Goodbye to All That*. London: Cassell, 1957.

Graziosi, Andrea. *The Great Soviet Peasant War: Bolsheviks and Peasants, 1917–1933*. Cambridge, MA: Harvard University Ukrainian Institute, 1996.

Gregory, Paul. "Grain Marketings and Peasant Consumption in Russia, 1885–1913." *Explorations in Economic History* 17 (1980): 135–64.

Gregory, Paul. "1913 Russian National Income." *Quarterly Journal of Economics* 3 (Aug. 1976): 445–49.

Gregory, Paul. *Russian National Income 1885–1993*. Cambridge: Cambridge University Press, 1983.

Grunt, A. I. *Moskva 1917: Revolutsiia i kontrrevoliutsiia*. Moscow: Nauka, 1976.

Gurevich, V. *Madzhel': Soiuz mladshikh agentov dvizheniia zheleznykh dorog 1917–1919 gg*. Moscow: Izd TsKZhD, 1925.

Haimson, Leopold. "The Problem of Social Stability in Urban Russia, 1905–1917." *Slavic Review* 4 (1964): 61-91; 1 (1965): 1–25.

Haimson, Leopold. *Russia's Revolutionary Experience 1905–17*. New York: Columbia University Press, 2005.

Haimson, Leopold, and G. Sapelli, eds. *Strikes, Social Conflict, and the First World War: An International Perspective*. Milan: Feltrinelli, 1992.

Haimson, Leopold, and Charles Tilly, eds. *Strikes, Wars, and Revolutions in International Perspective*. New York: Cambridge University Press, 1989.

Harrison, Mark, and Andrei Markevich. "Russia's Home Front and the Economy, 1914–1922: The Economy." In *Russia's Home Front in War and Revolution, 1914–1922*, bk. 3, edited by Christopher Read, Peter Waldron, and Adele Lindenmeyr, 1–22. Bloomington, IN: Slavica, 2018.

Hasegawa, Tsuyoshi. *The February Revolution: Petrograd 1917*. 1981. Leiden: Brill, 2018.

Hausman, Daniel M. "Are Markets Morally Free Zones." *Philosophy and Public Affairs* 18 (Fall 1989): 317–33.

Healy, M. *Vienna and the Fall of the Hapsburg Empire: Total War and Everyday Life in World War*. Cambridge: Cambridge University Press, 2004.

Hellbeck, Jochen. *Revolution on My Mind*. Cambridge, MA: Harvard University Press, 2006.

Heywood, Anthony. "Imperial Russia's Railways at War, 1914–17: Challenges, Results, Costs, and Legacy." In *Russia's Home Front in War and Revolution*, bk. 3, edited by Christopher Read, Peter Waldron, and Adele Lindenmeyr, 45–64. Bloomington, IN: Slavica, 2018.

Heywood, Anthony "Liberalism, Socialism and 'Bourgeois Specialists': The Politics of Iu. V. Lomonosov to 1917." *Revolutionary Russia* 17, no. 1 (2004): 1–30.

Heywood, Anthony. "The Militarization of Civilians in Tsarist Russia's First World War: Railway Staff in the Army Front Zones." *Military Affairs in Russia's Great War and Revolution 1914–22*, bk. 1, edited by Laurie Stoff, Anthony Heywood, John Steinberg, and Boris Kolonitskii, 327–67. Bloomington IN: Slavica, 2019.

Heywood, Anthony J. *Modernizing Lenin's Russia: Economic Reconstruction, Foreign Trade and the Railways*. Cambridge: Cambridge University Press, 1999.

Heywood., Anthony J. "Spark of Revolution? Railway Disorganisation, Freight Traffic and Tsarist Russia's War Effort, July 1914–March 1917." Unpublished ms.

Kazakov, D. N. "Slovo o 'Stepanovskom' miatezhe." *Innakar* 1, no. 18 (2014): 100–12. https://cyberleninka.ru/article/n/slovo-o-stepanovskom-myatezhe.

Hickey, Michael C. "Local Government and State Authority in the Provinces: Smolensk, February–June 1917." *Slavic Review* 4 (1996): 863–81.

Hickey, Michael C. "Peasant Autonomy, Soviet Power, and Land Redistribution in Smolensk Province, November 1917–May 1918." *Revolutionary Russia* 1 (June 1996): 19–32.

Hickey, Michael C. "The Provisional Government and Local Administration in Smolensk in 1917." *Journal of Modern Russian History and Historiography* 1 (2016): 251–74.

Hickey, Michael C. "Who Controls These Woods? Forests and *Mnogovlastie* in Smolensk in 1917." *Revolutionary Russia* 2 (2019): 197–225.

Hogan, Heather. "Conciliation Boards in Revolutionary Petrograd: Aspects of the Crisis of Labor-Management Relations in Russia." *Russian History* 1 (1982): 49–66.

Hogan, Heather. *Forging Revolution: Metalworkers, Managers, and the State in St. Petersburg, 1890–1914.* Bloomington: Indiana University Press, 1993.

Holmes, Larry. *Revising the Revolution: The Unmaking of Russia's Official History of 1917.* Bloomington: Indiana University Press, 2021.

Holmes, Richard. *Acts of War: The Behavior of Men in Battle.* New York: Free Press, 1986.

Holquist, Peter. "'Information Is the Alpha and Omega of Our Work': Bolshevik Surveillance in Its Pan- European Context." *Journal of Modern History* 3 (Sept. 1997): 425–50.

Holquist, Peter. *Making War, Forging Revolution: Russia's Continuum of Crisis, 1914–1921.* Cambridge, MA: Harvard University Press, 2002.

Holquist, Peter. "Violent Russia, Deadly Marxism? Russia in the Epoch of Violence, 1905–21." *Kritika* 3 (2003): 627–52.

Husband, William B. "Local Industry in Upheaval: The Ivanovo-Kineshma Textile Strike of 1917." *Slavic Review* 3 (1988): 448–63.

Husband, William B. *Revolution in the Factory: The Birth of the Soviet Textile Industry 1917–1920.* New York: Oxford University Press, 1990.

Hynes, Samuel. *The Soldiers' Tale: Bearing Witness to Modern War.* New York: Lane, 1997.

Immonen, Kh. *Mechty o novoi Rossii: Viktor Chernov (1873–1952).* St. Petersburg: EUSP Press, 2015.

Isupov, V. A. *Demograficheskie katastrofy i krizisy v Rossii v pervoi polovine XX veka.* Novosibirsk: Sibirskii Khronogaf, 2000.

Itkin, M. L. "Tsentry fabrichno-zavodskikh komitetov Rossii v 1917 godu." *Voprosy istorii* 2 (1974): 21–35.

Jahn, Hubertus. *Patriotic Culture in Russia during World War I.* Ithaca, NY: Cornell University Press, 1995.

Jenkins, Keith, ed. *The Postmodern History Reader.* London: Routledge, 1997.

Kaplan, Steven L. *Farewell, Revolution: Disputed Legacies, France 1789–1989.* Ithaca, NY: Cornell University Press, 1995.

Katsenelenbaum, E. S. *Denezhnoe obrashchenie Rossii 1914–1924.* Moscow: Izd. Ekon. Zhizn', 1924.

Keegan, John *The Face of Battle.* New York: Viking, 1976.

Kenez, Peter. "Pogroms and White Ideology in the Russian Civil War." In *Pogroms: Anti-Jewish Violence in Modern Russian History*, edited by John Klier and Shlomo Lambroza, 293–313. Cambridge: Cambridge University Press, 2004.

Kenez, Peter. "Russian Officer Corps before the Revolution: The Military Mind." *Russian Review* 3 (July 1972): 226–36.

Kerblay, B. H. *Les marchés paysans en U.R.S.S.* Paris: Mouton, 1968.

Khodiakov, M. V. *Den'gi revoliutsii i grazhdanskoi voiny 1917–1920 gody*. St. Petersburg: Izd. SPb State University, 2019.

Khromov, P. A. *Ekonomicheskaia istoriia SSSR: Period promyshlennago i monopolisticheskogo kapitalizma v Rossii*. Moscow: Vysh. Shkola, 1982.

Khromov, P. A. *Ekonomicheskoe razvitie Rossii*. Moscow: Nauka, 1967.

Khrushchev, A. G. *A. I. Shingarev*. Moscow: Kuchnerov, 1918.

Kingston-Mann, E., and T. Mixter, eds. *Peasant Economy, Culture, and Politics of European Russia, 1800–1921*. Princeton, NJ: Princeton University Press, 1991.

Kirianov, Iu. I. "Massovye vystupleniia na pochve dorogivizny v Rossii (1914–fevral' 1917 g.)." *Otechestvennaia Istoriia* 3 (1993): 3–18.

Kirianov, Iu. I. "Ulichnye besporiadki i vystupleniia rabochikh v Rossii." *Istoricheskii Arkhiv* 1–4 (1994): 91–99, 4–6; (1995): 62–105.

Kirianov, Iu. I. *Zhiznennyi uroven' rabochikh Rossii*. Moscow: Nauka, 1979.

Kitanina, T. M. *Khlebnaia torgovlia Rossii v kontse XIX–nachale XX veka: Strategiia vyzhivaniia, modernizatsionnye protsessy, pravitel'stvennaia politika*. St. Petersburg: Bulanin, 2011.

Kitanina, T. M. *Rossiia v pervoi mirovoi voine, 1914–1917 gg.: Ekonomika i ekonomicheskaia politika*. St. Petersburg: Nauka, 2003.

Kitanina, T. M. *Voenno-inflatsionnye kontserny v Rossii 1914–17 gg.* Leningrad: Nauka, 1969.

Kitanina, T. M. *Voina, khleb, i revoliutsii*. Leningrad: Nauka, 1985.

Klimokhin, S. K., ed. *Kratkaia Istoriia stachki tekstil'shchikov Ivanovo-Kineshmskoi promyshlennoi oblasti* Kineshma: Tip. Khoziaistvoi Sektsii Sov. Rab. i Krest. Deputatov, 1918.

Koenker, Diane P. *Moscow Workers and the 1917 Revolution*. Princeton, NJ: Princeton University Press, 1981.

Koenker, Diane P., and William G. Rosenberg. *Strikes in Russia 1917*. Princeton, NJ: Princeton University Press, 1989.

Kokhn, M. P. *Russkie indektsy tsen*. Moscow: Ekonomicheskaia zhizn', 1926.

Kolonitskii, Boris I. "Slukhi ob imperatritse Aleksandre Fedorovne i massovaia kul'tura (1914–1917)." *Voprosy Istorii* 1 (2005): 362–78.

Kolonitskii, Boris I. *Tovarish Kerenskii: Antimonarkhicheskaya revoliutsiia i formirovaniye kulta "Vozdya naroda" mart–iiun' 1917 goda*. Moscow: NLO, 2017.

Kolonitskii, Boris I. *"Tragicheskaia erotica": Obrazy imperatorkoi sem'i v gody pervoi mirovoi voiny*. Moscow: NLO, 2010.

Kondrat'ev, N. D. *Rynok khlebov i ego regulirovanie vo vremia voiny i revoliutsii*. Moscow: Novaia derevnia, 1922.

Korolev, G. *Ivanovo-Kineshemskie tekstil'shchiki v 1917 godu*. Moscow: Vserossiiskii Tsentral'nyi Soviet Professionalnye Soiuzy, 1927.

Kostrikin, V. I. *Zemelnye komitety v 1917*. Moscow: Nauka, 1975.

Larin Iu., and L. Kritsman. *Ocherki khoziaistvennoi zhizni i organizatisa narodnogo khoziaistva Sovetskogo Rossii*. Moscow: Gosizdat, 1920.

Laub, Dori. "An Event without a Witness: Truth, Testimony and Survival." In *Testimony: Crises of Witnessing in Literature, Psychoanalysis, and History*, edited by Shoshana Felman and Dori Laub, 78–85. New York: Routledge, 1992.
Leed, Eric. J. *No Man's Land: Combat and Identity in World War I*. London: Cambridge University Press, 1979.
Lih, Lars. *Bread and Authority in Russia 1914–1921*. Berkeley: University of California Press, 1990.
Lindenmeyr, Adele. *Citizen Countess: Sofia Panina and the Fate of Revolutionary Russia*. Madison: University of Wisconsin Press, 2019.
Lindenmeyr, Adele, Christopher Read and Peter Waldron, eds. *Russia's Home Front in War and Revolution 1914–1922*, bk. 2. Bloomington, IN: Slavica. 2016.
Litvin, A. *Krasnyi i belyi terror, 1918–1922*. Moscow: Isuza, 2004.
Liubichankovskii, Sergei. "Revolution and the Creation of the Volost' Zemstvo in Southeastern Russia (Spring–Fall 1917)." In *Russia's Home Front in War and Revolution*, bk. 1, edited by Sarah Badcock, Liudmila Novikova, and Aaron Retish, 45–66. Bloomington, IN: Slavica, 2015.
Lohr, Eric. *Nationalizing the Russian Empire: The Campaign against Enemy Aliens during World War I*. Cambridge, MA: Harvard University Press 2003.
Lohr, Eric. "The Russian Army and the Jews: Mass Deportation, Hostages, and Violence during World War I." *Slavic Review* 3 (July 2001): 404–19.
Lohr, Eric, Vera Tolz, Alexander Semyonov, and Mark von Hagen, eds. *The Empire and Nationalism at War*. Bloomington, IN: Slavica, 2014.
Lorenz, Konrad. *On Aggression*. Translated by Marjorie Kerr Wilson. New York: Harcourt Brace, 1966.
Lotman, Iurii. *Universe of the Mind: A Semiotic Theory of Culture*. Bloomington: Indiana University Press, 1990.
Lyandres, Semion. *The Fall of Tsarism*. Oxford: Oxford University Press, 2013.
Maksakov, V. V., and A. Turunov. "Vremennoe pravitel'stvo avtonomnoi Sibiri." *Krasnyi Arkhiv* 29 (1928): 86–138.
Malia, Martin. The *Soviet Tragedy: A History of Socialism in Russia, 1917–1991*. New York: Free Press, 1994.
Maliavskii, A. D. *Krest'ianskoe dvizhenie v Rossii v 1917 g*. Moscow: Nauka, 1981.
Malik, Hassan. *Bankers and Bolsheviks: International Finance and the Russian Revolution*. Princeton, NJ: Princeton University Press, 2018.
Malkov, V. L., ed. *Pervaia Mirovaia Voina*. Moscow: Nauka, 1998.
Malle, Sylvana. *The Organization of War Communism 1918–1921*. Cambridge: Cambridge University Press, 1985.
Manning, Bruce. *Bayonets before Bullets: The Imperial Russian Army, 1861–1914*. Bloomington: Indiana University Press, 1992.
Marks, Steven G. "The Russian Experience with Money, 1914–24." In *Russian Culture in War and Revolution, 1914–22*, vol. 1, edited by Murray Frame, Boris Kolonitskii, Steven Marks, and Melissa Stockdale, 128–40. Bloomington, IN: Slavica, 2014.
Markevich, Andrei, and Mark Harrison. "Great War, Civil War, and Recovery: Russia's National Income, 1913–1928." *Journal of Economic History* 3 (2011): 672–703.
Matsuzato, K. "Interregional Conflicts and the Collapse of Tsarism: The Real Reason for the Food Crisis in Russia after the Autumn of 1916." In *Emerging Democracy in Late Imperial Russia*, edited by Mary Schaeffer Conway, 243–300. Niwot: University Press of Colorado, 1998.
Matsuzato, K. "Prodrazverstva V. A. Rittikha." *Acta Slavica Iaponica* 13 (1995): 167–83.

Mayer, Arno. *Furies: Violence and Terror in the French and Russian Revolutions*. Princeton, NJ: Princeton University Press, 2000.
McAuley, Mary. *Bread and Justice: State and Society in Petrograd 1917–1922*. Oxford: Oxford University Press, 1991.
McCoy, D. *The National Archives*. Chapel Hill: University of North Carolina Press, 1978.
McDonald, D. M. *United Government and Foreign Policy in Russia, 1900–1914*. Cambridge, MA: Harvard University Press, 1992.
McMeekin, Sean. *The Russian Origins of the First World War*. Cambridge, MA: Harvard University Press, 2011.
Medvedev, Roy. *Let History Judge*. Edited by D. Joravsky and Georges Haupt. New York: Knopf, 1971.
Melancon, Michael. "Revolutionary Culture in the Early Soviet Republic: Communist Executive Committees versus the Cheka, Fall 1918." *Jahrbücher für Geschichte Osteuropas* 1 (2009): 1–22.
Melancon, Michael. "Trial Run for Soviet Food Requisitioning: The Expedition to Orel Province, Fall 1918." *Russian Review* 3 (July 2020): 412–37.
Mel'gunov, S. P. *Na putiiakh k dvortsovomu perevorotu*. Ann Arbor: University of Michigan Press, 1962.
Merridale, Catherine. "The Collective Mind: Trauma and Shell-Shock in Twentieth Century Russia." *Journal of Contemporary History* 1 (2000): 39–55.
Metel'kov, P. F. *Zheleznodorozhniki v revoliutsii: Fevral' 1917–iiun' 1918*. Leningrad: Lenizdat, 1970.
Michelson, A., P. N. Apostol, and M. V. Bernatskii. *Russian Public Finance during the War*. New Haven, CT: Yale University Press, 1928.
Michl, Susanne, and Jan Plamper. "Soldatische Angst im Ersten Weltkrieg: Die Karriere eines Gefühls in der Kriegspsychiatrie Deutschlands, Frankreichs und Russlands." *Geschichte und Gesellschaft* 2 (2009): 209–48.
Mikhailov, I. D. *Evoliutsiia Russkogo transporta 1913–1925*. Moscow: Ekonomicheskaia zhizn', 1925.
Mikhailov, I. D. *Osnovy voprosy transporta*. Moscow: Viksprod, 1918.
Miliutin, V. P. *Sovremennoe ekonomicheskoe razvitie Rossii i diktatura proletariata 1914–1918*. Moscow: Izd. IPK, 1918.
Mironov, Boris N. "Peasant Popular Culture and the Origins of Soviet Authoritarianism." In *Cultures in Flux*, edited by Stephen P. Frank and Mark D. Steinberg, 54–73. Princeton, NJ: Princeton University Press, 1994.
Mironov, Boris N. *Rossiiskaia imperiia: Ot traditsii k modernu*, 3 vols. St. Petersburg: Bulanin, 2014.
Mironov, Boris N. *The Standard of Living and Revolution in Russia 1700–1917*. New York: Routledge, 2012.
Moore, Colleen M. "Demonstrations and Lamentations: Urban and Rural Responses to War in Russia in 1914." *The Historian* 3 (2009): 355–75.
Moore, Colleen M. "Land for Service: Russian Peasant Views of a Postwar Land Settlement during World War I." In *Russia's Home Front in War and Revolution, 1914–1922*, bk. 3, edited by Christopher Read, Peter Waldron, and Adele Lindenmeyr, 297–320. Bloomington, IN: Slavica, 2018.
Moore, Colleen M. "'Vino kazennoe, i my kazennye': Krestiane-prizyniki i zapret prodazhi spiritnykh napitok v Rossii 1914 g." In *Malen'kii chelovek i bol'shaia voina v istorii Rossii*, edited by T. A. Abrosimova, 161–74. St. Petersburg: Bulanin, 2014.
Mosse, George. *Fallen Soldiers*. New York: Oxford, 1990.

Nabokov, Vladimir. "The Art of Translation." *The New Republic*, Aug. 4, 1941. https://newrepublic.com/article/62610/the-art-translation.
Nachtigal, Reinhard."Germans in Russia during World War I." In *Russia's Home Front in War and Revolution 1914–1922*, bk. 2, edited by Adele Lindenmyer, Christopher Read, and Peter Waldron, 327–42. Bloomington, IN: Slavica, 2016.
Narskii, I. V. "The Frontline Experience of Russian Soldiers in 1914–1916." *Russian Studies in History* 4 (Spring 2013): 32–34.
Narskii, I. V. *Zhizn' v katastrophe*. Moscow: Rosspen, 2001.
Nelipovich, S. G. *"Brusilovskii proryv": Nastuplenie Iugo-Zapadnogo fronta v kampaniiu 1916 goda*. Moscow: Tsikhgauz, 2006.
Norris, Stephen M. *A War of Images: Russian Popular Prints, Wartime Culture, and National Identity, 1912–45*. DeKalb: Northern Illinois University Press, 2006.
Nove, Alex. *An Economic History of the U.S.S.R.* New York: Penguin, 1982.
Osinskii, N. *Stroitel'stvo sotsializma*. Moscow: Izd. Kommunist, 1918.
Osipova, T. V. *Rossiiskoe krestian'stvo v revoliutsii grazhdanskoi voine*. Moscow: Izd. Strelets, 2001.
Oushakine, Serguei. *The Politics of Despair: Nation, War, and Loss in Russia*. Ithaca, NY: Cornell University Press, 2009.
Owen, Catherine. "A Genealogy of *Kontrol'* in Russia: From Leninist to Neoliberal Governance." *Slavic Review* 2 (Summer 2016): 33–53.
Pavlov, A. Iu. "Rossia na mezh-soiuzicheskikh konferentsiiakh v gody pervoi mirovoi voiny." *Voenno- istoricheskii Zhurnal* 2 (2010): 25–31.
Pershin, P. N. *Agrarnaia revoliutsiia v Rossii*. 2 vols. Moscow: Nauka, 1966.
Petrone, Karen. "I Have Become a Stranger to Myself": The Wartime Memoirs of Lev Naumovich Voitolovskii." In *Military Affairs in Russia's Great War and Revolution, 1914–22*, bk. 1, edited by Laurie Stoff Antony Heywood, Boris Kolonitskii, and John Steinberg, 199–218. Bloomington: Slavica, 2019.
Pipes, Richard. *The Russian Revolution*. New York: Knopf, 1990.
Plamper, Jan. *History of Emotions*. New York: Oxford University Press, 2015.
Plamper, Jan. "Fear: Soldiers and Emotions in Early Twentieth Century Russian Military Psychology." *Slavic Review* 68, no. 2 (2009): 259–83.
Plattner, Stuart, ed. *Markets and Marketing*. Latham, MD: University Press, 1985.
Pokrovskii, G. *Denikinshchina*. Berlin: Grzhebina, 1923.
Polanyi, Karl. "The Economy as Instituted Process." In *The Sociology of Economic Life*, 3rd ed., edited by Mark Granovetter and Richard Swedberg, 1–19. New York: Routledge, 2011.
Polanyi, Karl. *The Livelihood of Man*. New York: Academic Press, 1977.
Polner, T. J., *Russian Local Government during the War and the Union of Zemstvos*. New Haven, CT: Yale University Press, 1930.
Poovey, Mary. *A History of the Modern Fact*. Chicago: University of Chicago Press, 1998.
Porshneva, Olga S. *Mentalitet i sotsial'noe povedenie rabochikh, krest'ian, i soldat Rossii v period pervoi mirovoi voiny (1914–mart 1918 g.)*. Ekaterinburg: UrO RAN, 2000.
Poulantzas, N. *Political Power and Social Classes*. London: Verso, 1978.
Poulantzas, N. "Problemy voiny i mira v obshchestvennoi bor'be na urale, 1914–18." In *Pervaia Mirovaia Voina*, edited by V. L. Malkov, 467–70. Moscow, 1998.
Poulantzas, N. "Sotsial'noe povedenie soldat russkoi armii v gody pervoi mirovoi voiny." *Sotsial'naia Istoriia: Ezhegodnik* (2001–2): 355–98.
Poulantzas, N. *State, Power, Socialism*. London: NLB, 1978.

Pravilova, Ekaterina. *The Ruble: A Political History.* New York: Oxford University Press, 2023.
Prokopovich, S. N. *The Economic Condition of Soviet Russia.* London: P.S. King, 1924.
Prokopovich, S. N. *Voina i narodnoe khoziaistvo.* 2nd. ed. Moscow: Delo, 1918.
Pushkareva, I. M. *Zheleznodorozhniki Rossii v burzhuazno-demokraticheskikh revoliutsiiakh.* Moscow: Nauka, 1975.
Pyle, Emily. "Peasant Strategies for Obtaining State Aid: A Study of Petitions during World War I." *Russian History/Histoire Russe* 24 (1997): 41–64.
Rabinowitch, Alexander. *The Bolsheviks in Power.* Bloomington: Indiana University Press, 2008.
Rabinowitch, Alexander. *Prelude to Revolution:* Bloomington: Indiana University Press, 1968.
Rachinskii, V. *Zheleznodorozhnyi transport v 1913 g.* Moscow: Transpechat, 1925.
Radkey, Oliver. *The Elections to the Russian Constituent Assembly of 1917.* Cambridge, MA: Harvard University Press, 1950.
Radkey, Oliver. *The Sickle under the Hammer.* New York: Columbia University Press, 1963.
Raleigh, Donald J. *Revolution on the Volga: 1917 in Saratov.* Ithaca, NY: Cornell University Press, 1986.
Raleigh, Donald J. *Experiencing Russia's Civil War.* Princeton, NJ: Princeton University Press, 2002.
Rashin, A. G. *Fabrichno-zavodskie sluzhashchie v SSSR: Chislennost', Sostav, Zarabotnaia Plata.* Moscow: Voprosy Truda, 1929.
Rashin, A. G. *Formirovanie rabochego klassa Rossii.* 2 vols. Moscow: Izd. Sots. Ekon. Lit, 1958.
Read, Christopher, Peter Waldron, and Adele Lindenmeyr eds. *Russia's Home Front in War and Revolution, 1914–1922.* Bk. 3. Bloomington, IN: Slavica, 2018.
Remington, Thomas. *Building Socialism in Bolshevik Russia: Ideology and Industrial Organization, 1917–1921.* Pittsburgh, PA: University of Pittsburgh Press, 1984.
Remington, Thomas. "Institution Building in Bolshevik Russia: The Case of 'State Kontrol'." *Slavic Review* 1 (Spring 1982): 91–103.
Rendle, Matthew. "The Problem of the 'Local' in Revolutionary Russia: Moscow Province, 1914–1922." In *Russia's Home Front in War and Revolution,* bk. 1, edited by Sarah Badcock, Liudmila Novikova, and Aaron Retish, 19–44. Bloomington, IN: Slavica, 2015.
Retish, Aaron B. *Russia's Peasants in Revolution and Civil War: Citizenship, Identity, and the Creation of the Soviet State, 1914–1922.* Cambridge: Cambridge University Press, 2008.
Richardson, Frank. *Fighting Spirit: A Study of Psychological Factors in War.* London: Cooper, 1978.
Richardson, Frank. "The Izhevsk Revolt of 1918: The Fateful Clash of Revolutionary Coalitions, Paramilitarism, and Bolshevik Powers." In *Russia's Home Front in War and Revolution,* bk. 1, edited by Sarah Badcock, Liudmila Novikova, and Aaron Retish, 299–322. Bloomington, IN: Slavica, 2015.
Rieber, Alfred J. *Merchants and Entrepreneurs in Imperial Russia.* Chapel Hill, NC: University of North Carolina Press, 1982.
Rigby, T. H. *Lenin's Government: Sovnarkom 1917–1922.* Cambridge: Cambridge University Press, 1979.
Robbins, Richard. *Famine in Russia, 1891–92.* New York: Columbia University Press, 1975.

Romano, Claude. *Events and the World*. Translated by Shane Mackinlay. New York: Fordham University Press, 2009.

Romano, Claude. *L'événement et le monde*. Paris: Presses Universitaires de France, 1998.

Roosa, Ruth. "Russian Industrialists during World War I: The Interaction of Economics and Politics." In *Entrepreneurship in Imperial Russia and the Soviet Union*, edited by Fred V. Carstensen and Gregory Guroff, 59–90. Princeton, NJ: Princeton University Press, 1983.

Rosenberg, William G. "Les Liberaux Russes et le changement de pouvoir en mars 1917." *Cahiers du Monde russe et sovietique* 1 (1968): 46–57.

Rosenberg, William G. *Liberals in the Russian Revolution*. Princeton, NJ: Princeton University Press, 1974.

Rosenberg, William G. "Representing Workers and the Liberal Narrative of Modernity." *Slavic Review* 2 (1996): 245–70.

Rosenberg, William G. "The Social Background to the 'Tsektran' Controversy: Labor Conflict on the Railroads, 1920–21." In *Party, State, and Society in the Russian Civil War*, edited by Diane Koenker, William G. Rosenberg, and Ronald G. Suny, 349–71. Bloomington: Indiana University Press, 1989.

Rudd, C. A., and S. A. Stepanov. *Fontanka 16: The Tsar's Secret Police*. Montreal: McGill-Queens University Press, 1999.

Ruthchild, Rochelle. *Equality and Revolution: Women's Rights in the Russian Empire, 1905–1917*. Pittsburgh, PA: University of Pittsburgh Press, 2010.

Rybnikov, N. D., ed. *Massovyi chitatel'*. Moscow: Mysl', 1925.

Ryskulov, T. *Vosstanie tuzemtsev v Sredeni Azii v 1916*. Kzyl-Orda: Gosizdat K.S.S.R., 1927.

Sanborn, Joshua. *Drafting the Russian Nation: Military Conscription, Total War, and Mass Politics 1905–1925*. DeKalb: Northern Illinois University Press, 2003.

Sanborn, Joshua. "The Mobilization of 1914 and the Question of the Russian Nation: A Reexamination." *Slavic Review* 2 (2000): 267–89.

Schafer, Daniel E. "Bashkir Loyalists and the Question of Autonomy." In *Russia's Home Front in War and Revolution, 1914–22*, edited by Sarah Badcock, Liudmila Novikova, and Aaron Retish, 215–46. Bloomington, IN: Slavica, 2015.

Schapiro, Leonard. *The Origins of the Communist Autocracy*. Cambridge, MA: Harvard University Press, 1966.

Scott, James C. *Seeing Like a State*. New Haven, CT: Yale University Press, 1998.

Scott, James C. *Weapons of the Weak*. New Haven, CT: Yale University Press, 1985.

Semanov, S. N. *Kronshtadtskii miatezh*. Moscow: IKSMO, 2003.

Shanin, Teodor. *The Awkward Class: Political Sociology of Peasantry in a Developing Society: Russia 1910–1925*. Oxford: Clarendon Press, 1972.

Shanin, Teodor. "Nature and Logic of the Peasant Economy." *Journal of Peasant Studies* 1 (1973): 64–80.

Shatsillo, V. *Pervaia mirovaia voina, 1914–1918: Fakty, Dokumenty*. Moscow: Olma, 2003.

Shcherbinin, P. P. *Voennyi faktor v povsednevnoi zhizni russkoi zhenshchiny v XVIII–nachale XX v.* Tambov: Iulis, 2004.

Shmelev K. "Public Finances during the Civil War 1917–1921." In *Soviet Policy in Public Finance 1917–1928*, edited by G. Sokolnikov, 74–137. Stanford, CA: Stanford University Press, 1931.

Shmukker, M. M. *Ocherki finansov I ekonomiki zhel.-dor. transport za 1913–1922*. Moscow: NKPS, 1923.

Shtif, N. I. "Dobrovol'tsy i evreiskie pogromy." In *Revoliutsiia i grazhdanskaia voina v opisaniakh belogvardeitsev: Denikin, Iudenich, Vrangel*, 138–58. Moscow, 1991.
Siderov, A. L. *Ekonomicheskoe polozhenie Rossii v gody pervoi mirovoi voiny*. Moscow: Nauka, 1973.
Siderov, A. L. *Finansovoe polozhenie Rossii v gody pervoi mirovoi voiny*. Moscow: Nauka, 1960.
Siderov, A. L. "Zheleznodorozhnyi transport." *Istoricheskie zapiski* 26 (1948): 3–64.
Siegelbaum, Lewis. *The Politics of Industrial Mobilization in Russia 1914–1917*. London: Macmillan, 1983.
Siegelbaum, Lewis. "The Workers' Groups and the War-Industries Committees: Who Used Whom." *Russian Review* 2 (Apr. 1980): 150–80.
Sirotkina, I. "The Politics of Etiology: Shell Shock in the Russian Army, 1914–1918." In *Madness and the Mad in Russian Culture*, edited by A. Brintlinger and I. Vinitsky, 215–46. Toronto: University of Toronto Press, 2015.
Skinner, G. William. "Marketing and Social Structure in Rural China." *Journal of Asian Studies* 1 (1964): 3–43; 2 (1965): 195–228; 3 (1965): 363–99.
Smirnov, N. N. et al., eds. *Malen'kii chekovek i bol'shaia voina v istorii Rossii*. St. Petersburg: Bulanin, 2014.
Smirnov, N. N., ed. *Rossiia i pervaia mirovaia voina*. St. Petersburg: Bulanin, 1999.
Smele, Jonathan D. *The "Russian" Civil Wars, 1916–1926*. Oxford: Oxford University Press, 2015.
Smith, John T. "Russian Military Censorship during the First World War." *Revolutionary Russia* 1 (2001): 71–95.
Smith, Leonard V. *Between Mutiny and Obedience: The Case of the French Fifth Infantry Division during World War I*. Princeton, NJ: Princeton University Press, 1994.
Smith, S. A. *Red Petrograd: Revolution in the Factories*. Cambridge: Cambridge University Press 1983.
Sokol, Edward. *The Revolt of 1916 in Russian Central Asia*. Baltimore, MD: Johns Hopkins University Press, 1954.
Sokolov, A. S. "Prodovol'stvennoe snabzhenie i meshochnichestvo v Riazanskoi gubernii 1918–1919." *Ekonomicheskaia Istoriia* 4 (2019): 376–85.
Sokolov, K. N. *Pravlenie generala Denikhina*. Sofia: Rossiisko—Bulgarskoe knigo—izdatel'stvo, 1921.
Sokolnikov, G. Ia. *Soviet Policy in Public Finance 1917–1928*. Stanford, CA: Stanford University Press, 1931.
Sovetskii transport 1917–1927. Moscow: Izd. NKPS, 1927.
Stanziani, Alessandro. *L'économie en révolution: Le cas Russe, 1870–1930*. Paris: Albin Michel, 1998.
Stearns, Carol Z., and Peter N. Stearns. *Anger: The Struggle for Emotional Control in America's History*. Chicago: University of Chicago Press, 1989.
Stein, Margot B. "The Meaning of Skill: The Case of the French Engine Drivers, 1837–1917." *Politics and Society* 3–4 (1978): 399–428.
Steinberg, John W. *All the Tsar's Men: Russia's General Staff and the Fate of the Empire 1989–1914*. Washington, D.C.: Woodrow Wilson Press, 2010.
Steinberg, Mark D., and Valera Sobol, eds. *Interpreting Emotions in Russia and Eastern Europe*. DeKalb: Northern Illinois University Press, 2011.
Stepanov, Z. V. *Rabochie Petrograd v period podgotovki i provedeniia oktiabr'skogo vooruzhennogo vostaniia*. Moscow: Nauka, 1965.

Stites, Richard. *Revolutionary Dreams: Utopian Visions and Experimental Life in the Russian Revolution*. New York: Oxford University Press, 1989.

Stockdale, Melissa. *Mobilizing the Russian Nation: Patriotism and Citizenship in the First World War*. Cambridge: Cambridge University Press, 2016.

Stockdale, Melissa. "'My Death for the Motherland Is Happiness': Women, Patriotism, and Soldiering in Russia's Great War, 1914–1917." *American Historical Review* 1 (2004): 78–116.

Stockdale, Melissa. *Paul Miliukov and the Quest for the Liberal Russia, 1880–1918*. Ithaca, NY: Cornell University Press, 1996.

Stoff, Laurie. *Russia's Sisters of Mercy and the Great War: More Than Binding Men's Wounds*. Lawrence: University of Kansas Press, 2015.

Stoff, Laurie. *They Fought for the Motherland: Russia's Women Soldiers in World War I and the Revolution*. Lawrence: University of Kansas Press, 2006.

Stoff, Laurie, Antony Heywood, Boris Kolonitskii, and John Steinberg, eds. *Military Affairs in Russia's Great War and Revolution, 1914–22*. Bk. 1. Bloomington, IN: Slavica, 2019.

Stoler, Ann. *Along the Archival Grain*. Princeton, NJ: Princeton University Press, 2009.

Stone, David R. *The Russian Army in the Great War*. Lawrence: University of Kansas Press, 2015.

Stone, Norman. *The Eastern Front, 1914–1917*. London: Hodder and Stoughton, 1975.

Strakhov, V. V. "Vmitrennie zaimy v Rossii v pervuiu mirovuiu voinu." *Voprosy Istorii* 9 (2003): 28–43.

Strizhkov, Iu. K. *Prodovol'stvennye otriady v gody grazhdanskoi voiny i inostrannoi interventsii 1917–1921 gg*. Moscow: Nauka, 1973.

Struve, P. B., ed. *Food Supply in Russia during the World War*. New Haven, CT: Yale University Press, 1930.

Sumpf, Alexandre. *La Grande guerre oublié: Russie 1914–1918*. Paris: Perrin, 2014.

Taniaev, A. P. *Ocherki dvizheniia zheleznodorozhnikov v revoliutsiiu 1917 g*. Moscow: Istprofstran, 1925.

Tarasov, Konstantin. "Voennye zagovory, nastoiashchie i mnimye: Deiatel'nost' antibol'shevistskogo podpol'ya po organizatsii vooruzhennogo vosstaniia v Petrograde, mart–iiun' 1918 g." *Zhurnal Rossiiskikh I Vostochnoevropeyskikh Issledovaniy* 2 (2019): 32–69.

Tarasov, Konstantin. "Za predelami natsii: Krisiz rossiiskoi armii v 1917 kak sledstvie transformatsii imperskoi sotsial'noi sotsial'noi strukturi." *Ab Imperio* 2 (2020): 102–35.

Tsvetkov, V. Zh. *Belye armii iuga Rossia*. Moscow: Posev, 2000.

Tsvetkov, V. Zh. *Beloe delo v Rossii, 1917–1919*. Moscow: Iakor', 2019.

Tursunov, Kh. T. *Vosstanie 1916 v Srednei Azii I Kazakhstane*. Tashkent: Gos. izd-vo Uzbekskoï SSR, 1962.

Van Creveld, M. *Fighting Power: German and US Army Performance, 1939–1945*. Westport, CT: Greenwood, 1982.

van der Kolk, Bessel. *The Body Keeps Score: Brain, Mind, and Body in the Healing of Trauma*. New York: Penguin, 2014.

Vasil'ev, N. *Transport Rossii v voine 1914–18*. Moscow: Voenizdat, 1939.

Vasiliev, Pavel. "War, Revolution and Drugs: The 'Democratization' of Drug Abuse and the Evolution of Drug Policy in Russia, 1914–24." In *Russia's Home Front in War and Revolution 1914–22*, bk. 2, edited by Adele Lindenmyer, Christopher Read, and Peter Waldron, 411–30. Bloomington, IN: Slavica, 2016.

Viola, Lynne. *Best Sons of the Fatherland: Workers in the Vanguard of Soviet Collectivization.* New York: Oxford University Press, 1987.

Viola, Lynne. *Peasant Rebels under Stalin: Collectivization and the Culture of Peasant Resistance.* New York: Oxford University Press, 1996.

Viola, Lynne, ed. *The War against the Peasantry 1927-1940: The Tragedy of the Soviet Countryside.* Translated by Steven Shabad. New Haven, CT: Yale University Press, 2005.

Volkov, E. Z. *Dinamika narodonaseleniia SSSR.* Moscow: Gosizdat, 1930.

Vompe, P. A. *Tri goda revoliutsionnogo dvizheniia na zheleznykh dorogaku Rossisskoi Sovetskoi respubliki (1917-1920).* Moscow: Prodput', 1920.

Vorob'ev, N. Ia. "Izmeneniia v Russkoi promyshlennosti v period voiny i revoliutsii." *Vestnik Statistiki* 14 (1923): 115-54.

Wade, Rex. *Red Guards and Workers' Militias in the Russian Revolution.* Stanford, CA: Stanford University Press, 1984.

Wargelin, C. F. "The Economic Collapse of Austro-Hungarian Dualism, 1914-18." *East European Quarterly* 3 (2000): 261-88.

Watson, Alexander. *Ring of Steel.* London: Allen Lane, 2014.

Watson, Peter. *War on the Mind.* London: Hutchinson, 1978.

Wheatcroft, Stephen G. "Famine and Epidemic Crises in Russia, 1918-1922: The Case of Saratov." *Annales de démographie historique* (1983): 329-52.

White, Hayden. *Metahistory: The Historical Imagination in Nineteenth Century Europe.* Baltimore, MD: Johns Hopkins University Press, 1973.

Wildman, Allan. *The End of the Russian Imperial Army.* 2 vols. Princeton, NJ: Princeton University Press, 1987.

Winter, Jay. "Shell Shock and the Cultural History of the Great War." *Journal of Contemporary History* 1 (2000): 7-11.

Yarov, S. S. *Chelovek pered litsom vlasti 1917-1920 gg.* Moscow: Rosspen, 2014.

Yarov, S. S. *Gorozhanin kak politik.* St. Petersburg: Bulanin, 1999.

Yurchak, Alexei. *Everything Was Forever, Until It Was No More.* Princeton, NJ: Princeton University Press, 2005.

Za Piat' Let. Moscow: Gosizdat, 1922.

Zagorsky, S. O. *State Control of Industry in Russia during the War.* New Haven, CT: Yale University Press, 1928.

Zak, A. N. *Denezhnoe obrashchenie i emissionnaia operatsiia v Rossii 1917-1918 gg.* Petrograd: Svoboda, 1918.

Zaionchkovskii, A. I. *Pervaia mirovaia voina.* St. Petersburg: Poligon, 2002.

Znamenskii, O. N. *Iiul'skii krizis.* Moscow: Nauka, 1964.

Index

For the benefit of digital users, indexed terms that span two pages (e.g., 52–53) may, on occasion, appear on only one of those pages.
Figures are indicated by *f* following the page number

Admiralteiskii shipbuilding yards, 420
Adzhemov, Moisei, 255–56
Afghanistan War (1980s), 530, 534
Aivaz machine shops (Saint Petersburg), 74–75, 115–16
Aleksandrovsk railroad shops, 420, 438
Alekseev, Mikhail General
    Brusilov offensive and, 192, 194–95
    death of, 455
    Kerensky offensive and, 339–40
    Moscow State Conference (1917) and, 382
    Nicholas II's abdication and, 252, 254
    on prisoners of war and Russia's workforce needs, 188
    on Russian Army morale during World War I, 81, 288, 338
    Russia's World War I goals after February Revolution and, 288
    White Army forces commanded by, 420–21, 422, 455
Alexander II (tsar), 11–12, 451–52
Alexander III (tsar), 8–9
Alexandra (princess), 161–62, 220, 221–22
Alexandra Fedorovna (tsarina), 94–95
All-Russia Congress of Soviets (1917), 318–19, 331, 345, 398, 410
All-Russia Congress of Trade Unions (1917), 434–35
All-Russia Extraordinary Commission for Combatting Counterrevolution and Subversion. *See* Cheka
All-Russian Congress of Trade Industrialists (1917), 266–67
All-Russian Congress of Women, 250
All-Russia Railroad Union
    Bolsheviks' seizure of power (1917) and, 418–19
    Central Food Bureau of, 438–39
    Kornilov coup attempt (1917) and, 402
    Lenin and, 403
    local line committees' conflicts with, 357

    railroad democratization initiatives and, 366–68, 401
    Socialist Revolutionaries and, 401, 418–19, 437
    statization policies and, 376–77, 506
All-Russia State Conference (1917), 380–81
All-Russia Trade Union Conference, 333
Alperovich, Evgenii, 427–28
anarchists, 308, 331, 351–52, 387–88, 477
Andreev, Leonid, 34
Anfimov, A. M., 64–65
Anskii, S. (Solomon Rappoport), 55–56, 204
anti-Semitism. *See also* Jews
    accusations of espionage and, 107, 475–76, 484–85
    Baltic territories and, 128
    kulaks and, 471
    in Russian military and government, 103–6, 204, 478–79
    violence and, 23, 55–56, 360, 447, 466, 477, 484–85
    War Capitalism and, 152
    World War I and, 23, 48–49, 55–56, 107, 196–97, 360, 408
Antonov-shchina, 458, 489–92, 517
April Crisis (1917), 285–88, 307–10, 405–6
"April Theses" (Lenin), 285
Arendt, Hannah, 4, 25–26
Armed Forces of South Russia (AFSR). *See* White Army
Armenians in Russia, 150
Arsenii, Archbishop (Andrei Lvovich Chahovstov), 34
Article 87 (Fundamental Laws), 86–87, 88, 170–71, 173, 187, 189–90
Article Six (Soviet Constitution), 1–2
Astashov, A.B., 22–23, 49, 53–54, 359
Astrov, Nikolai
    Committee on Social Organizations and, 257
    Duma coalition politics and, 178–79
    July 8 declaration and, 352–53

Astrov, Nikolai (*cont.*)
   on price controls and rationing, 168–69
   Provisional Government position (1917) of, 223–24
   reform initiatives in South Russia and, 484
   Russian Civil War and, 487–88
   War Industries Committees and, 127
Austria. *See also* Galician Campaign (1914-1915)
   Brusilov Offensive and, 18
   Jews in, 23, 103–4
   military spending before World War I in, 62
   social stability before World War I in, 33
   speculation during World War I in, 149–50
   on price controls and rationing, 168–69
   "turnip winter" (1916) in, 157, 210
Avksent'iev, Nikolai, 309, 352, 420

Babel, Isaac, 462–63, 489–90
babi bunty ("women's' protests"), 520
Bachmanov, Andrei Arkad'evich, 396, 399–400
Badcock, Sarah, 213, 324–25, 329–31, 346, 362
Baker, Keith, 225–26
Baker, Mark, 213–14, 330
Baku, 72, 176
Baltic Ship Building plant, 321, 514
Baltic territories, 128
Bank for Trade, 149
Bark, Peter
   finance minister appointment of, 84, 86
   financial training of, 85–86
   financing of World War I and, 16–17, 86–87, 89, 91–92, 113–14, 170–72, 175, 200–1, 218–19
   gold standard financial system and, 164
   inflation during World War I and, 165
   military spending and, 185
   mobilization for World War I and, 30
   Nicholas II and, 85–86
   railroad bonds and, 149
   railroad tariffs and, 88, 174–75
   Russia's money supply in World War I and, 89
   State Bank position of, 86
   state ban on liquor sales during World War I and, 88
   tax reform proposals of, 86, 90, 91
   treasury notes for World War I and, 30
Barnaul draft riots, 36–37
Barzukov, V. S., 99
Beker (Becker) Shipbuilding, 91–92
Beliaev, M. A. General, 101
Beria, Lavrenti, 526
Berkhofer, Robert, 6–9

Berlin (Germany), 489, 523–24
Bernatskii, M. V., 169–70, 355, 363, 397–98
Bethmann-Hollweg, Theobald von, 149–50, 232–33
Beyrau, Dietrich, 478–79
black markets
   Babel's *Red Cavalry* and, 462–63
   Bolshevik era and, 415–16, 423, 429–30, 503
   Cheka's suppression of, 431–32
   hoarding and, 363–64
   the military and, 151, 338
   price controls and, 264
   railroads and, 112, 219
   war capitalism and, 149–50
Bloch, Ernst, 240–41
Bloody Sunday massacre (Petrograd, 1905), 231, 478
Bogdanov, Boris, 260
Bogorodsk, 158, 212
Bolsheviks
   All-Russia Congress of Soviets (1917) and, 331
   All-Russia State Conference (1917), 380–81
   Constituent Assembly dissolved (1918) by, 413, 431–32
   Constituent Assembly elections (1917) and, 419
   February Revolution (1917) and, 242–43, 248, 307
   grain requisition by, 488–89, 490, 491
   increasing support during World War I for, 144, 216–17
   July Days insurrection (1917) and, 344–45, 354
   Kornilov coup attempt (1917) and, 390
   land redistribution policies and, 422–23
   nationalization of private businesses by, 426–28
   nationalization of Russia's archives and, 14
   Ninth Party Congress (1920) and, 506–7
   "Peace, Land, and Bread" slogan of, 362–63, 414–15
   peace initiative to end Russia's involvement in World War I and, 421
   Petrograd and Moscow Soviet elections (1917) and, 390–91, 399–400
   Russia's participation in World War I opposed by, 32, 178–79, 332, 336–37, 340, 345, 408–9, 418
   scarcity as a source for political mobilization by, 236, 315, 409
   seizure of power (1917) by, 403, 410, 415, 416, 418–19

Seventh Party Congress (1918) in, 421–22, 439
Sixth Party Conference (1917) of, 415
socialist economic goals of, 415–16, 429, 433–34
State Bank and, 424–25, 427, 428
Tenth Party Congress and, 510, 512, 515–16, 517, 520–21
trade unions and, 434–35
underground movement during World War I of, 214–15
Brest-Litovsk fortress, 62
Brest-Litovsk Treaty (1918)
  accusations of betrayal regarding, 442–43, 447–48
  Don region and, 451
  Germany's demands in, 439
  Russia's ratification of, 439–40
  Ukrainian territories surrendered to Germany in, 413, 421–22, 439, 441–42, 447, 458
Brezhnev, Leonid, 528–29, 534
Brian, Eric, 214
Briukhanov, N. P., 459–60
Brover, B. I., 463–64
Brower, Daniel, 431–32
Brusilov, Aleksei General
  Brusilov offensive (1916) and, 18, 102, 192–96, 198, 199, 210–11, 311–12, 376
  on clothing scarcity among soldiers, 100
  early victories (1914) by, 57–58, 193
  on exhaustion among soldiers, 47–48
  Galician Campaign (1914-1915) and, 41, 59, 99, 193
  Kerensky Offensive (1917) and, 334, 335, 337, 339–40, 393
  military food supply issues and, 203
  Moscow State Conference (1917) and, 382
Bublikov, A. A., 173–74, 182–83, 320
Buchanan, Sir George 32–33, 34, 61–62, 146–47
Budberg, A. P., 483
Bukharin, Nikolai, 415, 421–22, 432, 439, 465–66, 520
Buldakov, Vladimir, 22–23, 37, 204, 474–78
Bulgakov, Mikhail, 487
Bulgakova, Liudmila, 213, 330
Burdzhalov, Eduard, 237
Bureau for Relations between Labor and Management, 320
Butler, Judith, 240

The Caucasus
  Cossack forces during Civil War in, 482–83

Muslim populations in, 475–76
nationalities questions in, 265, 342–43, 398–99
railroad labor armies in, 507–8
Russian soldiers' withdrawal during World War I from, 421
Russia's World War I battles in, 43–44, 60
shortages during World War I at, 207, 233–34
Central Conciliation Board, 400–1
Central Cotton Committee, 319–20
Central Land Committee, 327–28
Central Line Committee, 273
Central Soviet Executive Committee, 380–81
Central War Industries Committee (CWIC). See War Industries Committees (WICs)
Central Wool Committee, 319–20
Chaianov, A. V., 262–63, 267
Chaikovskii, N. V., 262–63
Chapaev, Vasili, 458
Cheka
  black markets suppressed by, 431–32
  Bolsheviks' political enemies suppressed by, 420–21, 432–33, 464
  brutality of, 453–54, 466–67
  deserters from Red Army targeted by, 491–92
  establishment of, 420
  Rabkrin and, 501–2
  railroad agents of, 444, 445–46, 453, 466–67, 504–5, 507–8
Chelnokov, M. V., 178
Cherevanin, F. A., 200
Chernev, Boris, 439
Chernigov, 103–4, 207, 471, 477
Chernov, Victor
  All-Russia Congress of Soviets (1917) and, 331
  April Crisis (1917) and, 309–10
  July Days insurrection (1917) and, 352–53
  land reform proposals and, 327–28, 362–63
  peasant advocacy of, 268–69, 309, 310
  railroads and, 274–75
  Russian Revolution history written by, 9
  seizures of privately held land and, 268–69
  Socialist Revolutionaries and, 11–12, 268–69
Chkheidze, Nikolai
  Duma coalition politics and, 178–79
  Duma dissolution in 1915 and, 132
  February Revolution (1917) and, 242–43
  food crisis of 1917 and, 263–64
  French Revolution and, 2–3
  Moscow State Conference (1917) and, 387–89, 404–5
  Petrograd Soviet and, 260

Chkheidze, Nikolai (*cont.*)
  political rights of workers and peasants supported by, 224–25
  Provisional Government (1917) and, 244, 259
  railroad workforce issues and, 174
  Russia's World War I goals after February Revolution and, 288
  subsistence riots of 1916 and, 215–16
  trade unions and, 180
Chuprov, A. A., 85–86, 113
Chuprov Society for the Development of Social Science, 113
Cohen, Aaron J., 52
Commission to Study the Current Cost of Living, 113
Committee for the Fight against Desertion, 491–92, 493–95
Committee for the Salvation of the Revolution, 418
Committee of Social Organizations, 257
Committee on State Security (KGB), 527
Communist Party (Soviet Union), 1–2, 530. *See also* Bolsheviks
Comte, Auguste, 9–10
Conference of Factory Representatives, 446–48, 450–51
Conference of Petrograd Factory Committees, 333
Conference of Railroad Engineers, 272–73
Conference of Representatives of Trade and Industry, 373
Conference of Trade Unions, 366
Conference on Supplying the Capital with Items of Primary Need (1916), 161–62
Constantinople, 81, 227, 245–46, 285–86, 287, 332, 342, 456, 482
Constituent Assembly
  Bolsheviks' dissolution (1918) of, 413, 431–32
  elections (1917) for, 380, 388–89, 413, 418–19
  July 8 Declaration (1917) and, 352–53
  land redistribution proposals and, 271, 327, 389
  nationality and federalism questions for, 341–42, 343, 398–99
  protests against the dissolution of, 449–51
Constitutional Democratic Party. *See* Kadets
Cossacks
  civilians abused during World War I by, 107, 383
  February Revolution (1917) and, 239–40, 241, 242–43
  July Days insurrection (1917) and, 348, 349–50, 389–90

refugees displaced by, 106–7
in Siberia, 477, 479–80, 485
subsistence riots (1916) suppressed by, 212
as White Army forces, 455, 456, 457, 479–80, 482–83, 484–85, 491–92
Council of Five. *See* Special Council of Five
Council of Industrial Congresses, 80–81, 112, 123–24, 188–89, 282, 372, 419, 453
Council of Ministers
  elected worker representatives at factories and, 143–44
  financing of World War I and, 89–90, 91–92, 173
  food supply issues and, 110
  fuel supply issues and, 137
  militarization of labor forces and, 142, 188
  military budgets and, 60
  new appointments (1915) at, 129
  Nicholas II's control of the military and, 130
  price controls during World War I and, 110–11
  "yellow workers" and, 187–88
Council of the Republic (1917), 405, 437–38
Council of Ural Mining Enterprises, 255–56
Crimea, 188, 203–4, 398–99, 489–90, 535
Cuban missile crisis (1962), 528–29
Czechoslovakia, 523–24, 528–29

Dan, Fedor, 224–25, 309, 349, 352
Daniels, Robert, 510–11
Danilov, N. A., 102–3
Dardanelle Straits, 77, 81, 227, 285–87, 342, 456
DDT (music group), 534
Declaration of Soldiers' Rights, 336–37, 385
Decree on Universal Obligatory Labor (1920), 500
Dement'ev, G. V., 377, 379
Democratic Conference (1917), 391, 404–5
Denikin, Anton
  atrocities by troops commanded by, 484–85, 486
  on insurrection in Russian army after Kerensky offensive, 341
  Kadets and, 455
  land reform policies and, 457
  requisition of food by forces of, 485
  retreat from Russian Civil War by, 490, 491, 497–98
  White Army forces commanded by, 420–21, 422, 453, 455–56, 482–83
Department for the Resolution of Conflict between Capital and Labor, 19–20, 312–13, 368, 434
Derrida, Jacques, 531

INDEX 569

Dolgova, A.V., 494
Donbas region, 72, 84, 128, 257-58, 441, 497-98
Donets region, 72, 183, 323
Doob, Leonard, 35-36
Dowling, Timothy C., 193
Dragomirov, Vladimir, 62
Dubcek, Alexander, 528-29
Dubnow, Simon, 105-6
Duma
  Budget Committee of, 88, 113-14, 165, 170-71, 215-16, 219-20
  election law (1906), 144
  establishment (1905) of, 10-11, 12, 38
  February Revolution (1917) and dissolving of, 237
  income tax passed (1916) by, 280
  military budgets and, 60
  session (1914) of, 29-32
  session (1915) of, 129-32
  session (1916) of, 216-17
Durnovo, Peter, 130-33
Dutov, Ataman, 482
Dzerzhinskii, Felix, 509, 511-12

East Prussia campaign (1914), 40-41, 42-43, 47-48, 57, 98-99, 106
Edelstein, Dan, 225-26
Eighth Army, 153-54, 193-94, 360
Eighth Congress of Representatives of Trade and Industry (1914), 64
Eighth Congress of Soviets, 511
Ekaterinburg, 169-70, 496-97, 507-8
Ekaterininskaia railroad line workers, 273
Elizabeth II (queen of England), 2
Enderlich, Paul, 34
Engel, Barbara, 210, 212, 213
Engelstein, Laura, 239
England. *See* Great Britain
Erikson, Erik, 44
Erikson Electric, 118, 177-78, 214
Erlikh, Henrykh, 260
Estonia, 398-99
Etkind, Alexander, 526-27
Everything Flows (Grossman), 526-27

Falkenhayn, Erich von, 193-94
famine of 1921-1922, 25, 463, 518-19, 521-23, 525
Farmborough, Florence, 55, 59, 93
February Revolution (1917)
  Bolsheviks and, 242-43, 248, 307
  Duma dissolution and, 237
  food protests and, 237-39
  land redistribution proposals and, 269

Nicholas II's abdication and, 8-9, 237, 242, 244, 252, 254
  Petrograd Soviet and, 15-16, 247
  Russia's involvement in World War I and, 252-54
  social identities and, 249-51
  women's involvement in, 238-39
Fel'zer and Co., 379-80
Fergana Valley, 204-5
Fifth Army, 41, 191
Fifth Congress of Soviets (1918), 451
Figes, Orlando, 394, 430-31, 458, 472, 492
Finland, 342-43, 398
First Army, 40-41, 47, 191
First Labor Army, 507-8
First Machine Gun Regiment, 344-45
First Moscow Food Brigade Regiment, 469-70
First World War. *See* World War I
Florinsky, Michael, 162-63
food crises in Russia (1916-1919)
  Bolshevik regime and, 429-30, 460-62
  grain requisitioning policies and, 264-68
  harvest levels and, 218-19, 261, 394, 440-41, 458-59
  hoarding and concealment during, 357, 440-41, 462, 468-70, 476-77, 502-3
  inflation and, 219-20, 314, 324, 328
  peasant activism and, 324-27, 328-29
  Russia's soldiers and, 307, 338
  strikes and, 314-17
formalist approach to economic development, 66-67, 76, 119
France
  anxiety among soldiers in, 48, 95
  financing of World War I in, 90-91
  French Revolution and, 2-3, 225-26, 237, 308-9, 413-14, 451-52, 529
  mutinies during World War I in, 234-35
  Russia's financing of World War I and, 89
  speculation during World War I in, 149-50
  war powers acts during World War I in, 36
  World War I patriotism in, 34
  World War I's Western Front in, 43-44, 48
Franco-Prussian War (1870-1871), 60
Fridman, M. I., 85-86, 397-98
Fukuyama, Francis, 8-9
Fundamental Laws, 86-87, 88, 170, 222, 225
Furet, François, 2

Gajda, Radola, 482
Galician Campaign (1914-1915)
  anxiety and exhaustion among Russian soldiers in, 47-49, 59, 93
  censorship of soldiers' views during, 57-59

Galician Campaign (1914-1915) (*cont.*)
  expropriation of property during, 111
  German reinforcements following early setbacks in, 58-59
  "Great Retreat" and, 58-59, 102, 105-6, 122, 130-31, 153-55, 190
  Jewish deportations during, 103-6
  Przemyśl fortress and, 57-59
  Russian prisoners of war during, 58-59
  Russia's early victories in, 57-58
  shortages among soldiers in, 48-49, 100-2
Galili, Ziva, 260, 309
Gallipoli, battle (1915) of, 77, 81, 163-64
gas warfare in World War I, 16, 45-47, 290*f*, 338-39
Gatrell, Peter, 16, 62-63, 64-66, 68-69, 106-7
Gaudin, Corinne, 22-23, 213
Geiferikh Sade plant (Kharkov), 378
Germany. *See also* Brusilov Offensive (1916)
  Brest-Litovsk Treaty and, 439
  East Prussia campaign (1914), 40-41, 42-43, 47-48, 57, 98-99, 106
  Galician campaign (1914-1915), 59
  gas warfare in World War I and, 45
  Jews in, 23
  military spending before World War I in, 62
  Nazi regime and World War II in, 523-25
  price controls during World War I in, 90-91
  rationing and food shortages in, 90-91
  social stability before World War I in, 33
  Soviet Union's trade with, 518-19
  speculation during World War I in, 149-50
  War Communism in, 265
Gerwarth, Robert, 475-76
Giddens, Anthony, 51
glasnost', 1-2
Glavpolitput', 445-46, 505-6
Glinka, G. V., 165-66
gold standard, 90, 164, 171-72
Golitsyn, Nikolai, 207, 231, 241-42
Golovin, N. N., 193
Gorbachev, Mikhail, 1-2, 532-33, 535-36
Goremykin, Ivan Logginovich
  Duma speech at beginning of World War I by, 29-30
  elected worker representatives at factories and, 143-44
  on labor unrest in Petrograd during World War I, 115-16
  militarization of labor forces resisted by, 142, 188-89
  Nicholas II's dismissal (1916) of, 161-62
  price controls in World War I and, 110-11
  Progressive Bloc and, 130-32
Got'e, Iurii Vladimirovich, 245
Government to Save the Revolution, 348, 351-53, 363-64, 368-69, 381
Grabar', Vladimir, 104
Graf, Daniel, 103
Graham, Stephen, 211
Graves, Robert, 108
Great Britain
  financing of World War I in, 90-91
  Ministry of Armaments in, 157
  Russia's financing of World War I and, 89, 91-92
  speculation during World War I in, 149-50
  war powers acts during World War I in, 36
  World War I and patriotism in, 34, 108
Great Reforms of 1861, 3, 12
Great Terror (1936-1938), 523-24
Great Turn (1929), 521
Great War. *See* World War I
Gribenchikov, Boris, 534
Groman, Vladimir
  April Crisis (1917) and, 309
  Commissariat of Food and, 428-29
  Commission to Study the Current Cost of Living, 113
  Economic Committee of, 19, 165-67
  food crisis of 1917 and, 242-43, 262-63, 264-66
  grain requisition policies and, 362, 443
  inflation and, 167, 328
  Petrograd Soviet and, 19
  price controls and, 19-20
  railroad workforce issues and, 174
  Special Council for Defense and, 19
  state regulation of the economy and, 168-69, 356-57, 396-97
  Union of Cities Conference (1916) and, 165-66, 200
  war communism and, 266-67
Gronskii, Paul, 255-56
Grossman, Vasili, 522, 526-27
Groznyi, 508
Guchkov, Alexander
  February Revolution (1917) and, 254, 256
  liberal reform proposals during World War I and, 130
  militarization of labor forces and, 142-43
  Moscow State Conference (1917) and, 384
  nationalization of military suppliers and, 17-18
  Octobrists and, 3-4
  Provisional Government (1917) and, 259

reforms of 1905 and, 124
resignation as war minister (1917) by, 310
War Industries Committees and, 124–25, 134–35, 145, 182–83
war planning after Galician retreat and, 122–24
Gulag prison camps, 526–27, 535
Gurko, V. I., 256
Guzhon metal works (Moscow), 350
Gvozdev, Kuz'ma
  as assistant minister of labor, 319
  Bolsheviks' criticisms of, 180
  labor mediation and, 320–21, 372, 402–3
  Petrograd Soviet and, 260
  political rights of workers and peasants supported by, 224–25
  Provisional Government (1917) and, 404–5
  railroads and, 174, 402–3
  trade unions and, 180–81

Haimson, Leopold, 33, 214
Harrison, Mark, 65–66
Hasegawa, Tsuyoshi, 237
Hegel, G.W.F., 2–3, 9–10, 12, 13–14
Heywood, Anthony, 219, 235–36
Hickey, Michael, 328–29
High Command (Stavka)
  anti-Semitism during World War I and, 105–6
  Brusilov Offensive (1916) and, 190, 192–93
  Caucus front in World War I and, 43–44
  contact with French and British military leaders and, 190
  directives to soldiers about correspondence and, 51
  Galician Campaign and, 57–58
  militarization of workforces and, 188
  price controls in World War I and, 110–11
  Russian loses in first months of World War I (1914) and, 42
Himmelfarb, Gertrude, 5–6
Hindenburg, Paul von, 194–95, 232–33
Hitler, Adolf, 489, 523–24
Hogan, Heather, 67–68, 321
Holmes, Richard, 108
Holquist, Peter, 455, 495–96
Hoover, Herbert, 6, 518–19
Horne, John, 475–76
Hungary, 195, 527–29
Hynes, Samuel, 23–24, 52, 195

Ianushkevich, Nikolai General, 103–4, 107, 122
Iaroslavl, 435

International Committee for Russian Relief, 518–19
International Women's Day protests (1917), 238–39
I. Stakheev & Company, 151
Isupov, V. A., 486
Italy, 58, 194–95
Iudenich, Nikolai General, 456, 482–83, 490
Iurenev, Peter, 371–72, 437–38
Ivanov, N. I. General, 41
Ivanovo
  labor unrest in, 117–18, 212, 403–4
  rationing in, 202–3
  shortages of industrial supplies in, 282
  textile production facilities in, 73, 403–4
Izgoev, A. S., 343

Jahn, Hubertus, 34
Jews. *See also* anti-Semitism
  civil rights proposals during World War I and, 133–34
  deportations during World War I of, 103–6
  expropriation of property during World War I from, 105, 204
  as merchants in Russia's peasant villages, 150
  Pale settlement and, 103–4
  as refugees during World War I, 106–7
  in the Russian military, 30–31, 103–4
July Days insurrection (1917)
  Bolsheviks and, 344–45, 354
  concerns about the harvest during, 350–51
  Cossacks and, 348, 349–50, 389–90
  July 8 Declaration and, 351–53, 362–63, 376, 387–88
  Moscow and, 346–47
  Nizhnii Novgorod and, 346
  opposition to Russia's participation in World War I and, 345
  Petrograd and, 344–47, 349
  strikes during, 350
  Tauride Palace occupation during, 349

Kadets (Constitutional Democratic Party)
  Constituent Assembly elections (1917) and, 419
  democratic self-determination and, 342, 343–44, 398
  Duma coalition politics and, 178–79
  Duma supervision over the military and, 130
  Eighth Party Congress (1917) of, 331, 332
  Kolchak regime and, 454–55, 457–58, 484
  land reform proposals of, 3–4, 271

Kadets (Constitutional Democratic Party) (*cont.*)
  liberal reform proposals during World War I and, 130
  Octobrists and, 3–4, 11
  Provisional Government (1917) and, 223–24, 255–56, 341, 347, 349–50, 385
  reforms of 1905 and, 124
  "revolution from above" philosophy and, 178
  Revolution of 1905 and, 3
  Sixth Party Congress (1916) of, 179–80
  Tenth Party Congress (1917) of, 405
Kafengauz, L. B., 397–98, 427–28
Kaledin, Aleksei General, 382–83, 385–86
Kalinin, M. I., 509–10
Kaluga, 315, 447, 448, 464–65, 469–70, 496–97, 501–2
Karpov, V. I., 185–86
Katzenellenbaum, Z. S., 85–86, 278
Kazakhstan, 521–22, 526–28
Kazan, 316, 362
Kenez, Peter, 483–84
Kerensky, Alexander
  All-Russia State Conference (1917) and, 380–81
  April Crisis (1917) and, 310
  Bolsheviks' seizure of power (1917) and, 415
  Duma dissolution in 1915 and, 132
  Duma speech at beginning of World War I by, 31–32
  February Revolution (1917) and, 242–43, 246–47
  flight from Russia (1917) by, 418
  French Revolution and, 2–3
  inflation and, 363
  July Days insurrection (1917) and, 344–45, 352–53, 359
  Kerensky Offensive (1917) and, 334, 335–37, 340–41, 376, 478–79, 484
  Kornilov coup attempt (1917) and, 390–91, 402
  on labor and economic conditions in Turkestan, 204–5
  Moscow State Conference (1917) and, 382–84, 388
  Petrograd Soviet and, 260
  political rights of workers and peasants supported by, 224–25
  Provisional Government (1917) and, 244–45, 248, 255, 259, 390–91, 397–98, 404–6, 410
  railroad labor negotiations and, 402–3
  Russian Revolution history written by, 9, 413–14

Russia's World War I goals after February Revolution and, 287
Ukraine and, 341–42
Khabalov, S. S. General, 239–40, 241–42, 243, 261
Kharkov region
  labor unrest in, 378
  locomotive works in, 364, 373
  military requisitions in, 183, 213–14
  pogroms in, 447, 466
Kherson province, 158, 264
Khrushchev, Nikita, 526–30
Khvostov, Alexander
  dismissal from interior minister post of, 183
  justice minister appointment (1915) of, 129
  on political instability under conditions of scarcity, 155, 158, 165–66, 176, 216, 406–7
  Special Council of Five and, 159, 160–61
  Special Council on Food and, 166
  Union of Russian People and, 162
Kiev province, 72, 102–3, 153, 268–69
Kirgiz region, 205
Kirianov, Iurii, 210–11
Kishinev, 392
Kishkin, Nikolai, 223–24, 255–56, 257, 261–62, 352–53, 390–91, 404–5
Kitanina, Taisia, 64–65, 151, 209
Kleinbort, L. M., 366
Kliuchevskii, Vasili, 502–3, 533–34
Knox, Alfred, 42, 98, 192–93, 195, 197, 335–36, 339–40
Kobozev, Peter, 445
Koenker, Diane, 431–32
Kokoshkin, Fedor, 420
Kokovtsov, Vladimir, 78, 84, 85–86, 89
Kolchak, Alexander General
  atrocities committed by troops under command of, 486
  Cossack forces and, 457
  Kadets and, 454–55, 457–58, 484
  Komuch overthrown by, 454, 484, 485
  land reform policies and, 456–57
  requisition of food by forces of, 485
  retreat from South and Central Russia by, 488–89, 490, 491
  White Army forces commanded by, 483
Koliubakin, M. A., 41–42
Kollontai, Aleksandra, 284–85, 315–16, 449–50
Kolomenskoe Locomotive and Car Shops, 185–86
Kolonitskii, Boris, 19, 312–13, 339
Kolpino, 447

kombedy (committees of the poor), 443, 452–53, 458–59, 461, 469–70, 479–80
Komuch (All-Russia Constituent Assembly), 454, 456–57, 458, 484–85
Kondrat'ev, Nikolai, 387–88
Konovalov, Alexander
 Bolshevik seizure of the textile firm of, 418–19
 Duma supervision over the military, 130
 elected worker representatives at factories and, 143–44, 145–46
 February Revolution (1917) and, 242
 mediation of worker-management conflict and, 182, 320–21
 militarization of labor forces and, 142–44
 Progressist Party and, 3–4
 Provisional Government (1917) and, 259, 281, 313, 333–34, 404–5
 state credits for industrial firms and, 281
 trade unions and, 181
 War Industries Committees and, 124–25, 126, 134–35, 145, 148, 181, 182–83
Kornilov, General Lavr
 April Crisis (1917) and, 308–9, 406
 commander in chief appointment (1917) of, 359
 coup plot (1917) of, 389–92, 394–95, 402
 death of, 422, 453, 455
 July Days insurrection (1917) and, 348–49, 351, 359, 389–90
 Kerensky Offensive (1917) and, 383
 Moscow State Conference (1917) and, 382–83
 Russia's World War I goals after February Revolution and, 288
 violence against Jews in Tarnopol (1917) and, 360
 White Army forces commanded by, 420–21
Kossior, Stanislav, 427–28, 463–64
Kostroma, 72–73, 117–18, 120–21, 125, 210
Kosygin, Aleksei, 528–29
Kovno fortress, 62
Kozakevich, P. P., 143–44
Krasin, Leonid, 505
Krasnov, Peter, 418, 455
Kritsman, Lev, 415, 465–66
Krivoshein, Alexander, 17–18, 110–11, 129, 152–53, 162–63
Kronstadt uprising (1921), 515–16, 517
Krupskaia, Nadezhda, 513–14, 519–20
Krym, Solomon, 255–56
Kuchin, Grigori Dmitrievich, 383–84
kulaks
 anti-Semitism among, 471
 Bolsheviks' efforts to identify and liquidate, 424–26, 452–53, 520, 521
 famine of 1921-1922 and, 522
 grain holdings and, 443, 458, 471, 520
Kurlov, Alexander, 243
Kuropatkin, A. N., 205
Kursk, 166, 378–79, 380, 395–96, 447–48, 523–24
Kutler, N. N., 112, 143–44, 277, 282, 356, 374
Kuz'min-Karavaev, V. D., 99, 218

Labour Party (United Kingdom), 157
Larin, Iurii (M.A. Lur'e), 428–29, 465–66, 500
Latvia, 234, 398–99
Laub, Dori, 481
Leed, Eric, 44
Lemberg, Austria (L'viv), 41, 58–59, 104
Lena massacre (1912), 32–33, 117, 118
Lenin, Vladimir. *See also* Bolsheviks
 All-Russia Congress of Soviets (1917) and, 331, 345, 378–79
 All-Russia Railroad Union and, 403
 anti-imperialism and, 217, 285, 286–87
 assassination attempts against, 451
 bourgeoisie power targeted by, 417
 Constituent Assembly and, 419, 420
 execution of brother (1887) of, 410
 February Revolution (1917) and, 248
 flight to Finland (1917) by, 348
 government relocated to Moscow (1918) by, 417
 grain requisition policies and, 443
 health problems of, 518, 519–20
 increasing support during World War I for, 144, 176–77
 July Days insurrection (1917) and, 344–45
 Kronstadt uprising suppressed (1921) by, 515
 Leninism and, 13–14, 61, 217
 liberal and social democratic opponents repressed by, 420
 mausoleum of, 1
 nationalization of private businesses by, 426
 nationalization of Russia's archives and, 13–14, 414
 "Peace, Land, and Bread" slogan of, 414–15
 peace initiative to end Russia's involvement in World War I and, 421–22
 return to Russia (1917) by, 285
 revolutionary intentions articulated by, 224–25, 226–27, 318–19, 345, 378–79
 Russia's participation in World War I opposed by, 32, 308, 332, 408–9

Lenin, Vladimir (cont.)
  scarcity as a source for political mobilization by, 236, 315, 409
  seizure of power (1917) by, 403, 410, 413–14, 415, 416
  Seventh Congress of Soviets remarks on food shortages (1919) by, 497–98
Leont'eva, Tatiana, 22–23, 37, 204, 474–75, 476–77, 478
Liberman, Evsei, 528
Liberty Loan bonds, 283–85, 334, 377, 386–87
Lih, Lars, 209, 270, 459
Likino, 365–66
Lithuania, 122, 398–99, 489–90
Lobanov-Rostovsky, Andrei, 50–51, 52–53
Lodz (Poland), 41, 106–7
Lohr, Eric, 103, 106, 204
Lomonosov, Iu. V., 275
loss
  historians' ability to analyze, 21–24
  of labor in rural Russia, 213, 329–30, 363
  Putin era and, 534–35
  Red Army casualties in civil war and, 305f, 486, 510, 513–14
  Russian casualties in World War I and, 16, 18, 41–42, 58–59, 93, 102, 107–8, 120–21, 122, 191–92, 194–96, 233, 239, 248, 271, 308, 329, 338–39, 340–41, 388, 407, 409–10, 414–15, 486, 519
  Russian casualties in World War II and, 523–25
  Russian Revolution's notions of sacrifice and, 285–87, 384–85, 409
  of Russian territory in World War I, 65–66, 72, 441–42, 458
  trauma and, 252–53, 388, 478–82
Lotman, Iurii, 51–52
Ludendorff, Erich, 57, 58, 232–33
Lunacharskii, Anatoly, 352, 513–14
Lutsk, battle (1916) of, 193–94
Luxemburg, Rosa, 249
L'viv. See Lemberg (Austria)
L'vov, Georgi (Prince)
  All-Russian Union of Zemstvos to Aid Sick and Wounded Troops and, 96–97
  April Crisis (1917) and, 310
  at the Duma at beginning of World War I, 30
  July 8 Declaration and, 351–52
  Provisional Government (1917) and, 250, 255, 259, 313, 351–52
  War Industries Committees and, 182–83
  war planning after Galician retreat and, 123–24

Lyandres, Semion, 220
Maidel, Wladmir Baron von, 138–39, 148–49
Main Artillery Administration (GAO), 60, 63–64, 109, 122–23
Main Economic Committee, 355, 357, 366, 371–72, 395–96, 397–98
Main Land Committee, 269, 350–51
Main Supply Administration, 189
Maiskii, I. M., 442–43
Makhno, Nestor, 477, 490
Maklakov, Nikolai, 109, 129, 142, 220, 244–45, 255–56, 384
Maklakov, Vasili, 3–4, 105–6
Malenkov, Georgy, 526
Malevich, Kazimir, 34
Malia, Martin, 5
Malle, Sylvana, 448–49
Manikovskii, Aleksei General, 99
Manuilov, Alexander, 3–4, 165–66, 255, 259, 313
Margulies, M. S., 128–29
Markovich, Andrei, 65–66
Marklov, Nikolai (Markov II), 30–31
Martov, Iulii, 11–12, 216–17, 224–25, 461–62, 465–66
Marxism, 2–3, 12, 13–14
Maslov, P. P., 165–66, 206–7, 218, 219–20
Masurian Lakes, battle (1914) of, 40–41, 42–44, 47, 87–88, 93, 191
Matsuzato, Kimitaka, 209
Mayakovskii, Vladimir, 34
Mayer, Arno, 2
McDonald, David, 130–31
McMeekin, Sean, 100–1
Medvedev, Roy and Zhores, 530
Mensheviks
  All-Russia Congress of Soviets (1917) and, 331
  April Crisis (1917) and, 309
  Cheka repression of, 464
  Constituent Assembly elections (1917) and, 419
  food crisis of 1916 and increasing support for, 216–17
  grain requisition policies and, 267
  Kornilov coup attempt (1917) and, 391
  Menshevik Internationalists and, 178–79, 216–17, 224–25, 284–85, 336
  political rights of workers and peasants supported by, 224–25
  Provisional Government (1917) and, 245
  Russia's participation in World War I and, 178–79, 336
  trade unions and, 180, 246–47, 434–35

Meserve, H. Fessenden, 148–49, 377–78
Metallists' Union, 499, 514
Metal Workers Union, 379–80
Michael (prince, brother of the tsar), 244
Michelson, Alexander, 277
Migulin, P. P., 63–64, 84–85, 91, 169–70, 283, 333–34
Miliukov, Paul
　April Crisis (1917) and, 309–10
　Bolshevik repression of, 420
　Daradanelle Straits and, 81
　death of son of, 178, 285–86, 478
　Duma session of 1916 and, 216
　Duma speech at beginning of World War I by, 30–31
　February Revolution (1917) and, 241–42, 243, 267–68
　Fundamental Laws and, 222
　inflation and, 113–14
　July Days insurrection (1917) and, 347
　Kadets' coalition politics and, 3, 11, 178–80
　liberal reform proposals during World War I and, 130
　Moscow State Conference (1917) and, 384–86
　Nekrasov and, 332–33
　Okhrana surveillance of, 38–39
　Provisional Government (1917) and, 242, 243, 244, 246, 255, 259, 307–8, 341
　Rasputin and, 231
　"revolution from above" philosophy and, 178
　Revolution of 1905 and, 31
　Russian Revolution history written by, 9
　Russia's World War I goals after February Revolution and, 285–86, 287–88
　statism and, 3–4
　Stiurmer and, 162
　subsistence riots of 1916 and, 215–16
　Ukraine and, 342–44
　war planning after Galician retreat and, 122
　White forces in Russian civil war and, 455
Miliutin, V. V., 441–42
Mirbach, Wilhelm von, 451
Mironov, Boris, 65–66
Molotov, Vyacheslav, 226–27, 527–28
Moscow
　economic activity during World War I in, 70, 75–76
　food shortages in, 160, 161–62, 210–11, 219, 235–36, 260–62, 423–24, 447
　government relocated (1918) to, 417
　July Days insurrection (1917) and, 346–47
　large percentage of Russian workforce in, 72
　refugees in, 153
　Society of Factory and Mill Owners in, 135, 350, 355, 369–70
　strikes and labor unrest in, 32–33, 116–17, 317, 370, 371, 417
Moscow-Kazan railroad line, 149, 273
Moscow-Kursk railroad line, 276–77, 512–13
Moscow Mechanical plant, 432–33
Moscow Soviet, 257, 283, 317, 346–47, 380–81, 390–91
Moscow State Conference (1917)
　Chkheidze's socioeconomic proposals at, 387–89, 404–5
　February Revolution discussed at, 384–85
　military discipline discussed at, 383
　problems of national scarcity and loss during, 386–88
　railroads discussed at, 386–87
　Russia's World War I goals discussed at, 382–83, 384–85
Mosse, George, 56–57
Murav'ev, N. L., 158
Muslim populations in Russia, 188, 203–6, 227, 475–76

Nabokov, V. V. (writer), 14–15, 475, 486–87
Nabokov, V. D. (Russian politician)
　assassination of, 489
　Bolshevism opposed by, 405
　capital punishment supported by, 403–4
　Kadets and, 3–4
　Moscow State Conference (1917) and, 384, 386
　on "patriotic anxiety" and World War I, 245
Napoleon's invasion of Russia (1812), 29, 33–34, 41–42
Naroch Lake, battle (1916), 190–91, 195–96
Narskii, Igor, 8, 55, 474–75, 488
National City Bank, 91–92, 148–49
Naumov, A. N., 159, 162–63
Nekrasov, Nikolai
　grain requisition policies and, 208
　imprisonment and execution of, 271–72
　industrial material shortages and, 374
　Miliukov and, 332–33
　Plekhanov Commission and, 19, 313
　Provisional Government (1917) and, 223–24, 255, 259, 262–63, 313, 353
　railroads and, 78–79, 81, 83–84, 87–88, 170, 271–72, 274–76, 313, 366–67, 376–77, 386–87, 401
　statization policies and, 376–77
　trade unions and, 179, 275
　Ukraine and, 343

neoliberalism in Russia during 1990s, 4, 25–26
Nevskii, V. I., 438–39, 445, 505
Nevskii Shipbuilding Plant, 115–16, 118
New Economic Policy (NEP), 25, 515–16, 519–21
Nicholas II (tsar)
  Bark and, 85–86
  beginning of World War I and, 29–30, 32, 33–34
  Brusilov Offensive (1916) and, 192–93
  domestic military production supported by, 63
  Duma appearance (1916) by, 170
  Duma established (1905) by, 10–11, 38
  Duma session (1915) and, 129–30, 132, 133–34
  February Revolution (1917) and abdication of, 8–9, 237, 242, 244, 252, 254
  liquor sales halted during World War I by, 86–88
  prime ministerial appointments by, 161–62, 207, 231
  Progressive Bloc and, 130–31
  war planning after Galician retreat and, 123
Nikolaev, N. N., 255–56
Nikolaevich, Nikolai (Grand Duke, Commander-in-Chief 1914-15), 33–34, 99, 122–23
Nikolaev railroad line, 273, 275, 321, 417, 420, 437, 447–48, 503–4, 512–13
Nikolaevsky, Boris, 393
Ninth Army, 193–94
Ninth Party Congress (1920), 506–7
Nixon, Richard, 527
Nizhnii Novgorod
  economic activity on eve of World War I in, 70
  food shortages in, 363, 423–24, 447, 472–73
  grain markets in, 128, 147, 470
  July Days insurrection (1917) and, 346
  state-owned factories in, 312
NKVD (Soviet secret police), 525–27
Nobel', Emanuel Liudvigovich, 135, 182–83
Nogin, Viktor, 435–36, 463–64
Nolte, Ernst, 2
Northern Front (World War I), 41, 47–48, 185–86, 194–95, 233–34, 359, 421
Northwestern Front (World War I), 44–45, 64–65, 93, 102–3, 125, 482–83
Novocherkassk, 455, 528
Novyi Lessner Shipbuilding Plant, 115–16, 118, 177–78, 200, 214, 374, 514

Obukhov Works, 420, 447, 448

October Manifesto (Nicholas II, 1905), 12, 122, 225
Octobrists, 3–4, 11, 33, 122
Odessa, 70, 127, 257–58, 395–96, 424–25, 427
Office of Military Transport and Communications, 79–80
Okhrana secret police, 38–39, 189, 221, 235–36
Old Believers, 150
Ol'ga (princess), 94–95
Omsk, 273, 374, 484–85
One Day in the Life of Ivan Denisovich (Solzhenitsyn), 526–27
Order 1042 (Ninth Party Congress, 1920), 506–7
Order Number 1 (Petrograd Soviet), 247–48, 251–52, 253–54
Osinski, Nikolai (V. V. Obolenskii), 426, 428–29, 441–42
Osipova, T. V., 430–31
Ottoman Empire, 43–44, 77, 204–5, 234–35
Oushakine, Serguei, 534–35

Pal'chinskii, A. I., 355
Pal'chinskii, P. I., 143–44, 182–83, 281, 283
Paleologue, Maurice, 29, 101, 106–7, 115–16
The Pale region, 103–4
Panina, Sophia, 3–4
Paraskeva, Nikitina, 115
Pares, Bernard, 100–1, 105, 162–63, 164–65, 170, 220–21
Paris Commune (1871), 349–50
patriotism in Russia, 33–38, 50–51
Peasant Congress, 327–28
Peasants Union, 265
Peoples' Bank of the Russian Republic, 299f, 429
Pepeliaev, Victor, 454–55
perestroika, 1–2, 532, 535–36
Peshekhonov, Aleksei, 325, 331, 343
Pétain, Philippe, 234–35
Peter the Great (tsar), 10, 38–39
Peter the Great Arsenal, 403–4
Petliura, Simon, 489
Petrichenko, Stepan, 515
Petrograd. *See also* Petrograd Soviet
  duma in, 389–90
  economic activity during World War I in, 70, 75–76
  February Revolution (1917) and, 238–40, 241–44
  food shortages in, 157, 159–60, 161–62, 219, 235–36, 256–57, 260–62, 297f, 423–24, 430–31, 447
  July Days insurrection (1917) and, 344–47, 349
  Kornilov's coup attempt (1917) and, 389–90

large percentage of Russian workforce in, 72, 75–76
metals syndicate in, 69–70, 73–74
rationing in, 202, 280
Stock Exchange in, 200
strikes and labor unrest in, 115–16, 177–78, 214–15, 315–16, 371, 514–15, 517–18
War Industries Committee in, 135
Petrograd Metals plant, 433–34
Petrograd Soviet
Declaration of Soldiers' Rights and, 336–37, 385
elections (1917) for, 390–91, 399–400
February Revolution (1917) and, 15–16, 247
food distribution by, 256–57
grain monopoly system and, 265
Ispolkom (Executive Committee) of, 19, 260, 262–63, 284–85, 318–19
mediation boards established by, 368
Order Number 1 and, 247–48, 251–52, 253–54
Provisional Government of Russia (1917) and "dual power dilemma" with, 245–46, 247–48, 254–55, 256–57, 260, 307
"revolutionary defensism" and, 285
trade unions and, 256–57
Petrograd Workers Group, 238
Petrone, Karen, 55–56
Pilnyak, Boris, 463
Pipes, Richard, 2, 5, 25–26, 118–19, 240–41, 252, 465–66
Plamper, Jan, 45, 51, 240–41
Plekhanov, Georgi, 19–20, 319
Plekhanov Commission, 19, 276–77, 313–14, 321–22, 401–2
Pokrovskii, N. N., 165–66
Pokrovskii, Viktor General, 482–83
Pokrovskii/Glinka Goup, 165–67
Poland
deportations during World War I from, 103–4
German occupation during World War I of, 64–66, 72
Progressive Bloc and, 133–34
self-determination and nationality claims in, 130, 341–43, 398, 475–76
uprising (1956) in, 527–28
Versailles settlement (1919) and, 489–90
World War I battles in, 41–42, 122
Polantzas, Nicos, 249–50, 312
Polanyi, Karl, 66–67, 92, 461
Polivanov, A. A., 60, 99, 136, 138, 140–41, 159, 163, 253
Poltava, 206, 264, 461–62, 463
Popular Socialists, 224–25

Porshneva, Olga
on peasants and instability of land communes, 22–23
on peasants and World War I, 37, 53–54, 176, 393
on security of communal ways of life, 69
on Stolypin reforms, 212–13
on uneven nature of mobilization, 213–14
postmodernism, 5–6
Postnikov, A. S., 350–51
posttraumatic stress disorder (PTSD), 46–47, 481–82. *See also* shell shock
Potemkin mutiny (1905), 39–40, 517
Potresov, Alexander, 224–25
Prague Spring (1968), 528–29
prisoners of war (POWs)
agricultural work by, 328
forced labor among, 112, 141–43, 188, 203–4, 328
overall numbers of, 16, 40–41
strikebreaking and, 177–78
Progressist Party, 3–4, 124
Progressive Bloc
Duma coalition politics and, 178–79
Duma session of 1915 and, 129, 133
February Revolution (1917) and, 242
liberal reform proposals during World War I and, 130–31, 147–48
Provisional Government (1917) and, 259
proguly (truancy), 116–17, 119–20, 235, 493, 498–99, 500
Prokovovich, S. N., 64–65, 85–86, 90, 165–66, 257, 355, 373
Protopopov, A. D., 220–22, 238–39
Provisional Government of Russia (1917)
April Crisis and, 310
civil rights promoted by, 254–55, 256
food supply commission and, 242–43
grain monopoly system and, 265
Kadets in the cabinet of, 223–24, 255–56, 341, 347, 349–50, 385
Kornilov coup attempt and, 389–92, 394–95, 402
land reform proposals and, 327–28
oath of allegiance and, 256
Petrograd Soviet's "dual power dilemma" with, 245–46, 247–48, 254–55, 256–57, 260, 307
railroad policy and, 275–76
"weighty actor thesis" and, 311
World War I and, 247, 256
Przemyśl fortress (Galicia), 41, 57–59, 62
Purishkevich, Vladimir, 220, 221–22
Putilov, A. I., 91–92, 123–24, 143, 187

Putilov Works (Petrograd)
  July Days insurrection and, 345, 349
  labor organizing and unrest at, 17–18, 177–78, 447
  militarization of workforce at, 180
  nationalization of, 17–18
  state financing guarantees and, 91, 148–49
Putin, Vladimir, 1, 8–9, 533–36

Rabkrin (Workers' and Peasants' Inspectorate), 499–503, 505, 507, 512–13
Radkey, Oliver, 490–91
Rafes, Moisei, 260
railroads in Russia
  black markets and, 112, 219
  Bolsheviks' establishment of dictatorial control (1918) over, 444
  Cheka agents on, 444, 445–46, 453, 466–67, 504–5, 507–8
  commercial goods transport during World War I and, 79–81, 201–2
  corruption and, 112, 159–60, 165, 174
  democratization initiatives regarding, 271–76, 366–67
  district-level administrations for, 78–79, 83–84
  European railroads compared to, 79
  expansion after Russo-Japanese War of, 84–85
  forced prisoner labor on, 78
  labor armies on, 507–8
  locomotives and, 78–79, 81
  maintenance of, 81
  militarization of labor forces and, 187
  military supplies and operations during World War I and, 77, 80, 84, 94
  national economic well-being during World War I, 77, 92
  private *versus* state-owned, 78
  profits at, 149, 163–64
  Railroad Management Committee, 137, 159–60, 186–87, 201–2, 207–8, 273–74, 366–67
  "railroad republic" and, 20, 367–68, 401, 418
  refugees and, 77, 106, 160–61, 294f, 295f
  state loan guarantees to private owners of, 78, 84–85
  tariffs during World War I on, 88, 174–75
  workforce of, 82–84, 174, 187
  wounded soldiers in World War I and, 94, 160–61
Raleigh, Don, 346, 369–70, 464–65
Ranke, Leopold von, 9–10

Rapallo Treaty (1922), 518–19
Rappoport, Shlomo (aka S. Anskii), 55–56, 204
Rasputin, 161–62, 163, 170, 220, 231
Red Army (Russian civil war)
  casualty and death totals among, 486
  demobilized World War I soldiers in, 479–80
  desertion from, 480, 491–96
  mobilization of soldiers into, 443, 453
  political sections of, 300f
  requisition of food by, 459–60, 469–70
  Volga region operations of, 458
Red Cavalry (Babel), 462–63
Reddy, William, 50–51, 55, 56
Red Guards, 357–58, 360, 390, 395, 418, 445, 479–80
Red Terror campaign (1918–1922), 451–52, 453, 464
refugees during World War I
  in Baltic territories, 128
  from Central Asian provinces of Russia, 205–6
  forced labor and, 188
  Galician Campaign (1915) retreat and, 153
  Jews as, 106–7
  overall numbers of, 16
  railroads and, 77, 106, 160–61, 294f, 295f
  zemstvos and, 96–97
Remarque, Erich Maria, 52–53
Remington, Thomas, 502–3
Rennenkampf, Paul von General, 40–42, 47–48, 62, 98, 191
Representatives of Industry and Trade, 123–24
Retish, Aaron, 37, 113, 120, 213, 324–25, 360–61, 463, 469–70
Revelstoke, Lord, 152
Revolution of 1905
  Bloody Sunday massacre and, 231, 478
  Duma established following, 10–11, 12, 38
  liberalism and, 3
  martial law declaration and, 12
  October Manifesto and, 12
  Potemkin mutiny and, 39–40, 517
  Russo-Japanese War and, 38
  Saint Petersburg Soviet and, 12
Riabushinskii, P. P.
  on "bourgeois" nature of February Revolution, 369
  Duma supervision over the military, 130
  reforms of 1905 and, 124
  trade unions and, 181
  War Industries Committees and, 126, 148, 181, 182–83
  warnings of financial collapse by, 358

war planning after Galician retreat
  and, 123–24
Riazan, 393–94, 429–30, 445, 448, 496–97
Riazan-Urals railroad line, 272
Rieber, Alfred, 124
Rittikh, Aleksandr
  February Revolution (1917) and, 241–42
  grain requisition system instituted by, 207–9,
    218, 235–36, 261, 264, 267, 394–95, 459
  minister of agriculture appointment (1916)
    of, 207
  subsistence riots of 1916 and, 216
Rodichev, Fedor, 342, 357–58
Rodzianko, Mikhail
  Central War Industries Committee and, 125
  on conditions of scarcity in World War I,
    163–64, 185–86, 236
  Duma dissolution in 1915 and, 132
  elected worker representatives at factories
    and, 143
  February Revolution (1917) and, 241–42
  liberal reform proposals during World War
    I and, 130
  militarization of labor forces and,
    142, 189–90
  nationalization of military suppliers
    and, 17–18
  Provisional Government (1917) and, 259
  "revolution from above" philosophy and, 178
  Stiurmer and, 162–63, 170
  war planning after Galician retreat
    and, 122–24
Romania, 194–95, 199, 232–35
Romanov dynasty, 8–9, 25, 130, 155, 231–33
Roosa, Ruth, 124
Rostov, 211–12, 257–58, 427, 464–65, 482–83
Rukhlov, S. V., 78, 137, 141–42, 187
Russian Red Cross, 94–95
Russko-Baltic Shipbuilding and Mechanical
  Works, 91–92
Russo-Japanese War (1904-1905)
  anxiety among Russian soldiers
    during, 45–46
  Baltic Fleet lost in, 38
  Bloody Sunday massacre (1905) and, 478
  military expenses during, 88–89
  mobilization for, 60
  mutinies during, 57
  peace settlement in, 60
  Revolution of 1905 and, 38
  Russian military updates following, 84–85
  suppression of dissent in Russia during, 36–
    37, 38, 159

Russo-Turkish War (1878), 60
Ruzskii, Nikolai, 41, 44–45, 58–59
Rykov, Aleksei, 464–65, 520–21

Saint Petersburg. *See* Petrograd
Sakharov, Andrei, 532–33
Samara, 169–70, 210–11, 430–31, 448, 466
Samsonov, Alexander General, 40–42, 47–48,
  87–88, 98, 190–91
Sanborn, Joshua, 36–37
Saratov
  city duma elections (1917) in, 354
  food shortages in, 458, 461–62
  harvest (1919) in, 460
  industrial material shortages in, 369–70
  nationalization of industrial plants in, 427
  regional peasant congress (1917) in, 268–69
Sazonov, S. D., 30
scarcity
  black markets and, 112, 149–50, 151, 219,
    264, 338, 363–64, 415–16, 423, 429–30,
    431–32, 462–63, 503
  Bolsheviks' political mobilization around
    issues of, 236, 315, 409
  Council of Ministers and, 110, 137
  famine of 1921–1922 and, 25, 463, 518–19,
    521–23, 525
  in Germany during World War I, 90–91
  grain requisitioning and, 119, 207–9,
    218–19, 235–36, 261, 264–68, 270–71,
    361–62, 394–95, 443, 459, 465–66, 488–89,
    490, 491
  hoarding and, 357, 363–64, 440–41, 462,
    468–70, 476–77, 502–3
  industrial supplies and, 282, 369–70, 374
  military incompetence and, 128–29
  in Moscow, 160, 161–62, 210–11, 219, 235–
    36, 260–62, 423–24, 447
  Moscow Conference (1917), 386–88
  price controls and, 17–18, 19–20, 90–91,
    110–11, 168–69, 202, 264
  in Nizhni Novgorod, 363, 423–24,
    447, 472–73
  in Petrograd, 157, 159–60, 161–62, 219,
    235–36, 256–57, 260–62, 423–24, 430–
    31, 447
  rationing, 168–70, 202–3, 280
  Russia's experiences in World War I and,
    48–49, 99–102, 128–29, 156, 157, 163–
    64, 185–86, 207, 223, 233–34, 236, 327,
    363, 408–9
  in Sartov, 458, 461–62
  Seventh Congress of Soviets and, 497–98

scarcity (*cont.*)
   as source of political instability, 155, 158, 165–66, 176, 216, 406–7
   Sovnarkhoz and, 440–41
   subsistence riots (1916) and, 210–16
   sugar riots and, 211–12
   in Viatka province, 448, 463, 471
   in Volga region, 430–31
   War Capitalism and, 149–50, 152, 169–70
Schapiro, Leonard, 510–11
Scott, James, 393, 399–400, 464–65
Second All-Russia Moslem Conference, 398–99
Second Army, 40–42, 87–88, 191
Second Congress of Soviets (1917), 416, 418
Second Labor Army, 508
Second World War. *See* World War II
"Secret Speech" (Khrushchev, 1956), 527, 530
Semashko, Nikolai, 508–9
Semipalatinsk food riots (1916), 211–12
Seventh Congress of Soviets (1919), 497–98
Shakhovskoi, V. N., 117, 159, 175
Shanin, Teodor, 69, 425–26
Shcherbatov, N. B., 354
Shchukin, D. V., 78–79
Shebeko, I. A., 189–90
shell shock
   brain injuries and, 45–46
   Brusilov offensive and, 233
   daily warfare conditions and, 46–47
   exhaustion and, 47–48
   gas warfare and, 45
   official Russian statistics regarding, 480
   Russian medical establishment's response to, 46
   treatment of Russian veterans for, 9–10
Shingarev, Andrei
   April Crisis (1917) and, 309–10
   attack on estate (1917) of, 308, 350–51, 393
   Bolsheviks' killing of, 420
   on conditions of scarcity and inequality during World War I, 156, 157, 223, 327, 363, 408–9
   Duma Financial Committee and, 86, 88
   Duma Military Supply Commission and, 127
   February Revolution (1917) and, 242
   financing of World War I and, 16–17, 170–72, 219–20, 278, 284–85
   food crisis of 1917 and, 263–66, 307
   Fundamental Laws and, 222
   grain requisition policies and, 208, 218–19, 264–65, 267–68, 270–71, 362, 465–66
   inflation during World War I and, 19–20, 113–14, 165, 328
   land redistribution proposals and, 269, 271, 326
   mediation of worker-management conflict and, 182
   Okhrana surveillance of, 38–39
   postwar reconstruction negotiations and, 173
   Progressive Bloc and, 133–34
   Provisional Government (1917) and, 256, 259, 262, 313
   Special Commission on Defense and, 139–40
   on state ban on liquor sales during World War I, 87–88
   state intervention in the economy and, 396–97
   tax policies during World War I and, 91
   War Industries Committees and, 134
Shkuro, General A. G., 482–83
Shliapnikov, Alexander, 226–27, 434–35
Shostakovich, Dmitri, 525
Shtil'man, G. N., 198
Shul'gin, Vasili, 162–63
Siberia
   civil war fighting in, 456–57, 485, 488, 491
   Cossack legions in, 477, 479–80, 485
   nationalities question in, 398–99
   Trans-Siberian railroad line and, 77, 81, 163–64, 186–87, 457, 485
Sidorov, A. L., 62, 64–65
Siegelbaum, Lewis, 181
Singer sewing machine workers' strike (1917), 370
Sirotkina, Irina, 46
Sivers, Thadeus von, 49
Sixth Finnish Rifle Regiment, 335–36
Skinner, G. William, 70–71
Skobelev, Matvei
   All-Russia Congress of Soviets (1917) and, 331
   April Crisis (1917) and, 309
   Department for the Resolution of Conflict between Capital and Labor and, 19–20, 312–13
   July Days insurrection (1917) and, 348, 349, 351
   Ministry of Labor position and labor mediation by, 19, 243, 310, 312–13, 319–20, 323, 372–73, 376–77, 400–1
   Petrograd Soviet and, 260
   Provisional Government (1917) and, 313, 404–5
   state labor exchange and, 366
   strikes and, 317–18
   unemployment problems and, 333
Skorokhod leather plant, 403–4, 430, 433–34
Smele, Jonathan, 482–83, 517–18
Smirnov, Vladimir, 426

Smolensk, 128, 464–65, 490–91
Socialist Party (France), 157
Socialist Revolutionaries
    All-Russia Congress of Soviets (1917) and, 331
    All-Russia Railroad Union and, 401, 418–19, 437
    Chernov and, 11–12, 268–69
    as coalition partners in Bolshevik-led government (1917), 418–19
    Constituent Assembly elections (1917) and, 413, 419
    Fifth Congress of Soviets (1918) and, 451
    Komuch and, 454
    land redistribution policies and, 422–23
    peasant mobilization to achieve political goals and, 11–12, 246–47, 268–69
    peasant support for, 33
    political rights of workers and peasants supported by, 224–25
    zemstvo elections and, 362–63
Society for the Sale of Metallurgical Products (Prodamet), 69–70
Society of Factory and Mill Owners
    Bolshevik regime's negotiations with, 434
    July Days insurrection (1917) and, 350, 369
    labor mediation and, 320–21
    Ministry of Trade and, 373–74
    in Moscow, 135, 350, 355, 369–70
    in Petrograd, 135, 320–21, 350, 355, 369–70, 373–74, 397–98, 434
Sokolov, Konstantin, 455
soldatki (soldiers' mothers and wives), 102, 120–21, 213–14, 277, 329–31, 449–50
Solzhenitsyn, Alexander, 49, 52–53, 525–27, 528, 530
Sormovo plant (Nizhnii Novgorod), 63, 212, 312, 323–24, 374, 420
Sotovskii plant, 117–18
Southeastern railroad line, 149, 223, 508
Southern railroad line, 288
Southwestern Front (World War I)
    agricultural land left fallow along, 64–65
    deportation of Jews near, 103–4
    exhaustion among soldiers and, 47–48
    food shortages along, 99–100, 233–34
    German reinforcements along, 58
    Kerensky Offensive (1917), 335–41
    military administrative control of territories near, 102–3, 338
    Russian military morale at, 196–97
    soldiers' concerns about family well-being and, 153–54
Soviet-Afghanistan War (1980s), 530, 534

Soviet Executive Committee (Ispolkom)
    July Days insurrection (1917) and, 344–45
    land reform proposals and, 327
    Provisional Government (1917) and, 317–18
    railroad policies and, 272–73
    Russia's World War I goals after February Revolution and, 287
Sovnarkhoz (All-Russia Council for the Economy)
    financial credits issued by, 499
    first meeting (December 1917) of, 428–29
    food shortages and, 440–41
    labor productivity goals of, 442–43
    nationalization of private businesses and, 432, 441, 443–44
Sovnarkom (Council of People's Commissars)
    Cheka and, 420
    demobilization from World War I and, 431
    establishment of, 416
    financial credits issued by, 468–69
    food shortages and, 440–41
    grain requisition policies and, 443
    nationalization of private enterprises and, 448–49
    workers' control affirmed by, 433
Special Commission on Restoration of Industry, 355
Special Committee on Metallurgy Production, 185
special complaint boxes (*iashchki zhalob*), 467
Special Council for Defense
    elected worker representatives at factories and, 143
    establishment of, 123
    financial credits for military production and, 185
    fuel supply issues and, 137
    local resistance to actions of, 139–40
    militarization of labor forces and, 142, 188–90
    Provisional Government (1917) and, 256
    requisition of equipment and supplies by, 136, 138
Special Council of Five, 159–62, 165–66
Special Council on Food
    data collection by, 136, 166–67, 184, 266
    food shortages in the Caucasus, 207
    grain requisition policies and, 207–8, 267
    Pokrovskii/Glinka Goup and, 165–66
    price controls and, 202
    Provisional Government (1917) and, 325
    railroads and, 137
Special Council on Fuel, 137, 319–20, 354, 356
Special Council on Transport, 137, 275

Spirodonova, Maria, 451
Stalin, Joseph
  collectivization and militarized industrialization policies under, 25, 521, 523
  death of, 525
  gulag prison system and, 535
  Khrushchev's denunciation of, 527–28
  political rivals in Communist Party and, 25, 518, 519–21, 523, 529–30, 532
  purges by, 527–28, 530
  Rabkrin and, 501, 502–3
  Ukraine famine and, 522–23
  World War II and, 523–25, 535
State and Revolution (Lenin), 415–17, 510–11
State Bank
  Bolshevik control after 1917 of, 424–25, 427, 428
  Liberty Loans and, 285
  Ministry of Finance and, 85
  money supply in Russia and, 90
  short-term treasury notes to support World War I costs issued by, 86–87, 89
  war financing bonds issued by, 278–79
State Committee on Food Supply, 262–63
State Council, 29–30, 141–42, 245
State Duma. *See* Duma
Stepanov, Vasili, 317–18, 350, 355, 455, 469–70
Stiurmer (Stürmer), Boris
  critics of, 162–63, 170
  financing of World War I and, 184–85
  interior minister appointment (1916) of, 163, 183
  militarization of labor forces and, 187, 188, 203–4
  Nicholas II's dismissal (1916) of, 207
  prime ministerial appointment (1916) of, 161–63
  Railroad Management Committee and, 186–87
  "yellow workers" and, 187–88
Stockdale, Melissa, 40
Stoff, Laurie, 40, 50–51, 94–95
Stoler, Ann, 23–24
Stolypin, Peter
  agrarian reforms under, 33, 61–62, 64, 69–70, 212–13, 266–67, 270, 326
  assassination of, 85–86
  martial law declared (1905) by, 12
Stone, David, 195
Stone, Lawrence, 5–6, 193
Strumilin, Stanislav, 64–65, 279–80
Struve, Peter
  food crisis of 1917 and, 264
  grain requisition policies and, 267, 362, 394–95
  inflation during World War I and, 167–68
  Kadets and, 167–68
  militarization of labor forces and, 188–89
  Pokrovskii/Glinka Goup and, 165–66
  price controls for food and, 17–18
  state regulation of the economy and, 168, 356–57
"subsistence riots" (1916), 210–16
substantivist approach to economic development, 67–68, 76
Sudetenland, 523–24
sugar riots, 211–12
Sukhanov, Nikolai, 239–40, 241, 415–16
Sukhomlinov, Vladimir, 62, 99, 103, 122, 129, 163, 239–40, 383–84
Sumpf, Alexandre, 22–23, 44
Syzran-Viazemskii railroad line, 512–13

Taganrog, 257–58
Tambov, 128, 151, 330–31, 490–91, 492, 517, 518–19
Tannenberg, battle (1914) of, 40–41, 42–44, 47, 93, 408
Tashkent, 204–5, 257–58
Tatiana (princess), 94–95
Tendriakov, V. F., 522
Tenth Army, 49, 57, 391–92
Tenth Party Congress (1921), 510, 512, 515–16, 517, 520–21
Tereshchenko, Mikhail
  financing of World War I and, 284–85
  minister of foreign affairs appointment (1917) of, 310
  Provisional Government (1917) and, 255, 259, 278–79, 313
  state credits for industrial firms and, 281
  trade unions and, 181
  War Industries Committees and, 181, 182–83
Ternopol', 311–12, 360, 393
Thirteenth Party Congress (1924), 526
Thomas, Albert, 157
Tol'stoi, Count A. N., 206
Tomsk, 36–37, 496
Torklus, General, 42–43
Trade Industrial Congress, 272–73, 282, 333, 355, 358
Trainin iron works (Petrograd), 400–1
Trans-Siberian railroad line, 77, 81, 163–64, 186–87, 457, 485
trauma
  neuropsychology research on, 481

posttraumatic stress disorder and, 46–47, 481–82
shell shock and, 9–10, 45–48, 233, 480
"trench psychoses" and, 95
war crimes and, 480
Trepov, Alexander, 159, 173–74, 186, 207, 231
Tretiakov, S. N., 182–83, 373
Treugol'nik rubber plant (Petrograd), 74–76, 372, 441, 443–44
Trotsky, Leon
  on dignity and workers, 315–16
  food requisition and, 417
  Glavpolitput' and, 505–6
  Jewish identity of, 466
  July Days insurrection (1917) and imprisonment of, 348, 404
  Kronstadt uprising suppressed (1921) by, 515
  labor brigades established by, 500, 507
  peace initiative to end Russia's involvement in World War I and, 421–22, 431
  Red Army organized and commanded by, 422, 452, 482, 491–92
  Russian Revolution history written by, 9
  Stalin and, 25, 518, 520–21
  Thirteenth Party Congress (1924) and, 526
  Tsektran and statization initiatives of, 367, 506–7, 508–9, 512–13
trudovaia povinnost' (universal obligation to work), 187, 396–97, 499–500
Trudoviks, 31–32, 224–25
Tsektran (Central Committee for Transport), 367, 506–7, 510–13, 516
Tsereteli, Irakli
  All-Russia Congress of Soviets (1917) and, 331
  April Crisis (1917) and, 309
  Bolshevik repression of, 420
  French Revolution and, 2–3
  July Days insurrection (1917) and, 344–45, 348, 349, 351–53
  Moscow State Conference (1917) and, 384–86
  Provisional Government (1917) and, 313, 404–5
  Russia's World War I goals after February Revolution and, 287–88
  state intervention in the economy and, 283
  Ukraine and, 343
Tsirupa, Alexander, 452–53
Tugan-Baranovskii, M. I., 64–65, 85–86
Tukhashevskii, Mikhail General (later Marshal), 458, 489–91, 515–16, 518, 523–24
Tula
  armaments complex in, 63–64, 142, 176–77, 199, 420, 447–48, 449, 496

food shortages in, 435
Russian Civil War and, 488–89
Turkestan, 204–5, 342–43, 398–99, 517–18
Tver, 211–12, 436, 448
Twenty Five Thousanders, 521
Tymashuk, Lydia, 526
Tyrkova, Ariadna, 465–66, 484–85

Ukraine
  Brest-Litovsk Treaty and surrendering of German acquisition of territory in, 413, 441–42, 458
  Denikin's forces during Russian Civil War and, 477, 488–89
  famine (*Holodomor*) in, 521–23
  July Insurrection (1917) and, 344
  military administrative control of territories during World War I in, 102–3
  military requisitioning of grain during World War I in, 119, 207
  Russia's War (2022–) in, 44, 535
  self-determination claims and nationality questions in, 128, 249, 341–43, 382–83, 398–99, 405–6, 475–76
  Stolypin agrarian reforms and, 70
  textile production in, 75–76
  World War I battles in, 43–44, 102–3, 231
Union for the Regeneration of Russia, 420–21
Union of Industrial Congresses, 350, 426
Union of Provincial Banks, 148–49
Union of Russian People, 158, 162
Union of Towns, 96, 165–66, 189–90
United States
  Cold War and, 527
  imperial foreign policies of, 342
  national archives in, 532
  presentism in, 8–9
  railroads and, 78–79, 456–57
  Russian Revolution and, 454
  Russia's financing of World War I and, 91–92
  World War I and, 157, 232–33, 336
  World War II and, 103, 523–24
Uritskii, Moisei, 451

Van der Kolk, Bessel, 481
Vanderlip, F. A., 149
Vasil'chikov, B. A., 94, 154–55
Verdun, battle (1916) of, 149, 190–91, 192, 194–95, 198
Verkhovskii, Alexander General, 346–47, 380–81, 390–91
Vernadskii, Georgi, 332–33

Viatka province
  divisions following February Revolution in, 360–61
  food shortages in, 448, 463, 471
  grain requisitioning policies in, 268, 361–62
  inflation during World War I in, 113
  internment camps in, 103
  mass mobilization of soldiers for World War I in, 120–21
  peasant activism in, 324–25, 327
  Red Army mobilization in, 453
Vikzhel. *See* All Russia Railroad Union
village sovereignty, 360–63
Vinaver, Maxim, 3–4, 105–6
Viola, Lynne, 521–22
Vladivostok, 132–33, 273, 517–18
Vlasov divisions, 489, 535
Voitolovskii, L. N., 55–56
Volga region
  autarkic agricultural practices after Russian Revolution in, 472
  Civil War and plundering in, 458, 483
  food shortages in, 301*f*, 430–31
  internment camps in, 103
  labor unrest and strikes in, 373
  low harvests (1916-1917) in, 394
  Red Army and, 458
  Stolypin agrarian reforms and, 70
Volodarskii, V., 445, 448
Vompe, Pavel, 503–4
Von Ditmar, Nikolai, 112, 182–83, 189–90, 282
Von Hötzendorf, Franz Conrad, 57–58
Vulkan machine works, 369–70
Vyshnegradskii, A. I., 123

Wade, Rex, 395
War Capitalism (World War I)
  anti-Semitism and, 152
  black markets and, 149–50
  corruption's impact on the military under, 153
  definition of, 147–48
  geographical concentrations of workforce and, 148
  inflation and, 169–70, 375–76
  July 8 Declaration (1917) and, 363
  peasant attitudes toward capitalism and, 150
  rationing and, 169–70
  requisition of goods under, 380
  scarcities and, 149–50, 152, 169–70
  speculation and, 149–52
  state financing guarantees and, 148–49, 363–64, 378

unemployment and, 365
War Communism (World War I and Civil War)
  compulsory labor and, 511–13
  end of, 25, 516
  in Germany, 265
  Gromov and, 266–67
  historical re-evaluations of, 510–11
  patriotism and moral obligation as tenets of, 209
  protests against, 513–14, 517
  Red Army's victory in civil war and, 510
War Industries Committees (WICs)
  All-Russian Workers Congress proposal and, 181
  Committee on Supply and, 127
  contract management and, 125, 134, 135
  defense industries' production levels and, 200
  defense production funding and finance guarantees by, 91, 134–35, 175–76, 185, 281
  elected worker representatives and, 143–44, 145–46
  first meeting of, 124–25
  inflation and, 127
  local branches of, 126
  mediation of worker-management conflict and, 182
  militarization of labor forces and, 142–43, 144–45, 188–89
  military procurement and, 125
  national conference (1915) of, 141
  in Petrograd, 135
  prisoners of war and, 142–43
  scarcities caused by military incompetence and, 128–29
  trade unions and, 181–82
  worker resistance to joining, 145–46
  Workers Group of, 180–81, 224–26, 428–29
War Industries Congress (1917), 338
Washburn, Stanley, 50–51, 52–53, 58
Watson, Peter, 46–47
Wheatcroft, Stephen, 486
White, Hayden, 6, 9, 12–13
  White Armies
  Alekseev and, 420–21, 422, 455
  atrocities committed by, 484–85, 486
  Cossacks and, 455, 456, 457, 479–80, 482–83, 484–85, 491–92
  demobilized World War I soldiers in, 479–80
  Denikin and, 420–21, 422, 453, 455–56, 482–83
  desertion from, 488–89, 491–92
  diverse leadership within, 483–84

land reform policies and, 457
Michigan National Guard's assistance to, 456
military advances (1919-1920) by, 25, 482–83
refugees to Europe from, 489
requisition of food by, 457, 485
Wildman, Allan, 392–93
Williams, Harold, 287
Wilson, Woodrow, 128, 199
Witte, Sergei, 69–70, 86, 92
women
  All-Russian Congress of Women and, 250
  babi bunty ("women's' protests") and, 520
  February Revolution (1917) and, 238–39
  International Women's Day protests (1917) and, 238–39
  in Russian workforce during World War I, 74–76, 146–47
  soldatki (soldiers' mothers and wives) and, 102, 120–21, 213–14, 277, 329–31, 449–50
  Women's Battalion of Death and 16, 40, 335
World War I. *See also specific battles and campaigns*
  casualty and death totals from, 16, 41–42, 108, 122, 233, 308, 329, 338–39, 407, 409–10, 414–15, 519
  demobilization following, 431, 442, 478–79
  desertion by Russian soldiers during, 49, 233, 335–36
  expectations of short duration of, 60
  February revolution (1917) and, 252–54
  financial costs of, 16–17
  gas warfare in, 16, 45–47, 290*f*, 338–39
  hospitals in, 93–96
  inflation in Russia during, 16–17, 76, 111, 113
  mobilization in Russia for, 16, 40, 60, 86–87
  monetary exchange restrictions in Russia during, 63–64
  "no man's zones" between lines in, 22–23, 44, 291*f*
  protests in Russia against, 36–37

Russian economic productivity during, 64–66, 69–76
Russian losses in early months (1914) of, 40–49
Russians' weapon quality during, 98
size of Russia's eastern front during, 43–44
soldiers' right to organize during, 22
strikes in Russia in the year preceding, 32–33, 36–37, 38, 117
surveillance to ensure loyalty in Russia during, 38–40
women in the Russian workforce during, 74–76, 146–47
World War II, 25, 523–25, 535
Wrangel, Peter, 482–83, 489–90

Yarov, Sergei, 510–11
"yellow workers" (workers from Asia), 112, 141–42, 187–88
Yurchak, Alexei, 533

Zabelin, A. F., 102–3
Zaionchkovskii, A. M., 193
Zaitsev, K. I., 394–95
Zasiadko, D. I., 159–60
zemstvos (quasi-democratic welfare organizations)
  data collection by, 184
  district elections (1917) for, 362–63
  liberalism and, 3
  Ministry of Agriculture and, 139
  refugees and, 96–97
  scarcity during World War I and, 126
Zemstvo Union (All-Russian Union of Zemstvos to Aid Sick and Wounded Troops), 96–97, 165–66, 338
Zenzinov, V. V., 244–45
Zhemchuzhina, Polina, 525
Zhukov, Georgy Marshal, 518
Zinoviev, Grigory, 445, 466, 515